CONFIDENT PUBLIC SPEAKING

SECOND EDITION

Deanna D. Sellnow

NORTH DAKOTA STATE UNIVERSITY

THOMSON

WADSWORTH

Australia | Canada | Mexico | Singapore | Spain | United Kingdom | United States

Publisher: *Holly J. Allen*
Editor: *Annie Mitchell*
Senior Development Editor: *Renée Deljon*
Assistant Editor: *Shona Burke*
Editorial Assistant: *Trina Enriquez*
Senior Technology Project Manager: *Jeanette Wiseman*
Senior Marketing Manager: *Kimberly Russell*
Marketing Assistant: *Andrew Keay*
Advertising Project Manager: *Shemika Britt*
Project Manager, Editorial Production: *Mary Noel*
Print/Media Buyer: *Doreen Suruki*

Permissions Editor: *Joohee Lee*
Production Service: *Robin Lockwood Productions*
Text Designer: *Robin West Morrow, Ox and Company, Inc.*
Photo Researcher: *Sarah Evertson, ImageQuest*
Copy Editor: *Anita Wagner*
Illustrator: *Hans Neuhart*
Cover Designer: *Patrick Devine*
Cover Image: *Getty Images/Daly & Newton*
Compositor: *Thompson Type*
Cover Printer: *Coral Graphic Services*
Printer: *Quebecor World/Versailles*

For more information about our products, contact us at:
Thomson Learning Academic Resource Center
1-800-423-0563
For permission to use material from this text or product, submit a request online at
http://www.thomsonrights.com.
Any additional questions about permissions can be submitted by email to thomsonrights@thomson.com.

Library of Congress Control Number: 2003116261

Student Edition: ISBN 0-534-55192-0

Annotated Instructor's Edition: ISBN 0-534-55197-1

Thomson Wadsworth
10 Davis Drive
Belmont, CA 94002-3098
USA

Asia
Thomson Learning
5 Shenton Way #01-01
UIC Building
Singapore 068808

Australia/New Zealand
Thomson Learning
102 Dodds Street
Southbank, Victoria 3006
Australia

Canada
Nelson
1120 Birchmount Road
Toronto, Ontario M1K 5G4
Canada

Europe/Middle East/Africa
Thomson Learning
High Holborn House
50/51 Bedford Row
London WC1R 4LR
United Kingdom

Latin America
Thomson Learning
Seneca, 53
Colonia Polanco
11560 Mexico D.F.
Mexico

Spain/Portugal
Paraninfo
Calle Magallanes, 25
28015 Madrid, Spain

I dedicate this book to Tim, Debbie (now 18), and Rick (now 14)

who continue to tolerate me as I pursue this project.
Your patience, endurance, sacrifices, and love keep me going.
I love you all very much!

BRIEF CONTENTS

CONTENTS

PART THREE
Considering Communication Contexts

Chapter 14
Informative Speaking   327

Chapter 15
Persuasive Speaking: Types and Designs   347

PREFACE

I wrote *Confident Public Speaking* because I believe anyone can become an effective public speaker, and that all of us can improve our public speaking skills. Effective public speaking is a process that improves as we cultivate it. Confident public speakers are not perfect at this craft but are effective at it, and effective public speakers are those who choose to work to develop their skills. Fundamentally, public speaking is a process that involves a series of steps focusing on aspects of content, structure, and delivery. That's why each chapter of this book teaches important concepts and then step-by-step methods for applying the concepts to a speech.

Communication can be defined as the sending and receiving of verbal and nonverbal messages to create shared meaning. Public speaking is one context for communication. It is not, however, simply linear, the mere sending of a message by the speaker to be received by the listener. It is actually transactional, because messages are sent and received simultaneously by both speaker and listener. Both therefore play important roles in creating shared meaning, and *Confident Public Speaking* carefully considers the role each plays in a presentation.

Because becoming an effective public speaker is an evolutionary process that requires continual development and adaptation of skills for diverse audiences that change not only in specific situations but with society and the times, treating public speaking as a fixed set of skills ignores the opportunity to grow through such changes. *Confident Public Speaking* embraces those opportunities by considering public speaking skills to be fluid and adaptive, and trusting that everyone is capable of developing the skills to address diverse audiences in American society and others. Confident speaking is a journey, not a destination.

About the Second Edition

The first edition of this book was called *Public Speaking: A Process Approach*. This edition's title, *Confident Public Speaking*, highlights the *result* of approaching public speaking as a process. Getting there is part of any journey's pleasure, but knowing where we're going can help us persist along the way.

This new edition retains and strengthens features that teachers and students thought helpful and offers many new features as well. The retained features include coverage of learning styles, speech anxiety, ethics, and diversity integrated throughout the book. The second edition also offers a thoroughly updated research base and new examples, along with expanded coverage of the narrative speech pattern, outlining, and purpose, and a greater emphasis on the relevance of public speaking in students' lives. Here are this edition's major new features:

ETHICS

- An **increased emphasis on ethics** in Chapter 1, Communication and Ethical Public Speaking, and a new marginal icon that flags relevant discussions of ethics throughout the text, ensure that this important topic remains in the foreground to prepare students to be ethical public speakers.

- **"Practicing the Process" boxes** highlight the text's focus on the process and active nature of public speaking. In each chapter these boxes provide step-by-step guides to and checklists for the process of preparing and delivering a speech, so that students can easily refer to ways to apply the strategies they're learning.

- **"Looking at the Learning Cycle" boxes** highlight key points pertaining to learning styles and the learning cycle, making it easy for students to find ways to apply the principles.

- **"Turning to Technology" boxes** present a collection of integrated activities that expand students' learning by directing them to the book's CD-ROM and Web site, and to diverse Internet resources.

- **Redesigned chapter-ending resources** further integrate the text's technology offerings. The "Returning to Technology" section now concludes each chapter to provide a starting point for using Speech Interactive on the book's CD-ROM, Speech Builder Express, and resources on the book's Web site, such as Key Terms, Activities, and InfoTrac College Edition exercises.

- **Speech Builder Express** prompts at the end of each chapter, flagged with a marginal icon, direct students to our groundbreaking (and award-winning!) Web-based program for outlining and developing speeches (discussed in detail below). The prompts help students know when and how to use this tool.

- **Increased and updated coverage of research** now reflects the fifth edition of the *APA Manual* and offers more documentation models as well as expanded discussions of online research and evaluating Web pages.

- **Streamlined discussions** further improve the readability of chapters by providing condensed explanations and a limited number of examples. The chapter on persuasion now focuses primarily on issues of particular importance to beginning speakers.

- A **new interior design,** more photographs, and updated art make the book easier and more enjoyable for students to use.

Overview of the Text's Contents and Organization

Confident Public Speaking is organized into three parts so that readers can strategically and easily locate information about preparing and presenting public speeches for diverse situations and audiences.

Part I: Understanding Communication Dynamics. Chapters 1 through 4 introduce foundational components of the communication process. These concepts are relevant not only to public speaking but to communication transactions generally. The chapters cover communication models, communication ethics, communication anxiety, listening, and evaluating.

Part II: Preparing and Presenting Public Speeches. Chapters 5 through 13 set forth the fundamental skills required to organize and deliver effective public speeches. The skills covered include topic selection, audience analysis, research and supporting material, organization, language, delivery, and presentational aids.

Part III: Considering Communication Contexts. Chapters 14 through 18 provide a basis for understanding why and how content, structure, and delivery might be unique, based on situation and audience. Various speech types are covered: informative, persuasive, special occasion, and group presentations.

Quick Review of Foundational Features

Confident Public Speaking is founded on several key features that have been designed to help students improve their skills as well as gain an appreciation for the public speaking process.

Materials for Speaking Right from the Start

Chapter 3, Your First Speech, helps get students up and speaking during the first weeks of class and provides experience-based context for the subsequent in-depth coverage of the entire process of public speaking. The chapter includes an example of a speech of introduction.

Exceptionally Thorough Coverage of Communication Apprehension

Public speaking anxiety is covered in Chapter 2, Coping Effectively with Public Speaking Anxiety, and whenever appropriate throughout the text, so that students have not just a general understanding of this topic but also practical, detailed strategies for reducing their communication apprehension.

Unique Coverage of Learning Styles and the Learning Cycle

Integrated throughout the text to address diversity issues without stereotyping, the twin concepts of learning styles and the learning cycle are discussed in the context of specific speaking skills, including audience analysis, supporting material, introductions, language, and reasoning. Students learn that effectiveness as a public speaker is enhanced by identifying and understanding one's own preferred learning style, and by addressing the diverse learning styles of the audience so that the speech rounds the entire learning cycle. Each chapter presents strategies to help achieve these goals. Chapter 1, Communication and Ethical Public Speaking, provides a solid introduction to learning styles and the cycle of learning, important topics researchers have studied for decades to increase our understanding of the relationship between ways of learning and information retention.

Emphasis on Cultural Diversity

Public speaking textbooks have addressed the important communication topic of cultural diversity since the early 1990s. Unfortunately, many of these books unintentionally marginalized or stereotyped certain cultural groups. To be more inclusive and to avoid stereotyping, *Confident Public Speaking* integrates these issues comprehensively in ways that acknowledge diversity without marginalizing and stereotyping individuals and groups. This improvement is achieved by addressing learning styles and through a somewhat unusual approach to demographic audience analysis (Chapter 6). Examples and photos from both popular culture and representing diverse students illustrate these concepts.

Focus on Critical Thinking

Confident Public Speaking encourages and supports critical thinking from cover to cover and on its CD-ROM and Web site. Many texts offer only an outline or set of learning objectives at the beginning of each chapter, but students rarely use them as intended, to focus their thinking as they read. Hence each chapter of this book opens with five Reflective Questions as well as chapter outlines under the heading "What's Ahead: Focusing Your Reading." The questions encourage students to become actively engaged by seeking answers as they read. Similarly, the chapters are interspersed with "What Do You Think?" boxes, which ask students questions that link the text's discussion to personal experiences to encourage critical thinking about the material. Finally, the "Turning to Technology" boxes integrated throughout every chapter direct students to Web sites and encourage them to think more deeply about direct applications for the concepts discussed in the text.

Emphasis on Ethics

Confident Public Speaking pays consistent attention to ethics, mindful that speakers make decisions at numerous points during the speech making process and that ethical considerations affect their decisions about choice of topic, audience analysis, research, organization, language, and delivery, and that listeners, too, make ethical choices in listening and evaluating.

Thorough Coverage of Technology

Throughout, *Confident Public Speaking* presents technology as a tool for both speech preparation and delivery, and offers practical advice for using technology effectively and ethically. Each chapter includes "Turning to Technology" boxes that direct students to online resources and activities and InfoTrac College Edition exercises, and indicate how Speech Builder Express supports completing the stage of the speech making process covered in each chapter. Chapter 7 contains abundant information on using the Internet to complete speech research and how to critically evaluate Web sources. Chapter 13 offers practical advice for creating presentations with PowerPoint or other computer slide programs.

Thoughtful and Engaging Pedagogy

Confident Public Speaking not only presents but uses the tenets of learning style theory: Concepts are explained in ways that attend to the "feeling, watching, thinking, and doing" dimensions of the learning cycle. As students read each chapter, they essentially "round the learning cycle." With its chapter-opening Reflective Questions, "What Do You Think?" prompts; step-by-step "Practicing the Process" guides to all stages of preparing and delivering speeches; integrated links (marginal prompts) to the Student Workbook; numerous speech outlines, full transcripts, and excerpts; and chapter-ending "Key Terms" lists and practical activities, *Confident Public Speaking* offers carefully designed and developed pedagogy to support its engaging, realistic approach. It also uses appropriate terminology from the communication field and defines terms simply and completely. The glossary at the end of the book contains all key terms and definitions, and interactive flashcards for the key terms are available on the book's Web site.

Resources for Students

This book's second edition offers a full complement of print and media resources, all integrated with the text to maximize usefulness:

* The ***Confident Public Speaking CD-ROM*** features Speech Interactive for *Confident Public Speaking* and is free with each new copy of the text. Packaged on the text's inside back cover, the CD also provides one-stop access to all of the text's technology components, including InfoTrac College Edition, Speech Builder Express, and links to chapter-by-chapter resources on the *Confident Public Speaking* Web site. Speech Interactive includes video of 10 student and 4 professional speeches, which are included or referred to in the text, along with interactive activities and evaluation guides. This multimedia tool makes sample speeches in the text come alive: Students maximize their experience by reading, watching, listening to, critiquing,

and analyzing the model speeches. By completing the speech evaluation checklists and speech improvement plans, students can compare their work to my suggestions. References to each component of the CD-ROM are flagged in the text with a CD icon.

- The *Confident Public Speaking* **Web site,** accessed through the book's CD-ROM, takes students to dynamic chapter-by-chapter and general text resources, including key term flashcards, speech transcripts, and interactive activities, many in addition to those in the book. Resources include live links for the URLs in the text and more InfoTrac College Edition activities. References to the Web site are flagged in each chapter with a combination CD/World Wide Web icon.

- **Speech Builder Express,** our groundbreaking speech outlining and development program, is a Web-based tool that coaches students through the speech organization and development process by guiding them through intuitively sequenced interactive sessions. This flexible program allows documents to be saved and returned to, exported to Word, and e-mailed to instructors. Links to InfoTrac College Edition, a dictionary, tutor comments specific to *Confident Public Speaking*, and video clips make this an invaluable and flexible tool. In the text, a Speech Builder Express icon appears with references to the program.

- **InfoTrac® College Edition.** This fully searchable online database provides students with access to articles from more than 4,000 scholarly journals and popular periodicals. Updated daily, and dating back 20 years, the database allows students to complete their speech research using articles from the best sources. A four-month subscription to InfoTrac College Edition is included in the price of every new copy of this book, and an InfoTrac College Edition activity is included at the end of each chapter, as well as in Turning to Technology boxes in selected chapters. Additional InfoTrac College Edition activities are available on the book's Web site. Look for an icon in the text.

- *InfoTrac College Edition Student Activities Workbook for Public Speaking,* by Nancy Goulden of Kansas State University, can be bundled with the text. The workbook features guidelines and an extensive selection of individual and group activities designed to help instructors and students get the most from InfoTrac College Edition.

- **Public Speaking Student Guide to the Opposing Viewpoints Resource Center (OVRC)** provides solid guidance for using this new online library, which was developed using the Greenhaven Press's acclaimed social issues series, as well as core reference content from other Gale and Macmillan Reference USA sources. The Center provides dynamic resources that range from the facts of controversies to the arguments of each topic's proponents and detractors. Special sections focus on critical thinking, walking students through the process of how to critically evaluate point-counterpoint arguments, and research and write source-based papers and speeches.

- The *Student Workbook for Confident Public Speaking,* which I wrote, features extensive individual and group activities to further enhance students' learning and support assignments suggested in the Instructor's Manual. Throughout *Confident Public Speaking*, workbook prompts appear in the margins to direct students to relevant activities in the workbook.

- *A Guide to the Basic Course for ESL Students,* by Esther Yook of Mary Washington College, is designed to assist the non-native speaker of

English. Features include FAQs, helpful URLs, and strategies for accent management and speech apprehension.

- *Service Learning in Communication Studies: A Handbook* by Rick Isaacson, San Francisco State University; Bruce Dorries, Radford University; and Kevin Brown, Montana State University, is invaluable for students (and instructors) in programs that integrate a service-learning component. The handbook provides guidelines for connecting service learning work with classroom concepts and advice for working effectively with agencies and organizations. It also provides model forms and reports and a directory of online resources.

Resources for Instructors

Confident Public Speaking features a full suite of resources for instructors. To request an examination copy of any instructor or student resources for full evaluation, please contact your local Wadsworth representative, contact our Academic Resource Center at 800-423-0563, or visit us at **http://communication. wadsworth.com**.

- **Annotated Instructor's Edition (AIE),** which North Dakota State University's Stephanie Ahlfeldt helped me prepare, is a student copy of the text with the addition in the margins of class-tested teaching tips and suggestions for integrating the extensive ancillary program. This teaching tool is a must-have for the first-time instructor or graduate teaching assistant and a great refresher for the veteran professor.
- The **Instructor's Manual/Test Bank to Accompany** *Confident Public Speaking* offers a wealth of suggestions for setting up the course, including various syllabi and daily schedules. The manual is filled with speech assignments, activities, extended chapter outlines, and sample lesson plans that include activities for all learning styles, allowing students to "round the cycle of learning." The manual's comprehensive "Test Bank" offers numerous test questions of various types—recall, conceptual, and application—in all formats for multiple cognitive levels. The Test Bank is also available in electronic format via ExamView.
- **ExamView® computerized testing.** Create, deliver, and customize tests and study guides (both print and online) in minutes with this easy-to-use assessment and tutorial system. ExamView offers both a Quick Test Wizard and Online Test Wizard that guide you step-by-step through the process of creating tests, while the unique "WYSIWYG" (What You See Is What You Get) capability allows you to see the test you are creating on the screen exactly as it will print or display online. You can build tests of up to 250 questions using up to 12 question types. Using ExamView's word-processing capabilities, you can enter an unlimited number of new questions or add existing questions.
- The instructor's password-protected *Confident Public Speaking* Web site, accessible directly through the book's CD-ROM or online at **http://communication.wadsworth.com/sellnow2**, contains the Instructor's Manual in electronic format, as well as additional resources such as PowerPoint slides, practice quizzes for students, and other activities and teaching tools.
- The **Student Speaker Video,** a 60-minute videotape, shows different types of speeches: self-introduction, informative, persuasive, special occasion, group symposium, and impromptu.

- A collection of **Overhead Transparencies** is available to demonstrate materials such as models, key charts, diagrams, and forms used in the preparation and presentation phases of public speaking.
- **Multimedia Presentation Manager: Microsoft® PowerPoint® Link Tool,** developed by Dan Cavanaugh, is a one-stop lecture tool that makes it easy to assemble, edit, publish, and present custom lectures for your public speaking course, both for students' reference and distance learning. The program offers predesigned PowerPoint presentations that contain both images and text, and includes a simple lecture-preparation wizard.
- **Public Speaking Instructor's Guide to the Opposing Viewpoints Resource Center (OVRC)** helps you take advantage of this new online library, which was developed using the Greenhaven Press's acclaimed social issues series as well as core reference content from other Gale and Macmillan Reference USA sources. The Center provides dynamic resources that range from the facts of controversies to the arguments of each topic's proponents and detractors. Special sections focus on critical thinking, walking students through the process of how to critically evaluate point-counterpoint arguments, and research and write source-based papers and speeches.
- **The Teaching Assistant's Guide to the Basic Course** is an exceptionally useful tool created by Katherine G. Hendrix of the University of Memphis. Based on leading training programs for communication teachers, the guide covers general teaching and course management topics as well as specific strategies for communication instruction, such as providing effective feedback on performance, managing sensitive class discussions, and conducting mock interviews.
- **CNN Today Videos** allow you to integrate the newsgathering and programming power of CNN into the classroom to provide students with additional information about recent and current events, which may help them identify speech topics. Divided into short segments, perfect for introducing a range of subjects, these high-interest clips are followed by questions designed to spark class discussion.
- **Student Speeches for Critique and Analysis** is a multivolume video series that offers both imperfect and award-winning sample student speeches. Selected speeches presented in the text are available in this series.
- **WebTutor™ Toolbox for WebCT and Blackboard** is a Web-based teaching and learning tool that takes a course beyond classroom boundaries to an anywhere, anytime environment. *WebTutor Toolbox for Confident Public Speaking* corresponds chapter-by-chapter and topic-by-topic with the book, including flashcards, practice quizzes, and online tutorials. Instructors can use WebTutor Toolbox to provide virtual office hours, post syllabi, set up threaded discussions, and track student progress on the practice quizzes.
- **MyCourse 2.0,** available with all Wadsworth titles, is an easy-to-use course management system that gives you a quick way to create a course Web site. It is free, PIN-less, and ready for you to populate with your own content.

Contact your Wadsworth/Thomson Learning representative for details, examination copies, or a demonstration of any of the teaching and learning resources, which are available to qualified adopters.

Acknowledgments

This book represents my growth and discoveries over the past three decades as a public speaker, teacher, director of the basic course, and author. To thank everyone who has played a part in my development along the way is impossible, but I would like to acknowledge a few: Howard Vallaincourt, my junior high school speech and debate coach; C. T. Hanson, Robert Littlefield, and Tim Sellnow, who inspired me to higher levels of skill and college competition; Bernard Brock, Professor Emeritus at Wayne State University, and Ivan J. K. Dahl, Professor Emeritus at the University of North Dakota, for their unrelenting belief in my abilities as a communication scholar and teacher; my father-in-law, Les Sellnow, who provided needed encouragement throughout this project; and for their unceasing, unconditional love and support, Grandpa Johnson and Grandma Miller, my inspirational mentors who, during the writing of this book, have gone to be with the Lord.

All of the professionals associated with Thomson Wadsworth have been marvelous to work with, providing information, encouraging me, and keeping the project on schedule: Annie Mitchell, acquisitions editor for communication studies; Renée Deljon, senior development editor; Mary Noel, production project manager; Robin Lockwood, production coordinator; Anita Wagner and Rick Reser, copyeditors; Kimberly Russell, senior marketing manager; Jeanette Wiseman, senior technology project manager; Shona Burke, assistant editor; and Trina Enriquez, editorial assistant. I would also like to thank the ancillary authors who've offered their expertise and time to this project: Stephanie Ahlfeldt, North Dakota State University, who helped prepare the annotated instructor's edition; Tamara Afifi, Pennsylvania State University, and Janice Stuckey, Jefferson State Community College, who together prepared the instructor's resource manual; and Dan Cavanaugh who prepared the Multimedia Manager.

I would like to extend special thanks to the many reviewers who helped us plan this new edition. Their time and energy, careful work, and thoughtful suggestions have made this book better than it otherwise would have been. Thanks go to Stephanie Ahlfeldt, North Dakota State University; Elizabeth R. Bernat, Plattsburgh, State University of New York; LeAnn Brazeal, Kansas State University; Lisa Darnell, University of North Alabama; Angela Gibson, Shelton State Community College; Dayle C. Hardy-Short, Northern Arizona University; Mike Hemphill, University of Arkansas at Little Rock; Mark E. Huglen, University of Minnesota, Crookston; Mary Austin Newman, Wharton County Junior College; Elaine VanderClute, Wor-Wic Community College; and Alaina Winters, Heartland Community College.

I would also like to renew the same special thanks to the reviewers of the book's previous edition: Jonathan Amsbary, University of Alabama, Birmingham; Linda Anthon, Valencia Community College; Dianne Lee Blomberg, Metropolitan State College of Denver; Tim Borchers, Minnesota State University, Moorhead; Joan Butcher, Louisiana State University; Jim Carlson, Jones County Community College; Rebecca Carrier, California State Polytechnic University, Pomona; Leah Ceccarelli, University of Washington; Della Dameron Johnson, University of Maryland, Eastern Shore; Lisa Darnell, University of North Alabama; Jill Davis, Mississippi State University; Lynn Disbrow, Sinclair Community College; Cynthia Galivan, Hudson Valley Community College; Darla Germeroth, University of Scranton; Tamara Golish, Luther College, Decorah, Iowa; Lisa Goodnight, Purdue University, Calumet; Jonathan Gray, University of Southern Illinois; Robert Greenstreet, East Central University, Oklahoma;

Charles Griffin, Kansas State University; Kelby Halone, Clemson University; Karin Hilgersom, Spokane Community College; Lawrence Hosman, University of Southern Mississippi; Mark Huglen, University of Minnesota, Crookston; Steve Hunt, Illinois State University; Rebecca Litke, California State University, Northridge; Steve Madden, University of Southern Mississippi; Mary Haslerud Opp, University of North Dakota; Nan Peck, North Virginia Community College; Norma Ragland, Norfolk State University; Amy Slagell, Iowa State University; Rick Soller, College of Lake County; Dick Stine, Johnson County Community College; Janice Stuckey, Jefferson State Community College; Rob Vogel, Spokane Community College; and Beth M. Waggenspack, Virginia Tech.

Finally, thanks to Tim and Debbie and Rick, not just for enduring me, but also for helping and encouraging me. You have supported me, guided me, and strengthened me, and will, I believe, continue to do so as we pursue our life journey together. I hope that I can do the same for each of you along the way.

To God be the glory.

Deanna Sellnow
North Dakota State University

ABOUT THE AUTHOR

 **Deanna D. Sellnow** is Associate Professor of Communication and Director of the Public Speaking Fundamentals Program at North Dakota State University, where she has taught since 1990. After finishing her master's degree at Wayne State University in Detroit, she completed the Ph.D. program at the University of North Dakota. She has received numerous honors for public speaking, teaching, and research, including the American Forensic Association's National Individual Events Tournament Champion in Communication Analysis, North Dakota Speech and Theatre Association's "Scholar of the Year," and "Outstanding Teacher" at North Dakota State University.

In addition to her teaching, Deanna is active in the National Communication Association, Central States Communication Association, and the North Dakota Speech and Theatre Association. She has served as Chair of the Basic Course Interest Group of the Central States Communication Association and Chair of the Experiential Learning Commission of the National Communication Association. She edited the *Basic Communication Course Annual,* a publication that focuses specifically on research related to the basic course, for three years. She has just been elected to serve as Vice President of the Central States Communication Association.

Deanna lives with her family in Fargo, North Dakota—husband Tim, daughter Debbie, and son Rick, along with their golden retriever, Trini, and cat, Oscar. She enjoys camping and traveling with her family, running marathons with Tim, directing the church choir, and playing a variety of musical instruments including the saxophone, piano, and guitar.

1

COMMUNICATION AND ETHICAL PUBLIC SPEAKING

REFLECTIVE QUESTIONS

1. In what specific situation would better public speaking skills benefit you?

2. In what contexts do you communicate with others? How are these contexts similar to one another? How are they different?

3. Have you ever thought of communication as a transaction? What are the elements of a communication transaction?

4. How do you like to learn? Is your preference different depending on the situation? Explain how you recently learned to do or understand something new.

5. What does it mean to be an ethical communicator? Discuss a time you felt that a speaker you were listening to was not being ethical.

WHAT'S AHEAD: FOCUSING YOUR READING

Why Study Public Speaking?

What Is Communication?

Models of Communication

The Seven Basic Elements of the Communication Process

Ethical Public Speaking

W ELCOME! IF YOU ARE READING this textbook, you probably recently enrolled in a public speaking course. Even before you start developing your public speaking skills, *congratulations!* A public speaking course may seem strange, but it can bring you enormous benefits.

If public speaking feels frightening, you are by no means alone. Most people feel the same way; surveys report that speaking in public is often feared more than flying, earthquakes, disease, or even death! Actor-comedian Jerry Seinfeld once put it this way:

> According to most studies, people's number one fear is public speaking. Number two is death. Death is number two. Does that seem right? This means to the average person, if you have to go to a funeral, you're better off in the casket than doing the eulogy. (Seinfeld, 1993, p. 120)

Surveys report that 70 to 75 percent of the adult population fears public speaking (McCroskey, 1993; Richmond & McCroskey, 1995). If you feel nervous, keep in mind that three out of four of your classmates do too. Even as many as 76 percent of *experienced* public speakers feel fearful before presenting a speech (Hahner, Sokoloff, & Salisch, 1993). Award-winning actor Meryl Streep's comments may represent the feelings of many successful public speakers:

> It's odd: I have this career that spans continents, but the pathetic thing is that I can't get up in front of people and speak. I get really, really nervous. (cited in Wasserstein, 1988, p. 90)

Other successful individuals who share Streep's feelings include singer Barbra Streisand, evangelist Billy Graham, former president Ronald Reagan, and former Chrysler Corporation chief executive officer Lee Iacocca.

So why do people make oral presentations at all? First, sometimes they have to. But second, it can be rewarding and even fun! That's why I usually enjoy reading student responses on the end-of-semester course evaluations for this class. They say things like the following:

- I thought I'd hate this class, but I'm actually going to miss it.
- I can't believe I'm saying this, but I enjoyed this class!
- This was the *best* class I've taken. Don't change a thing.
- It was *fun!*
- I've learned so much in this class. The skills I've learned here are already benefiting me in my other classes.
- I went to a job interview last week. I applied what I've learned in this class. I know it helped. P.S. I got the job!
- I was *terrified* about taking this class, now I can't figure out why I waited so long.

By reading this book, participating in your instructor's course, and applying what you learn to your own speeches, you too can become an effective public speaker and enjoy the gratification that can accompany it. This book will help you to (a) control speech anxiety and use it to your advantage, (b) approach your speech topics in ways that spark and maintain listener interest, (c) organize your ideas effectively, (d) present your speeches convincingly, and (e) integrate presentational aids appropriately.

This chapter begins by presenting several compelling reasons for studying public speaking. Next, we define public speaking and situate it within the bigger picture of the communication process. Finally, the chapter addresses ethical communication as it relates to public speaking.

Student Workbook

Review the syllabus in Chapter 1 of the workbook and identify which assignments you believe will be most beneficial to you and why.

What Do You Know about Communication?

www.queendom.com/tests/relationship/communication_skills_r_access.html

Go to this site and take the "Communication Skills Test" to see what you know (and what you don't) about communication.

WHY STUDY PUBLIC SPEAKING?

Over the years, other public speaking teachers and I have discovered that most students enroll in public speaking fundamentals because it is required (Trank, 1990; Trank & Lewis, 1991). But even if that's your situation, you will enjoy it and get much more out of it if you realize the benefits. Effective oral communication skills can improve your life in three crucial areas: personal relationships, college classes, and professional careers (Ford & Wolvin, 1993; Kramer & Hinton, 1996; Wolvin, 1998a, 1998b; Wolvin, Berko, & Wolvin, 1999).

WHAT DO YOU THINK?
Why did you enroll in this course? List two specific benefits you would like to achieve from taking it.

Personal Life Benefits

Do you have a friend who always seems able to convince you to see one movie instead of another? Most likely that's partly because he or she has effective oral communication skills. In this book you will learn which persuasive strategies work best when trying to convince friends and family, as well as to evaluate the merit of their attempts to persuade you. Similarly, do you have a certain friend or friends whom you are most likely to seek out for advice? They too probably employ effective oral communication skills. This book also clarifies how listening is a multifaceted skill that must be tailored to particular situations to be most effective (e.g., Halone et al., 1998). The communication skills you will learn in this course can help improve your personal interactions and relationships.

Communication scholars often look to popular culture as a guide to understanding the values and beliefs of a society. What might popular culture tell us about ourselves? Just think of the number of television sitcoms, soap operas, and talk shows, as well as comic strips, movies, and books, whose plots are based on miscommunication between people. It's a source of humor in television sitcoms such as *Home Improvement*, *Friends*, and *That 70s Show* and a source of drama and suspense in soap operas such as *Days of Our Lives* and *All My Children* (e.g., Brinson, 1992; Douglas, 1996; Honeycutt, Wellman, & Larson, 1997; Landay, 1999; Larson, 1991; "Nineteen-nineties," 1999). Television talk shows such as *Oprah*, *Ricki Lake*, and *Sally Jesse Raphael* often feature either guests whose personal relationships suffer from miscommunication or who are in some way experts at improving personal relationships through communication (e.g., Greenberg et al., 1997; Willis, 1996; Wilson, 1996). In comic strips, "Cathy," for example, often focuses on miscommunication between men and women, and "Dilbert" often deals with miscommunication in the workplace (e.g., Astor, 1999; Brown, 1997; Capowski, 1997).

WHAT DO YOU THINK?
Identify a recent frustrating discussion you had with a friend. Why did you feel frustrated? What communication skills can you focus on to improve your personal interactions?

That miscommunication is such a pervasive theme in popular culture suggests that effective oral communication skills are well worth developing.

College Education Benefits

The skills you learn in this class may benefit you throughout your college career. Jake, a student of mine, avoided taking the public speaking course until the last semester of his senior year. When asked whether this class could benefit students in their education, he exclaimed, "I can't believe I waited so long to take this class. So many of the classes in my major required graded oral presentations. I realize now how much better my grades could have been. If only I'd taken this class sooner." Jake is only one of many upper-class students to have offered this kind of insight.

Two trends that emerged in the 1980s and 1990s have made effective oral communication skills even more important to college students. These trends are the speaking-across-the-curriculum movement and the national assessment standards initiative. The first requires oral presentations to occur in all academic areas, not just in speech communication classes, and is growing in the United States. The national assessment standards initiative requires that standardized grading criteria be employed to measure speaker effectiveness. As a result of these two movements, oral presentations are now required in many classes ranging from English to science to engineering to architecture to agriculture to economics to psychology. Simply put, it is no longer possible to earn a bachelor's degree without delivering some graded oral presentations, usually both individual and group.

In addition to teaching you important skills in preparing and presenting effective public speeches, this course will also teach you other vital communication skills that are directly transferable to other academic areas. You will learn, for example, how to listen critically, take notes effectively, examine information analytically, and evaluate messages carefully. These will help you succeed throughout college.

WHAT DO YOU THINK?
Identify a favorite television program, comic strip, movie, or book. What skills does it reveal as important for effective communication in interpersonal relationships?

Professional Career Benefits

Finally, effective oral communication skills will help you succeed in whatever professional career you choose. For example, *Job Outlook 2004*, an annual forecast of hiring conducted by the National Association of Colleges and Employers, surveyed employers to find out what characteristics they sought most in new recruits. The following list indicates what employers identified, in rank order, from most to least important:

Top Ten Skills Employers Seek

1. Communication skills (verbal and written)
2. Honesty/integrity
3. Interpersonal skills (relates well to others)
4. Motivation/initiative
5. Strong work ethic
6. Teamwork skills (works well with others)
7. Analytical skills
8. Flexibility/adaptability

9. Computer skills
10. Detail-oriented

WHAT DO YOU THINK?

What career do you want to pursue? What are two ways effective oral communication skills will help you succeed in your career?

If you didn't realize just how important this class could be to your professional success, you should realize it now. In fact, communication skills have topped the list every year for the past five years! Notice where communication skills ranked compared to computer skills. Notice too that academic achievement (GPA) and proficiency in field of study didn't even make the list. These startling comparisons make sense when you think about it: Employers know they will train their employees again and again as new technologies emerge. Communication skills, however, are foundational. Once learned, they prove beneficial regardless of your role in an organization.

If this survey doesn't convince you, consider that communication training prepares a student for any entry-level position—not just in fields such as education, advertising, sales, and broadcasting, but in others such as accounting, computer science, and engineering (e.g., Bakos, 1997; Kramer & Hinton, 1996; Maes, 1997; Nagle, 1987; Peterson, 1997; Stinson & Asquith, 1997; Weitzel, 1987; Wolvin, 1998a, 1998b). Public speaking skills are important even in fields where you wouldn't expect them to be.

The bottom line is that these skills are important not just for success and promotion, but for getting a job in the first place. Employers receive numerous applications for each job vacancy and typically interview three or four applicants who appear most qualified. Who gets hired? Right! The person who communicates most effectively in the interview.

TURNING TO TECHNOLOGY

How Is Communication Important in Your Career Field?

Use the *Confident Public Speaking* CD-ROM to access InfoTrac College Edition and use as search terms the name of your chosen career field and "communication." In what ways is communication important in your chosen field? Take notes and bring them with you to class or post what you find on your class discussion forum.

WHAT IS COMMUNICATION?

We communicate in a variety of ways. We mail cards and write letters, send e-mail, talk on the telephone. Sometimes we communicate orally, other times in writing. Public speaking is simply another way. But what is **communication**? For our purposes we define it as *the process of sending and receiving verbal and nonverbal messages to create shared meaning.* Let's look at each part of this definition.

Communication is dynamic, meaning that both senders and receivers continuously formulate, send, and interpret numerous messages during an interaction. A **message** is simply any signal sent by one person **(sender)** and interpreted by another **(receiver).** The communication is successful when the sender and receiver achieve mutual understanding regarding the topic discussed. They may not agree about the merit of a topic, but they agree about the meaning of the message. For example, if you tell a friend that *South Park* is your favorite television show,

© Len Rubenstein/Index Stock

Effective public speaking skills will improve your communication skills when interviewing for a job.

your friend need not *agree* that it is the best program but will *understand* that it is *your* favorite.

Communication is both verbal and nonverbal. **Verbal messages** are made up of spoken words. **Nonverbal messages** are the signals sent by any other means, such as with our hands, body, face, and eyes. You might clench your fists as you talk about an issue that angers you, for example, or smile as you recount a pleasant experience. These are nonverbal messages that accompany the idea itself.

Finally, prior experiences and cultural background, as well as expectations, influence the meaning we attach to a particular message. For example, if you present a speech about the local rape and abuse crisis center and one of your audience members is a former victim of abuse (quite possible, given that one of every eight college women will be raped by the time she graduates), her experiences would influence the way she hears your speech (Jhally, 1995).

Communication Contexts

Public speaking is only one context where communication occurs. We also communicate in small groups, in one-to-one relationships, on the telephone, over the Internet, and on radio and television, as well as in newspapers, magazines, and newsletters. Communication research reveals five communication contexts: intrapersonal, impersonal, interpersonal, small group, and public (Littlejohn, 1989). Public speaking occurs in the public communication context. To select the most appropriate strategies for communicating in a public context, it is important to understand public speaking as it relates to the other contexts.

Although these contexts have similarities and are interrelated as forums for communication, they are also uniquely different. They differ in how formally you deliver your message, what kind of information you share, and how you transfer the information. But the various contexts blend together in certain ways. Let's look at each of them.

Intrapersonal

Intrapersonal communication is communicating with yourself. Usually this is not done orally but by thinking through choices, strategies, and the possible consequences of taking action. When you consider whether to tell your roommate that you are the one who broke her desk lamp, you are communicating intrapersonally. When you decide to replace the lamp before your roommate realizes it was broken, you are communicating intrapersonally. Much of this occurs subconsciously, without our being aware of the communication choices we make intrapersonally (Kellermann, 1992). When you head up the driveway "without thinking," for example, you are communicating intrapersonally on a subconscious level. Intrapersonal communication might occur within the public speaking context if, for example, you begin to wonder how you sound to your listeners while you're presenting your speech. Or you might notice confused looks on your listeners' faces as you explain a complex process and decide to rephrase your explanation.

WHAT DO YOU THINK?
Identify a situation when you communicate intrapersonally without really thinking about it. Have you ever wished you had been thinking more consciously to avert a consequence?

Impersonal

Impersonal communication is communication between two people about general information (Adler & Towne, 1996; Trenholm & Jenson, 1992). It is more intentional than intrapersonal communication but still fairly informal. Usually impersonal communication is with people we know relatively little about. When you say "hi" to a passing stranger, you are communicating impersonally. When you talk about the weather with the checker at the grocery store, you are communicating impersonally. Impersonal communication might occur within the public speaking context if, for example, you share introductory remarks related to current events or the weather or the occasion before you begin the main body of your speech. These impersonal comments don't relate directly to your speech but can signal your audience to get ready to listen.

Interpersonal

Interpersonal communication is communication between two people who already have an identifiable relationship with each other (DeVito, 1993). When you stop to chat with a friend between classes about weekend plans, how the kids are, or what you did last night, you are engaging in interpersonal communication.

When you have a heart-to-heart talk with a close friend or family member, you are engaging in interpersonal communication.

For example, interpersonal communication sometimes occurs within a public communication when a speaker tells a personal story about his or her experiences to support other points. Sharing personal information not generally known by others is **self-disclosure.** It establishes and maintains personal relationships and can act as a similar bond in a public communication context. For example, one speaker may talk about his reasons for returning to college as part of his recent calling to become a priest. Another might use self-disclosure during her speech about female bronco riders when she shows her own bruised knee (which she got from being bucked off a horse the night before). Both speakers have integrated interpersonal communication within the public communication context of presenting speeches.

Small Group

Small group communication is communication occurring in a group of about three to ten people (Poole, 1998, p. 94). The group might be meeting to perform a task, reach a common goal, share ideas, or simply engage in a social experience. There are many kinds of small groups; for example, a family, a group of friends, a group of classmates who work together on a class project, or a small group management team in the workplace (Ancona, 1990). In small group communication, individuals interact in such a way that "each person influences and is influenced by [the] other[s]" (Shaw, 1981, p. 10). Because more people are involved, small group communication is more complex than impersonal or interpersonal communication, but small groups are so important in personal and professional life that we need to be able to understand and deal with these complexities. Some research suggests that there are more small groups in the United States than there are people!

WHAT DO YOU THINK?
Identify a small group you've interacted in recently. It can be a family group, service group, social group, or business group. What communication-oriented issues can you identify that made interacting in that group rewarding or frustrating for you?

Small group communication occurs within a public communication context when groups of people are asked to make public presentations. When you are part of such a group, how effectively members work together throughout the process of developing ideas, as well as how effectively the group functions together to present them, reflects directly on your own success.

Public

Public communication takes place among audiences of more than about ten people. Public speaking is one form. **Public speaking** can be defined as a sustained formal presentation made by a speaker to an audience. When you give oral presentations in the classroom, you are engaging in public speaking. Teachers engage in public speaking when they lecture. So does a master of ceremonies, the actors who introduce award winners or accept awards, and corporate managers when they run large meetings. Presiding officers of clubs engage in public speaking when they conduct meetings; so do parents when presenting their ideas about educational issues to school boards or other officials. And the list goes on. Public speaking is much more prevalent in our day-to-day lives than most of us realize. Improving our ability to speak effectively in public is crucial to achieving important goals for ourselves, our families, and our communities.

Another form of public communication is **mass communication,** defined as communication produced and transmitted via media to large audiences. Newspaper and magazine journalists present written articles to large publics via mass communication. Television news anchors present information via mass commu-

Effective speakers can champion their goals to the public and to decision makers.

nication using a public speaking format. Radio morning shows where groups of three or four share ideas via mass communication use a small group communication format. Likewise, a televised debate between two presidential candidates is a mass communication form that utilizes elements of public speaking and interpersonal communication within it.

WHAT DO YOU THINK?

Identify an occasion when you spoke to a group of more than ten people. Were you effective? Why or why not?

MODELS OF COMMUNICATION

Linear

As scholars have learned more about the nature of communication, they have developed more detailed models of it. Some early models were linear—that is, communication was conceived of as a one-way process (Figure 1.1). According to a **linear model of communication,** a speaker sends a message to a listener who receives the message. The speaker's role, then, is to encode the message, and the listener's role is to decode it. **Encoding** is the process of putting ideas into symbols, in this case into words that the listener ought to understand. Conversely, **decoding** is the process of attaching meanings to the symbols we see or hear. For example, a child who tells his mother he is hungry is the sender of the message "I am hungry." The mother is the receiver. Although the communication occurs within a particular context, or **communication situation,** early scholars did not consider the situation to influence the interaction in any significant way.

Interactive

As communication scholars learned more about communication, they developed an **interactive model of communication.** This improved on the ideas expressed in the linear models, first by accounting for the feedback that receivers (listeners) return to senders, so that meaning is created by both (Figure 1.2). **Feedback**

Communication Situation

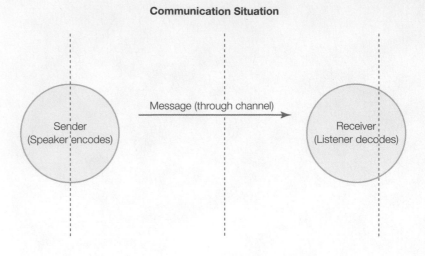

Message (through channel)

Sender
(Speaker encodes)

Receiver
(Listener decodes)

Figure 1.1   Linear model of
communication

consists of all those verbal and nonverbal messages receivers send back to senders during a communication interaction. Consider the hungry child and his mother again. If the mother responds with a comment like, "Oh, I didn't realize it was time for lunch already," she is giving verbal feedback. If she responds by shrugging her shoulders, it's nonverbal feedback.

An interactive model also accounts for internal and external interference. **Internal interference** is any distraction that originates in the thoughts of either participant. If the mother in the earlier scenario was worried about why her other child has such a high fever, that internal interference might distract her. **External interference** is any distraction that originates in the communication situation. If the telephone begins to ring during the conversation between the mother and her child, it is external interference. The communication situation is considered important in the interactive model primarily because external interference can arise in it. This two-way model of communication is more complete than the linear models, but is still limited.

Transactional

Recently, scholars developed a **transactional model of communication** to best describe the communication process. It expands on earlier models by accounting for the *simultaneous sending and receiving of messages* during a communication interaction as well as the *numerous ways in which the communication situation might influence the interaction*. During the conversation between mother and hungry child, for example, the mother's lack of eye contact and stern-looking facial expressions communicate messages at the same time her son is professing hunger. Likewise, her son might stomp his foot or pull on her arm while telling her he is hungry. All these messages occur simultaneously, and a transactional model accounts for the complexity.

To better understand the dynamics of the communication process, let's dissect this transactional model to discuss more fully each of its seven basic elements. These elements are the situation, the sender(s), the message(s), the receiver(s), the channel(s), the feedback, and the interference. Figure 1.3 illustrates this model. We'll look at each element as it operates generally in any communication interaction, as well as within the public speaking context specifically.

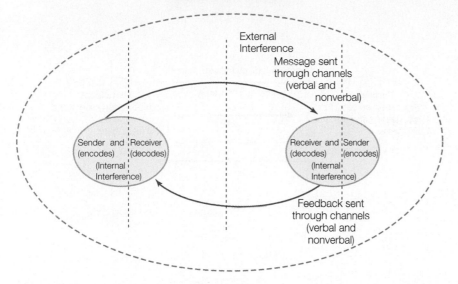

Communication Situation

External
Interference

Message sent
through channels
(verbal and
nonverbal)

Sender and | Receiver
(encodes) | (decodes)
(Internal
Interference)

Receiver and | Sender
(decodes) | (encodes)
(Internal
Interference)

Feedback sent
through channels
(verbal and
nonverbal)

Figure 1.2 Interactive
model of communication

Finally, we'll highlight goals public speakers ought to strive for based on the potential implications each element might have on the success of their message.

THE SEVEN BASIC ELEMENTS OF THE COMMUNICATION PROCESS

Situation

The situation is the place, time, occasion, and cultural context of the communication. The *place* of communication might be your home, office, car or bus, the park, a restaurant, or a classroom. The *time* might be early in the morning, late at night, right before class, or right after lunch. It might be Monday morning, Friday evening, or Saturday afternoon. And the *occasion* might be a board meeting, a social gathering, a special occasion such as a birthday or anniversary, or a ceremonial occasion such as a wedding, graduation, or funeral. These situational factors are all influenced by the *cultural context*. Culture has to do with the attitudes, beliefs, and values shared by a group, as well as their informal rules for behavior. The cultural context is important for public speakers to consider because it governs certain communication rules as we speak. We discuss cultural context in more detail in Chapter 6.

Considering the Situation

The communication situation is important because it can either help your message or hurt it. The kind of speech most appropriate for a graduation ceremony is not the same kind that ought to be presented at a funeral. Likewise, how you deliver a public speech in an outdoor amphitheater or large auditorium should probably differ from the way you do it in a small classroom. Even in the classroom, the arrangement of the furniture; number of listeners; time of day, week, or year; and context of recent events may potentially affect your success. How? Consider delivering your speech to classmates sitting in a circle rather than in a conventional classroom arrangement. How might they become more easily distracted

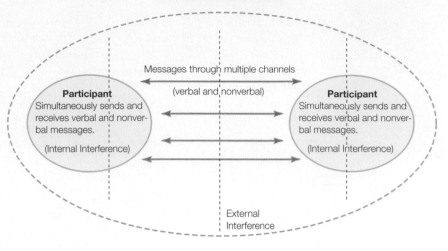

Communication Situation

Messages through multiple channels
(verbal and nonverbal)

Participant
Simultaneously sends and receives verbal and nonverbal messages.

(Internal Interference)

Participant
Simultaneously sends and receives verbal and nonverbal messages.

(Internal Interference)

External Interference

Figure 1.3 Transactional model of communication

from the message? How might a small and overcrowded classroom affect the attention span of listeners?

Considering Communication Rules

You need to determine the communication rules for a situation and then modify your message or the situation to allow you to adhere to the rules. **Communication rules** are guides for what is appropriate in a given place, time, occasion, and cultural context. These rules are implicit rather than explicit and thus are best determined by considering how you would react if you were the receiver of the communication.

Communication rules vary by culture. For example, I was recently introduced to a colleague from Kenya. As a friendly gesture, I asked him how many children he had. I later learned that my question would be inappropriate in Kenya, because referring to children in numbers devalues them as the unique God-given gifts they are believed to be. Cultural context can be global or conceived within the boundaries of a nation. A cultural group can be defined by age, race, ethnicity, gender, ability/disability, sexual orientation, geographic location, socioeconomic status, marital status, career, and religious beliefs when these dimensions shape an identifiable worldview. Thus the U.S. population might best be characterized as multicultural. For example, upon graduating with my bachelor's degree I landed a position that took me from a rural community in Minnesota to inner-city Detroit. I learned quickly that the communication rules of rural Minnesota were not necessarily appropriate in this urban setting. Among other things, avoiding eye contact when passing people I did not know in the city was better than smiling and saying "hi" to everyone.

Once you've determined the communication rules inherent in a situation, you might decide to modify the situation or the message. For example, in our culture you probably wouldn't talk with a close friend or family member about a serious personal conflict while having dinner in a restaurant with a group of business associates. You might modify the situation by waiting until you and your partner are alone to discuss the issue or, if you felt compelled to address it at the restaurant, you might modify the message to depersonalize it, making it a general statement not obviously connected to your partner.

When giving a public speech, you might also modify the situation or your message to adhere to communication rules. For example, if asked to introduce yourself in a classroom speech, beware of being too personal in discussing your lifestyle or background. I once had a student who told the class about his recent suicide attempt during such an introductory speech. That did not adhere to the communication rules for the situation. He could have modified the speech by talking about his background and lifestyle more generally. (If he felt compelled to talk about the suicide attempt as a plea for counseling, he could have modified the situation by talking with me individually after class or during my office hours.)

Sender

The sender is the person who initiates the communication. Although both sender and receiver(s) send verbal and nonverbal messages simultaneously, in public speaking the sender is the one who presents the actual speech. To be effective the speaker/sender must convey ethos. **Ethos,** in this sense meaning speaker credibility based on perceived competence and character, was originally conceived of more than 2,000 years ago by the Greek philosopher Aristotle. Because listeners often have a difficult time separating the message from the sender, good ideas can easily be discounted if the sender does not establish ethos via content, delivery, and structure. Conversely, weak ideas can seem more compelling when offered by a speaker who conveys ethos. For example, some critics argue that Ronald Reagan's ethos allowed him to make any idea sound good, whether or not it actually was. But Jesse Ventura was elected governor of Minnesota at least partly because the Republican and Democratic candidates unwisely disregarded him as a viable opponent, thinking that he lacked ethos. In the classroom, a student who presents a well-researched, structured, and delivered speech is likely to be more successful than one who does not, simply due to the ethos exhibited. Your goal as a public speaker is to convince listeners of your credibility. You can do this by stating your purpose clearly, conveying relevant knowledge about the topic, and portraying a positive self-concept while speaking.

WHAT DO YOU THINK?
Identify a speaker you heard who was really good. What did that speaker look like and act like? How did this contribute to your perception of the speaker's credibility?

PRACTICING THE PROCESS

Checklist for Conveying Ethos as a Public Speaker

☐ Look good. (Dress up.)
☐ Feel good. (Get plenty of rest and nutrition.)
☐ Sound good. (Research, organize, and rehearse.)

Message

The message is the ideas the sender (speaker) conveys to the receiver (listener). Listeners combine what they hear and see to determine the message. In other words, the message is not only what you say but also how you say it. The words you choose, the way you arrange them, the inflection of your voice, your posture and gestures, your facial expressions, your eye contact, and the presentational aids you integrate all are important contributors to the message.

For effective public speaking, make sure all of these messages fit together—that they all say what you want to say. Your nonverbal messages must emotionally or structurally reinforce your intended verbal message, making it more compelling to listeners. Do not send nonverbal messages—such as fidgeting, pacing, or playing with your glasses, hair, or notes—that distract from the verbal message. If listeners watch your distracting nonverbal messages rather than listen to what you have to say, your intended message is likely to be blocked. Also, avoid sending nonverbal messages that contradict the intent of your verbal message; don't slouch, sound or look bored, or keep your eyes focused on the floor or on your notes. Such nonverbal messages contradict the verbal message, and listeners will likely believe the nonverbal messages rather than the verbal one.

PRACTICING THE PROCESS

Guidelines for Safeguarding Your Message

- Choose your words wisely.
- Organize your ideas clearly.
- Stand up tall.
- Look at your listeners as you speak.
- Use gestures to reinforce key points or to clarify structure.
- Avoid fidgeting or playing with your glasses, hair, or notes.

Receiver(s)

The receiver is the listener, the person to whom the sender is communicating. Unfortunately, the speaker's intended message is not always what is received. We've already learned how nonverbal behavior can influence the message. It is also influenced by the receiver's frame of reference. Everything the speaker says and does is filtered through the listener's **frame of reference,** made up of his or her goals, knowledge, experiences, values, and attitudes.

Audience Analysis

No two people have identical frames of reference, but sometimes members of an audience share certain characteristics. Thus effective public speakers do two things: They appeal to the range of diversity represented in any audience and they

adapt their messages to the particular audience. This requires being audience centered, which is accomplished by audience analysis. **Audience analysis** is the process of finding out who your listeners are and then adapting your speech to make it relevant to their interests and desires. For example, if you present a speech about fire safety to a group of second graders, you might focus on the concept of stop, drop, and roll. But a talk on the same topic with the tenants in your apartment complex might better focus on where to place smoke alarms and fire extinguishers, how to test them, and how to use them effectively. Both speeches are on the same topic, adapted to be relevant to each audience.

The first goal cannot be emphasized enough. The United States is becoming ever more culturally diverse, to the point that it has been called the "first universal nation" (Wattenberg, 1991). To be on the safe side, assume that it is. In this way, you will make sure you're not appealing to too narrow a range and, more important, you will avoid the possibility of unintentionally offending or marginalizing listeners. **Marginalization** occurs when speakers discuss a topic from a majority perspective as though that perspective is the only legitimate one. It excludes some audience members from the exchange because their perspective is ignored as irrelevant or even nonexistent. As you prepare your speech, do not assume listeners' customs and beliefs are the same as yours. Show respect for other cultures and beliefs, and avoid **ethnocentrism**, the tendency to assume the values and beliefs of one's own culture are somehow better than those of other cultures.

Audience diversity is not just cultural. Failing to take into account diversity in sex, gender, and sexual preference also can marginalize listeners, for example. Consider Jim, who gave a speech on Elton John. At several points Jim sheepishly commented that Elton John was his role model because of his musical talent, *not* because of his sexual preference. Quite likely Jim's repeated comment offended or marginalized someone in his audience (*New York Times*, 1994). Or consider Luke, who gave a speech about collecting baseball cards. He exclaimed, "I don't know if many of the gals will be interested in this hobby, but I'll bet most of you guys will find it interesting." This offended some of the women in the class. Sexist language can also serve to exclude. Talking about the importance of fire fighters but repeatedly referring to them as *firemen*, for example, excludes women and may offend some listeners. Effective public speakers strive to use inclusive language, avoid ethnocentrism, and respect diversity.

Learning Styles and Audience Analysis

Another form of diversity to keep in mind is **learning style,** a person's preferred way of receiving information. If you vary the ways you present ideas, you address this diversity in your audience and thus are more effective. A number of

---

WHAT DO YOU THINK?

Were you raised in a city, in a suburb, in a small town, or on a farm?

Are you married? Single? Divorced? Widowed?

Do you have children? Grandchildren? If not, do you plan to have them someday?

What are your religious beliefs?

What are your career aspirations?

Do you belong to a political party? Why or why not?

Your answers to these questions reveal part of your personal frame of reference, which influences how you interpret messages.

scholars across disciplines have developed models for understanding learning styles (e.g., Barbe & Swassing, 1979; Canfield, 1980; Dunn, Dunn, & Price, 1975; Gardner, 1983; Kolb, 1984; McCarthy, 1980; Renzulli & Smith, 1978). One comprehensive model points out that, although most people have a preferred learning style, all people learn most effectively when ideas are presented in ways that round the entire cycle of learning (Kolb, 1984).

The learning process can be conceived as a four-stage cycle of feeling, watching, thinking, and doing (Figure 1.4). All people learn best when they move through all four stages because they are able to understand, retain, and apply the ideas and concepts offered. This means you should address all four stages in every public speech you present. Consider how your speech addresses each stage when organizing ideas, developing content, choosing supporting material, preparing presentational aids, and rehearsing delivery. Effective public speakers round the entire cycle of learning because it increases their likelihood of success.

People grasp ideas in particular ways, some relying more on one stage than on others. This reflects their preferred learning style. Your preferred learning style is likely to differ from that of many audience members, but make sure you prepare and present speeches that address all four stages of the learning process. Know what your preference is so that you won't overly favor it when presenting information to other people, whose preferred ways of learning may be different from yours.

The Stages of the Learning Cycle

Stage 1 of the cycle focuses on a combination of feeling and watching. If your preferred learning style falls in this stage, your strengths are imagination and the ability to view concrete situations, experiences, and examples from many perspectives. You enjoy brainstorming lots of ideas and hearing lots of concrete examples. You probably have broad cultural interests and like to gather information. You enjoy making personal connections with ideas and concepts. If you enjoy classroom experiences that focus on discussion more than lecture or activities, you might prefer Stage 1. In public speaking you are likely to prefer inductive organizational patterns and reasoning; listener relevance links focused on where things discussed in the speech have occurred; speaker credibility based on the speaker's experiences; supporting material focused on vivid descriptions and concrete examples as well as personal testimonies; presentational aids; rhetorical appeals to emotions; vivid and emotionally charged language; and vocally and visually expressive delivery. If your learning style preference does not fall in this stage, these items may not seem compelling at all (those with a Stage 3 preference are most likely to overlook Stage 1 when preparing speeches). It is still important to include these elements in your speech, however, not only to appeal to listeners with a Stage 1 preference but also because rounding the cycle of learning maximizes comprehension, retention, and application by all.

Stage 2 focuses on a combination of thinking and watching. If this is your preferred learning style, you are good at putting a wide range of information into logical, orderly form. You also enjoy critiquing the ideas of others. My mom, for example, tends to prefer Stage 2. She likes to make lists for everything—parties, vacations, groceries. She also likes to critique my ideas. For example, when I discussed how I planned to remodel my kitchen, she was quick to point out the cupboard space I would lose and how I should modify my plan to regain some. Public speakers who favor Stage 2 are likely to prefer very clear deductive organizational patterns and parallel structure; supporting material and visual aids that focus on facts, statistics, definitions, expert opinions, and detailed explanations; rhetorical

Student Workbook

Complete the Learning Styles readings and quiz in Chapter 2 of your workbook. Which dimensions do you prefer? Which dimensions will you need to make a special effort to include in your speeches and how?

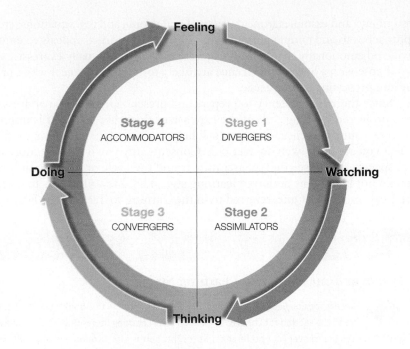

Figure 1.4   Kolb's cycle of learning

appeals to logic; language that focuses on accuracy and clarity; and intelligible delivery. If this is not your preference, be sure to include these elements not necessarily because doing so accounts for those with this learning style preference, but because doing so rounds the cycle of learning for everyone. Those with a Stage 4 preference are most likely to overlook Stage 2 when developing speeches.

Stage 3 focuses on a combination of thinking and doing. If this is your preferred learning style, your strengths are problem solving, decision making, and the practical application of ideas. You like to find the single best answer to a problem and to find it through deductive reasoning. You would rather deal with technical tasks than social or interpersonal issues and enjoy testing theories to see if they really work. If you cringe when faced with classroom experiences that focus on discussion more than lecture or applications, you might prefer Stage 3. You are likely to prefer speeches organized using a deductive pattern and deductive reasoning. You probably prefer clearly articulated plans for applying concepts and theories to real-life situations, and supporting material and presentational aids that focus on hands-on experiences, practical applications, experimentation, and results; rhetorical appeals to logic; language that strives for accuracy and clarity; and intelligible delivery. Those with a Stage 1 preference are most likely to overlook this stage when preparing and presenting their speeches and must take care to address it in order to effectively round the cycle.

Stage 4 focuses on a combination of doing and feeling. If this is your preferred learning style, your greatest strengths are carrying out plans and tasks, discovering hidden possibilities, taking risks, and getting involved in new experiences. You prefer input and information from other people to help solve problems and are good at synthesizing it. My Stage 2 mother has a Stage 4 daughter; I rarely make lists for anything and rarely stick to them when I do. That's not to say lists are bad—I can think of times when I've made return trips to the grocery store because I didn't use a list. In terms of public speaking, Stage 4 adherents are usually open to a variety of organizational patterns and types of reasoning. They enjoy hands-on experimentation; supporting material and presentational aids that rely on personal testimonies and examples from a variety of real people and real situations; creative approaches to and unique perspectives on topics; rhetorical appeals to emotion; vivid and emotionally charged language; and vocally and visually expressive delivery. Those with a Stage 2 preference are likely to overlook Stage 4 when preparing and presenting their speeches.

Since there is a tendency to prepare and present speeches that address one's own preferred learning style at the expense of the other stages, it is important to know your preference. Doing so will help you see which stage you prefer and which you are most likely to overlook. Consequently you'll prepare more effective speeches because you'll consciously round the cycle of learning in them. If you do not know your preferred learning style, take a few moments to complete the Learning Styles Quiz, referred to in the Turning to Technology box.

Consider how Barry rounded the cycle of learning in his informative speech about shamans (medicine men among certain North American Indians). He prefers Stage 2, so he took care to offer something to address Stage 4 as well. Before he knew his own preference, he rarely offered testimonials or demonstrated applications in his speeches. This time, though, he offered testimonials and true stories to appeal to those who prefer to learn through feeling (Stage 1 and Stage 4). He engaged the group in a simple massage technique used to eliminate headaches to appeal to those who prefer to learn by doing (Stage 3 and Stage 4). He showed some of the herbs used in healing to appeal to those who prefer to learn by watching (Stage 1 and Stage 2). And he organized his speech systematically, using a clear preview, transitions, and summary to appeal to those who prefer to learn by thinking (Stage 2 and Stage 3).

WHAT DO YOU THINK?
What type of classroom experiences do you prefer? What type do you detest? What does this tell you about your learning stage preferences?

Looking at the Learning Cycle

Try to Not Overlook Others' Preferred Learning Styles

Which learning style stage do you prefer? What stage are you likely to ignore when preparing and presenting your speeches? How will you go about addressing it?

Channels

Channels are the pathways through which messages are communicated between sender and receiver. Oral communication uses multiple channels; however, the most common channels are the auditory channel and the visual channel. The **visual channel** is what the receivers see. Messages sent via the visual channel include eye contact, facial expressions, posture, gestures, and appearance, as well as visual aids such as objects, diagrams, charts, graphs, and sketches. Madeleine, who brought her dream catcher to show the class as she discussed its construction, used the visual channel. The **auditory channel** is what the listeners hear—that is, the words chosen to convey the message as well as the manner in which it is said (that is, inflection, rate, voice quality, and tone). When Martin Luther King, Jr., repeated the phrase, "I have a dream," in slightly different ways throughout his now famous speech, he was using the auditory channel. Your goal as a public speaker is to use these channels in ways that complement and reinforce each other to better ensure that listeners interpret the meaning in the way you intended.

Feedback

The creation of shared meaning would not be possible without feedback. Because the communication transaction consists of the simultaneous sending and receiving of multiple messages, feedback can come from both the sender and the receiver. In the public speaking context, however, feedback generally goes from receiver to sender—that is, messages that listeners send back to a speaker about the clarity and acceptability of the speech. Feedback might come in written or oral form, but it is usually conveyed via facial expression, eye contact, and body language.

Your goal as a public speaker is to interpret listener feedback and adjust your message accordingly. Sometimes your general purpose is to inform your listeners about a topic. In that case, you might adjust your message based on feedback that seems to indicate a lack of understanding. For example, as Jack tries to explain how to complete a financial aid application, he notices quizzical looks on the faces of several listeners. Before moving on, he explains the procedure again in another way. Jack interpreted the feedback (quizzical looks) and rephrased his ideas before moving on. Other times, your general purpose is to persuade others to agree with you about an issue or a course of action to be taken. If you are attempting to convince your listeners to join a fraternity, you might watch for encouraging facial expressions and head nods as you proceed. Such feedback indicates that your persuasion is succeeding with at least some listeners.

Interference

Interference is any barrier to the communication transaction. External or internal interference distracts listeners from the message. External interference refers to barriers occurring outside the speaker or listener, and may be auditory or visual. For example, your stereo is external auditory interference when it distracts you from what your roommate is saying. In the classroom, external *auditory* interference may be a result of loud fans, classmates whispering among themselves, traffic outside, an airplane flying overhead, or people talking in the hallway. External *visual* interference may occur when a classmate enters the room while you are presenting your speech, when a police officer makes an arrest outside your classroom window, or when audience members are passing notes.

It is not always possible to eliminate external interference, but effective public speakers attempt to reduce its potential impact. They might close the classroom door to reduce the level of noise coming from the hallway, speak louder above the noise of fans, or pause as the airplane flies over. Good speakers also modify their delivery to reduce the potential for internal interference, which may be physical or psychological and may occur within the speaker as well as within the listeners. Perhaps one of your listeners has a distracting headache, is worried

Student Workbook

Read the section preceding and do the library assignment in Chapter 2 of your workbook.

about a test coming up next period, or is looking forward to lunch. As the speaker, you may also experience internal interference. You may have stayed up late rehearsing the speech and your resulting fatigue may cause you to lose your concentration. Or you may be worrying about what you look or sound like to your listeners instead of focusing on your message.

Effective public speakers consider each element of the transactional model of communication and how it might help or hurt their presentation. They seek to adapt their message to the communication situation and audience, offer their ideas using multiple channels, read and adjust to feedback, and limit the potential of external and internal interference that can impede listeners' understanding.

ETHICAL PUBLIC SPEAKING

ETHICS

Kathie Lee Gifford is a generally respected television celebrity. Through the years, her popularity has resulted in other kinds of recognition as well. For example, she has sponsored different products, such as Carnival Cruise Line and Wal-Mart clothing. But later she was scorned by many fans because she endorsed her own line of apparel at Wal-Mart. Why? Because her adoring public learned that some Wal-Mart clothing was said to be produced in sweatshops. By endorsing the clothing, many of Kathie Lee's fans believed she also endorsed Wal-Mart's "unfair" business practices. Although she announced publicly that she was unaware of Wal-Mart's use of sweatshops, she had already been labeled unethical. Consequently, she would spend years proving to her fans that she is actually ethical and worthy of their respect.

The question of what constitutes ethical behavior also pervades popular culture. Movies like *The Truman Show* ask viewers to consider the degree of rightness or wrongness in controlling someone's experiences without the person's knowledge, even if doing so is somehow deemed to be for the individual's own good. Television cartoons like *The Simpsons* and *South Park* also focus on ethical issues, such as when it is okay to lie, harass someone in the name of humor, or even kill (as happens to Kenny in each episode of *South Park*). Contemporary music lyrics often focus on ethical issues such as when it is okay to lie, cheat, steal, and even kill or commit suicide. But what is ethical behavior?

Effective public speakers do more than sound good and be convincing. They also make wise ethical choices. Adolf Hitler was a very successful public speaker who convinced millions to fight for a cause, but few would contend that he was ethical because the cause was reprehensible and the tactics he espoused were despicable. In the 1990s, the NATO decision to use military force to stop Slobodan Milosevic's ethnic cleansing in Yugoslavia was rooted in similar concerns. And even more recently, the decision made by the United States and Great Britain to engage in war with Iraq has been questioned by individuals within each nation as well as other countries in the United Nations. Obviously, achieving your goal is not all there is to being an effective public speaker. You must also be ethical.

ETHICS

Ethics refers to principles about what is right and wrong, moral and immoral, honest and dishonest, fair and unfair (Johannesen, 1990; Nilsen, 1974; Wallace, 1955). Ethical choices differ from legal choices. Laws are rules by which we *must* abide; ethics are rules by which we *ought to* abide. Breaking a law warrants a certain punishment. If you are pulled over for driving faster than the speed limit, for example, you understand that you will have to pay a fine or go to court. A speed limit is a law. If you choose to break it, you know you may be punished.

Ethical choices, on the other hand, have no direct legal ramifications. They are guided instead by your values, conscience, sense of justice, and sense of fairness.

Credible arguments usually exist on both sides of an ethical issue, so you must choose between options that may result in both positive and negative implications for you and for others involved. In essence, my interpretation about the degree of ethical rightness or wrongness in a certain behavior might differ from yours, as well as from others in the room. Whether to spank children is a question of ethics. Whether we should clone living beings, whether television violence should be censored, and whether to tell the whole truth are all questions of ethics.

Because ethical judgments focus on degrees of rightness or wrongness in human behavior, no universal list of ethical standards exists. There are, however, general ethical codes of conduct based on some basic virtues. These virtues can be summarized as, first, demonstrating respect for ourselves and for others. In other words, we ought to conduct ourselves in ways that are tactful, civil, and sensitive to the needs, concerns, and beliefs of others. The second basic virtue that guides most ethical decisions is honesty: We ought to be truthful about our opinions, truthful in reporting information, and truthful about our feelings. Sometimes honesty and demonstrating respect seem to be in conflict. For example, when my daughter was quite young she baked me a birthday cake, but forgot to include a couple of ingredients. When she asked me how it tasted, how was I to respond? I really wanted her to know that I respected her efforts. But could I do that if I was completely honest?

These virtues also provide a basis for making ethical judgments as a public speaker and listener. (We focus here on several strategies for ethical public speaking; strategies for ethical listening are addressed in Chapter 1.) You can measure yourself as an ethical public speaker by considering five key criteria throughout the speechmaking process:

- Considering your topic and goals
- Acknowledging personal biases
- Choosing evidence
- Reporting sources of information
- Conveying your ideas orally

WHAT DO YOU THINK?

Consider a time when you chose to tell a close friend only part of the story about something you had experienced. If honesty is the best policy, why did you decide not to tell the whole truth?

ETHICS

WHAT DO YOU THINK?

Has a friend or loved one ever asked you how a favorite outfit looks on them when it doesn't really look good at all? How did you respond? Were you able to be both honest and respectful? Why or why not?

TURNING TO TECHNOLOGY

The Code of Ethics for Communication

http://www.natcom.org/conferences/Ethics/ethicsconfcredo99/htm

Consider the guidelines for ethical communication offered at this Web site. Which do you believe to be most important and why? Are there any you disagree with? If so, why?

Considering Your Topic and Goals

Think carefully about your speech topic in relation to yourself and to your listeners. What are you hoping to accomplish? Do you have a thorough knowledge of the subject and relevant issues related to it? How is it relevant to your listeners? What are the potential implications of your message? Is it something you believe in strongly yourself?

ETHICS

Ethical speakers select topics that matter to them. If you are going to persuade listeners to recycle, for example, you ought to care about recycling and do it yourself. But the selected topic must also matter to listeners. Make sure your speech will be *relevant* to your listeners and give them new insight. Talking about how to properly address envelopes is probably not an ethically sound choice if college students are your audience because most of them already know how to do so; thus your information isn't new. If you could demonstrate some new way to address envelopes, say for priority mail or express mail or delivery confirmation, your information might be new after all. Ethical speakers strive to ensure that listeners will go away from the speech better off for having heard it. Finally, you ought to have a *thorough knowledge* of your topic. This means researching and thoroughly thinking about your topic and the issues related to it. To check the completeness of your knowledge, ask yourself, "Can I answer honestly, without evasion, any relevant question a listener might ask?" If you can answer yes, you have satisfied this criterion.

Acknowledging Personal Biases

ETHICS

Ethical public speakers acknowledge their own motivations or biases with regard to the topic. For example, if you present a speech about drunk driving and have been the victim of a drunk driving accident yourself, say so up front. Or if you hope to persuade listeners that Chevrolet makes a better truck than Ford and you work for Chevrolet, you ought to acknowledge that. Listeners have the right to know if you have a bias or a personal investment in your topic. Acknowledging bias demonstrates respect and honesty. Likewise, if you share testimony from someone whose opinion may influence the way listeners should consider the information, admit it openly and honestly. Don't assume that not telling listeners won't hurt anything. If listeners figure out these biases on their own, they will lose respect for you as an ethical public speaker.

Choosing Evidence

ETHICS

Ethical public speakers select and present facts and opinions related to the topic fairly and accurately. Don't distort or conceal information that the audience ought to know in order to make a fair judgment. Consider the tobacco industry, which chose to conceal facts about the addictive nature of nicotine in cigarettes by framing their arguments in terms of individual rights to exercise free choice, avoiding the issue of whether choice can exist with regard to an addictive additive. This ambiguous message strategy, born of the industry's decision to place profit over social responsibility, is an example of unethical communication with regard to the fair and accurate reporting of information (Ulmer & Sellnow, 1997).

It is also important to consider the credibility of your sources of information. You can determine source credibility by asking yourself if it is relevant, impartial, and recent. If your speech is about smoking and health, the *American Journal of Medicine* would probably be more relevant than *Consumer Reports*. This is not to say you cannot cite *Consumer Reports* if it published an article about smoking and health; however, it is not a publication closely tied to health issues. Conversely, if attempting to persuade listeners to purchase the best-quality appliance for the price, *Consumer Reports* would be more relevant than the *American Journal of Medicine*.

Even if you are attempting to convince listeners that smoking is *not* addictive, the tobacco industry would not be the most credible source on which to rely because it has a vested interest in sales and profit, meaning its information about

the issue may be biased. To be ethical, consider the sources you select in terms of how impartial they may or may not be with regard to your topic.

Also consider how recently the information was released. A 1976 source on smoking and health may not be as accurate as one published in 1999. Depending on the topic, recency may be an important consideration when choosing your evidence.

To be ethical, you also ought to demonstrate respect for diverse opinions and opposing arguments raised in the research. Acknowledge opposing evidence and opinions even as you advocate your side of the argument. In this way, ethical communication fosters free and informed choice. In a speech supporting spanking as ethical, for example, a speaker can acknowledge research suggesting that spanking can harm a parent-child bond. Rather than avoid mentioning opposing arguments, the speaker might talk about them in relation to age appropriateness (spanking might be appropriate when confined to children between the ages of eighteen months and six years old, for instance). Some research suggests that spanking can be okay for young children and in addition to other methods of discipline (for example, "time-outs" or removal of certain privileges).

WHAT DO YOU THINK?
Consider a news report you've heard recently that seemed to leave you with more questions than answers. In what ways might knowing those answers have been important to you?

To check your fairness in reporting information, ask, "In the selection and presentation of materials, am I giving my audience the opportunity to make fair judgments?" Make sure you can say yes.

Reporting Sources of Information

Ethical public speakers reveal the sources of information or opinions drawn from others. Always avoid **plagiarism,** the act of presenting another person's ideas as your own. Plagiarism is plagiarism whether it is intentional or not, and claiming you didn't realize you were plagiarizing does not change the fact that you were. In its most blatant form, plagiarism occurs when you present a speech written by someone else, passing it off as though it were your own. For example, two students once presented the same speech in different sections of a public speaking fundamentals course. One student had composed the speech and the other had plagiarized it. But if the first student knew the other was plagiarizing, both acted unethically.

ETHICS

More often speakers plagiarize by presenting paragraphs, sentences, or even phrases as their own ideas, or by summarizing or paraphrasing other people's ideas without citation. Even these forms of plagiarism can damage your reputation. During the 1987 presidential primaries, for example, Democratic Senator Joseph Biden used passages from speeches by John F. Kennedy and Hubert Humphrey; he eventually had to withdraw his candidacy as a result (Coffey, 1987; Kaus, 1987).

At this point you might be wondering how you can avoid plagiarizing when your speech requires the use of external sources. Cite the sources of information as oral footnotes during the presentation, and as internal references and in a reference list accompanying a written formal outline. **Oral footnotes** are brief references to the original source of information, cited at the point in the speech where the information is given. For example, you might say, "According to an article by James C. Cooper and Kathleen Madigan in the July 29, 2003 issue of *Business Week*, Alan Greenspan's number one concern regarding economic recovery is corporate America's reluctance to spend." Just as you cite information within the text of a written composition (footnotes) as well as in the reference list at the end of the manuscript (references), you also cite reference material orally during your speech as well as in the text of the formal outline you develop. A formal outline is available to the audience upon request, and the attached reference list provides full bibliographic information on the sources cited in the oral presentation. Together the oral footnotes and reference list function just like the footnotes and reference list you would include in a written paper. They give listeners enough information to look up the sources themselves.

Conveying Ideas Orally

ETHICS

Ethical public speakers demonstrate respect for their audience when presenting a message by rehearsing delivery, using inclusive and tactful language, and conveying ideas in ways that round the cycle of learning. Consider times when you have listened to someone who was disorganized, boring, or unprepared. Did you go away feeling respected or disrespected? Ethical speakers respect their audience's time by offering messages that are organized effectively and presented fluently.

Ethical speakers also respect their audience by using inclusive and respectful language. Terms that exclude or defame certain groups should be avoided. For example, referring to mail carriers and police officers as "mailmen" and "policemen" would exclude women, as would using the generic "he" to represent everyone. Ethical public speakers avoid racist, sexist, ageist, and other kinds of abusive language, not just because avoiding such language is politically correct but because it is ethically correct.

WHAT DO YOU THINK?

Consider a speaker you've heard who seemed disrespectful. Why? Ethical speakers demonstrate respect for their audience.

Finally, ethical speakers respect their audience by presenting ideas in ways that address a variety of preferred learning styles. Recall that this means understanding your own preferred learning style and then preparing and presenting public speeches so that they address the other learning styles as well. To do so, you must use a variety of different supporting material; multiple rhetorical appeals; clear, accurate, inclusive, and vivid language; vocally and visually intelligible and expressive delivery; and clear and systematic organization. Ask yourself, "If I were a member of my audience, would I be compelled to listen to my speech?" If you are able to answer yes, you have satisfied this criterion of an ethical speaker.

Ethical communication is, at the core, a simple concept. It simply means respecting the other participants in the communication transaction. In practice, however, it requires conscious effort and strategic choices on the five criteria just discussed. Ethical communication is simple, but not always easy.

PRACTICING THE PROCESS

Questions Ethical Speakers Must Be Able to Answer

ETHICS

- Can I answer honestly any relevant question a listener is likely to ask?
- Have I acknowledged my personal motivations or biases regarding this topic?
- In the selection and presentation of materials, am I giving my audience the opportunity to make fair judgments?
- Have I acknowledged the sources of my information throughout the speech?
- If I were a member of my audience, would I be compelled to listen to my speech?

Even when protesting, you should use respectful language if you want to be an ethical communicator.

© David Wells/The Image Works

SUMMARY

This chapter explored a number of reasons for improving your public speaking skills, defined and explained the process of communication as it relates to public speaking, and illustrated what it means to be an ethical public speaker. It provides grounding for the remaining chapters as you continue to refine your skills in developing and presenting effective public speeches. First, we answered the question, "Why study public speaking?" We did so by considering benefits to you in your personal relationships, college education, and professional career. Second, we defined communication as the process of sending and receiving verbal and nonverbal messages to create shared meaning. We discussed the evolution of the models of communication as they explain this dynamic process. Finally, we explored what it means to be an ethical public speaker. We defined ethics as principles about what is right and wrong, moral and immoral, honest and dishonest, fair and unfair. These principles are based on our conceptions of human virtues such as respect and honesty. We focused on five key criteria that must be considered in order to be ethical. These include (a) considering the topic and goal, (b) acknowledging personal biases, (c) choosing evidence, (d) reporting sources of information, and (e) conveying ideas orally. We concluded that ethical public speakers demonstrate respect for other participants in the communication transaction. Ethical communication is essentially a simple concept, but it is not easy.

The *Confident Public Speaking* CD-ROM is your one-stop point of access for not just the content on the CD itself, such as Speech Interactive, but also the many other resources on the *Confident Public Speaking* Web site, Speech Builder Express, and InfoTrac College Edition. Note that this chapter's key terms and activities are among the resources available in electronic format online. Additional information is included below.

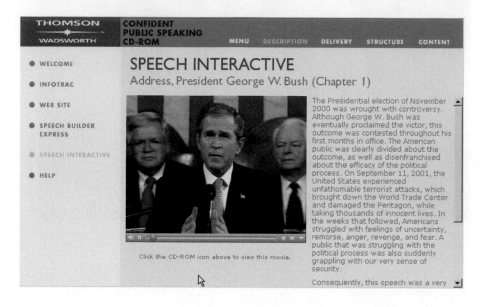

SPEECH INTERACTIVE
ON THE *CONFIDENT PUBLIC SPEAKING* CD-ROM

Speech Interactive is your link to this text's speech videos. Offering opportunities to practice critiquing speeches by students and other public speakers, these videos will help you prepare for providing effective feedback to your peers and evaluating your own speech performances.

SPEECH BUILDER EXPRESS

Access Speech Builder Express and set up your new student account so that you will be able to use this speech preparation tool. You will be asked to choose a user name and a password. Be sure to keep a record of the name and password that you enter; you might also want to check that you do want the program to remember your password when the password dialog box pops up. After setting up your account, explore the program by reading the introductory screens for starting a new speech and familiarizing yourself with the top and left-hand navigation buttons.

KEY TERMS

Interactive flashcards for these key terms are available on the *Confident Public Speaking* Web site. You'll find the "Flashcards" link under the resources for Chapter 1

ACTIVITIES

The activities below, as well as additional activities for this chapter, are available in electronic format on the *Confident Public Speaking* Web site. You'll find the "Activities" link under the resources for Chapter 1.

1. **Public Speaking Portfolio.** Purchase a composition notebook and begin documenting your experiences and growth as a public speaker throughout the course. Start by developing a one- to two-page paper articulating your communication goals for this semester. Eventually your portfolio will include (a) speech outlines, instructor evaluations, self and peer critiques for each speech you present in class; (b) a reflective question journal responding to the questions posed at the beginning of each chapter; and (c) other written assignments you complete throughout the semester.

2. **Interview a Professional.** Set up an interview with a personnel director from a company in your community. Ask the personnel director what the company looks for most in job applicants. What does the company look for on a résumé, in a cover letter, during an interview? How important is oral communication skill compared to other skills, including proficiency in one's field of study, technical skill, and academic achievement?

3. **Communication Process Analysis.** After having a conversation with a friend or family member, take a few minutes to write about it in your journal or draw a picture of what occurred using the transactional model of communication as a framework. What messages and feedback were being sent? What channels were employed? What forms of interference occurred? How did these elements influence the ultimate success of shared message creation?

4. **Determining Your Preferred Learning Style.** As was discussed in the chapter, everyone learns best by moving through all four stages of the learning cycle. Yet each of us tends to prefer one stage over the others (Kolb, 1984). This is what is referred to as your preferred learning style. To determine your preferred learning style, complete this twelve-point learning styles quiz. You can complete the Learning Styles Inventory on-line at the *Sellnow Connection* Web site at the Wadsworth Communication Café and in your Student Workbook.

INFOTRAC COLLEGE EDITION ACTIVITY

Locate and read one of the following three articles that include information about the need for communication, specifically public speaking skills, in the workplace: "A New Roadmap for Professional Advancement" by Richard J. Henley, "Are You a 'Great Communicator'?" by Peter Varhol, or "Don't Doubt Your Speaking Potential" by Roger Allen. (Hint: Use "career skills" as your search term.) Compare what you read with the public speaking skills you might need in your chosen career. Now, search InfoTrac College Edition to learn about the role of public speaking in your chosen career. You will probably want to search by the name of the career field (for example, nursing, mechanical engineering, agriculture, and so on). Take notes about what you find.

COPING EFFECTIVELY WITH PUBLIC SPEAKING ANXIETY

REFLECTIVE QUESTIONS

1. How would you define communication apprehension? Do you think a person can experience more than one form of communication apprehension? Why or why not?

2. What fears can lead to negative self-talk? Where might each come from?

3. What strategies can you think of that might help manage public speaking anxiety? Describe one situation in which such a strategy would have lessened your own or someone else's public speaking anxiety.

4. How might the way you breathe increase or decrease public speaking anxiety?

5. What negative self-talk do you engage in when faced with presenting a public speech and what positive coping statement could you replace it with?

WHAT'S AHEAD: FOCUSING YOUR READING

What Is Communication Apprehension?

Why Do We Experience Public Speaking Anxiety?

What Can Be Done to Reduce Anxiety?

L INDA HATES TO GIVE SPEECHES. IT'S not that she's bad at it, just that she gets so nervous she feels like she's going to explode. Even when she speaks for only a minute or two, time seems to stand still. She can't even recall the first time she experienced public speaking anxiety. She says she has always felt this way. While speaking, her voice gets tight and her palms sweat. It is so embarrassing that she dreads the experience from the moment the assignment is made until the entire ordeal is over. Linda is only one class away from earning her college degree—and she has been for two years now. That class is "public speaking fundamentals." If you're like Linda, you believe that you're more nervous than anyone else about public speaking and that your fear is insurmountable. You probably tell yourself, "That's just the way I am. I'm just not good at speaking in public." This chapter is designed to dissolve those myths, and show that you *can* overcome speech anxiety.

To better understand this, let's look more closely at the experience of others. First, they're nervous, too. More than half of all experienced public speakers feel nervous or fearful before presenting a speech (Hahner, Sokoloff, & Salisch, 1993). Here's what one such speaker, *Boston Globe* columnist Diane White, told her readers:

> There should be a public speaking horror movie—*Speechless in Seattle*, maybe, or *The Night of the Sweaty Palms*. I could write the screenplay. I have actually lied to avoid making speeches, and I hate to lie. But I hate public speaking even more. It makes me nervous. How nervous? Once, when called upon to introduce a speaker, I forgot my own name. Luckily, I remembered the name of the woman I was introducing. (White, 1998, p. 94)

Second, many people, regardless of how nervous they feel, have found ways to cope with their public speaking anxiety. Consider Roberta Perry, who was once so nervous about public speaking that "she made wild hand gestures as she spoke—with her hands jammed in her pockets!" After learning techniques like the ones you will read about in this chapter, she controlled her anxiety—and eventually went from being a secretary to cofounding an audiovisual company and serving as its senior vice president (Griffin, 1995, p. 65).

Perhaps you have intensively feared public speaking for as long as you can remember, and even tried techniques to reduce anxiety without success. But such fear is natural and can be overcome. This chapter is designed to help manage that fear.

TURNING TO TECHNOLOGY

Your Personal Report of Public Speaking Anxiety

Go to the *Confident Public Speaking* Web site. Look for the PRPSA (Personal Report of Public Speaking Anxiety) under the activities for Chapter 2. Complete this instrument, composed of thirty-four statements concerning feelings about communicating with other people, by indicating the degree to which the statements apply to you: Mark whether you (1) strongly agree, (2) agree, (3) are undecided, (4) disagree, or (5) strongly disagree. Work quickly; record your first impression. If you score between 111 and 170, you're like the majority of the United States population. If your score is lower than 111, you are part of the minority—the 25 percent who do not experience speech anxiety.

Peanuts reprinted by permission of United Feature Syndicate, Inc.

This chapter begins by giving you the background needed to understand public speaking anxiety. Then it discusses the reasons why people experience public speaking anxiety, a form of communication apprehension (CA), and how it can be controlled. To use this chapter most effectively, think about yourself and take notes as you read. Focus on the forms of communication apprehension that plague you most, the reasons for public speaking anxiety most similar to yours, and the anxiety-reducing techniques that might work best for you.

WHAT IS COMMUNICATION APPREHENSION?

Over the years, fear of public speaking has been given various names, including speech fright, speech anxiety, stage fright, and public speaking anxiety. All are essentially the same thing—anxiety associated with giving a public speech. As research on public speaking anxiety has developed over the past forty years, scholars have discovered that the fear of public speaking is actually only one type of anxiety housed within a general condition called communication apprehension.

Communication apprehension (CA) can be defined as "the fear or anxiety associated with real or anticipated communication with others" (McCroskey, 1977, p. 78). Uncontrolled communication apprehension can make life miserable, limiting a person's potential for success in both personal relationships and professional settings.

Thanks to research, however, communication apprehension can be managed effectively. The first step is to understand the forms of communication apprehension and the types of anxiety that fall within each form. This will help you identify what situations are most problematic for you and why, so that you can focus your reading and thinking effectively as we discuss specific anxiety reduction techniques. There are four forms of communication apprehension: traitlike, audience-based, situational, and context-based.

If you experience **traitlike communication apprehension,** you feel anxious about speaking in most situations— whether talking one-to-one, in a small group, or during a public speech. About 20 percent of all people experience this type of CA (Richmond & McCroskey, 1995). Even this form of CA, which affects so many of a person's interactions, can be managed effectively.

If you experience **audience-based communication apprehension,** you feel particularly anxious only about communicating with a certain person or group of people. For example, you might feel noticeably uncomfortable speaking to a certain professor or to your boss. Perhaps you feel anxious in front of a class because the focus is specifically on speechmaking, but you do not feel anxious when you're not being graded on your public speaking. Most of us can identify someone we feel anxious about communicating with, so this form of CA is quite common (McCroskey, 1984).

Student Workbook

Complete the PRPSA and readings in Chapter 2 of your workbook (or on this book's Web site). What is your score? If it's between 111 and 170, you're like the majority of the adult U.S. population.

Dilbert reprinted by permission of United Feature Syndicate, Inc.

Situational communication apprehension, also quite common, is a short-lived feeling of anxiety that occurs during a specific encounter (McCroskey, 1984). For example, you may feel particularly anxious while interviewing for a position you really want, while speaking with your professor about an assignment you thought you failed, or while telling your spouse that you wrecked the car.

If you experience **context-based communication apprehension,** you may feel anxious only in a particular setting (McCroskey, 1984). Four such settings have been identified: public speaking, meetings, group discussion, and one-to-one conversations. Public speaking is the one most strongly associated with communication apprehension (Richmond & McCroskey, 1995). Thus you may feel anxious about public speaking, but not about speaking in any of the other settings. To learn more about your own anxiety, see the two Turning to Technology boxes near here.

The rest of this chapter focuses on context-based CA in public speaking. The anxiety-reducing techniques presented, however, can help you deal with other forms of communication apprehension as well.

TURNING TO TECHNOLOGY

Your Context-Based Apprehension

Go to the *Confident Public Speaking* Web site. Look for the Personal Report of Communication Apprehension (PRCA-24) under the activities for Chapter 2. Complete this instrument, composed of twenty-four statements concerning feelings about communicating with other people, by indicating the degree to which each statement applies to you. Mark whether you (1) strongly agree, (2) agree, (3) are undecided, (4) disagree, or (5) strongly disagree. Work quickly; record your first impression. Based on your score, in which context(s) do you experience communication apprehension?

WHY DO WE EXPERIENCE PUBLIC SPEAKING ANXIETY?

Researchers have discovered a number of causes for public speaking anxiety. The causes vary by individual, so to develop a personalized plan for managing your anxiety effectively you'll need to find out what causes are relevant for you. There are three factors: socialized patterns of thinking and feeling, preferred learning styles, and self-talk.

TURNING TO TECHNOLOGY

Your Game Plan for Dealing with Anxiety

http://de.cstcc.cc.tn.us/anxiety/nature.htm

Explore this Web site. Does the "Speech Anxiety Cycle" make sense? Why or why not? Complete the steps described on the Web site to create your "Game Plan" for dealing with anxiety. Will the mental or physical plan be most difficult for you to achieve? Why?

Socialized Patterns of Thinking and Feeling

Socialized patterns of thinking and feeling are those we learned while growing up. **Socialization,** the process of learning to fit into society, is crucial to a society and its members. Unfortunately, not all such learning is useful. Some of us learned to be fearful of public speaking. Researchers contend that most communication apprehension is primarily a result of socialization (Richmond & McCroskey, 1995). The good news is that socialized behaviors can be unlearned. Diane White, the *Boston Globe* columnist mentioned earlier, explained how childhood socialization contributed to her public speaking anxiety: "In my family, looking for attention was one of the worst sins a child could commit. 'Don't make a spectacle of yourself' was a familiar phrase around our house" (White, 1998, p. 94). Research tells us we are socialized in two main ways: modeling and reinforcement. These are also the primary ways public speaking anxiety is learned—and can be unlearned. We will talk about specific techniques later in this chapter.

Consider your past. What was oral communication like in your home when you were a child? Did your parents talk freely with each other in your presence? Did family members talk with each other a great deal or were they quiet and reserved? What was it like around the dinner table? Consider anything you remember about public speaking experiences of members of your family. Did any of them do much public speaking? What were their experiences? Did they avoid public speaking if they could? If your family tended to be quiet and reserved, and avoided speaking in public or showed fear about it, your own fears may stem from **modeling,** the process by which we learn by watching and then imitating the behaviors and reactions of those we admire (Bandura, 1973).

Did you ever speak in front of a class in elementary or junior high school? What was the response? How did the teacher react? Did your classmates laugh at you or with you? Did they clap? Did they appear bored? How did you feel after the speech? If the experience was bad, your public speaking fear may stem from reinforcement.

Reinforcement is the learning process in which past responses shape future expectations and thus behavior (Daly & Stafford, 1984; McCroskey, 1982). If the first few speeches you give go well, you feel calm when speaking later because you learned that you will probably succeed. But if early audiences gave you negative responses, you may

WHAT DO YOU THINK?

Are there children in your life who view you as a role model? How might they be learning to imitate your behaviors and reactions about public speaking? Are the attitudes they're learning positive or negative? What might you do in the future to be a positive role model for them?

have learned to expect future failure and embarrassment and, thus, to feel anxious. As a result, you may be talking yourself into failure whenever you anticipate speaking in public. Just as reinforcement can train you to feel more anxious about public speaking, so too can it be used to train you to feel less anxiety. We will talk about specific strategies later in this chapter.

Preferred Learning Style

Public speaking anxiety might also be connected to your preferred learning style. If you tend to prefer to learn by watching and thinking (Stage 2), you might be more likely to experience high public speaking anxiety than if you prefer to learn by doing and feeling (Stage 4) (Bourhis & Berquist, 1990; Bourhis & Stubbs, 1991; Dwyer, 1998a). This relationship between high anxiety and learning style preference seems particularly true for women (Dwyer, 1998a). If high anxiety stems from preferred learning style, you can reduce it by approaching the public speaking process in ways that round the cycle of learning and by making extra efforts to understand clearly the requirements and grading criteria before you begin to prepare your speech (Dwyer, 1998b; McCarthy, 1987; Neer & Kircher, 1991). This cause of anxiety, like the others, can be overcome.

Looking at the Learning Cycle

Understanding Your Preferred Learning Style to Reduce Anxiety

Which stage of the learning cycle do you prefer? If you prefer Stage 1, using a variety of examples to support each main point might help reduce anxiety. If you prefer Stage 2, speaking from a clearly organized outline based on clearly articulated criteria might calm you. If you prefer Stage 3, providing clear listener relevance links for each main point regarding how listeners can benefit from listening might prove helpful. And if you prefer Stage 4, using inclusive "we" language throughout the speech will create a sense of participation with your listeners and thus reduce anxiety. Round the cycle of learning in your speech by adhering to all these suggestions and you should feel less anxiety overall.

Self-Talk

Public speaking anxiety is most commonly caused by negative self-talk (Ayres, 1986; Behnke & Beatty, 1981; Daly & Buss, 1984; Desberg & Marsh, 1988; Richmond & McCroskey, 1995; Pucel & Stocker, 1983). **Self-talk** is the thoughts about success or failure that go through your mind in a particular situation. It's a form of intrapersonal communication. Negative self-talk, which focuses on being unsuccessful, increases anxiety. Telling yourself that you can't possibly get through a presentation or are bound to fail when giving a speech is self-defeating because it increases your anxiety.

WHAT DO YOU THINK?

When you think about delivering a speech in front of a group, what thoughts run through your mind? Are they generally positive or negative? How might these thoughts influence your anxiety?

We engage in negative self-talk out of fear. Four major fears in particular can lead to negative self-talk in public speakers: fear of being stared at, fear of the unknown, fear of failure, and fear of becoming fearful. By recognizing and dealing with these fears in practical ways, we can reduce the negative self-talk and thus our anxiety.

It is human nature to enjoy being recognized for things we've done well; however, it is *not* human nature to enjoy being the center of attention all the time (Richmond & McCroskey, 1995). In public speaking this is exactly what happens: All eyes are focused on you and you feel conspicuous. Fear of being stared at in this way leads to negative self-talk and to feelings of anxiety.

There are several ways you can deal with this. Using presentational aids with your speech gives your audience something else to look at. Possibly the room might be arranged so that audience members will divert their eyes some of the time; you might arrange the seats into a semicircle or horseshoe pattern rather than rows, allowing audience members to naturally look at each other as well as at you. If the fear of being stared at has to do with the audience seeing your nervous bodily reactions, cover them up. Wear a long skirt or baggy slacks to hide shaky knees; wear a high-necked shirt or sweater to cover a blushing neck.

PRACTICING THE PROCESS

Managing the Fear of Being Stared At

- Use presentational aids.
- Rearrange audience seating.
- Check your appearance in a mirror before starting.
- Wear clothes that conceal bodily reactions.

The fear of being stared at arises because we know the audience will be looking at us. But not knowing what will happen can also increase anxiety. Speakers sometimes engage in negative self-talk about possible catastrophes. That's understandable if you have never seen the room, met the audience, or delivered the speech before, or don't know how large the audience will be or how listeners will react. Counter such anxiety by reducing the unknowns. For example, prepare adequately in advance. Do this by researching and organizing your speech thoroughly, practicing with your presentational aids, rehearsing the speech for a few close friends, and using an audio or video recorder so you can hear and see yourself before you get in front of the audience. You can also check the room where you will be speaking, and perhaps meet some audience members before the day of the speech.

PRACTICING THE PROCESS

Managing the Fear of the Unknown

- Research and organize your speech thoroughly.
- Practice in advance for a few close friends.
- Practice in the room where you'll be speaking.
- Meet some audience members in advance.

A third fear that can lead to negative self-talk is a fear of failure. This is not fear of flunking an assignment but of how your audience will react to your speech and whether you will meet their expectations. Will listeners be bored, fail to laugh at your jokes, or misunderstand what you are trying to say? To some speakers, making even one small mistake seems like failure. Those whose anxiety rises from a fear of failure tend to view public speaking from a performance orientation. They see themselves as performing before a hypercritical audience and feel that they must create a perfect speech and deliver it flawlessly (Motley, 1991).

Through negative self-talk, these speakers convince themselves that the audience will evaluate them poorly if they make any mistakes.

But public speaking is a process of communicating rather than performing, so these fears are irrational and can be overcome. One way is to deliver your speech from brief notes, not a complete manuscript or memorization. Doing so will help keep your focus on communicating, not performing. Also, try out your ideas on a few close friends. Ask them what they think about your jokes and about your speech in general.

The three fears just discussed can lead to a fourth form of negative self-talk: the fear of becoming fearful. That is, you convince yourself that these other fears are inevitable and that, consequently, you'll be overwhelmed by fear. You may find yourself worrying that your nervousness is going to show, that you could hyperventilate, or that you will look stupid. Speakers who worry about becoming fearful tend to engage in negative self-talk in all three areas, convincing themselves that doing a public speech at all is impossible. To combat this anxiety, realize that most nervous reactions are not visible to the audience. Listeners cannot see your heart pounding. For reactions that might be seen, however, cover them up strategically. Dress up a bit more than usual, and stop in a bathroom to check your face, hair, and clothing before entering the room where you will be speaking. You might rehearse your speech in a mirror or videotape yourself for similar reasons.

I don't know how you are feeling after reading about negative self-talk, but after writing about it, I felt more anxious than before. However, there are several techniques you can easily learn and employ that will reduce your public speaking anxiety. Consequently, you can learn to not only be an effective public speaker but also feel like one.

WHAT CAN BE DONE TO REDUCE ANXIETY?

Researchers have been studying communication apprehension and treatment methods for more than forty years, so we know of various effective methods for controlling public speaking anxiety regardless of how the anxiety developed. Most are techniques designed to be performed daily, as well as right before and during a speech. These methods are systematic desensitization, cognitive restructuring, and skills training.

Systematic Desensitization

Originally developed in 1958, **systematic desensitization** focuses on relaxation and visualization (Wolpe, 1958). Research indicates that this is the most widely used and most effective method used for treating communication apprehension (Hoffman & Sprague, 1982; McCroskey, 1972; McCroskey, Ralph, & Barrick, 1970; Richmond & McCroskey, 1995). More than 80 percent of those who try this method reduce their level of anxiety. Systematic desensitization is a three-step process that trains you to relax and maintain a state of relaxation, first while visualizing yourself in, and then while participating in, increasingly stressful speaking situations.

You can practice systematic desensitization on your own with the help of an audiotape or a friend. The most important element of this method is to begin with *daily practice* (twenty to thirty minutes) for about two weeks. Schedule it like you might schedule exercise or some other activity that is important to you. After about two weeks most people will have trained themselves to reach a relaxed state in a matter of minutes and remain there while delivering their speech. Hence, you can imitate this state during the moments before you get up to give your speech. The three steps of the systematic desensitization process are as follows:

1. Progressive relaxation activities
2. Progressive visualization activities
3. Progressive experiential activities

Step 1: Progressive Relaxation Activities

Relaxation exercises have been proven to reduce anxiety. They can help in and of themselves, as well as in Step 1 of systematic desensitization. For the exercises to be effective, however, you must dedicate yourself to doing them regularly. As with aerobics, inconsistent exercise is unlikely to have much lasting effect. Two kinds of relaxation exercises can be particularly helpful: breathing techniques and progressive muscle relaxation therapy.

Progressive muscle relaxation therapy is one technique that can help reduce public speaking anxiety.

WHAT DO YOU THINK?

Imagine you are about to get up to deliver a public speech. Does your breathing change? If so, how? Do any parts of your body get tense? If so, which ones?

Take a moment to focus on your breathing. When you inhale, do your shoulders rise? If so, you are engaging in shallow, or chest, breathing. This contributes to anxiety, depression, and fatigue (Bourne, 1990). To see why, think of your lungs as balloons that fill up with air and then release it. Shallow breathing is like filling only the top half of the balloon; to keep air from entering the bottom half you must close it off with your hand. The same thing happens to your lungs when you engage in shallow breathing. Like your hand on the balloon, your internal muscles must tighten in order to stop air from filling the bottom half of your lungs. When these muscles contract, you add unnecessary tension to your body, which increases anxiety.

We were all born breathing naturally from the abdomen, but many of us learned to breathe unnaturally from the chest. My childhood doctor asked me to breathe deeply, saying, "I want to see your shoulders rise." He didn't realize he was teaching me to breathe incorrectly. I began to believe that big breaths should make my shoulders rise. Unfortunately, after years of practice, shallow breathing feels natural to us. Through breathing techniques, you can retrain yourself to breathe from the abdomen and thereby reduce your anxiety.

If you breathe deeply and fill your lungs completely, your diaphragm moves down and pushes your stomach out of the way (Figure 2.1). You can practice and monitor deep breathing by breathing so that you see your stomach expand as you inhale and return to its normal resting position as you exhale (see activities 1 and 2 at the end of this chapter).

Another breathing exercise can be used immediately before giving a speech, when it is natural to feel a sudden rush of adrenaline. This nervous energy can actually improve performance, but you may misinterpret the adrenaline rush as anxiety; if so, your muscles tense up and you start taking shallow chest breaths. An effective response is to sigh. Physicians and psychologists have discovered that sighing is your body's way to release tension (Davis, Echelon, & McKay,

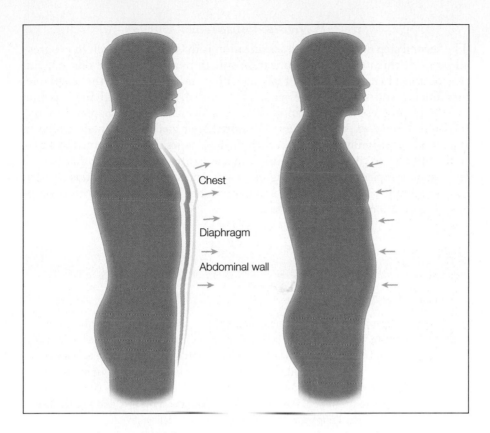

Figure 2.1
Upper body during deep breathing

1988). By sighing right before it is your turn to speak, you can lower your anxiety level (see activity 3 at the end of this chapter). Then the inevitable rush of adrenaline can work for you, not against you.

Along with learning to breathe deeply, teach your body to relax. This is where **progressive muscle relaxation therapy** comes in. The technique was developed more than sixty years ago and is still the most effective method for training one's body and muscles to relax (Jacobson, 1938). Progressive muscle relaxation therapy involves systematically tensing certain muscle groups for about ten seconds, then relaxing them for another ten seconds while focusing on what this relaxed state feels like (Friedrich & Goss, 1984). Usually each group is tensed and relaxed twice before the person moves on to the next group. The fifteen muscle groups isolated in this therapy are hands, biceps and triceps, shoulders, neck, lips, tongue, mouth, eyes and forehead, abdomen, back, midsection, thighs, stomach, calves, feet, and toes. (A progressive muscle relaxation exercise is included in the Chapter 2 Activities on the *Confident Public Speaking* Web site.) You will probably go through this process several times before you can maintain deep relaxation. Once you can, it's time to add the visualization step of systematic desensitization.

PRACTICING THE PROCESS

Progressive Relaxation Activities

- Breathe from your abdomen rather than your chest.
- Practice a heavy sigh right before you get up to speak.
- Practice progressive muscle relaxation techniques.

Step 2: Progressive Visualization Activities

The second step of systematic desensitization is to visualize yourself in progressively more threatening communication situations. Once you are relaxed, you may be asked to envision yourself talking with your best friend on the telephone, introducing yourself to a new acquaintance, and, ultimately, giving a public speech. (A progressive visualization exercise is included in the Chapter 2 Activities on the *Confident Public Speaking* Web site.) Your goal is to maintain a relaxed state while envisioning yourself in each of these types of communication situations. Initially, as you visualize yourself in a situation, you may feel that the relaxed state is replaced with a feeling of tension and anxiety. Your goal is to learn to maintain the relaxed state in that situation, then move on to a more anxiety-arousing situation and repeat the process.

TURNING TO TECHNOLOGY

Visualizing Success

Using InfoTrac College Edition, locate the articles "Visualization: The Mental Road to Accomplishment" by Dennis Best and "Do Try This at Home" by Wendy DuBow (Hint: Use "visualization" as your search term.) Read the articles and mentally revise them to fit the public speaking situation. Make a list of the parts of the speech presentation process you will visualize positively (for example, walking to the front of the room, looking listeners in the eye, and so on). Then practice visualizing yourself doing them without feeling anxious.

PRACTICING THE PROCESS

Progressive Visualization Activities

- Make yourself as comfortable and relaxed as possible.
- Envision yourself meeting one new classmate while remaining relaxed. Do not move on until you're successful.
- Envision yourself asking a question during class while remaining relaxed. Do not move on until you're successful.
- Envision yourself stating your name and major to the class while remaining relaxed. Do not move on until you're successful.
- Envision yourself walking to the front of the class and doing your speech of self-introduction while remaining relaxed.

Step 3: Progressive Experiential Activities

The final step is to engage in progressively more threatening communication situations. Over several sessions, for example, you may be asked to talk to a friend about yourself, then to introduce yourself to someone you don't know well, and, ultimately, to introduce yourself to a small group and then to a larger group. Your goal is to maintain a relaxed state in each of these progressively more threatening communication situations. (A progressive experiential activity is included in the Chapter 2 Activities on the *Confident Public Speaking* Web site.)

Systematic desensitization can help you in two ways. First, it reduces communication apprehension in general, including fear of public speaking. That is, you train yourself to relax in public speaking and other situations. Second, you can use many of the techniques to help yourself relax when you actually give a speech. For example, just before you get up to speak, take several deep breaths while focusing on your abdomen. You should feel yourself relax. Then close your eyes and visualize yourself giving a strong speech. When you walk to the front of the room, take three more deep breaths right before beginning your speech. While doing so, look at the first couple sentences to get them firmly in mind. Finally, jot down a few reminders on your notes to breathe deeply during the speech. Keep in mind, though, that this second use of systematic desensitization will help only if it reinforces, rather than replaces, regular systematic desensitization training.

Student Workbook

Complete the "Autograph Party" in Chapter 1 of your workbook. This activity will help desensitize you to your upcoming speeches by visiting informally with each of your classmates.

PRACTICING THE PROCESS

Desensitizing in the Moments before You Speak

- Do a cleansing sigh.
- Breathe from the abdomen.
- Visualize yourself walking calmly to the front of the room or group.
- Walk calmly to the front of the room or group.
- Plant yourself, pause, breathe, and look listeners in the eyes before starting to speak.

Cognitive Restructuring

Cognitive restructuring is a process designed to help you systematically rebuild your thoughts about public speaking. The goal is to replace anxiety-arousing negative self-talk with anxiety-reducing positive self-talk. The process consists of four steps:

1. Creating a negative self-talk list
2. Identifying the irrational belief or cognitive distortion embedded in each thought
3. Developing a coping statement for each irrational belief or distortion
4. Practicing coping statements until they become second nature

Step 1: Create a Negative Self-Talk List

To change your negative thoughts, you must first identify them. Write down all of the fears that come to mind when you know you must give a public speech. List as many as you can, regardless of what they are. Karna's list looked like this:

Negative Self-Talk List

- I'm afraid I'll forget my speech and look foolish.
- I'm afraid everyone will be able to tell that I'm nervous.
- I'm afraid my voice will crack.
- I'm afraid my audience won't believe me.
- I'm afraid I'll sound boring.

Create a Negative Self-Talk List

List the fears that come to mind when you think about giving a public speech.

*Step 2: Identify Irrational Beliefs and
Cognitive Distortions That May Guide Your Fears*

Most fears about public speaking are rooted in **irrational beliefs** (Ellis & Dryden, 1987), which project harm and danger onto an event that is neither harmful nor dangerous. Because public speaking is not life-threatening, fears of it are irrational. Look at Karna's list of negative self-talk again. She worried that she would forget her speech and look foolish. Is that life-threatening? No. She was also concerned that people could tell if she was nervous. Perhaps they might, but this too is not life-threatening. And if her voice cracks, if some listeners don't believe her, and if she sounds boring, she'll still live. She might tell herself "I'll just die if this happens," but she won't. Hence every negative thought on her list is an irrational belief that the event is in some way life-threatening.

> **WHAT DO YOU THINK?**
> Look at the list you generated in Step 1. If any of your fears actually comes true during your public speech, will it be life threatening? If not, the fears are based on irrational beliefs.

Knowing that most negative self-talk about public speaking is irrational, we can discuss how most of it is essentially a cognitive distortion. **Cognitive distortions** about public speaking are unrealistic, negative statements about yourself that lead you to judge your public speaking experience harshly even when it goes well (Ellis & Dryden, 1987). Like the irrational beliefs themselves, cognitive distortions increase anxiety and keep you from achieving your goals. As you read through this list, consider which of these cognitive distortions influence your self-talk about public speaking:

1. *The perfectionist.* "If I make even one mistake, I'll be a failure."
2. *The self-effacing phony.* "If someone compliments me, they're just being nice. That wasn't really me because I'm not that good."
3. *The thin skinned.* "They looked bored; I must be bad."
4. *The overgeneralizer.* "I got nervous. Getting nervous is bad. So I was bad."
5. *The psychic.* "My audience will be bored and so I'll be bad." "I always forget my speech, so I'll forget and be bad again." "I always get nervous, so I'll get nervous and be bad."
6. *The negativist.* "Even though I got many compliments, I forgot one part so I'm unworthy."

Negative self-talk that stems from cognitive distortions is often rooted in "must thoughts" that demand perfection (Dwyer, 1998b). Must thoughts may include (a) believing you must never make a mistake or people will think you're incompetent, (b) telling yourself that everyone in your audience must like your speech or you will fail, and (c) convincing yourself that you must not give a speech unless you feel perfectly calm. The goals implied are impossible for anyone to achieve. By allowing yourself to believe must thoughts, you set yourself up for inevitable failure.

Perfectionistic ideals stem from a performance orientation. As discussed earlier, a **performance orientation** leads you to think your speech must be presented flawlessly to be effective (Motley, 1991). But effective public speaking operates from a **communication orientation,** which focuses on the message and on helping your audience understand it.

Consider Karna's list of negative self-talk once again. Notice how the items stem from cognitive distortions such as the perfectionist, the thin skinned, and the psychic. She is not likely to forget the entire speech, but she might forget to mention *something* that she planned to say. Her negative self-talk, however, says doing so means she is a failure. This is an example of the perfectionist cognitive distortion being played out. The thin-skinned cognitive distortion is guiding her self-talk about boring her listeners, and the psychic is represented in several of her statements. No public speaker is perfect. We all make mistakes. We can all learn from our mistakes. Yet cognitive distortions act as barriers that keep you from attaining your public speaking goals. They set you up for failure by feeding your negative self-talk and increasing anxiety.

PRACTICING THE PROCESS

Identifying Irrational Beliefs and Cognitive Distortions

- Refer to the list of negative self-talk you identified in Step 1.
- Identify an irrational belief and cognitive distortions that fuel each statement.

Step 3: Develop Positive Coping Statements

Once you have analyzed and understand your negative self-talk, you can develop a list of positive coping statements to replace the negative statements. These statements must fit *your* concerns. There is no list of coping statements that will work for everyone. Only you can determine what your negative self-talk statements are, why each statement is irrational, what cognitive distortion guides it, and what positive coping statement you can use to replace it. Psychologist Richard Heimberg of the State University of New York at Albany approaches this step by asking clients to list all the things they are afraid listeners will think (negative self-talk list). He then asks them to estimate how many listeners in an audience of 100 would even notice, for example, sweaty palms or shaky knees (cognitive distortion identified) and how many would even care (again, cognitive distortion identified). He concludes by helping them generate a positive coping statement to replace the negative self-talk: "By the time we get to the end, it comes down to: Can you cope with the one or two people who [notice or criticize or] get upset?" (Griffin, 1995, p. 64).

Here is how Karna worked through the process of replacing her negative self-talk statements with positive coping statements. Rather than telling herself that she would forget the speech and look foolish, she began telling herself that forgetting a few details would not ruin her speech as long as she focused on getting the main points across to her audience. She also reminded herself most of her nervousness signs, such as sweaty palms and racing heartbeat, would not be noticeable, nor would most listeners focus on her shaky knees or a crack in her voice (and that those who do are really the ones with the problem, not her). She decided that though perhaps some listeners would not believe her she could convey her thoughts honestly after having conducted thorough research; beyond that, she can't control the beliefs of others. And as for sounding boring, she probably won't as long as she focuses on the message and not the performance. After all, she rehearsed out loud a lot. If a few listeners appear bored, that's their problem.

Step 4: Practice Your Coping Statements until They Become Second Nature

Memorize and practice your coping statements until they replace the old script of negative self-talk in your mind. Don't become discouraged when you begin to work on this step. It may feel awkward and even phony at first. Realize, though, that this restructuring process takes time and energy, because the negative self-talk has become a part of you. The more you read your list of coping statements, memorize them, and say them to yourself silently and aloud, the more natural they will become and the more unnatural the negative thoughts will seem.

Start by reading your coping statements at least once every day, and keep the list with you. When negative self-talk comes to mind, refer to your list and replace the old negative self-talk with the new positive coping statement. Also, set public speaking goals for yourself two or three times per week so you can practice your coping statements before speaking. These goals may include asking a question during class, introducing yourself to someone you don't know, or sharing a story with acquaintances between classes or during lunch. Any speaking situation that tends to make you nervous is appropriate. Review your list right before you give each speech. And, finally, practice positive coping statements after presenting each speech. Cognitive restructuring may sound almost too simple, but research proves it works. All that's required is committed practice on your part. Your fear and nervousness about public speaking will diminish.

Skills Training

The final method is based on a simple principle: The better you know something, the less anxious you feel about it. If you learn the skills involved in effective public speaking, you'll greatly reduce your fear of failure. In **skills training** the speechmaking process is broken into specific skills that can be mastered, first in isolation and then together.

This entire book is designed as a skills trainer. Each chapter introduces you to a component of the speechmaking process and asks you to practice the component through activities. By the time you finish reading this book you will have completed a session of public speaking skills training and should, as a result, feel less anxiety about presenting speeches.

To be successful, set specific goals as you work on each skill, practice each skill in isolation, and reward yourself for achieving the goals you set. For example, you might set a goal to use transitions that verbally tie two main points together. When you achieve that, reward yourself with positive self-talk rather than employing negative self-talk about something you hadn't yet set out to achieve. Upon achieving the goal and rewarding yourself for it, you might then set a goal of using colorful language choices in your transitions. After doing so, reward yourself again with positive self-talk before setting a higher goal. The idea is to set attainable goals, achieve them, and reward yourself with positive self-talk *before* aspiring to a new goal. Too often, anxiety is fostered because speakers employ negative self-talk for not achieving a skill they hadn't even set for themselves yet. And they do so while ignoring the skills they have achieved.

SUMMARY

In this chapter we talked about the nature of communication apprehension, why it exists, and how you can work strategically to overcome it. We discussed how public speaking anxiety is only one type of communication apprehension, but one that affects more people than any other. Some people claim to fear public speaking even more than death. We learned that public speaking anxiety stems from socialization, learning style preference, and self-talk. If you experience public speaking anxiety, it probably stems from negative experiences you have had, negative role models, or negative self-talk.

We also learned that public speaking anxiety can be reduced, and explored three methods that have proved effective in reducing it. Systematic desensitization focuses first on learning to relax. Then you strive to maintain a relaxed state while visualizing yourself in progressively more threatening communication situations. Ultimately, you try to stay relaxed while participating in increasingly more threatening communication situations. Cognitive restructuring is a process of replacing negative self-talk with positive self-talk. It involves identifying what negative self-talk statements shape your thinking about public speaking and analyzing those statements to discover the irrational beliefs and cognitive distortions that perpetuate them. This allows you to create alternative coping statements to replace each negative statement—coping statements that can be memorized and employed throughout the day, as well as right before and right after giving a speech. Finally, skills training breaks the speechmaking process into specific skills that can be mastered incrementally to ultimately reduce the fear of failure.

Ideally, public speakers will employ all of these methods in some form as they work to reduce public speaking anxiety. It is not possible to overcome public speaking anxiety overnight, but it can occur eventually by committing yourself to practicing relaxation and systematic desensitization, cognitive restructuring, and skills training in isolation as well as together.

RETURNING TO TECHNOLOGY

The *Confident Public Speaking* CD-ROM is your one-stop point of access for not just the content on the CD itself, such as Speech Interactive, but also the many other resources on the *Confident Public Speaking* Web site, Speech Builder Express, and InfoTrac College Edition. Note that this chapter's key terms and activities are among the resources available in electronic format online. Additional information is included below.

SPEECH INTERACTIVE
ON THE *CONFIDENT PUBLIC SPEAKING* CD-ROM

Speech Interactive is your link to this text's speech videos. Offering opportunities to practice critiquing speeches by students and other public speakers, these videos will help you prepare for providing effective feedback to your peers and your own speech performances.

SPEECH BUILDER EXPRESS

Select the "Create a New Speech" section of Speech Builder Express in anticipation of the first speech you'll prepare and present to your class. Once you've given your first speech a tentative title (such as "My First Speech"), select the Speech Timeline feature and try entering a fake due date. By providing structure and an easy way to monitor your progress, this feature, along with the step-by-step guidance the program provides through the navigation buttons on the left-hand side of the screen, can help minimize whatever public speaking apprehension you might have.

KEY TERMS

Interactive flashcards for these key terms are available on the *Confident Public Speaking* Web site. You'll find the "Flashcards" link under the resources for Chapter 2.

Audience-based communication
  apprehension 35
Cognitive distortions 46
Cognitive restructuring 45
Communication apprehension 35
Communication orientation 47
Context-based communication
  apprehension 36
Irrational beliefs 46
Modeling 37
Performance orientation 46

Progressive muscle relaxation
  therapy 43
Reinforcement 37
Self-talk 38
Situational communication
  apprehension 36
Skills training 49
Socialization 37
Systematic desensitization 41
Traitlike communication
  apprehension 35

ACTIVITIES

The activities below, as well as additional activities for this chapter, are available in electronic format on the *Confident Public Speaking* Web site. You'll find the "Activities" link under the resources for Chapter 2.

The exercises in activities 1–3 are designed to reduce public speaking anxiety. To be effective they must be practiced regularly outside the public speaking classroom. Then they can be adapted to help you during the minutes before you get up to speak, while you are speaking, and during the moments right after you finish.

1. **Controlled Deep Breathing Exercise.** If possible, lie on your back on the floor. Place a book on your stomach and take a breath. As you breathe in through your nose, watch for the book to rise. As you exhale through your mouth, watch for the book to lower. You may feel at first as though you are forcing the book to rise. With consistent practice, however, this breathing process will become more natural. You can practice deep breathing when you watch television or listen to the radio. Remember, though, that this retraining exercise must be practiced every day for about twenty minutes to be successful.

2. **Breathing in Transit Exercise.** You can also practice deep breathing while you're walking to and from class. As you walk, be sure that you are standing tall. Deep breathe at four-count intervals. For example, take four steps while inhaling through your nose to the count of four (think "1 - 2 - 3 - 4" as you inhale and walk). Then, take the next four steps while exhaling through your mouth to the count of four (think "1 - 2 - 3 - 4" as you exhale and walk). Not only will this improve your ability to breathe deeply, it will increase the oxygen supply to your brain and muscles, which will wake you up and give you more energy.

3. **Calming Sigh Exercise.** Use this exercise to reduce stress right before you get up to give your speech. First, inhale deeply but gently through your nose. Then slowly let the air out of your lungs while saying "Ahhhh." Finally, let your body go limp for a couple of moments. Do this two or three times in a row just before speaking. You will be surprised at how it relaxes you.

4. **Cognitive Restructuring Journals.** Cognitive Restructuring Journal entries occur in two phases. (1) Use the journal to identify communication situations where your anxiety level increases. Take it with you wherever you go so you can make a note whenever a situation increases your anxiety. Simply jot down the situation and the fears that immediately come to mind. Put the journal away until later. When you have some quiet time to reflect, complete the second phase. (2) Read the entry you completed earlier that day or week. Generate irrational beliefs and cognitive distortions linked to each fear. Finally, create a positive coping statement to replace each negative thought.

5. **Coping Statement Chart.** Create a list of (a) public speaking negative self-talk fears and (b) the irrational beliefs and cognitive distortions associated with each. Then develop a chart you can carry with you. Refer to this chart at least once every day to help yourself replace negative self-talk with positive coping statements and reduce your anxiety about public speaking.

6. **Portfolio Assignment.** Create a one- or two-page paper identifying two or three personal goals you have for coping with anxiety and why, as well as how you plan to achieve them. Finally, describe how you plan to reward yourself when you achieve them.

Find and read the article "Social Phobias" by Tamar Nordenberg. (Hint: Use "phobias" as your search term.) Compare your level of communication apprehension to the level of anxiety the individuals in the article experience. List any of the strategies under the category of "cognitive-behavioral therapy" that you think you would find helpful in reducing your anxiety about public speaking.

3

YOUR FIRST SPEECH

REFLECTIVE QUESTIONS

1. What ideas can you come up with for making the content of your speech interesting to your audience?

2. Why might clearly structured content be crucial to effective public speaking? And clearly signaled transitions from one section of content to the next—why might they be important?

3. Do you think having a creative attention catcher at the start of a speech and memorable clincher at the end is important? Why or why not?

4. Why is it so important to look audience members in the eye while speaking? What else should you do with regard to eye contact?

5. At what point(s) during the speechmaking process should you consider your audience?

WHAT'S AHEAD: FOCUSING YOUR READING

What Does It Mean to Be Audience-Centered?

What Does It Mean to Have Good Content?

What Does It Mean to Have Clear Structure?

What Does It Mean to Have Effective Delivery?

K RIS WAS ENROLLED IN PUBLIC speaking fundamentals, a general education core requirement at her university. She had enrolled in the course several times before, but had always dropped it after the first speech was assigned. She confided to her advisor that it seemed unfair to ask students to present a short speech introducing themselves before they had learned what an effective public speech looks like or how to prepare it. Kris made a lot of sense. It *is* unfair to expect students to stand up and present a speech, however short and simple, without some general guidance.

This chapter responds to Kris's concerns, which many of you may share. You can probably identify public speakers who seem to be good at it and others who are not so good. What's the difference? What makes for an effective speech? This chapter focuses on the key principles you should follow to develop and present a speech. There are three primary components of an effective speech, and some "glue" that holds them together. The components are content, structure, and delivery; the glue is being audience-centered or listener relevant. Consider the topic and requirements of your first speech assignment as you read the chapter so that you can apply the principles to it as you read. Kris's first speech is offered as an example throughout our discussion. You can also watch Kris's speech, "Mirror Image," on the Speech Interactive section of the *Confident Public Speaking* CD-ROM.

Your goal in public speaking exists on a continuum (Figure 3.1). A speech of self-introduction like Kris's is an informative speech. As an informative speaker, you intend to share knowledge and seek mutual understanding. Notice that as you move to the right on the continuum, the goals become loftier. We talk more about these in Chapters 14, 15, 16, and 17. For this chapter, simply realize that all public speeches have certain things in common, regardless of their primary goal: content, structure, delivery, and being audience-centered.

WHAT DOES IT MEAN TO BE AUDIENCE-CENTERED?

Student Workbook

Read through "Major Components of Public Speaking" in Chapter 2 or your workbook. Which component will you find most challenging and why?

ETHICS

WHAT DO YOU THINK?
Identify a public speaker you have heard who seemed to be really good at it. Why did you think so?

Effective public speakers are audience-centered. Listeners sense that the speaker cares about them enough to offer ideas in ways that (a) make sense, (b) are relevant, (c) reflect careful research, and (d) sound interesting. Being **audience-centered** means considering who your audience members are and how your message can best be tailored to their interests, desires, and needs (Reinard, 1988). Essentially, you demonstrate ethical speaking by demonstrating honesty and respect for your listeners. This requires analyzing the relationship between your audience and the message when selecting a topic, as well as *throughout* the speechmaking and presentation process. Always consider the audience

---

TURNING TO TECHNOLOGY

Becoming Audience-Centered

http://www.instantspeakingsuccess.com/tm.htm

Read about the four Cs to becoming a great public speaker. Which of the suggestions for connecting with your audience will you try? Why?

You can use analogies to support a main point, as Kris did about being a twin.

when selecting a topic and developing the *content*, when organizing the *structure*, and when rehearsing the *delivery*, as well as when actually presenting the speech.

Kris's first speech was a speech of self-introduction. Her audience was twenty to twenty-five college students also enrolled in the course, ranging in age from about eighteen to about fifty. Some were married, others not. Some had no children, some had young children, and some had grown children. The group included a single parent, a gay rights activist, a fellow who had recently returned to school to become a priest, and a migrant worker. In other words, Kris's audience was *demographically diverse*, differing in ages, experiences, attitudes, and values (Shaw, 1997). However, all were students at the same university taking the same required public speaking course.

From this cursory analysis, Kris decided her audience would be a supportive group, since they were all pretty much in the same boat, and that it would be important to respect the group's diverse perspectives and life experiences. Although her primary goal had been determined by the instructor—to present a self-introduction speech that was true to herself, her experiences, her beliefs, and her values—audience analysis helped her tighten her focus based on her listeners. For example, she would be careful to avoid presumptions that her beliefs, values, and experiences were better than those of others. She would also try to address ways in which this audience might benefit from learning about her and her experiences. Hence, she would honor the virtues of honesty and respect for herself and her audience.

PRACTICING THE PROCESS

Analyzing Your Audience

Who is in your audience? What are some of their similarities and differences? How might knowing this help you develop an audience-centered speech?

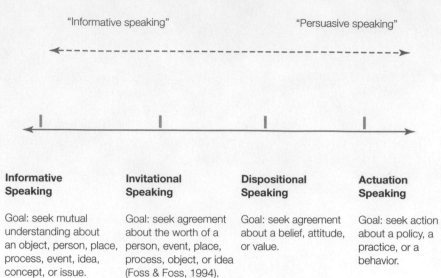

Figure 3.1 The public speaking continuum

"Informative speaking"   "Persuasive speaking"

Informative Speaking

Goal: seek mutual understanding about an object, person, place, process, event, idea, concept, or issue.

Invitational Speaking

Goal: seek agreement about the worth of a person, event, place, process, object, or idea (Foss & Foss, 1994).

Dispositional Speaking

Goal: seek agreement about a belief, attitude, or value.

Actuation Speaking

Goal: seek action about a policy, a practice, or a behavior.

WHAT DOES IT MEAN TO HAVE GOOD CONTENT?

Content is the actual ideas in your speech: the main topic and purpose, the ideas and information you include to support each main point, and the connections you make directly to listeners throughout. The **main topic** is the subject of the speech—the assigned main topic of Kris's first speech, for example, was herself. An important aspect of the main topic is the purpose, which has two parts: the general purpose and the specific purpose. The **general purpose** of any speech is to inform, persuade, or entertain. The **specific purpose** answers the question "about what?" Kris's general purpose was *to inform* and her specific purpose was to tell them a bit *about herself*.

The ideas and information you offer to support your topic and purpose are your main points and supporting material. It is a good idea to limit your speeches to two, three, or four main points. More could be difficult for listeners to keep track of. Kris's instructor advised students to consider their personal backgrounds, unique characteristics, and professional goals to develop their first speech. To introduce herself, then, Kris decided to talk about where she grew up (background), what makes her unique (characteristics), and why she chose North Dakota State University for her college education (professional goals). These three ideas became the main points of her speech. Cara, another student in the course, talked about her childhood adoption (background), her passion for sports (unique characteristics), and her dream of becoming a high school teacher and soccer coach (professional goals) in her speech "Left on a Doorstep."

ETHICS

Each main point is developed with evidence. **Evidence** is any information that clarifies, explains, or supports your main point. To be effective, evidence needs to have sufficient breadth and depth. **Breadth** refers to the amount and types of evidence. You can use such things as facts, statistics, definitions, descriptions, explanations, examples, testimonies, and analogies. These can come from your own experiences or from external research you collect from interviews or surveys, books, magazines, newspapers, journals, or the Internet. To be both ethical and effective, you should use many types of evidence to round the cycle of learning. **Depth** is the level of detail you provide from each piece of evidence. Usually you will offer two or three pieces of evidence to develop each main point and describe one of them in detail.

Kris used personal experiences as evidence. To support her first main point, she described the small town where she grew up, how long she lived there, and the school she attended and graduated from. Doing so added depth to her description. To support her second main point, she explained what growing up with a twin sister was like and how that shaped who she is today. She mentioned being exactly three minutes older than her sister and used the analogy of "good" and "evil" twins in her explanation, again adding depth. To support her third main point, Kris talked about her academic experiences, employment experiences, and future goals and explained how all these led her to NDSU to earn her degree. She used a variety of facts and statistics to add breadth. Thus, she rounded the cycle of learning by offering personal stories, analogies, facts, statistics, explanations, and descriptions.

Looking at the Learning Cycle

Types of Supporting Material

- To address Stage 1, use a variety of examples from real life.
- To address *watching,* use visual aids and offer vivid descriptions.
- To address Stage 2, use definitions and explanations.
- To address *thinking,* use facts and statistics.
- To address Stage 3, use expert testimony.
- To address *doing,* offer processes, procedures, or action plans.
- To address Stage 4, use analogies or hypothetical or actual examples.
- To address *feeling,* use emotional stories and sensory examples.

Content should also include **listener relevance links**, which are statements of how and why the ideas you offer might benefit your listeners. Include them when introducing your topic and when discussing each main point. Although listener relevance links are sometimes difficult to formulate, they are crucial to an audience-centered speech.

Kris offered a general listener relevance link in her introduction by talking about how important it is to forge new friendships. In discussing her first main point, she talked about her hometown as a place her classmates might consider visiting. In discussing her second main point, she talked about how easy it can be for anyone to take family for granted. And in discussing her third main point, she talked about reasons NDSU is a good school for her and, perhaps, for others as well.

PRACTICING THE PROCESS

Questions for Planning the Content of Your First Speech

- What are the topic and purpose of your next speech?
- What will be your main points?
- What specific pieces of evidence will you include to support each main point?
- What evidence will you talk about in detail for depth?
- What will you offer for listener relevance under each main point?

Content is the stuff of which speeches are made—a main idea and purpose, supporting ideas or main points, evidence to support each main point, and listener relevance links. But good content is not the only foundation of effective public speeches: Content must be structured so it can easily be followed and must be delivered compellingly.

PRACTICING THE PROCESS

Content Checklist for Your First Speech

- ❑ Do your topic and purpose meet the expectations of the audience?
- ❑ Have you limited your main points to between two and four?
- ❑ Do you offer different kinds of evidence for each main point?
- ❑ Do you go into detail on one piece of evidence under each main point?
- ❑ Do you provide a listener relevance link in the introduction and for each main point?

TURNING TO TECHNOLOGY

Considering Ethical Speechmaking

ETHICS **http://www.smsu.edu/com/com115/ethics.html**

Read the Web site authors' suggestions for ethical speechmaking. Which tips surprise you and why? Which will be most challenging for you and why?

WHAT DOES IT MEAN TO HAVE CLEAR STRUCTURE?

The **structure** of a speech is the framework that organizes the content. A clear structure guides your listeners as you talk so they can make sense of your ideas, and it demonstrates respect for your listeners (Jensen, 1985). Clear structure includes macrostructure and microstructure.

Macrostructure

Macrostructure refers to the general framework for the content. It usually consists of an introduction, a body, a conclusion, and transitions. In a clearly organized speech, each of these serves a particular function:

1. *Introduction.* Tells the audience what you're going to tell them.
2. *Body.* Tells them.
3. *Conclusion.* Tells them what you told them.
4. *Transitions.* Words or phrases that show the relationship between two main points and let the audience know you have completed one main point and are moving on to another.

Beginning speakers sometimes complain that this approach seems redundant and likely to bore listeners. On the contrary: It is crucial for an effective public

Student Workbook

Read through "Generic Public Speech Structure" in Chapter 2 of your workbook. Why is this called the "golden rule" of public speaking?

speech. The reason is that public speaking is transitory. Listeners can hear the message only once. Unlike readers, they cannot go back to an idea that confuses them. So extra care must be taken to ensure that listeners do not get lost along the way. Help your listeners by previewing main points in the introduction and restating them in the conclusion. Also, offer transitions to let them know when you've finished talking about one main point and are moving on to another. Although it may feel awkward to you at first, listeners appreciate clearly organized macrostructural elements.

The Introduction

The **introduction** gains the attention of your audience, announces your topic, and provides a brief road map of how you will proceed. In other words, you tell them what you're going to tell them. An introduction should include an **attention catcher**—something that both grabs attention and tunes listeners in to the topic. You might use a *rhetorical question* (one that requires no direct response), a *personal anecdote* (a short story about an experience you have had), a *famous quotation* related to your speech topic, or a *humorous* (yet tactful) *story*. Since listeners tend to be apathetic unless their curiosity is aroused, take the extra time to come up with a compelling attention catcher. A **thesis statement** is a one-sentence summary of the speech. It lets listeners know your general and specific purpose. A **preview** briefly mentions the two to four main points you will explain in the body of your speech. Remember, finally, that your introduction should also include a general listener relevance link connecting your topic and purpose to your listeners and a **speaker credibility statement** letting them know what makes you an authority on the topic. Kris's basic introduction looked like this:

I. **Attention catcher:** Have you ever looked into a mirror, seen your reflection, and then realized that the reflection in the mirror wasn't really you? (Rhetorical question) This may seem a little strange to all of you, but this has actually happened to me many times throughout my life. (Personal anecdote)

II. **Listener relevance:** As you listen to my speech today, I believe you'll begin to understand how important I believe it is to forge friendships with ourselves, with our families, and with others.

III. **Thesis statement:** Today, I'd like to inform you a little bit about who I—Kris Treinen—am. (One-sentence summary letting listeners know the general and specific purpose)

IV. **Preview:** More specifically, let's talk about where I grew up, what makes me unique, and why I chose to come to NDSU for my college degree. (Brief mention of three main points)

You may notice that Kris did not include an explicit speaker credibility statement. This is optional in a speech of self-introduction because listeners accept the speaker as an authority on him or herself. Kris used two attention-catching devices in her attention-catcher to make it even more compelling. Cara, on the other hand, used a personal anecdote for her attention catcher:

Student Workbook

Read through the section in Chapter 3 of your workbook that discusses how to create a preparation outline for your "Self-Introduction" speech, and then use the included form to work on your outline.

I. **Attention catcher:** Since birth, I've had a unique childhood. It began when I was abandoned on a police station doorstep with a note from my birth mother. I spent the next five months in an orphanage in Seoul, South Korea, where I was fed five times daily by a bottle propped up with a sponge.

II. **Speaker credibility:** Perhaps knowing this about me will help you understand why I believe my seemingly unorthodox adoption ordeal was one of the best experiences of my life.

III. **Listener relevance:** Although my life began in an unusual manner, you might be surprised by how much you all and I have in common.

IV. **Thesis statement:** I'm Cara Langaas, and I'd like to introduce myself to you by sharing some of the experiences I've been through as they have shaped who I am today.

V. **Preview:** We'll talk about my childhood adoption experience, my passion for sports, and my goals for the future.

Students say that creating an effective attention catcher is the most difficult part of developing their introduction. Here are examples from some of my students. Perhaps reading them will help brainstorm when creating yours. One student used both a hypothetical example and rhetorical questions when she asked her listeners to "sit back and picture this . . . a young girl standing in the middle of a large group of adolescents who are teasing her and laughing at her. They are shouting nasty things about her race, her weight, and even her clothes. How do you suppose this young girl feels? Why doesn't anybody help her?" Another quoted a phrase of welcome in Mandarin Chinese, which was her first language. Still another used a famous quotation. There are many types of attention catchers; your goal is to create one that sparks curiosity and tunes listeners in to your topic.

PRACTICING THE PROCESS

Guidelines for Creating Your Introduction

- Create a one-sentence summary for your speech (thesis statement).
- Identify your two, three, or four main points (preview).
- Create a statement or question to spark curiosity about yourself and your speech (attention catcher).
- Decide what can you offer to create a sense of connection with your listeners on this topic (listener relevance).
- Decide what makes you an authority (speaker credibility).

The Body

The body of your speech is where you explain what you mean by each main point—that is, develop each main point with sufficient evidence and a listener relevance link. Within the body of the speech, successive main points are tied together by transitions. A **transition** is a statement that ties together main points by both providing verbal closure for one main point and introducing the next. Beginning speakers sometimes neglect the closure function of a transition statement, and this hurts the fluency of their message. "Next, I'll talk about . . . " is not effective because it does not tie two points together. Transition statements can be very simple, but they must serve both functions to be effective. Kris, for example, offered this transition statement between her first and second main points:

Transition: Now that you know where I grew up (first main point), let's talk about what it is about my reflection in a mirror that makes me unique (second main point).

Because she mentioned the first main point and sparked curiosity about the second, Kris's transition statement was effective. Cara used a more creative approach but was also successful because she mentioned the main point she had finished talking about and introduced the second:

Transition: My early childhood was unique (first main point) and sometimes I wonder what role it had in shaping my love for sports (second main point).

PRACTICING THE PROCESS

Writing Effective Transitions

- Jot down each main point for your next speech.
- Identify the connection between each main point based on your thesis.
- Identify the best way to close the discussion of each preceding point and introduce the next one.
- Write transitions between them.

The Conclusion

In the conclusion, you give listeners a sense of closure in a way that might help them remember your main topic and ideas. Hence the conclusion restates the thesis statement, briefly summarizes main points, and offers a clincher. In its simplest form, a **thesis restatement** merely reiterates the thesis statement in past tense. The **main point summary** reminds listeners of the two to four main points of your speech. The **clincher** is a final sentence or series of sentences that reinforces your main ideas in a memorable way. When speaking to persuade, you may offer a call to action as part of the clincher. When speaking to inform, however, as in most speeches of self-introduction, you offer a round off—a statement that provides closure to the speech creatively to foster retention and ties back to the introduction. The same techniques appropriate for attention catchers also work for clinchers: a rhetorical question, direct question, story, startling statistic, or quotation. In a conclusion, then, you "tell them what you told them." Kris's conclusion was this:

I. ***Thesis restatement:*** Today, I've offered some insight into who I—Kris Treinen—am.

II. ***Main point summary:*** We've talked about where I grew up, what makes me unique, and why I chose to come to NDSU.

III. ***Clincher:*** So now I hope you see why I have learned to look beyond the reflection I see in the mirror to understand who I am.

Cara's conclusion was this:

I. ***Thesis restatement:*** So now you understand how all my experiences have shaped who I am today.

II. ***Main point summary:*** My childhood adoption ordeal, my love for sports, and my dreams of becoming a high school teacher and soccer coach all contribute to my character.

III. ***Clincher:*** It might sound odd, but I am actually grateful for being left on that police station doorstep so long ago. It was the first of many exciting experiences that have shaped my life and who I am today.

The student who talked about a girl being teased closed her speech this way: "Remember that girl on the playground, the one who was being teased and nobody helped? Well, that girl was me." The woman who quoted the phrase in Mandarin did so again, but also translated it in her clincher. Another student quoted the end of the speech that he had quoted in the beginning. Although it takes creativity to come up with effective clinchers, it can make all the difference in whether your listeners remember your speech.

PRACTICING THE PROCESS

Creating Your Conclusion

- Write a thesis restatement for your speech.
- Write a main point summary for your speech.
- Write a clincher using any of the devices suggested in this chapter. Make sure it is creative so that it heightens retention, and that it ties back to the introduction in some way.

Develop the macrostructure of your public speech by using three kinds of outlines. Begin with a **preparation outline,** a rough draft of your speech ideas. In it list first versions of your thesis, preview, main points, and supporting material. Preparation outlines usually use key phrases rather than complete sentences. You'll revise the preparation outline several times as you consider breadth, depth, listener relevance, and the learning cycle. Next, develop a **formal outline,** which uses complete sentences, internal references, and a complete reference list of any external sources used to develop the speech. Kris's formal outline was this:

MIRROR IMAGE

—Kris Treinen

Introduction

I. ***Attention catcher:*** Have you ever looked into a mirror, seen your reflection, and then realized that the reflection in the mirror wasn't really you? This may seem a little strange to all of you, but this has actually happened to me many times throughout my life.

II. ***Listener relevance:*** As you listen to my speech today, I believe you'll begin to understand how important I believe it is to forge friendships with ourselves, with our families, and with others.

III. ***Thesis statement:*** Today, I'd like to inform you a little bit about who I—Kris Treinen—am.

IV. ***Preview:*** More specifically, let's talk about where I grew up, what makes me unique, and why I chose to come to NDSU for my college degree.

Body

I. ***First main point:*** I spent most of my life before coming to NDSU growing up in the Brainerd Lakes area. Perhaps you'll want to visit this area after you hear about it today. (Listener relevance link)

   A. I grew up in a small town called Nisswa, MN.

     1. I moved to Nisswa when I was three years old.

     2. We lived in a house that is very special to me.

   B. As I grew up, I attended different schools.

     1. I went to elementary school in Nisswa.

     2. I then attended and graduated from Brainerd High School with 424 other students.

Transition: *Now that you know where I grew up, let's talk about what it is about my reflection in a mirror that makes me unique.*

II. ***Second main point:*** Well, I had a mirror image while growing up and still have her today. Her name is Karla and she is my twin sister. Every day I am away from her, I realize how easy it was to take her and my family for granted. (Listener relevance)

   A. My sister and I were born right here at a local hospital in Fargo, North Dakota.

     1. We were born three minutes apart.

     2. I was born first, so I'm the oldest.

   B. We were known as the "good" twin and the "evil" twin.

     1. Here is a story about me as the "good" twin.

     2. Here is a story about Karla as the "evil" twin.

Transition: *Now that you know about my unique characteristic—my role as a twin and my twin sister Karla—let's talk about why I chose to come to NDSU to earn my degree.*

III. ***Third main point:*** I chose to further my education at NDSU. NDSU is a reputable school offering a variety of reputable degrees. (Listener relevance)

   A. I earned my first degree in 1992.

     1. I earned this degree from Concordia College.

     2. I realized I loved to learn and knew I wanted to learn more.

(continued)

B. I worked in various jobs.

    1. I was in customer service.

    2. I did radio broadcasting.

C. I knew I wanted to do something more and NDSU was right for me.

    1. NDSU has a reputable program.

    2. NDSU is close to home.

    3. I have friends at NDSU.

Conclusion

  I. ***Thesis restatement:*** Today, I've offered some insight into who I—Kris Treinen—am.

  II. ***Main point summary:*** We've talked about where I grew up, what makes me unique, and why I chose to come to NDSU.

  III. ***Clincher:*** So now I hope you see why I have learned to look beyond the reflection I see in the mirror to understand who I am.

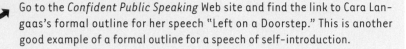

TURNING TO TECHNOLOGY

Cara Langaas's Formal Outline

Go to the *Confident Public Speaking* Web site and find the link to Cara Langaas's formal outline for her speech "Left on a Doorstep." This is another good example of a formal outline for a speech of self-introduction.

From your formal outline, develop a **speaking outline**—a brief outline that you'll refer to while presenting the speech. Write it down on index cards or paper using key words and phrases rather than complete sentences. Include delivery cues. Kris, for example, reminded herself on her speaking outline to slow down, look up, and pause (Figure 3.2). The speaking outline provides only the information you need to present the speech, not every word. Notice how Kris was able to use the same card for both her introduction and conclusion by merely color-coding her attention catcher and clincher. Presenting your speech from a speaking outline rather than a formal outline helps you speak extemporaneously and communicate with your listeners rather than perform for them or read to them.

TURNING TO TECHNOLOGY

Kris's Self-Introduction Speech

Go to Speech Interactive on the *Confident Public Speaking* CD-ROM to watch Kris present her speech.

What evidence does she offer for breadth under each main point? For depth?

What does she offer for listener relevance links under each main point?

Are her transitions clearly and correctly constructed? Are they creative?

Does her attention catcher serve its purpose?

Does her clincher serve its purpose?

PAUSE (1-2-3) BREATHE-----SMILE!!! ☺ ☺   1

ATTN C: HAVE YOU EVER LOOKED INTO A MIRROR...

LR: FORGE FRIENDSHIPS, FRIENDS, FAMILY...   *SLOW DOWN*

TODAY, I'M—INFORM YOU—WHO I // KRIS TREINEN // AM. ///

1-WHERE I GREW UP //

2-WHAT MAKES ME UNIQUE ///   *PAN ROOM*

3-WHY I CHOSE NDSU ///

                    LOOK UP

CLINCHER: (☺ ☺   PAUSE) SO, / NOW I HOPE YOU SEE WHY I'VE

LEARNED TO LOOK BEYOND THE REFLECTION IN THE MIRROR.... WHO

I AM (PAUSE!! SMILE!!!)

        I. BRAINERD LAKES AREA   *EYE CONTACT*   2

            NISSWA / SPECIAL HOUSE // DIFFERENT SCHOOLS

    TRANSITION: KNOW WHERE -----: REFLECTION IN THE MIRROR

        II. KARLA -- MIRROR

            BIRTH STORY /// GOOD AND EVIL TWINS

    TRANSITION: KNOW UNIQUE CHARACTERISTICS // WHY NDSU? //

        III. NDSU REPUTABLE SCHOOL AND DEGREES

            CONCORDIA / 1992 .... JOBS .... NDSU   *PAN ROOM*

    WAIT! PAUSE! ☺

Figure 3.2   Kris's speaking outline

Microstructure

Microstructure refers to language and style choices you make to convey ideas. In making these choices, strive for language that is clear, inclusive, and vivid.

There are no second chances with oral presentations, so they must be understood completely on first hearing. This requires choosing words that are familiar, concrete, and simple rather than unfamiliar, abstract, or complex. This isn't talking

Calvin and Hobbes   by Bill Watterson

Panel 1: I USED TO HATE WRITING ASSIGNMENTS, BUT NOW I ENJOY THEM.

Panel 2: I REALIZED THAT THE PURPOSE OF WRITING IS TO INFLATE WEAK IDEAS, OBSCURE POOR REASONING, AND INHIBIT CLARITY.

Panel 3: WITH A LITTLE PRACTICE, WRITING CAN BE AN INTIMIDATING AND IMPENETRABLE FOG! WANT TO SEE MY BOOK REPORT?

Panel 4: "THE DYNAMICS OF INTERBEING AND MONOLOGICAL IMPERATIVES IN DICK AND JANE: A STUDY IN PSYCHIC TRANSRELATIONAL GENDER MODES." / ACADEMIA, HERE I COME!

down to the audience, just an attempt to be as precise as possible for the sake of clarity. But even precise words aren't clear to a listener who doesn't understand their meaning. Kris talked about seeing her reflection in the mirror rather than merely seeing her face. That's okay because the word "reflection" is more precise than "face" and is still likely to be familiar to everyone in her audience. Had she used the word "visage," however, clarity might have suffered. For the same reason, avoid jargon or slang unless truly needed, and if you do use it define the words the first time you use them so all members of the audience will understand what you mean.

ETHICS

Since public speaking is a context for communication, use ethical language that demonstrates respect for listeners. Strive to be inclusive. First, whenever possible use "we" language rather than "I" or "you" language. "We" language acknowledges the role listeners play in creating shared understanding (Gorham, 1988; Powell & Harville, 1990). Kris, for example, offered "we" language at various points in her speech. Notice how her transitions incorporate it: "Now that you know where I grew up, *let's* talk about what it is about my reflection in a mirror that makes me unique." Second, avoid biased language that might marginalize some members of the audience and prevent you from reaching everyone with your message.

Finally, try to paint word pictures by offering vivid descriptions. Use descriptive language that enables listeners to see in their minds precisely what you see in yours. Kris referred to her reflection in the mirror rather than her face because "reflection" is not only more precise but more vivid. At minimum, the microstructure of an effective public speech is clear, inclusive, and vivid.

PRACTICING THE PROCESS

Guidelines for Incorporating Microstructure

- Go through your preparation outline and circle any words that might be unclear.
- Replace them with more concrete choices or define them using clear language.
- Incorporate inclusive "we" language wherever possible in your introductory statements, transitions, and concluding statements.
- Find one piece of evidence under each main point that you can embellish with descriptive language and word pictures.

PRACTICING THE PROCESS

Structure Checklist for Your First Speech

- ❏ Does your attention catcher tune listeners in to the topic?
- ❏ Do you offer a clear preview of your main points?
- ❏ Does each transition verbally tie the two points together?
- ❏ Do you restate your thesis statement and summarize your main points?
- ❏ Does your clincher tie back to the introduction?
- ❏ Is your language clear yet precise?
- ❏ Are your word choices vivid?
- ❏ Do you use inclusive language?

- Clear language appeals to the **thinking** dimension and the bottom half of the cycle.
- Inclusive language appeals to the **feeling** dimension and the top half of the cycle.
- Vivid language appeals to the **feeling** dimension and the top half of the cycle.

WHAT DOES IT MEAN TO HAVE EFFECTIVE DELIVERY?

To be effective, a public speech must also be delivered compellingly. Listeners often are more persuaded by the manner in which a speech is delivered than by the words used (Decker, 1992). Untrained listeners tend to focus almost entirely on delivery. **Delivery** refers to how you present your message. Using nonverbal cues such as the voice and body can help, but you must eliminate any nonverbal communication cues that might distract from your message or contradict the message. Integrate nonverbal cues that reinforce important points or clarify structure (Whalen, 1996). You can achieve this by carefully considering how you use your voice and body.

TURNING TO TECHNOLOGY

Delivery Tips

http://www.ukans.edu/cwis/units/coms2/vpa/vpa8.htm

At this Web site, read through the tips for presenting your speech. Do you agree? Why or why not? Which tips will be most difficult for you to achieve? Why?

Use of Voice

To deliver your first public speech, strive to be intelligible, conversational, and expressive. Speaking intelligibly means speaking in a way that is understood easily by all. This generally means speaking at a rate that is neither too fast nor too slow, a volume that is neither too loud nor too soft, and a pitch that is neither too high nor too low, thus allowing your ideas to be understood easily by all.

Conversational delivery sounds as though you are talking with listeners rather than reading to them or merely presenting in front of them. Beginning speakers are usually advised to speak extemporaneously from notes that consist of key words and phrases rather than from memory or from a manuscript. That's because it is extremely difficult to sound conversational when reciting from memory like an actor or reading from a script like a television news anchor (National Speakers Association, 2003). To be conversational, you must sound spontaneous no matter how many times you rehearsed the speech and no matter how much of it you memorized or are reading from notes.

Expressiveness is a matter of vocal variety. To be expressive, vary your voice over the course of the speech so you sound a bit more dramatic than you would in casual conversation, without sounding melodramatic. To do this, vary your rate, pitch, and volume to underscore your attitudes and emotional convictions; stress

WHAT DO YOU THINK?

Identify a public speaker who has what you consider a beautiful oral style (a preacher, a teacher, a television news broadcaster, an actor, and so on). Does the speaker sound conversational? Intelligible? Expressive? Describe why you think his or her oral style is beautiful.

key words and phrases; and pause strategically before, during, or after important ideas to make them stand out. Kris, for example, paused during her thesis statement to help make her name stand out. She said, "Today (pause), I'd like to inform you a little bit about who I (pause) Kris Treinen (pause) am." She also stressed key words when describing herself as the "good" twin and her sister as the "evil" twin. She exclaimed, "*Luckily* for *me* (pause), *I* was labeled the *good* twin. Unfortunately, though, this meant my sister was saddled with the label (pause) the *evil* (pause) twin."

An intelligible, conversational, and expressive voice is similar to the voice used in casual conversation because it sounds spontaneous but is actually *heightened* and *flexible* in ways that make the message sound more compelling.

PRACTICING THE PROCESS

Incorporating Vocal Delivery Cues

- Create a speaking outline of key words and phrases as described earlier in the chapter.
- Add slash marks (//) to remind yourself of places to pause for emphasis.
- Use a highlighter or underscore words or phrases you'll stress by speaking louder or by changing pitch.
- Use arrows above phrases where you want to increase or decrease your rate.
- Practice delivering your speech out loud.

Use of Body

To deliver an effective public speech you must also consider how your eyes, face, stance, and hands communicate. **Eye contact**—that is, looking at the audience—is crucial. First, use your notes only as references; refer to them less than 10 percent of the time. To convey commitment to your audience, you need to show them that they are more important to you than your notes. Do this by looking up from your notes at least 90 percent of the time. Second, pan the entire audience. Be sure to look not just at listeners in the center of the room, but also at those seated in far corners or in the front or the back. If you don't, some listeners might feel ignored or marginalized. Finally, to create a sense of connection with your listeners, look them in the eyes until you feel a sense of response in return. Because much of communication occurs with the eyes, your listeners need to feel this connection to you. It is generally a good idea to remind yourself in your notes to make eye contact. Kris, for example, reminded herself to "look up," "make eye contact," and "pan the entire room" on her speaking outline.

Try to make your facial expressions reflect your conviction about the topic. As with your voice, don't exaggerate. But speaking without much facial expression conveys a lack of commitment to the topic and occasion.

Your stance should express poise. Plant yourself firmly before beginning to speak, maintain this stance throughout the speech, and when finished wait a moment or two before returning to your chair. Poise can be shown by keeping your feet about shoulder width apart, not leaning on either leg, and keeping knees

Eye contact, facial expressions, and gestures contribute to a speech's effectiveness.

slightly bent. You might remind yourself about stance with a delivery cue on your speaking outline.

Make sure any gestures you use reinforce an important point or clarify structure. Kris gestured as she previewed each main point of her speech. Doing so helped clarify her structure. Plan and practice these gestures in advance. Practice your gestures while seated at a table to make sure they extend from the elbow rather than from the wrist. Also, be sure to avoid putting your hands in your pockets, fidgeting with your notes, or playing with your hair. These behaviors distract listeners from the ideas you are trying to convey. The key is to let your hands rest on your notes or at your sides unless you are using them to emphasize an important idea.

Beginning speakers are often more anxious about delivery than about structure or content. This is usually rooted in a fear of the unknown. The only way you can eliminate it is to practice. You might ask a few close friends to listen and offer suggestions. You might present your speech in front of a mirror. You might even videotape yourself. But you must rehearse to be effective.

TURNING TO TECHNOLOGY

Spontaneous Gestures

Access InfoTrac College Edition through the *Confident Public Speaking* CD-ROM. Locate and read "Capturing Feelings on Film: Natural Gestures Work Best" by Philip N. Douglis (Hint: Use "gestures" as your search term.) What kinds of messages do natural gestures convey? How can you make your planned gestures appear spontaneous to your audience? Is it appropriate for a speaker to adapt to audience responses to his or her gestures during the speech? Why or why not?

PRACTICING THE PROCESS

Incorporating Body Delivery Cues

- Put a reminder in your notes to *pause* before beginning and after finishing your speech.
- Put similar reminders for eye contact in your notes.
- Place reminders where you plan to gesture to emphasize important points or to clarify structure.
- Practice delivering your speech using your body cues to a few close friends or videotape yourself to discover whether you appear poised, spontaneous, and motivated.

PRACTICING THE PROCESS

Delivery Checklist for Your First Speech

- ❑ Do you sound conversational?
- ❑ Do you stress key words?
- ❑ Do you incorporate pauses to reinforce the message?
- ❑ Do you look up 90 percent of the time?
- ❑ Do you connect with your listeners?
- ❑ Do you pan the entire room?
- ❑ Do you plant yourself firmly before beginning and throughout the speech?
- ❑ Do your gestures extend from the elbow?

Kris's Delivery

Watch the video of Kris's speech again and focus on her presentation.

- Is she intelligible? Is she easy to understand?
- Does she sound conversational?
- Does she sound sincere? Do you believe her?
- Does she demonstrate good eye contact?
- Does her facial expression enhance her believability?
- Is she poised?
- Do her gestures emphasize important points or clarify structure?
- Does she display any distracting gestures or movement?

Delivery Tips

http://www.school-for-champions.com/speaking/using_notes.htm

Read through the tips offered for delivery. Take the Mini-quiz at the end to see what you've learned.

SUMMARY

The elements of content, structure, and delivery are the basis upon which all effective public speeches are built. As you develop your first speech, take time to consider your listeners as they relate to each of these three elements and your first speech will be successful. Key principles to guide content include selecting your topic and purpose, choosing kinds of evidence, and providing listener relevance links throughout. The key to effective structure focuses on the macrostructural elements in the introduction, body, and conclusion as well as the microstructural elements of language and style. The key to effective delivery is to convey your ideas in ways that reinforce the verbal message without distracting or contradicting it. You do so by considering your use of voice and body. Chapters 4–18 are devoted to deeper discussions of each of these basic principles of effective public speaking—that is, audience-centered content, structure, and delivery.

The *Confident Public Speaking* CD-ROM is your one-stop point of access for not just the content on the CD itself, such as Speech Interactive, but also the many other resources on the *Confident Public Speaking* Web site, Speech Builder Express, and InfoTrac College Edition. Note that this chapter's key terms and activities are among the resources available in electronic format online. Additional information is included below.

SPEECH INTERACTIVE
ON THE *CONFIDENT PUBLIC SPEAKING* CD-ROM

Speech Interactive is your link to this text's speech videos. Offering opportunities to practice critiquing speeches by students and other public speakers, these videos will help you prepare for providing effective feedback to your peers and your own speech performances.

SPEECH BUILDER EXPRESS

Use Speech Builder Express to prepare the self-introductory speech for which activity 1 below asks. Be sure to select "Introductory" from the drop-down menu of speech types on the Setup page. You might also want to use the Speech Timeline feature to help you manage your time (and possible anxiety about the project).

KEY TERMS

Interactive flashcards for these key terms are available on the *Confident Public Speaking* Web site. You'll find the "Flashcards" link under the resources for Chapter 3.

ACTIVITIES

The activities below are available in electronic format on the *Confident Public Speaking* Web site. You'll find the "Activities" link under the resources for Chapter 3.

1. **Speech of Self-Introduction.** Prepare and present a two- to three-minute speech introducing yourself to the class. Develop your main points around aspects of your personal background, some unique characteristic or experience, and professional goals. Evidence to support each main point can come from personal life experiences you've had. Deliver your speech from a speaking outline on index cards.

2. **Introduce a Classmate.** Interview a classmate to discover his or her personal background, a unique characteristic or experience, and professional goals. Evidence to support each main point can come from personal life experiences your classmate has had. Introduce him or her to the class in a two- to three-minute speech using a speaking outline on index cards.

3. **Personal Significance Speech.** Prepare and present a three- to five-minute speech informing your class about an object, a person, an event, or a belief that has helped shape who you are today. Main points should focus on specific values you hold that are somehow represented by that object, person, event, or belief. Evidence to support each main point should come from personal life experiences. Listeners should leave knowing why the topic is significant to you. Deliver your speech using a speaking outline on index cards.

INFOTRAC COLLEGE EDITION ACTIVITY

Locate and read the following article. "Capturing Feelings on Film: Natural Gestures Work Best" by Philip N. Douglis. (Hint: Use "gestures" as your search term.) What kinds of messages do natural gestures convey? How can you make your planned gestures appear spontaneous? Is it appropriate for a speaker to adapt to audience response communicated by their gestures while giving a speech? Why or why not?

CHAPTER

4

LISTENING AND CRITIQUING COMMUNICATION

REFLECTIVE QUESTIONS

1. What is the difference between listening and hearing? Why are listening skills important?

2. What is critical listening? What are some other purposes for listening?

3. What bad habits hurt effective listening? How might they be overcome?

4. What does it mean to be an ethical listener?

5. In what ways is critiquing more than listening? What does it mean to be an ethical critic?

WHAT'S AHEAD: FOCUSING YOUR READING

What Is Listening and Why Is It Important?

Types of Listening: Considering Your Purpose

The SIER Model of Critical Listening

The Ethical Listener: Tips for Improving Critical Listening Skills

The Ethical Critic: Tips for Improving Critiquing Skills

Examples of Content, Structure, and Delivery Critiques

BEKKA WAS EXCITED TO BE STARTING college. She had saved for a long time to make her dream of earning a college degree a reality. As she sat in class, she noticed the beautiful view. She hadn't thought about how much facilities managers do to make a campus beautiful.

The instructor went over the syllabus and major requirements for the course. He spoke in a soft voice for such a large room and Bekka strained to hear. She wondered why there was no microphone in the room. Oh well. Bekka decided to telephone her mother that evening to tell her how perfect college was turning out to be.

The professor explained that each student would be part of a team that would do a service learning project as a major part of the course requirements. The final project would be a paper and presentation to be delivered to employees of the organization where the student was placed. Bekka noticed that the professor's speaking style was poor. It reminded her of a boring high school teacher she once had. She worried that she was not going to like this section and wondered if there might be openings in another one. The person sitting next to Bekka was chewing gum. It annoyed her. She made a mental note *not* to chew gum in class. Bekka hoped she would not be teamed with slackers. She usually hated working on teams because it seemed like she had to do most of the work.

As the professor continued, Bekka felt her stomach grumble. She made another mental note: don't skip breakfast. Suddenly she noticed the room was quiet. She looked around to discover that all eyes were on her. The professor was waiting for her answer. The problem was that she didn't know the question. Bekka felt her face flush as she replied, "I'm sorry. Could you repeat the question?"

Bekka did telephone her mother that evening. But she didn't say that college was perfect.

Although Bekka had good intentions and wanted to make a favorable first impression, she was a poor listener. She is not alone. Research suggests that even when trying to listen carefully, most people remember only about 50 percent of what they hear shortly after hearing it and only about 25 percent two days later (e.g., DeWine & Daniels, 1993; Steil, Barker, & Watson, 1983).

TURNING TO TECHNOLOGY

Test Your Listening Skills

http://www.esl-lab.com/

At this Web site, listen to some of the EASY, MEDIUM, and DIFFICULT listening excerpts and take the quizzes that follow. Record the number of answers you get right and wrong. Why weren't you able to answer them correctly?

Unfortunately, most people are poor listeners even though it can hurt them personally and professionally. Most of us can identify at least one time when ineffective listening caused us such problems. If effective listening is so important to personal and professional success, why aren't we better at it? In this chapter, we explore that question.

The chapter starts with a discussion of what listening is and why it plays such an important role in communication transactions. Then it examines the types of listening and how understanding them can help us become more effective listeners. The SIER model provides a four-step process for critical listening. The

There are many potential distractions in any listening situation.

fourth section highlights what it means to be an ethical listener and provides specific strategies for improving listening skills. As noted in Chapter 1, ethical decisions are rooted in the virtues of respect and honesty, which provide the basis for our ethical decisions not only as public speakers but as listeners and critics. The chapter ends with a discussion of the characteristics of a critique, what it means to be an ethical critic, and one method for critiquing.

WHAT IS LISTENING AND WHY IS IT IMPORTANT?

People sometimes make the mistake of thinking that listening and hearing are basically the same. They are not. **Hearing** is a physiological process, whereas listening is a psychological process. Hearing is simply a biological function, but listening occurs only when we choose to attach meaning to what we hear. In other words, I can *hear* you without *listening* to you. It's true I must be able to hear you before I can listen to you, which means that hearing is a necessary component of listening, but listening adds the dimension of psychological processing (e.g., Halone et al., 1998).

Where I live, for example, emergency sirens are tested at 1:00 p.m. on the first Wednesday of each month. People can hear them throughout the city whether they're at home, the office, or outdoors. If I hear the sirens and continue doing what I'm doing without thinking about what they mean, I have merely *heard* them. But if I also consider whether they indicate just a test or a real emergency, I add the dimension of mental processing. Hence I not only hear the sirens but listen to them. **Listening** is the psychological process of receiving (hearing), attending to, constructing meaning from, and responding to spoken or nonverbal messages (International Listening Association, 1996).

TURNING TO TECHNOLOGY

The International Listening Association

http://www.listen.org

This is the official Web site of the International Listening Association. Look at the quotations offered and select two or three that you might use in a speech someday.

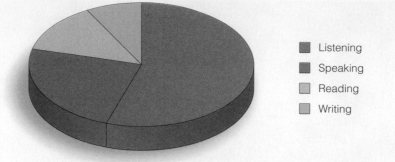

Listening
Speaking
Reading
Writing

Figure 4.1 Communication process breakdown

Listening skills are vitally important to our relationships because so much of our communication time is spent listening. We communicate by speaking, listening, reading, and writing, and as Figure 4.1 reveals we spend more time listening than on all other forms of communication combined: 55 percent on listening, 24 percent on speaking, 13 percent on reading, and 8 percent on writing (Watson & Barker, 1984). In college you spend about 90 percent of your class time listening (Coakley & Wolvin, 1991). Not surprisingly, studies show that students who listen more effectively learn better and, as a result, earn better grades than those who don't (Barker et al., 1980; Hunsaker, 1991; Legge, 1971).

Effective listening skills are also vital for you as a professional. Research suggests that employees spend 55 to 60 percent of their time listening and that poor listening skills can lead to billion-dollar mistakes. Many employers recognize this and offer listening training to employees (e.g., Hiam, 1997; Linowes, 1998; Wolvin & Coakley, 1991). Moreover, a survey of top-level North American executives revealed that 80 percent believe listening is one of the most important skills needed in the corporate environment (Salopek, 1999). It simply makes sense to improve listening skills.

WHAT DO YOU THINK?

Consider the classes you are currently taking. How often do you speak and for how long? Do you ask questions or discuss issues? How often do other students speak? How much time is spent listening to the professor and to other students?

TYPES OF LISTENING: CONSIDERING YOUR PURPOSE

Whether communicating with others at home, school, work, or someplace else, you can be sure that most of your time will be spent listening. To listen effectively, you must consider the listening purpose for that situation. For example, you might listen to a friend give you directions to a favorite restaurant, or vent about a recent argument, or even rehearse an upcoming public speech. In each case, your listening purpose differs.

There are five types of listening based on different purposes: discriminative, comprehensive, appreciative, empathic, and critical (Wolvin & Coakley, 1992). Each type demands a different degree of psychological processing. The most demanding type is critical listening. Critical listening requires us to hear, understand, evaluate, and assign worth to a message. Because we spend so much time listening, it is not feasible or necessary to engage in critical listening all the time. Consider your purpose and then engage in the most appropriate type of listening for a given situation.

Discriminative listening is "listening between the lines" for meaning conveyed other than through the words themselves. It has to do with being attentive to what is said via verbal and nonverbal cues such as rate, pitch, inflection, volume, quality, inflection, and so forth. Discriminative listening also includes considering the meaning behind behaviors accompanying the message, such as laughing, sighing, and yawning.

Paying attention to slips of the tongue and vocalized pauses like "ums" and "uhs," which might indicate deception, is also an aspect of discriminative listening. Parents trying to resolve a conflict between their children sometimes decipher meaning as much from what is *not said* as what *is said*.

Business executives also often engage in discriminative listening to determine underlying issues when dealing with employees (Linowes, 1998). Likewise, citizens listening to political speeches sometimes make inferences about unstated matters based on what the speaker *does* offer.

Comprehensive listening is listening for understanding. It is appropriate when your purpose is to gain knowledge and retain it. You concentrate on the message in order to understand it, not to judge it. Realize, though, that you must physically hear as well as psychologically discriminate verbal and nonverbal messages in order to understand the meaning accurately.

We engage in comprehensive listening frequently in our personal and professional lives. For example, in professional life we listen comprehensively to speakers at seminars, conferences, and symposiums, as well as to lecturing professors. In personal life we listen comprehensively to broadcast news reporters talk about recent events. We listen comprehensively to family members describe their day. We listen comprehensively to physicians explain a diagnosis. And the list goes on.

Appreciative listening is listening for enjoyment through the works and experiences of others (Wolvin & Coakley, 1992). It can include listening to music, environmental sounds, or a public speaker's oral style. When you engage in appreciative listening, your purpose is to savor the power and beauty of well-chosen and articulated spoken words or music.

Listening to music is a prime example of appreciative listening. Whether you enjoy rock, pop, hip-hop, country, classical, or some other genre, the fact that you have preferences suggests you engage in appreciative listening. Some people listen appreciatively to environmental sounds. I enjoy camping with my family every summer; one reason is the sounds I get to hear—birds and crickets and even the breeze whistling through the trees. You can also listen appreciatively to the oral style of public speakers. Consider that of Martin Luther King, Jr., as he delivered his famous "I Have a Dream" speech. I enjoy listening to the *Prairie Home Companion* radio program because I love Garrison Keillor's oral style. My friend Kathy enjoys listening to baseball games on the radio for similar reasons. She doesn't listen to understand who's winning and losing, but for the sound of a game being announced.

WHAT DO YOU THINK?
Identify a time when someone lied to you. Did you suspect they were lying before you found out? What specific things about the way they talked or behaved led you to your assumption?

WHAT DO YOU THINK?
Do you ever turn on the radio or television in the morning to decide what to wear that day? If so, why? If not, have you ever wished you had known to bring an umbrella or a jacket?

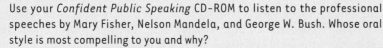

TURNING TO TECHNOLOGY

Appreciative Listening

Use your *Confident Public Speaking* CD-ROM to listen to the professional speeches by Mary Fisher, Nelson Mandela, and George W. Bush. Whose oral style is most compelling to you and why?

While perhaps more rousing than relaxing, listening to entertainers such as comedians can be a form of appreciative listening.

© The Everett Collection

Empathic listening is listening to support, help, and empathize with the speaker. It's what you do when you listen to a friend vent about a problem or concern. You are essentially a sounding board as he or she sorts through an issue out loud. Usually the goal of empathic listening is to lend support, not advice. This requires a good deal of psychological processing on your part because you must initially discriminate the verbal and nonverbal messages being sent and then comprehend them.

Empathic listening occurs most often in interpersonal relationships. Therapists, counselors, psychologists, and psychiatrists also engage in empathic listening with their clients. So do those who answer telephone hotlines to support troubled people (e.g., Gunderson, 1999; Morgan, 1983).

WHAT DO YOU THINK?

Have you ever vented to a close friend about someone or something that was bothering you? Were you seeking advice or seeking support? How did your friend respond and what was the result?

TURNING TO TECHNOLOGY

Empathic Listening

http://www.adv-leadership-grp.com/programs/evaluations/listening.htm

Go to this Web site and respond to the listening scenarios provided. Then submit your responses to see how you did. Which empathic listening tips did you have the most trouble with? How will you use this information to improve your listening skills?

Critical listening is the process of hearing, understanding, evaluating, and assigning worth to a message. It is appropriate when your goal is to think deeply and react analytically to a message. For example, you'll want to use critical listening when someone seeks your opinion, when asked to assume responsibility, or when trying to become an expert on an issue. To listen most effectively to public speakers you should also engage in critical listening, including when professors lecture. Why? Well, research suggests students who listen comprehensively without evaluating or reacting will forget most of the material shortly after completing the course (Luiten, Ames, & Ackerman, 1980).

Because so much time is spent listening and because critical listening demands so much effort, it is not possible to engage in it all the time. Hence, examine the situation and decide on the most appropriate type of listening for your purpose.

WHAT DO YOU THINK?
Identify a time when you should have engaged in critical listening. Did you do so? Were you successful? Were you satisfied with the result?

THE SIER MODEL OF CRITICAL LISTENING

The **SIER model** (Ross, 1983, p. 99) shows how critical listening depends on a four-step process that begins with hearing. As Figure 4.2 highlights, the four steps are *sense, interpret, evaluate,* and *react.* Let's discuss each of them and the potential obstacles you may have to overcome (*Active Listening,* 1997).

The first step is sensing, or simply hearing, the message. Several potential obstacles may be encountered here before it's possible to proceed to the next stage. These obstacles may originate in the speaker, environment, or listener. One obstacle might be inadequate volume by the speaker. Debbie, for example, is very articulate but so quiet that only those sitting in the first few rows can hear her. Another obstacle might be environmental sounds such as loud ceiling fans, radios, or traffic noises that can overpower the message. When one public speaking class

© Rhoda Sidney/Stock Boston, LLC

Hotline telephone volunteers engage in empathic listening.

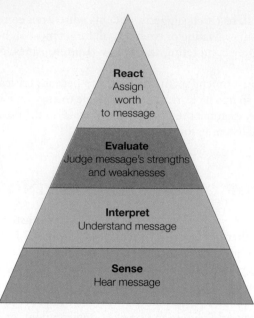

Figure 4.2 The SIER model of critical listening

took advantage of a nice day to go to a park, students discovered how difficult it was to be heard over the roar of traffic. Yet another obstacle might be a hearing disability in the listener. Any of these potential obstacles could inhibit hearing the message and, ultimately, make it impossible to listen critically.

If you can hear the message, the second step is to interpret—that is, understand it. This involves listening comprehensively. One potential obstacle to interpretation is not knowing the language being spoken, or the dialect or accent used. Unfamiliar slang or technical jargon can impede understanding too. Have you ever sat through a lecture where the professor used jargon without defining it or assumed you understood basic principles when you didn't? I remember being placed in a senior-level political science course as a first-year undergraduate. The professor assumed all the students had a fundamental understanding of political science concepts, but I didn't and could not interpret what he was telling us.

Sometimes a speaker's failure to enunciate clearly can act as a barrier to interpreting a message. **Enunciation** is how crisply we form vowels and consonants. Imagine the following conversation:

Ben: D'ja wannuh glassuh waduh?
Lars: Don'go'time. Gottuh goduh work cuz I owe my dad a hunner bucks.
Ben: Wha'duh ya owe yer dad a hunner bucks fer?
Lars: I dunno. I guessee thinks I shoulduh botmah ohn fishin' license er somepin.

Sloppy enunciation in informal conversations is common and generally doesn't matter. But use it in a public speech and listeners might have problems interpreting your message.

If you can hear (sense) and understand (interpret) the message, you can move to the third step, which is to evaluate the message. To do this you judge its strengths and weaknesses, determine whether you agree or disagree, and decide whether you like or dislike it.

Critical listening sometimes breaks down at this step because we prejudge the speaker as lacking credibility. Have you ever decided a teacher was not very intelligent because he or she appeared disheveled or disorganized? If so, you encountered an obstacle at the evaluation step: Your feelings about the speaker prevented you from judging the message fairly. Strong feelings about the message can also be an obstacle, tempting you to mentally argue with the speaker instead of evaluating the message. For example, Lenny disagreed with Jill's argument that alcohol should be allowed in campus dorms. There is nothing inherently wrong with disagreeing, but Lenny chose to mentally defend his own position throughout the speech rather than to listen open-mindedly to Jill's reasons and then formulate a response. Had Lenny listened first and judged later, he could have engaged in effective evaluation.

Once you have evaluated a message, you can move to the final step in the SIER model of critical listening: react. When you react to a message, you assign worth to it. You go beyond merely judging its strengths and weaknesses to determine the ways in which you and others who hear the message are better off for having heard it. In other words, you answer the following questions:

1. In what way or ways am I better off for having heard this message?

   And when the message is delivered to others as well as you:

2. How might this message benefit others in this room?

The potential obstacle you must overcome is the tendency to conclude that the communication was of no value to you, and maybe even not to anybody else. Effective critical listeners ask, "What's in it for me?" and *find something*.

Often you'll discover at least some benefit. For example, you might have learned about a new concept, idea, or process. Or the speaker might have presented statistics or evidence you had not been aware of or addressed a familiar topic in a new way. It's possible you will gain no new information or insight. This happened to Wanda when she listened to Marcus talk about how to change a flat tire; she was working her way through school as an automobile mechanic and the content of Marcus's speech was familiar. But Wanda could also *react* by considering how the audience might benefit. She decided that because most of her classmates had probably never changed a flat, the content was worthwhile because it benefited them.

You can also react by assigning worth based on the speaker's delivery. You might decide you're better off for having heard a speech because the delivery was effective. Marcus, for example, used eye contact and facial expressions in ways that made it seem like he was sincerely talking to each member of his audience. Wanda made a mental note to try to emulate his use of eye contact and facial expressions.

Likewise, you can decide you're better off for having heard a speaker use effective structure. Wanda liked how Marcus tied together his attention catcher and clincher by using a hypothetical story as the opening attention catcher and offering an ending to the story in his clincher. She decided she'd try to do something just as clever in her own speech.

You might also decide you're better for having heard a speaker whose delivery or structure was ineffective. Wanda had a difficult time following Marcus's organization because his transitions did not verbally tie his points together. She made a mental note to use transitions that verbally tie together her points. These kinds of reactions about a speaker's ineffective delivery or structure are also legitimate answers to the reaction questions in the SIER model of critical listening.

By representing critical listening as a four-step process, the SIER model provides several important insights: It shows how hearing is only the first step in the process of listening, and how we can listen to different extents, as well as where and why our efforts to listen critically may break down.

Once you see the steps involved in critical listening and the obstacles to it, you can understand why we don't always succeed as critical listeners. Add the percentage of communication time we spend listening and the task might seem rather daunting. Indeed, we'd burn out if we engaged in critical listening all the time. However, critical listening is not always necessary. An effective listener considers the purpose and employs the most appropriate type of listening to achieve that goal.

THE ETHICAL LISTENER: TIPS FOR IMPROVING CRITICAL LISTENING SKILLS

ETHICS

Research shows that critical listening is both important and difficult—that we grasp only about 50 percent of what we hear. Fortunately, it also suggests that we can improve our ability to listen effectively by employing certain strategies. Ethical listeners constantly strive to improve their listening skills. Why? As discussed in Chapter 1, an ethical choice is something we believe we "ought" to do rather than something we "have" to do. We talked about two fundamental virtues that guide ethical decisions: respect and honesty. You must strive to improve your listening skills to honestly demonstrate respect for yourself and the speaker.

This section discusses six of the most common bad habits that may hurt your ability to listen effectively. For each, we look at reasons people fall victim to the bad habit and offer a strategy to eliminate it. As you read, consider which habits plague you most often and situations where they tend to occur. Highlight at least one strategy you might use to improve your critical listening skills with regard to that habit.

Bad Habits

1. Becoming distracted
2. Faking attention
3. Being unprepared
4. Prejudging the speaker
5. Mentally arguing and jumping to conclusions
6. Listening too hard

Bad Habit Number 1: Becoming Distracted

This is probably the most common bad habit that results in poor listening. Distractions may be mental, physical, auditory, or visual. Consider again the story of Bekka from the beginning of this chapter. Bekka's poor listening came as a result of becoming distracted.

While listening to the professor, Bekka became distracted when she contemplated telephoning her mother and then again when she wondered who her team members would be. **Mental distractions** are simply the wandering thoughts you have when you ought to be listening instead.

Bekka was physically distracted when she felt her stomach grumble because she had skipped breakfast. **Physical distractions** are those associated with body aches, pains, and feelings. Bekka was visually distracted by the view from the classroom window. And Bekka experienced both a visual and an auditory distraction when she became annoyed with the person chewing gum. **Visual distractions** are those associated with something you see, and **auditory distractions** are those associated with something you hear.

The main reason we become distracted so easily has to do with the speed at which we speak and process information. Most people speak at a rate of 120 to 150 words per minute, yet our brains can process between 400 and 800 words per minute (Wolvin & Conkley, 1992). This means that listeners usually assume they know what a speaker is going to say before she or he finishes saying it. Because you are able to comprehend so quickly what a speaker is saying, your mind has time to wander. As a result you may lose your focus on the message.

The problem is compounded when the speaker talks even more slowly (Mayer, 1996). Have you ever tried to listen carefully to someone who speaks slowly? If you are like me, you want to finish their sentences for them. In any case, the chances for becoming distracted by a slow speaker are even greater.

The media may aggravate this problem. Changes in television programming and the format of commercials are causing us to have shorter attention spans and less patience. Commercials last about fifteen seconds today compared to one to two minutes in the 1950s and 1960s. Likewise, sitcom plots move very quickly. Hence people tend to become distracted more quickly now than twenty years ago (Stephens, 1999).

A Strategy: Expend Energy

Perhaps the most important strategy used to improve listening skills is to expend energy (e.g., Horowitz, 1996; Kaye, 1998; Mulvany, 1998). That means sitting up straight, leaning forward, and maintaining eye contact. Since the brain processes information more quickly than we speak, listeners must do whatever possible to stay focused. Expend energy at the beginning of the speech and then periodically check to make sure you have not started to relax. If you have, reel yourself back in. Even these behaviors can't prevent all distractions, but becoming distracted is less likely when you make a conscious attempt to be alert rather than slouch, lean back, or close your eyes.

As Marsha's classmate presented an informative speech about the Amish, for example, Marsha rested her head in her hands and closed her eyes. When the professor asked her to pay attention, she responded, "I am listening. I'm just resting my eyes." Perhaps Marsha was trying to listen, but her lack of energy would likely allow her mind to wander.

PRACTICING THE PROCESS

Expend Energy

The next time you feel your mind wander while a professor is lecturing, take these steps:

- Sit up straight.
- Lean forward.
- Maintain eye contact.
- Regain focus by expending energy to avoid missing important information.

Bad Habit Number 2: Faking Attention

Experienced listeners look the speaker in the eye, nod periodically as he or she speaks, lean forward a bit in their chair, and so forth. Our parents and teachers told us that practicing these confirming behaviors demonstrates respect for the speaker (Cissna & Sieburg, 1981). They were right. Unfortunately, many of us have learned to do this even when we are not really listening. In other words, we fake it. Although faking attention is useful on occasion, it also can lead to missing important information and even to botching a personal or professional relationship.

> **WHAT DO YOU THINK?**
> Recall a time when you ought to have been listening but faked paying attention instead. What was the situation? What were the consequences?

Consider this conversation between Davey and Brad. Davey had just engaged in a terrible argument with his girlfriend, and she had broken off their engagement, claiming he was insensitive and didn't respect her freedom. He decided to consult his best friend, Brad.

Davey: Brad, I don't know what to do. I feel awful.
Brad: [*Nods*]
Davey: I want Carol to know I respect her freedom, but she needs to know I don't think I can live without her.
Brad: [*Nods again and leans forward.*]
Davey: Maybe I should just let her go. If she really cares she'll come back. Or maybe I should go to her place and try to talk to her again. What do you think?
Brad: Sounds like a plan to me.

Brad practiced confirming behaviors but had not really listened to Davey at all.

Engaging in this bad habit can also result in missed information. Recall that this happened to Bekka, who appeared to be listening to her professor because she looked attentive and nodded during the lecture. But because she was faking attention, she was forced to ask, "Could you repeat the question?"

A Strategy: Take Notes

One way to avoid faking attention is to take notes (Bostrom, 1990; Kiewra et al., 1988; Messmer, 1998). This can help in a number of other ways as well: It can re-

PEANUTS reprinted by permission of United Feature Syndicate, Inc.

duce your tendency to become distracted from the message and make you more aware of the organizational patterns of the speech. For these and other reasons, effective note taking can increase the probability that you'll remember the information later.

Unfortunately, ineffective note taking can do more harm than good and few people are taught how to take effective notes. Good note takers are flexible and thus can adjust to the speaker's presentational style and connect ideas to their own experiences. If a speaker makes a claim and supports it with examples from his or her life, your notes might be more helpful if you embellish some of the examples with your own. When you review your notes later, examples that relate the ideas directly to your life might better crystallize the speech for you (Miccinati, 1988).

Because each method of taking notes has strengths and weaknesses, experiment to discover which is most helpful to you. The most common method is outlining (Figure 4.3). This is effective if the structure is clear. If it's not, consider using the precis method (Figure 4.4) or the organizational mapping method (Figure 4.5). With the precis method, every few minutes you mentally summarize what you've listened to and write it down. Record your summaries quickly, using short phrases and incomplete sentences, so you won't miss an important idea while writing. You can always go back to your notes and complete the sentences later. With the organizational mapping method, write down each main idea as it is presented and draw a circle around it. When a significant detail, example, or piece of evidence is offered to support a main idea, write it on a line extending from the circled main idea.

WHAT DO YOU THINK?

Have you ever tried to take notes by outlining when a professor did not use clear structure? How helpful were your notes later on?

PRACTICING THE PROCESS

Take Notes

The next time you feel yourself faking attention during a lecture, experiment by doing the following:

- Outlining the professor's information
- Recording quick key-word summaries of his or her information
- Mapping the ideas with circles and lines

Which of these methods seems most effective for following the professor?

Bad Habit Number 3: Being Unprepared

Good critical listening demands effort, not only during the communication event but also beforehand. It requires physical, mental, and intellectual preparation.

Introduction

I. *Thesis:* The SIER model of critical listening

II. *Preview:* It has four steps

Body

I. *Main point number 1:* First step is to sense
- **A.** *Supporting material:* This means you can physically hear it
- **B.** *Supporting material:* Obstacles occur in the speaker, listener, or environment

II. *Main point number 2:* Second step is to Interpret
- **A.** *Supporting material:* This means you understand it
- **B.** *Supporting material:* Obstacles include . . . etc.

Figure 4.3 Outlining method of note taking

- Listening is more than hearing.
- SIER model (four steps).
- Sense/hear.
- Interpret/understand.
- Evaluate/judge.
- React/assign worth.

Figure 4.4 Precis method of note taking

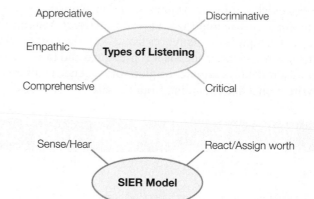

Figure 4.5 Organizational mapping method of note taking

But most people today juggle many roles and responsibilities. You might be a college student, an employee, a parent, and a volunteer. Consequently you might need to complete readings and assignments, complete your shift at work, transport children to and from after-school activities, and mail out a newsletter all in one evening before class. In our efforts to meet so many demands on our time, we run the risk of failing to prepare adequately. If you are not prepared to listen, you may lose concentration, become distracted, fail to understand information, or even fall asleep.

WHAT DO YOU THINK?

Consider a time when you went to class overtired or hungry. How much of the information did you remember later?

A Strategy: Prepare Yourself

This strategy is simple but not always easy. To engage in effective critical listening, prepare physically by getting plenty of rest and eating a healthy meal. Prepare mentally by clearing your mind of competing concerns; to do this, you might try aerobic activity or meditation. Prepare intellectually by completing any assigned reading *before* it is to be discussed so you'll have the background needed to understand what you hear. If you are planning to attend a professional lecture, read something the speaker wrote. This will give you ideas that you can expand on as you listen. Preparation is not necessarily easy, but if you take it seriously you will be a more effective listener.

PRACTICING THE PROCESS

Prepare Yourself

When you want to get the most out of a lecture, try this:

- Read up on the topic in advance.
- Take care of other business that might cause you to worry during the lecture.
- Go to bed early the night before.
- Get some exercise to clear your mind on the day of the event.
- Eat a healthy meal before the event.

Bad Habit Number 4: Prejudging the Speaker

Prejudging the speaker is an obstacle to critical listening, but it's common. Have you ever walked into a classroom on the first day of class and, based just on the way the instructor looked, decided it was going to be a waste of time? Perhaps you thought the instructor looked too young, or too old, too casual, too formal, too unstylish, or too eccentric. Research suggests that students do indeed determine whether they like the teacher very quickly (Kearney, 1994; Kearney, Plax, & Wendt-Wasco, 1985). Perhaps you fell victim to inaccurate assumptions based on cultural stereotypes (Kiewitz, 1997). Whatever the reason you doubt you'll learn much from a speaker, you will probably listen ineffectively.

According to a theory known as **impression formation and management,** we form first impressions of people based on how they look. Research suggests that we respond more favorably to formally dressed people than to casually dressed people (Ritts, Patterson, & Tubbs, 1992). We tend to think they are more intelligent. When the speaker is a woman, such prejudgments about intelligence based on attire are especially likely (Temple & Loewen, 1993; Treinen, 1998).

WHAT DO YOU THINK?
Identify a speaker who you believe is very effective and one who you think is very ineffective. What role does their appearance play in forming your impression?

A Strategy: Hear the Speaker Out

To be an effective listener, consciously avoid prejudging the intelligence of speakers based on appearance or manner (Adler & Towne, 1996). Instead, listen to them with an open mind and try not to evaluate the strengths and weaknesses of their messages until they have finished speaking (Gitomer, 2000). I've heard that a former president of a national sociology association, a very reputable man in the field, always presented his formal public speeches barefooted. It would be easy to prejudge him as an eccentric fool, but that would likely result in ineffective listening.

Hear the Speaker Out

When each classmate gets up to give a speech, ask yourself, "What assumptions am I making about this person before they even begin to speak? Why?" Then put the assumption aside and listen to the entire speech before making an evaluation of it.

Bad Habit Number 5: Mentally Arguing and Jumping to Conclusions

We've already touched on the subject of mentally arguing with the speaker and jumping to conclusions. Sometimes we mentally argue with claims being made, noticing that the speaker is making contradictory claims or ones we know to be inaccurate. Even if that's true, mentally arguing about it can keep us from listening to the rest of what the speaker says and the loss is ours. Sometimes we stop listening because we jump to conclusions about what the speaker's ultimate point is going to be. Right or wrong, we may miss important information.

People have probably always engaged in this bad habit, but modern technology has exacerbated it. We can get information about nearly any topic in seconds thanks to cable television and the Internet, and we tend to know a little bit about a lot of different topics. As a result, we're more likely to get hung up on the details of a speech because we've learned something a bit different about the topic.

A Strategy: Find Value in Every Speech

When you mentally argue with specifics in the speech or jump to conclusions about what the speaker is going to say, you make negative judgments and cannot reach the highest level in the SIER model, which is critical listening. To fight this bad habit, consciously force yourself to find value in every speech. For example, rather than dwell on a detail that you disagree with, make a mental or written note of it and move on to find something of value in the rest of the speech.

Find Value in Every Speech

When a classmate gives a speech, ask yourself these questions:

- Considering content, what new information—even if based on only one piece of evidence—can I learn from this speech?
- Considering structure, what can I learn about what to do or not do concerning their use of previews, transitions, summaries, and language choices?
- Considering delivery, what can I learn to do or not do concerning conversational style, vocal expression, poise, eye contact, facial expression, or gestures?

Answering these questions will help you find value in every speech.

Bad Habit Number 6: Listening Too Hard

Oddly, another bad habit is listening too hard. When you try to retain every detail of a speaker's message, you experience *listening overload*—you lose the main ideas and remember even less information than if you had not tried so hard.

A Strategy: Listen Analytically

To overcome the bad habit of listening too hard, try to listen analytically—that is, analyze the speech as you listen in ways that focus on the speaker's main point and general ideas. Ask yourself: What is the main point the speaker is trying to make? What are the main ideas supporting it? With this focused approach you'll retain more information than if you tried to remember every statistic or example. Round the statistics off if it helps. To use an example from this chapter, instead of trying to remember that 55 percent of our communication time is spent listening, 24 percent speaking, 13 percent reading, and 8 percent writing, you might just try to remember that more than half is spent listening, more than in all the other modes combined.

This section discussed six bad habits that hurt your ability to listen critically and six strategies you can use to avoid falling victim to them. These strategies will help you in any situation that requires effective critical listening, including public speaking.

PRACTICING THE PROCESS

Checklist for Effective Listening

- ❏ Expend energy.
- ❏ Take notes.
- ❏ Prepare yourself.
- ❏ Hear the speaker out.
- ❏ Find value in every speech.
- ❏ Listen analytically.

THE ETHICAL CRITIC:
TIPS FOR IMPROVING CRITIQUING SKILLS

ETHICS

A critique is based on critical listening—on hearing, comprehending, judging, and assigning worth—but goes beyond it. Based on your critical listening, your critique gives the speaker feedback, including suggestions for improvement. To be an ethical critic, however, your feedback must honor the virtues of respect and honesty. You must be *honest* about what you believe the speaker did both effectively and ineffectively. You must phrase your comments in ways that demonstrate *respect* for the speaker and his or her efforts. To be an effective critic, you need to be thorough—touching on content, delivery, and structure—as well as detailed and specific. You also need to provide both positive and negative comments. A critique that meets these criteria is ethical and effective. You'll have done your best to make your comments fair and useful to the speaker.

Characteristics of Ethical and Effective Critiques

ETHICS

In an ethical and effective critique, comments are phrased as **constructive criticism.** This means they are positive as well as negative, are specific, are accompanied by a rationale, and are phrased in terms of the listener's perception.

An effective critique offers specific opinions about what the speaker did not do well in terms of content, structure, and delivery. But negative comments must do more than merely list things the speaker did poorly. Comments like "slow down," "hard to follow," "too soft," and "confusing" are too vague to help the speaker improve much. Instead, be specific. What part of the speech was too fast, hard to follow, too soft, or confusing? To be specific, you might even suggest how it was confusing or how it could be changed.

Being ethical also means explaining. The reason you cite for each statement that you think falls short is also known as a rationale. If you believe the preview was too soft, for example, say why. If you simply couldn't hear it, say so.

To be ethical, phrase your comments as personal perceptions—which other listeners may or may not share—rather than as facts. One way is by using "I" rather than "you" language. For example, it is more ethical to say, "I couldn't hear your preview. It would help me follow the structure of your speech better if you

Student Workbook

Read "Critiquing Public Speeches" in Chapter 2 of your workbook. Why is it important to be specific in the comments of your critique? If possible, attend a round of competitive speeches and complete the provided "Forensics Speech Critique Form."

would speak louder" than to flatly state, "You need to slow down on your preview or your structure won't be clear." Offering a rationale phrased as a personal perception demonstrates that you respect the speaker's ability to decide whether a change will improve his or her overall effectiveness in future speeches.

For example, change the statement "great gestures" into an effective and ethical critique by:

- Making it specific: What, where, and how were the effective gestures used?
- Providing reasons: Why did the gestures make the speech better?
- Using "I" language: What made it helpful to you as a listener?

As another example, change the statement "slow down" by:

- Making it specific: What, where, and how in the speech did the speaker need to slow down?
- Providing reasons: Why did the fast rate hurt the speech?
- Using "I" language: What would slowing down this part of the speech do to help you as a listener?

A critique also includes comments about what the speaker did well in terms of the content, the structure, and the delivery. These positive comments help speakers improve by identifying specific things that work and that they ought to continue doing in future speeches. Like negative comments, positive comments should be specific, include a rationale, and be phrased as personal opinion. Comments like "good job" and "fine" and even "great transitions" or "good eye contact" are too vague to indicate what worked. A more effective and ethical comment would be, "Good eye contact. You spanned the entire room so no one seemed left out of the communication transaction." This lets the speaker know what the critic believes should be continued in future speeches, how, and why. Figure 4.6 provides a sample classmate critique form.

PRACTICING THE PROCESS

Checklist for an Effective and Ethical Critique

ETHICS ❑ Did you offer specific comments about what the speaker did not do well? (Consider what, where, and how.)
❑ Did you offer specific comments about what the speaker did do well? (Consider what, where, and how.)
❑ Did you provide reasons for each comment you made?
❑ Did you phrase each statement as a personal perception using "I" language?

You can help other speakers improve by offering effective critiques. You can also help yourself by completing a self-critique after each speech you give, using the same approach you use to critique others. Note things you believe you did effectively in addition to those you believe you did ineffectively. This can also reduce public speaking anxiety because it is a form of cognitive restructuring. Engaging in negative self-talk after a speech increases public speaking anxiety. A self-critique forces you to temper negative self-talk with positive criticism. If your anxiety is rooted in a fear of failure, this cognitive restructuring technique will eventually reduce it. Figure 4.7 provides a sample self-critique form.

Elements of Speech	Critique (Identify one thing the speaker did well and why. Identify one thing the speaker could do to improve, why, and how.)
Delivery	
Use of Voice	
Intelligible?	
Conversational?	
Expressive?	
Use of Body	
Attire?	
Poise?	
Eye contact?	
Facial expressions?	
Gestures and movement?	
Structure	
Macrostructure	
Introductory elements?	
Transitions?	
Concluding elements?	
Microstructure	
Language?	
Style?	
Content	
Analysis	
Focus?	
Breadth?	
Depth?	
Listener relevance?	
Learning styles?	
Support Material	
Relevant?	
Recent?	
Credited?	
Varied?	
Distributed?	

Figure 4.6 Sample class-mate critique form

PRACTICING THE PROCESS

Videotape Yourself

Videotape yourself giving a speech. Watch your speech and complete the sample self-critique form provided in Figure 4.7. What do you do well and why? What can you improve on? How?

Evaluate your own speech performance based on these guidelines. The focus is on redefining your self-talk and offering yourself specific and constructive suggestions rather than on criticism.

Elements of Speech	Positive critique: For each item, identify one or two things you did well and why.
Delivery Use of voice Use of body	
Structure Macrostructure Microstructure	
Content Analysis Support material	

To improve: Identify one thing you will try to do differently to improve the delivery, structure, and content of your next speech. Be sure to indicate why and how.

Delivery:

Structure:

Content:

Figure 4.7   Sample self-critique form

Looking at the Learning Cycle

Consider Your Own Preferred Learning Style

Consider your preferred learning style.

- What types of things are you most likely to notice in terms of a speaker's delivery? Structure? Content?
- What types of thing are you least likely to comment on in terms of a speaker's delivery? Structure? Content?

EXAMPLES OF CONTENT, STRUCTURE, AND DELIVERY CRITIQUES

Having looked at the characteristics of effective and ethical critiques, let's turn to the content of critique comments in terms of the three major aspects of public speeches: content, structure, and delivery. Consider all three as you listen to a speech. In order to critically listen as well as critique each section, it is usually most effective to jot short notes during the speech. Later you can enhance these to make an effective critique. By the time you present your critique to the speaker, make sure each comment is phrased as constructive criticism.

Comments on content focus on the speaker's analysis and supporting material. You might address breadth and depth of evidence or use of listener relevance links. You might talk about how the speaker used reasoning to connect evidence to main points. Or you might talk about how relevant, recent, or credible the evidence seemed to be. Did the speaker offer a variety of evidence to support the main points? Did the speaker offer sufficiently detailed evidence? Did the speaker address the relevance of the topic to listeners' lives? Figure 4.8 provides some examples of content critique statements.

Comments on structure cover both macrostructure and microstructure. To comment on macrostructure, you focus on such elements as the attention catcher, thesis, preview, transitions, thesis restatement, main point summary, and clincher. To comment on microstructure, you focus on aspects of language and style such as accuracy, clarity, inclusion, vividness, and novelty. Content comments focus on the speaker's topic and supporting ideas, but structure comments focus on the way the speaker puts those ideas together—in the outline, the language choices, and the style. Figure 4.9 provides examples of structure critique comments.

Comments on delivery focus on how the speaker uses his or her voice and body. When you comment on voice, for example, you might address intelligibility. How easily could you understand the message? Did the speaker's rate, vol-

ETHICS

Ineffective	Effective and Ethical
Interesting stories	I liked the story about your trip to the carnival. The depth of details you provided made it sound really fun.
Boring stories	The speech would have kept my interest better if I knew how each main point relates to me.
Too short	I would have liked to hear another example under each main point. This would have helped me to understand why the carnival was so significant to you.

Figure 4.8   Examples of content critique statements

ETHICS

Ineffective	Effective and Ethical
Disorganized	I had trouble knowing when a new main point was starting. It would have been helpful to me to hear clear transitions that tied the two main points together verbally.
Bad introduction	I would have tuned in to the speech quicker if you had used a creative attention catcher instead of starting immediately with the thesis statement.
Dull	I would have stayed tuned in to the speech better if you had used more colorful word pictures when describing the carnival.

Figure 4.9   Examples of structure critique statements

ume, and enunciation help or hinder your understanding? You might address whether the speaker has a conversational style. Did the speaker sound as though he or she was talking with you rather than reading to you or presenting in front of you? You might also address emotional expression. Did the speaker vary her or his rate or volume, stress key words and phrases, or incorporate pauses to reinforce an attitude?

When you comment on the speaker's use of his or her body, you might mention attire. Did the speaker's attire convey a sense of commitment? Or you might address poise and mannerisms. Did the speaker distract, such as by fidgeting with notes, playing with his or her hair, or shifting weight back and forth? Eye contact is another area you might address. Did the speaker look up from his or her notes at least 90 percent of the time? Span the entire audience? Look you in the eye? Finally, you can consider use of facial expressions and gestures. Did these nonverbal signals reinforce the verbal message? Figure 4.10 provides delivery critique comment examples.

Constructing effective and ethical critiques is not easy; it takes a good deal of critical thinking. With practice, however, you can learn to help speakers by focusing on what they did well and what they might do to improve their delivery, structure, and content, and why they need to work on them. Such critiques can help you improve as a speaker as well.

Student Workbook

Attend a presentation conducted by a professional public speaker. Answer the questions on the "Professional Speaker Critique" and "Audience Assessment" forms in Chapter 2 of your workbook. Then, prepare a 1–2 page typed critique based on delivery, structure, and content.

ETHICS

ETHICS

Ineffective	Effective and Ethical
Good rate	Rate was appropriate to easily follow your ideas. Intelligible.
Good gestures	I liked your gestures in the introduction because they helped clarify your main points for me.
Too fast	It would have helped me if you slowed down more while discussing the technical information in the first main point. I needed more time to process what you were saying.
Boring	I would have liked to hear more emotional expression in your voice. More enthusiasm when talking about the carnival would have kept my interest better.

Figure 4.10 Examples of delivery critique statements

PRACTICING THE PROCESS

Critique Your Classmates

Use the classmate critique form provided in Figure 4.6 to critique your classmates' next speech. Be sure to follow the guidelines of effective and ethical critiques:

- Be specific (what to improve and how).
- Provide reasons (why).
- Use "I" language.

Quiz Yourself

Go to the *Confident Public Speaking* Web site.

- Click on the Tutorial Quiz in the red box for Chapter 4.
- Take the quiz to help review what you've learned.

Did you retain more than 50 percent of the material on the first try?

At your instructor's request, submit your results.

SUMMARY

The psychological process of listening depends on, but is different from, the physiological process of hearing. Improved listening skills benefit you in both personal and professional life. As the SIER model makes clear, critical listening involves hearing, understanding, evaluating, and assigning worth to a message.

It is not possible to engage in critical listening all the time, so determine which type of listening is most appropriate in a particular context. In addition to critical listening, these types include discriminative listening (listening "between the lines"), comprehensive listening (listening to understand), appreciative listening (listening for pleasure), and empathic listening (listening as a sounding board).

You can improve your listening skills by becoming aware of six bad habits and the strategies for dealing with them. To overcome the bad habit of becoming distracted, expend energy throughout the speech. To avoid faking attention, take notes. To avoid being unprepared for the speech, prepare yourself physically, mentally, and intellectually. Avoid prejudging speakers by hearing them out before evaluating their message. Avoid mentally arguing and jumping to conclusions by finding value in every speech. Finally, don't try to remember every detail by listening too hard. Rather, listen analytically for main ideas.

A critique that is effective and ethical offers the speaker suggestions for improvement, accompanied by a rationale and phrased as a personal perception. Effective critiques can help speakers improve because they focus on the speech and not the speaker, describe specific aspects of the speech, and include both strengths and weaknesses in the areas of delivery, structure, and content. In addition to critiquing others, you can critique yourself, both to improve and to replace negative self-talk with positive coping statements.

RETURNING TO TECHNOLOGY

The *Confident Public Speaking* CD-ROM is your one-stop point of access for not just the content on the CD itself such as Speech Interactive, but also the many other resources on the *Confident Public Speaking* Web site, Speech Builder Express, and InfoTrac College Edition. Note that this chapter's key terms and activities are among the resources available in electronic format online. Additional information is included on the next page.

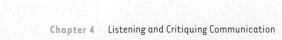

MENU   DESCRIPTION   DELIVERY   STRUCTURE   CONTENT

- WELCOME
- INFOTRAC
- WEB SITE
- SPEECH BUILDER EXPRESS
- SPEECH INTERACTIVE
- HELP

SPEECH INTERACTIVE
Glory and Hope, Nelson Mandela (Chapter 4)

After years of fighting for justice in South Africa, President Nelson Mandela delivered this speech to the nation's people in Pretoria on May 10, 1994. He lauded the South African nation for rejecting racism and racial oppression and argued that the nations of the world would now accept them as a result. He also used this opportunity to challenge the nation to continue the fight to promote peace, prosperity, democracy, human dignity, and freedom for all.

Pres. Nelson Mandela
South Africa
CNN LIVE

Click the CD-ROM icon above to view this movie.

SPEECH INTERACTIVE
ON THE *CONFIDENT PUBLIC SPEAKING* CD-ROM

Speech Interactive is your link to this text's speech videos. Offering opportunities to practice critiquing speeches by students and other public speakers, these videos will help you prepare for providing effective feedback to your peers and your own speech performances.

SPEECH BUILDER EXPRESS

If you would like to practice some of the listening and critiquing techniques presented in this chapter, log on to Speech Builder Express and open the file you created for your first speech so that you can watch the video clips of various speeches that are part of *Speech Builder Express*. You'll find video clips within the Introduction, Conclusion, and Visual Aids sections.

KEY TERMS

Interactive flashcards for these key terms are available on the *Confident Public Speaking* Web site. You'll find the "Flashcards" link under the resources for Chapter 4.

ACTIVITIES

The activities below are available in electronic format on the *Confident Public Speaking* Web site. You'll find the "Activities" link under the resources for Chapter 4.

1. **Resisting Distractions.** Form a three-person group. Designate two people as "senders" and one as a "receiver." One sender is to sit on the receiver's right and the other is to sit on the receiver's left. The two senders discuss *different topics* simultaneously for three to four minutes. The listener tries to focus on one sender's message. Afterward, the receiver reports all she or he can remember.

2. **Listening Analytically.** Listen to a radio news broadcast. Summarize the main ideas in a few short sentences.

3. **Effective and Ethical Critiquing.** Attend a speech by a professional and complete the "Professional Speaker Critique" and the "Audience Assessment Form" in Chapter 2 of your workbook. This exercise will give you practice in writing positive and negative critique statements about delivery, structure, and content that are both effective and ethical.

4. **Sandwiching Critique Technique.** Together with two other people, attend a professional lecture or watch one on television. One person should focus on the speaker's content, another on structure, and another on delivery. Employ the sandwiching technique for your designated aspect of the speech. To do so, begin by mentioning a specific thing the speaker did well and why you believe it is something the speaker should continue doing. Next, offer a suggestion for improvement, explain why it would improve the speech, and recommend how the speaker might incorporate the suggestion. Finally, provide another positive critique. This positive-negative-positive approach couches suggestions within a framework of praise, which can be more comfortable for both the beginning speaker and the beginning critic.

5. **Sandwiching Self-Critique.** Critique your own speech based on content, structure, and delivery using the sandwiching technique described in activity 4.

INFOTRAC COLLEGE EDITION ACTIVITY

Locate and read the following articles: "Is Anyone Listening?" by Jennifer J. Salopek and "A Manager's Guide to Effective Listening" by Robert C. Boyle. (Hint: Use "listening" as your search term.) List the reasons why people are poor listeners. Name the three poor listening behaviors you use the most often.

SELECTING AND NARROWING YOUR TOPIC

REFLECTIVE QUESTIONS

1. How might your favorite television programs, movies, comic strips, songs, hobbies, and interests help you select a speech topic?

2. In what ways could searching the Internet help you generate potential topics?

3. How might you narrow a broad topic to create an appropriate thesis statement for your speech?

4. Why might it be important for you to consider your audience when narrowing your speech topic?

5. How might your beliefs, attitudes, and values influence the topic you select?

WHAT'S AHEAD: FOCUSING YOUR READING

Preliminary Considerations for Selecting a Topic

Generating Potential Topics

Choosing a Topic

Narrowing Your Topic

W HILE HAVING LUNCH WITH HER friend Maria, Holly was trying to come up with a topic for the informative speech she would present in class next week. Holly had a long list of topics she'd thought up but discarded. Exasperated, she exclaimed, "Every idea I come up with seems so boring. Everybody must know about all this stuff already! I can't think of anything that's new and original."

After glancing at Holly's list, Maria said, "You have plenty of topics here I'd like to learn more about. You worked in a day care center—I'd love to know about that. Sometimes I wonder if my own kids are in the best environment. And I see you took some life-saving courses. I bet you know what to do if someone is choking. A major in child development and family science, day care experience, life-saving classes—most people don't know much about any of those."

"Maybe you're right," Holly said. "I do know some things that a lot of other people don't. I wonder what would be most interesting to the class?" Holly's process of selecting a topic now began in earnest.

Your first task as a public speaker is to select a topic. Students often say it's difficult. When I ask why, they respond that listeners are not going to be interested in anything they have to say, or that they don't know anything new and interesting to talk about. Many people feel that way, and it's a primary reason that anxiety levels begin to rise (Richmond & McCroskey, 1995).

You *do* have new and interesting ideas and you *can* approach your speech in ways that will be interesting to listeners. It requires generating a variety of potential topics, choosing one from the list based on your interests, and narrowing the topic based on your audience and purpose.

WHAT DO YOU THINK?

When you think about selecting a speech topic, what typically goes through your mind?

PRELIMINARY CONSIDERATIONS FOR SELECTING A TOPIC

You must select and narrow your speech topic in light of the **rhetorical situation**—that is, the circumstances under which you will deliver the speech. As Figure 5.1 illustrates, the circumstances are the speaker (you), the audience (your classmates), and the occasion (purpose). In other words, selecting and narrowing a topic is based on what interests you and how that can be adapted to address audience interests and expectations.

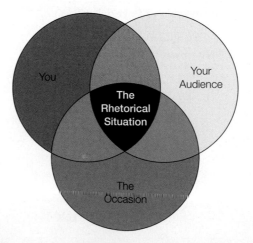

Figure 5.1 The rhetorical situation

Sometimes we fail to realize that our experiences, such as this woman's study of martial arts, are unusual and potentially interesting to our listeners.

The audience is crucial, so topic selection must include **audience analysis**—the process of understanding who your listeners are and adapting your speech to meet their needs, interests, and expectations. By considering your audience and speaking on a topic that is relevant to them, you demonstrate respect for your listeners, which helps them perceive you as more ethical. Because audience analysis is so important, it is treated separately in Chapter 6 and discussed in later chapters. Audience analysis must occur throughout speech preparation and presentation. By following the advice laid out here and in Chapter 6, you will be able to select interesting and relevant topics and do so with much less anxiety.

ETHICS

GENERATING POTENTIAL TOPICS

The first step in selecting and narrowing a topic is to generate a list of ideas to choose from. You can generate potential topics by brainstorming and by researching.

Brainstorming

A good way to begin this process is by **brainstorming**—that is, generating as many ideas as possible (Weiten, 1986). To brainstorm, set a time limit of fifteen to twenty minutes and write down every topic that comes to mind. Don't rule anything out at this point. Topics can be things you know a good deal about or things you'd like to learn more about. For now, just get as many possibilities on paper as you can (Clark, 1958).

Sometimes it is easier to brainstorm by thinking of categories—places, people, events, organizations, hobbies, television programs, books, personal goals, professional goals, opinions, beliefs, attitudes, and values. You might write these categories down as column heads on a sheet of paper and brainstorm each category for five minutes before moving on to the next.

Sometimes your instructor might simply assign a topic, such as your professional interests, or public policies, or social issues. You can still brainstorm different aspects of or perspectives on the assigned topic.

TURNING TO TECHNOLOGY

Brainstorming Topics

http://www.jpb.com/creative/brainstorming.php

Using the steps provided at this Web site, brainstorm topics and identify two or three that you might use for an upcoming speech.

Researching

Another way to generate topic ideas is to do research. Whereas brainstorming requires you to focus on your own knowledge and experiences, researching allows you to look at external resources for ideas.

You might, for example, browse through several magazines and make note of articles that interest you. These might be added to the list developed while brainstorming. Look through different types of magazines. *Time*, *Newsweek*, and *U.S. News and World Report* focus on different kinds of topics than do *People*, *Good Housekeeping*, or *Glamour*. *Business Week*, *Forbes*, and *Consumer Reports* focus on different topics than do *Runners World*, *Sports Illustrated*, or *National Geographic*. The more kinds of magazines you consider, the easier it will be to expand your list.

The same goes for newspapers. Try local papers as well as national publications such as *USA Today*, the *New York Times*, and the *Wall Street Journal*. For example, one student, Jenni, got her idea for a speech about the overuse of antibacterial products from an editorial cartoon in *USA Today*.

Reference books and indexes can also help generate topic ideas. Try opening an encyclopedia, dictionary, or the *Reader's Guide to Periodical Literature* at random. Skim through the topic headings. When something catches your interest, add it to your list under the appropriate column. You can skim CD-ROM encyclopedias in a similar fashion. I tried opening my dictionary to one page at random. Here's what I came up with:

- Gravure (method of printing with etched plates or cylinders)
- Gray's Inn (one of the four legal societies forming the Inns of Court in England)
- Great Salt Lake (Utah)
- Grecism (the style or spirit of Greek culture, art, or thought)

In addition to scanning printed materials, you can also browse the Internet (Siau, 1999) using any of a number of search engines such as WebCrawler, Yahoo!, Google, or Excite. Each allows you to brainstorm a topic, and from one site you can often link to other pages that interest you. Link from site to site, jotting down ideas as they reveal themselves. If you decide to surf for additional topic possibilities, however, it's generally best to limit how much time you spend doing so. An hour should be sufficient; much more is probably a waste.

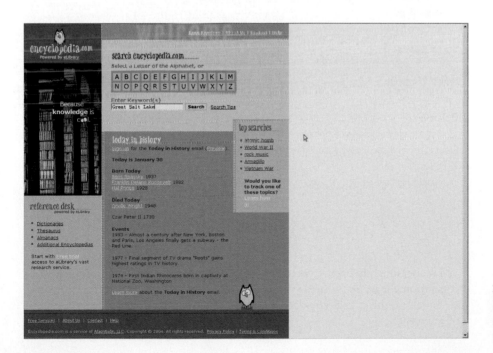

You might decide to use an online encyclopedia or Internet search to brainstorm speech topic ideas.

By the time you've finished brainstorming and researching, you will have a **personal inventory**—a list of all the topics you can think of that interest you in some way. Here's Holly's personal inventory:

 Holly's Personal Inventory of Topics and Ideas

Places
Bermuda Triangle
Trinidad
New Orleans
Rape and abuse crisis center
Day care centers

Events
Shooting at Columbine High
My annual family reunion
The birth of my first child
The Stanley Cup games

Hobbies
Playing piano
Running
Going to movies
Swimming

Books
Backlash
Boxcar Children
The Bible

Professional Goals
Earn at least $30,000/year
Managerial level
Graphics industry

Social Issues
Cost of prescription drugs
Health insurance
Teen suicide

Opinions
Women should be able to be priests.
Elementary and secondary school day should
   be lengthened.
Gun control is needed.

People
My grandmother
High school teacher
The pope

Organizations
Lion's Club
Church choir
Humane society

TV Programs
Seinfeld
20/20
South Park
Days of Our Lives

Personal Goals
Own a home
Have a dog
Graduate from college

Beliefs
Death penalty is wrong
Heaven exists

Public Policies
Affirmative action
Title IX

Values
Higher education
Christianity
Family

The personal inventory you create serves two purposes: It generates a host of diverse topic ideas, and it helps you begin to understand why each topic interests you. Together, these help you determine the direction you might take for a speech on each topic.

CHOOSING A TOPIC

Once you have generated a personal inventory, choose a topic for your speech. There are a number of ways to explore potential topic ideas, including expanding your personal inventory, creating a concept map, and doing research.

Expanding Your Personal Inventory

Create an **expanded personal inventory** by broadening your list to include a statement of why each topic interests you—personal experiences, cultural background, religious beliefs, ethnicity, gender, socioeconomic class, birth order, and so forth. Some of the categories on Holly's expanded list were these:

Holly's Expanded Personal Inventory

TOPICS/IDEAS	WHY?
Places	
Trinidad	Neat music
New Orleans	Love the Cajun food
Rape and abuse crisis center	My best friend was raped
Day care centers	I work at one
People	
My grandmother	She's blind and lives alone, gardens, and sews (amazing)
My high school teacher	Respected students as intelligent people
Events	
Shooting at Columbine High	Points to a much larger problem in our society. People need to feel needed. How can we change the direction of our country?
The Stanley Cup games	I wish I could have played hockey as a kid
Hobbies	
Playing piano	I taught myself to play
Going to movies	Entertainment; helps us think about important social issues
Swimming	I'm a senior lifesaver
TV Programs	
Seinfeld	Funny; about people and relationships
20/20	Newsworthy topics; seems somewhat sensationalized
South Park	Do kids learn to be violent?
Days of Our Lives	Sex on TV—is it okay?
Personal Goals	
Have a dog	My childhood dog was my best friend
Professional Goals	
Earn at least $30,000/year	I was raised in middle-class home; hope to stay there
Graphics industry	That's my major; I love to draw

(continued)

Social Issues

Cost of prescription drugs	Seniors shouldn't have to go to Canada or Mexico for these
Health insurance	I'm bothered that some people don't have access to quality health care

Public Policies

Affirmative action	I want to get a job because I'm most qualified
Title IX	I'm so glad young girls today have the opportunities I didn't have

Expanding your personal inventory this way is beneficial not only because it allows you to explore potential directions for each topic but because it helps you learn more about why you think and believe the way you do. A **belief** is a thing you think is true or false, an **attitude** is a predisposition to like or dislike something, and **values** are the enduring set of principles that shape your beliefs and attitudes. Understanding your own beliefs, attitudes, and values is crucial in topic selection because it is integral to effective audience analysis, as Chapter 6 discusses.

TURNING TO TECHNOLOGY

Considering Your Beliefs, Attitudes, and Values

http://www.nralive.com/index2.cfm

Go to this Web site and play the most recent video message posted by the NRA. How much do your values, beliefs, and attitudes about gun control influence your reaction to the message?

By expanding her personal inventory this way, Holly realized that her religious beliefs shape much of her thinking. She also recognized the value she places on nurturing interpersonal relationships. Hence she might hold a negative attitude toward the animated comedy *South Park* because of the value she places on civility. Knowing what you think and believe about topics and issues ultimately provides you with a perspective from which to examine your audience and adapt your speech effectively to it. Chapter 6 explores this in more detail.

Concept Mapping

Another strategy you might use to choose a topic is **concept mapping,** a visual means of exploring connections between a topic and related ideas (Callison, 2001). To discover connections, you might ask yourself questions about the topic—questions focused on who, what, where, when, and how. Figure 5.2 is an example from Holly's list.

Create Your Own Concept Map

http://www.coun.uvic.ca/learn/program/hndouts/map_ho.html

Go to this Web site and create a concept map following the step-by-step directions offered there.

Researching

You might go to the library or visit one online to read about a topic in more detail and make an informed choice. Sometimes your expanded personal inventory or concept map will lead you to the library to learn more about a possible speech topic. In Holly's case she might use the library to find more tips for parents who are selecting a day care center.

WHAT DO YOU THINK?

Consider a commercial you have seen that made you think the product was worth purchasing. Why? Do you think the commercial told you everything about that product? Could you create a speech on that topic? Why or why not?

Topic: Day Care

Figure 5.2 Holly's concept map

NARROWING YOUR TOPIC

Once you've selected a topic, narrow its focus based on the rhetorical situation and purpose. As discussed earlier, the rhetorical situation is the circumstances under which you will deliver the speech: the speaker (you), the audience (your classmates), and the occasion (purpose and constraints). By now you have generated topic ideas based on your interests and chosen one for your speech, so you have satisfied the first circumstance of the rhetorical situation. Now consider your audience, purpose, and constraints to ensure that what you say will be suited to the occasion and will meet the expectations of the audience. Research suggests that public speeches that make a tightly focused, simple point are most successful (Lamb, 1991; Suskind & Lublin, 1995).

WHAT DO YOU THINK?

Consider a teacher, religious leader, or other speaker you have heard who seemed to talk on and on. Can you identify what the main point was? What do you remember most about the speech? Why?

The Funnel Method for Narrowing Your Topic

The constraints of the rhetorical situation can be met by narrowing your focus using the funnel method. It helps you adapt to your audience and refine your purpose through a five-step process to formulate an effective **thesis statement**—a one-sentence summary of your speech (Figure 5.3).

Step 1: Select Your General Topic

In the first step of the funnel method you select a general topic from your personal inventory. Holly, for example, selected day care as her general topic. It wasn't the only good topic idea she had generated and placed in her personal inventory, but she chose it because she had experience working in a day care center and wanted to make wise day care choices for her own children. When she chose a topic from her personal inventory, she completed the first step in the funnel method.

Step 2: Determine Your Topic Area

In the second step, narrow your general topic based on the needs and interests of the audience (Trocco, 2000). Holly discovered that most of her classmates either have children or plan to have them someday. She decided that knowing more about day care choices would benefit most listeners. Therefore, she narrowed her general topic of day care to focus on the subtopic of day care choices. (This step is based on audience analysis, discussed in detail in Chapter 6.)

Step 3: Consider Your General Purpose

In the third step, decide on the general purpose of your speech. For assigned classroom presentations this is usually specified by the instructor, but in other settings you must decide the general purpose yourself. There are three types of **general purpose:** to inform, to persuade, and to entertain.

When your general purpose is to *inform*, the goal is to increase listeners' knowledge about and understanding of the topic. Chapter 14 is devoted entirely to informative speeches. In an informative speech, you are a teacher attempting to create shared understanding. Colleges and universities often invite guest lecturers to speak on campus; they usually present informative speeches about their areas of expertise. If Holly decides to inform her listeners, she might talk about the factors to consider when selecting a day care option.

WHAT DO YOU THINK?

Have you ever been assigned a research project for class but didn't know where or how to begin? Following the steps of the funnel method will help you narrow research project topics as well as speech topics.

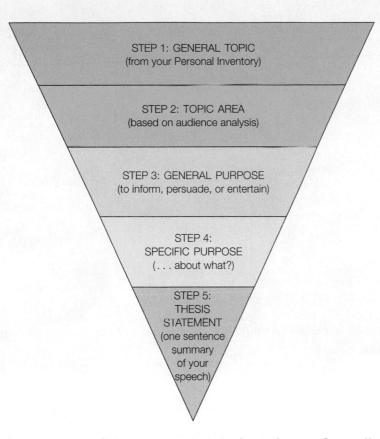

STEP 1: GENERAL TOPIC
(from your Personal Inventory)

STEP 2: TOPIC AREA
(based on audience analysis)

STEP 3: GENERAL PURPOSE
(to inform, persuade, or entertain)

STEP 4:
SPECIFIC PURPOSE
(. . . about what?)

STEP 5:
THESIS
STATEMENT
(one sentence
summary
of your
speech)

Figure 5.3 The Funnel Method

When your general purpose is to *persuade*, the goal is to influence listeners' beliefs or behaviors. Here too you provide information, but your purpose in doing so is to change listeners' beliefs or behaviors. Religious leaders often present sermons that can be classified as persuasive speeches. So can television infomercials, which attempt to convince viewers to buy something. If Holly decides to persuade her listeners, she might focus on why one day care option is better than others. She'll talk about the factors to consider when evaluating day care options just as she would in an informative speech, but with the goal of persuading listeners that one option is best.

When your general purpose is to *entertain*, the goal is to use humor to make a point. You might share information as in an informative speech, and try to win listeners over to your point of view as in a persuasive speech, but above all you entertain listeners through humor. Speeches to entertain also make a serious point. For example, Billy Crystal's humorous opening monologue at the 1998 Academy Awards ceremony ended with a serious point that all nominees are "winners."

If Holly decides to entertain her listeners, she might prepare a speech to entertain by focusing on the experiences of being a day care center employee. She might conclude, however, with a serious point about the importance of parent involvement in any kind of day care setting.

WHAT DO YOU THINK?

Identify a time when you heard a professional speaker give a keynote address, banquet speech, motivational speech, or the like. Was the general purpose to inform, to persuade, or to entertain? Did it seem appropriate to you as a listener? Why or why not?

Step 4: Determine Your Specific Purpose

Once you know whether you are going to inform, persuade, or entertain, you must answer the question "About what?" The **specific purpose** is expressed by

Although a comedy, *Daddy Day Care* addresses several factors parents might consider when evaluating day care options.

© Columbia/Courtesy Everett Collection

a single phrase that identifies precisely what you hope to accomplish in your speech. To determine your specific purpose, select one aspect of the topic as your precise focus and decide what you hope the audience will know or feel about it by the time you finish.

To ensure that your specific purpose statement is precise, you must also consider time constraints and audience expectations. Can you cover the topic thoroughly in the time allotted? Is the specific purpose relevant to the audience—not too technical or too superficial? For Holly's informative speech, the specific purpose is to identify the factors to consider when selecting a day care option. For Holly's persuasive speech, the specific purpose is to show how and why one option is better than the others. And for her speech to entertain, the specific purpose is to make her audience laugh about the experiences of a day care center employee and allude to the importance of parental involvement in any kind of day care setting.

TURNING TO TECHNOLOGY

Analyzing a Speech

Go to the *Confident Public Speaking* CD-ROM and click on the "Speech Interactive" link. Watch George W. Bush's Address to Congress and the American People (9/20/01). Using the funnel method, identify his general purpose, specific purpose, and thesis statement. Do you think his speech focused appropriately on the needs and interests of this audience (the American people) at the time? Why or why not?

Step 5: Create Your Thesis Statement

In the fifth and final step of the funnel method, create a *thesis statement* (Ball, 1999)—a one-sentence summary of your speech. It modifies the specific purpose from what you hope to accomplish to what you will say in your introduction. At this point, you may generate a thesis statement by simply combining your general purpose and specific purpose in a way that clearly declares the main point of your speech. As you work on the speech, you will probably want to modify the wording of the thesis statement. That's okay as long as it leads to further narrowing your general topic into a manageable main idea appropriate to the audience and the occasion. A manageable main idea is one you can cover thoroughly within the time allotted. Thesis statements that are too broad or too narrow fail to demonstrate the ethic of respect for your listeners.

Follow three key guidelines as you shape your thesis statement. Phrase it as a complete, declarative sentence; focus on one main idea; and use concrete language and style.

Complete, Declarative Sentence.   Phrase your thesis statement as a complete, declarative sentence, not as a question or a fragment. Questions allude to the topic but do not provide enough direction about what you hope to accomplish in the speech, and fragments are not complete thoughts but merely ideas.

Ineffective thesis statement: How do you select a day care provider?
Ineffective thesis statement: Choosing a day care provider
Effective thesis statement: There are three key factors to consider when selecting a day care option.

Ineffective thesis statement: Why earn a college degree?
Ineffective thesis statement: Benefits of a college degree
Effective thesis statement: Earning a college degree will enhance your professional life in three ways.

One Main Idea.   You cannot cover more than one idea thoroughly in the short time available for most public speeches. Although topic exploration may direct you to many interesting ideas, select only one and make sure the aspect of it you decide to focus on is worded precisely in your thesis statement. Ambiguous thesis statements don't clearly reveal what dimension of a topic you plan to discuss.

Ineffective thesis statement: France is a great place to visit.
Effective thesis statement: There are three significant historical sites known for their unique architecture you'll want to see when visiting France.

Ineffective thesis statement: Choosing day care can be difficult and many different options are available.
Effective thesis statement: A professional day care center provides more benefits to children than any other option.

Ineffective thesis statement: The Japanese culture is very interesting.
Effective thesis statement: Traditional Japanese clothing represents three important values of the Japanese culture.

Ineffective thesis statement: We are destroying our environment.
Effective thesis statement: Water pollution is a serious environmental problem in our country.

Concrete Language and Style. Phrase your thesis statement using concrete language and style. For listeners to comprehend your main point in one sentence, that sentence must be concise and use concrete terms. Inflated language and complex sentence structure might make your main point difficult to decipher.

Ineffective thesis statement:	The growing number of violent crimes in high schools across the United States points to a problem embedded in our cultural values.
Effective thesis statement:	The growing number of violent crimes committed in U.S. high schools is a serious problem.
Ineffective thesis statement:	A social movement that is becoming stronger and growing in number throughout our country is the neo-Nazi Skinhead movement.
Effective thesis statement:	Society should be alarmed by the fact that the violent hate group known as neo-Nazi Skinheads is growing rapidly.

PRACTICING THE PROCESS

Checklist for Using the Funnel Method to Create an Effective Thesis Statement

To test whether your thesis statement is effective, ask yourself the following questions:

❑ Does my thesis statement focus on the needs and interests of my particular audience?

❑ Does it reflect the general purpose I've selected?

❑ Does it address my specific purpose in a single, declarative sentence?

❑ Does it focus on a single main point?

❑ Is it phrased using concrete language and style?

Applying the Funnel Method

Narrowing the focus of your speech using the funnel method turns broad topics like those in your personal inventory into manageable speech topics by considering your audience, general purpose, and specific purpose.

Here are some examples of how Holly and others narrowed their speech topics using the funnel method:

General topic:	Day care
Topic area:	Day care options
General purpose:	To inform
Specific purpose:	I want to inform my listeners about the factors they should consider when selecting a day care option.
Thesis statement:	There are three key factors to consider when selecting a day care option.

Student Workbook

Read through "The Speech of Personal Significance" assignment and sample outlines in Chapter 3 of your workbook. Select a topic for your speech of personal significance, narrow it using the Funnel Method, and create an effective thesis statement for it.

General topic:	Higher education
Topic area:	Benefits of a college degree
General purpose:	To persuade
Specific purpose:	I want to persuade high school students to attend college.
Thesis statement:	Earning a college degree will enhance your professional life in three important ways.

General topic:	Japan
Topic area:	Japanese culture
General purpose:	To inform
Specific purpose:	I want to inform listeners about how traditional Japanese clothing represents certain aspects of Japanese culture.
Thesis statement:	Traditional Japanese clothing represents three important values of the Japanese culture.

PRACTICING THE PROCESS

Using the Funnel Method to Narrow Your Topic

- Select a general topic from your personal inventory.
- Consider your audience. Refine your topic to an aspect that is likely to focus on its needs or interests.
- Determine whether your general purpose is to inform, to persuade, or to entertain.
- Create a single phrase that answers the question "About what?"
  —Be sure to consider whether you can cover the topic thoroughly in the time allotted.
  —Be sure to consider whether the specific purpose you have identified is relevant to your audience—not too technical or too superficial.
- Create a one-sentence summary of your speech (thesis statement).
  —Does your thesis statement address your specific purpose in a single, declarative sentence?
  —Does it focus on a single main point?
  —Is it phrased using concrete language and style?

Looking at the Learning Cycle

Using the Whole Cycle in Topic Selection

Consider how the process of selecting and narrowing your topic rounds the cycle of learning:

Stage 1: Brainstorming and creating a personal inventory

Stage 4: Expanding your personal inventory

Stage 2: Narrowing the topic using the funnel method

Stage 3: Creating a one-sentence summary of your speech (thesis statement)

SUMMARY

Selecting and narrowing a topic into an effective thesis statement is a three-part process. Begin by brainstorming and researching to create a personal inventory—a list of places, events, people, organizations, hobbies, books, television programs, opinions, beliefs, values, and goals that interest you. Next, choose a topic and explore the different directions you might go with it. You can do this by expanding your personal inventory with "why" statements, creating a concept map, and doing additional research. Finally, narrow the focus of your topic to speak appropriately and thoroughly in the time allotted.

The funnel method is a five-step process designed to narrow a general topic into an appropriate thesis statement. In the first step, choose a general topic from your personal inventory. This general topic can be anything that interests you, either because you know a lot about it or because you'd like to learn more about it. In the second step, narrow your general topic into a topic area by considering how you might funnel it to address the audience's needs and interests. (See also Chapter 6.) In the third step, determine the general purpose of your speech—to inform, to persuade, or to entertain. In the fourth step, narrow your topic further by determining the specific purpose. The specific purpose focuses on what you hope to accomplish in the speech. In the fifth and final step, develop your thesis statement— a one-sentence summary of the speech. Your thesis statement should be phrased as a complete, declarative sentence; focus on one main idea; and use concrete language and style.

An appropriate speech topic is one that interests the speaker and is relevant to listeners. You can develop an appropriate speech topic by considering what interests you and why, and then narrowing your focus by considering your audience and purpose.

RETURNING TO TECHNOLOGY

The *Confident Public Speaking* CD-ROM is your one-stop point of access for not just the content on the CD itself, such as Speech Interactive, but also the many other resources on the *Confident Public Speaking* Web site, Speech Builder Express, and InfoTrac College Edition. Note that this chapter's key terms and activities are among the resources available in electronic format online. Additional information is included below.

SPEECH INTERACTIVE
ON THE *CONFIDENT PUBLIC SPEAKING* CD-ROM

Speech Interactive is your link to this text's speech videos. Offering opportunities to practice critiquing speeches by students and other public speakers, these videos will help you prepare for providing effective feedback to your peers and your own speech performances.

SPEECH BUILDER EXPRESS

The Goal/Purpose and Thesis Statement sections of Speech Builder Express provide another sequence of questions and steps that may help you select and narrow topics for introductory, informative, persuasive, and invitational speeches. You'll find the Goal/Purpose and Thesis Statement buttons on the left-hand navigation menu.

KEY TERMS

Interactive flashcards for these key terms are available on the *Confident Public Speaking* Web site. You'll find the "Flashcards" link under the resources for Chapter 5.

Attitude   112
Audience analysis   107
Belief   112
Brainstorming   107
Concept mapping   112
Expanded personal inventory   111

General purpose   114
Personal inventory   110
Rhetorical situation   106
Specific purpose   115
Thesis statement   114
Values   112

ACTIVITIES

The activities below are available in electronic format on the *Confident Public Speaking* Web site. You'll find the "Activities" link under the resources for Chapter 5.

1. **Personal Inventory and Reaction Paper.** Create a list of your own interests and reasons for them. Then select one or two topics about which you feel strongly. Discuss these topics individually with two or three significant people in your life, perhaps a parent, a grandparent, a sibling, a good friend who seems very similar to you, or a good friend who seems quite different from you. Based on these discussions, write a one- to two-page reaction paper highlighting the opinions and attitudes that emerged.

2. **Group Concept Map.** In groups of three or four, select a topic from one member's personal inventory list. Then do a concept map by passing the paper around the group. Each person adds a related idea until everyone has participated at least twice. Then talk as a group about the various directions this topic could take.

3. **Funnel Method Group Exercise.** In groups of three or four, select a topic from one member's personal inventory list. Then use the funnel method to narrow the general topic into a thesis statement.

INFOTRAC COLLEGE EDITION ACTIVITY

With your Expanded Personal Inventory at hand (see pages 111–112), log on to InfoTrac College Edition. Select one of your topic/ideas to use as your search term and type it into the Keyword Search entry box. Select where you want to search for the term (in the title, citation, or abstract, or entire article content), and then click on "search." Browse the articles the search returns to see if you find anything interesting that expands on the reason the topic is important to you. Before leaving the program, scroll to the end of one of the articles to find the section "View other articles linked to these subjects," and consider the related search categories. Do any of them help you further narrow the general topic you started with?

UNDERSTANDING YOUR AUDIENCE

REFLECTIVE QUESTIONS

1. What characteristics do you and your classmates have in common? What don't you have in common? How might these similarities and differences be important as you prepare a speech?

2. What could you do to learn about the characteristics and interests of your audience? When do you think doing so might be best?

3. How might the time of day or week affect the attention span of your listeners? What other environmental characteristics could you consider when preparing your speech? Why?

4. What might motivate your audience to listen to your speech?

5. Why is it important to consider the learning cycle as a part of audience analysis?

WHAT'S AHEAD: FOCUSING YOUR READING

Why Analyze Your Audience?

What Is Audience Analysis?

Analysis of Demographic Characteristics

Analysis of Psychological Characteristics

Audience Analysis and the Learning Cycle

Analysis of Environmental Characteristics

Methods for Audience Analysis

Considering Ethics: Integrating Audience Analysis

I N MANY WAYS, DUANE WAS A SUCCESS story for the university. He worked his way through college by waiting tables at a local restaurant and typing papers for his classmates. Even as a full-time student working two part-time jobs, he was active in several campus organizations and managed to graduate with a 3.8 grade point average. After earning his bachelor's degree, Duane completed medical school and was hired as an orthopedic specialist at a respected local medical facility. He never expected to end up back in this city, but he was happy and his family seemed to be adjusting well too.

The university orientation organizer thought Duane would be a good role model for incoming students and asked him to speak during Orientation Week about "Making the Most of Your College Experience." Duane was delighted to have the opportunity; there were certainly things he would do differently—or not do at all—in college if he were starting again today.

Duane decided to talk about academic and social life at college. He planned to discuss the importance of keeping up with assignments and attending class, pointing out that even though it's fun to be away from parental guidance students still need to be responsible for their education. He planned to talk about becoming involved in organizations, and how the friendships made there can keep a person in school when the going gets tough. He wanted to caution students against some of the local nightlife, which although fun can hurt students academically at a time when education should be the top priority.

Duane worked hard on his speech, and even prepared a slide show. But walking up to the lectern, he noticed that the first-year students in the audience weren't all 18 years old and fresh from high school, as he had expected. The secretary at the elementary school where he had just enrolled his daughter was a first-year student, for example, as were the stylist who had cut his hair yesterday and the mechanic who changed the oil in his car recently. Many in the audience were at least as old as he was; several had brought their young children along. One student was an orderly at the medical facility where he had just been hired! First-year students sure have changed, he thought to himself. Where were the kids who just graduated from high school? Well, at least they would enjoy the slide show, he thought. Just then, a first-year student and his seeing-eye dog entered the auditorium. As Duane arranged his notes, the only thought he had was "Help!"

Duane had worked hard to prepare his speech, but he neglected an important step in the process—analyzing his audience. Effective public speakers are audience centered: They learn who their listeners are and adapt the speech to reflect the listeners' interests and concerns. This is known as **audience analysis** (Reinard, 1988). As discussed in Chapter 5, effective speakers first conduct audience analysis as a part of selecting and narrowing a topic. But it doesn't stop there. The best speakers employ audience analysis throughout the speechmaking process.

This chapter discusses why audience analysis is important and looks closely at three general areas within which you can analyze your audience as well as specific methods for doing so. It concludes with a discussion about the role of audience analysis throughout the speechmaking process, beginning with topic selection.

WHY ANALYZE YOUR AUDIENCE?

Sometimes students become anxious about audience analysis because it can sound complex. Actually, audience analysis is one of the most important steps in the speechmaking process for *reducing* anxiety. For one thing, it will ensure that your topic is relevant to your listeners, and this will make you feel more confident about giving your speech. Second, through audience analysis you can develop your speech so that it addresses audience expectations and motivations. This, too, should increase confidence and reduce anxiety. Finally, once you have analyzed your audience the listeners are no longer total strangers, and research suggests that anxiety levels are highest when speaking to strangers. Speaking to people you know—even if only a little bit—reduces anxiety (Richmond & McCroskey, 1995).

Audience analysis may sound difficult, but it doesn't have to be. Indeed, you probably do it every day without applying the label to the process. Consider the different people with whom you interact—perhaps your parents, children, spouse, coworkers, neighbors, close friends, and casual acquaintances. If each of these people were to ask how you were feeling or how your day was going, would you respond exactly the same way to each? If you wouldn't, the modifications you would make are essentially the result of audience analysis.

Why do you explain things differently to different people? It's because you want your message to succeed—you want the listener to be able to make sense of your explanation. Similarly, if you want to persuade different people to go somewhere or do something, you'll phrase your argument in different ways to make it effective.

When giving speeches, you use a more formal version of the audience analysis used in daily life but for much the same reason: Audience analysis helps your message succeed. It helps you achieve the goal you set for the speech.

Furthermore, audience analysis boosts your own ethos. As discussed in Chapter 1, ethos has to do with your credibility in terms of perceived competence and character. It is crucial to the success of your speech because when listeners think positively of a speaker, they are more likely to think positively of the message as well.

Audience analysis helps you understand how listeners' attitudes, beliefs, and values are similar to and different from your own, so that your speech can be modified to demonstrate respect for those similarities or differences. Doing so helps you sound knowledgeable rather than arrogant or condescending, competent rather than naïve or misguided, and open-minded rather than intolerant. If you keep the speech true to your own attitudes, beliefs, and values but also modify it to reflect understanding and respect for those of your listeners, it conveys ethos and makes listeners more receptive.

WHAT DO YOU THINK?
Have you ever taught a group of children, for example a Sunday school class, Boys and Girls Club program, or a swimming class, or conducted meetings for a group such as 4-H, Scouts, or Future Business Leaders of America? If so, was your level of anxiety different on the first day you spoke compared to later days? Explain.

TURNING TO TECHNOLOGY

Understanding Your Audience

http://www.ljlseminars.com/audience.htm

Consider the elements of audience as provided at this Web site. Do any of the elements surprise you? If so, why?

WHAT IS AUDIENCE ANALYSIS?

Understanding audience analysis today requires understanding what it used to be. In the past it was usually limited to making generalizations about the audience based on **demographic characteristics** such as age, sex, gender, race, and sociocultural background that can be observed or readily ascertained. The purpose was to categorize listeners as belonging to a particular group, determine its profile, and then make a speech relevant to the majority of the group's members. For example,

Student Workbook

Read "Cultural Diversity" in Chapter 2 of your workbook. How is cultural diversity defined? Do you agree or disagree with this definition? Why or why not?

speaking to a group of women, you might create a profile of what you believe to be the typical needs and interests of women and adapt the speech accordingly.

But there are inherent problems with this approach that have become more obvious with increasing diversity in classrooms and communities. When a speaker focuses the message toward a particular group, some listeners are **marginalized**—that is, excluded from the communication transaction because their experiences, values, needs, and interests are ignored. The group has been **stereotyped** by the assumption that all members of a group behave or believe alike simply because they belong to the group. Stereotypes can be both inaccurate and damaging: Duane's assumption that first-year college students are unmarried, young, recent high school graduates led him to develop a speech largely irrelevant to many members of his actual audience.

Today's audiences are often *demographically diverse*. For example, a public speaking classroom is likely to include men and women, heterosexuals and homosexuals, people who are married, in other long-term relationships, or single, traditional students and older students, people of various ethnicities and perhaps nationalities, and people with a range of religious beliefs. Given this diversity, the traditional approach to audience analysis not only marginalizes and stereotypes but in most cases is not even possible.

Effective audience analysis today focuses on demographic characteristics from the perspective of demographic diversity, in conjunction with psychological and environmental characteristics. Speakers consider first whether any demographic characteristics unite all audience members. Even if so, they avoid assuming too much based on that, as doing so might result in stereotyping. If the analysis reveals few or no shared demographic characteristics, speakers try to reflect an understanding of and respect for the diversity of knowledge, values, and attitudes represented by individuals in the audience.

Consider Duane once more. One demographic characteristic shared by everyone in his audience was their status as first-year students at the same university. Duane read too much into this, however, and made stereotypical assumptions about their needs, interests, and expectations. Thus he failed to adapt the speech to their actual needs and interests. Had he considered this characteristic from a perspective of demographic diversity, he might have focused on the different majors from which to choose at this institution rather than assuming students would skip classes. Likewise, he might have revealed where students can go to learn about campus organizations without assuming that students who don't join them will get caught up in nightlife instead.

Effective audience analysis today also means going beyond demographic characteristics to also consider the psychological and environmental characteristics of the audience. **Psychological characteristics** are those that motivate people to listen to and retain ideas—tendencies to respond to human needs, rhetorical appeals, and preferred learning styles. **Environmental characteristics** are those that influence why listeners attend and what they expect from a particular speech—expectations about time, setting, and occasion.

ANALYSIS OF DEMOGRAPHIC CHARACTERISTICS

Audience analysis used to focus almost exclusively on demographic analysis. It is still important but now takes a different form. Its goal is to help a speaker deter-

Even in casual conversation, we explain things differently depending on whom we're talking to.

mine audience diversity and discover major patterns that could influence the speech. That is, through demographic audience analysis you will be able to make informed inferences about who the listeners are and what interests they have so you can focus on aspects of them that are relevant to your topic. Based on these inferences, you can shape a speech to acknowledge and respect listeners and their various values, beliefs, and attitudes. Where possible, try to discover connections between yourself and your listeners, and between your values and theirs—connections that you can highlight as listener relevance links throughout the speech.

Demographic analysis cannot provide you with definite answers, although it can be the basis for useful inferences about the audience (Berko, Wolvin, & Ray, 1997; Brumfit, 1993; Iino, 1993). The only way you can know for certain what listeners believe about a topic or expect from you as a speaker is to ask them. Unfortunately, this is rarely feasible or even possible. Hence speakers must rely on inferences they can draw based on demographic audience analysis.

What might your demographic audience analysis consist of and how might you use it? It can focus on a range of characteristics, such as age, sex, gender, sexual orientation, group affiliations, socioeconomic factors, and sociocultural background. Identify any characteristics that could be relevant to your topic and adapt your approach accordingly while taking care not to stereotype the audience.

> **WHAT DO YOU THINK?**
> Have you ever made an assumption about someone only to discover later that you were wrong? If so, what were the results?

Age

Will listeners be older or younger than you on average? What is the age range of the audience? Will your listeners include children, teenagers, young adults, middle-aged people, or seniors? Finding out can help you shape the speech, because age often influences attitudes, beliefs, and values as well as interests and knowledge (Caplan, 1999; Hummert et al., 1998; Hummert, Wieman, & Nussbaum, 1994; Kemper & Harde, 1999; Nussbaum & Coupland, 1995; Thimm, 1998; Williams, 1997).

© Mark Richards/CORBIS

The experiences of audience members can influence their attitudes about your topic.

Aristotle claimed that younger listeners tend to be more optimistic and trusting, as well as easier to persuade, than older listeners (McGuire, 1985). This is a broad generalization. Older people can be very trusting and open-minded, and younger people can be very distrusting and close-minded. Nonetheless, if you're giving a persuasive speech to an older audience you might want to make sure you have strong evidence to support your claims.

Age can also affect people's basic concerns. At different points in life, we have different goals. Thus a speech about career planning might be compelling to listeners under thirty, whereas it would be less likely to interest those over fifty, who are probably more concerned about career changing or retirement planning.

Age also influences experience, which in turn influences knowledge and opinions. Listeners who lived through the Depression, World War II, and the Cold War are likely to view topics related to economics, the military, and national security differently than those who didn't. Consider how a speech about the need for more U.S. military involvement in the Middle East or Indonesia might be perceived by listeners who fought or lost loved ones in the Vietnam War. How might their experiences influence their attitudes regarding the topic? How might you adapt a speech to demonstrate respect?

So be sure to consider the age range of the audience when developing your speech. Had Duane done so, he could have adapted his message to demonstrate respect for the breadth of experiences and values represented. Ian, another novice public speaker, did consider age range for his speech about fire safety. His audience included students ranging in age from eighteen to forty. For the younger students, Ian offered examples of safety measures to take in residence halls and apartments. In addition, he addressed key concerns for people who own their own homes. This added relevance for many of the older students in the class, as well as for the instructor. Because Ian took age into account, he was able to make his speech audience-centered for all. Far from stereotyping his listeners, Ian demonstrated respect for their demographic diversity.

Sex, Gender, and Sexual Orientation

Sex is the biological differences between males and females. Occasionally a topic—for example, medical topics such as hysterectomies or prostate cancer—is more relevant to one sex than the other. If you're interested in such a topic, figure out how knowing about it may benefit both sexes. A persuasive speech about the alarming number of unnecessary hysterectomies performed in the United States may seem less relevant to men than to women, but you could highlight how males are also harmed by the phenomenon through increased insurance rates and the emotional trauma experienced by family members. There's no reason to discard a topic because it seems to apply more directly to one sex, but you must find a way to make it relevant to both.

A more complex concept than sex, **gender** is the socialized tendency of men and women to perceive, believe, and behave differently (Wood, 1994, pp. 21–26). Gender is not innate like sex, but is learned behavior. Although these tendencies cannot be universally attributed to men or women, research reveals that by the time girls and boys are four or five years old, they already understand what "gender-appropriate" tendencies are and often act accordingly (Plotnik, 1993; Tannen, 1992).

What are the socialized tendencies of masculine and feminine gender? Essentially, "to be feminine is to be attractive, deferential, unaggressive, emotional, nurturing, and concerned with people and relationships," whereas "to be masculine is to be strong, ambitious, successful, rational, and emotionally controlled" (Wood, 1994, p. 21). Although the concept of what constitutes appropriate gender behavior changes over time, the basic blueprint is fairly consistent (Faludi, 1991; Kirtley & Weaver, 1999; McAdoo, 1999; Reisman, 1990; Sellnow & Golish, 2000).

Contemporary research suggests, however, that both males and females possess feminine and masculine tendencies (Ivy & Backlund, 1994). Thus the public speaker should avoid making assumptions about the males and females in the audience (Canary & Dindia, 1998; Canary & Hause, 1993; Reeder, 1996; Weatherall, 1998). Don't presume women are more emotional and men more logical, or that women prefer testimonials and men statistics, and so on.

Avoid gender stereotypes about the attitudes, interests, or likes and dislikes of audience members. Brad, for example, fell into this trap when he presented an informative speech about why growing up on a farm was significant to him. He made comments such as "Although the gals might not relate to the hard work of baling hay, I'm sure many of the guys know what I mean." As it turned out, several of the women in the classroom had grown up on farms and baled hay. Brad's comments stereotyped and marginalized some listeners and failed to reflect and build on reality. His ethos as a speaker was diminished and, consequently, so was the success of his speech.

As you prepare a speech, also be sensitive to the diversity of sexual orientation in the audience. Sometimes heterosexual speakers presume all listeners are heterosexual. This happened to Jim in his speech on Elton John's music (see Chapter 1). At several points he distanced himself by making clear that it was solely for the music that he admired Elton John. Jim had no way of knowing whether any of his listeners were homosexual and could be offended by his remarks. Likewise, when Kari talked about the important role of fathers in raising emotionally stable children she unknowingly marginalized Ryan, who—along with his little brother—was raised by a lesbian couple. Effective speakers respect the diversity of the audience by avoiding remarks that assume all intimate relationships and family systems are heterosexual.

PRACTICING THE PROCESS

Considering Listeners' Sex, Gender, and Sexual Orientation

Consider the topic and audience for your speech:

- How will you make sure to include both males and females?
- What can you speculate about them regarding gender? Sexual orientation?
- How will you make sure to demonstrate respect to all with regard to sex, gender, and sexual orientation?

Cathy © Cathy Guisewite. Reprinted with permission of Universal Press Syndicate. All rights reserved.

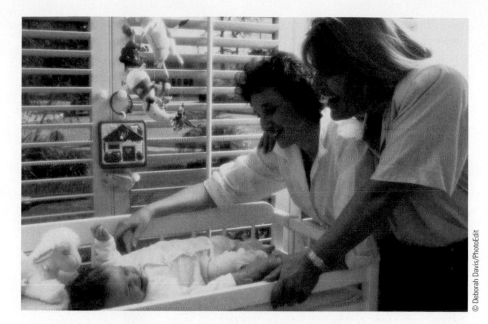

© Deborah Davis/PhotoEdit

Avoid gender role and sexual orientation stereotypes about the attitudes, interests, or likes and dislikes of your audience members.

Group Affiliations

We belong to many groups, such as political, religious, and social groups. These affiliations sometimes influence or reflect our views. Conscious affiliation with groups together with the value we place on the affiliation affects how we perceive experiences and events in our lives (Di Santa Ana, 1996; Gudykunst et al., 1996; Petronio et al., 1998; Suzuki, 1998). It's worth speculating about how affiliations might influence the way listeners may perceive your message. If you plan a speech about a controversial social issue on which Republicans and Democrats tend to disagree, for example, you will fare better if you know the political affiliations of the audience. Unless you're speaking at a political rally, listeners are unlikely to belong to the same party, but even if they are, not all are likely to be committed to the same ideals. When politics are relevant, a good speaker attempts to learn as much as possible about the political affiliations of listeners.

TURNING TO TECHNOLOGY

Considering Political Affiliations

Go to the *Confident Public Speaking* CD-ROM and click on Speech Interactive. Watch Mary Fisher's "A Whisper of AIDS" speech, delivered at the 1992 Republican National Convention. How did she demonstrate respect for the Republican Party as she talked about this controversial topic?

The United States is religiously very diverse, including Protestants of many denominations, Roman Catholics, Jews, Muslims, Buddhists, Hindus, Mormons, and people of numerous other religions, as well as atheists and agnostics. If your topic touches on religious beliefs, consider how religious affiliation might influence the perception of your topic, and communicate respect for diverse religions.

A persuasive speech on abortion rights, for example, will be better received if you adjust the language and limit the stridence of your attempt to persuade because you learned that most of the listeners are strict Roman Catholics who don't believe in birth control, let alone abortion.

Social groups include school clubs, volunteer organizations, professional groups, and many others that people join to engage in their interests. If you'll be giving a speech to a particular group, knowing its mission and goals can help you adapt your speech accordingly. A speech about drinking and driving, for example, should differ depending on whether it will be presented to a college fraternity, a PTA group, or a high school sports team. Usually listeners won't all share a social group affiliation, in which case you should simply demonstrate respect for their diverse affiliations.

Socioeconomic Factors

Socioeconomic factors include occupation, income, and education. Each can influence how listeners interpret your message.

We spend so much of our adult life working that occupation can have a significant effect on interests and experiences, as well as attitudes and beliefs. If speaking to a group whose members are in the same occupation—whether doctors, teachers, lawyers, sales representatives, farmers, or construction workers—they will have similar experiences, skills, and perspectives that you should allude to and build on in your speech. If you talk about gender and communication to a group of dental assistants, for example, you might use examples that are likely to occur in a dental office or discuss misinterpretations that can arise between a dental assistant and a patient of different genders.

If listeners work for a single company they may have even greater similarities of experiences and perspectives for you to take into account. Communication consultants, for example, often meet with company employees prior to speaking to them, so they can make their examples relate directly to the employees and their experiences.

How much money listeners earn can also influence their beliefs and attitudes, as income pervades most aspects of life. A speech about universal health care coverage, for example, may be perceived differently by low-income workers than by high-income professionals, as the latter are far more likely to receive medical insurance from their employers. Giving a speech to the latter group, you might address the advantages of universal health coverage over other plans; to the former group you might reveal steps these individuals can take to make universal coverage affordable.

As with all demographic factors, however, avoid stereotyping listeners based on their income. Don't assume, for example, that high-income people are always uninterested in, or even opposed to, universal health care coverage.

The education level of listeners might well affect the way you approach your topic. More education may mean more knowledge about a variety of topics, so if speaking to a highly educated audience, consider sharing an unusual insight or perspective on your topic. An informative speech on how to make an apple pie might provide new information to a group of elementary students, but probably not to college students. However, teaching how to make an apple pie over a campfire might provide new insight to the college students.

Of course, there are many kinds of educational experiences, and a person might lack formal education but be widely read, like Will in the Academy Award–winning film *Good Will Hunting*. So, avoid overgeneralizing about listeners based on educational level.

Even a well-educated audience may know little about your particular topic. What do you know that the audience doesn't? For example, Susan, a junior engineering major, realized that however much her public speaking classmates and instructor knew about other topics, when it came to engineering she knew more. Hence her speech on thermodynamics would likely be new to her audience.

If your audience is classmates it should be fairly homogeneous in level of education, but there is probably some variety. Students may be in their first year or their fourth or fifth year, and their majors will differ. Thus even if you're speaking in class, consider levels of education, especially regarding the topic of your speech. By comparing how much you and your listeners know about the topic, you can present a speech that respects listeners for what they already know while offering perspective or ideas they have not considered.

PRACTICING THE PROCESS

Considering Socioeconomics of Listeners

Consider the topic and audience for your speech:

- What are the education levels of your audience members?
- What are their majors (for students) or occupations (for nonstudents)?
- How might you adapt your speech to make it relevant to their needs and interests in this regard?

Sociocultural Background

Sociocultural background is determined largely by the family and groups we grow up in—the context in which we are raised. As members of a culturally diverse nation, listeners in the United States will likely vary in ethnicity and religion, and may be from different regions and from urban, suburban, and rural areas. Be aware of listeners' sociocultural backgrounds, because where and how they were raised has shaped their values, beliefs, and attitudes (e.g., Bashi & McDaniel, 1997; Donavan & Rundle, 1997; Gudykunst et al., 1996; Kim et al., 1996; Lustig & Koester, 1993; Masterson, Watson, & Cichon, 1991).

As discussed in Chapter 5, *values* are broad concepts we consider important and desirable in life. They are the basis of beliefs and attitudes. *Beliefs* are judgments about what is true or false. *Attitudes* are tendencies to respond negatively or positively to persons and things. All three are crucial to listeners' perceptions of a speaker's message.

A speech about gun control, for example, is likely to be perceived differently by classmates who grew up in an urban environment where gang violence is a problem than by those who grew up in a suburb where crime is rare or in a rural area where many people are hunters. The attitudes of urban-raised listeners, for example, might reflect their belief in a need for self-protection; the attitudes of students raised in the country might be quite different from those of students raised in the suburbs. If you were advocating gun control in your speech, you might address alternative methods of self-protection for the urban-raised listeners, and how your gun control plan could take into account hunters' rights for the country-raised listeners. You must do more than just shape your speech so that it takes into account how your listeners' backgrounds differ from your own; you also need to make sure it respects their diverse backgrounds.

Analyzing the audience based on demographic characteristics helps you realize similarities and differences among listeners as well as between them and yourself, which is key to being an effective public speaker. At the very least, conducting effective demographic audience analysis helps ensure that you'll avoid making inappropriate assumptions that could marginalize or offend listeners. In all likelihood, it will also increase the impact of your speech.

ANALYSIS OF PSYCHOLOGICAL CHARACTERISTICS

Examining the psychological characteristics of listeners helps you make a speech relevant to them and thus motivate them to listen and retain ideas. These characteristics fall into three categories: human needs, tendency to respond to rhetorical appeals, and the learning cycle.

Most people have various needs, respond to various appeals, and (as discussed in Chapter 1) tend to prefer different learning styles. So the key is to be aware of the range of psychological characteristics and to draw on them when possible throughout your speech. This will likely motivate your audience to listen and maintain its interest throughout.

Maslow's Hierarchy of Needs

Advertisers use the concept of needs every day as they attempt to sell products to consumers. They claim we'll be more attractive if we buy toothpaste that makes our teeth whiter, body lotion that makes our skin look younger, and of course, the right brand of jeans. This appeals above all to our need for love and belonging. Public speaking and advertising are quite different, but good speakers examine how the speech could enhance audience members' lives—how it could address their needs.

You may find it useful to think of the hierarchy of human needs outlined by A. H. Maslow (1970). As shown in Figure 6.1, Maslow's hierarchy has five levels: physiological needs, safety needs, love and belongingness needs, esteem needs, and self-actualization needs—physiological needs being the most basic. According to Maslow, we are motivated by our most basic unmet need. In public speaking, this means an audience is motivated to listen, learn, and respond to speeches that address some unsatisfied need. Consider what these needs might be, and remembering the diversity of your audience, incorporate appeals focused on more than one need.

WHAT DO YOU THINK?

Consider a television commercial that made you want to buy a product. What made the product appealing?

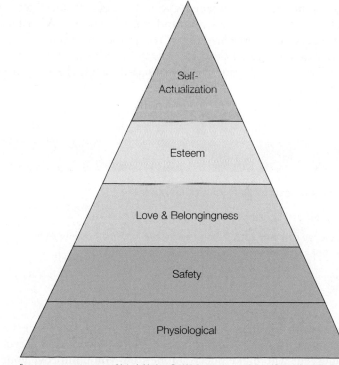

From *Motivation and Personality*, 3/e by A. Maslow, © 1997. Reprinted by permission of Pearson Education, Inc. Upper Saddle River, NJ.

Figure 6.1 Maslow's hierarchy of human needs.

Physiological needs are related to self-preservation—the need for air, food, water, rest, and avoidance of pain. Can you tie your speech to people's needs for bodily comfort, physical pleasure, sexual gratification, food, or sleep? College students, who are often strapped for money, might be more likely to listen to your speech about recycling if you can demonstrate how it can raise some extra spending money.

Safety needs relate to the desire for order, stability, and security. We often resist change if we think it violates our safety. To appeal to audience members' safety needs in a speech about recycling, you might talk about how recycling enables sanitation departments to deal with garbage in ways that are safer for our environment and thus how it makes us and future generations safer.

Love and belongingness needs reflect the desire to share our lives with others. We want approval and acceptance and don't like feeling isolated or alone. In a recycling speech, you might suggest that listeners join with neighbors or others, or that residence hall or apartment dwellers join forces to collect and dispose of recyclable trash. Talking about recycling as a group effort might motivate your audience to listen and act.

Esteem needs have to do with the desire for recognition and self-respect. How might your speech appeal to listeners' desires to improve their reputation, achieve more power, gain a sense of personal achievement, and so forth? In a recycling speech, you might describe a program that recognizes those who meet a certain level of recycling success. Perhaps an award can be created to honor businesses whose employees implement laudable recycling programs in the workplace.

Self-actualization needs reflect the desire to realize personal potential. Whereas esteem needs are most often externally defined by the perceptions others have of us, self-actualization needs are defined by our own perceptions of our abilities. How this manifests itself depends on the individual, but you might try to address it by thinking about what listeners might value most. For example, you might highlight where to take recyclables to benefit social service organizations such as homeless shelters, rape and abuse crisis centers, or Head Start programs. Listeners might not earn formal recognition for their efforts but will feel good about themselves by doing it. In my community, for example, bins where we can dispose of soda cans are plentiful and the proceeds go to arts programs in public schools.

PRACTICING THE PROCESS

Using Maslow's Hierarchy to Motivate Listeners

Consider the topic and audience for your speech.

- Identify how you can motivate them at each level on Maslow's hierarchy.
- Ask a friend or classmate to help if there are levels that stump you.

As you can see from the recycling example, a speech can address a variety of needs. You might emphasize the personal financial benefits of recycling to a group of young kids who'd like pocket money, but you'll improve your potential for success by addressing as many levels as possible.

Rhetorical Appeals

Ever since Aristotle explained the three rhetorical appeals—ethos, pathos, and logos—effective public speakers have used them to motivate audiences. Rhetorical appeals work because they appeal to something humans tend to respond to psychologically.

Ethos refers to appeals to the speaker's credibility in the sense of competence and character. Listeners more often listen seriously to a speaker who projects a competent and trustworthy image. You can foster ethos by your attire and appearance, delivery skills, and use of credible supporting material. (Supporting material is discussed further in Chapter 7 and delivery skills in Chapter 12.)

Pathos refers to appeals to the emotions. Listeners are more likely to retain ideas that touch their emotions. Consider public service announcements that appeal for money to help starving children. Would those announcements be as effective if viewers did not *see* the starving children they could save for the price of a cup of coffee?

Logos refers to appeals to logic. Listeners are more likely to be convinced by a speaker who arranges ideas systematically and articulates how and why evidence supports his or her claims—that is, by connecting each piece of evidence to the main ideas they support through reasoning.

Because different listeners are differently compelled by rhetorical appeals, employ all of them in your speeches. If talking about drinking and driving, for example, you could quote several sources on the number of deaths that occur from drinking and driving to boost your ethos. Using statistical evidence, you could employ logos by calculating how many fatalities occur each day and how likely someone in your audience is to eventually become a victim. You could share testimonies from people who lost loved ones to drinking-and-driving accidents, appealing to the emotions (pathos) of listeners. Use a variety of rhetorical appeals throughout your speech—appeals to competence and credibility, to emotions, and to logic.

TURNING TO TECHNOLOGY

Examining Rhetorical Appeals

http://www.inform.umd.edu/IAW/RhetoricalExercises/17appeals.html

Complete the questionnaire at this Web site by identifying which rhetorical appeal is being addressed with each statement. Discuss your answers with a friend or classmate.

AUDIENCE ANALYSIS AND THE LEARNING CYCLE

Chapter 1 explains that we all learn best by rounding the entire cycle of learning, but individuals tend to prefer one stage over the others. This is their preferred learning style (de Ciantis & Kirton, 1996; Kolb, 1984). When your speech addresses a listener's preferred learning style, he or she will pay attention (Dunn & Dunn, 1979; Magolda, 1989, Marshall, 1990; Rogers, 1983; Sprague, 1993). You'll need to address four primary learning modes: watching, doing, feeling, and thinking (Figure 6.2).

To address the watching mode, use visual aids such as objects and photographs. Recall that Duane (see chapter opener) offered a slide show in his speech. Visual aids are discussed in detail in Chapter 13.

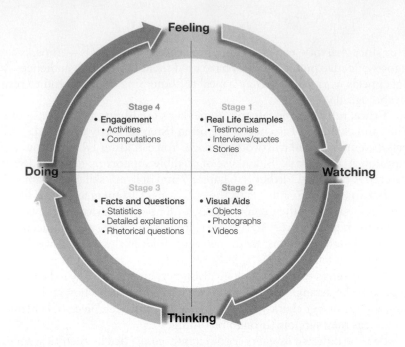

Figure 6.2 Audience analysis and the learning cycle

To address the doing mode, you might ask listeners to engage in an activity or to complete a computation as you speak. For example, if you inform listeners about appropriate body fat for good physical health you might explain how to compute their body fat based on height, weight, age, and body type. Better yet, display the formula on a visual aid as you explain it. This appeals to both watching and doing.

To appeal to the feeling mode, try to use examples from real life. Include a range of examples, testimonials, and interviews from experts in the field. In your speech about body fat, you might videotape testimonials from individuals who reduced their body fat as they talk about ways their lives have changed as a result. Showing people speaking for themselves appeals to feeling, because the people are real, and to watching, because audience members can actually see them.

To address the thinking mode, offer facts, statistics, and detailed explanations. In the body fat speech, you might cite facts and statistics about body fat and physical health, as well as insert rhetorical questions for students to ponder later.

TURNING TO TECHNOLOGY

Rounding the Cycle of Learning

http://www.presentersuniversity.com/courses_content_connect.php

At this Web site, consider the tips offered for rounding the learning cycle in your speeches. Which ones will you try for your next speech and why?

Return to the recycling speech and consider how you could address each preferred learning style. You might bring samples of different types of recyclable materials—grade 1, 2, and 3 plastics and so on (watching). You might discuss examples of the kinds of recyclable products college students tend to buy (feeling). You

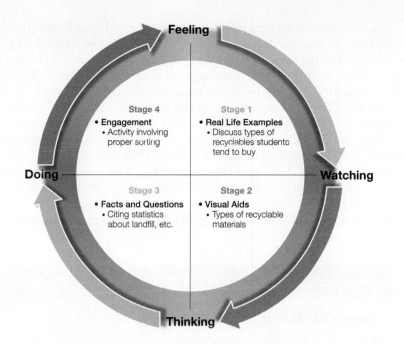

Figure 6.3   Addressing each learning style for the recycling speech

might cite facts and statistics pointing to the potential consequences of not recycling (thinking). And you might engage listeners in a recycling activity such as proper sorting (doing). These tactics address the entire learning cycle, motivating all audience members to listen to and retain the ideas you share (Figure 6.3).

Looking at the Learning Cycle

Your Next Speech

Consider the topic and audience for your next speech: Where and how will you address watching? Thinking? Feeling? Doing?

ANALYSIS OF ENVIRONMENTAL CHARACTERISTICS

Environmental characteristics are the factors that influence why listeners attend and what they expect from a particular speech—expectations about time, setting, and occasion. Analysis of environmental characteristics should not be overlooked. Fortunately it is perhaps the easiest of the characteristics to analyze and to adapt your speech to.

Chronemics

Chronemics are considerations related to time and expectations about time. Think about how listeners might be affected by the time of the day and week when you will present the speech. For example, if you speak at 8:00 on a Monday morning, listeners might well be tired. Perhaps you should begin your speech with an activity to wake them up. This could be as simple as asking for a show of hands or for them to repeat a simple action after you model it. The same is true if your speech is scheduled right after lunch. If asked to present a speech late on a Friday afternoon, keep it short: Listeners are probably looking forward to the weekend.

Time constraint expectations are also important. If you finish your presentation more quickly than listeners anticipated, they may feel cheated. (If a concert by your favorite band ended in less than an hour, would you feel you had gotten your money's worth?) If you speak longer than expected, however, listeners may feel disrespected. I have friends, for example, who get upset when the pastor's sermon takes longer than anticipated and they miss the start of a ballgame on television.

Note that these examples reflect conceptions of time that predominate in our culture. Traditionally, Americans tend to view time as a commodity that can be bought, sold, wasted, and saved (Merriam, 1982). This perception is not universally shared. In many Native American, Mediterranean, Asian, and Middle Eastern cultures, time is not something that can be manipulated at all (DiMartino, 1989; Lee, 1990). To be an effective public speaker in our culture, however, you must adhere to time constraints.

PRACTICING THE PROCESS

Considering Time Factors

- When will you present your speech?
- How will you adapt it with regard to time of day and week?
- What adaptations will you make for specific time constraints?

Physical Setting

In analyzing environmental characteristics related to physical setting, look at whether the speech will be presented indoors or outdoors, in a large or small space, in a room with comfortable or uncomfortable seating, and in front of a large crowd or a small group. All these factors can have significant repercussions for your speech.

Speaking outside may mean competing with a host of distractions, such as passersby, traffic, wind, or heat. To compete, you must speak louder and perhaps employ some novelty to maintain listeners' attention.

If you speak in a large room, speak louder and present material more formally than if you were in a smaller venue. If the room is crowded or the furniture uncomfortable, limit how long you speak because listeners' attention spans are likely to be shorter than in a sparsely populated room with comfortable furniture.

But if the furniture is too comfortable, listeners may relax to the point that their minds wander. In this case, engage them in an activity or use visual and audio aids to help them stay focused on you and your message.

PRACTICING THE PROCESS

Considering the Physical Setting of a Speech

- What is the room like where you will present your speech?
- What is the furniture like?
- Will there be distractions?
- How might you adapt your speech as a result?

Occasion

Ask yourself, "Why have I been requested to speak here and now?" It is crucial to understand what the audience expects to hear and then to adhere to expectations. For example, you may be asked to present an informative speech about a significant person in your life. If you instead give a persuasive speech about the need to have yearly physical examinations, it will not meet audience expectations. And if listeners expect an informative speech about where their college tuition goes and you instead try to persuade them to boycott college until tuition gets lowered, the speech will not meet expectations. Michael Moore's acceptance speech at the 75th Academy Awards in March of 2003 did not adhere to audience expectations. Rather than merely express thanks for the award, he expressed his opposition to President Bush and his political decisions. As a result, he alienated many of his audience members.

TURNING TO TECHNOLOGY

Honoring Occasion Expectations

http://www.oscar.com/oscarnight/winners/win_32297.html

ETHICS

- Read through the transcript of Michael Moore's acceptance speech. Did he honor the expectations of the occasion? Why or why not?
- Watch the video clip of the press conference held after the ceremony. Based on his answers to the reporters' questions, do you think he was ethical that night? Why or why not?

Consider your topic in relation to recent speeches and events. Your speech will be more audience-centered if it links to these when appropriate. For example, say you plan to speak about the need for a balanced diet. Earlier in the class period, someone spoke about the need to engage in aerobic activity. You might create a link by showing how your speech builds on the ideas offered in the earlier presentation, maybe explaining that aerobic activity alone is not enough to achieve good health; a balanced diet is equally important. Likewise, if you plan to persuade classmates to use the designated driver system when drinking, you might mention an alcohol-related traffic accident that occurred recently in your community.

Student Workbook

Attend a professional speech and complete the "Audience Assessment Form" in Chapter 2 of your workbook. Do you think the speaker adapted effectively to the audience? Why or why not?

METHODS FOR AUDIENCE ANALYSIS

We have talked about analyzing the audience to discover demographic, psychological, and environmental characteristics to consider as you adapt your speech to address the interests and needs of listeners. But knowing what to analyze is not enough. The question that remains is how. Following are direct and indirect methods you can use to analyze an audience (Figure 6.4). Direct methods solicit information from those who will be in the audience and are the most accurate, but time, resource, or access limitations may prevent you from employing them. Hence indirect methods must often suffice. Indirect methods require speculation about listeners' interests and attitudes toward your topic. You must draw inferences based on information you are able to obtain about them.

Direct Methods	Indirect Methods
Conduct interviews	Observe your audience
Do focus groups	Ask others
Conduct a survey	Read written resources
Do a poll	

Direct Methods

The most common direct methods are interviews, focus groups, and surveys. In an **interview,** you ask individuals questions to obtain the information you need about group affiliations, sociocultural backgrounds, and attitudes and beliefs about your topic. Questions should be developed in advance and include both closed-ended and open-ended varieties. With a **closed-ended question,** respondents choose from a small range of specific answers supplied by the interviewer. Often these require just a simple yes or no answer. For her speech about unidentified flying objects (UFOs), Michelle asked, "Do you believe in UFOs?" **Open-ended questions** require a response in the interviewee's own words. Michelle also asked respondents, "What are your feelings about UFOs?" Interviews can provide a wealth of precise information about listeners' interests and attitudes about your topic. Unfortunately, time constraints often prevent conducting interviews prior to developing a speech.

The **focus group** approach means you talk to a small group rather than to individuals. This allows you to gather information from more people in less time. The participants also talk among themselves, which can provide more descriptive information about their interests and attitudes. However, some people may be inhibited about talking in a group setting, so the information you get might be less accurate than in individual interviews.

A **survey** gathers information quickly from a large pool of respondents. Respondents often complete a **questionnaire,** which may have open-ended as well as closed-ended questions. Often responses are written. This maximizes efficiency, but you don't have the opportunity to ask respondents to expand or clarify their answers. Sometimes a survey can be a simple poll. A **poll** is a quick method to find out where listeners stand on your topic. Michelle could have asked her listeners through use of a poll whether they believe in UFOs, which would have surveyed listeners in much less time than interviews with each person.

PRACTICING THE PROCESS

Using Direct Methods

Consider the topic and audience for your speech:

- Develop several questions to ask in interviews, focus groups, or a survey that will help determine the focus of your speech.
- Which method will you use and why?

Indirect Methods

Although interviews, focus groups, and surveys allow you to find out directly about audience characteristics, attitudes, and beliefs, you may not have the time or resources to conduct them. But you can find out a lot by using indirect methods such as observing the audience, asking other speakers, and reading written resources.

If audience members will be your classmates or another familiar group, observe them and think about who they are and what they talk about. Ask yourself: How many people will there be in the audience? What is their age range? What sorts of information have they shared in previous class discussions and speeches? How might what they've talked about relate to my topic? Critical thinking about who your listeners are and what they have shared in the past can be very useful for audience analysis.

If you know other people who have spoken to the group you will address, you might ask them for information about the group. How did the audience react to humor, the length of the speech, and the kinds of stories and examples? Did any issues seem to make the audience uncomfortable? If you know someone who belongs to the group, you might ask that person for his or her observations and insights as well.

In many cases you might be able to read brochures, newspaper articles, organizational bylaws, or industry abstracts to learn about the group you will be addressing. Often an organization has a Web page that can tell you a great deal about what it is, its mission and goals, how it operates, and what it has achieved. When I was asked to present a motivational speech about success to the Society of Women Engineers (SWE), a student organization on our campus, I read its Web page to learn about its purpose and membership and tailored my speech to address the members' unique goals and accomplishments. I learned that members must maintain a high GPA, volunteer to help public service organizations in the community, and act as leaders in campus government. I adapted my speech to focus on success as more than earning good grades and achieving professional goals. Being a success also means making a difference in the lives of those around you.

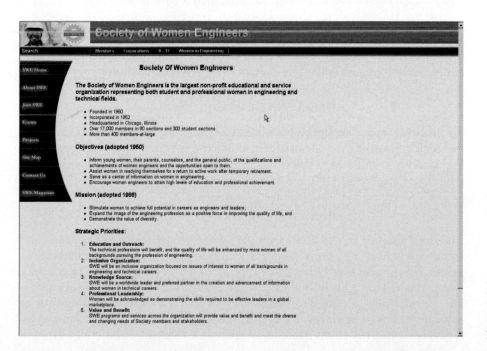

Organizations' Web sites can be an excellent source of useful information when you're analyzing audiences.

CONSIDERING ETHICS:
INTEGRATING AUDIENCE ANALYSIS

ETHICS

Audience analysis is a formidable but crucial task for public speakers. To demonstrate genuine respect for your listeners, you must integrate audience analysis throughout the speechmaking process—when you select and narrow your topic, when you choose supporting material, when you structure your ideas, and when you deliver the speech. Audience analysis begins with topic selection, but it is important throughout the preparation and presentation process.

Audience Analysis and Topic Selection

In the funnel method described in Chapter 5, the second step is to narrow your general topic to an area based on the needs and interests of listeners. Holly discovered that most of her classmates either have children or plan to someday. She learned this through audience analysis. Hence she molded her general topic of day care to focus more specifically on making educated day care choices.

Audience Analysis and Supporting Material

To effectively appeal to diverse human needs, tendencies to respond to rhetorical appeals, and preferred learning styles, offer listeners a variety of types of evidence throughout your speech—such as facts, statistics, testimonies, examples, analogies, descriptions, and definitions (Chapter 7 discusses this thoroughly).

Audience Analysis and Structure

To effectively appeal to diverse learning styles preferred by listeners and to round the cycle of learning for all, structure your messages to address feeling, thinking, watching, and doing. You can do this in your macrostructure and microstructure; Chapters 8, 9, 10, and 11 address the strategies.

Audience Analysis and Delivery

Audience analysis should come into play when you rehearse your speech and when you deliver it to the audience. By addressing psychological characteristics such as human needs, rhetorical appeals, and the learning cycle in your delivery, you will more likely attain and maintain listener interest. Likewise, adapting your delivery to adhere to environmental characteristics regarding time of day and week, as well as setting and occasion, improves your chances for success. Delivery strategies in light of audience analysis are considered in more detail in Chapter 12.

Audience Analysis and Presentational Aids

Audience analysis also ought to come into play when selecting, constructing, and integrating presentational aids. By addressing diverse human needs, rhetorical appeals, and the learning cycle in presentational aids, you can improve the chance for success in reaching your diverse audience. Chapter 13 deals with this concept.

TURNING TO TECHNOLOGY

Applying Audience Analysis to Your Speeches

http://www.ukans.edu/cwis/units/coms2/vpa/vpa4.htm

This virtual presentation assistant offers tips and strategies for using audience analysis to create and present the most effective speeches. Which tips will you try in your next speech? Why?

Looking at the Learning Cycle

Ethics and Audience Analysis

ETHICS

- How does rounding the learning cycle demonstrate ethical audience analysis
- With regard to topic selection?
- With regard to supporting material?
- With regard to structure?
- With regard to delivery?
- With regard to presentational aids?

SUMMARY

Through audience analysis, a crucial step in developing and presenting successful public speeches, you examine the demographic, psychological, and environmental characteristics of the audience in order to adapt your speech to be relevant to, and effective with, your listeners.

Demographic characteristics include age, sex, gender, sexual orientation, group affiliations, socioeconomic factors, and sociocultural background. Psychological characteristics include human needs as expressed in Maslow's hierarchy; the rhetorical appeals of ethos, pathos, and logos; and the learning cycle. Environmental characteristics include chronemics (time factors), the physical setting, and the occasion. The goal is to develop and present a speech tailored to the needs of your specific audience while respecting its diversity.

Audience analysis may be conducted through direct and indirect methods. Direct methods include interviews, focus groups, and surveys. Indirect methods include observation, discussion with other speakers, and use of written resources, including Web sites.

To demonstrate respect for listeners, integrate audience analysis throughout the speechmaking process. Consider the audience when selecting and narrowing your topic, when conducting research to collect supporting material, when structuring ideas, when rehearsing as well as delivering the speech, and when selecting and constructing presentational aids.

The goal of audience analysis is to find out who your listeners are and adapt your speech to address their interests, needs, and desires. To do so effectively, you must first understand who you are and what you value and believe. Then you can develop an understanding of and respect for the diverse knowledge, values, beliefs, and attitudes of your listeners.

RETURNING TO TECHNOLOGY

The *Confident Public Speaking* CD-ROM is your one-stop point of access for not just the content on the CD itself, such as Speech Interactive, but also the many other resources on the *Confident Public Speaking* Web site, Speech Builder Express, and InfoTrac College Edition. Note that this chapter's key terms and activities are among the resources available in electronic format online. Additional information is included below.

SPEECH INTERACTIVE
ON THE *CONFIDENT PUBLIC SPEAKING* CD-ROM

Speech Interactive is your link to this text's speech videos. Offering opportunities to practice critiquing speeches by students and other public speakers, these videos will help you prepare for providing effective feedback to your peers and your own speech performances.

SPEECH BUILDER EXPRESS

The Goal/Purpose and Thesis sections of Speech Builder Express can help you answer key questions about your audience. You'll find links to each section on the left-hand navigation menu.

KEY TERMS

Interactive flashcards for these key terms are available on the *Confident Public Speaking* Web site. You'll find the "Flashcards" link under the resources for Chapter 6.

Audience analysis   126
Chronemics   141
Closed-ended question   144
Demographic characteristics   127
Environmental characteristics   128
Ethos   139
Focus group   144
Gender   131
Interview   144
Logos   139

Marginalized   128
Open-ended question   144
Pathos   139
Poll   144
Psychological characteristics   128
Questionnaire   144
Sex   131
Sociocultural background   135
Stereotype   128
Survey   144

ACTIVITIES

The activities below are available in electronic format on the *Confident Public Speaking* Web site. You'll find the "Activities" link under the resources for Chapter 6.

1. **Focus Group Belief and Attitude Analysis.** Form a small group with three or four classmates. Each group member should select a topic from the personal inventory you created after reading Chapter 5. Each should select a topic about which she or he has strong feelings. Talk about each topic in terms of the beliefs and attitudes of each group member. As a group, select one topic from each list about which you all hold similar values/attitudes/beliefs and one topic about which you all have different values/attitudes/beliefs. Discuss how you might approach each topic based on the environmental, demographic, and psychological characteristics of the class.

2. **Conduct a Survey.** Prepare a short questionnaire based on the topic of your next speech to discover the values, beliefs, and attitudes of your audience members regarding it. Administer the survey at the outset of the next class period.

3. **Indirect Audience Analysis.** Consider the topic you have selected for your next speech. Speculate about your listeners' interests, beliefs, and attitudes about the topic. Note your generalizations on a piece of paper with two columns next to each item. Write a heading of "yes" or "no" above each column. Pass the paper around the room and ask classmates to mark a slash in the appropriate column next to each generalization. Once everyone has marked the paper, review the responses and adapt your speech based on what you learn.

INFOTRAC COLLEGE EDITION ACTIVITY

Log on to InfoTrac College Edition and, in the keyword search entry box, enter a search term for a topic that interests you, possibly one you plan to use for an upcoming speech or one related to an area of study for another of your courses. Identify two or three articles on the same aspect of the topic that were published in clearly different types of magazines, newspapers, or journals—for example, in scholarly or popular publications. After considering the articles' titles and reading a few introductory paragraphs or the abstract for each article, jot down some of the assumptions you think each article's author might have had about her or his audience.

SUPPORTING YOUR SPEECH: EVIDENCE AND RESEARCH

REFLECTIVE QUESTIONS

1. Why might it be important to use different types of supporting material when developing your main points?

2. Where might you locate evidence to support your speech?

3. What is the difference between facts and statistics? How might you use statistics effectively?

4. What questions might you ask to evaluate evidence?

5. Why could it be important to orally cite footnotes during your speech?

WHAT'S AHEAD: FOCUSING YOUR READING

Why Is Supporting Material Important?

Types of Supporting Material

Locating Supporting Material: Research

Conducting Ethical Research

ONCE YOU HAVE SELECTED AND narrowed a topic, you are ready to develop it with supporting material. This may seem difficult. In Holly's case, she first thought she couldn't come up with a topic before realizing she knew quite a lot about day care options, as described in Chapter 5. Her initial doubts returned when she thought about developing her topic. "There's not that much to say about day care options. I can't possibly fill even five minutes on this topic," she told me. But after we discussed types of supporting material she could use to develop her speech and research she could conduct, she was encouraged.

If you feel like Holly did, don't give up. This chapter will teach you how to turn a topic and thesis statement into a speech by developing ideas with **supporting material,** or **evidence,** which is information that clarifies, explains, or otherwise adds depth or breadth to a topic. Evidence comes from **research,** the process of gathering supporting material to better understand and develop a subject. You conduct research by asking questions about the topic and seeking the answers.

The focus here is on how to support your speech with evidence. We talk about why supporting material is important, identify the types of supporting material available, discuss where to locate them, and consider what it means to do ethical research. This will prepare you to develop main points effectively and ethically by using a variety of supporting material.

WHY IS SUPPORTING MATERIAL IMPORTANT?

Supporting material is crucial to effective speechmaking. Without it you have no speech, just a statement or opinion in the form of a thesis statement. The goal of every speech is to get listeners to understand and retain your message, and supporting material plays a primary role in achieving that goal. Advertisements use supporting material to develop their messages. For example, a company will try to prove that its product makes your teeth whiter by offering statistics about how much whiter they'll be after a few weeks and how easy the product is to use, sometimes offering testimony from satisfied customers. We certainly remember some ads because they are funny or sexy, but the ones most likely to compel use a variety of supporting material. The same is true for a speech: The supporting material used to develop your main points can mean the difference between success and failure. This shouldn't increase your anxiety; all you need to do is choose your supporting material carefully.

TURNING TO TECHNOLOGY

Evidence in Advertisements

http://www.vsvideoproductions.com/

Click on the "Corporate Samples" link at this site. What kinds of supporting material are used to compel viewers to use this company's services? Which were most compelling to you? Why?

Why is supporting material so important? First and foremost, it gives your speech breadth and depth. Second, it goes a long way in ensuring that your speech appeals to a diverse audience. And third, it can bolster your ethos as a speaker.

Add Breadth and Depth

Like Holly, beginning speakers often become anxious about whether their speech will be long enough. Adding breadth and depth can diminish this problem.

Main points are necessarily general. Supporting material is specific, so listeners can understand points more precisely and see their validity. When you clarify a point with different pieces of evidence, you add **breadth.** Holly did this by describing several day care settings in her community rather than only the center where she works. Clarifying a point by offering detailed evidence adds **depth.** Holly did this by providing an hour-by-hour schedule for a typical day at a day care center, rather than merely talking about general activities that occur. Breadth and depth clarify your message, incidentally making your speech longer and perhaps reducing your anxiety.

WHAT DO YOU THINK?
Consider an argument you had with a friend recently. What sorts of supporting material did you use to help make your point? How did this add breadth and depth to your position? What role did supporting material play in your success or failure?

Appeal to Your Diverse Audience

Speeches offering a variety of supporting material are more likely to appeal to diverse audiences. Different listeners may be more or less compelled by different kinds of evidence based on their preferred learning style. Hence you can reach more people when supporting material appeals to doing, feeling, watching, and thinking. Beginning speakers tend to include only supporting material that addresses their own preferred learning. But this comes at the expense of clarity and retention for all because it fails to round the entire cycle of learning (Figure 7.1).

Consider how Holly might vary the supporting material for her speech. Stories about her experiences at a day care center appeal to the feeling dimension. Statistics on how well children do in different day care settings appeal to thinking. Graphs and charts depicting these statistics, as well as pictures and diagrams of different day care settings, address the watching dimension. Finally, explanations about how to do some of the activities offered to children in different day care settings address the doing dimension.

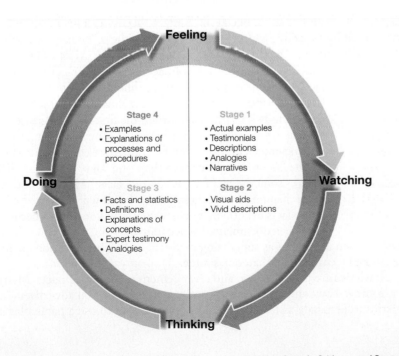

Figure 7.1 Supporting material and the learning cycle

Consider a speech you heard recently, perhaps from a teacher, a preacher, a motivational speaker, a comedian, a community leader, or a politician. Did the speaker's supporting material address your preferred learning style? How? How did this influence your opinion of the speech's overall effectiveness? Did the speaker's supporting material round the entire learning cycle? How? How might this thoroughness have made the speech more effective?

Bolster Speaker Ethos

When you offer various types of evidence drawn from a number of different sources, you convey competence and credibility. Listeners are more likely to find your speech compelling if you explain why you are an expert and how your ideas are supported by other experts. Holly bolstered her ethos when she explained her credentials as a day care center employee, when she quoted community providers she had interviewed, and when she cited federal day care regulations she found on a government Web site. (As explained later, using external sources to bolster your ethos requires citing their credentials.)

TYPES OF SUPPORTING MATERIAL

You can support your ideas with facts and statistics; definitions, descriptions, and explanations; examples; narratives; and testimony. Some beginning speakers think that facts and statistics are the *best* forms of evidence, but in reality there is no best form; each has its uses. One main point in your speech might best be supported by examples, another by statistics, and another by testimony. Recall too that different listeners tend to be persuaded by different kinds of evidence, so effective speeches use various types of supporting material.

Facts and Statistics

A **fact** is information that has been established as accurate. This means it must be documented by a credible source, perhaps an eyewitness, a journalist, or a historian. Facts usually concern events, times, people, and places. Most listeners require some factual information to accept a speaker's claims, although facts appeal most to the thinking dimension of the learning cycle (Reinard, 1991). If a fact can't be documented , it's merely an opinion. If Holly said where and when the first day care center was established, for example, many people won't consider it a fact unless she documents it. Moreover, facts are more compelling when they can be documented by more than one source, because different sources sometimes offer conflicting "facts." Hence if you can cite more than one source to support a fact it will be more believable. Some facts eventually become common knowledge because they have been documented as accurate over and over. You will be most effective when using facts as supporting material, then, when you document them as accurate by citing more than one source.

Statistics are the collection and arrangement of numerical facts. Many people are swayed by numbers. Consider, for example, how often advertisements use statistics to persuade us to buy products. We are told to use a particular tooth-

WHAT DO YOU THINK?

Consider a television program you might see on the History Channel, such as *Modern Marvels,* or the Discovery Channel, such as *FBI Files* and *New Detectives.* Do the facts offered seem believable? Based on what we have talked about in this chapter, why or why not?

paste because "three out of four dentists surveyed" recommend it. We are urged to eat a certain cereal because it has "100 percent" of the recommended daily allowance of essential vitamins. We are encouraged to purchase a certain brand of soup because it is "97 percent" fat free. And we are persuaded to drink a certain brand of soda pop because nationwide surveys show that "most people like it better" than other brands.

Statistics can be used effectively as supporting material to describe quantities, demonstrate trends, or infer relationships. Like facts, statistics tend to appeal to the thinking dimension of the learning cycle. When newspaper stories talk about the number of troops deployed in Iraq or killed in combat, they are offering statistics about quantities. When television reporters talk about rising unemployment rates, they are offering statistics that demonstrate trends. Laura D'Andrea Tyson (2003), dean of the London Business School, used statistics to help make her point clear:

> By the end of 2002, the U.S. current-account deficit—the gap between the nation's income from abroad and its spending overseas—hit 5.2% of gross domestic product. And for the first time in its history, the U.S. began paying more to the rest of the world than it received in interest, dividends, and other investment income. By comparison, the current-account gap at the end of the Gulf War was only about 2% of the gross domestic product. . . . It's much more likely that a prolonged current-account gap over 5% will trigger a drop in the dollar's value and higher interest rates. .
> . . Although the dollar is still over 20% above its mid-1990s level, it has fallen by over 25% against the euro in the past year. The course of the American economy now depends critically on how the rest of the world responds to the U.S.'s growing budget and current-account deficits. (p. 26)

If Holly were to talk about the percentage of children under age five who participate in each day care option, she would be describing quantities. If she showed the percentage who participate in these day care options as infants, toddlers, preschoolers, and school-aged children, she would be demonstrating trends. If she compared the academic achievement levels of children who had participated in each day care option, she would be inferring relationships.

TURNING TO TECHNOLOGY

Locating Statistical Evidence

http://www.ojp.usdoj.gov/bjs/nibrs.htm

Go to this site to find everything from the most recent Department of Justice crime statistics to statistics on how many students speak English as a second language. Compare the crime statistics for your community to those for your state and the nation. Are you surprised? Why or why not?

To use statistics effectively, follow a few simple rules:

- *Understand what the statistics mean and explain them.* When reading, consider not only the numbers presented but how these relate to the whole. Likewise, use visual aids to help make the statistics more concrete for listeners. If Holly learned that 60 percent of children under age five participate in licensed day care, for example, she should not assume that all 60 percent are enrolled in day care *centers*, nor should she assume that the other 40 percent receive care from parents. She would need to do additional research to discover the breakdown of child care for both the 60 percent and 40 percent figures. Not doing so would risk being misleading and unethical.

- *Round off statistics.* This might sound inaccurate and unethical, but it is better to help listeners retain key concepts rather than specific details.

  Let's say Holly's information revealed that 61.3 percent of children under age five participate in licensed day care. Later, she learned that 48.7 percent of those children participate in day care centers. The main ideas—*"about 60 percent* of the children" and *"nearly half* of those children"—are more likely to be retained by listeners than the exact percentages.

- *Limit how many statistics you offer.* Statistics should only be offered as they relate to the message you are trying to convey. You may find a lot of interesting statistical information, but if you use too much of it listeners may not remember any of it, let alone your main point. Holly, for example, learned how many children under age five participate in day care today as compared to previous decades. Although interesting, this did not relate to her goal so she left it out of her speech.

- *Remember that statistics are biased.* Mark Twain once said there are three kinds of lies: "lies, damned lies, and statistics." Not all statistics are lies, of course, but consider the source of the information, what that source may have been trying to prove, and how that might have influenced the way the data were collected and interpreted. No statistic can represent the truth perfectly; some bias is always involved (Frances, 1994). This doesn't mean statistics are useless, just that they are open to interpretation and require thoughtful evaluation before using them. Consider how the information was collected, whether the source is credible, and whether the organization that collected the information is partisan. For example, if Holly's statistics about the relationship between day care and academic achievement had been reported by an outspoken day care advocacy group, she might choose to discard them as potentially too biased.

WHAT DO YOU THINK?

Consider a time when you heard a speaker use a lot of detailed statistics. It may have been a teacher, a professional speaker, a politician, or the like. What do you remember from the statistics? From the speech?

TURNING TO TECHNOLOGY

Understanding Statistics

http://www.robertniles.com/stats/

At this site, explore the different types of statistics you could use in a speech and what they mean. What is the difference between *median* and *mean*? *Rate* and *per capita*? *Normal distribution* and *standard deviation*? Why should you know these terms when using statistics in your speech?

Evaluating Your Statistics

Consider the topic of your speech:

- What kinds of statistics might help clarify your main ideas?
- Where might you find them?
- How will you decide whether they are appropriate to your main ideas?
- How will you decide whether they are relatively unbiased?
- How will you make them clear to your listeners?

Definitions, Descriptions, and Explanations

Definitions, descriptions, and explanations are forms of supporting material you may need in order to clarify your topic or some aspect of it, particularly when you're talking about something unfamiliar or unique.

A **definition** is a statement that clarifies the meaning of a word or phrase. Definitions tend to appeal to the thinking dimension and serve three primary purposes in public speeches. First, they clarify the meaning of terminology that is specialized, technical, or otherwise likely to be unfamiliar. For example, when Dan talked about bioluminescence, he clarified the meaning of the word with the following definition: "Bioluminescence is the emission of visible light by living organisms like fireflies." Dictionaries and encyclopedias contain definitions, but depending on your speech topic, you might go to prominent researchers or professional practitioners. For example, for a speech on eating disorders you might examine the Web site of the American Dietetic Association for an accurate definition.

Second, definitions clarify terminology that has more than one meaning and might be misconstrued. For example, "child abuse" is a term that encompasses a broad range of behaviors. You might define it so that your listeners understand which behaviors you intend to talk about in your speech.

Third, definitions are used, especially with controversial subjects, to reflect your stance on a subject in an attempt to draw listeners to interpret it as you do. For example, in a speech about domestic violence against women, former U.S. Secretary of Health and Human Services Donna Shalala defined such violence as "terrorism in the home" (Shalala, 1994, p. 451). She did so in an attempt to entice her listeners to interpret domestic violence against women in the same way she does.

> **WHAT DO YOU THINK?**
> Consider a time when a speaker used unfamiliar terminology without defining it. Did you understand the message? Why or why not?

A **description** goes beyond a definition in that it attempts to create a picture in the minds of listeners. The best descriptions are vivid: They allow listeners to see, hear, smell, touch, or taste the thing you are describing. For these reasons, descriptions tend to appeal most to the watching and feeling dimensions of the learning cycle. Dan described the firefly as it illuminates the pitch-black night sky, darting quickly from one spot to another on an otherwise still summer evening. By creating vivid pictures, descriptions touch on emotions, so they can be an effective way to integrate pathos into your speech. Vivid descriptions can make an otherwise dull speech come to life, but be careful to avoid descriptions that are irrelevant to the topic or that may offend some listeners, such as vulgar or distastefully graphic descriptions.

An **explanation** goes beyond a definition to provide details related to *how* and *why*—hence appealing to the thinking and doing dimensions of the learning cycle. To explain how the firefly is bioluminescent, Dan talked about the way its abdominal organs produce a flashing light. To explain why the firefly is bioluminescent, he talked about its evolution to survive in its environment. As with definitions and descriptions, use explanations only to clarify details that are relevant to your topic and probably unfamiliar to listeners.

PRACTICING THE PROCESS

Clarifying Aspects of Your Topic

Consider the topic and audience for your speech:

- Identify any terminology you might need to define.
- Identify concepts or terms you might describe in more detail.
- Identify any concepts you might explain in terms of "how" or "why."

Examples

An **example** is a specific case used to illustrate a concept, condition, experience, or group. Examples tend to appeal most directly to the feeling dimension of the learning cycle. Dan used the firefly as an example of a bioluminescent organism. Examples can be brief like Dan's, or extended. A **brief example** is short and specific; an **extended example** is developed at some length. To provide the greatest impact, brief examples are usually used in a series to demonstrate either the magnitude or a trend. In her speech about the need to help the nation's independent farmers survive, Debbie offered a series of examples of farm foreclosures around the Midwest. "These are not isolated incidents," she concluded. "The problem is widespread and demands our attention." In her speech about day care options, Holly used an extended example to illustrate what goes on at day care centers before the children arrive:

> " Employees arrive by 7:00 a.m. each day. They use the thirty minutes before children start arriving to plan the morning activities. This means they organize snack-time materials, play-time materials, outdoor toys, and indoor toys, as well as straighten the coat room and restrooms. By 7:30 the children begin to arrive. That's when employees must tune out all distractions and focus on each child as they arrive. This can make or break the success of each day. When children do not feel welcomed, parents suffer, children suffer, and employees suffer. The only way to make it work is to use those thirty minutes wisely.

Examples can be factual or hypothetical. A **factual example** is an instance that actually occurred. Holly's extended example was factual. Factual examples can be based on events experienced by the speaker, someone the speaker knows, or someone the speaker learned about through research.

A **hypothetical example** is imaginary. These can't prove a point, but may engage listeners by asking them to imagine themselves in a certain situation. Hypothetical examples are not meant to trick anyone into believing a falsehood, so tell listeners at the outset that the story is fictitious yet plausible. Hypothetical examples can enhance a speech by allowing the audience to identify with someone else. Holly offered one in her speech:

> Imagine yourself in the living room of your dream home. What do you see? Perhaps you have a fireplace, or a computer, or a home entertainment system. The point is that your dream home is equipped with all the amenities you could possibly desire. Well, that's exactly what day care centers are designed to be for young children—a dream home. They have activity centers, art centers, physical recreation centers, reading centers, and the list goes on. Day care centers are dream homes for preschoolers!

Examples can be brief or extended, hypothetical or factual, based on your experiences or the experiences of others. They can be effective supporting material when they clarify what you are talking about, help listeners grasp the magnitude of a situation, or encourage them to identify with someone else. Thus examples can make your speech more compelling.

Narratives

A **narrative** is a story used to support a point. Narratives primarily appeal to the feeling dimension of the learning cycle, but they can also appeal to the visual dimension, as most narratives include description. Because narratives illustrate points and place the listener in the situation being presented, they can also appeal to the doing dimension. Sometimes you might tell a story about your experiences using the pronouns *I* or *we*, which is a **personal narrative.** Holly offered a personal narrative when she described an encounter she had with a group of children:

> I will never forget having lunch my first day on the job at the day care center. You see, I was not familiar with what the children were expected or able to do. I watched in awe as three-year-old children poured their own milk and passed the pitcher along to the next child at the table and, likewise, dished up their own macaroni and cheese, green beans, and so on. The children visited cordially with me as we ate. When everyone was finished eating, each child at the table helped to clear the dishes away. To my amazement, these three-year-olds were behaving in a more civil manner than my roommates do! I cannot help but wonder whether my friends and I could have benefited from learning the social skills these children had mastered as a result of their experiences at a day care center.

A **third-person narrative** is a story about what occurred in someone else's life, told using the pronouns *he*, *she*, or *they*. When Debbie described how a family in her community rebuilt their lives after losing their farm, she was sharing a third-person narrative. The most effective narratives use emotional appeals to spark audience interest or foster listener relevance. Debbie's story was particularly compelling because she developed it in ways that helped listeners imagine themselves in a similar situation.

Using Examples and Narratives

Consider your speech topic:

- Where could you use examples to help clarify a main point?
- Where could you use a factual example? A hypothetical example?
- Where could you tell a personal story? A third-person story?

Testimony

A **testimony** is a quotation or paraphrase used to support a point. Testimony can come from experts or from peers. **Expert testimony** is a quotation or paraphrase from a recognized professional in the field. Students are usually not experts in any field, so citing expert testimony can add credibility to your opinions. This can bolster your ethos, which will motivate listeners who prefer learning by thinking. Even professionals gain credibility by citing expert testimony. Holly cited her boss at the Wee Care Day Care Center, who holds a degree in child psychology, regarding child development as it relates to day care options.

Finding Quotations from Experts

http://www.bartleby.com/63/ or http://www.quoteland.com/

These Web sites contain more than 10,000 quotations and speeches from a variety of sources that you can search by subject, author, or title. Select two or three quotations you could use in your next speech.

Peer testimony is a quotation or paraphrase from someone who has firsthand experience. Hence, peer testimony tends to appeal to those who prefer the feeling dimension on the learning cycle. Infomercials rely heavily on peer testimony to compel viewers to purchase their products. Consider how "Hooked on Phonics," "The Total Body Trainer" from Body by Jake, and the "Miracle Blade III" knife set, for example, rely on testimony from ordinary people to persuade viewers. Holly talked with some of the children and parents involved in different day care settings to develop her speech. Likewise, Debbie talked with several farmers who had lost their farms to add credibility to her speech.

Using Peer Testimony

http://www.isawitontv.info/motor-millions.html

 ETHICS Go to this site and watch the short video designed to convince viewers to purchase Dean Graziosi's "Motor Millions Kit." How many testimonies are included? Were some more convincing to you than others? Why or why not? Do you think this marketing strategy is ethical? Why or why not?

Any forms of supporting material can be used effectively in speeches, but it's best to use a variety. This is because different points might be best supported by different types of evidence. One point might best be supported with facts or statistics, another with definitions, descriptions, or explanations, and another with examples, narratives, or testimony. And doing so ensures that you round the cycle of learning in your speech, increasing clarity and fostering retention.

LOCATING SUPPORTING MATERIAL: RESEARCH

Just as there are many types of supporting material, there are many places to locate it. Beginning speakers often make the mistake of going to their favorite search engine and rely only on that. Or they use the library research databases, but only Lexis-Nexis or InfoTrac College Edition because they are the easiest to use. Limiting research this way seriously reduces speech quality. There are many other ways to find evidence to develop your points: Your own knowledge and experience is one. So is the knowledge and experience of others, which you can glean from interviews and surveys, a range of library resources, and the Internet.

Drawing on Personal Experience

Begin research by thinking about your topic in connection with yourself. You might be surprised how productive this can be. Students often fail to give themselves credit for their own experience. Holly, who did her speech on day care centers, drew on her experience of working in one, particularly when she developed her extended examples. Dan, who had written his senior paper on bioluminescence, drew on his academic work for evidence. Debbie, who grew up on a farm

"First, they do an on-line search."

and witnessed her uncle's family farm foreclosure, also drew on personal experiences. Personal examples and stories are especially effective in adding human interest to speeches. To bolster the credibility of personal examples, however, be sure to state your **credentials**—that which qualifies you to speak as an authority. Holly's credentials include her years of professional service in a day care center. Dan's are his years of studying bioluminescence as part of his major. And Debbie's lie in her experiences growing up and watching family members lose their farms.

PRACTICING THE PROCESS

Considering Your Personal Experience

Consider your speech topic:

- What personal experiences have you had with the topic?
- How could you include them in your speech?
- How would you let listeners know your credentials?

Research Interviews

Sometimes you may have to present a speech on a topic about which you have limited personal experience. It may be difficult or impossible to cite yourself as an expert or to offer examples from your own experiences. Yet, knowing that insights from experts and personal examples can both be compelling, you want to offer some sort of personal testimony or example. Consider conducting an interview, which can help you learn information you cannot readily get from other resources. A **research interview** is one conducted with an expert to gather information.

Remember that experts exist on a continuum, however. The highest quality experts are more difficult to reach but most impressive to the audience. For example, quoting an interview from the county district attorney would probably be more compelling than quoting your uncle who is a lawyer (unless your uncle *is* the county district attorney). Beginning speakers sometimes think they won't be able to find or gain access to an expert, but the highest authority may not be necessary. Don't overlook experts who work on campus and in the community. An expert is anyone who possesses a high degree of skill in or knowledge of a subject. Dan's adviser, for example, had published several journal articles about bioluminescence, and he could interview her as an expert in the field. Holly interviewed her employer at the day care center, Mr. Glass, to gain an expert's perspective. The key to selecting someone to interview is to make sure that person is truly an expert. For example, Holly would not interview her public speaking teacher, who is certainly an expert in communication-related subjects but not in anything related to Holly's speech topic.

Just as it is necessary to cite your credentials when offering personal experience as evidence, so must you cite the credentials of the experts you interview. Listeners will not know that Dan's adviser is an expert unless he mentions her credentials. To do so, Dan might say:

> I have the privilege of having as my adviser one of the nation's leading bioluminescence scholars. In an interview with my adviser, Dr. Susan Stromme, professor of biogenetics right here at our university, I learned that some mutant frogs have been discovered that also exhibit this ability.

Likewise, in citing her boss, Holly might say:

> In a recent interview with Mr. Bill Glass, owner and director of four Wee Care Day Care Centers right here in our community, I learned that most children who attend his day care centers on a full-time basis exhibit outstanding social skills by the time they enter kindergarten. The skills Mr. Glass has observed include empathy, cooperation, and sharing. Mr. Glass told me, "Because I have been so impressed with the skill development of children in the Wee Care Day Care Centers, I have enrolled my own children, even though they could be provided for in my own home."

You can conduct an interview in person, by telephone, or by e-mail. Usually an in-person interview is preferable, but sometimes it's more practical to use the phone or e-mail, particularly if the expert is not local or is eminent and has little time to see you in person. If you conduct an interview, demonstrate respect by arriving promptly, and being precise, courteous, and concise. To maximize the effectiveness of your interview, develop a plan, implement it appropriately, and provide closure.

PRACTICING THE PROCESS

Guidelines for an Effective Research Interview

Before the interview:
- *Do preliminary research.* The interview should expand on what is available in the library and Internet resources.
- *Determine a specific purpose for the interview.* Your purpose might emerge from questions that arose while you were researching the topic.
- *Select an appropriate expert.* Choose someone who can likely answer the questions you are trying to answer.
- *Prepare a list of questions,* both open-ended and closed-ended. Prioritize them so that if you run out of time you will have asked the most important questions.
- *Set up an interview.* You can usually do this by telephone. Introduce yourself, explain why you are asking for the interview, and if the person is willing to be interviewed, agree on a time.

During the interview:
- *Dress professionally and bring a notebook and several pens.*
- *Arrive five to ten minutes early.*
- *Introduce yourself and repeat the purpose of the interview.*
- *Keep the interview on track.* Ask the questions on your list, departing from them as other relevant issues arise, but then returning to them.
- *Listen critically and take notes.* Use brief words and phrases while listening. If a particular quotation strikes you, ask the expert to repeat it as you transcribe it.
- *Finish within the allotted time.*
- *Thank the expert for his or her time.*

After the interview:
- *Review your notes as soon as possible.* If you wait too long, you might have trouble interpreting some of your notes and remembering what was said. Expand on ideas you jotted down. Circle quotations that may be useful in your speech.
- *Send a thank-you note to the expert.*

Perhaps the most important factor determining the effectiveness of your interview is the list of questions you develop. Don't ask questions to which you already know the answer. The purpose of the interview is to learn information you could not readily find through other resources. Also, avoid **leading questions**—those phrased to prompt a certain response. Holly would have been guilty of asking a leading question had she asked Mr. Glass, "You *do* believe most children who participate in day care centers are well adjusted, don't you?" This could insult the person being interviewed, and it undermines your goal of learning what the expert knows and thinks.

Develop both open-ended and closed-ended questions. As noted in Chapter 6, closed-ended questions are stated so that the respondent chooses from a finite group of answers (such as "yes" or "no"). Closed-ended questions are quick, whereas open-ended questions invite the respondent to speak freely and may produce a great deal of information. As an open-ended question, Holly might ask Mr. Glass, "What would you identify as benefits for children who participate in organized day care and why?"

WHAT DO YOU THINK?

Consider a television news program such as *20/20, 60 Minutes, Dateline, Good Morning America,* or the *Today Show,* where hosts interview experts. How do they demonstrate respect for the experts? What kinds of questions do they ask? How do they provide closure with each guest?

Surveys

As discussed in Chapter 6, a **survey** is a research tool designed to provide information from a large number of people. Surveys, generally conducted through questionnaires, are especially effective in discovering the attitudes, values, and beliefs generally held by people in your community. Holly might survey college students to see whether they believe organized day care is harmful or helpful to child development and why. Depending on her purpose, she might also distribute a questionnaire to day care providers, parents of day care children and other parents, members of her local church, child-development professors, and so on. The data so gathered might provide information about local opinions that Holly could compare to national surveys during her speech.

PRACTICING THE PROCESS

Conducting a Survey

Consider your speech topic:

- What would you like to know about the attitudes, values, and beliefs held about it?
- Who could you survey to help find these answers?
- Create a short questionnaire and conduct a survey.

Library Resources

Many students cringe when told they must do library research or consult with a reference librarian for an upcoming speech. Apparently they have come to think that the library is a troublesome place that should be avoided whenever possible. But libraries and librarians are your friends, not your enemies. If you are having trouble finding resources, it is your *responsibility* to ask a reference librarian for help. If information in any format exists on your topic the librarian will likely know where to find it, because that's a major part of a librarian's job.

You can find supporting material in a variety of library resources: books, general and specialized reference works, magazines and newspapers, government documents and academic journals, and maps, images, videos, and recordings. These and other resources can be unearthed by searching the library's catalog, searching indexes and databases such as EbscoHost, Academic Search, LexisNexis, ERIC, and InfoTrac College Edition, or talking with a reference librarian.

Books

Books can be excellent sources because they allow authors to discuss topics in depth. Unlike many Internet sources, whose reliability may be questionable, books are generally credible; publishing a book usually involves editorial review and possibly expert peer review. Sometimes a book offers multiple perspectives on a topic, as in edited collections such as "opposing viewpoints" series, whereas it may require finding several magazines to get multiple perspectives. The disadvantage of books is that they are sometimes outdated. It can take years for a book to be written, edited, and delivered to bookstores and library shelves, so even books with a recent copyright date may be outdated. Books about how to use the Internet, for example, deal with technology that is expanding so rapidly that books published even a few years ago may not be helpful now. But for most topics this isn't a problem. For example, Dan gathered information from books published many years ago to describe bioluminescence. For his purpose, their age didn't matter.

The library's catalog is a record of all the books it owns. Previously housed in card files but now maintained almost exclusively in databases, catalogs can be searched by *author*, *title*, and *subject heading*. As Figure 7.2 shows, catalog entries include substantial information you can use to determine whether finding the book itself would likely be worthwhile. Most notable are the relevance of the book's title and year of publication, and possibly the author's name, as it may help you to determine the author's credibility. The library's unique ID for the book is its call number, which you will need to locate the work.

Search Result – Quick Search

Viewing record 1 of 4 from catalog.

☐ Check here to mark this record for Print/Capture

Call number →
Title and author →

E185.86.R35 2003
Rap and hip hop / Jared Green, book editor.
Green, Jared.

Year and place of publication, publisher →

Title: **Rap and hip hop / Jared Green, book editor.**
Publication info: **San Diego : Greenhaven Press, c2003.**
Physical description: **175 p. ; 23 cm.**
Series: **(Examining pop culture)**
Bibligraphy note: **Includes bibliographical references (p. 162-167) and index.**
Contents: **Bring the noise: the roots of rap and hip hop – Blowing up: the rise of the hip-hop nation – Does rap glorify sex and violence? – Case study in controversy: Eminem and gay bashing.**

	COPY MATERIAL	LOCATION
CALL NUMBER		
1) E185.86 .R35 2003	1 Book	STACKS

Adapted from Foothill College's **Web**Cat ® library catalog.

Figure 7.2 Sample catalog entry

Reference Works

These include encyclopedias, dictionaries, yearbooks, atlases, almanacs, and biographical aids such as the *Who's Who* series. They can often help you find descriptions and data quickly. The kinds of information they provide is limited, however, so use them as a starting point or to supplement other resources. Debbie, for example, researched the history of farming trends by looking through the *Farmer's Almanac* year by year. Dan used a dictionary that defined bioluminescence and an encyclopedia that provided a simple explanation of it. Many reference works are now available in printed and CD-ROM or DVD formats. As with books, however, these reference works can be outdated.

TURNING TO TECHNOLOGY

Online Encyclopedias

http://www.encyclopedia.com/

Search this online encyclopedia for information on your next speech topic. What does the site tell you? Will any of the information be useful? Why or why not?

Magazines and Newspapers

Magazines and newspapers are great resources for current information. Because they are published often (monthly, weekly, or daily), the information in recent issues is usually up to date. Remember, however, that authors of magazine and newspaper articles may be journalists who are drawing on the work of others, rather than as experts themselves. Hence the information these periodicals provide can be useful but should not be used exclusively. Also, alternative press sources cover the same topic differently than mainstream media. It may be useful to consult both kinds.

TURNING TO TECHNOLOGY

Online and Alternative Newspapers

ETHICS

- Go to http://www.newspapers.com/. Many of the world's leading newspapers appear on this site. Visit three newspapers that offer something about your next speech topic.
- Now go to http://newslink.org/alter.html. This site lists many alternative newspapers. Visit three newspapers that offer something about your next speech topic.
- Is the information in mainstream and alternative newspapers similar or different? How will you use what you've learned, then, to create an ethical speech that demonstrates honesty and respect?

Most libraries have printed and computerized indexes to help search these resources efficiently. One of the most common indexes for searching magazines is the *Readers' Guide to Periodical Literature*, which is available in both printed and CD-ROM formats. Most colleges and universities also have an online catalog such as WebPals or GaleNet, which can expand your search to a network of catalogs and the services' databases. Many major newspapers are now specifically indexed. The *New York Times*, the *Wall Street Journal*, and *USA Today*, for example, each index their back issues and content. Holly found interesting articles about different day care options in magazines such as *Child* and *Parenting*; these articles cited the research of important experts, giving Holly a starting point for searching appropriate academic journals.

Like reference works, many popular magazines and newspapers are also available on the Internet. Most of these publications include the Web address on each hard copy. This address is usually on the front page of newspapers and inside the front cover of magazines. The online address for the local newspaper in my community, for example, is www.in-forum.com and for *Consumer Reports*, a popular magazine, is www.ConsumerReports.org.

Government Documents and Academic Journals

Government documents and academic journals are valuable because they often provide information directly from those doing the research. Quoting them can boost your credibility as a speaker, but there are drawbacks: You may have to decipher technical jargon, and it may take considerable time to retrieve the resource. Many indexes to these journals are now available online via the World Wide Web, however, making it much easier and quicker to access them.

Government documents are published by the federal government and address a wide range of topics. Often the information provided is not available elsewhere, and citing it can boost your ethos. Try consulting the CIS/Index (published by the Congressional Information Service) and the *Monthly Catalog of United States Government Publications* (published by the Government Printing Office). They are available in print and CD-ROM formats as well as online (Whitely, 1994). Also online are information from the Government Printing Office (www.gpoaccess.gov/index.html), federal agency indexes such as FedWorld (www.fedworld.gov) or the Federal Web Locator (www.infoctr.edu/fwl/), or the Library of Congress (www.loc.gov) (Basch, 1996). A good starting point for any U.S. government-related search is the official federal Web portal, www.firstgov.gov, a gateway to a vast array of information, services, and resources covering all branches of the federal government as well as state, local, and tribal governments.

Academic journals publish articles by professional researchers and educators. The focus of each academic journal is very specialized and not necessarily intended for the general public. As such, they are often riddled with technical jargon that can be difficult to decipher. However, the conclusions typically reflect the most recent research in a field. Indexes to academic journal articles are available in printed form, through your library's online catalog, and sometimes on CD-ROM. Some of these specialized indexes include the following:

- Education Index
- Business Index
- Communication Index
- Index to Legal Periodicals

Many specialized indexes are available on the Internet as well. For example, *Business Sources on the Net (BSN)*, which categorizes business-related sources by topics such as environment, finance, accounting, and marketing, can be accessed at www.hbg.psu.edu/library/ (click the links labeled "Research Tools and Resources," "Web Resources," and "Business and Economic Resources").

After locating books on bioluminescence, Dan searched their authors in the *Expanded Academic Index*, his library's online index, and found recent journal articles to update his information. Holly supplemented her interviews with articles she found by searching *ERIC* (Education Resources Information Center), a computerized research service focused on education-related topics, with terms such as "day care," "preschool," and "early childhood education."

Internet Documents

The **Internet** is a worldwide network of computers that links resources and people at colleges and universities, government agencies, libraries, corporations, and homes (Quaratiello, 1997). It provides access to huge amounts of information that can support your research. For example, you can find the most recent information about your topic, communicate directly with authors of important sources or with experts in a particular field, or even discuss your topic with others interested in it (Kent, 1998; Munger et al., 1999; Reddick & King, 1996; Young, 1998). The variety of resources for researchers to draw on, once limited by inaccessibility, is now nearly limitless. Conducting thorough research today usually includes searching the Internet. Remember, however, that you must consult more than just the Internet to research your topic thoroughly.

Although the Internet was created in 1969, it didn't become readily available to the general public until the 1990s when the World Wide Web was created. The **World Wide Web** is a software system that makes accessing information on the Internet as simple as using a Windows program on your personal computer. Although there are still racial and economic inequities that limit some people's access to the Internet, the disparities shrink as more schools, homes, and public libraries go online. Because the Web allows you to wander easily throughout the Internet, however, it is easy to lose sight of your purpose while "surfing." Try to follow eight research strategies while online, as listed in the Practicing the Process box below and described on the following pages, so that the time and energy you spend researching on the Internet efficiently provides you with supporting material for your speech. An excellent resource for college researchers is the Librarians' Index to the Internet (http://lii.org), which provides detailed guides to the Internet and Internet search tools as well as a comprehensive subject index.

PRACTICING THE PROCESS

Conducting Internet Research

- Access the Internet through a *browser*.
- Search your subject by key words using a *search engine*.
- If the search engine results are too broad, try using a *directory*.
- If the searches are too narrow, try using a *metasearch engine*.
- If necessary, access *other* Internet resources.
- Consider embellishing your information by searching *electronic discussion lists*.
- Keep track of your search terms and search engines so you don't lose track of information and waste time.
- *Evaluate* the reliability of Internet sources before including any of them in your speech.

Browsers

To access the Internet through the Web, your computer must have a **browser,** which is a doorway into the Web. The three most common browsers are Netscape Navigator, Internet Explorer, and Mosaic. To enter the World Wide Web, simply double-click on one of these icons on your computer's main screen.

Search Engines

Search your subject by key words on a **robot-generated index,** also called a search engine. This is a comprehensive program that automatically visits a multitude of Web sites and generates an index of those that match (or link to) key words. Access these **hyperlinks** (connections between two Web documents) by double-clicking on them. Hyperlinks can provide you with a lot of information (hits), but be aware that much of it may be irrelevant to your speech. Some of the most popular robot-generated indexes are the following:

- Google—www.google.com
- Lycos—www.lycos.com
- All the Web—www.alltheweb.com
- AltaVista—http://altavista.com
- WebCrawler—www.webcrawler.com

Directories

If a search on a robot-generated index is too broad and offers too many Web sites irrelevant to your topic, try searching by key words on a **human-edited index,** also called a **directory**—a search index edited by a person trained in library or information sciences. Only prospective sites that pass the editor's scrutiny are added to these. The following offer human-edited indexes:

- LookSmart—www.looksmart.com
- Yahoo Directory—www.dir.yahoo.com
- Galaxy—www.einet.net
- Open Directory—dmoz.org, or access it through directory options on Google, All the Web, or other engines
- Google Directory—www.google.com, click on the Directory tab to access Google's enhanced version of Open Directory
- MSN Search—search.msn.com (MSN's blend of LookSmart's directory and Inktomi's robot search)

Metasearch Engines

A **metasearch engine** searches for key words through several search engines at once. The following are a few popular metasearch engines:

- Metacrawler—www.metacrawler.com
- HotBot—www.hotbot.com
- Super Searcher—www.iquest.net
- Search.com—www.search.com
- Dogpile—www.dogpile.com

Other Resources

You can also access other Internet resources that are not on the World Wide Web. These include Gopher sites, Telnet sites, and Usenet news postings.

Electronic Discussion Lists

You can locate electronic discussion lists related to your topic. Perhaps the easiest way is to search **discussion boards,** online "bulletin boards" where people post, read, and respond to messages, at a site like *eWeek* magazine's at http:// discuss.eweek.com. This site allows you to conduct advanced searches by topic.

Evaluate Resources

Finally, evaluate the Internet resources you have selected. The Internet has no gatekeeper, so anyone can create a Web site. This is exciting because previously marginalized voices can be heard. However, researchers must figure out how valid and reliable the resources they locate on the Internet are. Here are key questions to ask yourself (Munger et al., 1999) before using a document from the Internet:

- Who is the author and what are his or her credentials?
- Does the author have an academic or professional affiliation?
- Is a link to the author's home page or e-mail contact information provided?
- Who is the sponsor of the resource and what are the sponsor's credentials with regard to the topic?
- Is the resource updated regularly?
- What potential biases or hidden agendas might the author or sponsoring organization have?

ETHICS

Some Internet documents that do not indicate an individual author instead indicate an organization (such as a government agency, business, or nonprofit) as author. As long as you're sure of or can verify the organization's credentials, you can use the information in your speech. Citing the organization will add to your credibility just as citing an individual author would. But if you can't determine the credentials of the individual author or organization, don't use the material. This is ethically crucial because an unverifiable document may have been written by someone with little expertise and citing it would do a disservice to you and potentially to your listeners.

Consider accessing the Virtual Reference Desk at http://thorplus.lib .purdue.edu/reference/index.html. This resource was created to assist researchers in locating the credentials of Web page authors. ProfNet's Expert Database (www.profnet.com), which profiles more than 2,000 authors who have been identified as experts in their fields, can also help. Or check out the Using Cybersources Web site at www.devry-phx.edu (click the links labeled "Educational Resources," "Online Writing Support Center," and "Using Cybersources").

CONDUCTING ETHICAL RESEARCH

ETHICS

Effective public speakers collect various types of supporting material from diverse sources, including their own experiences, interviews, surveys, and library

Checklist for Gathering Support Materials

- ☐ Consider and draw on your personal experience.
- ☐ Plan and conduct research interviews.
- ☐ Design and conduct surveys.
- ☐ Work with a reference librarian to find materials in or accessible through the library (books, reference works, magazines, newspapers, government documents, academic journals, databases).
- ☐ Use the Internet to obtain additional materials that are appropriate and reliable. Specifically, consider the credentials and possible biases of the Web page author and sponsoring organization, whether contact information is provided for them, and how up-to-date the resource is.

Evaluating Internet Source Material

http://www.uwec.edu/library/Guides/tencs.html

This site offers ten C's to consider as you evaluate the quality of Internet source material. What tips does it suggest? Do you agree with them? Why or why not?

and Internet research. They also conduct ethical research by evaluating the evidence and documenting it appropriately. Some of the same steps that make your speech effective also help make it ethical by demonstrating the virtues of honesty and respect.

Evaluating Your Evidence

Nearly any topic is likely to be discussed in numerous resources, so consider which pieces of evidence actually contribute to your purpose. Ask yourself whether the evidence is relevant, credible, and current. This is a practical matter (you don't want to write a speech that's unfocused or too long), but also a matter of ethics: By using evidence that does not meet these criteria, you risk misleading your audience and failing to demonstrate honesty or respect. Recall that alternative press sources cover a topic differently than mainstream media. Also consider whether the evidence you have collected is thorough by asking whether it answers all important questions, whether you've consulted a variety of resources, and whether you've used different kinds of supporting material. This gives the audience a balanced and full picture of your topic.

Is It Relevant?

During research you will likely come across a great deal of interesting information. Whether it is appropriate for your speech is another matter. **Relevant evidence** is information directly related to your topic. Irrelevant evidence confuses listeners because it doesn't address your point. Don't include it in your speech.

As Dan researched bioluminescence, for example, he learned that bioluminescent mutant frogs have been found only near the Sheyenne River in North Dakota. Some researchers speculate that the polluted river in some way causes the mutation. Moreover, these frogs appear to have a significantly shorter life than other frogs. Some environmental groups are protesting against the local power plant for continuing to pollute the river. This is certainly interesting, but little of it is related to Dan's main point on how bioluminescence works.

Is It Credible?

ETHICS

Credible evidence is information that seems both believable and reliable. Information is reliable if it's true not just in a few cases but in many similar ones. To be credible, supporting material should come from respected sources, people who are experts on your topic. Dan's professor is credible because she is an expert in bioluminescence. Holly's experience working in day care centers qualifies her as an expert of sorts on her topic, but to base her speech only on her own experience would not be ethical because her experience is limited and may not be reliable (generalizable). Keep in mind, especially with Internet documents, that unless the author or sponsoring organization can be identified the source cannot be considered credible and should not be used.

Is It Current?

Because the world we live in is rapidly changing, so is the information about it. **Current evidence** is that which is not outdated. What's current depends on the topic. For many topics, the most recently published evidence is required; for others, research from the past continues to be valid. For example, Dan might rely on older sources to explain how bioluminescence works because there haven't been any recent relevant discoveries, whereas Holly should look for the most recent statistics about day care facilities, because these statistics are constantly changing.

Does It Answer All Important Questions?

ETHICS

An ethically researched speech covers the topic thoroughly in the time allotted. You ought to be able to answer the questions posed by your thesis statement. If any questions remain unanswered, continue researching. Holly should be able to identify the factors to consider when selecting a day care option and why they are important before she stops researching. She will likely know more about day care options than merely selection factors, but selection factors is what her thesis statement says she will cover. Dan's research is not complete until he understands all aspects of how bioluminescence works.

Have You Consulted a Variety of Resources?

ETHICS

Ethical researchers use many resources, including interviews, newspapers and magazines, academic journals, books, and Internet documents. Each has strengths and weaknesses, but a combination of types enables a speaker to present a fuller picture and to round the entire cycle of learning. Holly conducted interviews and surveys, consulted magazines and academic journals, and offered personal stories. Dan consulted reference books, conducted interviews, and cited Internet documents. Both speakers referred to a variety of resources to support their ideas.

Do You Use Various Types of Supporting Material?

ETHICS

Using various types of supporting material is both effective and ethical. By including personal experiences and testimony, facts and statistics, visual representations, and practical applications, you will have the greatest impact on listeners because your main ideas will have breadth and depth and will round the entire learning cycle (see Figure 7.1).

PRACTICING THE PROCESS

Checklist of Ethical Considerations for Evaluating Evidence

- ❏ Is your evidence relevant?
- ❏ Is your evidence credible?
- ❏ Is your evidence current?
- ❏ Does your evidence answer all important questions?
- ❏ Have you consulted a variety of resources?
- ❏ Do you use various types of supporting material?

Documenting Your Evidence

ETHICS

Ethical public speakers document their sources in a reference list at the end of their formal outline, internally within the text of the formal outline, and orally throughout the presentation. Failing to do this is plagiarism (presenting another person's ideas as your own). Documentation is as indispensable to an oral presentation as it is to a written essay. It makes certain that you are not plagiarizing and also enhances your credibility (ethos).

A widely used format for documenting sources is that of the American Psychological Association (APA). The *Publication Manual of the American Psychological Association* (2001, 5th ed.) provides guidelines, and additional information about APA style is available online at www.apastyle.org. Other widely used formats are those of the Modern Language Association (MLA) and the *Chicago Manual of Style* (University of Chicago Press). Additional information about these is available online at www.mla.org and www.press.uchicago.edu/Misc/Chicago/cmosfaq/. MLA and CMS style are generally used in the humanities, whereas the APA style is generally used in the social sciences. Because the APA format has been adopted by the National Communication Association, the major academic organization for public speaking teachers and scholars, it is introduced here in some detail. However, you should ask your instructor's preference regarding citation format.

TURNING TO TECHNOLOGY

MLA and APA Style Guides

http://www.stylewizard.com/

This site offers guidelines, tutorials, and worksheets to help you build a reference list using APA or MLA formats. You might want to use it as you prepare citations for your next speech.

APA Style Reference List

The APA's reference list guidelines apply to sources of all types. Start the reference list on a new page. Double-space all entries. Alphabetize the entries by the authors' last names. Begin the first line flush left to your margin. Indent the subsequent lines of each entry five spaces (in word processing, use a one-half-inch hanging indent). On the first line, provide the author's last name, followed by a comma and one or more initials. Use "&" rather than "and" when citing multiple authors. Provide the date of publication in parentheses after the author's name and use a period after the parentheses. Space once (not twice) after the period. In italics, provide the work's title, and capitalize only the first word, proper nouns (names of specific people, places, and so on), and the first word after a colon. Unless the work's publisher is based in city not widely recognized, indicate only the city (not the state or country) of publication, followed by a colon, and then provide a shortened form of the publisher's name (that is, do not include unnecessary publishing information such as "company" or "incorporated").

The following list shows the basic form and an example of a proper citation for some of the sources most often cited by public speaking students. For a complete listing and explanation, consult the *Publication Manual of the American Psychological Association* (5th ed.).

Books

Last name, Initial(s). (year). *Title of book*. City: Publisher.

Maclean, N. (1992). *Young men and fire*. Chicago: University of Chicago Press.

Journal Articles

Last name, Initial(s). (year). Title of article. *Title of Journal, volume number*, pages.

Ayres, J. (1991). Using visual aids to reduce speech anxiety. *Communication Research Reports, 8*, 73–79.

Magazines

Last name, Initial(s). (year, month). Title of article. *Title of Magazine*, pages.

Franklin, D. (1998, May/June). Germ crazy. *Health*, 95–101.

Newspapers

Last name, Initial(s). (year, month and day). Title of article. *Title of Newspaper*, pages.

Froslie, E. (1998, May 1). Religious addiction. *The Forum*, p. B1.

Television Programs

Last name, Initial(s). (Name of producer or director). (year, month and day). Name of segment (if available). *Title of program*. City: Distributor.

Crystal, L. (Executive Producer). (1993, October 11). *The MacNeil/Lehrer news hour*. New York and Washington, DC: Public Broadcasting Service.

Music Recordings

Last name of writer, Initial(s). (Date of copyright). Title of song [Recorded by Last name, Initial(s) (if recording artist is different from writer)]. On *Title of album*.

[Medium of recording]. Location: Label (Recording date if different from copyright date).

> Branch, M. (2003). Are you happy now? On *Hotel paper* [CD]. Los Angeles: Maverick.

Internet Articles Based on Print Source

> Last name of author, Initial(s). (date of publication). Title of article. [Electronic version (if you viewed the article only in its electronic form)]. Name of publication. Page number (if indicated).

Note: If you believe that the online version of the article is different from the print version, or if page numbers are not provided, add the date you retrieved the document and the URL after the page number (if known) or, without a page number, the publication's name: Retrieved Month, day, year, from URL (do not end the entry with a period when the URL is the last piece of information).

> Udovitch, M. (2003, October 19). The sobering life of Robert Downey Jr. [Electronic version]. *The New York Times Magazine.* Retrieved October 22, 2003, from http://www.nytimes.com

Articles in Internet-Only Publications

> Last name of author, Initial(s). (date of publication). Title of article. *Name of Publication, volume* (issue) (if provided), Article number (if provided). Retrieved Month, day, year, from URL

> Forliti, A. (2003, October 22). Hasbro files suit against Ghettopoly maker. *Salon.* Retrieved October 22, 2003, from http://www.salon.com

Electronic Articles Retrieved from Database

> Last name of author, Initial(s). (date of publication). Title of article. *Title of Journal, volume* (issue), pages. Retrieved Month, day, year, from Name of Database.

> Cockburn, A. (2003, July 7). My life as a rabbi. *The Nation, 277*, 9. Retrieved October 20, 2003, from InfoTrac College Edition.

Other Internet Sources

> Last name of author, Initial(s). (date of publication). Title of document. Name of Sponsoring Organization. Retrieved Month, day, year, from URL

Note: If no author is listed, identify the organization posting the information. Also, if no publication date is provided, use "n.d."

> Def Jam Recordings. (n.d.). Biography of L.L. Cool J. Retrieved September 17, 2003, from http://www.defjam.com/llcoolj/

The fifth edition of the APA publication manual includes formats for many other types of sources. When in doubt, consult the manual, which you should be able to find in your school's library.

Within the Formal Outline

Like a written paper, a formal public speaking outline ought to include, along with a reference list, internal references at the points where information is based on

Student Workbook

Read through the formal outline samples for the "Information and Diversity Speech" in Chapter 3 of your workbook. Do the outlines cite sources correctly in the reference list and within the formal outline? Explain.

external research. According to the APA publication manual, when summarizing results you may simply include the author and year in parentheses at the end of the last sentence. For example, Holly explained that asking a grandma to babysit is not always the best solution, and she based this explanation on an article she read in *Parents* magazine. Therefore she concluded the relevant material in her outline with the following citation: (Ogintz, 1994).

If there is no author, include a shortened version of the article's title and its date. Holly cited several criteria that she learned about in a newspaper article titled "Studies Identify Criteria for Better Day Care." She concluded with the following citation: ("Studies Identify," 1995).

When using a **direct quotation,** you must indicate the page from which the quotation is drawn. This is included in the parentheses after the year. Quotations of fewer than forty words are part of the text line; quotations of at least forty words are set off as a block quotation. If you mention any citation information, such as the author's name, before the quotation, you do not need to repeat it in the parentheses. Again, see the APA manual for information on citing other kinds of sources.

Oral Citations During the Speech

ETHICS

To be an ethical public speaker, you must cite sources orally throughout your presentation. **Oral footnotes** are references to the original source made at the point in the speech where information from that source is presented.

Oral documentation is necessary to avoid plagiarism, and it enhances your ethos. Beginning public speakers sometimes have difficulty understanding the reasons for citing references orally. The reason is that those who hear your presentation don't see your outline or your reference list (except perhaps your instructor). They won't know where your information comes from unless you tell them. Because public speaking is oral rather than written, you must provide internal references orally as well as writing in-text citations and a reference list in the formal outline.

ETHICS

To be ethical, provide oral footnotes whenever you include information drawn from another source. These give listeners the name and credentials of the author and enough bibliographic information so that they could look up the source themselves. It is not necessary to include page numbers. Oral footnotes help ensure that the speaker is not fabricating information or offering his or her unsubstantiated opinions. It also lets listeners know that the speaker is not plagiarizing.

The following discussion illustrates oral footnotes for the types of sources most often cited by public speaking students. For each type, some information *should* be included and other information *may* be included, especially if it will enhance your credibility.

Books. Usually you need identify only the name of the author and title of the book, perhaps including the date of publication or credentials of the author if it will enhance your credibility (that is, if the author is well known or the date is very recent). Here are two possibilities:

> In his book *Young Men and Fire*, author Norman Maclean recalls his experiences fighting the deadly forest fire of August 5, 1949, in Mann Gulch, Montana.

> Norman Maclean recalls the haunting deaths of several firefighters in the Mann Gulch, Montana, forest fire in 1949 in his book *Young Men and Fire*.

Journal or Magazine Articles. For journal and magazine articles, include the name and date of the publication. You may also include the author and/or title of the article.

> Ayres wrote, in a 1991 article published in *Communication Research Reports*, that using visual aids during public speaking presentations may actually reduce speech anxiety.

> According to a May/June 1998 article in *Health* magazine titled "Germ Crazy," not all antibacterial products actually help prevent disease. In fact, some can even make the germs more resistant.

Newspapers. For newspaper articles, include the name of the newspaper and date of the article. You can also include the name of the author, but citing the newspaper is more likely to boost your credibility.

> According to a May 1998 article in the *Wall Street Journal*, religious addiction can be as damaging to relationships as drug or alcohol addiction.

Interviews. To cite information from an interview you conducted, include the name and credentials of the person interviewed and the date the interview took place. If you draw on the interview more than once during the speech, you need only cite the person's name in subsequent oral footnotes.

> In a telephone interview with Dr. Susan Nissen, physician for physical medicine in Kansas City, Kansas, on September 29, 2003, I learned that most Americans will break a toe or a finger at some point during their life.

Television Programs. For television programs, include the name of the program and date of the original broadcast. You may also include the name of the reporter.

> According to a May 1995 CNN special broadcast called "Cry Hatred," neo-Nazi skinhead hate crimes can be linked directly to the "Oi" music skinheads listen to.

Internet Documents. For Internet documents, include the author and her or his credentials and the date of the most recent revision. If there is no author, include the credentials of the sponsoring organization instead. Do not include the URL path as part of an oral footnote.

> The surgeon general warned in an article published on the Internet in 2002, "35% of normal dieters will become obsessive, unhealthy dieters."

The key to preparing oral footnotes is to include enough information for listeners to access the sources themselves and to offer enough credentials to enhance your credibility as a speaker on the topic. Ethical oral footnotes, then, help speakers enhance ethos and avoid plagiarism.

PRACTICING THE PROCESS

References and Oral Footnotes

Select one reference you have collected for your speech:

- Create a reference in correct APA style for the reference list.
- Create an internal reference note as it might appear in your formal outline.
- Create an oral footnote you could use during the speech.

Test Yourself

Go to the *Confident Public Speaking* Web site and access the student resources for Chapter 7. Take the Tutorial Quiz to see how much you've retained about supporting and researching your speech.

SUMMARY

Supporting material adds breadth and depth to speeches and helps round the cycle of learning.

You can and should draw on various types of supporting material. Use facts to support claims about events, times, and people; use statistics to demonstrate the significance of a problem or to highlight trends over time. Definitions, descriptions, and explanations help clarify aspects of your topic that may be unfamiliar to listeners. Examples—brief or extended, hypothetical or factual—help illustrate or represent concepts, groups, and so forth. Narratives are stories that pique audience interest and enhance listener relevance. Testimony from peers or experts is used to provide personal support for points, increasing pathos.

You can and should find supporting material in various types of sources. Draw on your own experience and expertise and that of others. Consider conducting research through interviews and surveys and using library resources and the Internet.

Your research must be ethical. To evaluate supporting material, ask yourself these questions: Is it relevant? Is it credible? Is it current? Does it answer all important questions? Have I consulted a variety of resources? Do I use various types of supporting material? Document your evidence in your outline and during the speech to enhance ethos and avoid plagiarism. Follow the APA format or another format to document the sources in your reference list and formal outline; use oral footnotes during your presentation.

Supporting material brings a speech to life for listeners and makes it compelling. By using various types of supporting material and resources and documenting them thoroughly, you'll make your use of supporting material maximally effective and ethical.

RETURNING TO TECHNOLOGY

The *Confident Public Speaking* CD-ROM is your one-stop point of access for not just the content on the CD itself, such as Speech Interactive, but also the many other resources on the *Confident Public Speaking* Web site, Speech Builder Express, and InfoTrac College Edition. Note that this chapter's key terms and activities are among the resources available in electronic format online. Additional information is included on the following pages.

SPEECH INTERACTIVE
ON THE *CONFIDENT PUBLIC SPEAKING* CD-ROM

Speech Interactive is your link to this text's speech videos. Offering opportunities to practice critiquing speeches by students and other public speakers, these videos will help you prepare for providing effective feedback to your peers and your own speech performances.

SPEECH BUILDER EXPRESS

The Supporting Material and Works Cited sections of Speech Builder Express provide sequences of prompts that can help you determine the best support materials for your main points and help you keep a thorough record of the sources you decide to use.

KEY TERMS

Interactive flashcards for these key terms are available on the *Confident Public Speaking* Web site. You'll find the "Flashcards" link under the resources for Chapter 7.

ACTIVITIES

The activities below, as well as additional activities for this chapter, are available in electronic format on the *Confident Public Speaking* Web site. You'll find the "Activities" link under the resources for Chapter 7.

1. **Interview Role-Play.** Form a group with four of your classmates. One student is the interviewer, one is the interviewee, and the other two critique the interview based on the information in the text. The interviewee is an "expert" on the topic of the interviewer's upcoming speech. As a group, come up with a list of open- and closed-ended interview questions. The two critics should take notes and share their observations after the mock interview is completed. Then switch roles and repeat the process.

2. **Small-Group Brainstorming.** In groups of four or five students, brainstorm a list of possible places to find supporting material for each member's upcoming speech topic. Use the categories of (a) personal experience, (b) interviews, (c) surveys, (d) library resources, and (e) Internet documents.

INFOTRAC COLLEGE EDITION ACTIVITY

Locate and make a copy of the speech "The Rap of Change" by Suzanne Morse. (Hint: Use the speaker's full name as your search term.) As you read, mark the statistical information used in the speech. Make a list of the strategies the speaker used to make each of the statistical facts more meaningful to the reader. Choose two or three strategies you'll use to help your audience understand the statistics in your speech.

ORGANIZING YOUR MAIN IDEAS

1. Why is clear organization essential to an effective public speech?

2. Is it important to organize ideas before outlining your speech? Why or why not?

3. How might organizational patterns make speeches on the same topic different from each other?

4. What questions could you ask yourself to decide which kinds of material to use to support your main points?

5. What ways might you be able to tie main points together?

WHAT'S AHEAD: FOCUSING YOUR READING

What Is Organization?

Why Is Organization So Important to Public Speaking?

Developing the Body of Your Speech

Selecting a Pattern for Your Main Points

Integrating Supporting Material

Incorporating Connectives

J ULIE'S INSTRUCTOR HAD ASKED students to prepare their next informative speech. Julie chose alternative methods of healing as her topic. She spent a good deal of time on research and had collected a lot of supporting material. But as Julie sat staring at a stack of books, journal and magazine articles, and Internet printouts, she thought, "Now what?" The more she read, the more anxious she became. "There are so many interesting things to say. But how? I don't want to ramble. Where do I go from here?"

Julie's anxiety stemmed from fear of the unknown. Her negative self-talk indicated worries about how to organize her ideas coherently and concern that she wouldn't make sense to her listeners. Julie is not alone; uncertainty about how to organize information is a common reason for public speaking anxiety (Dwyer, 1998). But by following a few guidelines, you can organize your ideas in a way that listeners will be able to follow.

This chapter explains basic elements that make up speech organization (macrostructure), why macrostructure is crucial to effective public speaking, and what is involved in organizing the body of a speech—that is, patterning main points, integrating supporting material, and incorporating connectives.

WHAT IS ORGANIZATION?

Organization is the process of putting your ideas and information together in a way that will make sense to listeners. Such a structure is one of the three components of an effective speech, as discussed in Chapter 3; the others are content and delivery. Effective structure is achieved through clearly articulated macrostructure, which is the general framework for ideas, and microstructure, which is thoughtfully selected language and style. Good organization leads to effective macrostructure and microstructure.

WHAT DO YOU THINK?
If you asked a friend for a recipe and you received a list of ingredients, would the recipe make sense? Why or why not?

Macrostructure consists of the elements that provide a general framework for ideas. Without it a speech is like a recipe without directions. Just as a list of ingredients makes no sense without directions, a string of ideas makes no sense without a general framework. Chapters 8, 9, and 10 all focus on macrostructure.

The most effective macrostructural pattern known for conveying ideas in a speech was developed more than 2,000 years ago by Aristotle and still works well today (Connor & McCagg, 1987; Darnell, 1963; Smith, 1951; Thompson, 1967). It's the arrangement of ideas into an introduction, body, and conclusion. Thus effective speakers organize their main points logically, develop their introduction and conclusion thoroughly, and outline the speech comprehensively. This reduces rambling and increases your chances of making sense to listeners.

Microstructure, the language and style choices you make, is the other key component to structuring your message. Microstructure is discussed in detail in Chapter 11. Microstructure and macrostructure are compared in Table 8.1.

WHY IS ORGANIZATION SO IMPORTANT TO PUBLIC SPEAKING?

Because the goal of any communication transaction is to make sense to the receivers, clear organization is always important, and public speaking is no exception. Because listeners must understand you based on hearing your ideas only once, it is crucial that they can follow you throughout the presentation—they

Macrostructure		Microstructure
Follow the Golden Rule		*Language and Style*
Introduction	Tell them what you're going to tell them	Clarity
Body	Tell them	Vividness
Conclusion	Tell them what you've told them	Inclusion

Table 8.1 Comparison of Macro- and Microstructure

do not have the luxury of rereading a paragraph. Consequently, speech organization has a unique set of guidelines, which are detailed in this chapter.

Organizational skills will improve not only your public speeches but also your personal and professional life. For example, imagine that Anita and Andrew, candidates for a job as public relations director for actor Jim Carrey, have the same college degree and the same level of experience. However, Anita spent a lot of time organizing what she planned to say in the interview, and Andrew didn't. Anita's organized answers would probably land her the job and Andrew would continue working his college job as a checker at the deli.

Clear organization also helps reduce public speaking anxiety. By now you probably realize that anxiety can increase at any point in the speechmaking process. Knowing why your anxiety is rising makes it possible to develop strategies to overcome your fear. If you find your anxiety increasing while organizing your ideas, you are probably engaged in negative self-talk focused on a fear of the unknown.

Perhaps you worry about "what ifs" like these: What if listeners cannot figure out what I'm trying to say? What if they can't follow my organization? What if I ramble? What if listeners can't tell when I'm finished? What if I lose my place or forget what comes next? If so, the skills you learn about organization in the next three chapters will help. Here we focus on organizing the body of your speech.

DEVELOPING THE BODY OF YOUR SPEECH

The first step in organizing macrostructure is to develop the body of your speech. Do this before developing your introduction and conclusion. This might seem odd, but it's like what you do when you give someone an outfit as a gift: Before you wrap it up, you select the items that go together. Similarly, develop the body of your speech before tying it together with an introduction and conclusion. Start by selecting a pattern for your main points, integrating supporting material to augment each main point, and creating connectives that glue together the main points and supporting material.

SELECTING A PATTERN FOR YOUR MAIN POINTS

Listeners find it difficult to keep track of more than two to four main points in an oral presentation. How do you determine what those main points ought to be? Consider what specific questions must be answered for others to understand your thesis statement. Ask yourself what listeners must know in order *to understand* the thesis of an informative speech, *to agree* with the thesis of a persuasive speech, or *to act* in the way advocated in a persuasive speech. Tiffany, for example, had to consider what questions must be answered for listeners to understand why living a vegetarian lifestyle is so important to her. Jaime had to determine what questions must be answered for listeners to agree that cloning is good for society (for him, this also meant considering why people might disagree so he could refute those beliefs). And for Richard, who wanted to convince listeners to try shopping online, it meant answering questions about the risks of online shopping and offering a strategic plan for doing so wisely.

Once you've determined the questions that must be answered, look for relationships among them so you can select an appropriate pattern for arranging them. Two possible methods are organizational mapping and card playing.

Organizational mapping is a process of brainstorming as many ideas as you can think of related to your thesis as well as to each other (Figure 8.1). Holly used this to narrow down her day care centers topic, as described in Chapter 5. It can also help in selecting main points because it provides a visual means for determining which ideas support a thesis statement, as well as which ideas go together.

Because Jamie's purpose was to gain the agreement of his audience that cloning is good for society, his main points had to include refuting the opposite view.

© RELTERS/Anthony P. Bolante/CORBIS

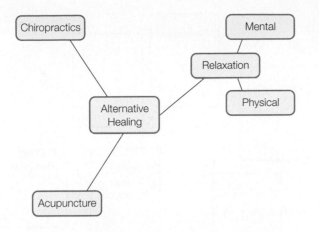

Figure 8.1 Organizational mapping

TURNING TO TECHNOLOGY

Organizational Mapping

http://www.coun.uvic.ca/learn/program/hndouts/class1a.html

Practice organizational mapping on this Web site. Then see the organizational map that the author created. Is yours similar? Why or why not?

Card playing is similar to organizational mapping. Put each idea on a separate index card or slip of paper (Figure 8.2). All the ideas are in some way related to your thesis statement, but the goal is to discover whether some are related to each other as they explain the thesis statement. Hence, rearrange the cards as they might go together. Eventually relationships among some of them become clear and the tangential nature of others becomes evident. You can then discard the less relevant cards (Foss & Foss, 1994).

PRACTICING THE PROCESS

Discovering Relationships

- Create an organizational map.
- Try the card playing approach.
- Which one worked better for you and why?

Whether or not you use one of these methods, the goal after discovering which ideas go together is to select a pattern for arranging your main points so your speech is orderly and the audience can follow as they listen. Some of the most common patterns are chronological, narrative, causal, spatial, topical, and comparison and contrast. Other patterns are used exclusively in persuasive speeches: problem with no solution, problem and solution, problem-cause-solution, refutative, comparative advantages, and Monroe's motivated sequence (see Chapter 15 for details).

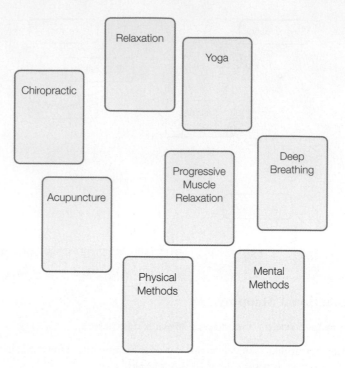

Figure 8.2   Relationship cards

Chronological Pattern

In a **chronological pattern,** main points follow a time sequence. You might try this when you want to narrate a series of events as they occurred, usually from past to present or from present to past. Lonna used a chronological pattern to arrange the main points in her narrative story about her life with AIDS:

I.   My life before I contracted AIDS was pretty typical.

II. My life today is no longer typical because I have AIDS.

III. My life plans for the future are also unique because I have AIDS.

Other times, main points demonstrate a process or procedure, such as demonstrating how to change a flat tire by offering a series of chronological steps as main points. Sometimes you can arrange main points chronologically by season of the year, time of day, life cycles (infant, child, teen, adult), months, years, or decades. You might use the 1960s, 1970s, 1980s, and 1990s in a speech about the history of rock and roll. Chronological patterns like these are especially suited for informative speeches.

Narrative Pattern

A **narrative pattern** conveys ideas through a story or series of stories. It's similar to a chronological pattern but the entire speech consists of a story or stories complete with characters, setting, and plot. It may entertain, inform, or persuade, but it is particularly effective when the stories are emotionally compelling. The goal is

An effective narrative, such as Jeffrey Taylor's "The Sacred Grove of Oshogbo," brings an experience to life and helps audience members see the event being presented.

for listeners to accept your conclusion by showing them through description rather than simply telling them. Lonna could use a narrative pattern for her speech about AIDS by sharing her story along with those of others she knows who have the disease:

I. Robert is 27 years old. He has AIDS. Let's learn his story.

II. Emma is 3 years old. She has AIDS. Let's learn her story.

III. My name is Lonna. I'm 20 years old. I, too, have AIDS. Let me tell you my story.

Jeffrey Tayler used a narrative pattern in his essay "The Sacred Grove of Oshogbo," published in 1999 by *Atlantic Monthly*. It recounts his visit to an area in the Nigerian town of Oshogbo, north of Lagos, where a collection of statues of ancient deities can be found. The following excerpt introduces a main character and is an example of vivid description (the complete essay is available online at http://www.theatlantic.com/unbound/abroad/jt990526.htm):

> As I passed through the gates I heard a squeaky voice. A diminutive middle-aged man came out from behind the trees—the caretaker. He worked a toothbrush-sized stick around in his mouth, digging into the crevices between algae'd stubs of teeth. He was barefoot; he wore a blue batik shirt known as a *buba*, baggy purple trousers, and an embroidered skullcap. I asked him if he would show me around the shrine. Motioning me to follow, he spat out the results of his stick work and set off down the trail. (Used with permission from *The Atlantic Monthly*.)

Speeches about natural disasters often use a causal pattern.

Causal Pattern

A **causal pattern** organizes main points to show a cause-and-effect relationship—how a cause eventually results in an effect. Hence the pattern typically consists of two main points, the cause and the effect. If Lonna were to do the speech about AIDS using a causal pattern, she might use these main points:

> I. Researchers have discovered three major causes of AIDS.
>
> II. There are also three primary effects of AIDS.

Medical topics may work with this pattern because the symptoms (effects) and causes of a disease are linked. Speeches about natural phenomena such as earthquakes, tornadoes, floods, and hurricanes also lend themselves easily to this pattern. Causal patterns can be used to organize the main points for both informative and persuasive speeches.

TURNING TO TECHNOLOGY

Causal Reasoning

http://commfaculty.fullerton.edu/rgass/newpage113.htm

This Web site poses a number of questions that could be addressed in a speech using a causal pattern. Identify one or two that you might consider for a speech.

Spatial Pattern

A **spatial pattern** is used to create a mental picture of what an object or a place looks like based on location or direction—north to south, near to far, top to bottom, or left to right. Flight attendants do this when they present preflight instructions to passengers by talking about where exits, flotation and oxygen devices, and restrooms are located. To explain where the library is located in relation to the rest of the campus, or how the components of a camera work when you snap a picture, your main points would employ a spatial pattern. If you talk about where various Native American Indian reservations are located, a spatial pattern would also work to arrange your main points. If Lonna were to use this pattern for her speech on AIDS, she might talk about which parts of the world are experiencing the most rapid growth of AIDS cases and why. Spatial patterns are most often used for informative speeches.

WHAT DO YOU THINK?
Consider a time when someone gave you directions to someplace. Were the directions described spatially? Were visual aids used? Were you able to find the location easily? Why or why not?

Topical Pattern

A **topical pattern** divides a topic into subtopics or categories. If speaking about the qualities of a fine diamond, the subtopics you would use as main points are cut, clarity, color, and carat.

The topical pattern can be used to discuss different viewpoints on a concept, idea, or problem, thus exposing listeners to many ways of looking at an issue. Eric, for example, talked about methods of discipline using these main points:

I. One method of discipline is based on a Skinnerian perspective.

II. Another method of discipline is based on a Freudian perspective.

III. Yet another method of discipline is based on a cognitive perspective.

For the AIDS speech, Lonna could arrange the main points topically by talking about AIDS experiences from the perspective of the person with the disease, of family and friends, and of health care providers.

Subtopics can also be arranged by gradation using a topical pattern. You might discuss main ideas from small to large, familiar to unfamiliar, simple to complex, least expensive to most expensive, and so forth (Foss & Foss, 1994). In her speech about alternative methods of healing, Julie began by talking about relaxation therapy as a simple, natural method of healing. She then talked about chiropractic therapy as a more complex approach. And she concluded by discussing acupuncture as an even more complex form of natural healing. Her main points were arranged by gradation using a topical pattern. Because it can be used for almost any topic and for any type of speech, the topical pattern is used more often than any other (Hoffman, 1992).

Compare-and-Contrast Pattern

This pattern is particularly useful for speeches about an unfamiliar concept, event, belief, or process. Shannon's speech about traditional Japanese clothing compared it to various kinds of Western clothing, making the following main points:

I. Some items of traditional Japanese attire evolved out of necessity, much like winter outerwear in cold-weather climates.

II. Some items of traditional Japanese attire have symbolic meaning, as does a white wedding gown for many people in this country.

III. Some items of traditional Japanese attire represent degrees of honor or status much like military clothing, stripes, and badges in this country.

This pattern helped make an unfamiliar topic more familiar to his listeners. For the AIDS speech, Lonna could use a compare-and-contrast pattern to illustrate the experiences of AIDS victims and those of victims suffering with terminal cancer. The pattern is most useful for informative speeches about unfamiliar topics, but it is sometimes used for persuasive speeches as well.

TURNING TO TECHNOLOGY

Organizational Patterns

http://www.angelfire.com/ks/teachme/patterns.html

This Web site offers explanations and examples of many common organizational patterns. Would any work well for your next speech? Why or why not?

Any of these patterns can be used to organize your main points. Selecting one to arrange the ideas and information in the body of your speech increases the likelihood that listeners will be able to follow you.

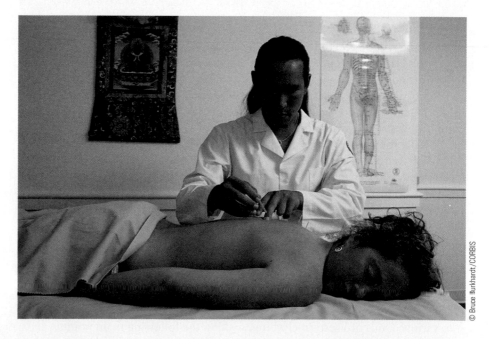

For her speech on alternative healing methods Julie used a topical pattern arranged by gradation, with acupuncture at the more complex end of the range.

© Bruce Burkhardt/CORBIS

Student Workbook

Read through the "Speech of Personal Significance" description, sample outlines, and grading criteria in Chapter 3 of your workbook. Which outline seems to best meet the criteria for this speech and why?

INTEGRATING SUPPORTING MATERIAL

Once you have arranged main points within a specific pattern, integrate supporting material under each one. Base your selection of supporting material on four key questions.

Sort Supporting Material among the Main Points

Ask yourself which main point each piece of supporting material you've collected relates to. Repeat this sorting process with each piece of evidence until you've considered them all. You might discover supporting material that doesn't relate directly to any of your main points; if so, discard it. Or you might find you need to do more research to find additional supporting material for a main point. As a general rule, you should have at least two pieces of supporting material for each main point.

Add Subdivisions Where Necessary

Next, ask yourself whether the supporting material lends itself to further subdivision of the main point. When Julie looked at her supporting material for her speech on alternative forms of healing, she discovered that her first main point—relaxation therapy—could be subdivided into two methods, psychological and physical. Then she organized the supporting material for her first main point once again as each piece fit within one of these subdivisions.

Consider the Learning Cycle

Now ask whether the supporting material you've chosen appeals to more than one dimension of the learning cycle. Remember that the most effective retention occurs when your speech rounds the entire cycle of learning. Do you offer something for thinking, doing, feeling, and watching? Do you focus on facts and statistics at the expense of personal stories and testimonies? Do you provide definitions and explanations at the expense of concrete examples? You probably won't have supporting material that addresses every dimension of the cycle for each and every main point, but the speech as a whole should address all four dimensions.

Looking at the Learning Cycle

Considering Supporting Material

- *Thinking:* definitions, descriptions, explanations, facts, statistics
- *Feeling:* hypothetical and factual examples, narratives, expert and peer testimonies
- *Doing:* action plans, strategies, formulas, processes, procedures, applications
- *Watching:* vivid descriptions, visual and audiovisual aids

Consider Relevance to Listeners

Finally, ask whether your supporting material can serve as listener relevance links for each main point. Although introductory comments offer a statement that relates your speech to listeners, make sure such connections occur throughout the speech. Doing so better ensures that you regain and sustain listener interest and motivation.

PRACTICING THE PROCESS

Guidelines for Integrating Your Supporting Material

- Sort the evidence for your next speech among the main points.
- Discard any evidence that does not relate directly to any of the main points.
- Collect additional evidence for any main points that do not have at least two items of support.
- Add subdivisions under main points if necessary.
- Label each piece of evidence as it addresses feeling, watching, thinking, or doing.
- Collect additional evidence if any of the dimensions are missing.
- Label each piece of evidence that could serve as listener relevance.
- Collect additional evidence if a main point is lacking listener relevance.

INCORPORATING CONNECTIVES

Once you have selected a pattern for ordering your main points and integrated appropriate supporting material under each main point, link them in ways that make your speech flow well. Do so by incorporating **connectives,** words or phrases that hold your speech together. Connectives include transitions, internal previews and summaries, and signposts.

Transitions

Transitions are words or phrases that show the relationship between two main points and let the audience know you have completed one main point and are moving on to another. The most effective ones tie the main point just completed to the next one and clarify the relationship between them. This reminds the audience where you've been and where you're going, as if you are saying, "Now that we've talked about this, let's discuss that."

Transitions may be a single sentence, or perhaps two or three. As part of macrostructure, however, they always connect two main points, the introduction to the body, or the body to the conclusion.

You can make transitions more creative and accurate by developing them in ways that reinforce the pattern of your main points. If, for example, the main points use a chronological pattern, you might try a time change pattern for the transitions. Use words like the following:

> until, previously, later, earlier, in the past, in the future, meanwhile, before, after, at present, today, eventually

Lonna used this transition in her speech: "*Before* I had AIDS, my life was pretty typical, but *today* my life is definitely not typical. My life today is different because I have AIDS."

Transitions that reinforce a causal pattern use words like the following:

therefore, consequently, thus, so, as a result, hence, since, due to, accordingly, because of

In the causal speech about AIDS, Lonna might say, "Now that you realize what causes AIDS, let's look at the effects that arise *as a result* of contracting the disease."

Transitions that reinforce a spatial pattern use words like the following:

above, below, in front of, in back of, to the east, to the west, to the right, to the left, just behind, nearby, in the distance, next to, furthest from

In a preflight presentation, a transition might be: "Although emergency exits are located only *in the front and back of the aircraft*, oxygen and flotation devices are located *above and below* each seat."

Transitions that imply comparison use words like the following:

compared with, likewise, similarly, just as, much like, in comparison

Shannon offered this transition: "*Just as* some traditional Japanese attire carries symbolic meaning, so does some traditional attire represent degrees of honor and status *much like* military clothing does in our country."

Transitions that illustrate contrast use words like the following:

but, yet, however, on the other hand, in contrast, rather than, on the contrary

Transitions that build an argument incrementally use words that signify additions like the following:

moreover, in addition, not only, also, furthermore, besides

In each of the three main points in Julie's speech about alternative methods of healing she used transitions that reinforced her continuum pattern:

I. Relaxation therapy

   Transition: *Not only* is relaxation therapy a natural healing method you can consider, but *also* chiropractic therapy is something you might choose.

II. Chiropractic therapy

   Transition: *In addition* to relaxation therapy and chiropractic therapy, another more complex natural healing method is acupuncture.

III. Acupuncture

She verbally tied her main ideas together using a strategy that reinforced the gradation approach she took using a topical pattern.

Internal Previews and Summaries

Internal previews and summaries connect pieces of supporting material to the main point or subpoint they address. Internal previews do so before offering the supporting material, whereas internal summaries do so afterward. This helps listeners understand how the supporting material supports the main point. You can develop internal previews and summaries by considering *why* you've included the supporting material. Julie used an internal preview before talking about psychological methods as an alternative form of healing. She said, "I'm sure most of you have heard the concept of 'mind over matter.' Well, 'mind over matter' is actually a psychological method you can use as a form of relaxation therapy. For example . . ."

Signposts

Signposts are words or short phrases that mark where you are in the speech or help move it forward. Usually they highlight numerical order: "first," "second," "third," and "fourth." Signposts can also be used to focus the audience on a key idea—"foremost," "most important," and "above all." Some signify an explanation—"to illustrate," "for instance," "in other words," "essentially," "in essence," and "to clarify." Sometimes they signal that an important idea or even the speech itself is ending: "in short," "finally," "in conclusion," "to summarize," and "in sum."

PRACTICING THE PROCESS

Guidelines for Incorporating Connectives

- Create transitions for the main points of your speech that reinforce the organization pattern you have selected.
- Integrate internal previews or summaries between subdivisions within your main points.
- Offer signposts to help move your speech forward among pieces of evidence.

TURNING TO TECHNOLOGY

Test Yourself

Go to the *Confident Public Speaking* Web site and click on the Tutorial Quizzes link to test yourself on what you have learned in Chapter 8. How did you do?

SUMMARY

Effective public speech organization is the process of arranging the macrostructural part of speech structure, which can reduce speaking anxiety that is rooted in a fear of the unknown. The macrostructural components of a public speech consist of the introduction, body, and conclusion. Because listeners must follow your organization as they listen, public speech structure must follow specific guidelines. This chapter focuses on the first set of guidelines, those associated with organizing the body of a speech—patterning main points, integrating supporting material, and incorporating connectives.

The body should consist of two to four main points that follow one pattern. The most common patterns for arranging main ideas are chronological, narrative, causal, spatial, topical, and comparison and contrast. Each main point is developed by integrating supporting material, rounding the learning cycle, and highlighting listener relevance. The elements of the body are further tied together with connectives. Transitions tie together main points in ways that reinforce the pattern as well as the relationship between them. Internal previews and summaries tie together supporting material with the main point or subpoints they augment. Signposts mark where you are and move the speech forward with short words or phrases. The most common signposts highlight numerical order. Others focus the audience on a key idea, signify an explanation, or signal that the idea or the speech itself is ending.

Developing the body of a speech is the first important step in organizing macrostructure. The equally important step of creating effective introductions and conclusions is the focus of Chapter 9.

RETURNING TO TECHNOLOGY

The *Confident Public Speaking* CD-ROM is your one-stop point of access for not just the content on the CD itself, such as Speech Interactive, but also the many other resources on the *Confident Public Speaking* Web site, Speech Builder Express, and InfoTrac College Edition. Note that this chapter's key terms and activities are among the resources available in electronic format online. Additional information is included below.

SPEECH INTERACTIVE
ON THE *CONFIDENT PUBLIC SPEAKING* CD-ROM

Speech Interactive is your link to this text's speech videos. Offering opportunities to practice critiquing speeches by students and other public speakers, these videos will help you prepare for providing effective feedback to your peers and your own speech performances.

SPEECH BUILDER EXPRESS

The Organization and Transitions sections of Speech Builder Express provide sequences of prompts that can help you organize your main ideas, and transition from one to the next, as effectively as possible. You'll find the links to these sections on the main navigation menu, found on the left-hand side of the screen.

KEY TERMS

Interactive flashcards for these key terms are available on the *Confident Public Speaking* Web site. You'll find the "Flashcards" link under the resources for Chapter 8.

Card playing 187	Narrative pattern 188
Causal pattern 190	Organization 184
Chronological pattern 188	Organizational mapping 186
Connectives 194	Signposts 196
Internal previews and summaries 195	Spatial pattern 191
Macrostructure 184	Topical pattern 191
Microstructure 184	Transition 194

ACTIVITIES

The activities below are available in electronic format on the *Confident Public Speaking* Web site. You'll find the "Activities" link under the resources for Chapter 8.

1. **Patterning Main Points.** Form a group with two or three classmates. Select a topic from the list that follows or come up with your own. Create three sets of main points for the same general topic based on three different patterns. Select from chronological, narrative, causal, spatial, topical, or comparison and contrast. Topic examples for this activity should be fairly broad and could include the following:

   - Teen suicide
   - Gambling
   - Rugby
   - Body piercing
   - Holidays
   - Cloning
   - Home schooling
   - Birth control
   - Skydiving
   - Chocolate chip cookies
   - Exercise
   - Restaurants

2. **Creating Transition Statements.** Continuing from activity 1, create transition statements for the main points of each of the three patterns you developed for your topic.

3. **Rounding the Learning Cycle.** Form a group with two or three classmates. Find three or four resources (such as magazine articles, newspaper stories, books, and Internet printouts) focused on one topic. It can be the same topic you arrived at for activity 1. Locate supporting material for the topic that addresses each of the four learning cycle dimensions: feeling, doing, watching, and thinking.

Go to InfoTrac College Edition and click on PowerTrac. Enter "Vital Speeches" in the Journal Name entry box. Select two speeches to look at. Print them out. Analyze them to discover (1) what organizational pattern each one used, (2) their transitions, (3) their internal previews and summaries, and (4) their signposts. Which speech seemed to flow best and why?

MAKING LASTING IMPRESSIONS:

INTRODUCTIONS

AND CONCLUSIONS

REFLECTIVE QUESTIONS

1. Why might it be important to devote time to developing your introduction and conclusion?

2. What do you think an introduction should accomplish? Is "My topic is . . ." an effective introduction? Why or why not?

3. What do you think a conclusion should accomplish? Is "thank you" an effective ending? Why or why not?

4. Why might it be important to provide a clear preview and summary of your speech to the audience?

5. In what ways could your introduction's attention catcher and your conclusion's clincher work together?

WHAT'S AHEAD: FOCUSING YOUR READING

Why Are Introductions and Conclusions Crucial?

Developing Effective Introductions

Developing Effective Conclusions

TIFFANY HAD WORKED HARD ON her speech about being a vegetarian. Because she had grown up on a cattle ranch, her decision to become a vegetarian had significant implications for her and her family and she wanted to convey this. She had organized her main points chronologically: her decision, her family's reactions, and the effects of her decision on her life today. She planned to talk first about when she made her decision, then how her family reacted, and finally how her decision impacts her life today. She felt good about this organizational pattern and about the details and facts she'd chosen to support her main points.

The body of Tiffany's speech was clearly organized, but her work was far from finished. Recall that listeners typically remember only about 25 percent of what they hear. Tiffany wanted her audience to listen to and remember her ideas. She knew she needed to create an introduction that would entice the audience to listen and a conclusion that would make her ideas memorable. The question was how.

Once you've developed the body of the speech—selected a pattern for main points, integrated supporting material that enhances each main point, and incorporated connectives—it's time to construct the introduction and conclusion. This chapter presents strategies you can use to develop effective introductions and conclusions. We begin by looking at why introductions and conclusions are crucial. Then we look specifically at the major functions of introductions and conclusions and how to fulfill them.

WHY ARE INTRODUCTIONS AND CONCLUSIONS CRUCIAL?

How your speech begins and ends can make or break it. One reason is what psychologists call the **primacy-recency effect:** We are more likely to remember the first and last items conveyed orally in a series than the items in between (Trenholm, 1989). Thus listeners are more likely to remember the beginning and end of your speech than what you say in the body. So make sure the introduction and conclusion are strong.

WHAT DO YOU THINK?

Consider a speaker you heard who seemed really good. Did she or he say or do something in the introduction or conclusion to influence your perception? Explain.

Another reason stems from the need for listeners to grasp the topic and main points as they listen to the speech. You can give listeners a framework by clearly and precisely highlighting the topic and main points in your introduction, and you can reinforce what they grasped by clearly and precisely reminding them of your topic and main points in the conclusion.

A clearly developed introduction and conclusion reduce public speaking anxiety. You can give yourself positive self-talk about creating a strong first and last impression. The introduction in particular can increase confidence by getting you off to a good start. Likewise, as the introduction has a precise main point preview, you can return to it as a reminder if you get stuck in the body. It can help you recall what major points you want to get across and why, getting you back on track.

DEVELOPING EFFECTIVE INTRODUCTIONS

The introduction serves five key functions and should do so in no more than ten to fifteen percent of the allotted speaking time. That's less than a minute in a six-minute speech. The five basic functions of an introduction are:

- Capturing audience interest
- Establishing a rapport with the audience
- Establishing your credibility
- Stating the speech topic
- Previewing the main points

Capturing Audience Interest

Use your first sentences to capture the interest of the audience. Because listeners are likely to be distracted by external or internal interference, grab them early by immediately arousing their curiosity. In developing an **attention catcher,** you can draw on various techniques including questions, quotations, stories or examples, startling statistics, action, and humor. The attention catcher must always relate to your topic, though, or it will confuse and distract the audience.

The attention catcher needs to be clever and entice listeners' curiosity; otherwise it will have no power. Advertisers are masters at this. How do television and magazine ads grab your attention? One popular lure is sex. Why, for example, does the model in the Herbal Essences commercial act like she's having an orgasm while shampooing her hair? Why is Cindy Crawford's sweater unbuttoned to the navel in her picture on the box of Special K cereal? And why do magazine ads for lotions, perfumes, and makeup almost always portray scantily clothed women? Although the ethical nature of such advertisements could be questioned, they do grab viewers.

Another popular technique used by advertisers is humor. The "Got Milk?" ads are a prime example, as are the Budweiser commercials hosted by frogs and the Taco Bell commercials hosted by a Chihuahua. But be careful. Some uses of humor confuse rather than promote.

Let's look more closely at some attention-catching techniques.

ETHICS

WHAT DO YOU THINK?

Consider a television commercial you thought was particularly funny. Did you realize what product was being promoted? Did the commercial achieve its purpose? Why or why not?

Questions

A question or series of questions can capture an audience if they are directly related to the audience and the topic, because they build suspense and arouse curiosity. You can use a rhetorical question or series of rhetorical questions, or a direct question or series of direct questions.

A **rhetorical question** is intended to stimulate thought but not an overt response. Sonja spoke about the experience of moving to a new place for the first time and began with this rhetorical question: "Have you ever packed up everything you owned, said good-bye to all of your friends, and moved to a place where you knew no one?" This question simply asked listeners to consider whether they had experienced such an event. Sometimes speakers begin with a series of rhetorical questions. For example, Sonja could have begun like this:

> 66 Have you ever taken a trip to a place you'd never been before? How did you feel before you left? Did you travel alone? How did you feel when you arrived? Were friends or family there to greet you? Can you imagine packing up everything you own, saying good-bye to all of your friends, and moving to live someplace where you know no one? Well, that is exactly what I did.

Humor, when used carefully, can be an effective attention catcher.

A series of rhetorical questions can be especially effective at arousing the curiosity of the audience by creating a climactic effect. They tend to appeal to both the feeling and thinking dimensions of the learning cycle by encouraging listeners to apply their own experiences to the speaker's ideas in a way that stimulates critical thought. But the questions must indeed arouse curiosity. In her speech about dog grooming, Jennifer asked, "Have you ever had a dog?" Although this is a rhetorical question that demands no answer, it does little to stimulate audience curiosity.

Direct questions, unlike rhetorical questions, demand a response and are thus more difficult to use effectively. This could increase your anxiety or get your speech off to a bad start. Using a direct question might require encouraging listeners to respond by saying something like "Come on now. I really want an answer," or by raising your hand as you ask the question and pausing until listeners respond. The pause can seem like a long time. Sonja could have begun her speech like this: "I'd like to see a show of hands. How many of you have ever packed up everything you owned and moved to a place where you knew no one?"

Although they pose challenges, direct questions *physically* involve listeners in the communication transaction by appealing to the doing dimension of the learning cycle and thus making listeners more alert. This may be particularly helpful if you must speak at, say, 8:00 on Monday morning. Also, the responses might help you make the body of the speech more relevant. For example, if one of Sonja's main points was her experiences adjusting to a new climate, she might have asked listeners if any had traveled to a new climate. If few had, she might provide more detail. And she might insert statements acknowledging similarities as listener relevance links.

TURNING TO TECHNOLOGY

Questions to Consider

http://www.gadzillionthings.net/

This Web site offers hundreds of clever rhetorical questions arranged by topic. Find one or two questions you could use in your next speech.

Quotations

If you find a short and effective quotation, consider using it as an attention catcher. For example, since Sonja's speech focused on the importance of courage and taking risks, she could have begun with Franklin D. Roosevelt's "The only thing we have to fear is fear itself," a well-known quotation by a famous person. Or she could have used a less known quotation by a famous person, such as Gertrude Stein's "Considering how dangerous everything is, nothing is really very frightening." Or she could have used a quotation by someone "famous" only to her. For example:

> " "No one ever said it would be easy. But you'll never know what you can do until you try." These are the words my grandmother used to tell me every time I told her I was afraid to try something new. She told me this when I was five years old and afraid to ride my bicycle without training wheels. She told me this when I was twelve years old and afraid to start junior high. And she told me this last year when I was afraid to move to a new city where I had never lived and where I would know no one.

A quotation can be a clever means of sparking the interest of listeners, but only if it relates significantly to the topic of the speech.

TURNING TO TECHNOLOGY

Finding Good Quotations

http://www.quoteland.com/

This Web site contains quotations indexed by author and subject. Find two or three quotations you could use in your next speech.

Stories

Because people are naturally interested in stories, one that serves as an example, whether actual or hypothetical, can be an effective attention catcher. Television advertisements, for example, can be very effective when they begin with a person sharing a story.

An **actual example** may be something that happened to you or a friend or family member; or something you learned about in a magazine, newspaper, or television news program. Actual examples tend to appeal to the feeling dimension of the learning cycle, since they focus on real people and events. Sonja elaborated on the quotation by her grandmother with actual examples from her own life.

A **hypothetical example** can take the form of asking listeners to imagine themselves in a certain situation, or it can be a story made up about an imaginary character in the situation. Again, this is particularly suited to the feeling dimension of the learning cycle. In this case, however, you need to immediately state that the story is not true.

Tiffany used a combination of examples in her attention catcher:

WHAT DO YOU THINK?
Consider a television commercial that uses a story to draw you in. Does it succeed? Why or why not?

> **"** With Thanksgiving just around the corner, many of you are probably anticipating a feast complete with a flavorful, juicy turkey as the main course. I, however, plan to bring my own addition to my family dinner—a rice pilaf, with grilled vegetables and garlic-roasted tofu.

She began with a hypothetical example about her listeners and followed with an actual example from her own life.

Startling Facts or Statistics

A **startling fact or statistic** is a little-known and shocking piece of information. In conducting research, you may read something surprising, something you did not know was so devastating, so widespread, or so common. If so, make note of it as a possible attention catcher. In her speech about eating disorders, for example, Marcia began her speech like this:

> **"** Who are five of the most important women in your life? Your mother? Your sister? Your daughter? Your wife? Your best friend? Now which one of them has had or will have an eating disorder? Before you disregard my question, listen to what research tells us. One in every five women in the United States has an eating disorder.

Startling facts and statistics caught the attention of Marcia's audience much more effectively than simply stating that "Eating disorders are an epidemic in this country."

Advertisers often startle viewers by using sex as an attention catcher. Models wearing scanty clothes or engaged in sexually illicit behavior do tend to startle and draw viewers in. Has this technique become overused and thus less effective? Apparently not, given that it is still so widely used. But ethically, where should advertisers draw the line in order to demonstrate respect and honesty for themselves and their viewers? Certainly, this question is being examined as a result of the breast-bearing event by Justin Timberlake and Janet Jackson during the 2004 Super Bowl halftime show.

Action

Action can also gain audience attention. You can demonstrate the action yourself or show it on video, which would appeal to the watching dimension of the learning cycle. Or you could ask for a volunteer from the audience, or ask all audience members to participate, appealing to the doing dimension. In a speech about bungee jumping, for example, you could show a videotape of someone doing it. Juan split a stack of bricks with his hand to catch the audience's attention in his speech about karate. And in her speech about ballet, Cherise asked for a volunteer who helped her demonstrate a simple dance. As with direct questions, however, asking for audience participation could increase anxiety if nobody volunteers or if the audience is reluctant. To reduce this possibility, you might do what Cherise did and secure a "volunteer" in advance.

Humor

Humor—a joke, anecdote, or story with a humorous twist—can also be used to catch attention. For example, a businessperson had to give a speech to an audience that was part Japanese and part American. He had learned that the Japanese always expected an apology at the beginning of the speech and that Americans expected a joke. So he apologized for not having a joke. If you use humor, however, be sure it adheres to the three-R test: It must be realistic, relevant, and repeatable. In other words, it can't be too far-fetched, unrelated to the point of the speech, or potentially offensive to some listeners (Humes, 1988). If you aren't sure if your humor might offend someone or some group, ask several friends who belong to different racial, ethnic, gender, or special-needs groups for their opinions.

Because your goal is to get through to listeners rather than turn them off in the first sentences, follow this general rule: When in doubt, leave it out. If you do use humor, consider how you will handle the situation if your audience doesn't laugh. You may simply decide to avoid using humor in your attention catcher (Slan, 1998).

TURNING TO TECHNOLOGY

Finding Good Jokes

http://dir.yahoo.com/Entertainment/Humor/Jokes/

ETHICS This directory links to several Web sites where you can find jokes about many different topics. Select one or two jokes that you could use in your next speech. Be sure to consider ethics as you decide.

© CBS/EC/Everett Collection

Using inappropriate humor (far-fetched, irrelevant, or potentially offensive) as an attention catcher may turn off your audience.

All effective public speeches begin with an attention catcher—a question, quotation, example, startling fact or statistic, action, or humor. Chuck used a combination in his speech on hate crimes:

 Murder. Simply the word itself can send chills through your body, but what if the only reason you were killed was because of something you had no control over? That's where the term *hate crime* comes in.

An attention catcher may be as brief as one sentence or as long as five or six sentences. In any case, it must not only arouse interest but relate directly to the topic of the speech.

Student Workbook

Look at the "Point-Counterpoint Dispositional Speech" sample outlines in Chapter 4 of your workbook. What device does each one use for the attention catcher? Which one is most compelling to you and why?

PRACTICING THE PROCESS

Guidelines for Creating Effective Attention Catchers

To generate a host of attention catchers, consider the topic of your speech and:

- Create a rhetorical question or series of questions.
- Create a direct question or series of questions.
- Identify a quotation.
- Identify a story (actual or hypothetical).
- Identify a startling fact or statistic.
- Come up with some kind of action.
- Identify a tasteful joke.

Which one seems most effective as an attention catcher for your speech? Why?

Establishing Rapport with the Audience

The introduction also should help establish rapport—a connection—with your audience. The best way is to show listeners that your speech not only will interest them, but interest them personally. Thus the introduction should include a **listener relevance link,** a statement of why your speech relates to or might affect listeners. This addresses the feeling dimension of the learning cycle. Sonja, for example, offered a statistic on how many people relocate and used it to point out that even those listeners who had never relocated before probably would someday. Tiffany talked about how many people are choosing to become vegetarians for health reasons and Chuck talked about how many people are victims of hate crimes or know someone who has been a victim of one.

As you work on the speech, ask yourself questions like these: Why should listeners care about this? In what way(s) might they benefit from hearing about it? How might they relate to my topic? You might focus in particular on how your speech relates to listeners' needs for health, wealth, well-being, self-esteem, success, and so forth. Generate ideas about listener relevance by recalling what you learned about your audience's psychological and demographic characteristics during audience analysis. Doing so essentially demonstrates respect for your listeners. Levi, who spoke against the use of road salt to remove ice from streets and highways, included

WHAT DO YOU THINK?

Think of a speaker who got your attention right away. What attention catcher did he or she use? Was the attention catcher connected to the topic of the speech? Was the attention catcher ethical? Why or why not?

in his introduction a reminder that road salt rusts automobiles and thus limits how long they last. In this way, he established that his message could have a positive impact on listeners' wealth. Likewise, Marcia established rapport by talking about health and well-being when she said:

> If the research is correct, then one in every five women in this room will likely be afflicted with an eating disorder. So if it's not you, then perhaps it's the person sitting next to you. And according to a July 1998 issue of the *Washington Post,* more than 90 percent are adolescents and young women. Although the majority are women, an October 1999 news report by the British Broadcasting Company reveals that one in ten people diagnosed are men. Even children as young as three have been treated. And only 60 percent ever recover—that is, many will die.

You should, of course, include listener relevance links throughout your speech. For your introduction, choose a link that you find especially compelling and that will be general and brief enough for this point in the speech.

Establishing Your Credibility

Let listeners know that you are a credible source, that they can trust what you are going to say. Doing so addresses the thinking dimension of the learning cycle. To do this, include in your introduction a **speaker credibility statement,** a brief statement clarifying why you are an authority on the topic. Answer unspoken listener questions such as "How do *you* know more about this topic than I do?" and "Why should I listen to *you?*"

Students sometimes have a hard time believing that they are an authority on a topic. But you don't need to be a Pulitzer Prize–winning poet to be credible on the topic of why poetry is significant to you. Nor do you have to be a well-known biotechnologist to be credible on the advantages and disadvantages of cloning. Perhaps your authority can come from your academic major, as it did for Jaime, a senior majoring in biotechnology who presented a speech on cloning. Jaime simply said:

> I have been interested in the subject of cloning ever since the story about Dolly, the sheep, hit the news. As a student majoring in biotechnology, I have taken several classes related to this subject and have done a good deal of research to educate myself about this scientific breakthrough.

Or your authority can come from personal experience, as it did for Tiffany, who talked about vegetarianism. Tiffany explained, "About five years ago, I made a decision to stop eating meat. This decision has changed my life in several ways." Chuck revealed that his close friend had recently fallen victim to a hate crime. The amount of research you do on the topic can also make you an authority. Jaime drew on both his academic experience and research efforts for his speaker credibility statement. In short, to be ethical you have to show that you are a credible source, not that you are *the* final authority or even *a* final authority.

Student Workbook

Look at the 'Point-Counterpoint Dispositional Speech' sample outlines in Chapter 4 of your workbook. What does each one say to establish credibility in the Introduction? Which one is most compelling to you and why?

ETHICS

Steps for Establishing Your Credibility

- Step 1: Consider the subject of your speech.
- Step 2: Ask yourself what personal experience, academic background, or research efforts of yours make you an authority on the subject?
- Step 3: Create a speaker credibility statement you can use in your introduction.

Stating the Speech Topic

No matter how interesting the introduction, it cannot be effective unless it gives listeners a clear sense of your topic. The introduction must include a **thesis statement,** a one-sentence summary of the speech. This addresses the thinking dimension of the learning cycle. For maximum clarity, word your thesis statement simply and precisely. Remember that if your listeners don't grasp the thesis firmly at the outset, they will have difficulty following the rest of your speech. They do not have the luxury of rereading as in a written composition. This might mean providing background information about the topic, such as short definitions or explanations. For example, a speech about CDs should make it clear that you are talking about compact discs and not certificates of deposit. Likewise, depending on the topic, you might need to provide a brief historical background.

Tiffany's thesis statement was simply "Living a vegetarian lifestyle is an important aspect of who I am." Marcia's was "Eating disorders are a serious problem in our society today." To provide necessary background, she added a short statement clarifying what she meant by eating disorders. Jaime's thesis statement was "If our scientific decisions about cloning continue to disregard ethical issues, I fear the consequences will be disastrous." He added a brief statement defining cloning as he would use it in his speech. And Sonja's thesis statement was "Relocating to a new state has taught me many lessons and, in fact, helped shape who I am today." By being both simple and precise, these statements clearly tell listeners what they will hear.

Previewing the Main Points

By the end of the introduction, you should have accomplished the first part of the golden rule of public speaking: Tell them what you are going to tell them. You will have done so by following the thesis statement with a **preview,** a brief statement of the main points of the speech. This gives listeners a sense of what you will say and in what order, so that they will more readily understand the body of the speech. Like the thesis statement, and for the same reasons, the preview should be simple and precise. Don't provide a lot of information. Sometimes a beginning speaker provides so much information in the preview that listeners think the body of the speech is now under way. The goal is to tell them what you're going to tell them, *not* to actually tell them.

One way to keep a preview simple and clear is to condense each main point to a phrase. Marcia's preview, for example, was "To help you realize the magnitude of the eating disorder problem in our society, I'll reveal just who is at risk, how severe the effects can be, and why it has become an epidemic." You might further clarify the preview with signposts, as Sonja did: "I learned valuable life lessons: first, by facing the challenges of finding a part-time job; second, by learning to use the public transportation system; and third, by meeting new people." Or you might use parallelism to emphasize the content in your preview, as well as make it more simple and clear. **Parallelism** involves repeating words or grammatical structures within or across sentences. Tiffany, for example, used parallelism in her preview:

> I'll talk specifically about how I made this choice to live meat-free. Next, I'll share some of the family issues that arose as a result of this choice. Finally, I'll discuss some of the ways this choice affects my life today.

Notice that Tiffany's preview is simple, clear, and precise and that the use of parallelism emphasizes and further clarifies what her main points will be. Her preview gives a clear sense of the speech's structure.

PRACTICING THE PROCESS

Checklist of Elements for an Effective Introduction

Make sure that your introduction includes the following elements, usually in this order:

- ❏ Attention catcher
- ❏ Listener relevance link
- ❏ Speaker credibility statement
- ❏ Thesis statement
- ❏ Preview

Including each of these elements fulfills each of the functions of an introduction. Moreover, it rounds the entire cycle of learning (Figure 9.1), motivates the audience to listen, and puts listeners in a position to understand the speech. And remember: Effective introductions are quick.

TURNING TO TECHNOLOGY

Chuck's Introduction

 Go to Speech Interactive on your *Confident Public Speaking* CD-ROM and watch Chuck's "Anatomy of a Hate Crime" speech. Is he successful at arousing your interest, establishing rapport and credibility, stating the topic and previewing the main points? Could some element have been stronger? If so, which one and why?

The introduction should clearly highlight the macrostructure for a speech, but at its best it does much more. It also arouses listeners' curiosity, motivates them to listen, and establishes your credibility. Here is Tiffany's whole introduction:

> **Attention catcher:** With Thanksgiving just around the corner, many of you are probably anticipating a feast complete with a flavorful, juicy turkey as the main course. I, however, plan to bring my own addition to my family dinner—a rice pilaf, with grilled vegetables and garlic-roasted tofu.

Notice how Tiffany combined a hypothetical example with a personal example to arouse the curiosity of her listeners in a creative way.

> **Listener relevance link:** Although a diet rich in eggs, meat, and potatoes was once the norm in our country, more and more Americans are choosing a vegetarian lifestyle, and many are doing so for health reasons. In fact, the American Dietetic Association, also known as the ADA, maintains that vegetarianism is not only healthful and adequate, but also helps in the prevention and treatment of certain diseases (www.eatright.org).

Here, Tiffany tied her topic to the basic human desire for good health as an appeal to motivate her audience to listen. She strengthened the credibility of her appeal by citing a reputable source.

> **Speaker credibility statement:** About five years ago, I made a decision to stop eating meat, which has changed my life in several ways.

Tiffany further strengthened her credibility by revealing personal experience—that she herself is a vegetarian.

> **Thesis statement:** Living a vegetarian lifestyle is an important aspect of who I am today.

Notice how simply and precisely Tiffany's thesis statement is worded. Listeners realized very easily that Tiffany was going to talk about the ways in which living a vegetarian lifestyle shapes who she is today.

> **Preview:** I'll talk specifically about how I made this choice to live meat-free. Next, I'll share some of the family issues that arose as a result of this choice. Finally, I'll discuss some of the ways this choice affects my life today.

Again, Tiffany simply and precisely highlighted what would be the three main points of her speech. She fulfilled the first step in the golden rule of public speaking: Tell them what you're going to tell them.

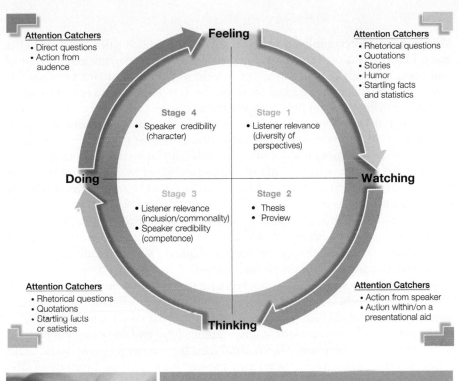

Figure 9.1 Speech introductions and the learning cycle

Feeling

Attention Catchers
- Rhetorical questions
- Quotations
- Stories
- Humor
- Startling facts and statistics

Stage 4
- Speaker credibility (character)

Stage 1
- Listener relevance (diversity of perspectives)

Doing

Watching

Stage 3
- Listener relevance (inclusion/commonality)
- Speaker credibility (competence)

Stage 2
- Thesis
- Preview

Attention Catchers
- Direct questions
- Action from audience

Attention Catchers
- Rhetorical questions
- Quotations
- Startling facts or satistics

Thinking

Attention Catchers
- Action from speaker
- Action within/on a presentational aid

TURNING TO TECHNOLOGY

Tiffany's Speech

Go to Speech Interactive on your *Confident Public Speaking* CD-ROM to watch Tiffany give her speech, "Meat Free and Me." Consider what tools she uses in her introduction. Is she effective? Why or why not?

DEVELOPING EFFECTIVE CONCLUSIONS

Recall that an introduction should take no more than 10 to 15 percent of the allotted speaking time. Likewise, your conclusion should be brief—no more than 5 to 10 percent of the allotted time. That means the conclusion for your six-minute speech should take only twenty to forty seconds! It is crucial to develop your conclusion in a way that leaves a positive lasting impression in listeners' minds. Hence, an effective conclusion for any type of speech serves three primary functions:

- Reinforcing the main ideas
- Motivating listeners to remember
- Providing a sense of closure

The goal is for listeners to remember what you've discussed. Chapter 4 notes that people typically retain only about 25 percent of what they hear. Whether you've informed, persuaded, or entertained them, you want what you said to be part of that 25 percent. Because of the primacy-recency effect discussed earlier, the conclusion is a central piece of what your listeners will remember, and it's the last chance you have to reinforce ideas. Hence, as with your introduction, spend time developing your conclusion.

WHAT DO YOU THINK?
Consider a speech that you remember well. Did you think it was effective or ineffective? Do you remember the conclusion? Why or why not?

Reinforcing the Main Ideas

Your conclusion accomplishes the final part of the golden rule: Tell them what you told them. Just as the introduction contains a thesis statement and preview of main points, so the conclusion contains a thesis restatement and a main point summary. Some beginning speakers think this is redundant or even an insult to listeners' intelligence. But public speaking is a one-time affair and you want to be assured that listeners remember your main points. A **thesis restatement** is a re-iteration of the thesis statement, usually offered in past tense. It is sometimes nearly verbatim, although it doesn't have to be. It can be more developed than this, but does not have to be. Tiffany's thesis restatement was nearly the same as her original thesis statement, but phrased in past tense: "Now you know why my vegetarian lifestyle is such an important aspect of who I am." Jaime's thesis restatement was less similar, but still restated his main thesis: "We must ground our scientific decisions about cloning in ethics or face the disastrous consequences of not doing so." Whether they are nearly verbatim or slightly modified, effective thesis restatements are still simple and precise.

A **main point summary** is a brief statement reminding listeners of the main points in the speech. It is usually shorter than the preview of main points, but can sometimes be embellished with a point or points that could not be mentioned in the preview. It is typically only one sentence long and sometimes combined with the thesis restatement. Marcia combined her thesis restatement and main point summary into a single sentence by stating "Now that you are aware of who is at risk and how severe the effects can be, you realize, as I do, that the eating disorder epidemic in our society cannot be ignored." Tiffany's main point summary was a single sentence that followed her thesis restatement:

> **Thesis restatement:** Now you know why my vegetarian lifestyle is such an important aspect of who I am.
>
> **Main point summary:** I talked about why I made *this choice* to be a vegetarian, how *this choice* has impacted my personal relationships, and how *this choice* continues to affect my life today.

Student Workbook

Look at Denelle's 'My Aunt Barb' speech outline in Chapter 3 of your workbook. What type of attention catcher does she use? How does she tie back to it in her clincher? Does her clincher help motivate you to remember? Why or why not?

Notice that Tiffany used parallelism in her main point summary. Use of parallelism further increases the likelihood that listeners will remember the main points.

As the preceding examples show, the thesis restatement and main point summary help provide closure. They do so by mirroring the introduction while signaling, through use of past tense and phrases like "Now that you realize," that the content has been presented and the speech is ending.

Motivating Listeners to Remember

A clear summary of the thesis and main points helps listeners remember them. But they will be even more likely to remember if you follow the summary with a **clincher:** a final sentence or series of sentences that reinforces your main ideas in a memorable way. Speakers who have no clincher sometimes try to provide closure by saying "thank you." There is nothing inherently wrong with this, but it's not a clincher. A clincher provides closure in a memorable way without a need to say thanks. You might motivate your listeners to remember the speech by using any of the techniques discussed for capturing audience interest: a rhetorical or direct question, a quotation, a hypothetical or actual story, a startling fact or statistic, action, or humor. As with your attention catcher, be sure to consider the ethical consequences of your choices.

Moreover, an effective clincher often refers back to the introduction, especially to the attention catcher used there. This is what Tiffany did in her speech:

> **Attention catcher:** With Thanksgiving just around the corner, many of you are probably anticipating a feast complete with a flavorful, juicy turkey as the main course. I, however, plan to bring my own addition to my family dinner—a rice pilaf, with grilled vegetables and garlic-roasted tofu.
> **Clincher:** As a vegetarian, I've discovered a world of food I never knew existed. Believe me, this Thanksgiving, my mouth will water, too, as I sit down hungrily before my rice pilaf with grilled vegetables and garlic-roasted tofu.

Notice how she referred back to the attention catcher. You might also use the clincher to issue a challenge based on the attention catcher as Marcia did:

> **Attention catcher:** Who are five of the most important women in your life? Your mother? Your sister? Your daughter? Your wife? Your best friend? Now which one of them has had or will have an eating disorder? Before you disregard my question, listen to what research tells us. One in every five women in the United States has an eating disorder.
> **Clincher:** I urge you to do your part to stop the rapid growth of the eating disorder epidemic in our country. This problem belongs to all of us and will take the efforts of all of us to solve. Perhaps then you will be able to confidently respond that not a single one of those five important women in your life has had or will have an eating disorder.

Or you might simply answer the rhetorical question posed in the attention catcher as Sonja did:

> **Attention catcher:** Have you ever packed up everything you owned, said good-bye to all of your friends, and moved to a place where you knew no one?
> **Clincher:** So, when the opportunity presents itself to pack up everything you own, say good-bye to all of your friends, and move to a place where you know no one, I hope you'll remember how my move has influenced who I am today. Perhaps then you too will accept the challenge and make the move!

A number of techniques are suited to clinchers, such as a rhetorical question, a direct question, a story, a startling statistic, or a quotation. The most effective clinchers often tie back to the attention catcher in a way that provides a sense of closure to the speech. You might answer the question you asked or issue a challenge, but you should do so in a creative and ethical way that motivates your listeners to remember your speech.

Providing a Sense of Closure

Ultimately the conclusion should provide a sense of closure. Some speakers simply stop when they finish the body of the speech. Listeners are left to tie the main ideas together themselves, something they may or may not be able to do. Sometimes speakers try to cover up this lack of closure by saying "thank you" or asking if there are any questions. Although there is nothing wrong with doing either, doing so should not replace providing a sense of closure with the conclusion to the actual speech.

Some speakers, on the other hand, don't know how or when to stop talking. They might signal that the speech is concluding with remarks like "In conclusion" or "In closing" or even "Let me end by saying." Hence, listeners expect to hear one or two final thoughts but instead get a conclusion that goes on and on and on, much like the Energizer bunny or the familiar children's song "that never ends. It goes on and on my friend."

You can avoid these problems by creating conclusions that adhere to the functions described here. Signal closure by verbal and nonverbal cues. Verbally, beginning your conclusion with a short phrase like "In conclusion" can be effective—as long as you then stick to the 5 to 10 percent time-limit rule for your remaining remarks.

Nonverbal cues may include gradually slowing down your rate and pitch as you move through the concluding remarks, perhaps stressing key words a bit more than you did during the body of the speech. Or you might incorporate pauses that allow time for each concluding point to sink in before moving on. It also might help to allow eye contact to linger a bit longer on each audience member before moving on to the next point. Or move a step or two closer to the audience. Any of these nonverbal behaviors can help provide a sense of closure. Effective public speakers incorporate several.

To be effective, then, conclusions remind listeners of the main ideas, motivate them to remember the speech, and provide a sense of closure. You can do it all quickly using three elements: thesis restatement, main point summary, and clincher.

Here is Tiffany's whole conclusion:

> **Thesis restatement:** Now you know why my vegetarian lifestyle is such an important aspect of who I am.

Notice how Tiffany merely restated her thesis in past tense. Doing so made it simple and precise.

> **Main point summary:** I talked about why I made *this choice* to be a vegetarian, how *this choice* has impacted my personal relationships, and how *this choice* continues to affect my life today.

Tiffany used parallelism to very clearly remind listeners of the main points of her speech.

> **Clincher:** As a vegetarian, I've discovered a world of food I never knew existed. Believe me, this Thanksgiving, my mouth will water, too, as I sit down hungrily before my rice pilaf with grilled vegetables and garlic-roasted tofu.

Tiffany's clincher tied back to the hypothetical and actual examples she used in her attention catcher. This time, however, she talked about how her mouth would water as she anticipated her vegetarian meal just as others' mouths would water for the traditional turkey dinner. Doing so provided a sense of closure.

Looking at the Learning Cycle

Your Introduction and Conclusion

Label where you address feeling, thinking, watching, and doing in the introduction and conclusion you developed for your next speech. Have you addressed all four? If not, revise them.

TURNING TO TECHNOLOGY

Beginning and Ending Your Speech

http://webclass.lakeland.cc.il.us/cyberspeech/beginning.htm

Read through the tips this Web site offers for beginning and ending your speech. Select one thing you might try in your next speech. Do you disagree with any of the tips? If so, which ones and why?

PRACTICING THE PROCESS

Checklist of Elements for an Effective Conclusion

❑ Thesis restatement
❑ Main point summary
❑ Clincher

SUMMARY

To write effective public speeches, take extra care to develop strong introductions and conclusions. These are crucial because of the primacy-recency effect: Listeners tend to remember best the beginning and end of what they hear. They are also crucial because public speaking is a one-time affair, so listeners need the help of being told what they will hear and what they have heard. Finally, knowing you have developed a strong introduction and conclusion will reduce speech anxiety.

Effective introductions serve five important functions: capturing audience interest, establishing rapport, establishing credibility, stating the topic, and previewing the main points. The elements of an introduction that help you do this are the attention catcher, listener relevance link, speaker credibility statement, thesis statement, and preview. The most effective introductions include all of these elements briefly, taking no more than 10 to 15 percent of the allotted speaking time.

Effective conclusions serve three important functions: reinforcing the topic and main points, motivating listeners to remember what you've said, and providing a sense of closure. The elements of a conclusion that help you do this are the thesis restatement, main point summary, and clincher. Like introductions, the most effective conclusions are brief, simple, and precise.

One of the most important aspects of effective public speaking is clear structure. The introduction, body, and conclusion combine to form the macrostructure of your speech. The introduction and conclusion are crucial because they reinforce for your listeners—and for you—the structure of the body of your speech. By applying what you've learned in this chapter—together with the lessons in Chapters 8, 10, and 11—you can create clearly organized speeches that will motivate listeners to attend to and retain your ideas.

RETURNING TO TECHNOLOGY

The *Confident Public Speaking* CD-ROM is your one-stop point of access for not just the content on the CD itself, such as Speech Interactive, but also the many other resources on the *Confident Public Speaking* Web site, Speech Builder Express, and InfoTrac College Edition. Note that this chapter's key terms and activities are among the resources available in electronic format online. Additional information is included below.

SPEECH INTERACTIVE
ON THE *CONFIDENT PUBLIC SPEAKING* CD-ROM

Speech Interactive is your link to this text's speech videos. Offering opportunities to practice critiquing speeches by students and other public speakers, these videos will help you prepare for providing effective feedback to your peers and your own speech performances.

SPEECH BUILDER EXPRESS

The Introductions and Conclusions sections of Speech Builder Express provide sequences of prompts that can help you prepare effective introductions and conclusions for your speech. You'll find the links to these sections on the main navigation menu, located on the left-hand side of the screen.

Interactive flashcards for these key terms are available on the *Confident Public Speaking* Web site. You'll find the "Flashcards" link under the resources for Chapter 9.

Actual example   205
Attention catcher   203
Clincher   214
Direct question   204
Hypothetical example   205
Listener relevance link   208
Main point summary   214
Parallelism   211

Preview   210
Primacy-recency effect   202
Rhetorical question   203
Speaker credibility statement   209
Startling fact or statistic   206
Thesis restatement   214
Thesis statement   210

ACTIVITIES

The activities below are available in electronic format on the *Confident Public Speaking* Web site. You'll find the "Activities" link under the resources for Chapter 9.

1. **Listener Relevance Links.** Identify a favorite hobby. Form a small group of four or five students. Brainstorm to come up with a listener relevance statement for each hobby.

2. **Connecting Attention Catchers and Clinchers.** Alone or in a small group, come up with an attention catcher and a related clincher for each of the following topics:
   - Peanut butter and jelly sandwiches
   - Spring break
   - Depression
   - Television violence
   - Women in the military

3. **Introductions and Conclusions.** In a small group of four or five students, make up an introduction and conclusion for one of the following topics. Be sure to include all five elements in your introduction and all three elements in your conclusion.
   - Oral hygiene
   - Aerobic exercise
   - Pet care
   - Attitude

4. **Advertisement Analysis.** In a small group of four or five students, analyze a television or magazine advertisement. Try to locate each of the components of an introduction in your advertisement:
   - Attention catcher
   - Listener relevance
   - Speaker credibility
   - Thesis
   - Preview

   When you've completed the task, share your discoveries with the rest of the class.

INFOTRAC COLLEGE EDITION ACTIVITY

Go to InfoTrac and then click on PowerTrac. Enter "Vital Speeches" in the Journal Name entry box. Select two speeches to look at. Print them out. Analyze them to discover what they used for the elements of the introduction (attention catcher, listener relevance link, speaker credibility statement, thesis statement, and preview) and the conclusion (thesis restatement, main point summary, and clincher). Which one seems most effective and why?

OUTLINING

YOUR SPEECH

REFLECTIVE QUESTIONS

1. Why might it be important to outline your public speech?

2. Do you think public speakers should create more than one kind of outline? If so, what kinds?

3. What do you think a "preparation outline" is, and why might it be important?

4. Do you think effective public speakers include delivery cues on one of their outlines? Which one?

5. Do you think it's a good idea for a speaker to put the final outline on index cards?

WHAT'S AHEAD: FOCUSING YOUR READING

Why Is Outlining Important?

The Process of Outlining Your Public Speech

I T WAS LATE IN THE EVENING, BUT Tiffany was finished. She had chosen vegetarianism as the topic of her next speech. Based on audience analysis and guidelines posed by her teacher, she decided to talk about the ways a vegetarian lifestyle affects her. She had collected lots of supporting material, including personal stories, definitions, explanations, facts, and statistics. And she had organized main points and developed an introduction and conclusion. Yet as Tiffany looked at her notes, somehow she just didn't think she was done. She was right: She hadn't finished organizing the speech. But she was ready to begin the final step in organizing its macrostructure: preparing outlines.

WHAT DO YOU THINK?

How do you think a television news anchor would feel if the news broadcast wasn't clearly organized? How would that affect you as you watched? Why?

That's outlines, not outline. Just as an effective writer prepares a series of rough drafts on the way to completing a final manuscript, so does an effective public speaker develop a series of outlines on the way to preparing the final speech. **Outlining** is a systematic process of placing ideas in a recognizable pattern that listeners can easily follow. This chapter begins by discussing why outlining is so important. Then it gives a step-by-step guide to the process of developing a preparation outline, a formal outline, and a speaking outline.

TURNING TO TECHNOLOGY

The Importance of Outlining beyond the Classroom

http://www.school-for-champions.com/writing/outlining.htm

This Web site explains why outlining is essential in all creative activities, not just for classroom public speeches. Read the article and take the mini quiz. Which argument is most compelling to you? Why?

WHY IS OUTLINING IMPORTANT?

Outlining is important for four reasons:

- It places content into a recognizable pattern for listeners to follow.
- It allows flexibility to adjust the message as you speak.
- It provides an opportunity for you to critique your speech.
- It can reduce public speaking anxiety and bolster ethos.

Arranging Your Ideas within a Recognizable Pattern

Outlining arranges ideas so that listeners can follow. Failing to do so increases the chance of rambling as you speak. Even if you don't ramble, listeners may think you are if they cannot see a logical order to the information you provide. Research suggests that organization is the most important factor in determining how well listeners understand a speech (Thompson, 1960).

Over time, outlining practice improves the ability to think on your feet about organization. As a result, you'll discover it takes less time to prepare outlines and you'll need fewer notes to speak from.

In regard to the learning cycle, outlining addresses the second stage (watching and thinking)—that is, putting a wide range of information into concise, logical form. If you fail to outline, you will fail to reach listeners fully because you won't address this stage. In addition, different parts of the outline address the various stages.

Looking at the Learning Cycle

Outlining

- *Stage 1:* Subpoints and sub-subpoints
- *Stage 2:* Overall outline macrostructure
- *Stage 3:* Thesis, internal summaries, conclusion
- *Stage 4:* Attention catcher, creative microstructure, clincher

Providing Flexibility As You Speak

It is more effective to outline a speech than to write it out word for word, because an outline provides some flexibility as you speak. You can take more time to develop an idea if listeners seem confused, or move more quickly when listeners seem to have a firm grasp of what you mean. Thus speaking from an outline is better than reading from a manuscript (which might also follow a recognizable pattern) because it more fully respects the role listeners play in the communication transaction. Also, with an outline you'll be more likely to communicate using a conversational style instead of sounding memorized, mechanical, or like you're reading.

WHAT DO YOU THINK?
Consider a speaker you have heard recently. Did the speaker seem to be talking with you or reading to you? How did this affect the speaker's success or failure in communicating to you? Why?

Providing an Opportunity to Critique Your Speech

Outlining allows you to organize your ideas visually, and then add, delete, regroup, expand, or condense them where necessary. Once you see what you've got, you can self-critique by asking questions like: Am I trying to cover too much material under one main point? Am I repeating things my audience already knows? Does the supporting material make sense where I've placed it under the main points? Is the amount of information included under each main point fairly balanced—will I spend a similar amount of time discussing each? Have I included a listener relevance link for each main point? Do I address each stage in the learning cycle somewhere in my speech? Once you can visually see what you've got, you can make adjustments that will improve the effectiveness of the speech.

Reducing Public Speaking Anxiety and Bolstering Ethos

One of the primary reasons for public speaking anxiety stems from a fear of failure, the concern that listeners won't understand what you are trying to say. Outlining can reduce negative self-talk rooted in a fear of failure because it helps you make sure that your ideas are arranged logically, that supporting material under each main point makes sense, and that main points are balanced. Moreover, an outline is shorter than a complete manuscript, so it's easier to keep your place when referring to it while speaking. In essence, outlining gives you confidence that you have a thorough and well-ordered speech. It thus enhances your ethos because listeners perceive you as more credible if your speech is organized (Sharp & McClung, 1966).

THE PROCESS OF OUTLINING
YOUR PUBLIC SPEECH

Outlining consists of three phases, each ending with the completion of a particular type of outline. Phase 1 leads to the preparation outline, Phase 2 to the formal outline, and Phase 3 to the speaking outline.

Your Preparation Outline

A **preparation outline** is a working rough draft of speech ideas. It may or may not be typed, but if it is, avoid the tendency to let it pass as the formal outline just because it already looks good. You will need to critique and revise the preparation outline several times before moving on to a typed formal outline. The revision process has six steps.

Steps 1, 2, and 3

You actually began working on a preparation outline and the six-step process of putting it together when selecting and narrowing a topic (Chapter 5), organizing main ideas (Chapter 8), and creating an introduction and conclusion (Chapter 9). The first step of the preparation outline is creating a thesis statement and main points. Developing the body of the speech by adding supporting material to each main point is Step 2. Step 3 is expanding the preparation outline by jotting down ideas for developing each element of the introduction and conclusion. At this point, only three steps remain: placing content into standard outline format (Step 4), integrating internal reference citations and a reference list (Step 5), and critiquing the outline for balance (Step 6).

Step 4

The fourth step is to place ideas into a proper outline form, most commonly by using the alphanumeric system. Roman numerals are used to identify major points; then a consistent pattern of letters and numbers follows beneath the major points. Let's break this down.

First, label the introduction, body, and conclusion in the far left margin:

Introduction

Body

Conclusion

Second, use a Roman numeral and label for each element in the introduction and conclusion, as well as for each main point in the speech body. This ensures an introduction and a conclusion that accomplish all their purposes (Chapter 9). The Roman numerals are also placed at the far left margin:

Introduction

  I. Attention catcher:

  II. Listener relevance link:

  III. Speaker credibility statement:

  IV. Thesis statement:

  V. Preview:

Body

I. First main point:

II. Second main point:

III. Third main point:

Conclusion

I. Thesis restatement:

II. Main point summary:

III. Clincher:

Third, add subpoints under each main point by using capital letters. The capital letters are indented five spaces from the left margin or aligned with the first letter of the label directly above it. Subpoints typically consist of supporting material. For a speech that tells a chronological story, for example, you might offer an extended example for each subpoint. Sometimes there may be subpoints of subpoints; if so, use Arabic numbers:

Body

I. First main point:

    A. Subpoint:

        1. Sub-subpoint (if used):

        2. Sub-subpoint (if used):

    B. Subpoint:

        1. Sub-subpoint (if used):

        2. Sub-subpoint (if used):

II. Second main point:

    A. Subpoint:

        1. Sub-subpoint (if used):

        2. Sub-subpoint (if used):

    B. Subpoint:

        1. Sub-subpoint (if used):

"He has the rough outline of a good body but none of the details."

    2. Sub-subpoint (if used):

  III. Third main point:

    A. Subpoint:

      1. Sub-subpoint (if used):

      2. Sub-subpoint (if used):

    B. Subpoint:

      1. Sub-subpoint (if used):

      2. Sub-subpoint (if used):

Finally, add transition statements between main points. Align each transition label with the far left margin, since they are not actually part of the body content but rather the structural glue that holds the main points together. Including transitions on the outline is optional but increases the likelihood that you'll remember to use them as you speak:

Body

  I. First main point:

    A. Subpoint:

      1. Sub-subpoint (if used):

      2. Sub-subpoint (if used):

    B. Subpoint:

      1. Sub-subpoint (if used):

      2. Sub-subpoint (if used):

Transition

  II. Second main point:

    A. Subpoint:

      1. Sub-subpoint (if used):

      2. Sub-subpoint (if used):

    B. Subpoint:

      1. Sub-subpoint (if used):

      2. Sub-subpoint (if used):

Transition

  III. Third main point:

    A. Subpoint:

      1. Sub-subpoint (if used):

      2. Sub-subpoint (if used):

    B. Subpoint:

      1. Sub-subpoint (if used):

      2. Sub-subpoint (if used):

Step 5

After arranging ideas into the standard outline form, integrate external source citations. Read through the outline once again, this time adding internal reference citations where appropriate. As you do, place the source citations in the reference list as well. This way, you'll be less likely to inadvertently leave out a source when typing the formal outline. A reference list is an alphabetical listing of the complete source citations for every external source on which the speech is drawn. Use the format required by your instructor; most require either APA or MLA style. Chapter 7 explains how to write a complete bibliographic citation.

TURNING TO TECHNOLOGY

Creating Your Reference List

http://www.stylewizard.com

This Web site may help you create a reference list, as it provides Wizards to assist in using several different style guides including APA and MLA.

Step 6

The final step in developing a preparation outline is to critique and revise it for balance. This requires examining and revising the outline several times.

Consider Sources. Begin by examining external sources. Are they evenly distributed throughout the speech? If not, where might additional ones be needed? Also consider whether you rely too heavily on one or two resources and adjust the balance if needed, perhaps by conducting additional research to find more sources. When Tiffany examined her preparation outline, she realized that her third main point (disadvantages and advantages) relied only on personal experiences and beliefs. She went back to the library to find articles in reputable publications to support her beliefs that low-fat diets are healthy and that vegetables cost less than meat.

WHAT DO YOU THINK?
Consider a newspaper story written by the Associated Press versus a letter to the editor on the same topic. Or consider a news story published in a magazine like *Newsweek* or *Time* compared to one published in a tabloid like the *National Enquirer* or the *Globe*. Which stories would you be more likely to believe and what role might source credibility play in your decision?

PRACTICING THE PROCESS

Checklist for Choosing the Best Sources for Your Speech

- ❑ Do you rely on a variety of different sources?
- ❑ Do you rely too heavily on one or two of them?
- ❑ Are your external sources evenly distributed among your main points?
- ❑ Is there a main point that could use an additional external source?

Identify Listener Relevance Links. Now go through the outline to identify listener relevance links under each main point. A **listener relevance link** is a statement that reveals how and why the ideas offered might benefit listeners, such as how the topic is something they will experience someday. As you find listener relevance in the outline, label it. If you can't find it for a particular point, add it. Remember, these links maintain listeners' interest. Tiffany provided listener relevance for her first main point by talking about how her childhood was probably similar to that of many of her classmates. In her second main point, she talked about how family conflicts are normal for young adults learning to separate from older family members to begin making their own decisions. And for the third main point, she alluded to the menu options seen in popular restaurant chains.

PRACTICING THE PROCESS

Ensuring Listener Relevance

Identify and label listener relevance for each main point of your speech. If you can't find listener relevance for a point, come up with a statement to help listeners see how that point might relate to them.

Examine Learning Styles. Next, identify in the outline the points where you address different stages on the learning cycle. The simplest way is by labeling points and subpoints as they appeal to the dimensions of watching, thinking, doing, or feeling. If you discover that a stage was missed, integrate something to address it. Tiffany, for example, realized she needed something visual in her presentation, so she added a visual aid depicting one of her favorite vegetarian recipes. She also included facts and statistics about healthy eating habits from the American Dietetic Association to address the thinking dimension and a visual aid of the vegetarian food pyramid to address watching. An application, action plan, or activity may be needed to address the doing dimension, or personal stories or testimonials for the feeling dimension. Tiffany addressed these with the step-by-step plan she engaged in to adjust her eating habits (doing) and sharing a story about her pet cow, who eventually became a steak on her plate (feeling).

"Don't you see—we could all be free-range!"

© The New Yorker Collection 1995 Al Ross from cartoonbank.com. All Rights Reserved.

When Tiffany realized that her speech was missing a visual component, she added a photo of a favorite vegetarian dish.

Revising the outline to address the entire learning cycle improves presentation effectiveness by appealing to all preferred learning styles. This gives everyone their best chance to retain your message.

Looking at the Learning Cycle

Assessing Your Outline

- Go through the outline for your speech and label where you address feeling, watching, thinking, and doing.
- Are any dimensions missing or inadequately addressed? If so, add elements to account for them.

Check Supporting Material. Go through the outline one more time to check the balance of supporting material under each main point. If any main point offers one subpoint, it must also include a second; you cannot have an A without a B or a 1 without a 2, and so forth. If you have no second point, revise the outline to include all the information within the main point. Tiffany did so for her second main point. She added a subpoint under her discussion about how her immediate family felt betrayed by going on to talk about the concerns her grandparents expressed about her becoming anemic.

Check for Symmetry. Does the introduction or conclusion take too much time? Is about the same amount of time spent on developing each main point? If not, you might need to delete from or add to them. Tiffany timed her introduction and found that it took more than a minute of her four- to six-minute speech. So she removed the video she had originally planned to show as an attention catcher and replaced it with a photograph transferred to an overhead transparency.

Checkpoints for Achieving Symmetry

Keeping in mind the time constraints for your speech, ensure that:

- ❏ The introduction and conclusion seem neither too short nor too long.
- ❏ The treatment of each main point seems similar in length.

Add a Title.　This isn't mandatory, but if you apply a title make it brief, no more than three to five words. Make sure it captures the essence of the speech, and doesn't mislead the reader about the focus of your speech. As with the attention catcher, use figurative language that might entice the reader to want to know more. Tiffany, for example, chose the title "Meat-Free and Me."

Once you have finished critiquing and revising according to the procedure just described, the preparation outline is complete. It is comparable to the rough draft of a written composition but is not the final product. It contains editorial comments regarding listener relevance, learning style stages, and presentational aids. All the macrostructural elements are included, although rarely as complete sentences. In addition, internal reference citations and a reference list are included so you remember which pieces of evidence came from which sources.

Figure 10.1 provides a completed preparation outline for Tiffany's speech on vegetarianism. A preparation outline is crucial because it is the working draft, which is usually critiqued and revised several times before your ideas are thoroughly covered and logically ordered.

What is Tiffany's title? Is it brief? Does it capture the essence of her speech?

Notice how Tiffany includes her external sources on the outline where she is drawing from them. In the introduction, she references the American Dietetic Association and includes the Web address in parentheses. Look for her internal references to the book *Diet for a New America* and to the *Vegetarian Times* under her first main point. List the other internal citations she provides. Now, look at her reference list. Are they all included? Which style guide does she use?

MEAT-FREE AND ME

—Tiffany Mindt

Introduction

I. ***Attention catcher:*** Talk about anticipating typical Thanksgiving food and what I will eat (feeling) (maybe show a slide or photograph for watching).

II. ***Listener relevance link:*** Eating habits are changing across the country for health reasons. Cite the American Dietetic Association (ADA) (www.eatright.org) (thinking).

III. ***Speaker credibility statement:*** I've been a vegetarian for five years now.

IV. ***Thesis statement:*** Living a vegetarian lifestyle is an important aspect of who I am today.

V. ***Preview:*** How I made this choice, family issues as a result, ways this choice affects my life today.

Body

I. ***First main point:*** How I made this choice.

    A. ***Subpoint:*** Personal childhood experiences not unlike yours (listener relevance), story about my pet cow Charlie (feeling) and picture (watching).

B. **Subpoint:** Book I read as a young adult thanks to my friend Amy: *Diet for a New America* (thinking).

C. **Subpoint:** Steps I went through to adjust my eating habits and still be healthy, *Vegetarian Times*, Jan. 1997 (thinking and doing).

Transition: The decision to become a vegetarian not only affected my own life, it also created some interesting issues within my family.

II. **Second main point:** Family conflicts (listener relevance—young adults separating from family to make our own decisions).

A. **Subpoint:** Family felt betrayed.

1. **Sub-subpoint:** My rancher father didn't understand (feeling).

2. **Sub-subpoint:** Grandparents worried I would become anemic (feeling); myths listed in *Tufts University Health and Nutrition Letter*, April 1998 (thinking).

B. **Subpoint:** Family learned more about vegetarianism.

1. **Sub-subpoint:** Some books and articles I've shared with them (*Vegetarian Times*, April 1999; *Runners World*, April 1997; *Dr. Spock's Baby and Child Care*, 1998) (thinking).

2. *Better Homes and Gardens*, June 1996 (thinking); presentational aid (watching).

3. **Sub-subpoint:** Grandma now prepares vegetarian dishes for me when I visit (feeling); show a couple of recipes to the audience on a transparency (watching and doing) (recipes in *Vegetarian Times*, Jan. 1999).

Transition: I'm glad my family has adjusted to my choice to be a vegetarian; however, this choice continues to affect my life today.

III. **Third main point:** I deal daily with both disadvantages and advantages as a result of this choice.

A. **Subpoint:** Disadvantages.

1. **Sub-subpoint:** Limited choices at restaurants.

a. **Sub-sub-subpoint:** Menu options from popular restaurant chains (listener relevance and thinking); show items on a transparency (watching).

b. **Sub-sub-subpoint:** Personal story from Indianapolis (feeling).

2. **Sub-subpoint:** Limited choices at grocery stores.

B. **Subpoint:** Advantages.

1. **Sub-subpoint:** Low-fat diet is good for you and vegetables are naturally low in fat.

2. **Sub-subpoint:** Vegetables cost less than meat; *Vegetarian Times*, April 1999 (thinking).

3. **Sub-subpoint:** Personal satisfaction of living a lifestyle that matches my beliefs (feeling).

Transition: Although being a vegetarian is not always easy, it is worth the struggle because it is true to who I am.

(continued)

What are Tiffany's listener relevance links for each main point? Do they seem effective? Why or why not? If not, what could she say to make them more effective?

How many times does Tiffany do something to address each dimension of the learning cycle? Should she do more to address one of them? If so, which one and how?

What types of supporting material does Tiffany use? Does she rely too heavily on one type (that is, facts, statistics, definitions, explanations, examples, narratives, etc.)? If so, which type and what might she replace with what and where?

Does Tiffany's outline appear symmetrical? Why or why not?

Figure 10.1 Sample preparation outline

Is Tiffany's conclusion effective? How does her clincher tie back to her introduction?

Conclusion

I. **Thesis restatement:** This afternoon, I discussed why a vegetarian lifestyle is important to who I am.

II. **Main point summary:** How I made this choice, family issues, and impact on my life today.

III. **Clincher:** Talk about Thanksgiving dinner again to tie back to attention catcher.

References

American Dietetic Association. (2003). Vegetarian diets. Retrieved October 17, 2003, from http://www.eatright.org/Public/GovernmentAffairs/92_17084.cfm

Applegate, L. (1997, April). Vegetable matter. *Runner's World, 32*, 26–27.

Beard, C. H. (1997, January). Become a vegetarian in 5 easy steps. *Vegetarian Times, 223*, 74–79.

Dworkin, N. (1999, April). 22 reasons to go vegetarian right now. *Vegetarian Times*, 90–97.

Farell-Kingsley, K. (1999, January). Low in fat, high in flavor. *Vegetarian Times*, 41.

Friedman School of Nutrition Science and Policy. (1998, April). Clearing up common misconceptions about vegetarianism. *Tufts University Health and Nutrition Letter, 16*, 4–6.

Hubbard, M. (1996, June). Scaling the vegetarian pyramid. *Better Homes and Gardens*, 96–98.

Robbins, J. (1998). *Diet for a new America* (2nd ed.). Tiburon, CA: H. J. Kramer.

Spock, B. (1998). *Dr. Spock's baby and child care* (7th ed.). New York: Pocket Books.

What kinds of sources does Tiffany rely on? Do they seem credible and ethical for her topic? Does she rely too heavily on any source? If so, which one(s) and why?

TURNING TO TECHNOLOGY

Developing Your Outline

http://owl.english.purdue.edu/handouts/general/gl_outlin.html

This Web page, hosted by the Purdue University Online Writing Lab, provides steps for writing effective outlines and a sample outline. Does the site propose any suggestions you hadn't considered before? Does it leave any out? If so, what are they? What will you do in your outlines? Why?

Student Workbook

Read through the speech assignment in Chapter 3 of the workbook. Create your preparation outline. Be sure to label listener relevance links and learning cycle dimensions.

Your Formal Outline

Once you've developed, critiqued, and revised the preparation outline to your satisfaction, translate this working draft into a formal outline. If the preparation outline is thorough, the formal outline is fairly easy to prepare. A **formal outline** is a typed outline that labels and applies all the macrostructural elements in the speech using complete sentences. Here you hone language and style choices, which is the focus of Chapter 11. This version also includes a speech title, your name, and internal reference citations, as well as a complete reference list. The reference list should begin on a separate page immediately following the formal outline and include a title (that is,

WHAT DO YOU THINK?

What problems might you encounter if you deliver your speech using a formal outline as your notes? Why? How might this impact your effectiveness?

Works Cited, References, Bibliography) as dictated by the style used (refer to Chapter 7). Labels for learning style and listener relevance are not necessary on the formal outline, although you may include them. The formal outline is like the final draft of a written composition—that is, a reader could just as easily use it to develop a thorough manuscript as you can use it to deliver your speech. Figure 10.2 shows Tiffany's formal outline. Other examples of formal outlines are in Chapters 3 and 14 and on the *Confident Public Speaking* Web site.

MEAT-FREE AND ME

—Tiffany Mindt

Introduction

I. ***Attention catcher:*** With Thanksgiving just around the corner, many of you are probably anticipating a feast complete with a flavorful, juicy turkey as the main course. I, however, plan to bring my own addition to my family dinner—a rice pilaf, with grilled vegetables and garlic-roasted tofu.

II. ***Listener relevance link:*** Although a diet rich in eggs and meat was once the norm in our country, more and more Americans are choosing a vegetarian lifestyle, and many are doing so for health reasons. In fact, the American Dietetic Association, also known as the ADA, maintains that vegetarianism is not only healthful and adequate, but also helps in the prevention and treatment of certain diseases (www.eatright.org).

III. ***Speaker credibility statement:*** About five years ago, I made a decision to stop eating meat, which has changed my life in several ways.

IV. ***Thesis statement:*** Living a vegetarian lifestyle is an important aspect of who I am today.

V. ***Preview:*** I'll talk specifically about how I made this choice to live meat-free. Next, I'll share some of the family issues that arose as a result of this choice. Finally, I'll discuss some of the ways this choice affects my life today.

Body

I. ***First main point:*** I made this choice for several reasons.

A. ***Subpoint:*** One reason comes from my childhood. Many of my childhood experiences are probably similar to yours. I lived on a ranch with my family and my many pets. One of my pets was my cow, Charlie. His mother died giving birth to him, so I had to feed him with a bottle. As you can probably guess, Charlie and I became very close friends. We had lots of fun together. That is, until one day when my pet Charlie became the steak on my plate.

B. ***Subpoint:*** Another reason I made this choice comes from what I learned in a book I was given by my friend Amy. In *Diet for a New America,* author John Robbins taught me that eating meat is not as "healthy" as we've been led to believe, nor is meat an efficient food source.

C. ***Subpoint:*** Finally, I was able to make this choice because I learned a simple five-step method to adjust my eating habits: (1) chart what you eat right now,

(continued)

Notice how Tiffany describes Thanksgiving in her attention catcher as a "feast" complete with "flavorful, juicy turkey." How does this appeal to your senses? How does the word picture change for you when she brings up "rice pilaf, with grilled vegetables and garlic-roasted tofu"? Identify another place where Tiffany uses vivid language or descriptions to make her speech more memorable. Does it work for you? Why or why not?

Notice how Tiffany uses complete sentences in this outline. How does that help or hurt you as a reader? How might it help or hurt you as a listener if she were to read these sentences word for word in her speech?

Notice how Tiffany's childhood story serves as supporting material and a listener relevance link, and also appeals to the feeling dimension of the learning cycle.

Figure 10.2   Sample student formal outline

(2) categorize your diet, (3) rethink the categories, (4) add new foods, and (5) make the change. (Christine Beard, *Become a Vegetarian in 5 Easy Steps*, 1997).

Transition: The decision to become a vegetarian not only affected my own life, it also created some interesting issues within my family.

II. **Second main point:** I decided to become a vegetarian about the same time I moved away from home to attend college. This was tough on my family, partly because we were experiencing a number of other "growing pains" associated with my new role as an adult member of the family. These kinds of conflicts are pretty common. Perhaps you can relate.

> A. **Subpoint:** My family felt I had betrayed them.
>> 1. **Sub-subpoint:** My father, who was a rancher by trade, didn't understand.
>> 2. **Sub-subpoint:** My grandparents tried to understand, but worried I would become anemic. They believed several myths about vegetarianism ("Clearing Up Common Misconceptions," 1998).
> B. **Subpoint:** Eventually, my family learned more about vegetarianism.
>> 1. **Sub-subpoint:** Learning about the vegetarian food pyramid helped (Hubbard, 1996).
>> 2. **Sub-subpoint:** Since my family respects Dr. Benjamin Spock, reading about his fervent support of a vegetarian diet also helped (Spock, 1998).
>> 3. **Sub-subpoint:** My grandma learned how to prepare several vegetarian dishes (Farell-Kingsley, 1999).

Transition: I'm glad my family has adjusted to my choice to be a vegetarian; however, this choice continues to affect my life today.

III. **Third main point:** I deal daily with both disadvantages and advantages as a result of this choice.

> A. **Subpoint:** There are some disadvantages related to being a vegetarian.
>> 1. **Sub-subpoint:** Sometimes, my options are limited at restaurants.
>>> a. **Sub-sub-subpoint:** My options at places like McDonald's or Burger King are limited to a garden salad and a soda.
>>> b. **Sub-sub-subpoint:** My options at most formal restaurants are also pretty limited (Cole, 1999). Let me tell you a personal story about dining in Indianapolis with friends.
>> 2. **Sub-subpoint:** Although it is certainly getting better, my choices are somewhat limited at grocery stores as well.
> B. **Subpoint:** There are some definite advantages to being a vegetarian, advantages that—for me—outweigh the disadvantages.
>> 1. **Sub-subpoint:** A low-fat diet is good for you and vegetables are naturally low in fat.
>> 2. **Sub-subpoint:** Vegetables cost less than meat (Dworkin, 1999).
>> 3. **Sub-subpoint:** I feel a sense of personal satisfaction knowing that my lifestyle as a vegetarian matches my beliefs.

Transition: Although being a vegetarian is not always easy, it is worth the struggle because it is true to who I am.

Notice how Tiffany's transition statements verbally tie the main point she has just completed to the upcoming point to create a fluent sense of forward motion.

Notice how Tiffany's formal outline uses internal references within the text to enhance credibility and avoid plagiarism.

Consider Tiffany's three main points. What organizational pattern does she use? How does this pattern help sustain listener attention?

Conclusion

I. ***Thesis restatement:*** Now you know why a vegetarian lifestyle is such an important aspect of who I am.

II. ***Main point summary:*** I talked about why I made this choice, how this choice has impacted my personal relationships, and how this choice continues to affect my life today.

III. ***Clincher:*** As a vegetarian, I've discovered a world of food I never knew existed. Believe me, this Thanksgiving, my mouth will water, too, as I sit down hungrily before my rice pilaf with grilled vegetables and garlic-roasted tofu!

References

American Dietetic Association. (2003). Vegetarian diets. Retrieved October 17, 2003, from http://www.eatright.org/Public/GovernmentAffairs/92_17084.cfm

Applegate, L. (1997, April). Vegetable matter. *Runner's World, 32,* 26–27.

Beard, C. H. (1997, January). Become a vegetarian in 5 easy steps. *Vegetarian Times, 223,* 74–79.

Dworkin, N. (1999, April). 22 reasons to go vegetarian right now. *Vegetarian Times,* 90–97.

Farell-Kingsley, K. (1999, January). Low in fat, high in flavor. *Vegetarian Times,* 41.

Friedman School of Nutrition Science and Policy. (1998, April). Clearing up common misconceptions about vegetarianism. *Tufts University Health and Nutrition Letter, 16,* 4–6.

Hubbard, M. (1996, June). Scaling the vegetarian pyramid. *Better Homes and Gardens,* 96–98.

Robbins, J. (1998). *Diet for a new America* (2nd ed.). Tiburon, CA: H. J. Kramer.

Spock, B. (1998). *Dr. Spock's baby and child care* (7th ed.). New York: Pocket Books.

> Look at Tiffany's reference list. She used APA style (5th edition). Notice how this style does not use the first names of authors. Does anything else surprise you about what is or is not included in a reference list citation using APA?

> Notice that three of Tiffany's references are the same magazine, *Vegetarian Times.* Do you think this is effective for Tiffany? Why or why not?

PRACTICING THE PROCESS

Guidelines for Completing Your Formal Outline

Use your preparation outline to create a formal outline for your next speech. Be sure to:

- Use complete sentences.
- Include internal source citations throughout
- Create a reference list on a clean page after the formal outline using an accepted style guide.
- Label learning styles and listener relevance (optional).

Your Speaking Outline

A **speaking outline** is a condensed outline used solely as a memory aid when presenting the speech. It is similar to the preparation and formal outlines in certain ways, but it is unique.

Like the preparation outline, the speaking outline uses key words and phrases rather than complete sentences. The formal outline helps shape the language you'll use to express ideas (Chapter 11). To help you maintain a conversational style, however, the speaking outline should include only brief notes to jog your memory. The only exceptions have to do with the attention catcher and clincher, as well as direct quotations used as supporting material. Because the opening and closing statements are crucial to establishing your initial and terminal credibility, write them out word-for-word, or commit them to memory, or both (Beatty, 1988). This can also reduce the initial anxiety you might feel at the outset of speech delivery. Since you want to be accurate in restating direct quotations, write them out word-for-word as well. Like the preparation outline, the speaking outline includes notes about when and where to share presentational aids to ensure that you'll remember to use them during the speech. Figure 10.3 is Tiffany's speaking outline for "Meat-Free and Me."

Like the formal outline, the speaking outline includes internal references throughout. These are needed in the speaking notes so you remember to cite them orally during the presentation, avoiding plagiarism and enhancing ethos. The information in the speaking outline might differ somewhat from that in the formal outline. For example, if a magazine or newspaper is well known and credible, and if the author is merely reporting rather than interpreting data, you might just cite the magazine or newspaper title orally and omit the author. Citing both is usually better, however, as is citing the credentials of an otherwise unfamiliar author.

The speaking outline uses a format similar to the formal outline. This helps you see instantly where you are in the speech as you present it. Because you look only momentarily at the notes while speaking, you don't want to spend much time finding your place.

Speaking outlines differ from preparation and formal outlines in four important ways. First, they often use abbreviations to keep the outline brief. Tiffany used ADA on her speaking outline because she knew it stood for American Dietetic Association. As long as you know what the abbreviation stands for and use the complete term when you speak, abbreviations are fine in a speaking outline.

Second, speaking outlines include delivery cues that remind you *what* you plan to say and *how* you plan to say it. You might jot down words like "PAUSE," "SLOW DOWN," "GET LOUDER," "DISPLAY THE VISUAL AID," or "PLAY THE VIDEO NOW" at key places. Rather than words as reminders, you might try a symbol system or color coding. For example, a series of slash marks (/ / /) could indicate pauses of various lengths. "Greater than" and "less than" symbols could be reminders to get louder (>) or softer (<). A series of arrows could remind you to gradually increase your rate (→→→→), and a series of ellipsis points could remind you to gradually slow down (. . .). Likewise, you could underline key words or phrases to stress or mark them with a highlighter. Delivery cues remind you how to deliver the speech effectively, whether you are a beginning speaker or a professional.

Third, the speaking outline includes actual supporting material you plan to cite. Quotations, statistics, and specific definitions or explanations are often provided in detail here so you don't inadvertently misrepresent information.

Fourth, the speaking outline is usually typed or printed in large neat letters on one side of a few three-by-five-inch or four-by-six-inch index cards. The number of cards used depends on the length of the speech. Index cards are better than sheets of paper because they are smaller and stiffer, and thus less distracting to listeners. Also, you can hold them in one hand, leaving the other hand free to gesture. Sometimes, particularly when using a lectern, you may use paper for the speaking outline, but the same general rules apply: Use large type and a simple font, triple spacing, and clearly numbered pages. Simply slide each sheet of paper to the side as you finish with it.

Card 1:

INTRO   1

PAUSE! (IN THE EYE)

I. WITH THANKSGIVING ...

II. EGGS, MEAT, NORM ... CHOOSING A **VEGETARIAN** LIFESTYLE
FOR HEALTH REASONS ... ADA MAINTAINS THAT "VEGETARIANISM IS NOT ONLY
HEALTHFUL AND ADEQUATE, BUT ALSO HELPS IN THE **PREVENTION** OF
CERTAIN DISEASES." //

III. 5 YEARS AGO

IV. VEGETARIAN WHO I AM TODAY

V. **PREVIEW!!!**   HOW I MADE, ///FAMILY   ISSUES, ///
AFFECTS MY LIFE TODAY ///

Notice Tiffany does not write out her attention catcher. Does this adhere to the chapter suggestions? Do you suppose she has committed it to memory?

Card 2:

         2

I. SEVERAL REASONS

       →   →

   A. CHILDHOOD EXPERIENCES, PETS, PET COW CHARLIE (☺)
      LOTS OF FUN. BECAME THE STEAK / ON MY PLATE //

   B. DIET FOR A NEW AMERICA JOHN ROBBINS TAUGHT ME
      NOT HEALTHY AND NOT EFFICIENT FOOD SOURCE

   C. SIMPLE / FIVE-STEP METHOD CHRISTINE BEARD, AUTHOR OF
      BECOME A VEGETARIAN IN FIVE EASY STEPS

           (SHOW VISUAL AID !)

TRANSITION: THE DECISION VEGETARIAN NOT ONLY AFFECTED
MY OWN LIFE, ALSO MY FAMILY.

Notice the delivery cues Tiffany offers herself to pause, look listeners in the eye, show visual aids, speed up or slow down, and smile. Should she have reminded herself when to conceal her visual aids as well? Why or why not?

Card 3:

         3

II. DECISION, COLLEGE, GROWING PAINS, CONFLICTS AS ADULT

   A. FAMILY FELT BETRAYED   (EYE CONTACT!!)

     1. DAD, RANCHER

     2. GRANDPARENTS ... ANEMIC.   BELIEVED THE MYTHS
       APRIL 1998 TUFTS UNIVERSITY HEALTH AND NUTRITION LETTER
      (SHOW AID)

   B. FAMILY LEARNED

     1. VEGETARIAN FOOD PYRAMID (SHOW AID)

     2. DR. SPOCK 1998 EDITION OF DR. SPOCK'S BABY AND CHILD CARE:
      // "RAISING YOUR KIDS VEGETARIAN IS THE BEST THING
      YOU'LL EVER DO FOR THEM." ///

Notice that Tiffany's outline format is the same as the format of her formal outline. This will help her find her place quickly and maintain more eye contact with her audience. Why is this a good idea?

Figure 10.3 Sample student speaking outline

Notice that Tiffany used only key words and phrases. How might this help her eye contact, conversational style, and ethos? Why?

Look at Tiffany's fifth index card. Notice how she wrote out her direct quotations word for word. Why is this a good idea?

Notice that Tiffany wrote out her clincher word-for-word. Based on what you've learned in the chapter, why is this a good idea?

4

    3. GRANDMA LEARNED RECIPES (SHOW AID: RECIPE FOR
       TAMALE PIE FROM JAN 99 <u>VEGETARIAN TIMES</u> MAGAZINE.)

TRANSITION: // I'M GLAD MY FAMILY HAS ADJUSTED TO MY CHOICE,
CONTINUES TO AFFECT MY LIFE TODAY.

III. DISADVANTAGES AND ADVANTAGES
   A. DISADVANTAGES
     1. LIMITED AT RESTAURANT OPTIONS
      FAST FOOD AND FORMAL DINING, (INDIANAPOLIS)
     2. GROCERY STORE LIMITATIONS

5

   B. ADVANTAGES
     1. LOW-FAT DIET = HEALTH MARION NESTLE, CHAIR, NUTRITION DEPT. AT NYU,
      SAYS "THERE'S NO QUESTION THAT LARGELY VEGETARIAN DIETS ARE
      AS HEALTHY AS YOU CAN GET" WALTER WILLETT, CHAIR, NUTRITION
      DEPT., HARVARD SCHOOL PUBLIC HEALTH "A DIET RICH IN FRUITS &
      VEGETABLES PLAYS A ROLE IN REDUCING THE RISK OF ALL THE
      MAJOR CAUSES OF ILLNESS AND DEATH" (NUTRITION ACTION
      NEWSLETTER, OCT. 1996).
     2. VEGGIES COST LESS THAN MEAT. ACC. TO NORINE DWORKIN, APRIL 1999
      VEGETARIAN TIMES "REPLACING MEAT WITH VEGETABLES AND FRUITS
      IS ESTIMATED TO CUT FOOD BILLS BY AN AVERAGE OF // $4,000 //
      A YEAR."
     3. PERSONAL SATISFACTION, <u>NOT EASY</u>, <u>WORTH</u> THE STRUGGLE ///

CONCLUSION   (PAUSE—EYE CONTACT—SLOW!!)   6
   I. NOW YOU KNOW <u>WHY</u> A VEGETARIAN LIFESTYLE IS SO IMPORTANT TO WHO I AM,

   II. WHY I MADE <u>THIS CHOICE</u> //

      HOW THIS CHOICE HAS IMPACTED MY PERSONAL RELATIONSHIPS //

      AND HOW <u>THIS CHOICE</u> CONTINUES TO AFFECT MY LIFE TODAY. ///
   III. AS A VEGETARIAN, I'VE DISCOVERED A WORLD OF FOOD I NEVER KNEW
      EXISTED // (SMILE) BELIEVE ME (SMILE)_THIS THANKSGIVING / MY MOUTH WILL
      WATER TOO, AS I SIT DOWN HUNGRILY BEFORE MY RICE PILAF WITH GRILLED
      VEGETABLES AND GARLIC ROASTED TOFU.
     (PAUSE EYE CONTACT SMILE!)

Tips for Preparing Your Speaking Outline

- Unless you're using a lectern, use three-by-five-inch or four-by-six-inch index cards.
- Number your cards or pages.
- Use an outline format.
- Use abbreviations, key words, and brief phrases.
- Type or print in large, neat letters.
- Write out your attention catcher and clincher and commit them to memory.
- Write out quotations, statistics, definitions.
- Include internal references.
- Include delivery cues.

Tiffany's Speech

Go to Speech Interactive on your *Confident Public Speaking* CD-ROM. Click on Tiffany's speech. Watch her deliver her speech while you follow along with her outlines in this chapter.

- Did she leave anything out?
- Did she add anything?
- Did she adhere to the delivery cues on her speaking outline?
- How successful was she in following her outline and what role did that play in your understanding of her message? In her ethos? In how well you'll remember her speech? Why?

SUMMARY

Outlining is important to a public speech for four primary reasons: It places content into a recognizable pattern for listeners to follow; allows flexibility to adjust the message as you speak; provides an opportunity for you to critique your speech; and can reduce public speaking anxiety and bolster ethos.

Outlining is best done in three phases: the preparation outline, the formal outline, and the speaking outline.

A preparation outline is a working draft of speech ideas. It evolves through a six-step process: selecting and narrowing a topic, organizing main ideas and supporting material, developing the introduction and the conclusion, placing the major elements, main points, subpoints, and transition statements into proper outline form, integrating internal reference citations, and critiquing and revising the outline according to listener relevance links, the learning cycle, and supporting material, as well as creating a title.

A formal outline is a typed version that labels and applies all content using complete sentences. It also includes a speech title, the speaker's name, internal reference citations, and a complete reference list.

A speaking outline is a condensed outline used solely as a memory aid while speaking. Like the preparation outline, it uses key words and phrases rather than complete sentences. Like the formal outline, it includes internal references throughout and uses a proper outline format. But speaking outlines often use abbreviations, include delivery cues and the actual content of supporting material to be cited, and are usually typed or printed in large neat letters on one side of a few numbered index cards. The exception to the last rule is when speaking from a lectern, when the speaking outline is usually printed or typed on regular sheets of paper.

Speakers who expend the effort to complete the entire three-phase process of outlining reap the rewards. Their speeches are clearly organized, well documented, and thorough.

RETURNING TO TECHNOLOGY

The *Confident Public Speaking* CD-ROM is your one-stop point of access for not just the content on the CD itself, such as Speech Interactive, but also the many other resources on the *Confident Public Speaking* Web site, Speech Builder Express, and InfoTrac College Edition. Note that this chapter's key terms and activities are among the resources available in electronic format online. Additional information is included below.

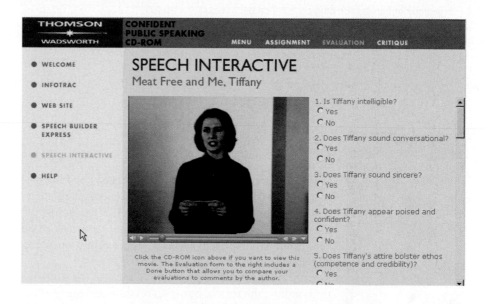

SPEECH INTERACTIVE
ON THE *CONFIDENT PUBLIC SPEAKING* CD-ROM

Speech Interactive is your link to this text's speech videos. Offering opportunities to practice critiquing speeches by students and other public speakers, these videos will help you prepare for providing effective feedback to your peers and your own speech performances.

SPEECH BUILDER EXPRESS

The Outline, Supporting Material, and Transitions sections of Speech Builder Express provide sequences of prompts to help you ensure that your outlines are well structured and effective. You'll find links to these sections on the main navigation menu, located on the left-hand side of the screen.

KEY TERMS

Interactive flashcards for these key terms are available on the *Confident Public Speaking* Web site. You'll find the "Flashcards" link under the resources for Chapter 10.

Formal outline   233
Listener relevance link   227
Outlining   222

Preparation outline   224
Speaking outline   236

ACTIVITIES

The activities below are available in electronic format on the *Confident Public Speaking* Web site. You'll find the "Activities" link under the resources for Chapter 10.

1. **Group Outline.** Form groups of four or five people. Make up a word like "spoophoni" or "aberambolt." Then decide as a group what it means. Create a preparation outline for a speech describing what it is.
2. **Reformat a Message.** Form groups of four or five people. Select an article from a magazine or a newspaper. Reformat the article into a preparation outline as described in this chapter. If the article does not offer a particular component, create one.
3. **Speaking Outline.** From the preparation outline created in activity 1 or 2 above, construct a speaking outline as a group and present it to the class.
4. **Listen to and Evaluate a Message.** Listen to a commentary on a television or radio program. Try to identify the main points. Did the speaker offer a preview or a summary? What impact did this have on your ability to figure out the main points? Prepare a one-page critique based on your reaction.

INFOTRAC COLLEGE EDITION ACTIVITY

Use "public speaking" as your search term to find the article "How to Be a Successful Presenter" by Michel G. Hypes, Edward T. Turner, Charlotte M. Norris, and Linda C. Wolfferts.

- What do the authors suggest regarding organization?
- What do you think about the recommendations to include *estimated times* for each section of the speech on your preparation outline?
- Name one recommendation they offer that you could use to make your speaking outline more useful and explain why.

LANGUAGE AND STYLE CHOICES IN YOUR SPEECH

REFLECTIVE QUESTIONS

1. What might the term "inclusive language" refer to? Explain. Give some examples of language that might be considered inclusive.

2. Should you avoid using slang or jargon in a public speech? Why or why not?

3. What does "vivid language" mean? Explain. Give examples of language that might be considered vivid. How might you integrate it into your public speech?

4. How does spoken language differ from written language, and what might account for those differences?

5. What points should you consider if incorporating humor into a public speech? Why are these considerations important?

WHAT'S AHEAD: FOCUSING YOUR READING

Why Are Language and Style Important?

The Symbolic Nature of Language

Strategies for Effective Language and Style

Integrating Language and Style

As her speech went on, Cindy was clearly losing her classmates. Her thesis—that anyone can use art therapy to reduce stress—was interesting and relevant. Her speech was well organized. But in planning her speech, Cindy had never thought specifically about its language and style. She used many long sentences, more appropriate to a paper than to a speech, and many technical terms used by art therapists. The content was interesting; the way she conveyed it was not. She settled for abstraction instead of vividness, so the audience found the speech difficult and boring.

Speeches have both macrostructure and microstructure. Ideas must be organized into main points that support a thesis, but must also be expressed in phrases and sentences. One idea can be expressed using different language and style, so your choices in these matters are essentially part of the structure—the overall framework—of your speech. The language and style choices are the **microstructure** of the speech.

This chapter explores why language and style are so important. Specifics of the nature of language and its implications for speakers are given by looking at three major goals of language and style—clarity, vividness, and inclusion—and strategies that can help achieve them. When and where language and style choices should be integrated during speech preparation is considered. By applying what you learn in this chapter, you can make speeches interesting and memorable for listeners.

WHY ARE LANGUAGE AND STYLE IMPORTANT?

Effective microstructure helps maintain listener interest and thus makes a speech memorable. Classic speeches are usually characterized by language and style choices that make them forever memorable, such as the repetition of "I have a dream" in Martin Luther King, Jr.'s famous speech and John F. Kennedy's "Ask not what your country can do for you—ask what you can do for your country." Carefully chosen words maintain audience interest by increasing the clarity of ideas, arousing emotions, and fostering a sense of inclusion. All this can help reduce public speaking anxiety as well. It's a matter of using language and style to round the entire cycle of learning (Figure 11.1).

Increasing Clarity

Language either increases clarity through concrete and descriptive word choices or confuses listeners by being abstract and ambiguous. Used properly, it's like painting word pictures in the minds of listeners.

Why is a beautiful painting beautiful? Is it the color choices, brushstrokes, attention to detail? These distinctions maintain interest and make the painting memorable. Just as artists clarify their perspective of an object or scene through detail and color, so do effective speakers paint word pictures in the minds of listeners through carefully selected language. The descriptive words you choose add color to your ideas.

Consider, for example, the picture you get from the description of a sunny day as "bright, warm, and friendly" as opposed to "blinding, scorching, and wicked." The day is sunny, either way, but the word picture describing it differs considerably. The details color the basic idea.

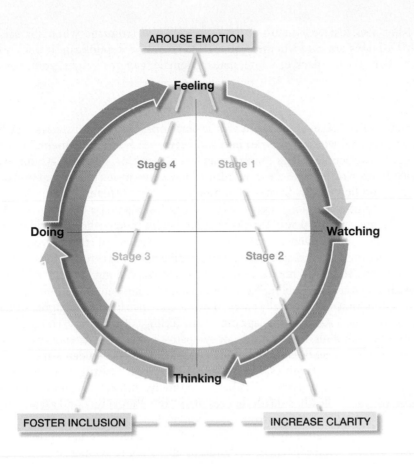

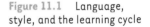

Figure 11.1 Language, style, and the learning cycle

Fostering Inclusion

Carefully selected language and style foster inclusion with your listeners. Since public speaking is communication, effective speakers create a sense of connection with listeners by using "we" rather than "I" or "you" language and by avoiding biased terms. It's a subtle reminder that listeners play an important role in the communication process. Mary Fisher, in her "Whisper of AIDS" speech delivered at the 1992 Republican National Convention, united her audience periodically through "we" language choices like this:

> Adolescents don't give each other cancer or heart disease because they believe they are in love. But HIV is different. And we have helped it along—we have killed each other—with our ignorance, our prejudice, and our silence. (Fisher, 1994)

Fisher's statement would have been much less effective had she distanced herself from her audience with "you" language choices. Here's how it might have sounded:

> Adolescents don't give each other cancer or heart disease because they believe they are in love. But HIV is different. And [you] have helped it along—[you] have killed each other—with [your] ignorance, [your] prejudice, and [your] silence.

Fisher also fostered inclusion through unbiased language when she said, "It [AIDS] does not care whether you are Democrat or Republican. It does not ask whether you are black or white, male or female, gay or straight, young or old."

Arousing Emotion

Language and style choices can arouse emotions. "Sticks and stones may break my bones, but words will never hurt me," says the childhood lament, but it's not true. What people tell us can make us feel miserable—or great. As our experiences with words make clear, words can have enormous emotional power. Effective public speakers harness that power to inspire listeners.

Sometimes emotionally charged words can foster a desire to know more. Geoff used language in this way in his speech about Venice by appealing to feelings of happiness, love, and romance: It is "the city of love, the city of romance, and the city of my dreams," he said, and went on to describe traveling through the city in gondolas rather than automobiles as being "romanticized along" as you "glide imperceptibly forward" and feeling "completely happy because life is beautiful and good."

Other times, emotionally charged words convince listeners to agree with a position or to take action. Language can arouse feelings of adventure, companionship, curiosity, fear, guilt, loyalty, pride, or sympathy, convincing listeners to agree and act because of it. In her speech about how students are harmed by fraternities, for example, Kris described Rutgers University student James Callahan's "untimely, unfortunate, and unnecessary death: a death that resulted from chugging kamikazes—a nerve-numbing mixture of vodka, triple sec, and lime juice—at a college fraternity party." Kris carefully crafted this description to influence listeners' emotions by appealing to sympathy.

Politicians and political activists often use emotionally charged language to arouse emotions. Consider again the language in Mary Fisher's speech that appeals to fear, guilt, and sympathy:

WHAT DO YOU THINK?

Identify an argument you've had recently. What words did the other person use that increased your anger? What words did you use for similar reasons? How did the dispute end? What role did language choices play in how the argument ended?

> " The lesson history teaches is this: If you believe you are safe, you are at risk. If you do not see this killer stalking your children, look again. There is no family or community, no race or religion, no place left in America that is safe. Until we genuinely embrace this message, we are a nation at risk.
>
> Tonight, HIV marches resolutely toward AIDS in more than a million American homes, littering its pathway with the bodies of the young. Young men. Young women. Young parents. Young children. One of the families is mine. If it is true that HIV inevitably turns to AIDS, then my children will inevitably turn to orphans. (Fisher, 1994)

TURNING TO TECHNOLOGY

Mary Fisher's Speech

Go to the Speech Interactive section on your *Confident Public Speaking* CD-ROM and listen to Mary Fisher's "Whisper of AIDS" speech. You can also read a transcript of her speech that appears in Appendix B of this book. Identify how she used language to foster inclusion with her audience. Also identify several places where she used language to arouse emotion. How effective was she? Why?

Thinking carefully about the language and style of your speech should make you feel more confident because you'll keep listeners interested. That reduces anxiety and negative self-talk. Most important is using inclusive language. "I" and "you" distance the speaker from the audience; "we" creates a sense of connection. "We" language reduces the perception that the speaker is in this transaction alone. The right language choices persuade the audience that you are *communicating* rather than *presenting* to them. This reduces anxiety because it helps you focus on communication rather than performance (Motley, 1991). In addition, some figures and structures of speech—such as alliteration, assonance, and onomatopoeia—can be easy to remember, thus reducing anxiety. Choosing words by considering how they increase clarity, foster inclusiveness, and arouse emotion gives you more confidence.

TURNING TO TECHNOLOGY

The Nuts and Bolts of Language Style

http://www.nutsandboltsguide.com/style.html

This site, sponsored by Hackett Publishing, offers some tips about writing style. What do you agree with and why? What do you disagree with and why?

THE SYMBOLIC NATURE OF LANGUAGE

To make wise language choices, you must first understand the nature of language. Language is symbolic. We use words as symbols to represent things, ideas, events. For example, the word "dog" stands for a four-legged domesticated mammal. But the word "dog" is not the animal. The *word* is not the *thing*.

A word has no tangible meaning in and of itself; we simply construct meaning based on prior experiences with it (Duck, 1994; Shotter, 1993). The same word might be interpreted differently by different people. To the public speaker, this means that listeners may misinterpret your meaning unless your words are concrete and precise. For example, we probably agree that a dog is a domesticated four-legged mammal, but I envision a fun-loving, rambunctious golden retriever. Probably you don't. The word *dog* is abstract; the phrase a "mangy hound with tangled and matted fur and a face gray from age" is more concrete.

Language is thus symbolic but also arbitrary. We simply agree to call a dog "dog," as a matter of social construct. Because language is arbitrary, meanings can change over time and differ across cultural groups. So speakers must make language choices that enhance their message rather than hinder it.

STRATEGIES FOR EFFECTIVE LANGUAGE AND STYLE

Several strategies can help ensure that your message will be understood and memorable. To fully understand how these strategies work in public speeches, let's start by discussing how oral style differs from written style. Then we'll discuss the strategies of accuracy, clarity, inclusion, and vividness in detail.

Oral versus Written Style

Oral style differs from written style; at least it ought to. **Oral style** tends to be less formal than written style. Because a primary goal of the speaker is to establish a relationship with listeners, language choices must reflect a personal tone that encourages listeners to feel important to the speaker and the occasion. To develop this sense of relationship, the best oral styles differ from written style in four ways.

First, good speakers tend to use personal pronouns, which acknowledges listeners and creates a sense of relationship with them. In writing a paper about gun control, for example, this might be the thesis statement: "The issue of gun control is currently being debated on a number of fronts." In an oral presentation, you might say: "I'd like to talk with you today about gun control, an issue that is currently being debated on a number of fronts." This better acknowledges the audience; even better would be this: "Let's talk today about gun control, an issue that is currently being debated on a number of fronts and deserves our attention." Using personal pronouns such as "we," "us," and "our" creates a stronger sense of relationship. Mentioning audience members by name can also help. For example:

> Last week, Georgia talked with us about teen violence and what we can do about it. Let's take that discussion further today by talking about gun control. Gun control is currently being debated on a number of fronts and deserves our attention.

Referring to listeners by name, in addition to using personal pronouns, fosters an even stronger sense of relationship between speaker and audience.

Second, effective speakers tend toward short sentences and familiar language because they know listeners must grasp meaning upon hearing ideas only once. Long sentences may sound like you are reading to listeners instead of talking with them. Contractions, for example, work well when spoken: "let's" rather than "let us," "we'll" rather than "we will," "won't" rather than "will not," and so forth.

Third, repetition works well in a speech because listeners can't reread a passage they don't understand. Repeating yourself is discouraged in a written composition, but an oral presentation can benefit from the redundancy of previews, transitions, summaries, and stating important points in more than one way. Mary Fisher used repetition to help listeners grasp the main point of her message:

> **❝** To the millions of you who are grieving, who are frightened, who have suffered the ravages of AIDS firsthand: Have courage and you will find comfort.
>
> To the millions who are strong, I issue this plea: Set aside prejudice and politics to make room for compassion and sound policy.

Fourth, good oral presentations use descriptive words more often to sustain listener interest. Colorful adjectives and adverbs draw listeners into your message, but don't get carried away. Using too many reduces their effectiveness.

Writing styles vary, and so do oral styles. The style depends on the personality of the speaker, the subject of the speech, and the audience, among other things. But if you pick the right oral style for your speech, you'll grab your audience.

Guidelines for Integrating Oral Style

Working with the formal outline that you prepared for your speech,

- Insert personal pronouns wherever possible.
- Simplify language choices wherever clarity might be an issue for some listeners.
- Break complex and compound sentences into two or more shorter sentences.
- Use, but don't overuse, colorful descriptors.

Another important distinction is between conversation and public speaking. Although both use oral styles, they are not quite the same. Public speaking has fewer interruptions, is more formal in tone, has more constraints, uses more repetition, and stays on topic longer.

Now let's look more closely at the language and style strategies of accuracy, clarity, inclusion, and vividness.

Accuracy

Accuracy means using words that precisely convey your meaning. The most important requirement for a public speaker is to be **intelligible**—clear enough to be understood. If listeners don't understand you, your attempt to communicate is doomed. There are several aspects of intelligibility, including pronunciation, enunciation, rate, volume, and so forth. Chapter 12 deals with those. Other aspects have to do with language and style, and accuracy is one of these. Let's look at accuracy in terms of denotations, connotations, and standard English.

Denotations and Connotations

To understand denotations and connotations, consider the words "feminist" and "feminism." If someone asks if you are a feminist, what would you say? It probably depends on how you define "feminism." Words have both denotative and connotative meanings. A **denotation** is the dictionary definition of a word. For feminism, that's "a doctrine that advocates for women the same rights granted to men." But some people agree that women should be granted the same rights as men without considering themselves feminists. The reason might be the connotations attached to the word. A **connotation** is what the word suggests or implies. Different words can have similar denotations but different connotations.

Calvin and Hobbes © Watterson. Reprinted with permission of Universal Press Syndicate. All rights reserved.

For this reason, many people who support equal rights for women now use the term "feminism" rather than "feminist." Connotations can be neutral, positive, or negative and can be quite different for different people. Thus, some might attach negative connotations to the word "feminist," such as "male basher," "radical," or even "feminazi."

Words have connotations based on our experiences. Exposure to negative portrayals of "feminists" in the media might explain why the word has negative connotations for some people. Others have had bad experiences with people who called themselves feminists. Connotative meanings give emotional power to words; people will even fight and die for them. Speakers can use connotative meanings to increase the emotional appeal (pathos) of presentations, but the words must be carefully chosen so as to help, not hinder, the message. Avoid words that arouse unintended connotations, or at least define them in ways that reduce negative emotional responses.

Use words correctly. If you are not certain of the meaning of a word, look it up. Words often have multiple meanings, and the meanings attached to them can change over time. "Gay," for example, once meant "happy and lighthearted." It still does, but now it also commonly means "homosexual." Today's "slide show" may be a computer-generated PowerPoint presentation, and "networking" may mean connecting your computer to others rather than making personal contacts. Sometimes entirely new words or phrases are coined. "Channel surfing," for example, came about with the invention of remote control devices. Computers and the Internet have given rise to countless new words and phrases, such as "surfing the Web," "WBASAP," "scrolling," and "bugs" and "worms" that aren't biological. As recently as twenty years ago, one might have guessed that cyberspace was a place where Captain Kirk took his crew on *Star Trek*, rather than the place where information is exchanged over the Internet. Use a good up-to-date dictionary to make sure that the intended meaning of the words you choose adheres to today's reality.

Sometimes a **thesaurus** helps. Look up the word you've thought of and see if another one better fits your purpose. Godzilla was certainly "big" and "large," but a thesaurus gives synonyms such as "enormous," "sizable," "massive," "great," "appreciable," "bulky," "ample," "giant," "gigantic," "immense," and "extensive." Some of these may be more precise for your purpose. Others—like "appreciable," "bulky," and "extensive"—are inappropriate because they might confuse listeners. A thesaurus is an effective tool if used for intelligibility rather than phony sophistication.

Standard English

Accuracy relies on vocabulary and grammar. To ensure that your listeners will understand your intended meaning, use **standard English,** the language preferences described in the dictionary. Be aware that your **dialect,** a regional variety of a language, may influence your tendency to use certain vocabulary and grammar. In some places a car's turn signal is called a blinker, a seesaw is a teeter-totter, and a soft drink is a pop or a coke. Regional dialect may also influence pronunciation, as when "wash" is pronounced "warsh" and "creek" becomes "crick." Avoid regional pronunciations because they can hurt intelligibility as well as credibility.

Likewise, poor grammar—"he don't," "I says," "this here book," "them cars," "on account of he was sick," "beings as he was sick," and so forth—can be rooted in dialect and reduce speaker intelligibility or credibility. If you have reason to be concerned about your use of standard English, consult a handbook and place delivery cue reminders on your speaking outline.

WHAT DO YOU THINK?
Do you think Black English is appropriate for a formal public speech? Why or why not?

Checklist for Ensuring Accuracy

When you prepare and practice your speech:

- ❏ Consult a dictionary to check the denotations of word choices.
- ❏ Consult a thesaurus only for more precise language.
- ❏ Avoid using words that might arouse unintended emotional responses.
- ❏ Use standard English.
- ❏ Avoid vocabulary and grammar tendencies that are rooted in a particular dialect.

Clarity

Intelligibility also requires clarity. Use familiar terms, concrete words, simple language, and the active voice, and avoid vocalized pauses.

Use Familiar Words

Effective public speakers use words that are familiar to their audience. Listeners won't hear your speech again, so speak plainly. Don't use a thesaurus just to find more sophisticated words. And try to avoid jargon or slang. **Jargon** is the terminology of a trade or profession that is not generally understood by outsiders because it is unique to the users' field of practice. That's fine when it describes concepts or functions precisely for an insider, but to those outside or new to the organization it is usually just confusing.

What are a "hail Mary," a "blitz," a "bomb," and a "shotgun"? Football fans probably know; others don't. The computer industry has a staggering host of technical terms that insiders need, but not everyone knows what RAM, megabytes, and gigabytes are. Most disciplines have jargon that is understood by others in the field but not by general public. And the words may not be in a standard dictionary.

Take care when using jargon. It's okay to use some if you define it clearly, and it can even empower listeners by letting them in on private codes—especially students working to learn about the field in question. This book tries to do that: It uses the terminology of the field and defines it in simple terms in order to avoid a potential language barrier between academicians and students.

If you use jargon, define it the first time it is used. The same goes for abbreviations and acronyms. It's fine to talk about the NCA, for example, but only if it is defined as the National Communication Association at first use. Here's what Larissa did when using the acronym STDs:

By permission of John L. Hart FLP, and Creators Syndicate, Inc.

The use of **slang**—words arbitrarily assigned meaning by a social group or subculture—may also harm credibility and clarity. The word "good," for example, has been expressed as groovy, super, cool, rad, and bad in various times and by various groups. Using "bad" as meaning "great" might well be misunderstood.

Public speakers should normally avoid using slang because it may be misinterpreted. And it can hurt speaker credibility (ethos) because it doesn't sound professional.

TURNING TO TECHNOLOGY

Internet Jargon

http://info.astrian.net/jargon/

This jargon dictionary reveals the meanings for much of the newest hacker jargon used on the Internet. It also provides several tips about how jargon works. Read through the tips. Did any of them surprise you? Why or why not?

Use Concrete Words

Concrete words paint a clear, vivid picture for listeners. "Collie" is more concrete than "dog," and "the heroic, friendly, television collie we all know as Lassie" is even more concrete. Including adjectives, adverbs, and examples helps. In her speech advocating aerobic exercise, Julie made "aerobic activity" more concrete by talking about "aerobic activity like running, jogging, swimming, or bicycling."

Use Simple Language and Sentence Structure

Even if an idea is complex, explain it simply. Think about the structure of your sentences. Keeping them simple helps listeners understand and focus on your ideas. For example, in her speech about toughening environmental standards, the administrator of the U.S. Environmental Protection Agency, Carol M. Browner (1998), said this:

> And there is little doubt as to where Americans stand. They want clean air. They want the public health to come first in setting clean air standards. They want their children protected.
>
> They want the EPA to do its job—which is ensuring that the air they breathe is safe and healthy.

These simple words are powerful and her message was clear as a result. Had she attempted to sound more sophisticated, she might have said this:

And there is relatively little doubt as to where Americans stand with regard to environmental issues and standards. Americans desire perfectly purified air, as well as clean air standards that are developed by focusing first and foremost on public health. And they also yearn for protection from environmental hazards for their children.

They hope that the Environmental Protection Agency will do what it was created to do, which is to ensure in every way possible that the air they breathe is both safe and healthy for them.

That's not as clear and not as powerful. In general, favor simple words and sentences over complicated words and sentence structure.

Use Active Sentences

In an **active sentence,** the subject *performs* the action. In a **passive sentence,** the subject *experiences* the action (Legette et al., 1991). Active sentences are usually clearer and more concrete:

Passive: Food and clothing items were donated to the shelter by us.
Active: We donated food and clothing items to the shelter.

Avoid Vocalized Pauses

Vocalized pauses such as "like," "you know," "really," "well," "and," "basically," "um," and "uh" are verbal garbage that sometimes creep in while you formulate your next thought. They are unnecessary and disrupt the fluency of your message, making it less clear. It's a bad habit that crops up when a speaker fears silence. But silent pauses are less likely to disrupt the flow of ideas than are vocalized pauses.

PRACTICING THE PROCESS

Checklist for Ensuring Accuracy and Clarity

To achieve intelligibility via language and style, check your speech to ensure the following statements are true:

- ❏ I use familiar words.
- ❏ I avoid slang.
- ❏ I define jargon the first time I use it.
- ❏ I use concrete words that paint clear pictures.
- ❏ I use simple sentence structure.
- ❏ My denotations are accurate.
- ❏ My connotations are intended.
- ❏ I use standard English.
- ❏ My sentence structure is simple.
- ❏ I use active sentences.
- ❏ I avoid vocalized pauses.

Inclusion

Inclusion means making language choices that show respect for your audience and for all types of people. To be inclusive, use "we" language, use bias-free language, and avoid inappropriate humor.

Use "We" Language

To make all listeners feel included and important, demonstrate verbal immediacy with "we" language. **Verbal immediacy** is the use of language to reduce the psychological distance between you and the audience. Using "we" instead of "you" or "they" conveys a sense of connection with listeners and involves them in the topic and occasion. "We" language can often be incorporated into the macrostructural elements of your speech, such as the thesis statement, preview, and transitions. Here's how Pete did it:

> **Thesis statement:** Today we'll see why Tok Pisin of Papua New Guinea should be considered a legitimate language.
>
> **Preview:** We'll do this by looking at what kind of language Tok Pisin is, some of the features of the Tok Pisin language, and why this language is necessary in New Guinea.
>
> **Transition** (*between the first and the second point*): Since Tok Pisin is essentially a combination of languages, let's look more specifically at some of its unique features.

Used appropriately, "we" language helps build verbal immediacy. The more "immediate" you are, the more likable, friendly, and understandable your listeners find you to be (Gorham, 1988; Powell & Harville, 1990).

Use Bias-Free Language

Bias-free language is also inclusive. **Bias-free language** demonstrates through word choices an ethical concern for fairness and respect for groups based on race, gender, or ethnicity as well as different identities and worldviews (Grabmeier, 1992). Do you know, for example, that many people with disabilities prefer not to be called disabled because they find the term dehumanizing (Braithwaite & Braithwaite, 1997)? Likewise, words such as "fireman," "mailman," and "mankind" have generally been replaced with the more inclusive terms "firefighter," "postal carrier," and "humanity."

Some people mock such language choices as "politically correct" word substitutions. They argue that bias-free language is an overreaction to insignificant problems, or that other language choices don't always imply disrespect. One student said, "Just because I referred to medical doctors as 'he' in my speech did not mean I believe only men can be medical doctors," and another remarked, "How am I supposed to know whether to call them 'Indians' or 'Native Americans.' I think people need to get less bent out of shape. I do not intend to be offensive." Regardless of intent, however, to be an effective public speaker you must demonstrate respect with regard to race, ethnicity, and gender, and that means using bias-free language (Strossen, 1992).

Avoid stereotypes based on race, ethnicity, gender, age, sexual orientation, or any other characteristic. Biased language is not only inaccurate and unethical but is likely to marginalize, alienate, or offend listeners. Thus, using bias-free language simultaneously improves your speech and your chances of connecting with your audience. Several reference books can help you with this (including Maggio, 1988; Miller & Swift, 1991).

Consult one of these references when you are uncertain about a word or phrase. If bias-free language is new for you, don't feel badly when you slip up

---

Student Workbook

Read through the sample outline for Shannon's personal significance speech titled "Japanese Clothing" in Chapter 3 of your workbook. Circle each instance where he uses inclusive (i.e., "we" and bias-free) language.

WHAT DO YOU THINK?

Does the term "political correctness" have positive, negative, or neutral connotations for you? Why? Can you identify experiences you've had that contribute to your personal connotation?

© Jeroboam

Effective public speakers use inclusive language.

occasionally. With practice it becomes easier. And if you use bias-free language generally, listeners are less likely to be offended by a lapse because they can more easily see that it was not intentional.

Four simple strategies can help you achieve bias-free language: Don't use irrelevant descriptions related to the group a person belongs to, gender-linked terms, or masculine pronouns to represent both men and women. Do use parallel treatment when referring to males and females. Let's consider these four guidelines in more detail.

First, if the group a person belongs to isn't relevant to your point, don't bring it up. Concrete descriptions are useful, of course, but only when they are relevant. For example, if you are speaking about Sandra Day O'Connor as the first woman appointed to the Supreme Court, then the fact that she is a woman is central to your speech. If, however, you are speaking about outstanding Supreme Court justices, the fact that she is a woman is irrelevant and should not be mentioned. And in a talk about teachers who influenced you, probably it is not relevant that one of them was Asian American. Some beginning public speakers add unnecessary descriptions of people, especially those who are not white males. It's not necessary to say "woman doctor" nor "male nurse," for example. The intention might be to show inclusiveness but the actual effect can be the opposite (Treinen & Warren, 2001).

Second, avoid using **gender-linked terms,** which imply exclusion of males or females. "Chairman," "fireman," "mailman," "spokesman," and "mankind" tend to exclude women. Use "chairperson," "firefighter," "mail carrier," "speaker," and "humanity" instead. Although people claim that they mean both men and women when they use gender-linked terms, research shows that when people hear them,

WHAT DO YOU THINK?

Is it appropriate to call sports teams "Sioux," "Braves," "Blackhawks," "Indians," and so forth? Why or why not?

they think of men and not women (Wood, 1994). Say "server" not "waitress" and "flight attendant" not "stewardess" to include men. And instead of "unwed mother" and "maternity leave," use "single parent" and "parental leave."

Third, don't use "he" and "him" to represent both males and females; it causes some listeners to perceive that only males and not females are included (e.g., Gastil, 1990; Hamilton, 1991; Switzer, 1990). Instead of "he" use "he or she." Better yet, make the sentence plural by using "they," or rephrase the sentence:

Problematic: Today, the typical college student knows what he wants from his education.
Preferred (use both pronouns): Today, the typical college student knows what he or she wants from his or her education.
Preferred (make it plural): Today, most college students know what they want from their education.
Preferred (rephrase the sentence): Today, students expect certain things from college.

Fourth, use **parallel treatment**—similar labels—for the genders when referring to them together: "men and women," "husband and wife," and "boys and girls." Don't call women of all ages "girls" if you refer to males as "men." Also avoid statements that make assumptions about inequality. For example, the phrase "doctors and their wives" assumes that all doctors are male. Say "doctors and their spouses" instead.

Avoid Inappropriate Humor

ETHICS

Demonstrate respect for your audience by avoiding inappropriate humor. Dirty jokes, sexist remarks, or profanity may not be intended to be offensive or disrespectful, but some listeners will disagree. Chris Rock did this many times during his remarks as host of the 2003 MTV music awards. For example, he introduced rapper Eminem this way: "Our next presenter saves a lot of money on Mother's Day. Give it up for Eminem!" This might have been funny to some but certainly offended others. Later in the program, Rock introduced P. Diddy as "being sued by more people than the Catholic church." Catholics in the audience may have been offended by this (MTV Video Music Awards, 2003). To be most effective and ethical in your formal public speeches, avoid humorous comments and jokes that might offend some listeners. In general, when in doubt, leave it out. Being inclusive means demonstrating respect for all listeners.

"We're trying to come up with a less offensive term for 'political correctness.'"

PRACTICING THE PROCESS

Guidelines for Being Inclusive

When preparing and practicing your speech:

- Use "we" language wherever possible, particularly in your thesis, preview, transitions, thesis restatement, and summary.
- Avoid irrelevant descriptions related to the group a person belongs to.
- Avoid gender-linked terms.
- Avoid masculine pronouns to represent both men and women.
- Use parallel treatment when referring to males and females.
- Avoid inappropriate humor, particularly profanity.

Student Workbook

Read through the sample outline for Peter's "Teen Suicide" actuation persuasive speech titled "Teen Suicide" in Chapter 4 of your workbook. Circle each instance where he uses vivid language. Identify spots where he could adjust his language to be more vivid.

Vividness

Make your speech memorable by **vivid language and style,** which evokes feelings and images in listeners' minds and thus invites them to internalize your ideas. This appeals to different dimensions of the learning cycle (watching, feeling, doing, and thinking) in ways that make your ideas memorable. You can increase vividness by appealing to the senses and by using figures and structures of speech.

Use Sensory Language

Appeal to listeners' senses of seeing, hearing, touching, tasting, smelling, and feeling. Consider how you can re-create what something, someone, or some place *looks like.* Consider too how you can help listeners imagine how something *sounds.* How can you use language to convey the way something feels (textures, shapes, temperatures)? How can language re-create a sense of how something tastes or smells?

To achieve this, use colorful descriptors. They make your ideas more concrete and can arouse emotions. They invite listeners to imagine details. Here's an example about downhill skiing:

Sight: As you climb the hill, the bright winter sunshine glistening on the snow is blinding.

Touch and feel: Just before you take off, you gently slip your goggles over your eyes. They are bitterly cold and sting your nose for a moment.

Taste: You start the descent and, as you gradually pick up speed, the taste of air and ice and snow in your mouth invigorates you.

Sound: An odd silence fills the air. You hear nothing but the swish of your skis against the snow beneath your feet. At last you arrive at the bottom.

Smell and feel: You enter the warming house. As your fingers thaw in the warm air, the aroma from the wood stove in the corner comforts you. And you sleep.

By using colorful descriptors that appeal to the senses, you maintain the interest of listeners and make your ideas more memorable.

Use Figures and Structures of Speech

Figures of speech make striking comparisons between things or ideas that are not obviously alike and so help listeners visualize or internalize what you are saying. **Structures of speech** combine ideas in a particular way. Following are some examples.

Alliteration is the repetition of sounds at the beginning of words that are near one another. In her speech about the history of jelly beans, Sharla used alliteration when she said, "And today, there are more than fifty fabulous fruity flavors from which to choose." Used sparingly, alliteration can catch listeners' attention and make the speech memorable, but overuse can hurt the message because listeners might focus on the technique rather than the content of your message.

Assonance is the repetition of vowel sounds, as in "she said *ouch* with an *outhouse mouth*," or "*how now brown cow*." As with alliteration, this can make your speech more memorable as long as it's not overused.

Onomatopoeia is the use of words that sound like the things they stand for, such as "buzz," "hiss," "crack," and "plop." In the speech about skiing, for example, the "swish" of the skis is an example of onomatopoeia. Again, don't overuse it.

Personification attributes human qualities to a concept or an inanimate object. When Linda talked about her car, Big Red, as her trusted friend and companion, she used personification. Likewise when Rick talked about flowers dancing on the front lawn he used personification.

Repetition is restating words, phrases, or sentences for emphasis. Martin Luther King, Jr.'s use of "I have a dream" is a classic example:

You can help listeners remember by appealing to the senses.

© Ken Redding/CORBIS

> " I say to you today, my friends, so even though we face the difficulties of today and tomorrow, I still have a dream. It is a dream deeply rooted in the American dream.
>
> I have a dream that one day this nation will rise up and live out the true meaning of its creed: "We hold these truths to be self-evident: that all men are created equal."
>
> I have a dream that one day on the red hills of Georgia the sons of former slaves and the sons of former slave owners will be able to sit down together at the table of brotherhood.
>
> I have a dream that one day even the state of Mississippi, a state sweltering with the heat of injustice, sweltering with the heat of oppression, will be transformed into an oasis of freedom and justice.
>
> I have a dream that my four little children will one day live in a nation where they will not be judged by the color of their skin but by the content of their character. I have a dream today.

Reprinted by arrangement with the Estate of Martin Luther King, Jr. c/o Writers House as agent for the proprietor New York, NY. Copyright 1963 Dr. Martin Luther King, Jr., copyright renewed 1991 Coretta Scott King.

TURNING TO TECHNOLOGY

"I Have a Dream"

Go to the Speech Interactive section on your *Confident Public Speaking* CD-ROM and watch Martin Luther King, Jr.'s "I Have a Dream" speech. Which phrases does he repeat and how does this strategy make the speech more memorable? You can also go to this book's appendix, where you'll find the transcript of the speech if you want to follow along as you listen.

Antithesis is combining contrasting ideas in the same sentence, as when John F. Kennedy said, "Ask not what your country can do for you—ask what you can do for your country." Likewise, Jesse Jackson used antithesis to close his Rainbow Coalition speech powerfully when he said, "We've come from disgrace to Amazing Grace. Our time has come."

Simile is a comparison between two unlike things using the words "like" or "as." If you've seen the movie *Forrest Gump*, you might recall Forrest's use of similes: "Life is like a box of chocolates. You never know what you're going to get" and "Stupid is as stupid does." Neil used a simile in his student speech when he said, "The fireflies lit the sky like strings of thousands of holiday lights." Similes can be effective because they make ideas more vivid in listeners' minds. But they should be used sparingly or they lose their appeal.

Metaphor is an implied comparison between two unlike things without using "like" or "as." Socrates' statement, "fame is the perfume of heroic deeds," is a metaphor. Metaphors can be effective because they make an abstract concept more concrete, strengthen an important point, or heighten emotions. Sometimes similes and metaphors become overused and trite. "Fit as a fiddle," "hungry as a bear," "busy as a bee," and "light as a feather" are **clichés** that should be avoided because their predictability makes them ineffective.

Analogy is an extended metaphor. Sometimes you can develop a story from a metaphor that makes a concept more vivid. If you were to describe a family member as the "black sheep in the barnyard," that's a metaphor. If you went on to talk about other members of the family as different animals on the farm and the roles ascribed to them, you would be extending the metaphor into an analogy. An analogy can be effective for holding your speech together in a creative and vivid way. Analogies are particularly useful to highlight the similarities between an unfamiliar concept or object with one that is familiar. For example, if you were explaining the concept of bioluminescence, you might talk about it as a miniature flashlight, which is something familiar to most listeners. Analogies also appeal to both the thinking and the feeling dimension of the learning cycle, making it more memorable.

Looking at the Learning Cycle

Round the Cycle with Your Language Choices

- Feeling: *vividness* (also connotations, sensory language, metaphor, analogy, personification, bias-free language)
- Watching: *clarity* (also sensory language, onomatopoeia, repetition, concrete words, simple language and sentence structure, parallel phrasing)
- Thinking: *accuracy* (also denotations, standard English, familiar words, metaphor, analogy, antithesis, repetition)
- Doing: *inclusive* (also humor, active sentences, "we" language, bias-free language, sensory language, personification, simile, metaphor)

INTEGRATING LANGUAGE AND STYLE

Language and style form the microstructure of your speech. As such, you should consider language and style choices as you develop your formal outline, the one you phrase in complete sentences. Hence these choices should be considered specifically when transferring ideas from the preparation outline to the formal outline.

Also consider language and style choices when transferring ideas from the formal outline to the speaking outline. If you are concerned about forgetting to use certain language or style strategies, include them on your speaking outline as well. Tiffany did this with her preview and summary for the "Meat-Free and Me" speech, as shown in Figure 10.3. She didn't want to forget to use parallel phrasing in her presentation, so she worded her preview and summary quite specifically on her speaking outline.

SUMMARY

Language and style choices are crucial to effective public speeches because they can inspire audiences to listen and make the speaker's ideas memorable. They do so by increasing clarity, fostering inclusion, and arousing emotion. Consequently, effective language and style choices can reduce public speaking anxiety rooted in a fear of failure.

Language is symbolic—that is, words do not have any tangible meaning in and of themselves.

Oral style differs from written style in four general ways: It uses more personal pronouns, simpler language and sentence structure, more repetition, and more descriptors than written style. Oral style in public speaking differs from that in conversation; it has fewer interruptions, is more formal in tone, has more constraints, uses more repetition, and stays on topic longer.

There are four general strategies to consider when developing language and style for a speech: accuracy, clarity, inclusion, and vividness. For accuracy, use correct words by considering denotations and connotations, and use correct grammar based on standard English.

To ensure clarity, use familiar words that make abstract ideas and concepts concrete and precise. Use simple language and sentence structure, and active voice whenever possible. Avoid vocalized pauses such as "um," "uh," "really," "like," "you know," and "basically," which can distract listeners and disrupt the flow of your message.

Regarding inclusion, use "we" language in structural comments as opposed to "you" or "they" language. Doing so increases connection with listeners. Likewise, use bias-free language. That is, avoid using irrelevant descriptions related to the group a person belongs to, gender-linked terms, or masculine pronouns to represent both men and women. Use parallel treatment when referring to males and females. Finally, demonstrate respect for your audience by avoiding inappropriate humor. That means refrain from telling a dirty joke, making a sexist remark, or using profanity in the name of humor. Any of these is likely to offend some listeners.

Being vivid means using language and style that arouse emotions. Use descriptions that appeal to the senses of seeing, hearing, tasting, touching, smelling, and feeling, and be vivid by using figures and structures of speech. Effective techniques include alliteration, assonance, onomatopoeia, personification, repetition, antithesis, simile, metaphor, and analogy. These inspire audiences to listen and remember your ideas.

Effective public speech structure incorporates language and style that ensure understanding and inspire listeners by painting word pictures and arousing emotions. Integrate strategic language and style choices as you finalize your formal outline. You must consider both macrostructure and microstructure to achieve a truly effective public speech.

The *Confident Public Speaking* CD-ROM is your one-stop point of access for not just the content on the CD itself, such as Speech Interactive, but also many other resources on the *Confident Public Speaking* Web site, Speech Builder Express, and InfoTrac College Edition. Note that this chapter's key terms and activities are among the resources available in electronic format online. Additional information is included below.

SPEECH INTERACTIVE
ON THE *CONFIDENT PUBLIC SPEAKING* CD-ROM

 Speech Interactive is your link to this text's speech videos. Offering opportunities to practice critiquing speeches by students and other public speakers, these videos will help you prepare for providing effective feedback to your peers and your own speech performances.

SPEECH BUILDER EXPRESS

Speech Builder Express's sequenced prompts can help you pay closer attention to the language you use, so that you see the need for adjustments as early as possible.

KEY TERMS

 Interactive flashcards for these key terms are available on the *Confident Public Speaking* Web site. You'll find the "Flashcards" link under the resources for Chapter 11.

ACTIVITIES

The activities below, as well as additional activities, are available in electronic format on the *Confident Public Speaking* Web site. You'll find the "Activities" link under the resources for Chapter 11.

1. **Music Lyric Analysis.** Select a favorite song and examine the lyrics to discover what language and style strategies are used to (a) communicate inclusion or exclusion and (b) paint vivid word pictures and arouse emotions. Ask yourself: Does the song use "we" language? Bias-free language? Does it appeal to the senses? Does it use figures and structures of speech?

2. **Being Bias-Free.** Form pairs. With your partner, change the following terms and phrases to make them inclusive and less biased:
   - Manpower
   - Mothering
   - Male secretary
   - Men and ladies
   - Businessmen and their wives
   - Disabled person
   - Man (verb)

3. **Using Vivid Oral Style.** In groups of four or five students, select an article from a magazine or newspaper. Examine where the article attempts to be vivid by appealing to sense or using figures and structures of speech. Change some sentences to make them do so more effectively. Now, rephrase the article according to the three key components of oral style: (a) Use personal pronouns, especially "we" language. (b) Use simple language and sentence structure. (c) Use repetition. Have two volunteers from the group present the two versions of the article to the class. Discuss which version is more effective and why.

INFOTRAC COLLEGE EDITION ACTIVITY

Locate and read the following articles: "Sport Management Students' Views on Eliminating Sexist Language" by Janet B. Parks and Mary Ann Roberton; "Gender Issues in Advertising Language" by Nancy Artz; and "Does Alternating between Masculine and Feminine Pronouns Eliminate Perceived Gender Bias in Text?" by Laura Madson and Robert M. Hessling. (Hint: Use "sexism in language" as your search term.) What are some reasons for using bias-free language in your speeches? Why do some people continue to resist using bias-free language?

DELIVERING YOUR PUBLIC SPEECH

REFLECTIVE QUESTIONS

1. What is nonverbal communication? Why might it be important when delivering a speech?

2. What distance from the audience is optimal for speaking in public? What plans with regard to time would help a speaker?

3. In what ways might the speaker's body be used to enhance the verbal message? What body miscues could detract from the message?

4. What methods work best in practicing to make sure oral delivery is intelligible, conversational, and expressive?

5. How can all the above affect speech anxiety?

WHAT'S AHEAD: FOCUSING YOUR READING

Why Is Delivery So Important?

What Are the Characteristics of Effective Delivery?

Principles of Nonverbal Communication

Types of Nonverbal Cues

Effective Use of Voice

Methods of Delivery

Practicing the Speech

Delivery and Public Speaking Anxiety

T RINI HAD SPENT TWO WEEKS researching and preparing her speech. She wrote several drafts before finally deciding how to organize it and had even asked several friends to offer suggestions on her outline. She was certain that her speech was thoroughly prepared. But as soon as she walked to the front of the room her hands began to shake, and as she began to speak, her voice quivered. It seemed like everyone was watching her hands rather than listening to her message. The further she went, the worse her anxiety got, and she began to have difficulty focusing on the message. Ultimately she lost her place, skipped over most of her third main point, and finished in less time than required. Trini returned to her seat frustrated and disgusted.

Although Trini's research and structure were strong, she still wasn't thoroughly prepared because she hadn't practiced her delivery a number of times, including at least once in front of others. So she didn't feel comfortable with either her speech or the audience, and her fear of these unknowns increased her speech anxiety. As a result, despite all her other preparation, her speech was ineffective that day.

Speaking anxiety can occur at various points during speech preparation, but for most people it's most strongly associated with delivery. Yet delivery practice is the step most often neglected by beginning speakers. Taking time to practice your speech is the most important strategy to reduce your anxiety.

This chapter looks at why delivery is so important to effective public speaking. The characteristics of delivery, principles and types of nonverbal communication, and methods and strategies for effective delivery and reduced speaking anxiety are explained. These tips will improve your effectiveness in the classroom and beyond.

WHY IS DELIVERY SO IMPORTANT?

All the strategies we've discussed so far—analyzing the audience; determining a topic and purpose; and researching, preparing, and organizing ideas—go to waste if you can't communicate those ideas well. You must know what you want to say (content), organize it so it makes sense (structure), and communicate it so that it's compelling (delivery). **Delivery** is how a message is communicated orally and visually by your use of voice, face, and body.

TURNING TO TECHNOLOGY

Communicating in the Business World

http://cbpa.louisville.edu/bruce/lyle2.htm

Listen to what Lyle Sussman, from the College of Business at the University of Louisville, has to say about the importance of communication to your professional career. Do you agree? Why?

According to research, listeners are influenced more by delivery than by the content of speeches (Decker, 1992). Some 55 to 90 percent of the meaning they grasp is derived from delivery. This means you may construct an adequate speech that nevertheless seems great simply because you deliver it effectively. Conversely, poor delivery can cause listeners to miss the whole point you are trying to convey, even if the speech is otherwise excellent.

Thus, your goal is to construct an excellent speech *and* deliver it well. If you do, the message is likely to be remembered long after it's heard.

TURNING TO TECHNOLOGY

John F. Kennedy's Funeral

http://www.historychannel.com/broadband/

Go to this site and play the video clip of John F. Kennedy's funeral. What things does the narrator do with his voice to give the speech emotional impact and make it more compelling?

WHAT ARE THE CHARACTERISTICS OF EFFECTIVE DELIVERY?

In contrast to the words of a speech, which are conveyed through the *verbal channel*, delivery is conveyed through the *nonverbal channel*. **Nonverbal communication** is all speech elements other than the words themselves. These include your

THE FAR SIDE® BY GARY LARSON

© 1987 FarWorks, Inc. All Rights Reserved/Dist. by Creators Syndicate

The Far Side® by Gary Larson © 1987 FarWorks, Inc. All Rights Reserved. Used with permission.

"Fellow octopi, or octopuses … octopi? … Dang, it's hard to start a speech with this crowd."

voice, eye contact, facial expressions, gestures, body language, and even appearance. Effective delivery requires effective use of these nonverbal elements.

Effective delivery has two main characteristics. First, it is listener centered. In other words, it is focused on ways to nonverbally reinforce the verbal message, making it more compelling to listeners. A prerequisite is to avoid sending nonverbal messages that distract from or contradict the verbal message. If listeners notice how you pace back and forth or periodically brush the hair from your face, or even how you gesture for no apparent reason, they are momentarily distracted from the message itself.

Effective delivery is also conversational. It sounds and looks as though you are talking with listeners rather than making a presentation or reading to them. In other words, it's communication, not performance. The delivery is a bit more dramatic than in casual conversation, but it isn't theatrical. Appearing so natural, so comfortable and so sincere, ironically requires considerable planning and practice of where and how to gesture, pause, and so forth.

If delivery is listener centered and conversational, nonverbal elements appear spontaneous as they reinforce the verbal message. To achieve this, practice your speech sufficiently and, when you give it, concentrate on the message and on whether the audience appears to understand it, rather than on how you look or sound.

WHAT DO YOU THINK?

Consider a president you thought was a good speaker. Why do you remember him? What was most inspiring to you—the ideas conveyed or the manner in which he conveyed them? Why?

TURNING TO TECHNOLOGY

Delivery Tips

http://www.mtholyoke.edu/acad/intrel/speech/delivery.htm

This short Web page offers several tips on effective delivery. Which techniques seem most relevant to you? Why?

PRINCIPLES OF NONVERBAL COMMUNICATION

To use nonverbal cues to reinforce the verbal message, you need to understand four basic principles:

- Nonverbal communication is inevitable.
- Nonverbal communication is culturally and situationally bound.
- Nonverbal cues are believed.
- Nonverbal cues are seldom isolated.

Nonverbal Communication Is Inevitable

We cannot *not* communicate nonverbally (Watzlawick, Bavelas, & Jackson, 1967). You send nonverbal messages whether you intend to or not, whether speaking or silent, and whether or not others perceive them.

Consider, for example, the first day of this class. What did you wear? What might that have communicated about you to others? Did you think the class would be fun, boring, interesting, or difficult? How might the way you walked into the room and sat down have communicated your expectations? Did you look at your instructor as he or she talked? What might this eye contact or lack of it have communicated? Now consider your classmates on that day. What assumptions did you make about them and why? Similarly, consider a job interview you once had. What did you wear and why? What assumptions did you make about the employer and why? Were you more or less anxious to get hired after meeting your potential employer and why? Because we communicate nonverbally all the time, good speakers strive to make sure their nonverbal messages reinforce their verbal messages.

Nonverbal Communication Is Culturally and Situationally Bound

Very few nonverbal cues mean the same thing to everyone. Often the meaning varies by culture or even by situation. This chapter mainly discusses the nonverbal cues used in mainstream American culture, but if you speak to an audience primarily of another culture or culturally diverse, be aware of potential differences and adapt accordingly so you don't unintentionally offend anyone.

In mainstream American culture, for example, direct eye contact is usually a sign of respect. In many Native American cultures, however, it could be interpreted as disrespectful if the speaker is a superior. Likewise, the hand gesture commonly used in the United States to signal "okay" has a vulgar meaning in Mexico and means "I'll kill you" in Tunisia.

TURNING TO TECHNOLOGY

Cultural Diversity and Nonverbal Cues

http://www.unl.edu/casetudy/456/traci.htm

This Web site presents a number of nonverbal cues that mean different things in different cultures. Do any of the cues surprise you? If so, which ones?

Nonverbal communication is also situationally bound. Because they are ambiguous, nonverbal cues can mean different things in different situations. A furrowed brow could signify confusion, but in another situation it may indicate anger. Consider Jesse, who was presenting a speech about the civil rights movement in the United States. When he saw Byron put his head on the desk, he assumed Byron was bored. Actually, Byron had just pulled an all-nighter studying for an exam. In another part of the room, Monica was fidgeting and glancing at the clock. Jesse wondered if she was offended, but actually she was worried about getting to a job interview immediately following class. Jesse became unnecessarily nervous because he misinterpreted these ambiguous nonverbal cues.

WHAT DO YOU THINK?
Have you ever felt offended or insulted by someone from another culture? Was it something you said or did? Was it something they said or did? Do you think it was intended to offend? Why or why not?

Nonverbal Cues Are Believed

When verbal and nonverbal messages contradict each other, listeners are more likely to believe the nonverbal messages than the verbal ones. Have you ever asked a friend whether something looks good on you, gotten the response "Sure," and not believed it? Quite likely it was because something in his or her tone of voice, facial expressions, or body language contradicted the verbal message.

WHAT DO YOU THINK?
Consider a time when someone misinterpreted what you meant. What sort of nonverbal cues might you have sent that contributed to the misinterpretation?

This principle is crucial to public speaking. Isak, for example, began his presentation by saying, "Each of us is contributing to the destruction of the planet every time we throw a soda can or a newspaper in the garbage. I'm here to convince you to do your part to save the earth by making recycling a habit in your life." But when he delivered it he was barely audible, shifted from foot to foot, and never looked up from his notes. Although Isak is an ecology major convinced that recycling is important and his words made this clear, listeners were not persuaded because his voice and body language contradicted his verbal message.

In short: When verbals and nonverbals conflict, the nonverbals usually win.

Nonverbal Cues Are Seldom Isolated

Most nonverbal messages are simultaneously conveyed by several cues, which is why listeners tend to believe the nonverbal over the verbal when the messages contradict each other. Isak sent one verbal message: Recycling is important. But he sent several nonverbal cues, all of which contradicted the verbal message. As a result, listeners were unconvinced.

TYPES OF NONVERBAL CUES

There are six types of nonverbal communication cues for speakers to be aware of: space, time, appearance, eye contact, body, and voice. Many speakers are trained to consider only the use of body and voice. Certainly these are crucial. They are also relatively complex: Use of body includes facial expressions, gestures, posture, and body movement. Use of voice includes quality, rate, volume, pitch, pronunciation, enunciation, stress, and pauses. However, the other four types of nonverbal cues also have considerable impact.

Space

As a public speaker, you may or may not be able to influence how far you are from the audience or how listeners are seated. If it is possible, use space in the way that is most conducive to effective delivery. How space and distance communicate is sometimes known as **proxemics** (Hall, 1968).

Stand at a distance where you and listeners can easily and comfortably make eye contact. This appeals to Stage 4 of the learning cycle (feeling and doing) because it fosters a perception of inclusion between you and the audience. In general, the greater the number of people listening, the more space speakers need between themselves and listeners. Audiences of about ten to thirty people can be addressed effectively from four to eight feet away. This is usually the case for a public speaking class, for example. You can move around within that range while talking, but don't get farther away because you could appear too formal, cold, or distant, and avoid moving closer so listeners in the front won't feel you've come too close. Forty or more people are best addressed at a distance of more than eight feet. Closer contact, usually eye contact, is possible with a smaller audience, but with a large audience, such as in a lecture hall or auditorium, it is not possible to recognize all audience members as individuals. Instead you must try to create a general sense of audience contact without directly meeting every person's eyes (Barker et al., 1979).

WHAT DO YOU THINK?
Consider a time when you thought someone was lying to you. What sort of nonverbal messages contributed to your belief that they were not telling the truth?

Being close enough to your audience so that you can make eye contact is ideal.

© Dennis MacDonald/PhotoEdit

Ideal distances might be different if the audience is from another culture. For example, in many Latin American and Mediterranean countries people tend to stand closer to one another when interacting, and the distance between a public speaker and the audience might be less as well (Lustig & Koester, 1993). Context also counts; people tend to stand closer when communicating interpersonally than when speaking in front of a group and even closer to intimate partners. Most U.S. business relationships begin in the social zone, which is from four to twelve feet. Interacting with professional acquaintances less than four feet away might have negative consequences (Bremer, 2002).

TURNING TO TECHNOLOGY

Too Close for Comfort?

http://www3.azwestern.edu/psy/dgershaw/lol/proxemics.html

Read about the cultural differences regarding space as described on this Web site. Has something like this ever happened to you? Explain.

WHAT DO YOU THINK?

Consider a time when you observed what you assumed was a romantic couple in a public situation. What nonverbal cues made you think they were romantic? How do you feel about public displays of affection? Why?

WHAT DO YOU THINK?

Consider a class you've taken where the seats were arranged in a semicircle and one where they were arranged as in a traditional lecture hall. Which class had more discussion and interaction? What role might the seating arrangement have played?

Two other aspects of space may influence speech delivery: group density and seating arrangement. **Group density** has to do with how crowded the room feels to the audience. Generally, if listeners are seated at least one and one-half feet apart they'll be best able to attend to and retain your message. At less than a foot apart, they may be distracted and have a reduced attention span; if so, consider shortening your speech a bit and providing more variety in your delivery to help maintain interest. For most speeches in or out of the classroom, audience members sit in rows and face the speaker. This is especially common for formal speeches, as it focuses listeners on the speaker and his or her message. For small group discussions, audience members are often arranged in a semicircle in front of the speaker, which can encourage interaction and even reduce speech anxiety. The speaker is less afraid of being stared at because listeners look at each other as well as at the speaker.

TURNING TO TECHNOLOGY

Body Language and Territorial Space in the Workplace

http://members.aol.com/katydidit/bodylang.htm

This Web site talks about some important dos and don'ts with regard to space and territory in the workplace. Read through the short article. Do any of the tips surprise you? Why or why not? Have you experienced any of the personal space violations described here? If so, explain.

PRACTICING THE PROCESS

Guidelines for the Use of Space

- Consider the size of your audience.
- Consider the cultural context for your speech.
- Consider the size of the room where you'll speak.
- Consider group density: Will the room be crowded?
- Consider seating: How will the chairs be arranged?

Time

Like other nonverbal messages, how time is used should depend on cultural context. The meanings attached to time are **chronemics.** People from Western cultures tend to be very time conscious. We carry daily planners and wear digital watches so that we can arrive and depart at precisely the "right time." People from many other cultures are far less time conscious. In the Mexican culture, for example, it's rare to specify an exact time for guests to arrive for dinner. And American executives typically expect to take care of business quickly, whereas those in Europe and Japan expect to devote time to social interaction first. Strict punctuality might not be expected in some cultures, but mainstream Americans usually expect a speaker to finish and end on schedule. To promote a perception of respect for your

ETHICS

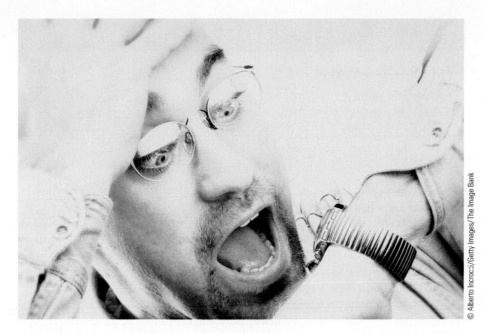

Be mindful of time on the day of your speech by arriving a bit early and adhering to time limits.

listeners, which appeals to Stage 4 (feeling and doing) of the learning cycle, don't disappoint them.

First, arrive a bit early for your speech. Just as it would at a job interview, a last-minute arrival tends to convey that you are unprepared, inconsiderate, incompetent, or uncommitted to the topic and occasion. This is due, in part, to the mainstream American perception of time rules for superiors and subordinates—the implicit understanding that subordinates wait for superiors, but superiors don't wait for subordinates. If you have a meeting set with a professor and show up late, it's best to apologize; but if the professor shows up late, don't expect an apology. (Did you know that former president Richard Nixon used to show up late to congressional meetings to demonstrate his power over them?)

TURNING TO TECHNOLOGY

Being "On Time" at Work

http://cbpa.louisville.edu/bruce/mgmtwebs/commun_f98/chronemics.htm

This short Web page offers tips to managers to ensure that employees arrive "on time." Do you agree or disagree with the suggestion offered? Why or why not?

Second, adhere to the time limit your audience expects. Some students argue that classroom time limits are unrealistic, pointing out that in the real world speakers are not penalized for running short or long. Actually, failing to adhere to time limit expectations sends the wrong message to listeners and thus detracts from the success of any presentation. If the talk is shorter than expected, listeners may feel cheated; if it's too long they may think the speaker is inconsiderate of their time. Did you ever have an instructor who repeatedly kept the class running beyond the scheduled time?

WHAT DO YOU THINK?
Can you think of someone you know who is perpetually late for engagements? How do you feel about your relationship with that person as a result?

Guidelines for the Use of Time

- Arrive a bit early.
- Adhere to time limit expectations by timing your speech during practice.

Appearance

Some students think what they wear shouldn't factor into the success of a speech. Yet studies show that a neatly groomed and professional appearance does send important messages about a speaker's commitment to the topic and occasion as well as about credibility (Bate, 1992; Cherulnik, 1989; Lawrence & Watson, 1991; Molloy, 1975; Temple & Loewen, 1993). Like the other nonverbal factors, appearance should reinforce your message and should certainly not distract from it. Appearance as a communication form is known as **object language.** Looking like a professional tends to improve speaker credibility (ethos). Would you wear jeans and a sweatshirt to a job interview? Probably not. Most business professionals realize the importance of appearance to help generate respect (Blouin et al., 1982; Drogosz & Levy, 1996). Furthermore, feeling good about how you look can reduce speech anxiety by reducing tension stemming from the fear of being stared at.

ETHICS

   Three general rules can help you decide how to dress and groom yourself for a presentation. First, avoid extremes. Consider the Mimi character on the *Drew Carey Show.* She wears flamboyant clothes and bright makeup and gets little or no respect from her colleagues. (Granted, she is also caustic, but the attire reduces her credibility even before she speaks.) For the public speaker, a tuxedo or evening gown, or large, dangling earrings and bright red lipstick are generally too extreme and likely to distract listeners. This rule applies even to attire related to the speech topic. For example, wearing a tutu to present your speech about ballet dancing is so extreme that it would probably distract listeners from your message. Wearing your postal carrier's uniform while delivering a speech about the postal service might work well, however, because it's not extreme to the point of distraction.

"Mimi" without Makeup

http://abc.go.com/primetime/drewcarey/lookandlisten.html

Watch the video of Kathy Kinney (Mimi) found at this site. Is your impression of her different when she isn't wearing her makeup and flamboyant clothes? Why?

   Second, consider the audience and occasion for the speech and dress a bit more formally than listeners are likely to be. Too formal equals untrustworthy and insincere (Phillips & Smith, 1992). Too casual equals lack of commitment to the topic and occasion (Morris et al., 1996). But dressing slightly better than the average audience member usually comes off quite well. Don't wear an evening gown for a classroom speech; save it for the after-dinner presentation at an honorary society banquet. Likewise, don't wear jeans and a flannel shirt for a classroom speech; save them for talking about fertilizers to area farmers. Dressing a bit more formally than listeners is the best way to boost your credibility and communicate a sense of commitment to the topic and occasion.

Finally, consider your topic and purpose. Some topics demand a more formal appearance. If describing how to succeed on a job interview, dress more formally than if talking about co-curricular activities on campus. You might dress even more formally if trying to convince listeners to support an important cause. Generally, the more serious your topic and purpose, the more formally you should dress.

TURNING TO TECHNOLOGY

Dressing for Success in the Business World

http://www.casualpower.com/

Read and view the before-and-after case studies offered. Do you agree with the suggestions made for dressing for success? Why or why not?

PRACTICING THE PROCESS

Guidelines for an Effective Appearance

- Avoid extremes.
- Be well-groomed.
- Consider the audience and occasion, and dress a bit more formally than your listeners are likely to be.
- Consider your topic and purpose. If your topic is quite serious or your purpose is to persuade, dress more formally.
- Double-check your appearance in the mirror before entering the room where you will speak.

"Tell me about yourself, Kugelman—your hopes, dreams, career path, and what that damn earring means."

From *Wall Street Journal*. Permission, Cartoon Features Syndicate. Reprinted by permission.

Eye Contact

Eyes are probably the most expressive source of nonverbal communication, and eye contact is an important way to include listeners in the communication transaction. Keeping in mind cultural orientations, consider three guidelines for maximizing eye contact.

TURNING TO TECHNOLOGY

Making and Sustaining Eye Contact

http://www.innerself.com/Lifestyle_Changes/eye_contact.htm

Read the suggestions for learning to make better eye contact offered by author Carlos Warter. Try the techniques. Do you think they work? Why or why not?

First, look at the audience at least 90 percent of the time. You may not achieve this goal, but set your standards high to increase the likelihood you'll make sufficient audience contact. Use your notes only as a reference; don't read directly from them, and refer to them only periodically. Because eyes express so much, the more you look at listeners instead of notes, the more you can support your message nonverbally.

WHAT DO YOU THINK?

Do you know which side you tend to favor when speaking? How might this affect contact with listeners seated on the other side of the room? What will you do to overcome this obstacle?

Second, scan the entire audience with your eyes. Beginning speakers tend to neglect listeners in the corners of the room, and we all tend to look at listeners on one side of the room more than the other. The latter often corresponds to the hand we favor; left-handers tend to look more to the left side than the right side. The only way to overcome this is through conscious effort.

Finally, look listeners in the eye. Some beginning speakers are concerned that this will increase anxiety and would prefer to gaze over everyone's heads, but looking listeners in the eye is much more effective for several reasons. First and foremost, most listeners will offer positive reinforcement when you look them in the eye—they'll nod and smile, perhaps—and that reduces speaker anxiety. Second, they tend to feel you are communicating with them and that they matter. Third, looking listeners in the eye gives you a chance to read their feedback and adjust your message as necessary. For example, Tasha noticed that several in the audience had quizzical looks as she explained external combustion. So she rephrased her explanation until those quizzical looks became affirming nods.

Before a large group you must create a sense of looking listeners in the eye even though you actually cannot. This is called **audience contact.** Television newscasters do this by making "eye contact" with the camera, creating a sense of connection with viewers at home.

TURNING TO TECHNOLOGY

Eye Contact Is Good for Your Audience and for You

http://www.speaking.com/articles_html/C.MikeJousan_588.html

Read C. Mike Jousan's suggestions about eye contact. Do you agree? Why or why not?

Guidelines for Eye Contact

- Look up from your notes 90 percent of the time.
- Scan the entire audience.
- Look listeners in the eye until a sense of connection is made before moving on.
- If the audience is large, create a sense of audience contact by simulating eye contact.
- If the audience is on the other side of a camera, make eye contact with the camera.

Body

The body communicates through facial expressions, gestures, posture, and body movements, cumulatively known as **kinesics.** Use your body in a way that appears appropriate, natural, and dynamic, and make sure all this is integrated with your verbal message.

Facial Expressions

Facial expressions can reinforce a wide range of verbal messages (Figure 12.1). For example, Nancy furrowed her brows and pursed her lips when she told the story of two young children who were abandoned in a parking lot. Her facial expression conveyed seriousness and disgust. Thad raised his eyebrows and smiled slightly as he talked about the many new forms of entertainment a domed stadium would bring to the city. His facial expression conveyed excitement. If you've ever watched the sitcom *Seinfeld,* you may recall that the Kramer character is a master at using facial expressions to make his messages more poignant, sometimes without saying a word. Beginning speakers may be reluctant to try emotionally reinforcing the verbal message through facial expressions, but it can dramatically increase a speech's appeal.

The most effective facial expressions are lively and yet appear natural and spontaneous even though they are not. They must be planned and practiced. Go through your speech outline and determine where a facial expression could reinforce an emotional stance, decide what that facial expression might be, make a note on the speaking outline, and practice your speech using that expression. Try it in front of a mirror so you can determine precisely what it looks and feels like when you achieve the effect you desire. This should make it easier to replicate during your actual speech.

The Use of Facial Expressions on *Seinfeld*

http://members.aol.com/artieman/entertainment/seinfeld/video.htm

Watch the *Seinfeld* video clip about the monkey and the banana peel. How do each character's facial expressions reinforce the verbal message and make the humorous point more successful?

© Columbia/The Kobal Collection

Exaggerated facial expressions are not necessary or desirable (except during a humorous speech).

Gestures

Gestures reinforce the verbal message by (a) emphasizing an important point, (b) referring to presentational aids, or (c) clarifying structure. As with facial expressions, effective gestures must appear spontaneous and natural but be carefully planned and practiced.

First, as you plan and practice your speech think about where gestures might serve a function. For example, you might extend an open palm to invite listeners to agree with you, or gesture with a closed fist to plead with them to do so. You might extend your arm toward a visual aid that explains a concept. And you might move your hand incrementally to reinforce the preview of main points. Regardless of the specific gestures, carefully plan and strategically place them so that they serve their purposes.

Second, eliminate gestures that don't reinforce the verbal message. Otherwise they will simply distract or even confuse listeners. Don't gesture so often that listeners await the next one instead of listening to what you have to say.

© Michael Newman/PhotoEdit

Strive for lively, natural expressions that convey true emotions.

Third, gesture from the elbow rather than the wrist. This looks more natural. Practice while sitting at a table, making your gestures above the table, not under it. (Thus you'll avoid the "penguin effect.") When using a gesture to point out a presentational aid, use the hand closest to the aid to keep from turning your back to the audience.

PRACTICING THE PROCESS

Guidelines for Gestures

- Place a note on your speaking outline where you'll gesture to reinforce points.
- Place a note on your speaking outline where you'll gesture to clarify structure.
- Place a note on your speaking outline where you'll gesture to refer to presentational aids.
- Practice the speech with your gestures until they feel spontaneous and natural, making sure they extend from the elbow.

Ensure that your gestures are purposeful and reinforce your message.

Some speakers get nervous about what to do with their hands as they speak. Planning and practicing gestures helps, because it ensures using the hands purposefully. For example, Mason's speech anxiety showed because he stuck his hand in a pocket and then removed it periodically. As listeners began watching the action rather than listening to him, his anxiety increased and yet he felt so awkward that he couldn't stop making the distracting gestures. Once Mason began planning gestures to reinforce certain points and practicing them in advance, his awkward feelings dissipated and the distracting gesture ceased.

Posture

You can convey confidence and commitment by your **posture**—how you stand and carry yourself. Use posture this way before you speak, as you speak, and as you conclude.

To send listeners an early message of calm confidence (regardless of whether you actually feel it), take your time approaching the front of the room and walk with your shoulders back, not slumped. Then pause for a moment or two and establish eye contact with a few listeners before beginning to speak. The pause creates a sense of **initial ethos,** or credibility.

During the speech, stand firmly on both feet, keeping them about shoulder width apart. Do not slouch or lean on one leg, which indicates a lack of commitment to the topic and occasion. Likewise, do not shift back and forth from one leg to the other or rock forward and backward on your heels, which communicates nervousness and can distract listeners. Don't lock your knees; it could cause your knees to shake and communicate nervousness. Standing firmly on both feet communicates confidence and commitment.

Finally, use posture to create a sense of **terminal ethos,** or closing credibility. Do this by pausing a moment or two and looking a few listeners in the eye upon finishing your conclusion. It might feel a bit awkward at first, but it leaves listeners believing in your commitment to the topic and occasion.

PRACTICING THE PROCESS

Guidelines for Posture

- Walk to the front of the room slowly and with your shoulders back.
- Pause and make eye contact with a few listeners before you begin to speak.
- Stand firmly on both feet throughout the speech.
- Don't lock your knees.
- Pause and look a few listeners in the eye upon finishing your speech.
- Walk back to your seat slowly and with your shoulders back.

Body Movement

Some people feel more comfortable speaking if they can move around, and doing so can also help maintain listener interest by appealing to the visual dimension of the learning cycle. If you choose to move, strive for **motivated movement,** which reinforces the verbal message by emphasizing important points, referring to presentational aids, or clarifying structure. As such, motivated movement is done along with a gesture to make the function even clearer. Movement is not appropriate unless it embellishes a gesture.

Movement thus operates much the same as gestures, and the same guidelines apply. Plan and practice movements that reinforce the verbal message; avoid those that do not, as they will merely distract.

To appear more natural, movement should be used together with gesture. For example, Leena's speech ended with a plea for more support from businesses for parental leave to care for sick children. She decided that this call to action would be enhanced by moving forward and at the same time gesturing with palms up. In this way, the movement would appear natural and her call to action would come across as a sincere plea and not a command. The combination of movement and gesture bolstered Leena's final emotional appeal.

It's important to remain "open" to the audience when moving from side to side so it doesn't look like you're turning your back to anyone. If you choose to move from one side of the room to the other, lead with the foot nearer your destination. If walking to the left, lead with your left foot and left hand simultaneously; if to the right, lead with your right foot and right hand simultaneously.

As with gestures, using your body effectively can reduce speech anxiety. If you often feel like you need to move while speaking, motivated movement may relax you as well as reinforce your message.

When moving during a speech, always remain "open" to your audience.

© Rick Friedman/CORBIS

TURNING TO TECHNOLOGY

Body Language in Interviews

http://cbpa.louisville.edu/bruce/mgmtwebs/commun_f98/kinesics.htm

Read about the tips suggested for body language in a job interview. Do any of these tips surprise you? If so, which ones and why?

PRACTICING THE PROCESS

Guidelines for Body Movement

- Use facial expressions that reinforce an emotional stance.
- Use gestures to emphasize important points, refer to presentational aids, or clarify structure.
- Stand firmly on both feet during the speech to communicate initial and terminal ethos.
- Use motivated movement with gestures to further reinforce the verbal message. Plan and practice where you'll move and why (to reinforce a point, clarify structure, refer to visual aids), so that during the actual speech your movement feels and looks natural and spontaneous.
- Remain open to the audience as you move.
- Make appropriate notes on your speaking outline.

Voice

Sending a verbal message with your voice also sends a nonverbal one. The verbal message is the actual words you say. Nonverbal use of voice refers to all elements of voice other than the actual words—rate, volume, pitch, quality, pronunciation, enunciation, stress, and pauses. It's *how* you say what you say. Such **paralanguage** contributes to meaning. For example, changing which words are stressed in a sentence can convey a very different meaning. Consider the sentence "Sally likes spinach." Saying "*Sally* likes spinach" means that Sally, not some other person, likes spinach. "Sally *likes* spinach" means that Sally likes rather than dislikes spinach, and "Sally likes *spinach*" means she prefers it to some other vegetable. If you ask "Sally likes spinach?" it means you didn't realize she likes spinach. It's the same three words in every case, but how they are spoken—the nonverbal component of the voice—makes a considerable difference in the meaning.

EFFECTIVE USE OF VOICE

The goal with regard to the nonverbal elements of voice is to be intelligible, vocally varied, and conversational. Intelligibility is a matter of quality, rate, volume, pitch, pronunciation, and enunciation. Vocal variation also requires considering rate, volume, and pitch, as well as stress and pauses. To be conversational means sounding spontaneous no matter how much you've practiced the speech or which delivery method you've chosen.

Intelligibility

Intelligibility is the capacity to be understood. If you are unintelligible, listeners are bound to struggle with your verbal message. Intelligibility is crucial to show that you are a competent and credible speaker. Let's look at each voice aspect that contributes to intelligibility.

Vocal quality, or **timbre,** distinguishes your voice from others. Although each voice is unique, strive for a pleasing vocal quality so as to be most intelligible. Otherwise listeners may focus on how you sound rather than on what you're saying. Practice the Deep Breathing and Controlled Exhalation activities at the end of this chapter, and employ them whenever you give a speech. Beginning speakers often have problems with breathiness, harshness, and nasality.

If too much air escapes noticeably through the vocal folds in your throat, you'll sound feathery, fuzzy, and whispery—that is, *breathy*. Marilyn Monroe was famous for this, and many think it made her sound sexy. Today actors such as Demi Moore, Goldie Hawn, Nicole Kidman, and Kathleen Turner sometimes use breathiness for the same purpose. But breathiness usually doesn't work for public speakers; it reduces ethos because it doesn't carry well and suggests immaturity, shallowness, and a weak, frail personality (Mayer, 1994). A breathy voice comes from improper breathing habits and too little tension in the vocal folds while speaking. To overcome it, in addition to deep breathing and controlled exhalation try the Cold Mirror Test activity at the end of this chapter.

Constricting the throat too much, on the other hand, sounds *harsh*—strident, tense, and shrill like Joan Rivers or Marge Simpson or Lucille Ball. This comes across as hypertense or abrasive. Or it might sound gravelly, guttural, and throaty like John Wayne, Nick Nolte, or Jack Nicholson, which may be perceived as cold and unsympathetic (Mayer, 1994). Either way, intelligibility suffers and listeners may focus on voice quality rather than the message. If you constrict your voice for long, hoarseness may result, further hurting your intelligibility. To improve, in addition to deep breathing and controlled exhalation, practice speaking with a relaxed and open throat (see the Open Throat exercise in Chapter 12 additional activities on the Web site).

If too much air passes through the sinuses and nose, the voice sounds *nasal*. This is associated with immaturity, lower-than-average intelligence, and a boring personality (Mayer, 1994). Country singers such as Dwight Yoakam, Dolly Parton, and George Strait are nasal, but for most speakers nasality simply hurts intelligibility and leads listeners to focus on it rather than the message. Nasality can be reduced by opening your mouth wider, relaxing your tongue in the rear of your mouth, and using crisper articulation for consonants. If you need to work on nasality, try the Nasality Reduction exercise in Chapter 12 additional activities on the Web site.

Rate is how fast you speak. Between 100 and 200 words per minute is right for most speeches. Most people naturally speak at about 120 words per minute. Speaking more slowly can hurt intelligibility because it's usually boring; speaking more quickly directly hurts intelligibility, especially if complex ideas and arguments are being presented.

Volume is how loudly or softly you speak. Speak loudly enough, with or without a microphone, to be heard easily in the back of the room but not so loudly as to bring discomfort to listeners seated near the front. Soft speakers run the risk of losing credibility because they appear timid and unsure of themselves. Speakers who are too loud also risk losing credibility because they may appear obnoxious or pushy.

Pitch is the highness or lowness of your voice on the musical staff. Pitch that is too high tends to communicate nervousness; too low tends to sound artificial and insincere. Intelligible pitch fluctuates as in normal conversation. A monotone pitch—one that does not fluctuate—usually hinders intelligibility.

WHAT DO YOU THINK?
What regional dialect do you have? What are some pronunciation and enunciation habits associated with it? Are any other dialects represented in your audience? Why is it important to use standard enunciations and pronunciations?

Pronunciation is how the sounds of a word are said and which parts are stressed. Think about pronunciation when you plan and practice your speech and again when you deliver it. In general, use standard dictionary pronunciation—and if you're not sure what that is for a given word, look it up and practice saying it aloud. People mispronounce words by omitting, adding, or changing the order of sounds, substituting one sound for another, and stressing the wrong syllables (Mayer, 1994). Some commonly mispronounced words are given in Table 12.1, along with the correct pronunciation. Poor pronunciation almost always harms credibility and intelligibility.

Sometimes students argue that dialect pronunciations such as "warsh" for "wash" or "mudda" for "mother" might be more conversational if listeners come from the same region. But there's almost always someone in the audience who is unfamiliar with the dialect. Wise speakers choose standard pronunciations, which everyone will recognize.

Enunciation is the act of speaking distinctly and clearly. In conversation, sounds are often dropped or run together, especially in common combinations of words, such as when saying *Ja-eet?* for *Did you eat?* A public speaker, however, usually is best off using a formal style, which includes clear enunciation. Sloppy enunciation is not the same as mispronunciation, but it too can affect credibility and intelligibility. So be aware of words or types of words you tend not to enun-

Word	Correct Pronunciation	Incorrect Pronunciation
athlete	a-thlete	ath-a-lete
creek	creek	crick
environment	environment	enviroment
escape	escape	excape
February	February	Febuary
government	government	goverment
hundred	hundred	hunderd, hunnert
library	library	libary
mirror	mirror	meer
picture	picture	pitcher
roof	roof	ruff
sandwich	sandwich	sanwich, samwich
wash	wash	warsh

Table 12.1 Commonly mispronounced words

PRACTICING THE PROCESS

Guidelines for Intelligibility

- Speak at a generally moderate rate.
- Speak loud enough for all to hear you easily, even in the back of the room.
- Check pronunciations and make notes on your speaking outline.
- Make notes on your speaking outline to enunciate certain words or phrases clearly if necessary.

ciate clearly. For example, you might tend to delete the first syllable of *because* (cuz), delete the *g* in the verb ending *ing* (goin', doin', walkin', talkin'), or combine *to* with a preceding verb (wanna, hafta). If you're aware of such patterns, you can work to enunciate the words clearly while practicing your speech.

Vocal Variety

Vocal variety refers to changing rate, pitch, and volume—three aspects of voice discussed in the previous section—as well as stressing certain words and using pauses. Vocal variety enables speakers to reinforce the emotional meaning of their message and to be dynamic.

Emotional intent can be reinforced by gradually speeding up or slowing down (varying rate), speaking higher or lower (varying pitch), or speaking louder or softer (varying volume). Generally, speeding up rate, raising pitch, or increasing volume can convey emotions such as joy, enthusiasm, excitement, fear, and anticipation, and a sense of uncertainty or urgency. Slowing down rate, lowering pitch, or decreasing volume can communicate peacefulness, resolution, remorse, disgust, or sadness. For example, Dalmus exclaimed:

> Millions of Americans suffer needlessly each year. These people endure unbearable pain needlessly because, although our government is capable of helping them, it chooses to ignore their pain. Our government has no compassion, no empathy, no regard for human feeling. I'm here today to convince you to support my efforts toward legalizing marijuana as a painkiller for terminally ill patients.

To reinforce the emotional elements of anger, disgust, and seriousness in this, Dalmus gradually slowed his rate, decreased his volume, and lowered his pitch as he exclaimed, "Our government has no compassion, no empathy, no regard for human feeling."

Stress is emphasis placed on words to indicate the importance of the ideas expressed. Stress can also be used for contrast, as in the examples of "Sally likes spinach" earlier. Consider a line from Dalmus's speech in which he stressed the key words to give the line even more weight: "Our government has no comPASSion, no EMpathy, no reGARD for HUMan FEELing."

Pauses, too, can be used to mark important ideas. If one or more sentences express an important idea, you can pause before each sentence to signal that something important is coming up, or afterward to allow the ideas to sink in. Pausing one or more times within a sentence adds further impact. Dalmus included several short pauses within and a long pause just after his line (pauses and their length are indicated by slash marks): "Our government has no comPASSion, / no EMpathy, / no reGARD for HUMan FEELing. / /"

As with the other aspects of delivery, plan where to vary rate, pitch, and volume, as well as where to stress key words and incorporate pauses. Place reminders on your speaking outline and practice thoroughly to achieve effective delivery in your actual presentation. Consider tape-recording or videotaping yourself practicing so you can critique whether you are actually conveying the vocal variety you intend.

PRACTICING THE PROCESS

Guidelines for Vocal Variety

On the speaking outline for your speech:

- Make notes to slow down at appropriate points to convey anger, disgust, or seriousness and practice doing so.
- Make notes to speed up your rate, raise pitch, or increase volume to convey uncertainty, urgency, excitement, fear, or anticipation. Practice doing so.
- Make notes to stress key words or phrases. Practice doing so.
- Make notes to pause before or after key phrases to help them stand out. Practice doing so.

Conversational Style

Being conversational is a major characteristic of effective delivery. If you are **conversational,** you sound spontaneous and natural despite thorough practice. Conversational style sounds as if you're talking *to* listeners rather than *at* them, sharing ideas *with* them rather than presenting a speech *in front of* them. One of the best ways to achieve this is to focus on sincerely trying to get your ideas across. It's also a great way to reduce speech anxiety, as getting a message across is usually less stressful than performing.

METHODS OF DELIVERY

Understanding the components of effective delivery is certainly the first step, but how do you meet all these criteria? The short answer is practice. However, the best way to practice depends on your method of delivery.

The four methods for delivering a speech are impromptu, manuscript, memorized, and extemporaneous. More than one can be drawn on for a single speech, but each delivery primarily follows just one method.

The Impromptu Method

The **impromptu method** involves speaking with limited preparation. Like any other speech it focuses on one general purpose (inform, persuade, or entertain) and is organized using clear macrostructure as well as accurate, inclusive, and vivid language. Unlike other speeches, however, preparation time for formulating and organizing ideas is limited to a few moments. Although most beginning speakers fear impromptu speaking, they probably do it often in many contexts. When television reporters interview people live, the interviewees are speaking impromptu. When people agree to share a few words at a banquet, they engage in impromptu speaking. When supervisors ask an employee for a brief project progress report at a meeting without forewarning, the response must of necessity be impromptu. Chapter 17 discusses occasions for impromptu speaking in more detail.

WHAT DO YOU THINK?

Have you ever been asked to tell a story on the spot, give a toast at the last minute, or explain a concept to the class in response to a teacher's question? If so, you've used the impromptu speaking method.

An advantage of speaking impromptu might be that you sound spontaneous and conversational, because you are forced to be. But your response probably won't be structured too clearly, so you might sound incoherent. You might also have trouble sounding fluent and expressive without practice, and you may find it difficult to come up with the best language and style choices. Thus public speakers avoid using the impromptu method for formal presentations.

The Manuscript Method

The **manuscript method** involves reading a speech that has been written out in its entirety. The president of the United States delivers important speeches such as the State of the Union address using the manuscript method. Television news anchors read much of the evening news from a manuscript via a teleprompter. An advantage is that you can carefully select words and phrases and then use precisely those when speaking, making it unlikely that you'll be misunderstood. This can be particularly beneficial if your speech is likely to be quoted later. But there are many disadvantages. Reading allows less eye contact with the audience and, in general, less sense of connection. You may sound mechanical rather than conversational and sincere. It is difficult to bring a manuscript to life without a lot of practice and work because you must make formal sentences sound informal. (The Ted Baxter character delivering the evening news on the *Mary Tyler Moore* show is a classic example of this problem.) Moreover, a speech read word for word makes it difficult to adapt to the feedback listeners may give as you talk. For these reasons, avoid the manuscript method except when reading direct quotations or statistics that must be accurate.

The Memorized Method

The **memorized method** is similar to the manuscript method in that the entire speech is written out but differs in that it is presented from memory. You don't even use notes. Professional speakers who use one speech on different occasions and for different audiences often do this.

Because the memorized speech was scripted first, this method has some of the same language and style benefits as the manuscript method, and it does allow a great deal of eye contact. However, unexpected audience feedback may throw you off or cause you to lose your place; with no notes or manuscript in hand it may be difficult to regain your composure and continue. It also takes a lot of practice and hard work to get a memorized speech to sound conversational. Thus beginning speakers usually should avoid the memorized method, though it's fine to memorize some important segments so you can maximize eye contact, facial expressions, and vocal variety. For example, speakers often memorize the attention catcher and clincher to create stronger initial and terminal ethos.

The Extemporaneous Method

The **extemporaneous method** requires that a speech be carefully researched and planned just like the manuscript or memorized method. However, you prepare and speak from a speaking outline rather than writing everything out. Thus each time you present the speech, the key concepts remain intact but the ideas are phrased somewhat differently. This has many of the advantages of the other methods and avoids the disadvantages: You can sound spontaneous and conversational, as with the impromptu method, and yet organized and coherent, as with the memorized and manuscript methods. Precisely because it can be thoroughly planned and practiced but sound spontaneous and conversational, the extemporaneous method is usually the best approach for beginning speakers (Table 12.2).

Looking at the Learning Cycle

Considering Delivery

Various aspects of delivery address the four dimensions of the learning cycle:

- *Feeling:* time, space, eye contact, facial expressions, vocal variety, conversational style
- *Watching:* appearance, facial expressions, gestures, motivated movement, posture
- *Thinking:* intelligibility, appearance, posture
- *Doing:* time, space, eye contact, gestures, motivated movement, conversational style

---

PRACTICING THE SPEECH

To gain the considerable advantages of the extemporaneous method, practice your speech out loud. Practice will make you more effective. It gives you the opportunity to experiment with each type of nonverbal cue. You can try various facial expressions, gestures, and movement; you can try saying words and phrases

Delivery Component	Impromptu	Manuscript	Memorized	Extemporaneous
Macrostructure	−	+	+	+
Language and style	−	+	+	+
Eye contact	+	−	+	+
Intelligibility	−	+	+	+
Vocal variety	−	−	+	+
Conversationality	+	−	−	+
Adaptability	+	−	−	+

+ = Potential strength of this method
− = Potential weakness of this method

Table 12.2 Delivery methods and their effects

in different ways in terms of rate, pitch, volume, stresses, and pauses. By experimenting strategically, you can figure out how to use your voice and body to reinforce your verbal message. Ultimately, you can make notes on your speaking outline to serve as reminders when you present the actual speech.

Practice has other important benefits, too. Most important, it reduces speech anxiety. Most speech anxiety is rooted in fear of the unknown, which arises when we ask ourselves "what if" questions. Practicing out loud eliminates some of those what-ifs because you prove to yourself that you can get from the beginning to the end. Practicing also reduces anxiety by increasing self-confidence. And it enhances your ethos. The more you practice, the more fluent you will sound and the more confident you will appear. Fluency and confidence improve credibility.

When Should You Begin Practicing Your Speech?

Don't fall into the procrastination trap, where practice always suffers. If you wait until the end to prepare your speech, you'll run out of time to practice. Like Trini's speech in the example at the beginning of this chapter, even the most clearly organized and thoroughly researched speech is likely to fail if the delivery is poor. Ideally, finish outlining your speech *at least three days before your assigned speaking day*, so you have time to practice. It's like piano lessons: The student who practices a little each day improves more than the one who crams it all into the few hours before the next lesson.

How Should You Practice Your Speech?

As you practice, focus especially on nonverbal cues related to use of voice and body, because these are the hardest to figure out. Also work on smoothly and effectively incorporating presentational aids.

Always practice out loud. Reading through notes silently and thinking about how you will deliver the speech is not good enough. You need to make sure that you will be intelligible and conversational, and to plan how to use vocal variety. As you practice, look for and work on mispronunciation and sloppy enunciation. Also, practice using vocal variety such as stresses, pauses, and changes in rate and volume at different points in your speech and in different ways. Choose the techniques that best support your ideas. Feedback from friends can be helpful here. The goal is fluent and conversational sentences that flow from a speaking outline. If you begin practicing with a manuscript, gradually reduce the written sentences to the key words and phrases of the speaking outline you will use during the actual presentation.

Mark delivery cue reminders on your speaking outline. For example, you might capitalize or highlight words you plan to stress. Recall that slash marks (/) can be used to signal pauses. Arrows pointing up or down can signal volume changes. You might also include short notes to remind yourself to SLOW DOWN or to LOOK AT THE AUDIENCE or to REFER TO THE PRESENTATIONAL AID. The coding system ought to be your own. What's important is using delivery cues and having some system for coding them. Even the most accomplished speakers use cues.

As with vocal cues, body cues for facial expressions, gestures, and movements may be developed by practicing in front of friends whose opinions you trust. Practicing in front of a mirror or videotaping yourself can also be helpful. While practicing, focus on whether facial expressions reinforce your verbal message, whether gestures and movements appear natural and spontaneous, and whether you

© Dwayne Newton/PhotoEdit

Practicing in front of a mirror can help you hone nonverbal aspects of your speech such as facial expressions and gestures.

remain "open" to the audience rather than turning your back. Natural-looking use of body is, in fact, well practiced.

Incorporate your presentational aids. Practice revealing and concealing them at the appropriate points. Practice gesturing toward them. Try to think of the worst that could happen while using presentational aids and plan what you'll do if it does happen. What will you do If the posterboard falls to the floor, the projector malfunctions, or the visual aids are in the wrong order? Although you should try to avoid such problems, have an alternative course of action ready. Chapter 13 provides more specifics on the use of presentational aids.

Make sure you practice enough times. The more you practice, the more techniques you can try and the more likely that you will find the ones that work and actually incorporate them when you present the speech. Make sure, also, that you practice fully enough. The more aspects of nonverbal communication you include in practicing, the less you'll fear the unknown and the less you'll feel anxiety.

DELIVERY AND PUBLIC SPEAKING ANXIETY

Remember that some anxiety is useful because it releases adrenaline, which helps you think faster and speak with more enthusiasm. The aim is **controlled nervousness**—anxiety that can be turned into positive energy and actually enhance

Rehearsal Guidelines

- Begin practicing at least three days before giving the speech.
- Focus on use of voice and body.
- Practice out loud.
- Include delivery cues on your speaking outline.
- Incorporate your presentational aids.
- Record and critique yourself.
- Solicit feedback from friends.

your delivery. What follows are two sets of tips, the first for use while practicing and the second for use when presenting the speech.

Anxiety Reduction While Practicing the Speech

1. *Speak extemporaneously.* We've seen the advantages of the extemporaneous method; to feel comfortable about using this method effectively, use it in practices as well.

2. *Concentrate on getting your ideas across.* In trying out various nonverbal cues, keep in mind that these should support your verbal message. Avoid flowery language or overly dramatic oral delivery. When all is said and done, the purpose of speaking is to share your message with listeners. You'll feel more relaxed about your speech if you've geared it to this purpose.

3. *Imagine yourself presenting an excellent speech.* Negative imaging and self-talk will most certainly hurt you by increasing anxiety. Positive imaging and self-talk might help you by reducing it. Imaging and self-talk tend to be self-reinforcing. Therefore, use positive imaging and self-talk throughout your speech practice.

4. *Devote extra time to practicing the introduction and conclusion.* Use practice to polish both the content and delivery of your introduction and conclusion. Not only does research show that listeners are most likely to remember the beginning and end of the message but, just as important, your confidence is usually enhanced when you feel good about how the first few lines go.

5. *Practice in the room where you will present the speech.* To reduce the fear of the unknown, try to practice where you'll present the speech. This gives a sense of how loudly or softly you need to speak and can help you prepare for possible environmental distractions that might occur there.

6. *Devote extra time to gestures.* Speech anxiety rooted in the fear of being stared at escalates when speakers start worrying about what to do with their hands. For this reason, it's especially important to develop gestures that are effective and to practice them in front of a mirror or in front of friends to reassure yourself that they look natural and spontaneous.

Anxiety Reduction While Presenting the Speech

1. *Employ mental and physical relaxation techniques before leaving your seat.* Use deep breathing exercises, muscular relaxation techniques, and positive self-talk to lower your pulse and help you feel calmer. Then, right before you

walk to the front of the room, take three deep breaths. Tighten your muscles while holding each breath; relax your muscles while exhaling each breath. This takes little time and can make a dramatic difference in lowering anxiety.

2. *Pause before beginning the speech.* Walk to the front of the room, organize your materials, and plant your feet firmly. Then force yourself to pause for three seconds before beginning. Count silently "one-one thousand, two-one thousand, three-one thousand" or look down at your notes and silently read the attention catcher you've prepared. This technique helps you appear confident and will help you feel more confident and calm as well. Moreover, reading over your attention catcher may help reduce the fear of failure because you'll have the chance to get those words firmly in mind.

3. *Focus on the message.* Communicate rather than perform. Public speaking is not acting. You have researched and organized a message that you believe will benefit your listeners, so focus on getting it across.

4. *Remember that everyone makes mistakes.* Keep the speech in perspective. When you make a mistake, as is inevitable, don't focus on the mistake and whether anyone noticed it. Instead, remind yourself that everyone makes mistakes and move on.

5. *Remember that most bodily reactions are not visible.* It may seem like everyone notices your wobbly knees or shaky hands, but usually that's not so. If your knees begin to wobble, remind yourself that it's probably not noticeable, and stay focused on your message.

6. *Never apologize for nervousness.* Never start out by saying how nervous you are. All it could do is cause listeners to focus on your potential jitters rather than on the message.

7. *Act poised.* Do this no matter how you feel inside. Act poised and most people will never know how you feel.

8. *Look audience members in the eyes.* Avoiding eye contact usually increases anxiety because your imagination tends to overestimate negative reactions, whereas most listeners will provide positive nonverbal feedback if given the chance. Looking listeners in the eye, then, not only reduces anxiety but, as you perceive listeners' smiles and nods, increases your confidence as well.

9. *Do not let individual listeners upset you.* If someone seems inattentive or even belligerent, remember it's his or her problem, not yours. Forget about it and focus instead on everybody else.

10. *Always remember, it is normal to be nervous.* The most effective public speakers are nervous. They simply learn how to control their anxiety and make it work for them. You can too!

SUMMARY

A speech is thoroughly prepared only if its delivery has been thoroughly practiced. Delivery is how you present a speech through use of voice, face, and body. These are nonverbal communications that have to do with *how* we say what we say. The two essential characteristics of effective delivery are being listener centered and sounding conversational. Delivery should be communication based, not performance based.

Nonverbal cues must be considered by how they reinforce your verbal message. Types include the use of space and distance, time constraints, appearance, eye contact, use of body, and use of voice. All six are important, but use of body and use of voice require extra attention. Use of body includes nonverbal cues related to facial expression, posture, gestures, and movement. Use of voice concerns intelligibility, vocal variety, and conversational style.

The four methods of delivery are impromptu, manuscript, memorized, and extemporaneous. Speeches may contain elements of various methods but belong primarily to one. The extemporaneous method, which involves speaking from an outline, combines the advantages of the other methods in that an extemporaneous speech is simultaneously prepared and conversational. It's generally the most effective choice for beginning speakers.

Practice the speech several times before actually giving it. This improves its effectiveness, and reduces your anxiety while increasing your ethos. Begin practicing at least three days before speech delivery. Work on nonverbal cues related to use of voice and body and on how to incorporate presentational aids. By following several tips given for managing speech anxiety while practicing and presenting the speech, you'll reduce anxiety and make it work for you.

RETURNING TO TECHNOLOGY

The *Confident Public Speaking* CD-ROM is your one-stop point of access for not just the content on the CD itself, such as Speech Interactive, but also the many other resources on the *Confident Public Speaking* Web site, Speech Builder Express, and InfoTrac College Edition. Note that this chapter's key terms and activities are among the resources available in electronic format online. Additional information is included below.

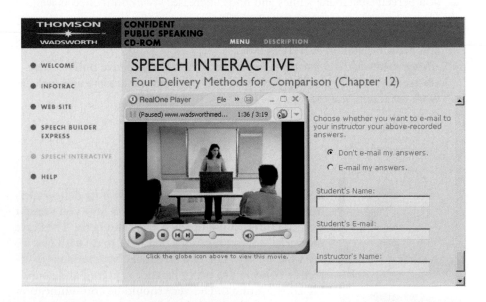

SPEECH INTERACTIVE
ON THE *CONFIDENT PUBLIC SPEAKING* CD-ROM

Speech Interactive is your link to this text's speech videos. Offering opportunities to practice critiquing speeches by students and other public speakers, these videos will help you prepare for providing effective feedback to your peers and your own speech performances.

SPEECH BUILDER EXPRESS

Use the Speech Timeline feature of Speech Builder Express to help you manage the time you have to prepare your speech. You may also want to watch some video clips of speeches included in the program to evaluate others' delivery.

KEY TERMS

Interactive flashcards for these key terms are available on the *Confident Public Speaking* Web site. You'll find the "Flashcards" link under the resources for Chapter 12.

ACTIVITIES

The activities below, as well as additional activities, are available in electronic format on the *Confident Public Speaking* Web site. You'll find the "Activities" link under the resources for Chapter 12.

1. **Music Lyrics Interpretation.** Bring the lyrics to a favorite song with you to class. In pairs, work to discover how to convey the emotional intent of the lyrics orally. Then consider how to further reinforce the emotional intent through use of body. Finally, read those lyrics to the group, employing the techniques for use of voice and use of body detailed in this chapter.
   Use of voice: Intelligible, vocally varied, conversational
   Use of body: Facial expressions, posture, gestures, movement
2. **Conveying Emotions Nonverbally.** Form a group with three or four classmates. As a group, identify a variety of emotions (sadness, excitement, worry, fear, and so on) and write them on index cards. Place the cards face down in a pile at the front of the room. One at a time, draw a card. Each student recites the same nursery rhyme or children's poem three times for the class, trying to convey the emotion on his or her card. The first time,

the speaker should try to convey the emotion through voice alone; the second time, the speaker should add facial expression; and the third time the speaker should add body language as well. After each recitation, the class tries to guess the emotion. When each speaker finishes, he or she should talk about what was done to convey the emotion vocally, facially, and bodily. Talk about the implications for public speakers.

3. **Deep Breathing.** First, lie flat on your back. Place a book on your abdomen, and place one hand on the upper part of your chest. Breathe in and out as naturally as possible. You should notice a slow and regular expansion and contraction in the area under the book and very little movement in the area under your hand. Practice doing this until it becomes second nature. Second, stand up and place one hand on the front of your abdomen and the other on your lower back. Breathe in and out as naturally as possible, trying to keep most of the movement in the center of your body.

4. **Controlled Exhalation.** Take a deep breath and release it slowly, making the sound "sssss." Keep it even and regular to the count of ten, then fifteen, and finally twenty. Repeat this process with the sound "fffff." Eventually, sustain the "ssssss" and the "fffff" sounds to the count of thirty.

5. **Cold Mirror Test.** Hold a very cold mirror about one-and-a-half inches from your mouth. Say "aaahhh." Check the mirror. If it's foggy, you're allowing too much breath to escape as you speak. Wipe the mirror off and try again, saying "aaahhh" much louder. There should be less fogging. Practice until you can keep the mirror from becoming foggy. Then repeat this activity with the sounds "oh," "ow," "ee," and "oo."

6. **Audio Self-Critique.** Record your delivery of an upcoming speech on audiotape and listen to it. Critique yourself according to intelligibility, vocal variety, and conversationality. Determine what specific things you can do differently to improve your use of voice. Indicate them on your notes, and practice the speech several more times. Then audiotape yourself again, comparing the two versions to assess effective change. Include this self-critique in your portfolio.

7. **Video Self-Critique.** Videotape your delivery of an upcoming speech and then watch the video without the sound. Critique yourself according to facial expressions, posture, gestures, and movement. Determine what specific changes you can make to improve your use of body. Indicate them in your notes, and practice the speech several more times. Then videotape yourself again, comparing the two versions to assess effective change. Include this self-critique in your portfolio.

INFOTRAC COLLEGE EDITION ACTIVITY

Use the search term "regional dialects" to locate and read articles about dialects spoken near where you live or elsewhere. What are some of the word choices or pronunciations that are unique to each dialect? How many different dialects do you think are represented in your public speaking classroom? Do you think public speakers should use standard English? Why or why not?

CREATING AND USING PRESENTATIONAL AIDS

REFLECTIVE QUESTIONS

1. How might presentational aids enhance your public speech?

2. How might you decide whether a line graph, bar graph, or pie graph is the most appropriate visual to illustrate a piece of evidence?

3. Why is it considered better not to pass photographs around the audience, and not to use the chalkboard as a presentational aid in a formal public speech?

4. Why should visual aids—even those presented via a program such as PowerPoint—be more than just a list of words?

5. What guidelines would you suggest for a speaker using a video or audio clip as a presentational aid?

WHAT'S AHEAD: FOCUSING YOUR READING

What Are Presentational Aids?

Why Use Presentational Aids?

Types of Presentational Aids

Media for Displaying Presentational Aids

Constructing Presentational Aids

Using Presentational Aids

IVY GAVE A SPEECH ABOUT RELIGIOUS rites of passage with a focus on the similarities and differences between the Jewish bar mitzvah and the Christian confirmation. She'd planned to use slides to illustrate aspects of each ceremony as she spoke, but after switching on the projector she discovered the lightbulb had burned out. The great deal of time she spent preparing and organizing the slides could not overcome this catastrophe. She gave the presentation without slides, trying her best to explain in words what the slides would have shown. But she could tell from her listeners' faces that much remained unclear.

Claus's speech compared the origins and rules of football and rugby. He had prepared charts to help listeners visualize differences between the sports. When he unrolled the first poster and placed it on an easel, however, the poster rolled back up and tumbled to the floor. Claus calmly picked it up and held it in his hands while he spoke. But holding the poster meant he could not make adequate eye contact or use gestures.

Ahmad's speech on how television sitcoms often stereotype African Americans featured portions of three programs he had videotaped to support his three main points. After showing the first clip, Ahmad noticed that he had only a minute left to complete his speech. He had to leave out the other two clips, and his speech was less compelling as a result.

These speakers would have benefited from knowing more about using presentational aids in a public speech. Ivy could have prepared for the worst by bringing an extra lightbulb, preparing a handout, or even arriving early enough to check her equipment in advance. Claus could have used sturdier posterboard for his charts. And Ahmad could have timed his speech, including the videotaped examples, to ensure that he would remain on schedule. Each speaker learned an important lesson about using presentational aids—but the lessons came late.

TURNING TO TECHNOLOGY

The Apollo 11 Moon Landing

http://www.historychannel.com/broadband/

Watch the "Apollo 11 Moon Landing" found through the "Video Clips" link at this site. How do the visuals make the message more concrete? Does the background music as a presentational aid help or hinder the message? How and why?

WHAT ARE PRESENTATIONAL AIDS?

Presentational aids help explain the ideas in a speech. They are usually visual, audio, or audiovisual. **Visual aids** include actual objects, models, photographs, drawings and diagrams, graphs, and charts. Ivy's photographs made into slides and Claus's charts were visual aids. **Audio aids** focus on sound and include things such as musical recordings, conversations, interviews, speeches, and environmental sounds. **Audiovisual aids,** such as videotapes and computer-generated slide show presentations, combine sight and sound. Occasionally, presentational aids appeal to the other senses of touch, smell, and taste.

By supplementing words, presentational aids make ideas more concrete and clear for listeners (e.g., Mitchell, 1987). Can you recall a time when someone

© Bob Daemmrich/Stock Boston, LLC

It would be difficult or impossible to learn how to tie a shoe without visual aids to demonstrate the process.

gave you directions that only confused you more? If they had shown you a map, perhaps it would have cleared things up. Imagine trying to teach a toddler how to tie shoelaces without demonstrating the process. Or trying to describe what your favorite musical group sounds like without playing a bit of their music. One reason schools perform fire drills, cities sound storm alarms, and radio stations test the emergency broadcast system is to give people a chance to hear what these alarms sound like so they will recognize them in a real emergency. We understand things better when we can actually see or hear them.

Presentational slide shows such as those constructed on software like PowerPoint have become essential for successful public speaking in business. Studies suggest that presenters who use good computer-generated slide shows are rated as 43 percent more persuasive than those who don't (Antonoff, 1990). The problem is that many people don't have the training to create effective slide shows (Booher, 2003). This chapter provides that know-how.

Here we discuss how presentational aids can enhance a speech, explore the types of aids you can choose from, consider various media for displaying these aids. We also examine factors you need to think about in order to construct effective presentational aids and use them well.

WHAT DO YOU THINK?

Consider a time when you tried to describe to someone what something sounded, smelled, or tasted like. Was it easy or difficult? How might a presentational aid have helped?

WHY USE PRESENTATIONAL AIDS?

The main purpose of presentational aids is to make verbal messages more concrete. Presentational aids also add variety to a speech, reduce public speaking anxiety, increase listener retention, convey information concisely, enhance persuasive appeals, and reach more listeners by rounding the cycle of learning.

Clarifying the Verbal Message

The best aids make the verbal message clearer so listeners better comprehend the speaker's meaning. For example, an informative speech on how to groom a dog might use slides to illustrate whisker trimming and toenail clipping. Seeing the process while it is described out loud makes the explanations more concrete. If an aid does not add concreteness, don't use it. Hence aids should never be a mere bulleted list of single words or topics; rather, they should supplement spoken words to make meaning more clear (Booher, 2003).

Adding Variety

Presentational aids add variety by giving the audience something new to look at or listen to. Listeners whose minds begin to wander can be drawn back into the speech when you introduce a presentational aid. Creatively constructed aids can prove especially effective for this purpose; they are even more important for long presentations such as those given at a business meeting or conference. Marjorie Brody (2003), award-winning author of fifteen books and internationally recognized expert on image/career enhancement, explains how to get a crowd of hungry or tired conference attendees interested in your presentation this way:

> Be daring and different. Seek untraditional methods to relate your information. Investigate all your options. Never rule anything out. (Brody, 2003)

Stephanie used a creatively constructed visual aid to add variety to her informative speech on the popularity of the Rolling Stones over several decades. She presented a bar graph depicting the sales of successive recordings. She added variety to it by using pictures of tongues—a bright red tongue is a symbol of the band—to represent numerical increments on the bars.

Reducing Public Speaking Anxiety

Presentational aids can help reduce public speaking anxiety. In the case of visual aids, listeners will be looking at the aid, not at you (Dwyer, 1998; Wangen, 1999). All presentational aids can reduce anxiety stemming from the fear of failure, be-

DILBERT reprinted by permission of United Feature Syndicae, Inc.

cause the information they contain jogs your memory about portions of the speech.

Increasing Listener Retention

Presentational aids increase listener retention, which is one of your main goals. If constructed well and integrated properly, aids help listeners remember key points after the speech is over. Some research suggests that people remember as little as 20 percent of what they only hear but more than 50 percent of what they both see and hear (Heinich, Molenda, & Russell, 1993). Other research suggests that retention increases fivefold (Long, 1997). Thus the cliché "A picture is worth a thousand words."

WHAT DO YOU THINK?

Can you recall a time when a speaker used a visual aid that confused you? Why was it confusing? What effect did it have on the success of the speech for you?

Conveying Information Concisely

Presentational aids convey information concisely. Some ideas or concepts are difficult to explain through words alone, or would require lengthy explanations that would tire listeners. Aids can clarify concepts in less time and with fewer spoken words. A fifteen- to twenty-second video clip, for example, can illustrate as much as ten minutes of verbal description or explanation (Currid, 1995). Television commercials in the 1950s and 1960s typically lasted about a minute; today, most are fifteen seconds or less. This shift came about in part because advertisers learned they can quickly get people to buy with the aid of visuals.

Increasing Persuasive Appeal

By adding impact to a speech, presentational aids can increase a speaker's credibility and, thus, persuasive appeal. In a study by the 3M Corporation, speakers who used visual aids in their presentations were almost twice as likely to persuade listeners than their counterparts who did not (Vogel, Dickson, & Lehman, 1986). Consider television appeals on behalf of needy children, for example. They are more persuasive when they show, not just talk about, how the children are struggling to survive. Of course, poorly constructed or poorly used presentational aids won't help and might hurt a persuasive appeal. For example, H. Ross Perot's infomercials for the 1992 presidential campaign included unprofessionally constructed and awkwardly used visual aids. *Saturday Night Live* and others poked fun at these aids, which suggests that Perot would have been better off not using them at all than using them ineffectively.

TURNING TO TECHNOLOGY

Save the Children

Go to http://www.compassion.com/sponsorachild/. View the slide show. How do the visuals make the message more compelling? What other strategies are used to compel viewers to sponsor a child?

Now go to http://www.compassion.com/dayinlife/. View this slide show. How does it differ from the previous slide show?

Finally, go to http://www.compassion.com/project/. Which of the three shows was more compelling to you? Why?

Rounding the Learning Cycle

Presentational aids can increase the number of listeners you are able to reach because they *address diverse learning styles.* Recall that individuals have different learning style preferences—feeling, thinking, watching, or doing. Some listeners might understand a message well merely by listening to it; others might need visual or other forms of reinforcement. Addressing all learning styles rounds the entire cycle of learning and benefits all listeners, because they will retain your message better regardless of their preferred learning style.

Consider, for example, how Andria used presentational aids in her speech on acupressure. Andria explained that acupressure is a natural method of relieving pain that is similar to acupuncture but relies on fingertip stimulation rather than needles. As she discussed the kinds of pain acupressure can relieve, she incorporated a video clip of a person experiencing a severe migraine headache. This real-life example especially appealed to the watching and feeling dimensions of the learning cycle.

She later showed a diagram of the human body, depicting pressure-point locations and the pains associated with each. This aid addressed the watching and thinking dimensions by offering logical explanations of abstract concepts visually.

Using herself as a sort of presentational aid, Andria demonstrated acupressure stimulation to reduce headache by applying pressure to one hand with the thumb and forefinger of her other hand. She asked listeners to also try it, thus addressing the doing dimension by experimenting with practical applications.

She concluded by showing another video clip of the same person whose headache had now been relieved. Andria increased her chances of reaching listeners by reinforcing her ideas with presentational aids that rounded the cycle of learning.

Looking at the Learning Cycle

Andria's Presentational Aids

- *Feeling:* Migraine headache video clip
- *Watching:* Migraine headache video clip, diagram of the human body and its pressure points, herself demonstrating a pressure-point stimulation procedure
- *Thinking:* Diagram of the human body and its pressure points
- *Doing:* Herself demonstrating a pressure-point stimulation procedure and asking the audience to try it

TURNING TO TECHNOLOGY

Tips for Effective Business Presentations

http://www.cpc.tcu.edu/resources/handouts/7HINTS.pdf

This site, sponsored by the M. J. Neeley Center for Professional Communication, offers several tips for effective business presentations. Do any of the tips surprise you? Why or why not?

TYPES OF PRESENTATIONAL AIDS

To determine what aids to use in your speech, you need to understand the advantages and disadvantages of each type and then think about which will work best to make your message concrete. Presentational aids are either actual objects or symbolic representations. Representations include models, photographs, drawings and diagrams, maps, graphs, charts, audio materials, audiovisual materials, and other sensory materials.

Actual Objects

Actual objects are the most concrete form of visual representation. They can be animate (people, animals, plants) or inanimate.

As Andria did, you can use yourself as a presentational aid. You might, for example, demonstrate sign language, ballet steps, yoga positions, or tennis strokes. Or you might dress in a Pakistani wedding gown or a postal uniform. You can also use another person as a presentational aid. Isaak, for example, used his roommate to demonstrate how theatrical makeup is applied to make actors appear old.

Using a person is often a good way to keep audience attention. Using a person to demonstrate a process especially benefits the doing and feeling dimensions of the learning cycle. One possible disadvantage is that those in the back of the room might not be able to see a demonstration (for example, demonstrating yoga positions while seated on the floor). Also, make sure that human visual aids aren't a distraction before or after the points they help clarify. In other words, there might be logistical problems to overcome.

Animals have similar advantages but greater logistical problems—that is, they are interesting to the audience, but often too interesting, and they are difficult to control. You may not be able to stop your puppy from pooping or your cat from clawing. These concerns may not only reduce the presentational aid's effectiveness but also increase your public speaking anxiety. When Josey used her cat in a speech about pet therapy, the cat was well behaved but some listeners found it more fun to watch the cat than to concentrate on Josey's speech. At best the disadvantages of using animals tend to outweigh the advantages.

A wide range of inanimate objects can be effective. For example, when giving an informative speech on golf, you could use golf clubs to show listeners the differences between woods and irons and to demonstrate drives and putts.

An advantage of inanimate objects is that listeners see precisely the thing you are talking about. Potential disadvantages include size, complexity, and danger. Randy realized his four-wheeled all-terrain vehicle was too large to fit through the doorway of the classroom, and Marjie foresaw that her diamond ring was too small to be seen from the back of the room. Shayla realized the miniature parts housed in her thirty-five millimeter camera were too complex (and too small) to make it an effective presentational aid. When Lana brought in a twelve-gauge shotgun, her instructor told her she couldn't use this presentational aid, which wasn't even allowed on campus.

What Randy, Marjie, and Shayla did—and what Lana should have done—was to bring a representation of the object, rather than the object itself: Randy brought a model of his vehicle; Marjie, an enlarged picture of her ring; and Shayla, a simplified diagram of her camera. When using the object itself presents problems, a representation is often a better aid. Because there are so many types of representations, they serve many functions as presentational aids.

WHAT DO YOU THINK?
Consider a time when you observed a speaker using an actual object for a presentational aid. Was it effective? Why or why not?

Models

Models are scaled-down or scaled-up versions of actual objects. Randy used a scaled-down model of an all-terrain vehicle. In a speech about ear infections, you could use a scaled-up model of the inner ear. Models can be effective because they are concrete representations of the object you are talking about. Sometimes, however, obtaining or creating models can prove costly or time-consuming.

Photographs

Photographs are an obvious alternative when neither objects nor models are feasible. However, for everyone to see them they must be enlarged, transposed into slides or transparencies, or used in a computerized slide show program such as Microsoft's PowerPoint, Lotus's Freelance Graphics, or Adobe's Persuasion (all discussed later).

Drawings and Diagrams

Drawings are yet another alternative to objects and models. A **diagram** is a type of drawing used to show a whole and its parts. Claus's representations of football and rugby fields were diagrams, as was Andria's representation of the human body and its pressure points (Figure 13.1). Drawings and diagrams are relatively simple and inexpensive to construct but do require some artistic ability. As with any presentational aid, poorly prepared drawings and diagrams can lessen your credibility and persuasive appeal.

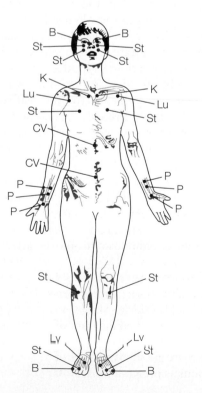

Figure 13.1 Sample diagram

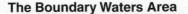

The Boundary Waters Area

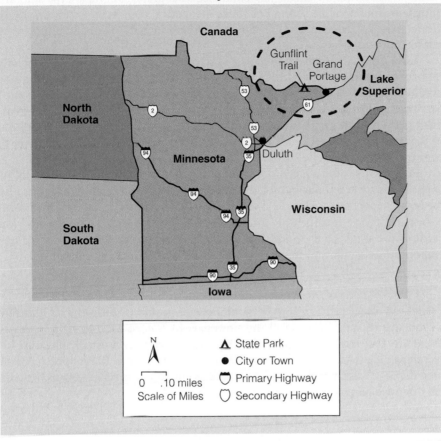

Figure 13.2   Sample map

Maps

Depending on your topic, a map of a campus, neighborhood, city, state, country, or the world might be a good presentational aid. **Maps** are schematic representations of real or imaginary geographic areas. They can show routes or where two or more places are in relation to one another. When Brian spoke on the boundary waters canoe area, between Canada and Minnesota, he used a map to show where and how big the area is (Figure 13.2). Angie's speech on her family's trip to the Grand Canyon used a map on which she'd outlined the route they took and highlighted the key places she discussed.

Graphs

Graphs are generally representations intended to make statistics, statistical trends, and statistical relationships clearer and more understandable. Graphs can make complex numerical trends and relationships more concrete because they allow numbers to be represented visually. Graphs are sometimes used unethically, however, particularly when they mislead the audience with distorted units of measure. There are several kinds of graphs.

ETHICS

Bar graphs consist of parallel bars with lengths proportional to quantities that highlight comparisons between two or more items. For example, Libby used a bar graph to compare the amounts of garbage produced by the United States, Japan,

England, Mexico, and Canada. Jaqueline used a bar graph to compare the amounts of caffeine found in one serving of chocolate, coffee, tea, and cola (Figure 13.3). Notice how Jaqueline used coffee cups as symbols in her bars to add interest and reinforce what the numbers mean.

Line graphs are especially useful for representing trends over time. Daily reports of the Dow Jones Industrial Average are usually reported with a line graph (Figure 13.4). Glynnis used a line graph to show the reduction of people's perceived public speaking anxiety each week over the course of a six-week treatment period. A line graph can also show two or more related trends, allowing you to make comparisons. Figure 13.5 shows how a line graph is used this way to compare projected public school enrollment trends in sections of a district.

Pie graphs show what proportion of a whole is represented by each of its parts. In his speech about balanced diets, Tim used the pie graph in Figure 13.6 to show the percentage of total calories that should come from the various components of foods. Ideally a pie graph has two to five "slices." More than eight clutter a pie graph, so use another kind of graph unless you can consolidate several of the less important items into the category of "other," as Tim did.

Charts

Charts can clarify relationships between steps or positions. **Flowcharts** illustrate a sequence of steps. Tim used the flowchart in Figure 13.7 to help listeners assess why they might be overweight. **Organizational charts** usually illustrate hierarchical relationships among positions in an organization. In his speech, Claus used the organizational chart in Figure 13.8 to highlight the relationships between the offensive players and the quarterback in football.

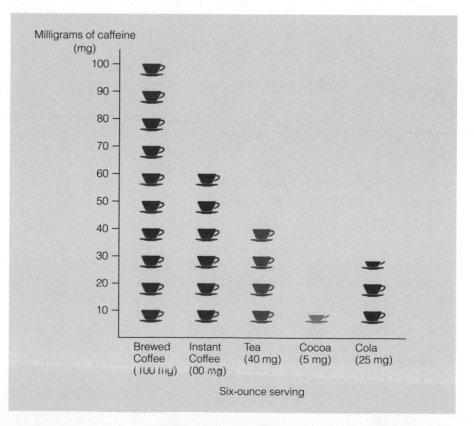

Figure 13.3 Sample bar graph

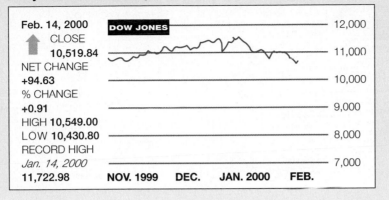

Daily markets roundup

Feb. 14, 2000
↑ CLOSE
10,519.84
NET CHANGE
+94.63
% CHANGE
+0.91
HIGH **10,549.00**
LOW **10,430.80**
RECORD HIGH
Jan. 14, 2000
11,722.98

DOW JONES

12,000
11,000
10,000
9,000
8,000
7,000

NOV. 1999   DEC.   JAN. 2000   FEB.

Figure 13.4   Sample line graph: One trend

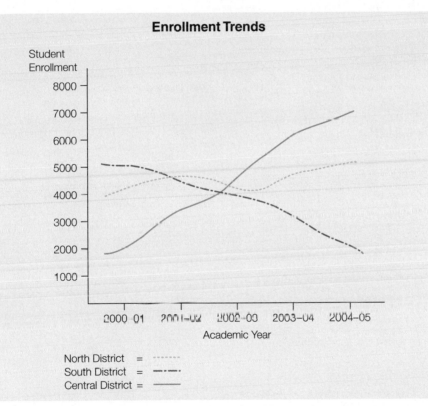

Enrollment Trends

Student Enrollment

8000
7000
6000
5000
4000
3000
2000
1000

2000–01   2001–02   2002–03   2003–04   2004–05

Academic Year

North District   = ...
South District   = –·–·–·
Central District = ———

Figure 13.5   Sample line graph: More than one trend

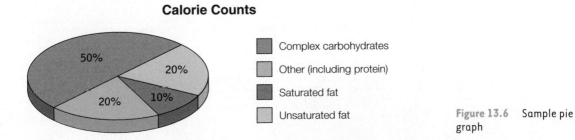

Calorie Counts

50%
20%
20%
10%

☐ Complex carbohydrates
☐ Other (including protein)
☐ Saturated fat
☐ Unsaturated fat

Figure 13.6   Sample pie graph

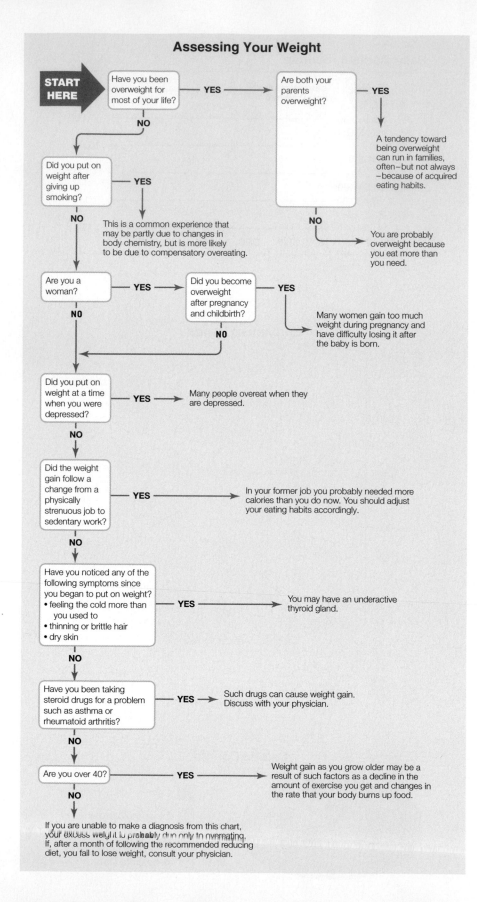

Figure 13.7 Sample flowchart

**Offensive Positions
on the Football Field**

Figure 13.8 Sample organizational chart

Audio Materials

There are times when an explanation or description is incomplete without sound. For example, David brought in his trumpet and three types of mutes to demonstrate what each sounds like. He asked listeners to close their eyes while he played each to see if they could identify the types. In a speech about New Age music as it represents a philosophy of inner peace, you could make the concept more concrete and compelling by playing an excerpt. Audio materials also include audiotaped excerpts of famous speeches, radio programs, and recordings of interviews, conversations, and environmental sounds. In her speech about whales, for example, Emily played a recording of them "singing." Before using audio material, however, make sure you have enough time to present it and that you have access to a high-quality cassette or CD player.

Audiovisual Materials

Materials that use both sight and sound include videotapes, films, and computer-generated slide shows. Ahmad knew that his explanation of television sitcom stereotypes of African Americans would be clearer if he showed some examples. Good idea, but as noted earlier it took too much of his speech time. Equipment needs can also be a disadvantage, especially for presentations before large audiences where multimedia projection units and a large screen or multiple viewing monitors might be required.

TURNING TO TECHNOLOGY

Great Video Clips

http://www.historychannel.com/broadband/

Click on the "Video Clips" link at this site to browse through a variety of clips you could use in your speeches.

Other Sensory Aids

Depending on the topic, other **sensory aids** that appeal to smell, touch, or taste may work well. A speech about perfume, for instance, might benefit from allowing listeners to smell scented swatches as you describe them. In other cases, having the audience feel fabrics or kinds of sandpaper might appeal to the sense of touch—in a speech about Braille, you might bring an example for listeners to touch. Greg focused on taste for his speech about generic foods, asking listeners to compare the taste of name-brand cereals to the generic counterparts and see whether they could tell the difference.

The many types of presentational aids each have advantages and disadvantages to consider in deciding which are most appropriate and effective for your speech.

WHAT DO YOU THINK?

Have you ever tasted the food samples offered in a grocery store while you're shopping? How do they function as sensory aids? Have you ever purchased the food after sampling it? Why or why not?

Looking at the Learning Cycle

Round the Cycle with Presentational Aids

- *Feeling:* actual objects, models, photographs, audio materials, audiovisual materials, sensory aids
- *Watching:* actual objects, models, photographs, drawings, diagrams, maps, graphs, charts
- *Thinking:* drawings, diagrams, maps, graphs, charts
- *Doing:* diagrams, line graphs, flowcharts, organizational charts, sensory aids

MEDIA FOR DISPLAYING PRESENTATIONAL AIDS

Media are the equipment used to display presentational aids. The nonelectronic variety includes chalkboards, flip charts, posterboards, and handouts. Electronic media include slides and slide projectors, transparencies and overhead projectors, cassette or CD/DVD players, VCRs used with LCD projectors or monitors, and computers used with LCD panels or projectors.

Nonelectronic Media

Chalkboard

The chalkboard might seem appealing because most classrooms have one, and it costs nothing and requires no preparation time. In reality, the chalkboard or white board is effective only when you want to encourage direct listener participation. In such a case, you don't know in advance what ideas will be raised. The chalkboard allows you to include these ideas and facilitates any related discussion. But formal public speeches seldom involve direct listener participation.

Other disadvantages: Few students can draw neatly enough on a chalkboard to enhance their credibility. Also, the speaker's back must be turned to the audience while drawing on the board, which limits eye contact and interrupts the flow of the speech. Except when soliciting listener participation, find another medium.

Flip Charts and Posterboards

Flip charts are large pads of paper displayed on easels. Professional trainers commonly use them in business and industry. **Posterboards** are large pieces of tag board or foam core displayed on easels. Both are relatively inexpensive and easy to work with. They can display a wide range of presentational aids, and if carefully prepared should enhance speaker credibility. Thus they're a good choice for beginning speakers and, for that matter, are highly effective in business presentations too, particularly if the speaker is a good illustrator (Brody, 2003). To avoid Claus's dilemma mentioned previously, however, use sturdy posterboard that won't roll up and fall on the floor.

Handouts

Handouts are an effective medium for anything you want listeners to refer to after the speech: a set of steps to follow later, useful telephone numbers and addresses, or mathematical formulas, among many other possibilities. Gail Zack Anderson (2003), president of Applause, Inc., suggests that handouts can also be an appropriate choice when speaking to small audiences. Tim used a handout to display his flowchart about determining reasons for being overweight. Professional speakers and salespeople often use handouts to get their phone numbers and e-mail and Web site addresses into the hands of listeners who might not take notes. But don't distribute handouts before or during a speech, as they can be distracting; listeners wind up reading the handout instead of listening to you. Distribute them at the end of the presentation instead. If you want to refer to information on the handout during the speech, create another visual aid that you can reveal only when discussing it for use during the actual speech.

> **WHAT DO YOU THINK?**
> When you receive a handout during a presentation, do you continue to listen to the speaker or find yourself reading the handout? Does this affect what you later remember from the speech?

Electronic Media

Electronic media can be more effective than nonelectronic media when they appear more professional, increasing your ethos and persuasive appeal. Unfortunately it can be difficult or impossible to get access to the equipment—and it is your responsibility to make sure you have the equipment you need in the room on the day you speak. As mentioned, electronic media include slides and slide projectors, transparencies and overhead projectors, audiocassette and DVD or CD players, VCRs and LCD projectors or monitors, and computers with LCD panels or projectors.

Slides and Slide Projectors

Photographs not originally shot on slide film can nevertheless be made into slides and projected onto a screen using a projector. Angie had several photographs from her trip to the Grand Canyon made into slides and displayed them this way. Slides are easy for the entire audience to see and are fairly concrete representations. However, getting access to a slide projector and paying the price for turning photographs into slides are disadvantages to consider.

Transparencies and Overhead Projectors

Showing transparencies with an overhead projector works for many types of visual aids—photographs, drawings, diagrams, maps, graphs, and charts. Transparencies can be particularly effective for illustrating layers of complexity. For example, three overlapping transparencies could display the line graph about public school enrollment projections (Figure 13.5). Each transparency could superimpose an additional line to the graph as you move into a discussion of the next district.

WHAT DO YOU THINK?

Have you ever tried to take class notes from information on a transparency that was too small or unclear? How did this affect your ability to focus in class? How much did you remember later on?

Transparencies are simple and inexpensive to create; almost any photocopier can transfer visual materials onto transparencies. They are also easy to transport and use. Most classrooms and meeting rooms have overhead projectors. Transparencies can be made to look professional by using computer software programs and photocopiers. Thus they are a good choice for many presentations. It is also a good idea to have transparencies as backup when using computerized slide shows in case the system crashes (Brody, 2003).

Audiocassette and CD/DVD Players

If you decide to use audio materials, make sure you have access to the media needed to play them and that the sound quality is sufficient. Audiocassette and CD/DVD players usually fit the bill; they are affordable and effective.

VCRs and LCD Projectors or Monitors

Video clips as presentational aids require access to a VCR and an LCD projector or a monitor. Ideally you can show examples using an LCD multimedia projector. An **LCD projector** connects to a VCR or computer and projects images onto a screen. LCD projectors can enlarge images so all audience members can see, but they are expensive and may not be readily available, especially to beginning speakers. Displaying video clips using a VCR connected to a television monitor or multiple monitors (depending on audience size) also suffices.

Computer and LCD Panels or Projectors

Computerized slide shows, such as those you can create using Microsoft's PowerPoint, Lotus's Freelance Graphics, or Adobe's Persuasion, are becoming increasingly popular to both prepare and display presentational aids. Such shows can be very effective because they often appeal to several learning cycle dimensions by integrating a wide range of presentational aids (Hotch, 1992). Most computer software programs allow you to integrate drawings, diagrams, maps, graphs, charts, lists, photographs, and video clips. You can include nearly anything you can imagine in a slide show by creating it yourself, using the folders of clip art included in the software, downloading materials from the Internet, or scanning data you find in various print resources into the system.

TURNING TO TECHNOLOGY

PowerPoint Tips and Tricks

http://www.microsoft.com/office/powerpoint/using/default.asp

This Microsoft Web site offer several tips and tricks for getting the most from the program. Identify two you might try in your next speech.

A major disadvantage is the need for a computer and LCD panel or projector to display the slide show. An **LCD panel** is a device connected to a computer and placed on top of an overhead projector that projects what is on the computer monitor to a screen in the front of the room. LCD projectors are similar but have their own light source. (As mentioned above, LCD projectors also work for enlarging video images onto a screen.) LCD panels are more portable and less expensive than LCD projectors, but they require overhead projectors with very bright projection lights. Also, a computer malfunction during the presentation can mean total disaster. Be sure that good quality equipment is available and, even so, prepare backup overhead transparencies or handouts.

TURNING TO TECHNOLOGY

Avoiding the Seven Deadly Sins of Visual Presentations

http://www.presentersuniversity.com/visuals_designforclose_visuals_7_Deadly_Sins.php

This short article highlights seven mistakes presenters make when using computerized slide shows. Do any of them surprise you? If so, why?

As discussed earlier, good presentational aids enhance a verbal message by making it more concrete, clear, understandable, interesting, credible, and memorable. Poorly constructed or ineffectively used ones do the opposite. To ensure that your presentational aids enhance rather than detract, let's turn to guidelines for constructing and using them.

CONSTRUCTING PRESENTATIONAL AIDS

Students are often apprehensive about constructing presentational aids, usually because they feel unsure about what makes them effective. Although computerized slide shows are increasingly popular, many people who use them neglect to follow the guidelines for effective presentational aids, so these are specifically addressed throughout the following discussion. We consider five key guidelines for constructing presentational aids: (a) The presentational aid should enhance the verbal message by presenting information in some other way. (b) The presentational aid should communicate ideas clearly. (c) The presentational aid should be worth the cost in terms of time and money. (d) The presentational aid should not take too much time to present. (e) The media needed to display the presentational aid must be accessible and manageable.

The Aid Should Enhance the Verbal Message

To enhance the verbal message, a presentational aid should consist of more than just words. Avoid visual aids that simply list phrases used in the speech. For all presentational aids—including those such as videotapes and CDs that are clearly not just words—make sure that the aid reinforces your verbal message and in some way goes beyond it.

Variety in Computerized Slide Shows

It's a common mistake in computerized slide shows to offer slides that are nothing more than a series of bulleted lists (Booher, 2003; Brody, 2003; Pearce, 2003; Tufte, 2003). Like all presentational aids, a computerized slide show must include more than words. Does yours contain, for example, charts, graphs, diagrams, and relevant clip art or pictures downloaded from the Internet or scanned in? If not, why not? Computerized slide shows make it easy to use a wide range of materials that round the cycle of learning, and professional-looking graphics can be made fairly quickly. But don't clutter your slides, go overboard with corny clip art graphics, or create more slides than truly necessary (Pearce, 2003).

The Aid Should Communicate Ideas Clearly

Like the verbal message, a presentational aid isn't effective unless it's clear. So make it large enough for the room and audience, keep it simple, and use color effectively.

Size

Visual or audiovisual aids should be large enough so that even those in the back of the room can see them. Enlarge photographs to at least ten by twelve inches. Better yet, convert them into slides or transparencies for projection or scan them into a computerized slide show. Flip charts or posterboards should be at least two by three feet. For video clip visibility, use at least a twenty-five-inch monitor for audiences of thirty or fewer people; for larger audiences use multiple monitors or an LCD panel or projector that can project images on a large screen.

For all types of visual and audiovisual aids, print titles and labels in large letters—at least two or three inches tall, or whatever it takes to see them easily from the back of the room. If possible, check this by placing a draft of the aid in the front of the room where you will be speaking and walk around to make sure it is legible from all parts of the room.

Simplicity

Keep presentational aids simple conceptually and visually so as to make understanding easier, not harder. Convey only one idea per aid and express it clearly in the title. Include no more than three or four points to support the idea, and express those clearly with single words or short phrases. If more seems needed, divide the material between two aids. This is of particular concern when using a computerized slide show. Be sure to use one background design for the entire presentation, limit your use of slide transition effects, and limit how much you include on each slide.

For visual clarity, draw neatly and spell correctly. Don't use all capital letters for labels and titles. It's easier for audience members to read a combination of capital and lowercase letters. If necessary use stencils, ask for help from a friend, or use a computer to create titles and labels. Use only one font, even if you have a series of aids. Choose a strong, straight font like Arial, Helvetica, or Times New Roman, and avoid thin, italicized, or shadowed fonts, as they are difficult to read (Figure 13.9). Include enough information so that the aid makes sense on its own, but not so much that it becomes cluttered: Remember that you'll be explaining the aid orally.

Color

Careful use of color can do a lot to make presentational aids clear. Use a single background color, even if you have a series of aids. Make sure there is sufficient contrast between the background and the labels and images. Generally, light colors such as white, tan, or a pastel work best for backgrounds, and bold colors such as black, blue, or purple work best for titles and labels, as they can be seen more easily from a distance. Avoid using more than two or three colors in an aid. And because about 8 to 12 percent of males and 1 percent of females are color-blind, avoid using red and green together (they are difficult for color-blind people to distinguish) (Shaw, 2003).

Graphic Design of Computerized Slide Shows

As with other presentational aids, use a type size large enough to be seen clearly from anywhere in the room. For audiences of forty or more, slide titles should be in 48-point type and labels in 36-point type; for audiences of twelve to forty people, titles should be in 36-point type and labels in 28-point type. For smaller audiences, titles should be in 36-point type and labels in 24-point type (Currid, 1995). Never use a size smaller than 20 points on a computer slide show slide.

Use a single font throughout; mixing fonts makes slides less clear. For the same reason, stick to two or three colors on a slide.

Software programs offer many slide background designs. Find one and stay with it for the entire show. Some backgrounds project better on a screen than others—light text on a dark background usually projects most clearly, but dark text on a light background may also work. Just make sure there is distinct contrast between the background color and the text and images. Avoid backgrounds that use pastels; these limit contrast and make projections less clear. If possible, experiment with designs in the room where you'll be speaking.

Slide show programs also offer many options for **slide transitions,** or ways to move from one slide to the next; for example, fade in, fly in, and checkerboard. Again, choose one and stick to it for the entire presentation to avoid distracting and confusing the audience.

Effective	Ineffective
This is Arial.	This Helvetica Neue Light Condensed is too thin.
This is Futura.	*This Goudy italicized font is hard to read.*
This is Helvetica.	*This Edwardian Script font is hard to read.*
This is Times New Roman.	

Figure 13.9 Effective and ineffective font choices

Use bullets to highlight key points, and try to use just one to three words per bullet. Never use more than six words per line or six words per slide, so that your slide show enhances the verbal message rather than replacing or repeating it (Kurnoff, 2003).

TURNING TO TECHNOLOGY

Generating Results with PowerPoint

http://www.presentersuniversity.com/visuals_designforclose_Visuals_generate_results.php

This short article provides excellent tips for preparing PowerPoint slide shows that will tell your story in a compelling way. What will you try to incorporate in the slide show for your next speech? What will you try to avoid?

The Aid Should Be Worth the Time and Money

Presentational aids need not take hours and hours to prepare. Save time by using, for example, maps, charts, or graphs on the Internet or in books or articles. Make sure you cite these sources as a footnote on the aid or orally as you discuss the aid. Soliciting help from friends might also help with time.

Try to hold down expenses. For example, don't pay a lot for permission to use a copyrighted aid if a free or cheaper one can be found. Rather than hire a professional graphic designer to construct diagrams, charts, or graphs, consider paying a graphic design or art student to help you.

Economics of Computerized Slide Shows

However professional and impressive computerized slide shows may look, creating them may be time-consuming if you're not familiar with the equipment and software. Perhaps a friend who is familiar with it can help. Or you might pay a computer science or communication student to help you, or enroll in a class or workshop to learn how yourself. Might several posterboard diagrams serve the same purpose?

Computer-generated visual aids, such as PowerPoint, must enhance the verbal message, not replace or repeat it.

© Romily Lockyer/Getty Images/The Image Bank

The Aid Should Not Take Too Much Time to Present

Remember how Ahmad's video examples consumed so much of his time that he was forced to eliminate a couple of examples and part of his verbal message? Be sure to consider how long it will take to present slides, video clips, cassette recordings, and so on. As a general rule, aids should take at most 15 to 20 percent of your total speaking time. For a four-to-six-minute speech, then, all aids combined should take less than one minute.

Presentation Time of Computerized Slide Shows

Computerized slide show aids should also not usurp your speech (Booher, 2003). Avoid using so many slides that they overtake what you have to say. Limit yourself to at most one slide for every two minutes of speech, and insert blanks between presentational slides to control listeners' focus on them. You can also temporarily conceal a slide and then reveal it once more (in PowerPoint, strike the "b" to conceal and again to reveal). To ensure that you don't spend too much time on one slide, use the automatic time-sequencing option in the software. This automatically moves to a blank slide after a certain number of seconds that you program in.

The Media Needed Must Be Accessible and Manageable

Make sure that you have access to the equipment needed to display your aids—slide projector, overhead, VCR, monitor, cassette player, computer, LCD panel, or LCD projector—that it is in working order, and that you know how to operate it. As illustrated by Ivy's predicament at the beginning of the chapter, it is important to have backup equipment or plans. Being prepared means abiding by Murphy's law: Anything that can go wrong will go wrong. By preparing backups, you can defeat Murphy if necessary.

Checking Equipment for Computerized Slide Shows

Equipment and its quality vary from facility to facility. Plan ahead by finding out whether the computer you will be using is a Macintosh or IBM compatible, and make sure the LCD panel or projector provides quality images. Verify that the room where you will speak has a screen and dimmable lights. Save your slide show on more than one disk, CD, or memory stick, and always bring handouts or transparencies as a backup.

Student Workbook

Read through the guidelines for constructing PowerPoint presentational aids in Chapter 2 of your workbook. Create a PowerPoint slide show for your next speech following the step-by-step guidelines provided.

PRACTICING THE PROCESS

Checklist for Constructing Presentational Aids

Regardless of the medium used, effective presentational aids:

❑ Enhance the verbal message by using another symbol system.
❑ Are large enough to see clearly from the back of the room.
❑ Are concise and simply composed.
❑ Incorporate bold colors (but do not combine red and green).
❑ Are short (if an audio or video clip).

And, if you're using a computerized slide show, the aid must:

❑ Be available to you in backup form.

USING PRESENTATIONAL AIDS

Your presentational aids will be effective if you adhere to five specific suggestions: (a) Practice with your presentational aids. (b) Position your presentational aids before beginning your speech. (c) Explain and integrate your aids at appropriate points during the speech. (d) Talk to your audience, not to the presentational aid. (e) Disclose and conceal your presentational aids when appropriate.

TURNING TO TECHNOLOGY

Presentational Aids in the Business World

http://www.presentersuniversity.com/courses_visual-aids_visuals_9mistakes.php

This article by Dianna Booher, president of Booher Consultants, identifies nine mistakes presenters make with visual aids. Read through the list. Do any of the mistakes surprise you? Why or why not?

Practice with Your Presentational Aids

Because presentational aids can hurt credibility if you fumble while using them, practice with them when you practice the speech. This is the best way to spot potential problems. Had Claus practiced with his posterboards, he would have found that they weren't sturdy enough. When practicing, make notes on your speaking outline to remind yourself where in the speech to present the aids.

WHAT DO YOU THINK?

Consider a career you would like to have. How might you use presentational aids in that career? What media are you likely to use to display them? Why?

Be aware of the challenges of each medium used to present your aids and practice accordingly. For example, practice smoothly revealing and concealing visual aids on posterboards. For audiotapes or video clips, practice to make sure they don't take too much time and to become comfortable with the equipment. Practice with overheads and transparencies to get used to placing them on and removing them from the projector, as well as to point to items on the screen rather than on the transparency itself. Practice using the computer-generated slide show and the LCD panel or projector you'll be using for the actual presentation so that you'll be familiar with the setup and operation of that particular unit. All this reduces anxiety by assuring you of proficiency—the aids will no longer be an unknown to be feared.

TURNING TO TECHNOLOGY

Presentations in Professional Settings

http://www.powerpointers.com/

This Web site offers tips for preparing and presenting to a variety of audiences and how to use PowerPoint effectively with them. They range from formal to informal presentations, and from sales presentations to presentations to the media. Select an article appropriate to your career choice. Identify one or two tips you didn't know before.

Still, plan for the unexpected as you practice with your aids. What will you do if equipment malfunctions or aids get lost or ruined on the way to class? By becoming aware of possible problems, you'll be fully prepared.

Position Presentational Aids before Beginning Your Speech

Before speaking, position all presentational aids and equipment where you want them and make sure everything is ready and in working order. This means checking that your posterboards or slides are in sequence and positioned where all audience members can see them. It means testing to make sure the equipment for video or audio aids works and that the excerpts are cued correctly. It also means testing the overhead projector, slide projector, computer, and LCD unit to make sure everything works and is visible throughout the room. Taking the time to position your aids will make you feel more confident and look more professional and at ease.

WHAT DO YOU THINK?
Imagine setting up your computer and LCD monitor or projector only to discover there are technical difficulties and your slide show won't work. What would you do?

Explain and Integrate Presentational Aids

Remember that aids cannot speak for themselves. You must explain them and integrate them fully and appropriately into your speech. Doing so means helping listeners understand why and how they support and enhance the verbal message. Follow five simple steps: announce each aid, explain and describe its purpose, refer and point to it, show its connection to the point you are making, and remove it from view or turn it off when it is no longer the focal point.

Include reminders about these steps in your speaking notes. The step of pointing to aids and items on them is important for helping listeners understand. Point with your hand or a pointer, and make sure listeners can tell what you're pointing to. Remember, if aids are projected onto a screen, point to content on the screen, not on the projector.

Talk to Your Audience, Not to the Presentational Aid

Rather than facing the aid as you explain it, face the audience; the aid doesn't care what you say but the listeners do. It's important not to lose connection with the audience. Stand to one side of a posterboard or flip chart and gesture with the hand closest to the aid so you can't turn your back to the audience. Stand to one side of the VCR/monitor or cassette player and operate the controls with the hand closest to the aid. Stand to one side of the projection screen and gesture with the hand closest to the screen.

Disclose and Conceal Presentational Aids When Appropriate

Show an aid only when you're about to discuss it, and remove it from view as soon as you've finished. Otherwise it may distract listeners from your speech. This principle applies to all types of aids.

With visual aids on a posterboard or flip chart, use a cover sheet that you can easily remove and replace, or simply turn the posterboard around on the easel. Turn off the video or audio player when not in use; don't let a video or song play in the background while you speak. Turn off the projector when you are through discussing a transparency, or use a cover sheet if you want to keep the projector on between transparencies. With computer-generated slide shows, blank slides between aids can function like a cover sheet. Distribute handouts only after a speech; if a handout contains material you want to discuss during the speech, consider displaying that material on a posterboard, transparency, or slide as well. This way, you can control where listeners place their attention and then provide the handout at the close of the speech.

Guidelines for Using Presentation Aids Effectively During Your Speech

1. *Reveal* the aid by disclosing it to the group.
2. *Explain* what the aid is by describing its purpose.
3. *Refer* to the aid by pointing to it and then to the images or details you are talking about.
4. *Integrate* the aid by showing its connection to the point you are making in your speech.
5. *Remove* the aid by concealing it from the group.

SUMMARY

Presentational aids—visual, audio, or audiovisual—are supporting materials that help explain ideas. Visual aids include actual objects, models, photographs, drawings and diagrams, maps, graphs, and charts. Audio aids can be anything from musical recordings to excerpts from famous speeches or even taped examples of environmental sounds. The most common audiovisual aids are videotapes and films. Other sensory aids include those that appeal to taste, touch, or smell.

Presentational aids enhance your speech by clarifying the verbal message, adding variety, reducing public speaking anxiety, increasing listener retention, increasing persuasive appeal, and rounding the cycle of learning.

Each of the many types of presentational aids has advantages and disadvantages to weigh when deciding which to use. Actual objects can be animate or inanimate. Also consider models, photographs, drawings and diagrams, maps, graphs, charts, audio materials, audiovisual materials, or other sensory materials.

Various types of media—equipment—are needed to display some presentational aids. Nonelectronic media include chalkboards, flip charts, posterboards, and handouts. Electronic media include slide projectors, overhead projectors, audiocassette and CD players, VCRs and LCD projectors or monitors, and computers and LCD panels or projectors. Sometimes cost and accessibility limit choices when selecting media.

When constructing presentational aids, consider whether they enhance the verbal message, communicate ideas clearly, are worth the time and money, and can be used effectively within the allotted time, and whether the equipment needed is accessible. When using presentational aids, practice in advance, position aids before beginning to speak, explain and integrate them during the speech, talk to the audience, and disclose and conceal the aids when appropriate.

Properly constructed and used, presentational aids make an excellent speech even better by making the message clearer and more memorable through addressing multiple learning styles.

The *Confident Public Speaking* CD-ROM is your one-stop point of access for not just the content on the CD itself, such as Speech Interactive, but also the many other resources on the *Confident Public Speaking* Web site, Speech Builder Express, and InfoTrac College Edition. Note that this chapter's key terms and activities are among the resources available in electronic format online. Additional information is included below.

SPEECH INTERACTIVE
ON THE *CONFIDENT PUBLIC SPEAKING* CD-ROM

Speech Interactive is your link to this text's speech videos. Offering opportunities to practice critiquing speeches by students and other public speakers, these videos will help you prepare for providing effective feedback to your peers and your own speech performances.

SPEECH BUILDER EXPRESS

The Visual Aids section of Speech Builder Express can help you decide which of your speech's points would benefit the most from an accompanying visual aid, and what kind of aid would be the most effective.

KEY TERMS

Interactive flashcards for these key terms are available on the *Confident Public Speaking* Web site. You'll find the "Flashcards" link under the resources for Chapter 13.

Audio aids 300	LCD panel 315
Audiovisual aids 300	LCD projector 314
Bar graphs 307	Line graphs 308
Diagram 306	Maps 307
Flip charts 313	Media 312
Flowcharts 308	Models 306
Graphs 307	Organizational charts 308

ACTIVITIES

The activities below are available in electronic format on the *Confident Public Speaking* Web site. You'll find the "Activities" link under the resources for Chapter 13.

1. **Who Can Follow Directions?** Find a partner. One partner should give the other directions to a familiar destination. You may not use gestures or other visual aids to clarify the directions. Once one partner has finished giving the directions, the other should try to guess the location. Discuss what made the task simple or difficult.

2. **Did You See What I Saw?** Form an observation team with two or three classmates. Locate five visual aids in magazines, newspapers, and books. Then critique each one based on how it addresses the learning cycle dimensions: feeling, watching, thinking, and doing. Select one visual aid that seems to best address each dimension and explain to the entire class why you picked that one.

3. **Visual Aid Workshop.** Form a group with two or three classmates. Select one of the topics listed below or come up with one of your own. Construct two different visual aids clarifying the same information. Use notebook paper and markers to construct your aids. When you've finished, show and explain each of the aids to the class. Ask the class to vote for the most effective visual aid and to explain why they voted as they did.

   - Your group is employed by *Rolling Stone* magazine. Construct two possible visual aids showing the three best-selling CDs of the year.
   - Your group is employed by a travel and tourism agency for your state. Construct two possible visual aids showing places visitors should see.
   - Your group is employed by the university relations department at your college or university. Construct two possible visual aids showing reasons students should attend your school.
   - You and your group are members of the film academy. Construct two possible visual aids showing the three best films of the year.

INFOTRAC COLLEGE EDITION ACTIVITY

Access InfoTrac College Edition and use "PowerPoint" and "presentations" as your search terms. Find at least three articles that present differing points of view about the pros and cons of using computerized slide shows in public speeches. What techniques might help you minimize the risks of using presentation software?

INFORMATIVE

SPEAKING

REFLECTIVE QUESTIONS

1. Why might public speaking anxiety increase when you are going to give an informative speech?

2. What do you think an informative speaker's goal is, and how might it differ from that of speakers presenting other types of speeches?

3. In what ways do you think speeches of description, explanation, and demonstration differ from one another?

4. Why might considering the cycle of learning while preparing an informative speech be especially important?

5. What key questions might you ask in preparing an effective informative speech?

WHAT'S AHEAD: FOCUSING YOUR READING

What Is Informative Speaking?

Types and Patterns of Informative Speeches

Guidelines for Effective Informative Speaking

A Sample Informative Speech

ERIC'S MOM TELEPHONED ONE MORNING to wish him a belated happy birthday. She asked *what* he had done to celebrate, *where* he celebrated, *who* he celebrated with, and *why* he hadn't come home to celebrate. He explained that he had celebrated in the park with his fiancé Mandy, who had made him a strawberry torte from a special recipe handed down from her grandmother. Mandy had been free during the day but had to work that evening, and because she could not come home with him, Eric had decided to stay at school with her. Eric's mom asked *how* Mandy made the torte, wondering whether to try the recipe for Eric's sister's graduation open house later that month. Finally, she asked Eric *what* he wanted for his birthday, as she hadn't yet bought a present. Eric mentioned some new computer software he wanted and its special features. In answering his mother's questions, Eric engaged in informative speaking.

When you talk with friends about people you know, places you've been, things you've done, or issues you're considering, you're practicing informative speaking. You do it all the time whether you realize it or not. You're also constantly on the receiving end of informative speaking, bombarded with news from people face to face or from television, newspapers, magazines, or the Internet. More information has been published in the past thirty years than in the previous five thousand, and the amount available is doubling every two and a half years (Banach, 1991). Thanks to the Internet, the quantity of information we have access to is immeasurable. Many refer to our era as the "information age."

This chapter is about the nature and purpose of informative speaking: the unique characteristics of informative speeches as they differ from other kinds of speeches, the types of informative speeches, the patterns most appropriate for each type, and guidelines for creating effective informative speeches. The chapter ends with a sample informative speech.

WHAT DO YOU THINK?
Consider the last conversation you had with a friend or family member. In what ways were you engaged in informative speaking?

WHAT IS INFORMATIVE SPEAKING?

The primary purpose when speaking to inform is to share knowledge and create mutual understanding. **Informative speaking** shares knowledge with listeners by answering questions such as "who," "when," "what," "where," "why," "how to," and "how does." Informative speakers are essentially teachers who answer questions about objects, events, places, people, processes, procedures, concepts, or issues.

Remember that all public speeches, including informative speeches, are based on goals. The informative speaker's goal is to help listeners understand a topic in the same way the speaker does by shaping their perceptions of the topic and what they need to know about it. This varies from the goals for other kinds of speeches, as shown in Figure 14.1. Success or failure is ultimately measured by how well listeners *understand*, *retain*, and *apply* topic ideas to their own lives. Notice how the goal becomes loftier as you move further to the right on the continuum depicted in the figure. The invitational speaker seeks agreement about the worth of a person, event, place, process, object, or idea; the dispositional persuasive speaker seeks agreement about a belief, attitude, or value; the actuation persuasive speaker seeks not only agreement but action. Chapters 15–17 discuss invitational and persuasive speeches in detail. The goal of the informative speaker is fairly modest in comparison—to achieve mutual understanding about an object, person, place, process, event, idea, concept, or issue.

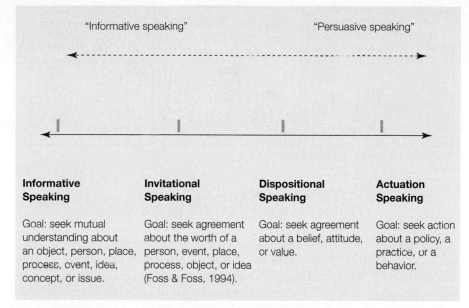

Figure 14.1 The public speaking continuum

Information Is Power?

http://www.publicus.net/present/public/

This article makes an argument that the ability to harness, understand, and re-present information is as important as being able to masterfully persuade. Which point or points are most compelling to you? Why? Do you disagree with any points? If so, which ones and why?

However modest its goal, informative speaking poses a unique challenge to speakers: It can be difficult to *gain the attention* of listeners as well as *sustain their attention* throughout a presentation. The persuasive speaker wants to influence listeners' dispositions or actions, but the informative speaker simply seeks to get listeners to learn (that is, to understand, retain, and apply). The consequences of not achieving mutual understanding are relatively insignificant, so listeners can easily become distracted or lose interest during the speech.

For some, speaking anxiety increases when thinking about preparing and presenting an informative speech. Usually this is from the speaker's fear of being boring—that listeners will be uninterested, will already know the information, and simply won't care about the topic. These are understandable concerns for those who themselves have had to listen to bad informative speakers. And by the time you graduate from high school, who hasn't?

Indeed, teachers are supposed to be informative speakers. You can probably easily remember one or two teachers you considered very effective and their opposites. In describing the bad ones, words such as "boring," "dull," "irrelevant," "disorganized," "confusing," "condescending," and "apathetic" probably come to mind. The prospect of sounding like them is not cheerful. Fortunately, there are ways to prepare and present effective and interesting informative speeches that will reduce such anxiety.

DILBERT reprinted by permission of United Feature Syndicate, Inc.

TYPES AND PATTERNS OF INFORMATIVE SPEECHES

Three types of informative speeches help create mutual understanding: speeches of description, explanation, and demonstration. Each results in a different kind of understanding. Most good speeches offer elements of all three, but the primary thesis focuses on only one. Determining which type of informative speech is best for your purpose helps shape your thesis statement.

WHAT DO YOU THINK?
Identify a former teacher who taught you a lot. What made you think he or she was a good teacher?

To determine which type of speech to present, ask what you want to clarify. Are you trying to paint a picture? Clarify a concept, issue, or idea? Outline a process, procedure, or function? For example, to explain how to change a flat tire, a speech of demonstration can be used to outline the procedure. To explain what tires are made of, a speech of description is better: It paints a picture in the listener's mind. To explain why certain tire treads provide better traction in different climates, a speech of explanation can clarify the concept. All three of these informative speeches are about tires, but as the goal differs so does the type of informative speech. Determining the speech type in turn helps narrow your focus and shape your thesis statement.

PRACTICING THE PROCESS

Checklist for Deciding Which Type of Informative Speech to Prepare

- ❑ Do you want to paint a picture in the minds of your listeners? [Description]
- ❑ Do you want to clarify a concept, issue, or idea? [Explanation]
- ❑ Do you want to outline a process, procedure, or function? [Demonstration]

Speeches of Description

Student Workbook

Read through the description and grading criteria for a "Speech of Narration" in Chapter 3 of your workbook. Brainstorm three possible topics for a speech of narration.

The intent of a **speech of description** is to create a clear picture in the minds of listeners. These speeches usually answer an overarching "who," "what," or "where" question. Answering "What is a tire made of?" requires a speech of description. So do most speeches about objects, people, events, or places. Examples include Ben's speech about items to include in a winter survival kit, Lynetta's speech about the life of Walt Disney, Lori's speech about the annual hometown potato festival, and Colleen's speech about inexpensive places to go for spring break.

Films and television programs often take the shape of speeches of description. For example, the movie *The Messenger* tells the story of Joan of Arc. It functions like a speech of description because it attempts to create in the viewer's mind a

© Bettman/Corbis

A speech telling about Joan of Arc paints a picture for listeners, so it is a speech of description.

clear picture of who Joan of Arc was. Likewise, a television program such as VH1's *Behind the Music* attempts to paint a picture of the personalities of musicians. Many programs on the Discovery Channel or History Channel also function like speeches of description. Programs about chimpanzees in the Congo, gorillas, sharks, crocodiles, disasters in America, military blunders—all paint pictures in the minds of viewers.

Because each speech topic is unique, it's not reasonable to say that any particular type of speech should follow a certain organizational pattern. Nonetheless, some patterns lend themselves more easily to speeches of description.

To describe people or objects, main points are usually placed in a chronological, topical, or narrative pattern. In a speech about Beethoven, a chronological pattern would first discuss his childhood, then his experiences as an adult before becoming deaf, and finally his experiences after becoming deaf. Or a narrative pattern of stories complete with characters, settings, and plots could be used. In a speech of personal significance about your dog, a topical pattern might be best to discuss how he taught you the importance of responsibility, unconditional love, and friendship.

TURNING TO TECHNOLOGY

Biographies

http://lifetimetv.com/shows/ip/

This site provides short biographies of thousands of people you might study for a speech. You can search alphabetically or by profession for athletes, actors, authors, comedians, musicians, politicians, and so forth. Select one or two that interest you.

Descriptions of places often use a spatial pattern. When Mike talked about the college library, he used a spatial pattern to explain where to find academic journals, books, and reference resources in relation to the main entrance and to each other.

Describing events may take a topical, comparative, chronological, or narrative pattern. For example, contrasting the rituals in an Amish wedding ceremony with those in a typical wedding ceremony of the dominant American culture would require a comparative pattern. A chronological pattern or narrative pattern could be used to talk about your trip to the Holy Land.

Speeches of Explanation

A **speech of explanation** is intended to generate a clear interpretation in the minds of listeners. Such speeches usually address an overarching "why" question and often focus on issues, concepts, ideas, or beliefs. Tiffany's speech about why she chose to be a vegetarian is an example. So are speeches about the advantages and disadvantages of home schooling or the different forms of sexual harassment. Just about any controversial issue or policy can be a topic for an informative speech if it stops short of trying to convince listeners that one perspective is better than the others. When informing, the goal is to provide information from all sides so listeners can make their own educated choices.

Television provides many programs that function like speeches of explanation. For example, when *20/20* aired a story on the differences between boys and girls, it was essentially a speech of explanation. When TV shows like *Seventh Heaven* or *Touched by an Angel* focus on complex issues such as premarital sex or teen violence, they usually attempt to explain what is occurring in society like a speech of explanation. So do satires such as *The Simpsons* and *South Park*. And in-depth segments on virtually all news programs do the same.

TURNING TO TECHNOLOGY

Identifying Issues

http://lii.org/search/file/society

This site offers a multitude of social issues and problems you might research for a speech. Identify one or two issues you might consider for your next speech.

Speeches of explanation often follow a topical, causal, narrative, or comparison-and-contrast pattern. For example, home schooling might be addressed with a topical pattern by talking first about its advantages and its disadvantages (in an informative speech the pros and cons must be balanced for objectivity). Another topical pattern is gradation, as when talking about degrees of sexual harassment from least severe (sexist jokes) to worst (coercion and threats). A speech about the negative effects of overexposure to the sun would probably follow a causal pattern. The narrative pattern was favored by Chuck, who told the story of Matthew Shepherd to explain hate crime. The compare-and-contrast pattern is common, as when speaking about the sparkling wines of France (dry, intense) and California (sweeter, more fruity).

Satirical television programs like *South Park* essentially function as speeches of explanation because they attempt to explain what is happening in society.

Speeches of Demonstration

A **speech of demonstration** clarifies a process or procedure. It answers an overarching "how" question about the way something works, functions, or is accomplished—for example, how to harvest wild rice, how to make chocolate chip cookies, how laser eye surgery works, how Doppler radar works, how to read food packaging labels, and how tattoos are applied.

This Old House, *While You Were Out*, and *Trading Spaces* on television consist mainly of demonstration speeches on how to remodel and repair one's home, just as *Sewing with Nancy* demonstrates how to sew, *Daily Workout* demonstrates how to exercise. And when *The Magic Schoolbus* demonstrates how the body functions, it's essentially a speech of demonstration about how something works.

Because speeches of demonstration are about processes or procedures, they most often use a chronological pattern in which the speaker reveals steps for the listener to follow in the given order.

Student Workbook

Read through the description and grading criteria for a "Speech of Demonstration" in Chapter 3 of your workbook. Brainstorm three possible topics for a speech of demonstration.

WHAT DO YOU THINK?
Consider one of your favorite television programs. Would you consider it more like a speech of description, explanation, or demonstration? Why?

GUIDELINES FOR EFFECTIVE INFORMATIVE SPEAKING

The general principles discussed earlier in this book are important for preparing and presenting informative speeches. However, certain guidelines are especially important when speaking to inform. Since the goal is essentially to teach listeners something, consider how the speech relates to the learning process and whether the information it contains is new, relevant, clear, and novel. You can check these aspects in the form of the five questions in the following sections.

The Everett Collection

Is My Speech New?

The intent of an informative speech is to share knowledge. But if listeners already have the knowledge, you have nothing much to share. The content of the informative speech—its main points and supporting materials—must help you break through the **apathy barrier,** the tendency of listeners to be indifferent toward your speech, partly as a result of their having heard over the years some informative speeches that were not very interesting. Without something new to share, this is a difficult barrier to overcome. New topics and new approaches are thus necessary.

Select a topic that is new to the audience. If listeners know relatively little about it, they are more likely to be interested. One student chose to inform listeners about the Ebola virus; most of them didn't know much about it, so the topic was new to them.

ETHICS

An entirely new topic is hard to find, but a topic somewhat familiar to listeners can also be interesting if you provide new developments or insights. Use audience analysis (Chapter 6) and ask yourself: What about my topic do listeners probably not know? Not only will this strategy help you find a way to hold listener interest, but it is crucial for ethical informative speaking when your primary goal is to share knowledge. Make your topic new by considering depth, breadth, or perspective.

Adding depth means going beyond people's general knowledge of the topic. Jen did this in an informative speech about psychics. Most listeners know that psychics claim to predict the future but little about the methods they use. So Jen focused on psychics' methods and their roots in astrology, astronomy, and numerology.

Adding breadth means looking at how the topic relates to associated topics. Larissa did this when she informed listeners about the effects of a hysterectomy. She discussed physical and emotional consequences for the individual having the operation, the emotional and relational effects on the patient's friends and family, and the financial costs to society.

Adding perspective means presenting a topic from a point of view listeners probably have never considered. For example, you could talk about issues facing migrant workers by discussing them from the perspective of the workers themselves.

Is My Speech Relevant?

Once you've found new information, relate it directly to listeners' needs and desires. Don't assume they will recognize the relevance of the information; use listener relevance links to show how each main point affects them. If you're proving how they can benefit from the information you offer, listeners will pay attention.

TURNING TO TECHNOLOGY

Brainstorming New Topics

http://www.projectcensored.org/

This site talks about important stories that are often overlooked by the popular press. Identify two or three topics you might consider for a speech.

One way to make a speech more relevant is to compare the new information you're presenting to things listeners are already familiar with. Andria, for example, compared the unfamiliar practice of acupressure to the more familiar practice of acupuncture. Amanda compared Islamic traditions with Judeo-Christian traditions more familiar to her audience. Such comparisons add not only relevance but clarity.

TURNING TO TECHNOLOGY

Combating Apathy

http://www.americanrhetoric.com/MovieSpeeches/moviespeechgoodwillhunting.html

Listen to this clip from the film *Good Will Hunting*. Identify two or three things in it that attempt to combat viewer apathy. To what extent do they keep your attention? To what extent do they make Will's point clearer? What is Will's point?

Is My Speech Clear?

Since your goal is to create mutual understanding, your meaning must be clear to listeners. Knowledge shared in writing can be reread, but in an informative speech listeners must understand you in one hearing; you have no rewind button. Hence it is crucial to convey the message clearly and immediately. The keys are to limit complex vocabulary and technical jargon, avoid abstractions, and explain thoroughly.

Use straightforward, concrete language in an informative speech. If complex or technical jargon is necessary, define the terms as simply as you can. Clarity is the goal, not impressing the audience with vocabulary. Not that jargon should never be used; when defined simply, it can actually make your message clearer. In his speech "Take a Test Drive on the Information Superhighway: Unmasking the Jargon," for example, Carl S. Ledbetter (1995) clarified technical jargon about the Internet throughout his speech. In doing so, he demystified it:

> **"** Let's start with "National Information Infrastructure." That means pork for every state. This is the only kind of infrastructure ever invented for which the construction workers are politicians.
>
> "Multimedia" means more than one medium—a fancy way of saying "Talkies"—movies with sound. Multimedia means mixing voice, video, image, and data in a single communication system.
>
> It's the difference between the records we played as teenagers, which we could only listen to, and the music videos our kids listen to and watch. (p. 567)

Avoid abstractions by preferring vivid imagery and detail (see Chapter 11) and by comparing unfamiliar ideas, objects, or concepts with those that your listeners are more familiar with. Carl Ledbetter did so by comparing multimedia to records and music videos.

Explain thoroughly. Don't overestimate what the audience knows. Beginning speakers whose topic is from the field they major in sometimes assume that their speech classmates are familiar with information from that field. But what's common knowledge in that field is probably not known by all. Likewise, information from your personal and professional experiences outside academia is probably not common knowledge. Surveying classmates before the speech can provide helpful data on what they already know, but if you can't do that then assume listeners will be hearing about your topic for the first time.

TURNING TO TECHNOLOGY

Being Clear

http://www.americanrhetoric.com/MovieSpeeches/moviespeechtokillamockingbird.html

Listen to the closing remarks given by Atticus Finch at the trial of Tom Robinson in *To Kill a Mockingbird.* Identify two or three things Atticus does to make his argument clear to the jury.

Is My Speech Novel?

Mutual understanding requires gaining and maintaining listeners' interest, and novelty can help. Creative flair can be applied to your primary structural elements, language choices, and delivery style.

Perhaps more importantly in an informative speech than in any other kind, start with an attention catcher that sparks listener interest. Be creative. For example, you might start with a physical activity, a startling fact or statistic, a story, or anything else that will make listeners curious and involved. Humor can serve as an attention catcher for an informative speech by lightening the atmosphere and making people more receptive to learning (Wallinger, 1997; Wanzer & Frymier, 1999), but avoid the offensive variety (Sev'er & Ungar, 1997; Swift & Swift, 1994). Although the attention catcher is especially important, think of ways to make each element of structure—listener relevance links, preview, transitions, and so on, all the way to clincher—work to sustain listener interest.

Use vivid language and style in an informative speech. Appeal to listeners' senses; help them see, hear, feel, taste, and smell what you are talking about. Where relevant, use emotional appeals. Be creative by using figures of speech (such as alliteration, repetition, similes, metaphors, and analogies, as detailed in Chapter 11) to reinforce some important points. As you prepare, continually ask, If I were in my audience, what sorts of language and style choices at this spot might gain and sustain my interest and help me remember the speech?

Use your voice to convey enthusiasm about the information being shared. As you practice, think how to change rate, pitch, and volume as well as pauses and stresses to reinforce your ideas (as discussed in Chapter 12).

Use facial expressions to further the enthusiasm and to reinforce the emotions in your verbal message. Pay attention to gestures and movement to emphasize the points you want listeners to remember and to help gain and sustain their attention. Because the eyes are attracted to moving objects, gesturing and using movement appropriately can draw listeners back into the speech.

WHAT DO YOU THINK?

Consider a television commercial you've seen that uses humor. To what degree does the use of humor grab your attention, maintain it, and help you remember the commercial?

PRACTICING THE PROCESS

Checklist for Preparing an Effective Informative Speech

Ask these key questions as you prepare your speech:

- ❏ Is my speech new?
- ❏ Is my speech relevant?
- ❏ Is my speech clear?
- ❏ Is my speech novel?
- ❏ Does my speech round the cycle of learning?

TURNING TO TECHNOLOGY

Novelty in Speeches

http://www.americanrhetoric.com/MovieSpeeches/moviespeechleanonme3.html

At this site, listen to the clip addressing the expulsion of students in *Lean on Me*. Identify language and delivery strategies used to gain and maintain listener interest. Do you think the use of profanity helps or hinders the message? Why?

ETHICS

Does My Speech Round the Cycle of Learning?

Research suggests that listeners vary in the kinds of supporting material that interest them. Some prefer facts and statistics; others, personal examples, or definitions and explanations, or presentational aids. By including different kinds of supporting

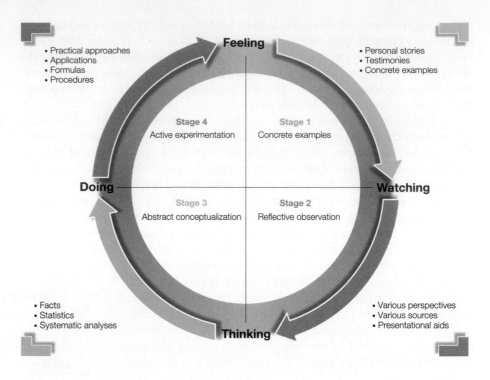

• Practical approaches
• Applications
• Formulas
• Procedures

Feeling

• Personal stories
• Testimonies
• Concrete examples

Stage 4
Active experimentation

Stage 1
Concrete examples

Doing

Watching

Stage 3
Abstract conceptualization

Stage 2
Reflective observation

• Facts
• Statistics
• Systematic analyses

Thinking

• Various perspectives
• Various sources
• Presentational aids

Figure 14.2 Informative speaking and the learning cycle

material, you'll be more likely to gain and maintain the interest of all listeners. The variety also rounds the entire cycle of learning, enabling listeners to better understand, retain, and apply the information because they experience it via all four dimensions of the cycle. For the same reason, present supporting material in different ways—verbally, visually, and audiovisually (Figure 14.2).

To address the feeling dimension, include supporting material that addresses *concrete experiences*. These are stories from people who have actually experienced what you're talking about. The experiences can be your own, those of people you've read about, or those of people you've interviewed. In her speech about acupressure, for example, Andria shared personal testimonies from several individuals who had been helped by the practice.

To address the doing dimension, include supporting material that addresses *active experimentation*. Offer practical applications and give examples. If relevant, provide a formula or procedure that audience members can complete for self-assessment. Andria demonstrated one simple acupressure procedure for relieving headaches and asked listeners to try it at the same time.

To address the thinking dimension, include supporting material that addresses *abstract conceptualization*. You might, for example, include a systematic analysis of some aspect of your topic or relevant facts and statistics. Andria shared statistics about the growing number of medical doctors who endorse acupressure as a viable option for pain relief. She also included facts that compared costs of over-the-counter pain medications with acupressure.

To address the watching dimension, include supporting material that addresses *reflective observation* from a variety of perspectives. Include research from different kinds of sources (books, journals, magazines, newspapers, government documents, and so forth) and identify them. Try to include opinions from academics and other professionals in the field, as well as from nonspecialists. You also might conduct a survey to get the opinions of a broad range of people on some aspect of your topic.

Presentational aids, too, should round the cycle of learning (as discussed in Chapter 13). These could be graphs and charts showing statistical relationships and trends (thinking), a video clip of someone experiencing the topic firsthand (feeling), and a diagram showing the relationships among a variety of perspectives (watching). As with the verbal part of your speech, variety in presentational aids helps all listeners understand, retain, and apply the information offered.

Looking at the Learning Cycle

Checklist for Informative Speeches

❑ Supporting material that addresses *concrete experiences* [Feeling]
❑ Supporting material that addresses *reflective observation* [Watching]
❑ Supporting material that addresses *abstract conceptualization* [Thinking]
❑ Supporting material that addresses *active experimentation* [Doing]

In short, you can shape the content, structure, and delivery of your informative speech in ways that will help you gain and sustain your listeners' interest. Consider how your topic or approach to your topic is new. Relate your speech directly to your listeners' needs and desires. Use clear language that limits complex vocabulary, defines jargon, and explains ideas fully. Work on an enthusiastic delivery style and novel language choices to maintain audience interest. Finally, use supporting material and presentational aids that address feeling, watching, thinking, and doing.

A SAMPLE INFORMATIVE SPEECH

Curt's speech, "The Illongot Headhunters" (Baker, 1998) provides an example of how to apply the guidelines offered in this chapter to an informative speech. His speech outline appears on pages 340–342, after an analysis of its introduction. After examining the introduction and its analysis, continue the process for the rest of the speech. Use these questions to guide your analysis:

- How is the speech made new?
- How is the speech made relevant?
- How are complex ideas made clear?
- How is the speech made novel?
- How does the speech address feeling, thinking, watching, and doing?

You can watch, listen to, and critique Curt's speech by going to Speech Interactive on your *Confident Public Speaking* CD-ROM.

Student Workbook

Read through Katherine's "Is that Kosher" Information and Diversity Speech outline in Chapter 3 of your workbook. How well does she meet each of the five requirements for an effective informative speech?

Line-by-Line Analysis of Curt's Introduction

- *Attention catcher:* Notice how Curt uses vivid language to add novelty and arouse curiosity right away.
- *Listener relevance:* Curt establishes listener relevance in his opening comments to draw listeners into his topic. He also appeals to fear by talking about killing people just for their heads.
- *Speaker credibility:* Curt establishes his credibility so listeners will be more inclined to believe that he has a degree of expertise.
- *Thesis:* Curt's thesis statement is somewhat blunt, reading more like a specific purpose than a thesis. Still, it clearly identifies the topic of his speech.

- *Preview:* Again, his preview is clearly stated. Listeners know he is doing a speech of description. We should have a clear picture in our minds when he is finished.

Challenge yourself to continue commenting on Curt's speech based on the guidelines offered in this chapter.

THE ILLONGOT HEADHUNTERS

—Curt Ziniel

Introduction

I. ***Attention catcher:*** In the spring, when the fire plant blooms, the gentle swinden farmers of the Philippines go mad with anger and turn into the ferocious headhunters of South Seas legend.

II. ***Listener relevance:*** Remember Robinson Crusoe, the Swiss Family Robinson, or even the swashbuckling or missionary stories of childhood about island savages? Well, headhunters of the Illongot tribe were still killing people for their heads just twenty years ago and there is no guarantee they won't start again.

III. ***Speaker credibility:*** My interest in the Illongot grew out of an anthropology course I took and research I've done into the history and culture of this hunter/gatherer tribe.

IV. ***Thesis statement:*** Today, I'd like to give you a glimpse into the lives of the Illongot headhunters.

V. ***Preview:*** To help you understand who these people are, I'll talk about the headhunting ritual itself, some important restrictions on it, and what caused the Illongot to stop the practice.

Transition: As I said, the Illongot are an indigenous tribe living in the jungles of the Philippine Islands subsisting on hunting, gathering, and swinden farming. "Indigenous" means original and usually tribal, and "swinden farming" is a kind of slash-and-burn agriculture where the people till the land until it doesn't produce well, and then they move on (Microsoft Corporation, 1995). Many jungle-dwelling tribes in the Philippines practice this kind of farming (National Geographic Special Publications Division, 1986). But "taking heads" is a special practice that is unique to the Illongot tribe.

Body

I. ***First main point:*** Headhunting was done by young, unmarried men as a manhood ritual. It was essentially a rite of passage from boyhood to manhood.

Listener relevance: This rite of passage concept is not unique to the Illongot tribe. It is actually quite similar to the sort of ritual of boys who go out on their first hunting trip with their fathers in this country.

A. ***Subpoint:*** Taking the head of an enemy was required before a young man could marry.

1. ***Sub-subpoint:*** Young women viewed more successful men favorably.

2. ***Sub-subpoint:*** Tribal leaders viewed more successful men favorably.

D. ***Subpoint:*** Headhunting was done when the bright red fire plant bloomed.

1. *Sub-subpoint:* The blooming plant was associated with overwhelming anger.
   2. *Sub-subpoint:* Some speculate that the plant actually has a chemical effect that intensifies feelings of anger when it blooms.
   3. *Sub-subpoint:* Although these connections are not fully understood, they have come about, in part, because the Illongot are typically known as a close-knit tribe who rarely show anger (M. Z. Rosaldo, 1980).

Transition: Because headhunting was a rite-of-passage ritual, several restrictions governing whose heads could be taken also existed.

II. *Second main point:* The most important restriction had to do with whose heads could be hunted.
   A. *Subpoint:* Only people who were members of other Philippine tribes could be headhunted.

   Listener relevance: As you can probably imagine, whether you are hunting gophers or gold or even heads, things don't always go as planned.
   B. *Subpoint:* Sometimes anthropologists would mistakenly be killed (R. Rosaldo, 1980).
   C. *Subpoint:* Sometimes missionaries who were trying to convert the people to Christianity would be killed (M. Z. Rosaldo, 1980).

Transition: Unfortunately, these murders of people who were not members of Philippine tribes resulted in some bad press for the Illongot and eventually led to the end of the practice.

III. *Third main point:* Why did the Illongot stop headhunting?
   A. *Subpoint:* Christianity actually had relatively little to do with it.
   B. *Subpoint:* The headhunting ritual ended primarily due to economics and politics.

   Listener relevance: It seems that money plays a major role, not only in our country, but in other countries as well.
   1. *Sub-subpoint:* When the government forced the Illongot to live in permanent compounds, they could no longer engage in swinden farming, which resulted in starvation (R. Rosaldo, 1980).
   2. *Sub-subpoint:* In order to receive government assistance, the tribe had to agree to stop engaging in the ritualistic practice of headhunting.
   C. *Subpoint:* Since the practice of headhunting did not end because of a change in Illongot beliefs, it may not be permanent.
   1. *Sub-subpoint:* It might depend on the government.
   2. *Sub-subpoint:* It might depend on the church.
   3. *Sub-subpoint:* It might depend on the blooming of the fire plant.

Conclusion
   I. *Thesis restatement:* Now I hope you have a clearer picture—more than just a snapshot—of who the Illongot headhunters of the Philippines are.

   II. *Main point summary:* We discussed the headhunting practice as a ritual, some of its unique restrictions, and why the tribe has stopped practicing it.

(continued)

III. **Clincher:** Whether they practice the ritual or not, we can assume that when spring is in the air and the fire plant blossoms are flaming red, young Illongot men continue to dream of taking heads and winning a wife. Today they dream. Tomorrow— who can tell?

References

Microsoft Corporation. (1995). Philippines. *Microsoft Encarta.*

National Geographic Special Publications Division. (1986). *Vanishing people of the earth.* Washington, D.C: National Geographic Society.

Rosaldo, M. Z. (1980). *Knowledge and passion: Illongot notions of self and social life.* Cambridge, England: Cambridge University Press.

Rosaldo, R. (1980). *Illongot headhunting 1883–1974: A study in society and history.* Stanford, CA: Stanford University Press.

SUMMARY

Informative speaking is the process of sharing knowledge to create mutual understanding. A speaker informs by answering questions such as "who," "when," "what," "where," "why," "how to," and "how does." Successful informative speakers help listeners understand their perspective, retain their ideas, and apply them after the presentation is over. Informative speakers are essentially teachers, answering questions about objects, events, places, people, processes, procedures, ideas, concepts, beliefs, or issues. Public speaking anxiety sometimes increases when preparing informative speeches due to a fear of boring listeners. These anxieties can be overcome.

There are three types of informative speeches: description, explanation, and demonstration. Most informative speeches offer elements of all three, but the primary thesis focuses on only one. Determining the type of informative speech helps narrow the topic and shape the thesis statement. To determine which type of speech to present, ask what you want to clarify. Are you trying to paint a picture; explain a concept, issue, or idea; or outline a process, procedure, or function?

Answer five key questions when preparing an informative speech: Is my speech new? Is my speech relevant? Is my speech clear? Is my speech novel? Does my speech round the cycle of learning by addressing feeling, watching, thinking, and doing? If the answer to each question is yes, the informative speech will share knowledge to create mutual understanding and listeners will retain and apply what they've learned.

RETURNING TO TECHNOLOGY

The *Confident Public Speaking* CD-ROM is your one-stop point of access for not just the content on the CD itself but also Speech Interactive and the many other resources on the *Confident Public Speaking* Web site, Speech Builder Express, and InfoTrac College Edition. Note that this chapter's key terms and activities are among the resources available in electronic format online. Additional information is included below.

SPEECH INTERACTIVE
ON THE *CONFIDENT PUBLIC SPEAKING* CD-ROM

Speech Interactive is your link to this text's speech videos. Offering opportunities to practice critiquing speeches by students and other public speakers, these videos will help you prepare for providing effective feedback to your peers and your own speech performances.

SPEECH BUILDER EXPRESS

At the Create a New Speech screen of Speech Builder Express, you are given the option of specifying the type of speech you are going to work on. From the drop-down menu, select Informative. Then, on the subsequent Setup screen, select the kind of informative speech you're starting. The program will provide prompts sequenced specifically for the kind of informative speech you indicated.

KEY TERMS

Interactive flashcards for these key terms are available on the *Confident Public Speaking* Web site. You'll find the "Flashcards" link under the resources for Chapter 14.

Apathy barrier   334
Informative speaking   328
Speech of demonstration   333

Speech of description   330
Speech of explanation   332

ACTIVITIES

The activities below, as well as additional activities, are available in electronic format on the *Confident Public Speaking* Web site. You'll find the "Activities" link under the resources for Chapter 14.

1. **Professional Speaker Analysis.** Attend a lecture on campus. Examine the speech in terms of the aspects discussed in this chapter. Answer the following questions and provide examples from the speech.

- Is it a speech of description, explanation, or demonstration?
- What kinds of supporting material are offered to appeal to thinking, doing, feeling, and watching?
- In what way or ways is the topic new?
- Does the speaker define technical jargon?
- What are some examples of vivid language?
- How does the speaker use his or her voice and body to sustain interest?
- What sort of presentational aids are offered and how do they address feeling, doing, thinking, and watching?

2. **Brainstorming Informative Speech Types.** Form a group with two or three of classmates. Generate several potential speech topics. Select one topic and do the following:
   - Create three purpose statements: one for a speech of description, one for a speech of explanation, and one for a speech of demonstration.
   - Next, select one of the statements and pattern the main points for it.
   - Share your results with the class.

INFOTRAC COLLEGE EDITION ACTIVITY

Access Infotrac College Edition and search for the following articles: "Is Experience the Best Teacher?" by Margaret A. Gallego and "How the Brain Learns Best" by Bruce Perry. Alternatively, use "learning styles" and "informative speeches" as keywords. After you've read the articles, consider which strategies may help you maintain listener interest in your informative speeches.

PERSUASIVE SPEAKING: TYPES AND DESIGNS

REFLECTIVE QUESTIONS

1. In what ways do you think a persuasive speech can be an argument? How might it differ from an informative speech? Do you think there's a point at which an attempt to persuade becomes coercion?

2. How might a dispositional persuasive speech differ from an actuation persuasive speech? Which do you think might include a call to action?

3. In what ways do you think the target audience might influence the way you should approach preparing a persuasive speech?

4. What do you think you might want to do to your speech if you expect your audience to be hostile, or when your speech is likely to be controversial?

5. How might you arrange main points to make an actuation persuasive speech as effective as possible? Why?

WHAT'S AHEAD: FOCUSING YOUR READING

What Is Persuasive Speaking?

Persuasive Speaking and Public Speaking Anxiety

Using Audience Analysis to Shape Your Speech

Persuasive Speech Types

Making a Claim in Your Thesis Statement

Organizing Your Main Points

M ADISON HAD HER HEART SET ON a good steak for her birthday dinner. It would have been a rare luxury, and she'd been looking forward to it for weeks. But nothing on the menu really appealed to her. Wondering how Rick had managed to convince her to go to an Italian restaurant, she finally ordered the chicken tetrazinni, wishing it were filet mignon.

Sherry stared at her returned exam in disbelief. How could she have earned such a low grade? She had answered every question correctly, but lost points on each one. What more could she have done? To make matters worse, her friend Dana had earned a higher grade with less complete answers! "Well," Sherry thought, "there's only one way to find out." She knocked on the professor's door. "Sherry, come in! What can I do for you?" "Well . . . the reason I came by . . . is . . . well, I really think I deserve a better grade on this examination. I've reviewed my notes and even talked with some classmates. I'm not one to complain, but I really think I've answered the questions completely. I guess I'm asking you to look at it one more time." "Sure, Sherry," her professor responded. "I admire your courage. I'll take another look."

Eric is the oldest of several children. Growing up, he saw his younger siblings argue and fight more after watching violent television programs. He wanted to do a speech on this topic, but realized the audience would likely disagree with him about censoring television. There must be a way to convince even this audience, he thought, but how? Amanda wanted to speak on domestic violence, but like Eric she worried that some classmates might oppose her views. She wondered if another topic would be better. Pete wanted to raise awareness about teen suicide and convince his audience to act to prevent it, but like Eric and Amanda he wondered if he could organize his thoughts well enough to convince the listeners.

Aware of it or not, we constantly send and receive persuasive messages. A friend convinces you to go to one movie instead of another. Your kids try to persuade you to let them go to a friend's house. A salesperson has plenty of reasons why you should buy that new car. And those are just the person-to-person pleas—then comes the bombardment from television, newspaper, magazine, and other media ads.

On the other hand, perhaps you have tried to convince a professor to change a grade, a spouse to go out to dinner, or a client to buy your widgets. Why do some messages convince but others fail? What is persuasive speaking and what makes it effective?

This chapter focuses on the characteristics of persuasive speaking and how to organize persuasive speeches. It examines the nature of persuasive speaking, its relationship to public speaking anxiety, dispositional and actuation persuasive speech types, and the organizational patterns that most effectively influence listeners based on target audience and goal. The next chapter focuses on strategies to make a persuasive speech successful.

WHAT DO YOU THINK?

Consider a time when someone convinced you to do something you had not planned to do. How did the person change your mind? Why was he or she successful?

WHAT IS PERSUASIVE SPEAKING?

Persuasion is the process of influencing other people's attitudes, beliefs, values, or behaviors. **Persuasive speaking** is the process of influencing attitudes, beliefs, values, or behaviors through a public speech. The persuasive speaker develops an argument in support of a position on a topic. In this context, **argument** means articulating a position with the support of evidence and reasoning, not "quarrel," "dispute," or "disagreement." Thus persuasive speakers "argue" a position (Perloff, 1993).

In addition to creating mutual understanding, persuasive speakers aim to gain listeners' agreement by influencing attitudes, beliefs, values, and behaviors.

ETHICS

The informative speaker seeks to create mutual understanding about a topic. So does the persuasive speaker, but in addition hopes to influence listeners to agree with a position and sometimes to take action as a result. For example, an informative speaker talks about how to set up a recycling center; a persuasive speaker does that too and goes on to try to convince listeners that recycling is crucial, and perhaps to start a recycling center or lobby Congress in support of recycling legislation. Informative speakers are *teachers*, persuasive speakers are *leaders*. Persuasive speakers want to lead listeners toward agreement (the strategies for doing this are discussed in Chapter 16). But the agreement must be voluntary and not based on threats; persuasion is ethical, but threats do not demonstrate respect for listeners' freedom to choose and are merely attempts at coercion. Persuasive speaking is the most complex and challenging kind of public speaking but potentially the most rewarding.

Persuasion is necessary only when there are two or more points of view on a topic; these may be directly opposed or differ only in degree. In a speech about television censorship, for example, you could favor or oppose it, seeking agreement with one of two opposing points of view. Or you could argue that television censorship should be more accessible to parents and guardians, in which case you seek to convince listeners only to a degree. Persuasion occurs any time you influence a listener's position in the direction you advocate, even if it's only a matter of degree. To be effective, learn the existing points of view on your topic and determine where your audience stands. This lets you create arguments by shaping the speech around reasons the audience is most likely to accept.

Effective persuasive speaking is important for you as a speaker and as a listener. As a speaker, you can learn to articulate your position about topics that matter to you with solid logic and reasoning. Consequently, you can make a difference by fostering positive changes to improve your school, community, and even society. As a listener, you can become aware of problems and ways to solve them as presented by speakers. Persuasive speaking can also force reevaluation of your positions, as well as improve your ability to defend them. And it can make you a better critical consumer of attempts made by others to influence you. Finally, being able to judge how well others use persuasive speaking techniques can help you improve your own effectiveness as a persuasive speaker.

TURNING TO TECHNOLOGY

Controversial Questions

http://www.valencia.cc.fl.us/lrcwest/kaysmith.html

This site poses numerous questions related to both sides of controversial issues. Use this site to brainstorm potential topics for your persuasive speeches. Which controversial questions interest you and why? Which ones might be most compelling for the audience of your persuasive speech and why?

PERSUASIVE SPEAKING AND PUBLIC SPEAKING ANXIETY

When you consider the challenges of persuasive speaking, it's not surprising that it can contribute to public speaking anxiety. It's one thing to talk to listeners about seat belt safety, quite another to convince them to wear seat belts. It takes more to motivate listeners to change their thinking or behavior than it does to motivate them to listen and retain information. Because the expectations you place on yourself are greater when speaking to persuade, fear of failure can also be greater, resulting in increased public speaking anxiety.

The best way to combat this fear is to make sure that the structure, language, content, and delivery of your speech are appropriate and serve your persuasive purpose. The earliest step, on which the success of all the others depends, is audience analysis. It helps eliminate speech anxiety, because the more you know about your listeners and where they stand, the more confident you can be that you know how to persuade them.

USING AUDIENCE ANALYSIS TO SHAPE YOUR SPEECH

Employ audience analysis to learn not only what listeners might know but also where they might stand. This input affects what kind of persuasive speech to give.

1. When your target audience agrees with you, seek action.
2. When your target audience is undecided, seek agreement.

3. When your target audience opposes your position, seek incremental change.

For most topics, even before audience analysis it's safe to assume listeners have different opinions. Some probably agree with you or already behave in the manner you desire; others don't have a firm position. Some probably disagree with you entirely. These situations suggest slightly different persuasive goals. If listeners agree, *reinforce* their point of view. If they're undecided, help them *form* a position. If they're opposed, try to *reform* their position. But in an audience with a range of positions, how do you know which goal to focus on? Analyze the audience to find a majority group that becomes your **target audience**—the people you most want to persuade. Then tailor your message accordingly. This does not mean that you ignore the rest of the audience, just that you aim primarily for the target group.

If most listeners already agree with you, *seek action*. If, for instance, most already believe recycling is important but few actually recycle much, these listeners are the target audience. Tailor your speech to further their behavior, perhaps by persuading them to help enact new recycling policies at the state or local level. Include steps for them to follow, which is a **call to action.** For example, Amanda learned that most of her classmates believed domestic violence is a problem and Pete discovered that most agreed that teen suicide is a problem. But their listeners didn't know what to do about it. Pete and Amanda gave them suggestions. Bottom line: When most listeners already agree with you, seek action.

If most listeners aren't sure where they stand, the best strategy is usually to *seek agreement*. In a classroom poll, for example, Eric discovered that seventeen of the twenty-two students were unsure whether television censorship is a good thing. So he decided to try to convince listeners to agree that censorship is necessary. When the target audience is unsure, use a persuasive speech to help them form a position.

TURNING TO TECHNOLOGY

Persuasive Speeches

Go to the *Confident Public Speaking* Web site and find the links to three outlines of persuasive speeches. "Domestic Violence" by Amanda Brown and "Teen Suicide" by Peter Klemin are calls to action. "Television Censorship Will Save America's Children" by Eric Gustafson seeks agreement.

If most listeners oppose your stand, seek **incremental change.** Try to move them even a small degree in your direction, hoping for further movement later. Begin by brainstorming objections, questions, and criticisms that might arise, then shape your speech around answers and responses to them. You might try the **coactive approach** for confronting reluctant audiences intelligently and constructively (Simons, 1986). It has five basic parts:

First, establish a welcoming, nonconfrontational climate. Don't use a startling statistic for an attention catcher; a reluctant audience must be eased into the speech gently.

Second, talk about beliefs, attitudes, and values that the audience is likely to share with you. The goal here is simply to get listeners nodding in agreement. Henrietta Lewis (1998) did this in her speech about how technology is taking away our rights:

> People do it every day. They walk in an airport through an electronic device; if it beeps, they walk back around, empty their keys and change and walk through it again. We accept these modern-day intrusions on our personal liberties because we recognize the need for ever tighter security in an increasingly dangerous world and we regard the resulting inconvenience as a small price to pay for our own safety and well-being.
>
> Video surveillance in public places is already here, and a new generation of sophisticated weapons and contraband devices is only a few years away. Today, I will be discussing this technology, how this technology can infringe on Fourth Amendment guarantees, and some solutions regarding how we can defend our constitutional rights.

Third, set modest goals, such as getting your audience to consider what you have to say. This goal might seem inappropriate to persuasive speaking, but if you can achieve it you might ultimately go further. For example, because of the **sleeper effect,** change may emerge later after listeners have absorbed your ideas and incorporated them into their own beliefs. Amanda hoped this would happen in her speech about a way to reduce violence by avoiding certain television programs. Or if your speech results in **raised consciousness,** the audience has been sensitized to the issue and will be more receptive to persuasion in the future (McCombs, 1981). Or you may have gained **situational acceptance,** where listeners agree that a policy, approach, or behavior is acceptable in some situations. Neil did this in his speech about abortion. He'd learned that most of his listeners opposed abortion, so he argued only that it might be justified when the mother's life is in danger. With this limitation, his target audience considered what he had to say and he may have gained situational acceptance.

Fourth, when persuading reluctant listeners, cite authorities they are likely to recognize and respect. In listeners' minds you are not an expert, particularly to those who oppose your position, so the more credible the external support you offer, the greater your chances for success.

Fifth, acknowledge the arguments of the opposing side as valid and understandable before identifying flaws in them. For example, in the speech about seat belt safety you might acknowledge that seat belt laws restrict rights, but then examine the need to balance rights with responsibilities.

Identifying the target audience allows you to tailor your persuasive approach to increase the potential for success and limit your anxiety. When most listeners already agree with you, seek action. When most are undecided, help them form a position by seeking agreement. When most oppose your position, seek incremental change, as by using a coactive approach. Once the target audience is identified and you've thought about how best to approach your topic, determine a thesis statement and organize main points.

PRACTICING THE PROCESS

Guidelines for Using the Coactive Approach

1. Establish good will early in the speech.
2. Start by talking about general areas of agreement rather than disagreement.
3. Set modest goals.
4. Cite authorities the audience will respect.
5. Acknowledge opposing arguments respectfully.

Dispositional speeches aim to influence listeners' disposition (beliefs, attitudes, and values) toward a topic.

PERSUASIVE SPEECH TYPES

Persuasive speeches take two main forms: dispositional and actuational. The goal of each depends on what you are trying to influence. As with types of informative speech, the type of persuasive speech you select helps determine its thesis statement.

Dispositional Persuasive Speeches

A **dispositional persuasive speech** is designed to influence listeners' disposition toward the topic—that is, their beliefs, attitudes, and/or values. Let's look at each of these targets more closely.

A **belief** is something accepted as true or false although it hasn't been or can't be proved. For example, you might believe that watching gratuitous violence or sex on television promotes teenage violence or sexual promiscuity. This is only a belief because, although you can support your position with evidence, other points of view are possible and defensible. In contrast, it's a fact, not a belief, that some television programs do depict violence and sex. Because people tend to consider their beliefs to be facts, you must offer a great deal of evidence to convince them to change their beliefs.

An **attitude** is the tendency to respond favorably or unfavorably to something, to like or dislike it. For example, you might strongly dislike television shows with gratuitous violence and sex. In a dispositional persuasive speech you might argue that such shows are vulgar or unappealing. Attitudes change fairly frequently and are easier to influence than beliefs or values.

A **value** is a deeply held concept about what is good, right, and important with regard to conduct and existence, such as honesty, respect, integrity, loyalty, freedom, justice, order, love, courage, and wisdom (Johannesen, 1990). In a dispositional persuasive speech you might argue that television violence and sex are wrong because they reflect a lack of respect for human beings. Eric's speech (located at the end of this chapter) is a dispositional speech grounded in a value.

WHAT DO YOU THINK?
Do you believe the gratuitous violence on television today promotes violent behavior in children? In teenagers? Why?

Actuation speeches aim to influence listeners' behavior.

Values, which are deeply held, are the most difficult dispositions to change. In a speech favoring capital punishment, for example, it would be easier to convince someone who opposes it on the grounds that it doesn't deter crime than someone who opposes it on the grounds that it is immoral and wrong.

Beliefs, attitudes, and values are often closely related. For example, people valuing wisdom and believing that older people are wise probably have a favorable attitude toward older people in the workplace. All three types of disposition are likely to be represented in a dispositional speech, but one will provide the grounding for your thesis statement. For example, Eric's speech on television censorship was grounded in the *value* of respect for human beings, specifically children. He also addressed the *belief* that censorship is necessary as a tool for parents and the *attitude* that television too often depicts acts of violence and sex that are graphic, vulgar, and brutal. Although the thesis is likely based on either a belief, an attitude, or a value, main points and supporting material usually reflect all three.

Actuation Persuasive Speeches

Actuation persuasive speeches are designed to influence behavior. To **actuate** means to move someone to action. So you seek to move listeners to action in an actuation persuasive speech. Advertisers engage in actuation persuasive speaking by trying to convince you to buy. Sherry engaged in actuation persuasive speaking to convince her professor to reconsider her grade. The action sometimes involves politics or policy. For example, you might urge listeners to vote for a candidate, write to their representatives in support of a bill, or demonstrate against a tuition increase. Josh did this by staging an all-night vigil outside the home of the college president. Or actions might concern individual behaviors, such as when encouraging listeners to wear seat belts, take multivitamins, or even floss their teeth regularly. Amanda did this when she urged boycotting certain television programs that depict domestic violence, and Pete when he beseeched listeners to watch for the signs of depression that often lead to teen suicide.

WHAT DO YOU THINK?

Consider a television commercial that made you want to buy the product. What made the product appealing to you? Did you actually purchase it? Why or why not?

A speech arguing that excessive television violence is wrong and harmful to society is a dispositional speech focused on a value.

Actuation persuasive speaking is the most challenging type of public speaking. To persuade listeners to act, you must be competent in all forms of public speaking. Consider the public speaking continuum illustrated in Figure 14.1. When speaking to inform, you merely share knowledge, with the goal of mutual understanding. When speaking to persuade about a disposition, you inform listeners, with the goal of agreement. When seeking action (actuation speaking), you inform listeners about aspects of the topic and seek agreement with your position so as to motivate them to act.

In Tammy's speech about dental hygiene her ultimate goal was to seek action—to get listeners to floss regularly so as to avoid gum disease. To do this, she had to inform her listeners about the nature of gum disease and seek agreement that it can cause life-threatening medical problems (belief), as well as about why most people don't floss (attitude). Then she could seek action by compelling listeners to promote expanded dental education programs, advertising campaigns, and personal behavior modification (Frisby, 1998). Amanda had to convince her audience of the magnitude of the problem of domestic violence as well as its most pervasive causes before she could advocate her solutions and seek action.

ETHICS

Another challenge of persuasive speaking is especially serious, particularly in calls to action. Although ethics are important in any type of public speech, the potential consequences of a successful persuasive speech can be more significant than those of an informative speech. After all, it's an attempt to convince listeners to change their thinking or behavior. So it's your ethical responsibility to thoroughly research content and to accurately and fully represent findings. Don't just rely on sources that support your argument. If you convince listeners to do something, the consequences are your responsibility.

If you convince listeners to stop taking over-the-counter drugs, what if someone stops taking an aspirin a day to help prevent heart disease? The implications are your responsibility. You would have been more ethical to acknowledge that some over-the-counter drugs are worth taking. Your evidence must have sufficient

WHAT DO YOU THINK?
Consider an infomercial you've seen that advocated a diet, dietary supplement, or piece of exercise equipment. What claims were made about what the product will do? Were the potential risks addressed? Do you think the infomercial was ethical? Why or why not?

Anti-smoking ads function like actuation persuasive speeches, as they try to convince people that smoking is harmful and persuade them to quit.

breadth and depth, and you must reason ethically with it. As discussed in Chapter 16, this includes avoiding faulty reasoning.

MAKING A CLAIM IN YOUR THESIS STATEMENT

As with any speech, narrow the persuasive speech topic to arrive at a manageable thesis statement. The process is somewhat different here, however: You must decide to make a claim of either fact, value, or policy on which to base your thesis statement.

Claim of Fact

A **claim of fact** states that something is true—it takes a position on something not known but that can be argued for. A thesis statement that makes a claim of fact seeks agreement about a belief. Claims of fact can concern the past, present, or future.

Claims of fact concerning the past can be on topics as different as whether Lee Harvey Oswald acted alone in shooting President Kennedy and whether birds evolved from dinosaurs. If something is already known or accepted as the truth by all, it cannot be the basis for a claim of fact. For example, you couldn't give a speech on whether Kennedy is dead—we all know he is.

Even though a claim of fact may or may not be true, phrase the thesis statement as though it is true. Your thesis statement might be, for instance:

* Although Lee Harvey Oswald shot President Kennedy, he was actually part of a larger conspiracy.

Or you might state:

* The birds that fly the earth today are actually the descendants of dinosaurs.

Claims of fact concerning the present are also possible. One fertile area is health, including new treatments, drugs, and substances. For example:

* The fat-free chemical used in some snack chips and known as olestra is harmful to one's health.
* Television violence promotes teen violence.

- Sugar is a better sweetener than NutraSweet.
- Sexual orientation is genetically determined.
- Distorted images of what constitutes an ideal female body promote eating disorders.
- There is life on other planets.

After years of research, many claims of fact about the present are eventually proved or disproved. At that point, a claim of fact and persuasive speech would no longer be possible. In the 1950s, for example, you might have presented a persuasive speech arguing that smoking does or does not cause lung cancer. Today, however, we know that smoking is a leading cause of lung cancer.

Claims of fact can also be focused in the future—that the Red Sox will win the next World Series, for example. Thus a prediction could serve as a thesis statement based on a claim of fact. Science fiction films and novels are often future-based claims of fact. Viewers and readers are enticed by them because they include an element of plausibility. For example:

- E-mail will eventually render traditional postal service obsolete.
- Global warming will eventually force us to live on water as well as land.
- Thanks to the Internet, paperbound books will eventually cease to exist.

Claims of fact can focus on the past by arguing that something did or did not exist or occur in a certain way; on the present by contending that something is or is not harmful, does or does not exist, or is or is not the cause of something else; or on the future by predicting what will or will not occur.

<aside>
WHAT DO YOU THINK?
Consider a science fiction film you've seen, such as *The Matrix, Waterworld, Alien,* or *The Terminator.* What claim of fact did it argue?
</aside>

Claim of Value

A **claim of value** judges whether a concept or action is good, right, moral, fair, or better than another. As with speeches based on claims of fact, agreement is sought from listeners—but here the agreement concerns a judgment of worth. Thesis statements that make claims of value are easy to generate; they are often rooted in personal positions about things we deem important. However, preparing and presenting an effective speech focused on them often takes more effort because values are hard to change.

Here are some examples of a claim of value.

- Jimmy Carter was an excellent president.
- Cloning is wrong.
- Spanking is not a good form of child discipline.
- Brisk walking is a better form of aerobic exercise than running.
- A low-fat diet is better than a fat-free diet.

Claim of Policy

A **claim of policy** states a position about whether a specific course of action should be taken. A thesis statement that makes a claim of policy leads to an actuation persuasive speech. The following questions could lead to such a claim, for example: "What should be done to improve the quality of education in the United States?" "What should be done to reduce the problems associated with nuclear waste?" "Should the legal age for drinking alcohol be changed?" "What should be done to improve recycling efforts?" "What should be done to deal with

Fact	Value	Policy
Past	Good/bad	Do it/don't do it
Did/did not occur	Moral/immoral	Should/shouldn't
Present	Fair/unfair	Must/must not
Does/does not exist		
Cause/doesn't cause		
Is linked/is not linked		
Future		
Will/will not occur		

Figure 15.1 Types of claims at a glance

the problem of domestic violence?" By brainstorming these kinds of questions, you can come up with a claim for a thesis statement:

- We must improve the quality of education in the United States.
- The legal drinking age should be lowered to 18.
- Government agencies, community organizations, and individuals must do more to foster the habit of recycling.

Amanda's thesis statement made a claim of policy: "Action must be taken to reduce domestic violence." Similarly, Pete's thesis was: "Teen suicide is a serious problem today, one we must take action to eradicate."

Figure 15.1 summarizes the three types of claims—fact, value, and policy. Narrow your persuasive speech topic by considering which type of claim to make. Dispositional persuasive speech thesis statements typically make a claim of fact or value. Actuation persuasive speeches make a claim of policy. Determine your claim based on what you learn through audience analysis about where the target audience stands on the issue.

ORGANIZING YOUR MAIN POINTS

Some of the organizational patterns discussed in Chapter 8 can be used in persuasive speeches (particularly topical, causal, and narrative), but others are uniquely suited to building persuasive speech arguments. Four that work particularly well for dispositional persuasive speeches are the refutative, comparative advantages, invitational, and problem (no solution) patterns. Four patterns that are particularly appropriate for actuation persuasive speeches are problem/solution, problem/cause/solution, modified comparative advantages, and Monroe's motivated sequence patterns (Figure 15.2).

WHAT DO YOU THINK?
Have you ever watched a political debate? Did you have an opinion about the issues or candidates before watching? Who was more convincing to you and why? What role did your preconceived notions play in your decision?

Organizing Main Points in Dispositional Persuasive Speeches

Usually several reasons emerge in support of your dispositional speech claim. In such cases, each will probably serve as a main point in the body of your speech.

Dispositional	Actuation
Topical	Problem/solution
Causal	Problem/cause/solution
Narrative	
Refutative	
Comparative advantages	Modified comparative advantages
Invitational	Monroe's motivated sequence
Problem (no solution)	

Figure 15.2 Main point patterns for persuasive speeches

Hence the main point pattern is essentially topical. Eric used this approach for the main points of his speech on television censorship:

> - Television censorship will soon be possible.
> - Television censorship is a necessary tool for today's parents.
> - Television censorship is beneficial to children.

Other times a causal design is most effective. For example, in a speech about olestra as harmful to your health, you might arrange your main points around causes and effects. A speech about media effects on eating disorders might also be arranged most effectively using a causal pattern.

Sometimes a narrative pattern can best achieve your purpose. For example, in a speech about spanking as a form of child discipline, you might share the stories of two adults, one who was spanked as a child and one who was not.

But sometimes none of these works well—for example, when the target audience opposes your position or when the points of view surrounding your topic vary merely in degree. In these cases, try a refutative, comparative advantages, invitational, or problem (no solution) pattern for the main points.

Some experts say that the strongest arguments should be placed at the beginning and end of the speech, based on the primacy-recency effect (the tendency to remember first and last items in a speech) (e.g., Cook, 1989). But others say the placement should depend on the audience, that the strongest argument should be first when the target audience opposes your position and last when the target audience is neutral (e.g., Sonnenberg, 1988). Best of all, however, is to order arguments by considering both topic and audience.

Refutative Pattern

The **refutative pattern** is a main point arrangement that persuades by both disproving the opposing position and bolstering your own. This is particularly effective when the target audience opposes your position. Begin by acknowledging the merit of opposing arguments and then showing their flaws. Once listeners understand the flaws, they are more receptive to the arguments presented to support your position.

This is not the only refutative strategy, but it is effective. Typically you follow a four-step process for each main point, although sometimes speakers use it to develop the four main points of their speech. Laine used a refutative pattern for her dispositional persuasive speech about school uniforms:

Student Workbook

Read through the description of and grading criteria for a "Point-Counterpoint Speech" in Chapter 4 of your workbook. Then critique Dixie's and Robert's speech outlines and delivery (on this book's CD-ROM) using the criteria.

Thesis statement: *School uniforms will not solve the problems in our school system.*

I. **First main point** *(State opposing argument):* Some people claim that school uniforms reduce violence.

   A. **Subpoint** *(State evidence to support the opposing argument):* This argument is based on beliefs regarding social comparison theory, child development, and socioeconomic status (explain each of these).

   B. **Subpoint** *(State and give evidence of the flaws in the argument):* Although these beliefs make sense to a certain degree, several studies have been conducted showing that schools which switched to uniforms actually experienced increased violence among students (cite some of the results and conclusions).

   C. **Subpoint** *(State your argument and evidence to support it):* When one looks at the evidence regarding school uniforms and violence, it is obvious that school uniforms will not reduce violence and may even result in more of it (cite examples again).

II. **Second main point** *(State opposing argument):* Some people claim that school uniforms will improve academic achievement and standardized test scores.

   A. **Subpoint** *(State evidence to support the opposing argument):* This argument is based on beliefs regarding social comparison theory, child development, and emotional intelligence (explain each of these).

   B. **Subpoint** *(State and give evidence of the flaws in the argument):* Again, these perceptions tend to make sense, that is, until one considers the research conducted that shows no significant improvement in test scores by students in schools where uniforms were made mandatory (cite some of the results and conclusions).

   C. **Subpoint** *(State your argument and evidence to support it):* Although there may be good reasons for mandating school uniforms, improving academic achievement and test scores are not among them.

III. **Third main point** *(State your argument and evidence to support it):* Schools where students wear street clothes do not have more problems than schools where students wear uniforms.

   A. **Subpoint** *(State your argument and evidence to support it):* Schools where students wear street clothes rather than uniforms do not necessarily engage in more violence (cite some of the results and conclusions).

   B. **Subpoint** *(State your argument and evidence to support it):* Schools where students wear street clothes rather than uniforms do not report significantly lower standardized test scores (cite some of the results and conclusions).

   C. **Subpoint** *(Show how your argument erodes the argument of the opposing side):* If this research is correct, then it is obvious that wearing uniforms will not solve problems of violence or academic achievement in our schools.

Laine concluded by restating her thesis statement, "School uniforms will not solve the problems in our school systems." She summarized her main points by reminding listeners that school uniforms "won't necessarily reduce violence among students or improve academic achievement," and clinched with "I'm not here to convince you that we shouldn't adopt a school uniform policy, but let's not do so for the wrong reasons."

PRACTICING THE PROCESS

Guidelines for Using the Refutative Pattern

Follow this four-step strategy to develop each of your main points:

1. State an argument typically used in support of the position you are refuting.
2. State and give evidence of the flaws in this argument.
3. State and give evidence to support your argument.
4. Show how your argument erodes the argument of the opposing side.

Comparative Advantages Pattern

The **comparative advantages pattern** is a main point arrangement that leads the audience to agree that one of two or more alternatives is best. You show that the advantages of your alternative outweigh the disadvantages, and that its advantages surpass the advantages of the other options (Ziegelmueller, Kay, & Dause, 1990, p. 186). You might also show how the disadvantages of other options outweigh their advantages. Because the goal in a dispositional speech is to seek agreement, stop short of advocating action. Instead, leave that decision to your listeners. This pattern can be very effective with target audiences that oppose your position because, unlike the refutative pattern, it acknowledges that both or all alternatives have merit. You are simply illustrating why one alternative is better. Salespeople use this approach when trying to convince you that their brand is best, but they take it a step further to convince you to purchase their product. This modifies the comparative advantages pattern to include seeking action (discussed later in this chapter). It is also how tourism ads market vacation destinations. Recall these thesis statement claims mentioned earlier: Brisk walking is a better form of aerobic exercise than running, and a low-fat diet is healthier than a fat-free diet. Each of these claims seeks agreement about one alternative over another and could be argued using the comparative advantages pattern. You could also use this pattern effectively to support no-alternative claims such as "Brisk walking is the best form of aerobic exercise."

John used this pattern to develop his speech that Chevrolet trucks are better than Ford trucks. He focused on comparative advantages and disadvantages regarding cost, dependability, and special features. He found supporting material in publications such as *Consumer Reports*, from interviews with local automobile mechanics and used-car dealers, by surveying a representative sample of the general population, and from personal experience. Dan also used the comparative advantages pattern to develop his speech about satellite television:

Thesis statement: *A satellite system is better than a cable subscription for getting television programming.*

I. **First main point:** Many people have cable television subscriptions because cable offers several advantages over rooftop antenna reception.

   A. **Subpoint:** One advantage is its consistently clearer reception than with a rooftop antenna.

   B. **Subpoint:** Another advantage is the ability to access a variety of programming, as opposed to merely two, three, or four local stations.

   C. **Subpoint:** Finally, it is possible to select from a variety of cable subscription packages, allowing one to access specialty programming like movies and sports.

II. **Second main point:** Satellite television is now another option from which to choose.

   A. **Subpoint:** Advantages include its excellent picture and sound quality, access to a plethora of movie and sports programming, customer service satisfaction, and value for the money.

   B. **Subpoint:** Some potential disadvantages include initial costs for the dish and installation, need for a clear southern exposure for your dish, limited access to local television stations, and the inability to watch two different satellite programs at the same time in your home.

III. **Third main point:** Comparative advantages and disadvantages illustrate that, unless your property does not have a clear view to the south, satellite is the better alternative.

   A. **Subpoint:** Cost issues ultimately weigh in favor of satellite television, particularly for sports and movie enthusiasts (cite ratings from *Consumer Reports*, December 1999).

   B. **Subpoint:** Picture and sound quality are better with satellite television.

   C. **Subpoint:** Customer service satisfaction is better with satellite television.

   D. **Subpoint:** Access to local programs can be easily obtained with a rooftop antenna, which is free to use.

   E. **Subpoint:** Ability to watch different programs on different television sets at the same time can be achieved with a rooftop antenna or by purchasing an add-on receiver (about $100) and paying an additional $5 per month.

   F. **Subpoint:** When all the inherent advantages and disadvantages of cable and satellite television options are compared, satellite television clearly provides the best value for your money.

WHAT DO YOU THINK?
Do you think butter or margarine is healthier? Why? What are the comparative advantages of the product you chose?

Dan concluded by restating his thesis statement claim that satellite is a better alternative than cable for receiving television programming. He summarized his main points and then clinched by reminding his listeners, "I'm not here to tell you what to do. I am here, however, to help you see why the advantages of a satellite system outweigh its disadvantages, as well as any potential advantages of cable television. My only hope is that I've made that point 'perfectly clear.' "

Invitational Pattern

The **invitational pattern** is a main point arrangement designed to invite rather than convince listeners to agree with a position. Although it can also be effective for organizing informative speeches, it is particularly useful for persuasive speeches where the target audience is opposed or even hostile to your position. The topic is first approached by recognizing other positions and their validity. Then you search for common ground and communicate on that basis. You focus on positive rather than negative aspects of a person or situation and encourage persistence of those positive behaviors rather than resisting or battling negative behaviors (Foss & Foss, 1994; Foss, Foss, & Griffin, 1999). The invitational pattern uses a three-step strategy for arranging main points: (1) offer your perspective and describe how it works for you; (2) create an atmosphere that encourages mutual understanding; and (3) focus on positive aspects of a situation and their persistence.

In a speech about wearing motorcycle helmets, for example, you might discuss the main points this way:

1. Your perspective and how it works for you: Wearing a helmet is safe. Talk about when, where, and why you wear a helmet. Perhaps explain why you decided to wear a helmet.
2. Create an atmosphere that encourages mutual understanding: People have many justifiable reasons for not wearing helmets. Acknowledge a variety of reasons.
3. Focus on positive aspects of a situation and persistence of them: Wearing a helmet promotes safety for ourselves and for others. Talk about the positive

aspects of wearing helmets for immediate safety, long-range enjoyment of riding, and to set a safety example for others.

4. End by inviting listeners to agree that wearing a helmet is, in fact, a good thing.

Recall that Tiffany did this to a certain extent in her personal significance speech, "Meat-Free and Me." She did not focus on the negative consequences of eating meat. Instead she created common ground by talking about her belief in a meat-free diet and why it works for her, telling her story about becoming a vegetarian, and focusing on positive aspects of her current situation and how she manages to continue the behavior. Ultimately, she invited listeners to agree that a vegetarian lifestyle can be both healthy and satisfying. She did not urge them to become vegetarians, but leaves the choice to them.

Thesis statement: *Living a vegetarian lifestyle is an important aspect of who I am today.*

I. ***First main point:*** I made this choice for several reasons.

II. ***Second main point:*** I decided to become a vegetarian about the same time I moved away from home to attend college. Perhaps you can relate.

III. ***Third main point:*** I deal daily with advantages and disadvantages of this choice, but the advantages outweigh the disadvantages.

Tiffany concluded by restating her belief in being a vegetarian and clinched with a positive visualization about her upcoming Thanksgiving dinner, inviting listeners to agree her meal will be both healthy and tasty without expecting them to become vegetarians.

TURNING TO TECHNOLOGY

Controversial Speech Topics

http://library.sau.edu/bestinfo/Hot/hotindex.htm

This site is a great place to brainstorm for controversial topics. Browse through the list and identify one or two topics you might use for a persuasive speech.

PRACTICING THE PROCESS

Guidelines for Using the Invitational Pattern

1. Offer your perspective and describe how it works for you.
2. Create an atmosphere that encourages mutual understanding.
3. Focus on positive aspects of a situation and persistence of them.

Problem (No Solution) Pattern

The **problem (no solution) pattern** is a main point arrangement that focuses on the depth and breadth of a problem to convince listeners that it is, in fact, a significant problem. This pattern is particularly useful for developing claim-of-fact speeches focused in the present or future, since the goal with them is to attain agreement about whether something exists or is likely to occur. It is also a good choice when the target audience is uncertain about or opposed to your position. Luke used this pattern in his speech about binge drinking on college campuses.

> Thesis statement: *Binge drinking is becoming a serious problem on college campuses across the United States.*
>
>   I. *First main point:* Binge drinking is common among college students.
>
> II. *Second main point:* Binge drinking causes serious problems for these students.
>
> III. *Third main point:* Binge drinking causes serious problems for society as well.

Each of these main point patterns can help you develop a convincing argument for a dispositional speech. Which one to choose depends on your topic, claim, and target audience.

Organizing Main Points in Actuation Persuasive Speeches

Because the goal in an actuation persuasive speech is to provoke action, you must offer a solution and a call to action. A **solution** is a way to solve the problem identified. It usually addresses multiple levels such as what ought to be done on a large scale and on a personal level. As mentioned, a call to action is a plea to take specific steps to solve the problem or satisfy the need. An effective call to action is immediate—something that listeners must do right now. It is specific in describing exactly what to do, meaningful in terms of helping to solve the problem or meet the need, and doable with relative ease. For example, listeners might be asked to write to their senators or representatives (immediate) and tell them to support a certain congressional bill (specific) that solves the problem at hand (meaningful), and to address the letter to a particular postal or e-mail address (ease). The actuation persuasive speech likely will be arranged according to one of four patterns—problem/solution, problem/cause/solution, modified comparative advantages, or Monroe's motivated sequence.

Student Workbook

Read through the "Problem-Cause-Solution Generic Outline" and Amanda's "Domestic Violence" outline in Chapter 4 of your student workbook. What does Amanda identify as the problem, the cause, and the solution for her speech?

TURNING TO TECHNOLOGY

Peace and Nuclear Disarmament

http://www.wagingpeace.org/articles/02.03/0325kucinichspeech.htm

At this site, read Ohio Representative Dennis Kucinich's call to action for nuclear disarmament. Does his call to action meet the criteria listed above? Is his call to action convincing? Why or why not?

Problem/Solution Pattern

A **problem/solution pattern** has two main points. The first examines the problem, the second presents a solution. This pattern is particularly useful for speeches where listeners are unaware or unconvinced that a problem exists. The problem is what you believe is wrong with present conditions and why. It should be examined in sufficient breadth and depth, as well as offer listener relevance. You might provide breadth, for example, by talking about the scope of the problem and the number of people it affects and by talking about trends over time, including trends likely for the future if the problem isn't addressed. You might provide depth by talking about harms—that is, people directly affected by the problem and how their lives are affected. In her speech about gang violence, for example, Karlie gave the problem breadth by talking about the wide range of people who join gangs and about the presence of gangs in communities across the country. She gave it depth by looking closely at the harmful effects of gangs on a particular community. She incorporated listener relevance by offering examples from her listeners' own community.

Thesis statement: *We must do something to squelch the alarming problem of gang violence in our country.*

I. **First main point:** We cannot deny the fact that gang violence is a serious problem.
   A. **Subpoint:** Gang violence occurs in urban, suburban, and rural communities and areas across the country. (Cite examples and statistics about growing numbers.)
   B. **Subpoint:** Gang violence occurs in our fine community as well. (Cite examples and statistics.)
   C. **Subpoint:** Contrary to what you might believe, gang members are not isolated to one ethnic or racial group, or from a particular social class. (Cite examples and statistics.)
   D. **Subpoint:** The consequences of gang violence include harassment, vandalism, dismemberment, and death. (Cite examples and statistics.)

The solution is typically multifaceted, indicating what listeners should do personally in a call to action, as well as what should be done on a larger scale. The latter might take the form of policies or regulations that different levels of government should enact, or strategies that businesses or local organizations could

II. **Second main point:** Although gang violence is too large a problem to eradicate with one simple solution, there are some issues that ought to be addressed to begin to deal effectively with it.
   A. **Subpoint:** Congress should pass gun control laws to limit gang member access to guns. (Explain the plan.)
   B. **Subpoint:** Schools and communities must implement programs that give kids positive alternatives to joining gangs and participating in gang activity. (Offer examples.)
   C. **Subpoint:** As parents and guardians, we must be accountable for the actions of our children.
      1. **Sub-subpoint:** This includes encouraging them to participate in healthy activities and taking an interest in them when they do.
      2. **Sub-subpoint:** This also means knowing where our children are and what they're doing during their free time.
      3. **Sub-subpoint:** And this means being responsible for and accepting certain consequences when they do engage in inappropriate, and perhaps harmful, activities.

A speech that identifies and then presents steps to improve a bad situation, such as Karlie's about gang violence in the U.S., employs the problem/solution pattern for actuation speeches.

use. In any case, leave listeners with a strategy they can implement personally to help solve the problem. Karlie posed this three-part solution:

Karlie's call to action came in her concluding remarks when she urged listeners to do the following:

> 66 Write to your representative today and urge them to pass gun control laws that will limit gang member access. You can do so by going to http://www.house.gov/ writerep/. It's simple. And it will make a difference. There's really no excuse not to do it. But that alone isn't enough. Be accountable for the actions of the children in your life. Know where they are. Ask them where they're going, what they'll be doing, who they'll be with, and when they'll be home. Ask them about their experiences when they do come home. These seemingly small actions can make a difference. I implore you. Do your part to make our world a better place.

TURNING TO TECHNOLOGY

Hot Topics in Congress

http://www.nwmissouri.edu/library/courses/english2/termindex.htm

Browse through these issues that are being debated today. Select one or two you could focus on for your actuation persuasive speech.

....

Problem/Cause/Solution Pattern

The **problem/cause/solution pattern** is a main point arrangement with the first main point articulating the problem, the second analyzing its causes, and the third presenting multifaceted solutions. This differs from the problem/solution pattern in that the addition of a main point on causes makes it possible to analyze the problem more thoroughly with regard to underlying reasons for its existence and then to tie the solutions directly to these causes. This is particularly useful for addressing problems that have been dealt with unsuccessfully in the past, usually because of lack of attention to the inherent causes of the problem.

Margaret, for example, discovered that people's failure to recycle stems mainly from their ignorance about recycling and the inconvenience of recycling. She was therefore able to present the causes of the problem and to offer solutions that directly address them. To address ignorance as a cause, she proposed community programs and promotional campaigns designed to clarify proper recycling procedures. To address inconvenience as a cause, she made two proposals: first, that public cafeterias and restaurants be required to have clearly labeled recycling bins wherever they have trash containers, and second, that city sanitation departments be expanded to provide curbside pickup of recyclable materials.

Thesis statement: *If we don't want garbage to overcome us and our world, we must make the habit of recycling the norm rather than the exception.*

I. **First main point** *(problem):* Waste disposal is a significant problem. (Here she addressed the breadth, depth, and relevance of the problem briefly but also with evidence.)

II. **Second main point** *(cause[s]):* Since most of us realize that waste disposal is a serious problem and recycling can be an effective solution, why aren't we better about doing it?

   A. **Subpoint:** One reason has to do with ignorance about recycling.

   B. **Subpoint:** Another reason has to do with inconvenience.

Transition: *I see many of you nodding your heads in agreement with me at this point— waste disposal is a serious problem that recycling could help solve if it weren't difficult or inconvenient to implement. But let's not stop there.*

III. **Third main point** *(solution):* Let me propose three solutions that will make recycling both easier and more convenient.

   A. **Subpoint:** We need to implement community programs and promotional campaigns that clarify proper recycling procedures. (Explain what these might look like and what audience members must do to make them a reality.)

   B. **Subpoint:** Public cafeterias and restaurants should be required to have clearly labeled recycling bins wherever they have trash containers. (Explain what audience members must do to make this a reality.)

   C. **Subpoint:** City sanitation departments must be expanded to provide curbside pickup of recyclable materials. (Explain what audience members must do to make this a reality.)

She then ended with a clear call to action urging her listeners to lobby state officials by e-mailing them and collecting petitions for curbside pickup of recyclables, form ad hoc committees to make recycling bins a reality in their workplace, and raise the issue for community programs at the upcoming city planning meeting (including where and when).

Modified Comparative Advantages Pattern

Recall that the comparative advantages pattern as a main point arrangement leads the audience to agree with you that one of two or more alternatives is better than the others (Ziegelmueller, Kay, & Dause, 1990, p. 186). In its purest form this pattern does not advocate action, though it is often implied. Sometimes the pattern is modified to offer an explicit plan and call to action, especially when more than one plan exists. The goal is to show why your plan is best and to convince listeners to act on it. In this case, arrange your main points to identify the problem and its significance, delineate other plan(s) proposed to solve the problem, and finally explain your solution and why it's better than the others. If Dan were to modify his comparative advantages speech about satellite television, it might look like this:

Thesis statement: *If you are looking for the best value and quality television reception available today, choose a satellite television system.*

I. **First main point** *(problem)*: We need to invest in some system for television reception if we want access to the information and entertainment it provides.

II. **Second main point** *(alternatives)*: There are several options available today.
   A. **Subpoint:** Using a rooftop antenna is one option.
   B. **Subpoint:** Subscribing to cable television is another option.
   C. **Subpoint:** Installing a satellite system is another option.

III. **Third main point** *(best plan and call to action)*: Choose satellite television.
   A. **Subpoint:** Here's why the satellite television system is the best plan available.
   B. **Subpoint:** Install a satellite television system in your home quickly and easily by following these steps.

Monroe's Motivated Sequence

Monroe's motivated sequence is a five-step approach for arranging main points. It was originally developed by Alan Monroe (1935) to account for what it takes to motivate listeners to take action by demonstrating how it will satisfy human needs. This pattern allows you to develop both the problem and solution, as well as illustrate in detail the consequences of implementing your plan or failing to do so. The steps are attention, need, satisfaction, visualization, and action. This approach differs from the others in having a visualization step that allows focusing on how your solution addresses innate human needs, which can help you overcome the apathy barrier. Typically you deal with the attention step in introductory comments, the action step (call to action) in concluding remarks, and the other steps as three main points.

Step 1: Attention.   Catch the attention of listeners. Although you should do this in any speech, spend a little more time on it here because you want to start motivating listeners not only to listen but also to internalize a sense of urgency to do something about a problem. You might present and explain two or three examples or startling statistics, capturing listeners' attention with your attention catcher, listener relevance, credibility, and other introductory comments.

In her speech about sexual assault policies on college campuses, Maria Lucia R. Anton's (1994) thesis statement was "Sexual assault has become a major problem on U.S. campuses today." She got attention this way:

> **Attention catcher:** "If you want to take her blouse off, you have to ask. If you want to touch her breast, you have to ask. If you want to move your hand down to her genitals, you have to ask. If you want to put your finger inside her, you have to ask."
>
> What I've just quoted is part of the freshman orientation at Antioch College in Ohio. In the sexual offense policy of this college, emphasis is given to three major points: (1) If you have a sexually transmitted disease, you must disclose it to a potential partner; (2) to knowingly take advantage of someone who is under the influence of alcohol, drugs, and/or prescribed medication is not acceptable behavior in the Antioch community; (3) obtaining consent is an ongoing process in any sexual interaction. The request for consent must be specific to each act.
>
> The policy is designed to create a "safe" campus environment, according to Antioch President Alan Guskin. For those who engage in sex, the goal is 100 percent consensual sex. It isn't enough to ask someone if they would like to have sex; you have to get verbal consent every step of the way.
>
> This policy has been highly publicized and you may have heard it before. The policy addresses sexual offenses such as rape, which involves penetration, and sexual assault, which does not. In both instances, the respondent coerced or forced the primary witness to engage in nonconsensual sexual conduct with the respondent or another.

Step 2: Need. This step is similar to the problem portion of the problem/solution and problem/cause/solution patterns. Show listeners that there is a serious problem with the existing situation or present conditions. Of course, some needs are not problems, just desires to improve our circumstances, situations, or world. Television commercials and print advertisements, for example, offer needs that are essentially desires:

- Buy this toothpaste and you'll have whiter teeth and more success with romance.
- Choose this automobile insurance and you'll save money, which you can use to take a vacation.
- Eat at this restaurant and you'll be more satisfied.
- Shop for your clothes at this store and you'll be "cool" and have more friends.

Develop the need for change with strong supporting materials, then demonstrate the depth and breadth of it as well as the impact it has on listeners. Never assume the need is obvious; develop supporting points by illustrating the need with specific incidents. You can highlight ramifications of the problem with facts, statistics, examples, and quotations. Or you can point to the direct relevance of the problem to the people in your audience. Maria developed the need in her speech by sharing specific instances, statistics, and effects:

> **First main point—Need:** Sexual assault has become a reality in many campuses across the nation. Carleton College in Northfield, Minnesota, was sued for $800,000 in damages by four university women. The women charged that Carleton was negligent in protecting them against a known rapist. From the June 1991 issue of *Time* magazine.

Amy had been on campus for just five weeks when she joined some friends to watch a video in the room of a senior. One by one the other students went away, leaving her alone with a student whose name she didn't even know. "It ended up with his hands around my throat," she recalls. In a lawsuit she has filed against the college, she charges that he locked the door and raped her again and again for the next four hours. "I didn't want him to kill me, I just kept trying not to cry." Only afterwards did he tell her, almost defiantly, his name. It was on top of the "castration list" posted on women's bathroom walls around campus to warn other students about college rapists. Amy's attacker was found guilty of sexual assault but was only suspended.

Julie started dating a fellow cast member in a Carleton play. They had never slept together, she charges in a civil suit, until he came to her dorm room one night, uninvited, and raped her. She struggled to hold her life and education together, but finally could manage no longer and left school. Only later did Julie learn that her assailant was the same man who had attacked Amy.

Ladies and gentlemen, the court held that the college knew this man was a rapist. The administration may have been able to prevent this from happening if they had expelled the attacker, but they didn't. My campus has no reports of sexual assault. Is the administration waiting for someone to be assaulted before it formulates a sexual assault policy? This mistake has been made elsewhere; we don't have to prove it again.

Perhaps some statistics will help you understand the magnitude of the problem. According to *New Statesman and Society,* June 21, 1991, issue:

> A 1985 survey of sampled campuses by *Ms.* magazine and the National Institute of Mental Health found that one in every four college women were victims of sexual assault, 74 percent knew their attackers. Even worse, between 30 and 40 percent of male students indicated they might force a woman to have sex if they knew they would escape punishment.
>
> In just one year from 1988 to 1989, reports of student rape at the University of California increased from two to eighty.
>
> These numbers are indeed disturbing. But more disturbing are the effects of sexual assault: a victim feeling the shock of why something this terrible was allowed to happen; having intense fears that behind every dark corner could be an attacker ready to grab her, push her to the ground, and sexually assault her; many waking moments of anxiety and impaired concentration as she remembers the attack; countless nights of reliving the traumatic incident in her sleep; mood swings and depression as she tries to deal internally with the physical hurt and the emotional turmoil that this attack has caused.

Step 3: Satisfaction. This step is similar to the solution portion of the problem/solution and problem/cause/solution patterns. Present your plan for solving the problem, providing enough detail so listeners have a clear understanding of how it will actually solve the problem. You might develop supporting points by explaining the proposal in an easily understood way, demonstrating precisely how the solution meets the need that was pointed out, citing examples of where this proposal has worked, and showing how your proposal overcomes potential objections. Maria offered her plan by indicating that it is only a first step, but a necessary one, and laying it out clearly:

> **Second main point—Satisfaction:** Many campuses are open invitations for sexual assault. The absence of a policy is a grand invitation. I have never been sexually assaulted so why do I care so much about a policy? You know why—because I could be assaulted. I won't sit and wait to be among one out of every four women on my campus to be assaulted. The first step to keep myself out of the statistics is to push for a sexual assault policy on my campus. One way to do this is through a petition to the university.
>
> Although the Antioch policy sounds a little far-fetched and has been the target of criticism in comedy routines such as those on *Saturday Night Live,* and although students feel that formalizing such a policy is unnatural, many campuses are taking heed and revisiting their own policies. Campuses like mine don't have a sexual assault policy to revisit. Does yours?
>
> By far the most controversial policy today is the one established at Antioch College. I'm not saying that we need one as specific as theirs, but every university has a responsibility to provide a safe environment for its students. Universities have an obligation to provide a sexual assault policy.
>
> The following points are fundamental to the safety of the students and need to be addressed by universities:
>
> 1. Every campus should have a sexual assault policy that is developed with input from the students, faculty, staff, and administration. The policy then needs to be publicized in the student handbook. The school newspaper should print and the campus radio broadcast the policy periodically to heighten awareness.
> 2. Campuses must institute programs to educate students and other campus personnel. Examples of these policies can include discussing the sexual assault policy during mandatory student orientation and conducting special workshops for faculty and other staff.
> 3. Campuses should outline a step-by-step written procedure to guarantee that sexual assault victims are assisted by the university. It is pertinent that they are not without support at this very critical time.

Step 4: Visualization.   Visualize the future in order to intensify listeners' desire to solve the problem, perhaps by describing what will happen if your plan is implemented. Picture listeners enjoying the benefits that acceptance of your proposal will produce. You might visualize a negative future by describing what will happen if today's situation continues, and picture listeners enduring the unpleasant effects resulting from failure to implement your proposal. You might provide both positive and negative visualization. This step is really the crux of the pattern. The goal is to develop within your audience an image of the consequences of their choices. Whereas you strive to get them to agree that the plan will work in the satisfaction step, you strive to get them to see it working for them in the visualization step. Advertisements do this very well when, for example, they get consumers to visualize themselves using the product and experiencing the positive outcomes.

The visualization step should be able to stand the test of reality—that is, the conditions you describe must seem realistic. The more vivid your visualization, the stronger the reaction it will evoke. Maria developed her visualization step first with positive and then with negative visualization:

> **Third main point—Visualization:** My vision is a campus where there is no place for any sexual assault. I want to leave the classroom at night knowing that my trip from the building to the car will not be one of fear for my personal safety.
>
> You may be saying to yourself that there are laws to handle crimes like these. In the *Chronicle of Higher Education,* May 15, 1991, issue, Jane McDonnell, a senior lecturer in women's studies at Carleton, says colleges cannot turn their back on women. "We'd be abandoning victims if we merely sent them to the police," she says. "The wheels of justice tend to grind slowly and rape has one of the lowest conviction rates of any crime."
>
> Without a policy, most institutions lack specific penalties for sexual assault and choose to prosecute offenders under the general student-conduct code. At Carleton College, for example, Amy's attacker was allowed back on campus after his suspension, and consequently he raped again.
>
> Although the policy may not stop the actual assault, would-be offenders will think twice before committing sexual assault if they know they will be punished. In addition, it guarantees justice for victims of sexual assault. We need to make it loud and clear that sexual assault will not be tolerated.

Student Workbook

Read through the "Monroe's Motivated Sequence" generic outline and the "Dirty Truth about Antibacterial Products" formal outline in Chapter 4 of your workbook. What do you identify as the attention catcher? The need? The satisfaction? The visualization? The Call to Action?

Step 5: Action. This step provides the basis for your conclusion. By now you have convinced the audience that the problem and its consequences warrant implementing your solution. Here you tell listeners what they should do and how to do it. Perhaps you provide them with addresses to write to or telephone numbers to call. Perhaps you give them names of organizations to join. Perhaps you hand them a petition to sign. Once you provide them with a specific call to action, conclude with a final appeal to reinforce their commitment to act. This is part of your clincher as you tie back to your attention catcher. Here are Maria's concluding remarks, including her call to action:

WHAT DO YOU THINK?

Consider an advertisement you saw where you could see yourself using the product. What made the visualization realistic for you?

> **Conclusion—Action:** Yes, universities have a big task in the struggle to prevent sexual assault.
>
> You and I can actively assist in this task and can make a giant contribution to move it forward. On my campus, students have not only voiced their concerns, but we have also started a petition demanding that the university formulate a sexual assault policy.
>
> The bottom line is that we need to prevent sexual assault on campus. The key to prevention is a sexual assault policy. If your university does not have a policy, then you need to petition your administration to have one. I know I won't stop my advocacy until I see a policy on my campus.

Actuation persuasive speeches are unique in that they seek action. Because they advocate a plan and make a call to action, they are arranged according to the problem/solution, problem/cause/solution, modified comparative advantages, or Monroe's motivated sequence pattern.

Guidelines for Using Monroe's Motivated Sequence

Step 1: Attention: Catch the attention of your listeners so that they not only listen to you but also internalize a sense of urgency.

Step 2: Need: Show listeners that there is a serious problem or inadequacy with the existing situation or the present conditions.

Step 3: Satisfaction: Present your plan for solving the problem, providing enough detail so listeners have a clear understanding of how your plan will solve the problem.

Step 4: Visualization: Visualize the future in order to intensify listeners' desire to solve the problem.

Step 5: Action: Tell your listeners what they should do and how they can do it.

A Motivational Persuasive Speech

http://www.speakerstevesiebold.com/video.htm

Listen to former professional tennis player and entrepreneur Dennis Siebold, now a million-dollar motivational speaker, talk about mental toughness. How does he get the attention of his audience? Establish listener relevance and need? What is his plan? What is his call to action? Is he convincing? Why or why not?

SUMMARY

Persuasion is the process of influencing the beliefs, attitudes, values, or behaviors of others. Persuasive speaking is engaging in persuasion within a public speaking context.

Persuasive speaking differs from informative speaking in that persuasive speakers are leaders rather than teachers. Hence they build arguments in support of a position. Because persuasive speeches attempt to influence listeners, they can be more difficult to prepare than informative speeches. Public speaking anxiety might increase as a result of not knowing where listeners stand on the issue. By analyzing the audience, you can discover a target audience, adapt your speech to it, and reduce anxiety while increasing effectiveness.

Dispositional persuasive speeches seek agreement about a position by focusing on a belief, an attitude, or a value. Actuation persuasive speeches seek action regarding a policy or behavior.

In a persuasive speech, the thesis statement makes one of three kinds of claims: a claim of fact for a dispositional speech focused on a belief, a claim of value for a dispositional speech focused on an attitude or value, or a claim of policy for actuation persuasive speeches.

The most common main point arrangements for dispositional persuasive speeches are the topical, causal, narrative, refutative, comparative advantages, invitational, and problem (no solution) main point patterns. The most common main point arrangements used in actuation persuasive speeches are the problem/solution, problem/cause/solution, modified comparative advantages, and Monroe's motivated sequence patterns.

RETURNING TO TECHNOLOGY

The *Confident Public Speaking* CD-ROM is your one-stop point of access for not just the content on the CD itself, such as Speech Interactive, but also the many other resources on the *Confident Public Speaking* Web site, Speech Builder Express, and InfoTrac College Edition. Note that this chapter's key terms and activities are among the resources available in electronic format online. Additional information is included below.

SPEECH INTERACTIVE
ON THE *CONFIDENT PUBLIC SPEAKING* CD-ROM

Speech Interactive is your link to this text's speech videos. Offering opportunities to practice critiquing speeches by both other students and public speakers who are not students, these videos will help you prepare for providing effective feedback to your peers and your own speech performances.

SPEECH BUILDER EXPRESS

At the Create a New Speech screen of Speech Builder Express, you are given the option of specifying the type of speech you are going to work on. From the drop-down menu, select Persuasive. Then, on a subsequent Setup screen, select the kind of persuasive pattern you want to use. The program will provide prompts sequenced specifically for the kind of persuasive speech you indicated.

KEY TERMS

Interactive flashcards for these key terms are available on the *Confident Public Speaking* Web site. You'll find the "Flashcards" link under the resources for Chapter 15.

ACTIVITIES

The activities below, as well as additional activities and sample persuasive speech outlines, are available in electronic format on the *Confident Public Speaking* Web site. You'll find the "Activities" link under the resources for Chapter 15.

1. **Identifying Your Target Audience.** Form small groups of four or five members each. As a group, come up with three different social issues that could be developed into a persuasive speech. Create a claim of fact or a claim of value for each issue. Speculate as a group about where the target audience in the class probably stands on the issue. Next, poll the audience by anonymous ballot to discover whether you were right or wrong. Finally, decide how you might approach the speech based on what you learn about your audience.

2. **Problems and Causes.** Form small groups of four or five members each. Brainstorm several problems on your campus, in your community, or in the country. Select one that continues to be a problem despite attempts to solve it. As a group, try to identify possible causes of the problem (reasons for its existence) that may, in fact, need to be dealt with in order to solve it.

3. **Group Commercial.** Form groups of five people. One person from each group selects an object from a bag of items the instructor brings to class. These items can be anything from the home or office. Each group develops a one- to two-minute "commercial" designed to sell the object to the class using Monroe's motivated sequence (attention, need, satisfaction, visualization, action). The object cannot be sold as what it actually is, but rather as fulfilling some need unique to college students. All students in the group must participate in the commercial, and all steps of Monroe's motivated sequence must be evident.

Locate and make a copy of the speech "The Dark Side of Technology" by William N. Joy. Use the speaker's full name as your search term. Read the article and answer the following questions: (1) What is the basic problem? (2) What is the nature of the problem (breadth and depth)? (3) What are the causes of the problem? (4) What solutions are recommended? (5) Were you convinced that these solutions will work? Why or why not?

Visit of Christopher Reeve to the Weizmann Institute of Science
July 29, 2003

PERSUASIVE STRATEGIES

REFLECTIVE QUESTIONS

1. Why do you think a speaker's credibility is so important in persuasive speeches?

2. How might you enhance credibility in the content, delivery, and structure of your persuasive speech?

3. What do you think the differences are among inductive, deductive, and analogical reasoning? How might you use each kind of reasoning in your persuasive speech?

4. What do you think reasoning (logical) fallacies are, and what might you look for to determine whether speakers are using them in their speeches?

5. Why might a speaker use emotion in a speech, and how might it best be used ethically?

WHAT'S AHEAD: FOCUSING YOUR READING

Strategies for Conveying Ethos

Strategies for Conveying Logos

Strategies for Conveying Pathos

A COUPLE OF YEARS AGO, MY HUSBAND and I bought a pickup truck. That's interesting because I really didn't want one—it just didn't make sense to me. Both Tim and I work full-time outside the home. We are also the parents of two wonderful children, each attending a different school and active in a number of extracurricular activities. We need two vehicles to juggle their transportation needs with our own. Because we try to carpool with other parents, it's also important to drive vehicles that can accommodate more than one or two children at a time. And we try to visit our extended families in different states several times each year. So it just makes sense to own vehicles that are comfortable, economical, and have room for several people. But we did buy a pickup eventually, and I supported the decision.

Why did I change my mind? Quite honestly, because Tim used several persuasive strategies during our discussions. He used effective reasoning. With regard to carpooling, he demonstrated how a cab-and-a-half pickup can safely transport up to four children (with seat belts). He reasoned further that we ought to drive a four-wheel drive vehicle during the winter months, as well as when driving in the Montana and Wyoming mountains. Then he talked about the times we had to borrow a pickup truck to haul various things. If we owned a pickup, he reasoned, we would reduce some of our emotional stress in these situations.

He also bolstered his credibility by citing numerous sources that depicted cost comparisons between pickups and cars over the life of the vehicle. He offered facts and statistics regarding purchase price, mileage figures, repair estimates, and durability. He then took me to several dealerships to show where the best deals were and why. He demonstrated that he'd really done his homework.

WHAT DO YOU THINK?
Consider a time when you were convinced to purchase a product that you didn't necessarily want or need. What persuaded you to buy it anyway?

Finally, he appealed to my emotions in a number of ways. He had me test drive several of his favorite choices. He talked about how he was reaching an age when some men wanted to get a motorcycle or a convertible, but all he really wanted was a pickup. He talked about how his desire for a truck was much more practical. He asked which one I liked the best and why. This made me feel included. Finally, he brought the children along to look at and ride in these trucks. Afterward he asked them whether they would like to own a truck. Of course they did! You bet! Because Tim effectively employed a number of persuasive strategies, I agreed that we ought to buy a pickup truck. And we did.

The strategies of persuasion include three types of appeals: to ethos (speaker credibility), logos (logic and reasoning), and pathos (emotions). First articulated by the Greek philosopher Aristotle in his book *The Rhetoric*, these appeals continue to guide communicators today. Although they can be useful in any public speech, they are particularly important to persuasive speeches. By shaping the content, language, and delivery of a speech this way, you greatly increase the chance of persuading listeners.

Ethos, logos, and pathos are motivational appeals (Chapter 6)—they compel listeners to believe and agree with you and to be impassioned about your topic. **Ethos,** or speaker credibility, is the sense of competence and character you convey. **Logos,** or logical appeals, is the systematic way you structure the argument and the way you use reasoning to build it and support your claims with evidence. Chapter 15 dealt with logos as ways to systematically structure arguments. This chapter looks at logos in terms of reasoning and evidence. **Pathos,** or emotional appeals, refers to attempts to evoke certain feelings in listeners.

Why are these motivational appeals crucial to the persuasive speech? Listeners must be motivated not only to listen and understand, but also to consider—and often reconsider—their attitudes, beliefs, values, and behaviors. Since they have

We and the people in our lives are frequently trying to convince each other to think or do certain things.

spent their life so far developing and solidifying their attitudes, beliefs, values, and behaviors, how can you influence them in a single speech? By integrating motivational appeals throughout your speech, which encourages listeners to believe in you, agree with you, and care about your topic. Influencing them requires appealing to their minds and hearts.

These appeals also allow you to round the cycle of learning by addressing all preferred learning styles. Incorporating all three kinds of appeals makes the speech more persuasive, for example, to learners who prefer logical explanations and to those who prefer stories with emotional import. Most important, all listeners will be more likely to internalize your message when you round the entire learning cycle (Figure 16.1).

WHAT DO YOU THINK?

Consider a television commercial you've seen recently that compelled you in some way. What elements of the commercial worked for you? Which were ethos strategies? Pathos? Logos?

TURNING TO TECHNOLOGY

Crimes of Persuasion

http://www.crimes-of-persuasion.com/

ETHICS Being aware of the principles of persuasion is important for public speakers and also in daily life. This site explains how unethical individuals use persuasion techniques to con unsuspecting consumers every day. Which of the crimes on this site disturbs you most? Why?

STRATEGIES FOR CONVEYING ETHOS

Not surprisingly, public speakers are more compelling when they seem credible (Benjamin, 1997). What can you do to convey credibility (or ethos) in a speech? There are two aspects of ethos, competence and character. **Competence** means being perceived as well informed, skilled, or knowledgeable about your subject—

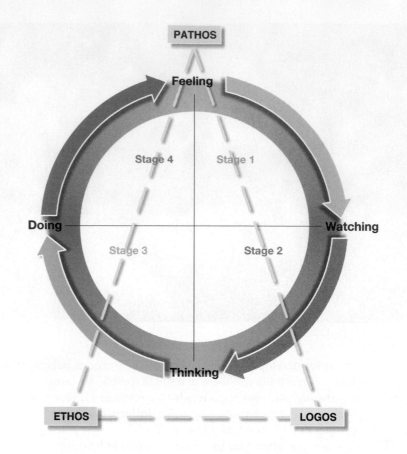

Figure 16.1 Rhetorical appeals and the learning cycle

in other words, as an expert of sorts. What academic credentials, personal or professional experience, or research makes you knowledgeable about the topic? **Character** means being perceived as trustworthy, honest, and sincere, as well as engaging, likable, and attractive (e.g., Booth-Butterfield & Gutowski, 1993; O'Keefe, 1990; Reardon, 1991). Notice that these definitions are in terms of listener perceptions. Credibility depends not on your actual knowledge and sincerity but on whether listeners perceive those qualities in you.

Credibility varies greatly. For instance, a speaker could be perceived as credible about one topic and not another. If Madonna came to your campus to talk about popular music, you'd probably perceive her as credible. If, for some unknown reason, she were to talk about pesticides, however, you'd probably question her credibility.

Credibility can also vary by audience. For example, some people said they voted for Jesse Ventura, former governor of Minnesota, in part because he did not have a college degree. For them, he seemed credible because he represents common folk rather than aristocracy. Other people were appalled when he was elected, in part because he did not have a college degree. For them, he lacks credibility because he hasn't earned what they perceive to be a necessary fundamental education.

Finally, credibility can vary over the course of a speech; this is what enables us to build ethos. Messages about credibility are sent before you even begin to speak. These give rise to **initial credibility**. Messages sent by the things you say and do during the speech result in **derived credibility**, which may be stronger or weaker than initial credibility. The sense of your competence and

WHAT DO YOU THINK?

Consider the election of Arnold Schwarzenegger for governor of California. Do you think his ethos helped win the election? Why or why not?

Arnold Schwarzenegger, shown here in his *Terminator* movie role, became the 38th governor of California in the fall of 2003. Some might question his ethos as an actor turned governor.

character that listeners have at the end of your speech is **terminal credibility.** How can you increase credibility throughout your speech? In a sense, everything you do well increases credibility, so the more effort devoted to preparing and delivering your speech, the more likely the audience is to perceive you as credible. However, several strategies can help; these involve content, language, and delivery.

TURNING TO TECHNOLOGY

Perspectives on Ethos and Persuasion

http://www.lcc.gatech.edu/gallery/rhetoric/terms/ethos.html

Read through this history of ethos as a tool to persuade listeners posted by Yasmin Hussain at the Georgia Institute of Technology. What is unique about ethos today compared to ethos in the days of Aristotle? Cicero? Quintilian? Martin Luther?

Strategies Involving Content

When developing content, keep in mind three strategies you can use to enhance credibility: explaining your competence, establishing common ground, and using strong evidence.

Explain Your Competence

As competence is a crucial part of credibility, tell listeners about your expertise. Do this during introductory comments and at appropriate places within the body of the speech (Stewart, 1994). If you've done a good deal of research on the topic, say so. Don't assume listeners know. If you have personal experience, say so; don't worry about sounding arrogant or conceited. This is especially important for student speakers, who probably haven't yet established a reputation that confers high initial credibility. It may also be especially important for women, because some research suggests that many women have been trained not to talk about their expertise and achievements (e.g., Murphy & Zorn, 1996). For example, Madonna seems credible about the music industry, not about pesticides. But what if at some point she had earned a degree in pest management? This would boost her credibility as a speaker about pesticides—but only if she tells listeners. Tell listeners about your expertise: It can't hurt, and it might boost your credibility (Miller et al., 1992).

Establish Common Ground

The **common ground** strategy works by enhancing character. Identify yourself with the audience by talking about shared beliefs and values related to the argument addressed in your speech (Perloff, 1993). By talking about these you demonstrate respect for your listeners and seem more likable to them. As with explaining competence, it's especially important to create common ground at the beginning of your speech, partly to overcome any biases listeners may have based on sex, race, ethnicity, and so on. If the topic is controversial or the target audience is opposed to your position, common ground is vital. In his speech arguing against the death penalty, for example, Lester used the common-ground technique in his introduction: "I'm sure that you, like me, value human life." If you can get listeners to nod in agreement at the beginning, they are more likely to be receptive to the rest of the speech as well (McCroskey & Teven, 1999).

Use Strong Evidence

Strong evidence is important in any speech, but particularly persuasive speeches. It's a crucial aspect of logos and also enhances credibility: The stronger the evidence, the stronger your credibility. It demonstrates that you've researched well and, in a sense, you're borrowing the credibility of your sources. Here are three ways of using evidence to enhance credibility:

1. *Use varied supporting material.* This addresses different learning styles and thus enhances your credibility and effectiveness with a range of listeners, as well as rounds the entire cycle of learning.
2. *Use qualified impartial sources.* Listeners are best persuaded by evidence from such sources (Perloff, 1993; Reinard, 1988). It demonstrates your competence, and listeners are better persuaded by sources that seem impartial. For example, in a persuasive speech on infant and toddler automobile safety standards, citing experts from the National Highway Traffic Safety Administration might be more persuasive than citing experts from the Ford Motor Company, whose remarks could be perceived as biased. Drawing on impartial sources and avoiding sources that could be perceived as biased demonstrates your character, particularly fairness.
3. *Use new evidence.* Supporting material that listeners don't already know is more persuasive (Morley & Walker, 1987). Commonly known facts and statistics won't persuade today if they didn't yesterday. But new evidence may get listeners to rethink the issue, and it shows you've done thorough research.

PRACTICING THE PROCESS

Guidelines for Using Evidence to Enhance Credibility

- Use varied supporting material.
- Use qualified, impartial sources.
- Use new evidence.

Strategies Involving Language

Use of language can enhance your character. Always use language that is respectful to listeners. In your introduction you might even express gratitude about the opportunity to speak. This fosters a sense of goodwill that not only enhances your character but reduces potential barriers. Humor can make you seem likable and increase receptivity to your message (Slan, 1998). (But avoid offensive humor, which detracts from your character.)

Strategies Involving Delivery

Attire, body language, and use of voice (see Chapter 12) can strengthen or weaken your credibility. Thus delivery is especially important to persuasive speaking. Conveying ethos through delivery is particularly complex due to cultural differences. For example, in the United States eye contact is about as basic as the firm handshake. I remember a song my children listened to when they were young: "You gotta stand up tall. Conjure up a smile. Take a big breath. Look 'em in the eye and say Hi!" (Grammer, 1986). But in Asia, Africa, and Latin America, direct eye contact is a sign of disrespect. Even within a country, people of different cultures use eye contact differently. African Americans tend to use more eye contact when talking and less when listening. People from Arab countries often use prolonged eye contact to gauge trustworthiness. Hence you must base delivery choices on the audience and the situation. What follows fits the mainstream American audience.

TURNING TO TECHNOLOGY

Cultural Differences

http://www.cnr.berkeley.edu/ucce50/ag-labor/7article/article01.htm

Read this article posted by the regents of the University of California. What are some differences the author discovered during her travels? How might you adjust your speech to convey ethos for these audiences and why?

Attractive people are generally perceived as more competent, well organized, and confident (e.g., Buck & Tiene, 1989; Cherulnik, 1989; Drogosz & Levy, 1996; Robinson et al., 1989). Attire contributes to this, and research suggests that persuasive speakers dressed formally are perceived as more credible than those dressed casually or sloppily (Morris et al., 1996; Treinen, 1998). Thus, persuasive speakers especially benefit from dressing neatly and professionally.

Body language can do a great deal to enhance credibility at all stages of your speech. Direct eye contact conveys self-confidence and an interest in others. Walk confidently to the front of the room, and pause a few moments and make direct eye contact with a couple of listeners before you begin speaking. Look listeners in the eye throughout the speech. When you finish, pause and make eye contact again. For a large audience, pause and make general audience contact before beginning and upon finishing.

Research shows that credibility is strongly influenced by use of voice. Speaking fluently, using a moderately fast rate, and expressing yourself with conviction makes you appear more intelligent and confident than losing your place, using lots of "ums" and "uhs," speaking too slowly, or sounding monotonous

AP/Wide World Photos

Being prepared for and offering a question-and-answer period at the end of your speech can bolster your credibility.

or unconvinced (e.g., O'Keefe, 1990; Perloff, 1993). Rehearse enough so that you can deliver the speech fluently and expressively. Likewise, use stresses and pauses that convey a sincere sense of urgency, and gestures and facial expressions should reinforce the conviction expressed in your voice.

Finally, consider offering a question-and-answer period at the end of your presentation. This bolsters ethos because listeners learn that you are willing to provide an opportunity to seek clarification from you and to engage in discussion about the ideas shared.

TURNING TO TECHNOLOGY

Doing Business across Cultures

http://www.media3pub.com/bizonline/articles/culture.html

Read through these delivery tips for doing business with people from different cultures. What surprises you? Why? Which of these tips might you consider for your persuasive speech? Why?

Student Workbook

Read through Amanda's "Domestic Violence" outline in Chapter 4 of your student workbook. Identify 4 or 5 strategies she uses to convey ethos.

STRATEGIES FOR CONVEYING LOGOS

Recall that logos refers to logical appeals—appeals to listeners' intellect. Thus you convey logos by building a strong argument. This means organizing your argument well, using strong evidence to support claims, and using clear and effective reasoning to tie the evidence to the claims. This makes for persuasive argument. Logos is conveyed in large part through structure (persuasive argument structure is discussed in Chapter 15) and to some extent through language and delivery. For example, you can word your argument clearly and use transition words effectively, and use gestures and movement to reinforce the structure of arguments. However, the most significant ways to convey logos lie in content—that is, in evidence and reasoning.

Boosting ethos requires credibility through strong evidence that is varied in type and comes from reliable sources. Such evidence enhances credibility partly because it conveys logos: Your evidence is sound. That means it is appropriate to the main points you're making. For each piece of evidence considered, decide whether it makes your argument more compelling. If not, don't use it. You must also decide *how* it makes your argument more compelling—how it supports your main points—and explain that link in your speech.

Reasoning is the process of supporting main points with evidence in a logical way. Rather than simply stating evidence, clarify how it supports your point. Beginning speakers sometimes assume that these connections will be obvious. Assume instead that they aren't obvious, and articulate them (O'Keefe, 1990). Connecting the main points to the evidence motivates listeners to agree with you through logos. For each piece of evidence, ask yourself these questions:

- How does this piece of evidence support my main point?
- How can I make this connection clear to my listeners?

Three types of reasoning are particularly useful: inductive, deductive, and analogical (Figure 16.2). Which type to use depends on the nature of your main point and evidence. In most persuasive speeches, using more than one type is best. But avoid *reasoning fallacies*, or flawed reasoning.

Inductive Reasoning

Inductive reasoning arrives at a general conclusion from a series of pieces of evidence. In daily life we often rely on inductive reasoning. For example, when I bought my Ford Escort, I reasoned as follows: (a) The previous two Escorts I owned were reliable. (b) *Consumer Reports* ranks Escorts consistently high across categories. (c) I see a lot of Escorts being driven around the city. Based on this, I concluded the Escort is reliable. College students often decide which classes to take (and *not* take) by applying inductive reasoning to evidence from course descriptions and other students about whether a class is fun, interesting, easy, boring, irrelevant, or difficult.

In a public speech, inductive reasoning can be effective in persuading others. You can base a conclusion on any kind of evidence—examples, statistics, testimonies, and so on. If a number of examples support a main point, you can report them and show how they support the point. For example, Julie offered several examples of people who had been healed of different physical ailments with the help of chiropractors and without medication. These came from her own experiences and those of friends, family members, and people she learned about through library research. She used these examples to support her conclusion that chiropractors can heal physical ailments effectively.

When you reason inductively, the persuasiveness of a conclusion depends on the strength of the evidence it's based on. To develop an effective inductive argument, therefore, consider three key questions:

- Do I have enough items of evidence to support my conclusion?
- Are my items typical?
- Are my items recent enough?

Let's look at each question in turn.

Generally it takes more than one or two instances to effectively support a conclusion. In her speech about chiropractors, Julie conducted library research because she realized that the few examples based on the experiences of people she knew would not be enough to persuade listeners that chiropractors are effective.

Even many examples aren't enough in themselves. You've also got to show that your evidence is typical, not isolated. One way is by backing up examples with statistical evidence. This is what Ajay Krishnan (1998) did in his speech about auto repair fraud. After sharing examples of people who had been victims of such fraud, he continued:

> The National Highway and Traffic Safety Administration reports that a whopping 40 percent of car repair costs last year were either fraudulent or unnecessary. But this 40 percent isn't just concentrated on a couple of gullible, exploitable consumers. Instead, as the *Orange County Register* of December 16, 1996, reveals, 90 percent of car owners are victims of such fraud. (p. 120)

Means of Reasoning	Starting Point	Resulting Conclusion	Source of Persuasive Power
Induction	Specific instances or facts	Formulation of a general principle	Strength and quality of evidence
Deduction	General premise	Applicability to a specific case	Supported major and minor premises
Analogy	Identifying that two things are alike in some ways	Believing the two things must be alike in other respects	Appropriate comparison

Figure 16.2 Types of reasoning.

Once he included these statistics, listeners couldn't dismiss the examples as aberrations and his conclusion was strengthened.

Depending on the topic, recency might be an issue as well. In a sense, this is related to whether the evidence is typical: if evidence is old, it may no longer be typical. It's fine to include older evidence, but supplement it with newer evidence or otherwise show that it is still valid.

PRACTICING THE PROCESS

Checklist for Using Inductive Reasoning

- ❑ Do these pieces of evidence support the main point?
- ❑ How can I make the connection clear to my listeners?
- ❑ Do I have enough items of evidence to support the point?
- ❑ Are the items typical?
- ❑ Are the items recent enough?

Deductive Reasoning

Deductive reasoning is reaching a conclusion by showing how a general premise applies to a single case. Inductive reasoning argues from specifics to a general conclusion, deductive reasoning from a general principle to a specific conclusion. Deductive reasoning starts with a **major premise,** a general principle that most people agree upon or that you provide support for. Then it moves to a **minor premise,** establishing that the specific point or example fits within that general principle. The conclusion states that the principle applies to the specific point or example. This three-part form of reasoning is called a **syllogism.** At its simplest, deductive reasoning looks like this:

Major premise: All opera singers can carry a tune.
Minor premise: John is an opera singer.
Conclusion: John can carry a tune.

Major premises often express commonly held beliefs, as in the previous example, or values, as in the following one:

Major premise: It is wrong to censor speech or other forms of expression.
Minor premise: Popular music is a form of expression.
Conclusion: It is wrong to censor popular music.

When using deductive reasoning, you'll usually need supporting material for your major or minor premises to make the argument more compelling. For example, Tammy Frisby (1998) used deductive reasoning embellished in this way in her speech about the need to floss regularly. In its most basic syllogistic form, it would look like this:

Major premise: Bacteria is generally unhealthy.
Minor premise: Our mouths are full of bacteria.
Conclusion: Bacteria in our mouths is unhealthy.

To determine whether to embellish a major premise with supporting material, consider whether the premise is something most listeners are likely to agree with. If not, provide evidence before moving on to a minor premise. In Tammy's case, there was no need for supporting material on her major premise; most listeners would agree that bacteria is generally unhealthy. If you think some might doubt your major premise, then offer supporting material. It certainly won't hurt your argument and will probably help. Even for Tammy, adding a statement about the kinds of antibacterial products on the market would have embellished her major premise. After all, if your major premise is rejected, your conclusion will be too. As with a major premise, bolstering a minor premise with supporting material cannot hurt your argument and will probably make it more compelling. Consider how much more persuasive Tammy was when she bolstered her minor premise, that a lot of bacteria grows in the mouth, with evidence about some of its harmful effects.

When you reason deductively, the persuasiveness of your conclusion also depends on the truth of your premises. If the premises are true, the conclusion should be true. To develop a strong deductive argument, consider three key questions:

- Is the major premise true?
- Is the minor premise true?
- Has anything been omitted from the premises that might affect the conclusion?

Consider this example:

Major premise: Calcium is an important part of a healthy diet.
Minor premise: Ice cream is high in calcium.
Conclusion: Ice cream is an important part of a healthy diet.

Although the major and minor premises are both true, the conclusion is not valid because important facts weren't taken into account—namely, that ice cream is high in unhealthy saturated fats and that there are many other sources of calcium.

PRACTICING THE PROCESS

Checklist for Using Deductive Reasoning

- ❏ Is the major premise true?
- ❏ Is the minor premise true?
- ❏ Has anything been omitted from the premises that might affect the conclusion?

Analogical Reasoning

Analogical reasoning, or reasoning by comparison, links two things together and claims that what is true of one is therefore true of the other. Advertisers do this to motivate consumers to purchase a product when they claim, "If you liked that other product, then you'll love this product." Movies are sometimes marketed this way as well: "If you liked *Ordinary People*, then you'll love *American Beauty*," and so on. (I often used it to get my children to try a new food by telling them, "It's good. It tastes like chicken!")

This strategy is particularly useful in persuasive speeches in which you advocate or oppose a solution that has been tried elsewhere. You can use analogical reasoning to point to the success or failure of earlier programs as a rationale to support or oppose a similar program (Ziegelmueller, Kay, & Dause, 1990). Administrators at our school, for example, are promoting the use of a computer networking system because it is working well in other state university systems. A group of students presented a speech about reversing the trend of declining population in North Dakota, focusing on (among other things) programs similar to those Michigan and South Dakota have successfully implemented to boost the economy and bring in new people. Similarly, Stephanie Hamilton (1999) discussed policies implemented by the International Council of Cruise Lines to ensure justice for passengers who become victims of violent crimes while on board their ships. She then proposed that all cruise lines adopt such policies.

To develop an effective analogical argument, consider two key questions:

- Are the similarities between the two cases relevant?
- Are any of the differences between them relevant?

First, think carefully about the similarities. Are they relevant to the argument you are making? Are they strong enough? The student speakers just mentioned talked about the need for high-paying jobs in the state. Then they illustrated how the programs in Michigan and South Dakota bolstered the economy and created higher-paying jobs. The results were similar to the goal the speakers had for North Dakota. The analogical argument becomes more compelling when more relevant and similar comparisons can be drawn.

Second, think carefully about the differences between the cases. Are they safe to ignore—that is, are they irrelevant to your argument? Or are they differences that should be taken into consideration in your speech, or that perhaps even make an analogical argument impossible? Had Stephanie tried to argue that existing victims' rights programs in the United States should also be implemented on cruise ships, she would have failed because the differences are relevant. Cruise ships often sail on international waters and many are registered in other countries, which makes U.S. laws and regulations inapplicable.

WHAT DO YOU THINK?
Consider a popular television program such as *Trading Spaces, Joe Millionaire,* or *The Simpsons.* What other shows have imitated them in hopes of attracting viewers? To what degree are these producers using analogical reasoning?

PRACTICING THE PROCESS

Checklist for Using Analogical Reasoning

- ❑ Are the similarities between the two cases relevant?
- ❑ Are any of the differences between them relevant?

Avoiding Reasoning Fallacies

Reasoning fallacies are flawed reasoning. They are sometimes used with the intent to deceive; other times they're simply the result of carelessness. Unfortunately, it is possible to persuade listeners based on flawed reasoning because fallacies often appear reasonable. Since they are not valid, however, the consequences of persuading listeners based on them can be harmful. To be ethical as well as effective, avoid flawed reasoning in your persuasive speeches. Fallacies can destroy the validity of an otherwise good argument (Ericson, Murphy, & Zeuschner, 1987). By knowing what they are and how they work, you can avoid them in your speeches and identify them in the speeches of others, improving yourself as both a persuasive speaker and a receiver of persuasive arguments. Among as many as 125 identified types of fallacies, the ten most common are hasty generalization, false cause, slippery slope, either-or, straw man, bandwagon, appeal to tradition, red herring, ad hominem, and non sequitur (*New York Public Library Desk Reference*, 1993). See Figure 16.3.

TURNING TO TECHNOLOGY

Reasoning Fallacies

`http://pertinent.com/pertinfo/business/nunleyP1.html`

This article discusses various fallacies found in everyday persuasive arguments. Which fallacy disturbs you most? Why? Which one seems to get used most often? Why and how?

Hasty Generalization

The **hasty generalization** fallacy is when a speaker draws a conclusion based on too little evidence. People who jump to conclusions are committing hasty generalizations. Robin did this when she said, "A child I know is being home schooled and can't read or write at grade level. Home schooling does not work." Robin was trying to use inductive reasoning, but did not offer enough evidence to support her conclusion. How much evidence is enough? Not every account you know of must be shared, just enough to let listeners know your examples are typical. Follow the guidelines discussed earlier regarding inductive reasoning.

False Cause

False cause is when a speaker claims that because one event follows another, the first caused the second. Another term for this fallacy is *post hoc, ergo propter hoc*, a Latin expression meaning "after this, therefore because of this." If you did well on a test you didn't study for, and claimed you did well *because* you didn't study, that's a false cause fallacy. When my mother reasoned that I'd caught a head cold because I didn't dress warmly enough when it was chilly, she engaged in this fallacy. (A virus caused the cold, not the weather.) If a speaker claims that violence among teenagers is caused only by television violence, that's also engaging in this fallacy. When one event follows another, there may be no connection at all or the first event might be just one of many causes that contribute to the second.

Slippery Slope

Like false cause, **slippery slope** is a fallacy involving cause and effect. Here it's the claim that one action will begin a chain of events inevitably leading to a certain result. For example, the claim that offering free contraceptives to teenagers will lead to more sexual activity among them, which will lead to the destruction of moral values, is a slippery slope fallacy. So is this argument by Kathy:

> If we begin to control the sale of guns by restricting the purchase of handguns, you can be certain that it won't end there. Next we'll be restricting the purchase of shotguns, and then hunting rifles. Eventually the right to bear arms will be eliminated from the Constitution altogether. Hunters—both men and women—will lose one of our basic freedoms.

There is a lot of ground between initial event and ultimate effect. Because situations are complex and involve many factors, it is unlikely that an event would lead inevitably to a certain result.

Either-Or

An **either-or** fallacy is the argument that there are only two alternatives when, in fact, others exist. Many such cases are just oversimplification of a complex issue. When Robert argued that "we'll either have to raise taxes or close the library," he committed an either-or fallacy. He reduced a complex issue to one oversimplified solution when there were many other possible solutions. Speakers who use this fallacy usually make one of the alternatives so undesirable that supporting their position seems vital. One can assume that few, if any, of Robert's listeners would want to close the library; however, raising taxes is probably not the only way to keep its doors open.

Straw Man

The **straw man** argument is when a speaker weakens the opposing position by misrepresenting it in some way and then attacks that weaker (straw man) argument. That is, a speaker distorts an opposing view in a way that makes it seem trivial or silly, then easily refutes it. For example, in her speech advocating a seven-day waiting period to purchase handguns, Colleen favored regulation, not prohibition, of gun ownership. Kathy argued against that by claiming "it is our constitutional right to bear arms." Colleen, however, did not advocate abolishing the right to bear arms. Hence, Kathy distorted Colleen's position, making it easier to refute—the straw man reasoning fallacy.

Bandwagon

The **bandwagon** fallacy is when something is presented as popular and therefore good or desirable. The speaker might say that everyone is doing something so you should too, or that everyone believes something so it must be true. He or she is trying to get you to jump on the bandwagon. Some people refer to this by its Latin name, *ad populum*. It is not necessarily wrong to talk about how many people support your position, but this support does not guarantee accuracy or worth. It is your ethical responsibility to articulate *why* so many people support it. This also supports your claim. Advertisers and salespeople often use the bandwagon fallacy to entice buyers, and politicians sometimes use polls this way. Just because 61 percent of those polled (even assuming they're representative of the population) support a candidate does not mean that he or she is the best person for the job. In her speech, Julie talked about the growing number of people using chiropractors for a variety of physical ailments. Had she stopped there, she would have been guilty of using the bandwagon fallacy. She went on, however, to discuss *why* more people are using chiropractors—citing research, for example, comparing the success rates of prescription drugs and chiropractic treatments.

ETHICS

WHAT DO YOU THINK?
Identify a television commercial that tried to convince you to purchase a product simply because it's the "cool" thing to do or because "everyone is doing it" (for example, clothes from a certain store or with a certain label, soft drink brands, and so on). Was this bandwagon appeal effective? Ethical? Why or why not?

Type of Fallacy	Description/Source of Flawed Reasoning
Hasty Generalization	A conclusion based on insufficient evidence
False Cause	Claiming that because one event follows another, the first caused the second
Slippery Slope	Claiming one action will begin a chain of events leading to a certain result
Either-Or	Arguing that there are only two alternatives when others exist
Bandwagon	Using popularity as evidence of something being good or desirable
Appeal to Traditional	Defending something based simply on the fact that it's the way things have always been
Red Herring	Using irrelevant evidence to divert attention from the real issue
Ad hominem	Attacking an opponent's character rather than dealing with the issue at hand
Non sequitur	Supporting an argument with irrelevant evidence or presenting a conclusion that does not logically follow from evidence

Figure 16.3 Reasoning fallacies

Appeal to Tradition

The **appeal to tradition** fallacy is a defense of the way things are simply because that's the way they've always been. Traditions may or may not be good, but they aren't in themselves reasons to oppose change. If the United States still followed its original practices, only white males with property would be allowed to vote. Likewise, as more people telecommute today, some employers maintain that work must occur in offices because that's how modern business has always been conducted. That's tradition but not a solid argument against change—in fact many employees are more productive working from home. The old ways are not always the best. In a speech about online courses, one student argued that taking them would not promote the best learning because students would miss out on classroom interaction with the teacher and other students. The appeal to tradition fallacy here is in assuming that "classroom interaction" can only occur as it traditionally has.

Red Herring

Also called a smoke screen, the **red herring** fallacy is use of irrelevant evidence or arguments to try to divert listeners' attention from the real issue. (The name comes from the English hunting practice of dragging a foul-smelling herring across a fox trail to divert the dogs who were sniffing out the trail.) When political candidates avoid answering questions by talking about something altogether different, they are employing a red herring fallacy—most often when questioned about highly controversial issues such as abortion, gun control, or censorship. Jeremy committed it in this case:

Many argue that marijuana must remain illegal because people die as a result of harm done to them while someone is high. Well, if that's the case, then alcohol ought to be illegal as well. Far more people are killed by drunk drivers than by drivers high on marijuana. Drunk drivers kill themselves. They kill others. It's certainly possible that by legalizing marijuana fewer people would be killed by drunk drivers.

Ad Hominem

Ad hominem is Latin for "at the person." Also known as mudslinging or name-calling, this is attacking an opponent's character rather than dealing with the issue. Senator Joseph McCarthy used name-calling to build his reputation after World War II, when many Americans feared Communism. He accused opponents of being Communists with no basis for his accusations. When Jon argued that Clara couldn't understand political issues because "she's an airhead," it was an ad hominem fallacy because he attacked her personal character rather than her stand on the issues.

Non Sequitur

ETHICS

Non sequitur is Latin for "does not follow." This fallacy is when a conclusion doesn't follow from evidence or when an argument is supported with irrelevant evidence. Advertisers do this when, for example, they show beautiful models using their products in hopes that consumers will reason that using the products will make them look like the models. If a speaker argues that public school standards must be raised, and supports that position by citing the growing number of kids joining gangs, it's a non sequitur fallacy. Although both statements might be true, the supporting material is not necessarily related to the argument.

To convey logos, organize your argument well, use strong evidence to support it, and use clear, effective, and ethical reasoning to tie evidence to claims through inductive, deductive, and analogical reasoning. Take care to avoid reasoning fallacies.

WHAT DO YOU THINK?

Consider the candidates running for the next election. Do you know where they stand on controversial issues such as abortion, gun control, and censorship? Do you know where they stand on issues important to you? If not, what can you do to find out?

TURNING TO TECHNOLOGY

Analyzing Arguments and Detecting Fallacies

http://www.drury.edu/ess/critthink.html

This Web page, developed by Charles Ess at Drury University, offers several useful suggestions for analyzing arguments. Which suggestions might you use in your daily life? Why?

Student Workbook

Read through the "Solving the Problem of Gang Violence in America" outline in Chapter 4 of your student workbook. Identify 4 or 5 strategies she uses to convey logos. Does the outline ever offer a reasoning fallacy? If so, where?

PRACTICING THE PROCESS

Checklist for Detecting Fallacies When Listening to Public Speakers

❑ Does the claim have anything to do with the main point?
❑ Is the claim relevant to the issue?
❑ Is the language clear and unequivocal?
❑ Is the speaker claiming as certain something that is only a possibility?

STRATEGIES FOR CONVEYING PATHOS

Pathos involves a wide variety of emotional appeals—to positive emotions such as love, pride, compassion, and reverence, as well as to negative emotions such as fear, anger, jealousy, shame, and guilt. For example, you might appeal to listeners' compassion to persuade them to volunteer at the local center for domestic abuse, or to their fear of contracting a sexually transmitted disease to persuade them to practice safe sex. Often positive and negative appeals are combined. For example, to convince listeners to exercise and eat right, you might appeal to both fear and pride. Emotional appeals can be highly effective tools for a persuasive speaker because they touch the hearts of listeners, making them far more likely to change their disposition or behavior (e.g., Eagly & Chaiken, 1993; Maloney, 1992). To add breadth, develop emotional appeals that address each level on Maslow's hierarchy of human needs (discussed in Chapter 6).

Many emotional appeals come when discussing positive and negative consequences related to a topic. Motivate listeners by demonstrating the desirable results of accepting your argument and the undesirable results of not accepting it. Weight loss programs, for example, often use a positive consequences motivational approach by showing before-and-after photographs of members. Environmentalists sometimes use a negative consequences motivational approach by describing what the world will be like if we continue to engage in destructive habits such as polluting the air and water and depleting natural resources.

ETHICS

Because appeals to pathos are directed at emotions and thus can be very influential, they are susceptible to abuse. All too often they have been used to promote religious intolerance, ethnic and racial hatred, and so forth. Take extra care to use emotional appeals ethically. Keep three crucial points in mind.

First, emotional appeals can be both effective and ethical when they are appropriate to your speech topic, goal, occasion, and audience. If inappropriate to any of these, don't use them. For example, don't share emotion-arousing photographs, videos, or music simply to get the attention of listeners if they are not related directly to your topic and goal. Even if they are related, don't appeal to disgust by showing vivid photographs of contaminated food products if you are speaking at a luncheon or dinner. Likewise, don't appeal to emotions by describing or showing graphic illustrations of illicit behaviors to a group of children. Consider what you're trying to accomplish, who the audience is, and where and when you'll be speaking; then integrate only those appeals to pathos appropriate to all four.

Second, emotional appeals can be both effective and ethical when they build on well-thought-out arguments. In other words, pathos can enhance an argument but should not itself make the argument (e.g., Waddell, 1990; Witte, 1992). Never substitute emotional appeals for evidence and reasoning.

Third, emotional appeals are most effective when they round the cycle of learning. To motivate listeners to internalize your message, appeal to their senses in ways that address feeling, watching, thinking, and doing. For example, in a speech about school violence you might address the feeling dimension by sharing a personal testimony from someone who lived through such an experience. You could address watching by showing photographs or a video clip of a school setting where violence has occurred or could occur. To address thinking, you could share startling statistics about the breadth and depth of school violence incidents today as compared to earlier decades. And you could address doing by describing what warning signs violators have provided prior to their acts of violence to help avoid future tragedies. To ensure that your appeals are ethical, ask three questions before integrating each emotional appeal into your speech: Is this emotional appeal appropriate to my speech topic, goal, occasion, and audience? Does my emotional appeal complement a thoroughly supported argument rather than attempt to replace it? Do my emotional appeals round the learning cycle?

Looking at the Learning Cycle

Considering Emotional Appeals

- How do you address feeling in your emotional appeals? Consider testimonials, personal stories, or vivid descriptions of actual incidents.
- How do you address watching in your emotional appeals? Consider using presentational aids.
- How do you address thinking in your emotional appeals? Consider startling statistics that address breadth and/or depth.
- How do you address doing in your emotional appeals? Consider describing processes or procedures undertaken prior to the problem.

TURNING TO TECHNOLOGY

Pathos

http://www.lcc.gatech.edu/gallery/rhetoric/terms/pathos.html

This site discusses historical and contemporary views on pathos. In what way will you incorporate pathos in your next speech? Why?

PRACTICING THE PROCESS

Checklist for Ethical Emotional Appeals

ETHICS

- ☐ Is this emotional appeal appropriate to my speech topic, goal, occasion, and audience?
- ☐ Does my emotional appeal complement a thoroughly supported argument rather than attempt to replace it?
- ☐ Do my emotional appeals round the learning cycle?

Strategies Involving Content

When developing the speech, include supporting material that will appeal to listeners' emotions. Include appeals that address a variety of human needs. Consider Maslow's hierarchy of human needs (Chapter 6) when developing content. Include stories and testimonials that personalize and dramatize the issue for listeners. You can also use startling statistics, because listeners are more affected by emotions accompanied by surprise, and listener relevance links because emotions are stronger when listeners feel personally involved. When possible, strengthen the emotional impact by reinforcing this supporting material with presentational aids. Remember that appeals can be positive or negative.

WHAT DO YOU THINK?

Consider a time when someone told a story or joke and you thought, "I can't believe she or he said that!" What made it inappropriate? Did it have to do with the topic, goal, occasion, audience, or something else?

David Slater (1998), for example, used a story to appeal to emotions in his speech about becoming a bone marrow donor. He could have conveyed the content by simply saying something like: "By donating bone marrow—a simple procedure—you can help save lives." Instead, he shared a vivid story about Tricia, Tommy, and Daniel:

> When Tricia Matthews decided to undergo a simple medical procedure, she had no idea what impact it could have on her life. But more than a year later, when she saw five-year-old Tommy and his younger brother Daniel walk across the stage of the *Oprah Winfrey Show,* she realized that the short amount of time it took her to donate her bone marrow was well worth it. Tricia is not related to the boys who suffered from a rare immune deficiency disorder treated by a transplant of her marrow. Tricia and the boys found each other through the National Marrow Donor Program, or NMDP, a national network which strives to bring willing donors and needy patients together. Though the efforts Tricia made were minimal, few Americans made the strides she did. Few of us would deny anyone the gift of life, but sadly, few know how easily we can help. (p. 63)

Notice how much more compellingly David made his point by sharing this story that appealed to listeners' emotions. In addition to being moved, listeners could readily see that the procedure was simple and its benefits dramatic. They were thus far more likely to be persuaded to become donors.

You can often strengthen emotional appeals by using different kinds of supporting material together. In his speech about shaken baby syndrome, Ryan Labor (1998) began with the following vivid story:

> Last winter, two-year-old Cody Dannar refused to eat or play. He had a headache. Doctors said he just had the flu. After a couple weeks home with this mother, Cody felt better. Days later, according to *Woman's Day* of October 7, 1997, Cody's headaches returned. Coming home from work the next afternoon, his parents found the baby-sitter frantically calling 911 and Cody lying rigid and unconscious on the floor. He didn't have the flu; in fact, he wasn't sick at all. The baby-sitter had caused his headaches. To quiet Cody down, she had shaken him, damaging the base of Cody's brain that now risked his life as he lay on the ground. (p. 70)

Ryan immediately followed with these startling statistics:

> Unfortunately, Cody isn't alone. Over one million infants and young children suffer from Shaken Baby Syndrome annually while thousands die. What's worse, these children are misdiagnosed by the majority of doctors. . . . The results are tragic. One quarter to one third of all SBS victims die within hours or days. Only 15 percent survive without damage. The remaining children suffer from blindness, learning disabilities, deafness, seizures, cerebral palsy, or paralysis. (p. 70)

By first sharing a vivid story and then building on it with startling statistics, Ryan made the topic personal and then demonstrated its significance as a problem. Using the two kinds of supporting material led to a stronger emotional appeal. At a later point, he appealed to emotions through listener relevance:

> Jacy Showers, Director of the first National Conference on Shaken Baby Syndrome, says "shaking occurs in families of all races, incomes, and education levels" and ". . . 81 percent of SBS offenders had no previous history of child abuse. The reason? The offenders were so young, either baby-sitters or new parents." (p. 71)

By making it clear to listeners that they couldn't dismiss the topic as irrelevant to themselves, he further strengthened the emotional appeal.

A personal testimonial, if appropriate, can also appeal effectively to emotions. Kristofer Kracht (1998) used a testimonial in his speech arguing for the inclusion of students with disabilities in all aspects of school life. As the following excerpts show, he threaded it throughout his speech:

> My brother, Joshua, who is mentally handicapped, is one of those born like a bird with a broken wing. . . . My parents have faced the problem of getting my brother included ever since he started school. . . . Just this year, my parents had to ask the physical education teacher if he would give Josh the opportunity to be in his class. The teacher's response was "no." . . . When *I* was in high school, my parents never had to ask a teacher if they wanted me in their classroom, so why should they have to ask for my brother? . . . It was easier in elementary school, but they are now faced with going to court. . . . I am holding a petition addressed to the NASSP [National Association of Secondary School Principals] and the NSBA [National School Board Association] as well as the North Central Accreditation Association and the Council of Chief State Officers. . . . Please sign this petition. (pp. 96–98)

By returning to this testimonial as one of the supports for successive main points, Kristofer gave his listeners an emotional motivation for signing the petition. Taken together with his arguments, this emotional appeal was compelling.

We're all aware of the potential emotional impact of photographs and other visuals and of music. For example, to reinforce her argument that television celebrities who embrace the "lollipop stick look" are contributing to the eating disorder epidemic among young girls, Jonna showed before-and-after photographs of Jennifer Aniston and Courtney Cox Arquette from *Friends*, as well as Calista Flockhart from *Ally McBeal*. These clarified the dramatic weight loss of all three women in an emotional way that words could not convey. Look for opportunities to further reinforce the impact of your emotional appeals by using presentational aids.

PRACTICING THE PROCESS

Content Strategies to Appeal to Emotions

- Use supporting material that will appeal to emotions through the senses, Maslow's hierarchy, or the learning cycle.
- Use supporting material that dramatizes the issue.
- Use listener relevance links to help audience members feel personally involved.
- Reinforce the material with presentational aids.

Presentational aids, such as these paired photos of Jennifer Aniston before and after losing weight, can reinforce the impact of your emotional appeals.

© Gregory Pace/CORBIS

© CORBIS

Strategies Involving Language

Many language choices are available for conveying content, as discussed in Chapter 11. In developing your speech, include **persuasive punch words**—words that evoke emotion. These must be used selectively, however, or they'll lose their impact. Concentrate them in important parts of the speech, such as the preview, transitions, and summary, as well as the supporting material where you make emotional appeals.

Here's how Ryan Mulholland (1998) used evocative language in the preview of his speech, "Nuclear Scare: What's Happening Out There?"

> Today, let's *examine* the *dangers* that exist because of stolen nuclear material, the reasons *such a frightening situation* has arisen, and the steps we *must take* to protect ourselves from this, the *worst of all possible dangers*. (p. 149)

Notice how much less compelling his preview would have been had he stated it like this:

> Today, let's *discuss what is happening* because of stolen nuclear material, why *this situation* has arisen, and what we *can do* to protect ourselves.

To see how persuasive punch words can be used to strengthen the emotional appeals in supporting material, consider this excerpt from Ryan Labor's (1998) speech:

> The *worst of all epidemics* is a silent one. With the majority of all *victims* either infants or young children, Shaken Baby Syndrome can be classified *a stealthy plague.* . . . When shaken, the brain is *literally ricocheted* inside the skull, *bruising the brain* and *tearing blood vessels* coming from the neck . . . *cutting off* oxygen and causing the *eyes to bulge.* (p. 70)

Persuasive punch words can effectively appeal to the emotions, but use them strategically—where it matters.

PRACTICING THE PROCESS

Guidelines for Using Language to Appeal to Emotions

- Incorporate persuasive punch words into your introduction, transitions, and conclusion.
- Incorporate persuasive punch words into supporting material used as an appeal to emotion.

Strategies Involving Delivery

Just as language can reinforce emotional content, so can delivery. Use stresses and pauses to signal the importance of content through which you make emotional appeals. Use vocal variety and, as much as possible, convey with your voice the emotions you want listeners to feel. Appropriate gestures and facial expressions can also help convey these emotions. Use gestures and facial expressions that emphasize a sense of urgency about the issue, such as clenched fists, fist to palm, and furrowed brows. Convince listeners that you feel the emotions yourself. Although effective use of delivery to convey emotions is subtle and far from easy, when done well it can truly heighten impact. But you must practice your delivery.

WHAT DO YOU THINK?
Consider a public service announcement you've seen on television (such as an appeal to listeners to help starving children or to refrain from smoking or drinking alcohol). How did the speaker's delivery (voice, face, gestures) help convey and reinforce the emotional appeals?

PRACTICING THE PROCESS

Guidelines for Using Delivery to Appeal to Emotions

- Use vocal variety that reinforces the emotional appeal you are making.
- Use facial expressions and gestures to reinforce the emotional appeal you are making.
- Practice delivery appeals to emotion using a mirror, audio recorder, or video camera and critique yourself.

© Bob Daemmrich/PhotoEdit

Appropriate gestures and facial expressions can also reinforce emotional appeals.

Student Workbook

Read through Peter's "Teen Suicide" outline in Chapter 4 of your student workbook. Identify 4 or 5 strategies he uses to convey pathos.

SUMMARY

Successful persuasive speakers prepare and present a speech that employs effective rhetorical appeals to credibility, logic, and emotion. This increases the chance of compelling listeners to believe and agree with you, and to be impassioned about your topic. Three types of appeals can be integrated into a persuasive speech. Ethos, or speaker credibility, is the sense of competence and character conveyed. Logos, or logical appeals, is the use of reasoning and evidence to build the argument. Pathos, or emotional appeals, involves evoking a range of emotions and feelings in listeners.

Bolstering ethos, or credibility, ensures that listeners will perceive you as competent—well informed, skilled, and knowledgeable about your subject—and as having character—trustworthy, honest, and sincere, as well as engaging and likable. To create a perception of high credibility—high initial, derived, and terminal credibility—use several specific strategies in planning the content, language, and delivery of your speech. With regard to content, explain your competence, establish common ground, and use strong evidence. With regard to language, use respectful language and be gracious about the opportunity to speak to the audience. With regard to delivery, choose appropriate attire, pause before and after the speech, use direct eye contact, and speak fluently and with conviction.

Convey logos by using strong evidence and logical reasoning. Reasoning is what makes arguments and supporting material logical; it shows listeners how evidence supports your claim. Employ inductive, deductive, or analogical reasoning to do this. Inductive reasoning is arriving at a general conclusion from a series of pieces of evidence. Deductive reasoning is reaching a conclusion by illustrating how a general premise applies to something specific. Analogical reasoning, or reasoning by comparison, links two things together and claims that what is true of one is therefore true of the other. To be most effective as well as ethical, avoid using fallacies, or flawed reasoning. Some of the most common errors to avoid are hasty generalization, false cause, slippery slope, either-or, straw man, bandwagon, appeal to tradition, red herring, ad hominem, and non sequitur.

Convey pathos by appealing to listeners' emotions. Pathos can include appeals to positive emotions such as pride and compassion and to negative emotions such as anger and fear. Shape content to generate emotional appeals by including vivid stories and testimonials, reinforced when possible by presentational aids. Startling statistics and listener relevance links can also evoke emotions. Persuasive punch words also evoke emotions; they work best in the preview, transitions, and summary, as well as in dramatic examples and stories included as supporting material. In delivering the speech, use stresses and pauses, as well as gestures and facial expressions, to reinforce the emotions you want to evoke and to convey a sense of sincerity and urgency about your topic.

RETURNING TO TECHNOLOGY

The *Confident Public Speaking* CD-ROM is your one-stop point of access for not just the content on the CD itself, such as Speech Interactive, but also the many other resources on the *Confident Public Speaking* Web site, Speech Builder Express, and InfoTrac College Edition. Note that this chapter's key terms and activities are among the resources available in electronic format online. Additional information is included below.

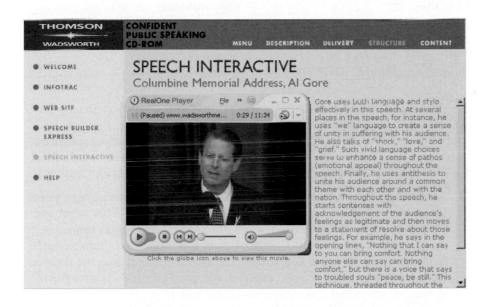

SPEECH INTERACTIVE ON
THE *CONFIDENT PUBLIC SPEAKING* CD-ROM

Speech Interactive is your link to this text's speech videos. Offering opportunities to practice critiquing speeches by both other students and public speakers who are not students, these videos will help you prepare for providing effective feedback to your peers and your own speech performances.

At the Create a New Speech screen of Speech Builder Express, you are given the option of specifying the type of speech you are going to work on. From the drop-down menu, select Persuasive. Then, on a subsequent Setup screen, select the kind of persuasive pattern you want to use. The program will provide prompts sequenced specifically for the kind of persuasive speech you indicated.

KEY TERMS

Interactive flashcards for these key terms are available on the *Confident Public Speaking* Web site. You'll find the "Flashcards" link under the resources for Chapter 16.

Ad hominem   395
Analogical reasoning   391
Appeal to tradition   394
Bandwagon   393
Character   382
Common ground   384
Competence   381
Deductive reasoning   389
Derived credibility   382
Either-or   393
Ethos   380
False cause   392
Hasty generalization   392
Inductive reasoning   388

Initial credibility   382
Logos   380
Major premise   389
Minor premise   389
Non sequitur   395
Pathos   380
Persuasive punch words   400
Reasoning fallacies   392
Red herring   394
Slippery slope   392
Straw man   393
Syllogism   389
Terminal credibility   383

ACTIVITIES

The activities below, as well as additional activities that include student speech outlines for analysis, are available in electronic format on the *Confident Public Speaking* Web site. You'll find the "Activities" link under the resources for Chapter 16.

1. **Analyzing a News Report.** Watch a television news human interest story. Listen carefully for strategies of ethos, logos, and pathos. What strategies within each type of appeal can you identify? Does the reporter rely more on one type of appeal than the others? If so, how does this influence you? Consider these factors as you watch: (1) Regarding ethos, does the reporter explain his or her competence, establish common ground, use strong evidence, use respectful language, dress appropriately, use direct audience contact, speak fluently and with sincere conviction? (2) Regarding logos, does the reporter use inductive, deductive, or analogical reasoning or commit reasoning fallacies? (3) Regarding pathos, does the reporter use positive or negative emotional appeals—such as stories, testimonials, statistics, persuasive punch words, presentational aids, and vocal variety—that are appropriate to the topic, goal, occasion, and audience?

2. **Advertisements and Persuasive Appeals.** Select two or three advertisements from a newspaper, magazine, or television that you find in some way

compelling. Identify strategies of ethos, logos, and pathos used in them. Which strategies do you find most persuasive? Why? Analyze the advertisements by considering these factors: (1) Regarding ethos, consider competence, common ground, strong evidence, and respectful language. If there are people in the advertisement, also consider appropriate attire, audience contact, vocal fluency, and sense of sincere conviction. (2) Regarding logos, consider inductive, deductive, or analogical reasoning, and reasoning fallacies such as hasty generalization, false cause, slippery slope, either-or, straw man, bandwagon, appeal to tradition, red herring, ad hominem, or non sequitur. (3) Regarding pathos, consider positive or negative emotional appeals—such as stories, testimonials, statistics, persuasive punch words, presentational aids, and vocal variety—that are appropriate or inappropriate to the topic, goal, occasion, and audience.

3. **Looking for Fallacies.** Read the letters to the editor in your local newspaper. See if you can identify examples of any of the ten reasoning fallacies discussed in this chapter (hasty generalization, false cause, either-or, slippery slope, straw man, bandwagon, appeal to tradition, red herring, ad hominem, and non sequitur).

INFOTRAC COLLEGE EDITION ACTIVITY

Using Infotrac College Edition, locate and make a copy of the speech "The Dark Side of Technology" by William N. Joy. (Hint: Use the speaker's full name as your search term.) Read the article and answer the following questions: (1) Which strategies for conveying ethos does the speaker use? (2) Which strategies for conveying pathos does the speaker use? (3) Which strategies for conveying logos does the speaker use? (4) Does the speaker rely most heavily on inductive, deductive, or analogical reasoning? (5) Does the speaker use any reasoning fallacies? (6) Which strategies did you find most compelling? Why?

SPEAKING ON
SPECIAL OCCASIONS

REFLECTIVE QUESTIONS

1. What do you think makes special occasion speeches different from other types of speeches?

2. How might speeches of introduction and of welcome differ from each other? How might they be similar?

3. What do you think is a key point to remember when giving a speech of acceptance?

4. When might a person give a speech of tribute?

5. In what ways do you think a speech to entertain is different from entertainment that is merely spoken?

WHAT'S AHEAD: FOCUSING YOUR READING

What Is Special Occasion Speaking?

Types of Special Occasion Speeches

L INDA OPENED THE ENVELOPE she had been waiting for so anxiously and read:

> The competition for this year's commencement address was extremely tough. All of the applicants were excellent. However, the committee has decided to ask you to represent the graduating class with your speech during the commencement ceremony.

It seemed too good to be true. The committee had chosen her!

Ben's grandfather had been more like a father to him. When Ben was growing up, he and his grandfather spent hours playing ball, fishing, or simply watching television together. Although his grandfather lived a long and fruitful life, Ben found it difficult to say goodbye. Still, he wanted to do the eulogy. He only hoped that his words would do justice to his grandfather.

Kim could hardly believe she would have the opportunity to hear in person the scholar on whose work she had based her thesis paper. He had agreed to present a guest lecture on her campus. Not only that, but Kim had been asked to introduce him. What an honor! Kim wondered, "How do you introduce someone who is so distinguished? What should I say?"

WHAT IS SPECIAL OCCASION SPEAKING?

Student Workbook

Read through Chapter 5 in your student workbook. Prepare and present speeches to the class as described in the "Award Presentation Activity."

Throughout life, many kinds of special occasions arise where you could be asked to speak. These range from commencement addresses at graduation ceremonies to presentations at awards banquets to toasts at weddings to eulogies at funerals. The speech you'd give on each of these occasions looks a bit different from the standard informative and persuasive speeches talked about earlier, as well as from other special occasion speeches. Linda's commencement address, for example, adheres to guidelines that differ from Ben's eulogy and from Kim's speech of introduction. They're different because each is intended for a different type of occasion. Yet they are similar because in each case the occasion is special—these are all **special occasion speeches.**

The situations Linda, Ben, and Kim face are far from uncommon. Most people at some point are asked to present some type of special occasion speech, so it's useful to know how to do it effectively. Before looking at the different types of speeches, let's look at special occasion speeches in general.

The goal of a special occasion speech lies somewhere between informing and persuading. You *invite listeners to agree with you* about the value of the person, object, event, or place the special occasion revolves around, so special occasion speeches resemble invitational speeches (discussed in Chapter 15). You do not merely inform, nor do you attempt to convince the audience; rather, you invite them to agree. Another characteristic most special occasion speeches share is brevity: They are generally less than five minutes long. Some, however, may be considerably longer, especially speeches of tribute such as eulogies and keynote, commencement, and commemorative addresses.

WHAT DO YOU THINK?

For what occasions in your personal and professional life have you been asked (or might you be asked) to give a special occasion speech? Explain.

TYPES OF SPECIAL OCCASION SPEECHES

This chapter discusses seven of the most common types of special occasion speeches: speeches of introduction, welcome, nomination, presentation, acceptance, tribute, and entertainment.

The Ethics of Humor in Special Occasion Speeches

http://www.squaresail.com/auh.html#intro

ETHICS At this site, read what Anthony Audrieth offers as tips for using humor appropriately in public speeches. What tips do you agree with and why? What tips do you disagree with and why? Do any tips surprise you? If so, which ones and why?

Speeches of Introduction

A **speech of introduction** is short, generally three to five minutes, and has the purpose of introducing the main speaker. To be effective it must achieve three goals: (1) establish a welcoming climate for the speaker, (2) highlight the speaker's credibility, and (3) generate enthusiasm for listening to the speaker and topic. These goals serve as guidelines as you prepare.

First, it is important to both the main speaker and the listeners that you create a welcoming and friendly atmosphere. Tell the audience how much you like or appreciate the speaker and why. Express sincere pleasure at having the privilege of introducing the speaker. You might also say the speaker's name several times during your speech to help familiarize listeners with it. And you might share personal facts about the speaker that audience members could identify with. (Of course, it is important not to share information that is too personal. If you are unsure about whether certain information is appropriate to share, ask the speaker in advance.) For example, Dr. Julia Wood, a noted scholar in interpersonal communication, spoke at North Dakota State University in April 1997 during a devastating flood. I'd asked her whether she was still willing to come, despite the flooding. During the speech of introduction, I shared her response. She'd said, "Of course. And I'll be sure to bring my boots!" This information, without being too personal, shared something about her that might have helped the audience relate to her.

Second, establish and boost the speaker's credibility. Tell listeners why they should listen to *this* speaker about *this* topic. Ask the speaker to provide a curriculum vitae, résumé, or biographical statement to help you generate this portion of the speech. (The most helpful resource is usually the curriculum vitae, which details the speaker's educational background, professional experience, publications, awards and honors, and so forth. A résumé is similar but far briefer, and a biographical statement limits itself to the speaker's most notable accomplishments.) Select information relevant to the topic of the speech and that will do the most to boost the speaker's credibility. Make sure not to set up unrealistic expectations; arouse the audience's expectations, but not to the point that the speaker cannot live up to them.

Finally, the speech of introduction should generate enthusiasm for the upcoming speech. If the title is cleverly worded or intriguing, state it. Share something unique about the speaker if it might spark audience curiosity. Above all, generate enthusiasm through your own delivery by sounding excited about what is to come.

See page 410 for a speech of introduction that Laura Bush delivered at the White House Conference on Missing, Exploited and Runaway Children on October 2, 2002. Notice how she established a welcoming climate by thanking everyone for attending and using "we" language to acknowledge that everyone in attendance wants the best for our children. Notice also that she mentions the speaker's name, President Bush, several times during her short speech (guideline 1).

Although talk show hosts don't deliver complete speeches of introduction when they introduce their guests, their brief introductions serve many of the same functions.

The Everett Collection

PRACTICING THE PROCESS

Checklist for a Speech of Introduction

A successful speech of introduction does the following:

❑ Creates a friendly atmosphere
❑ Establishes the speaker's credibility
❑ Generates enthusiasm for the speech

WHAT DO YOU THINK?

When have you heard a speaker introduced? Did the introduction build enthusiasm for the speaker? Why or why not?

Although she doesn't offer details from the president's vita, she establishes his credibility by saying that he speaks from his heart about children and that he believes there is no more important cause than protecting children (guideline 2). Finally, she generates enthusiasm by offering several examples of the president's love for children and ending with how proud she is to introduce him (guideline 3):

> ❝ Thank you. Distinguished guests, thank you for joining this important Conference on Missing, Exploited and Runaway Children. Everyone here believes that every child deserves to live in a loving, safe and secure home—because every child is precious. We are here today because we want the best for our children's future. We want every child to realize a life full of promise and potential. We all know that many major threats to our children today aren't a matter of chance, but a matter of choice. Today, we choose to join a concerted collaborative effort to save and improve young lives. President Bush and I want every child to have a life full of love and laughter; dreams and success. When President Bush speaks of children, he speaks from his heart. He believes, as all of us do, that there is no more important cause than protecting and preparing children for the rest of their lives. Ladies and gentlemen, I am proud to introduce my husband President George W. Bush. (Bush, 2002)

Speeches of Welcome

A **speech of welcome** is a formal, public greeting to a visiting person or group to make them feel comfortable and appreciated. It is typically presented by a **master of ceremonies,** an individual designated to set the mood of the program, introduce participants, and keep the program moving. Most year-end honorary banquets as well as award ceremonies such as the Academy Awards, the MTV Music Awards, the Emmy Awards, and the Tony Awards use a master of ceremonies for this purpose.

The speech of welcome invites listeners to agree that the occasion is friendly and indicates that their attendance is appreciated. Do this by respectfully catching their attention, graciously and thoughtfully setting a friendly tone, and providing information about the occasion and those in attendance. Typically, a speech of welcome is not more than two to four minutes long.

PRACTICING THE PROCESS

Checklist for a Speech of Welcome

A speech of welcome does the following:

❑ Catches attention respectfully
❑ Sets a friendly tone
❑ Provides information about the occasion and attendees

The master of ceremonies at a special event welcomes guests and introduces featured speakers, such as pilot and actor John Travolta, who spoke at the dedication of the Smithsonian Institution's National Air and Space Museum's new Steven F. Udvar-Hazy Center in Washington, D.C.

AP/Wide World Photos

The following example is from the National Sports Awards program aired on June 23, 1993 (as cited in Volunteer State Community College Humanities Department, 2003). Tom Brokaw, *NBC Nightly News* anchor, was master of ceremonies for this special event honoring five great athletes:

> Good evening and welcome. This is such a fitting national celebration because, after all, what would life be without the games that we play? The greatest athletes—the most memorable—are those who gave us a sense of exhilaration off the field as well as on. Heywood Hale Broun once said, "Sports don't build character; they reveal it." What you'll share here tonight is the essence of character as revealed by the lives of these great athletes.
>
> Sports are such an important part of our national culture, our language, our fantasies. Well, tonight the National Sports Awards honors those who played their games at the highest level—and lived their lives at the same heights. They lifted us all by their achievements and by their conduct. Four of them are here in Washington with us tonight; one of them, Ted Williams, has been asked by his doctor not to travel, so he's watching from his home. They were all nominated by a panel of leading sports journalists.
>
> The first that we honor tonight is a woman. When she was born, one of twenty-two children in a Tennessee family, no one could have guessed at that time that her story would echo over the decades, or that it would make even a big impression on the 1962 Middle Atlantic Conference High Jump Champion.

After Brokaw's brief speech of welcome, several individuals presented speeches of tribute to the first honoree, Wilma Rudolph. At that point, Brokaw presented her with the first National Sports Award.

TURNING TO TECHNOLOGY

Critiquing a Speech of Welcome

http://www.microsoft.com/billgates/speeches/2001/05-23ceosummit.asp

Read the transcript of Steve Ballmer's welcome remarks. Did he adhere to the guidelines for speeches of welcome as described in this chapter? How successful do you think he was in achieving the welcome speech goals? Why?

Speeches of Nomination

A **speech of nomination** proposes a nominee for an elected office, honor, or award. Every four years, political parties do this at national conventions. Those speeches are rather long, but most speeches of nomination are brief, lasting only about two to four minutes. The goal is to highlight the qualities that make this person the most credible candidate. It requires doing three specific things. First, clarify the importance of the position, honor, or award, perhaps by describing the responsibilities involved, related challenges or issues, and the characteristics needed to fulfill it. Second, list the candidate's personal and professional qualifications that meet those criteria. The goal is to link the candidate with the posi-

Actor Tommy Lee Jones nominated Al Gore for president at the 2000 Democratic National Convention.

tion, honor, or award in ways that make him or her appear to be a natural choice. Third, formally place the candidate's name in nomination at the end, creating a dramatic climax to clinch your speech.

PRACTICING THE PROCESS

Checklist for a Speech of Nomination

A speech of nomination does the following:

❑ Clarifies the importance of the position, honor, or award
❑ Lists the candidate's qualifications for it
❑ Formally places the candidate's name in nomination

A speech of nomination could be as simple and brief as this:

I am very proud to place in nomination for president of our association the name of one of our most active members, Ms. Adrienne Lamb.

We all realize the demands of this particular post. It requires leadership. It requires vision. It requires enthusiasm and motivation. And, most of all, it requires a sincere love for our group and its mission.

This candidate meets and exceeds each one of these demands. It was Adrienne Lamb who chaired our visioning task force. She led us to articulate the mission statement we abide by today. It was Adrienne Lamb who chaired the fund-raising committee last year when we enjoyed a record drive. And it was Adrienne Lamb who acted as mentor to so many of us, myself included, when we were trying to find our place in this association and this community. This association and its members have reaped the benefits of Adrienne Lamb's love and leadership so many times and in so many ways. We now have the opportunity to benefit in even greater ways.

It is truly an honor and a privilege to place in nomination for president of our association, Ms. Adrienne Lamb!

Speeches of Presentation

A **speech of presentation** is given to present an award to an individual or group and recognize the recipient's accomplishments. The Academy Awards, Grammy Awards, and MTV Movie Awards include speeches of presentation. They may be as brief as "And the winner is . . ." but are usually a bit longer, perhaps two to three minutes.

A speech of presentation invites listeners to agree that the person or group is worthy of receiving the award. Do this by pointing out relevant achievements. If listeners aren't familiar with the award and its purpose, include an explanation in your speech. Sometimes special achievement awards are given at the Academy Awards, for example, and are usually explained during the ceremony. If the winner was chosen from a group of candidates, acknowledge the worth of those not selected.

PRACTICING THE PROCESS

Checklist for a Speech of Presentation

A speech of presentation does the following:

❑ Stays brief (not more than two to three minutes)
❑ Points out relevant achievements
❑ Explains unfamiliar awards
❑ Acknowledges the worth of other candidates

The following example is a speech presenting Wendy Pearson with the Pioneer Award at the annual Science Fiction Research Association ceremony. Notice how the presenter explains the purpose of the award, acknowledges the other candidates, and points out the relevant achievements of the recipient, all in a relatively short amount of time:

> Deciding on the Pioneer Award for the one critical article in a year that does the most to advance SF criticism is both a pleasure and a challenge for the selection committee. Peter Lowentrout, Shelley Rodrigo Blanchard, and I looked for articles with the qualities we all admire: persuasive reasoning, grace and clarity of style, knowledge of the field of SF, and special insights into the particular subject of study. I'm happy to say there were many articles of that quality. What we also looked for in a Pioneer Award winner is the breadth of scope and innovation that mark a trailblazer, a piece that opens the field of SF criticism for further scholarly work. This will be the SFRA's tenth Pioneer Award. The winners have been illustrious: from Veronica Hollinger, Bruce Franklin, and Istvan Csiscery-Ronay Jr. the first three years to Carl Freedman last year; and the subjects have been wide-ranging: war, both historical and futuristic, outsiders figured in vampires and aliens, cyberpunk and other theoretical frontiers, science fiction cinema, science fiction endings, and the oft-proclaimed end of science fiction.

>   This year we award an honorable mention to George Slusser for "The Perils of an Experiment: Jules Verne and the American Lone Genius," published in Extrapolation. His article contrasted French and American attitudes toward scientific experimentation as expressed in the two national literatures and connected these attitudes with the different receptions of Verne's novels in the United States and France. Slusser's large canvas displays his command of the sociological and historical context of the literatures of two nations and their implications for science fiction. We admired the breadth and depth of his scholarship and the clarity of his style.
>
>   Despite our admiration for George's article and others, and surprisingly, really, we had no difficulty at all in agreeing on the winner of the Pioneer Award for 1999. There was one that stood out for all of us for the depth of its scholarship, the clarity of its argument, its illustrations drawn from a wide range of SF, its clear style enlivened by touches of wit, and, not least, for the fact that it brings a field of theory that took shape only a few years ago into the arena of SF scholarship, opening the way for future work. This year's winner which opens Science Fiction Studies' special issue on science fiction and queer theory, is Wendy Pearson's "Alien Cryptographies: The View from Queer."
>
>   Queer, Pearson tells us, reveals "the deeply un-natural and constructed nature of our understandings of biological sex, the performative nature of gender roles, and the sociocultural institutions founded upon this ideology." Such revelations may come from either a queer text or a queer reading. She offers four models for queer readings of a range of texts and concludes that "queer sf provides spaces to go beyond simply writing gay men and lesbians into uninterrogated heteronormative visions of both present and future," and queer readings employ strategies for "disinterring the many and peculiar ways through which the dominant twentieth-century Western conception of sexuality underlies, is implicated in, and sometimes collides with sf's attempt to envision alternative ways of being-in-the-world." Wendy's article is bound to give many of us a better sense of how queer theory can yield new insights into SF texts and how SF texts might extend the interrogations of queer theory.
>
>   Wendy is in Australia this year and could not be with us tonight, but I hope she'll be able to feel our appreciation for her contribution to SF studies halfway around the world. (Stratton, 2000)

Speeches of Acceptance

A **speech of acceptance** expresses appreciation for an award or gift received. The goal is to sincerely convey to listeners your appreciation for the honor and the recognition. You might also thank individuals who contributed to your success. To be effective, the speech should be brief, humble, and gracious. This is not the time to call attention to a political cause. Nor would it be appropriate to in any way be offensive, as was U2's lead singer, Bono, who accepted the best album award at the 1994 Grammy Awards by saying "we shall continue to abuse our position and f— up the mainstream" (Bellefante, 1994, p. 109). Remember that the goal in a speech of acceptance is to convey appreciation in a way that makes the audience feel good that you are receiving the recognition.

Acceptance speeches are a large part of awards shows such as the Grammy's.

© Marc Serota/CORBIS

WHAT DO YOU THINK?

Consider an acceptance speech you heard—for example, during an awards program on television or a ceremony you attended—that seemed inappropriate. Why did the speech seem inappropriate?

Here is a speech of acceptance given by Chris Cooper at the 75th Academy Awards ceremony. Chris won the Best Actor in a Supporting Role award for the character he played in the film *Adaptation*. Notice how he briefly thanked the Academy, which gave him the award, and those who contributed to his achievement, as well as acknowledged the competition:

> ❝ Take this in for one second. From the Academy to the womb that bore me, thank you. To all the nominees, it's a pleasure to be thought in your same company. To all the people in *Adaptation* who helped to make this the most enjoyable job I ever had, thank you. Charlie Kaufman, Spike Jonze, Nicolas Cage, the fabulous beautiful wonderful Meryl Streep. Working with this woman was like making great jazz. You had a lot to do with this, so I thank you. To my wife, Marianne, you took on all the burden, thank you. And in light of all the troubles in this world, I wish us all peace. Thank you. (Cooper, 2003)

"Don't go away...I'll go get my acceptance speech."

Copyright © 1992. Reprinted courtesy of Bunny Hoest and Parade Magazine.

TURNING TO TECHNOLOGY

Critique a Speech of Acceptance

http://oscar.com/oscarnight/winners.win_32290.html

ETHICS At this site, read through Adrien Brody's acceptance speech for his role in *The Pianist.* Do you think he met the guidelines described here for acceptance speeches? Why or why not? Watch the video clip of questions and answers. How do these answers influence your perception of his speech as ethical? Explain.

Speeches of Tribute

A **speech of tribute** praises or celebrates a person, a group, or an event. There are various types, including eulogies, toasts, farewells, dedications, commemorative addresses, and commencement addresses. Beyond informing listeners, the goal is to invite them to truly appreciate the person, group, or event by arousing their sentiments. To do this, focus on the most notable aspects of the person, group, or event—that is, on the most notable characteristics, achievements, and influences on others. For example, if the speech of tribute is for a person, select a few key aspects of his or her personality to share, along with stories to illustrate them. You might also share some of his or her most outstanding achievements, and several things he or she has done to make a difference in the lives of others and the community. A lengthy list would defeat your purpose, however, as listeners wouldn't be able to keep track. Being selective makes the speech of tribute more compelling.

A **eulogy** is a speech of tribute honoring someone who recently died. Eulogies are often delivered at funerals but can also be public events in themselves. For example, former President Reagan presented the following public eulogy after the *Challenger* space shuttle disaster in 1986. Notice how he focuses on a few notable aspects of those who died in the disaster by acknowledging each of them first by name and then as a group. He calls them heroes and brave and dedicated pioneers who are to be admired for their willingness to serve in spite of the dangers. Also take note of how he acknowledges the sentiments of the audience: "the families of the seven [who died]," "the schoolchildren of America who were watching the live coverage," "every man and woman who works for NASA or who worked on this mission," as well as "all the people of our country." Finally, notice his careful choice of stories, examples, and vivid language to arouse sentiments. He begins, for example, by talking about being "pained to the core by the tragedy," moves on to talk of "the courage it took for the crew of the shuttle," and ends with the honorable "manner in which they lived their lives . . . waved good-bye and . . . [went] to 'touch the face of God.'"

66 TRIBUTE TO THE *CHALLENGER* ASTRONAUTS

—Ronald Reagan

Ladies and gentlemen, I'd planned to speak to you tonight to report on the State of the Union but the events of earlier today have led me to change those plans. Today is a day for mourning and remembering. Nancy and I are pained to the core by the tragedy of the shuttle *Challenger*. We know we share this pain with all of the people of our country. This is truly a national loss.

Nineteen years ago, almost to the day, we lost three astronauts in a terrible accident on the ground. But we've never lost an astronaut in flight; we've never had a tragedy like this. And perhaps we've forgotten the courage it took for the crew of the shuttle; but they, the *Challenger* Seven, were aware of the dangers, but overcame them and did their jobs brilliantly. We mourn seven heroes: Michael Smith, Dick Scobee, Judith Resnik, Ronald McNair, Ellison Onizuka, Gregory Jarvis, and Christa McAuliffe. We mourn their loss as a nation together.

[For] the families of the seven, we cannot bear, as you do, the full impact of this tragedy, but we feel the loss, and we're thinking about you so very much. Your loved ones were daring and brave, and they had that special grace, that special spirit that says, "Give me a challenge and I'll meet it with joy." They had a hunger to explore the universe and discover its truths. They wished to serve, and they did. They served all of us.

We've grown used to wonders in this century. It's hard to dazzle us, but for twenty-five years the United States space program has been doing just that. We've grown used to the idea of space, and perhaps we forget that we've only just begun. We're still pioneers. They, the members of the *Challenger* crew, were pioneers.

> And I want to say something to the schoolchildren of America who were watching the live coverage of the shuttle's takeoff. I know it is hard to understand, but sometimes painful things like this happen. It's all part of the process of exploration and discovery. It's all part of taking a chance and expanding man's horizons. The future doesn't belong to the fainthearted; it belongs to the brave. The *Challenger* crew was pulling us into the future, and we'll continue to follow them.
>
> I've always had great faith in and respect for our space program, and what happened today does nothing to diminish it. We don't hide our space program. We don't keep secrets and cover things up. We do it all up front and in public. That's the way freedom is, and we wouldn't change it for a minute.
>
> We'll continue our quest in space. There will be more shuttle flights and more shuttle crews and, yes, more volunteers, more civilians, more teachers in space. Nothing ends here; our hopes and our journeys continue.
>
> I wish to add that I wish I could talk to every man and woman who works for NASA or who worked on this mission and tell them: "Your dedication and professionalism have moved and impressed us for decades. And we know of your anguish. We share it."
>
> There's coincidence today. On this day three hundred ninety years ago, the great explorer Sir Francis Drake died aboard ship off the coast of Panama. In his lifetime the great frontiers were the oceans, and an historian later said, "He lived by the sea, died on it, and was buried in it." Well, today we can say of the *Challenger* crew: Their dedication was, like Drake's, complete. The crew of the space shuttle *Challenger* honored us by the manner in which they lived their lives. We will never forget them, nor the last time we saw them, this morning, as they prepared for their journey and waved good-bye and "slipped the surly bonds of earth" to "touch the face of God." Thank you.

White House, Washington, D.C., January 28, 1986 (Transcribed from the video *Great Speeches*, Volume V).

TURNING TO TECHNOLOGY

Reagan's *Challenger* Address

http://www.historychannel.com/broadband/

At this site, click on the link for the "Reagan on the Challenger Disaster" video clip. Watch and listen to the speech. How does Reagan's delivery make his message more meaningful?

TURNING TO TECHNOLOGY

Tributes to the Victims of September 11, 2001

http://yosemite1.epa.gov/administrator/speeches.nsf/

At the Administrator Speeches menu, click on "Speeches by Date" to link to "Remarks by Marianne Lamont Horinko," delivered at the 9/11 Remembrance Ceremony in Washington, D.C., on September 11, 2003. Read this speech by an official of the Environmental Protection Agency (EPA) and evaluate how well it meets the guidelines for an effective speech of tribute.

Leading the nation on September 11, 2001 and in the days immediately following, former New York City mayor Rudolph Giuliani was widely praised for his response to the terrorist attacks in, among other situations, press conferences and speeches of tribute.

© CORBIS

TURNING TO TECHNOLOGY

Preparing Eulogies

http://www.powerpublicspeaking.com/Eulogies.htm

Read through the questions and answers offered about length, crying, what you should and should not talk about, and so forth. Do any answers surprise you? Do you disagree with any? If so, why?

WHAT DO YOU THINK?

Consider a funeral or memorial service you've attended. Was a eulogy offered? Were several offered? Identify one. Was it effective or ineffective? Why?

A **toast** is a very short speech of tribute, often delivered impromptu—that is, with little or no preparation. Toasts are often given at wedding receptions, graduation dinners, awards luncheons, holiday dinners, and so forth. The goal is to focus on some positive aspect of the person or group and to set a tone of goodwill. Remember that the most successful toasts follow this general rule: Be sincere. Be brief. Be seated. Weddings are the most common occasion for toasts. Typically at least three toasts (each not more than five minutes long) are given during the reception: one by the bride's father (or the person who "gave her away"); one by the groom; and one by the best man.

TURNING TO TECHNOLOGY

Preparing a Toast

http://www.weddinggazette.com/category/000820.shtml

Read through the tips provided for preparing each type of wedding toast, then try preparing one yourself.

Weddings are the most common occasion for toasts.

A **farewell** is a speech of tribute honoring someone who is leaving—perhaps retiring, resigning, relocating, or being promoted. The goal is to create a sense of appreciation of the honoree's fellowship and accomplishments. If you are both the speaker and the person who is leaving, express gratitude for the opportunities your tenure provided both professionally and personally. Here is Robert E. Lee's farewell speech to the Army of Northern Virginia (1865). Notice his gracious comments throughout:

> After four years of arduous service, marked by unsurpassed courage and fortitude, the Army of Northern Virginia has been compelled to yield to overwhelming numbers and resources.
>
> I need not tell the survivors of so many hard-fought battles who have remained steadfast to the last that I have consented to this result from no distrust of them; but feeling that valor and devotion could accomplish nothing that could compensate for the loss that would have attended the continuance of the contest, I determined to avoid the useless sacrifice of those whose past services have endeared them to their countrymen. By the terms of the agreement, officers and men can return to their homes and remain until exchanged.
>
> You may take with you the satisfaction that proceeds from the consciousness of duty faithfully performed, and I earnestly pray that a merciful God will extend to you his blessing and protection.
>
> With an unceasing admiration of your constancy and devotion to your country, and a grateful remembrance of your kind and generous consideration of myself, I bid you all an affectionate farewell.

A **dedication** is a speech of tribute that honors a worthy person or group by naming a structure such as a building, monument, or park after the honoree. The goal is to invite listeners to agree that the honor is deserved. Many campus buildings are named after someone and were probably dedicated. Here is a speech given by Senator Matt Matsumaga at the dedication ceremony of Spark M. Matsumaga Elementary School in Germantown, Maryland, on May 5, 2002. Notice how he invites listeners to agree that his father is worthy of this school dedication:

> 66 Thank you for your warm welcome and the kind words this afternoon. It's good to come back to Montgomery County . . . having grown up and gone to school here, there are a lot of memories here for me—and more than a few embarrassing moments that I chalk up to typical teenage behavior.
>
> Or maybe it was being the youngest of five children. I'm sure there were times I gave my parents fits. And here this afternoon, I see so many people who were friends of my parents, and I'm afraid they probably have a lot of stories to tell about us kids. It's a tribute to them that we've all done well, and that we're productive members of our society. That even applies to me, even as an elected government official. . . .
>
> My mother spent almost forty years here, and considers Montgomery County her home. I know she would have loved to be here today if she could. She sends her love and her regards, and I'll be sure to pass on to her all the good wishes from her friends back home.
>
> If she could be here, she would be humbled, as I am, that Montgomery County has honored my father in this way. And if he were here, he'd be embarrassed by all the attention, but I think he'd be secretly pleased that the County took this step to honor the diversity of its people and the contributions of the Asian-American community here.
>
> Before he went to Congress and the Senate, my father had plans to be a teacher. His plans were interrupted by the war . . . he fought with the 100th battalion, was awarded two Purple Hearts and the Bronze Star, and his war experience eventually led him to a career in public service.
>
> Still, he always maintained his commitment to the importance of education. Having five children probably played a part—he was always telling us how important a good education is. As a kid, of course, you get tired of hearing about it. But he sincerely believed it, and furthermore, he lived his commitment, and became known for his support of education at all levels.
>
> My father also had a passion for peace, and especially for peace education. "Blessed are the peacemakers" is a phrase that held special meaning for him. "Let Us Teach Our Children to Want Peace" is an essay he wrote when he was a freshman in college. And on this day, at this place, with your presence, it seems most appropriate to pay tribute to his fundamental belief that we can transcend our differences and overcome our counterproductive divisiveness through a focus on our shared ideals and common interests.
>
> He truly believed in communities and peoples at peace. And in tribute to that belief he so strongly held, I am grateful and so honored to be with you this afternoon.
>
> Thank you, and God Bless. (Matsumaga, 2002)

A **commemorative address** is a speech of tribute that inspires listeners by remembering accomplishments and setting new goals. Commemorative speeches might be given on occasions such as an anniversary party, a family reunion, or an honor society's annual banquet. Present some fact about the person, group, or event being celebrated and then build on it to create a desire for a new goal. Here is an excerpt from a commemorative speech I gave at a banquet of the Society of Women Engineers. Notice how I begin with the accomplishments that the group has achieved and then build on that to point to a new goal:

> When I was in high school, we used to shout a cheer to encourage our sports teams as they played. Perhaps some of you know it as well. It went something like this: "S-U-C-C-E-S-S. That's the way we spell success. Success! Success! Success!"
>
> Today, I've been asked to talk with you about success. First, I'd like to congratulate you for all your successes in life thus far. For example, you've graduated from high school. And you're in the process of earning your college degrees in a field that is not known for being welcoming to women, I might add! And you're learning about the joys of outreach and service to community, evidenced by your commitment to the goals of this organization. Congratulations on a job well done!
>
> Today, though, I want to move beyond the successes you've already achieved . . . to consider what it will mean to succeed tomorrow, next week, next year, and for the rest of your life. Actually, my specific goal is to challenge you to think differently about what "success" means. Then, I'll encourage you to live each day—no, each moment—of your life successfully. (Sellnow, 1999)

A **commencement address** is a speech of tribute praising graduating students and congratulating them on their academic achievements. Commencement addresses are generally delivered by the class valedictorian or another student, or by a guest speaker. If you give a commencement address, begin by praising the graduating class. Then point graduates toward future goals. Finally, inspire them to reach for those goals.

WHAT DO YOU THINK?
Do you remember a commencement speech you heard? What do you recall? What was good about it? How could it have been improved?

PRACTICING THE PROCESS

Checklist for a Commencement Address

A commencement address does the following:

❑ Praises the graduating class
❑ Points toward future goals
❑ Inspires graduating students to reach for those goals

Notice how foreign correspondent Georgia Anne Geyer includes each of these steps in her commencement address at the Saint Mary-of-the-Woods College:

Commencement speakers generally offer praise, congratulations, and inspiration to the graduating classes they address.

> ## ❝ JOY IN OUR TIMES: COMMENCEMENT ADDRESS, MAY 7, 1989
>
> *—Georgia Anne Geyer*
>
> Three months ago, I walked into my condominium in downtown Washington and happened to see the great Russian/American conductor Mstislav Rostropovich, standing at our front desk. We are proud that he lives there. He is always a man filled with life and spirit, but this day he had the most marked look of pure joy on his face that I had ever had the . . . well . . . joy of seeing.
>
> After greeting me, he stood for a few minutes at the desk and repeated several times, as if in sheer wonder, "Last night, I conducted two hundred fifty cellists. . . . Last night, I conducted two hundred fifty cellists. . . ." Ladies and gentlemen, at that moment I knew that I had seen as close to a beatific joy as I have ever seen, next to certain pictures of Christ. For I discovered then that this great musician, who is a cellist, had conducted at the world conference of five thousand cellists!
>
> That magical moment—that blessed moment—made me think of our younger generation today—of your generation—and I wondered if any of them, of you, would understand that kind of joy. For when I go around to schools—and to the very best and most serious schools—what even our best young people ask me is things like, "Miss Geyer, what are they looking for out there?" In short, in place of that inner joy of Rostropovich's which knew

" his love for music and for his cello, many young people of your generation instead are looking and waiting for some elusive and fickle "someone" out there to tell them what they are.

"What are they looking for out there?" That is one phrase that will warn you if you let it of what *not* to be thinking, even in today's often treacherous world. Some others? "How can I get ahead? What's in it for me? Let's get him." And, "How can I stop being bored? What company can I take over today? How much will I make? What's in it for me?"

Let us, for a moment, consider "Joy." My dictionary says that it is the "emotion excited by the acquisition or expectation of good." I like that. Not the acquisition of things, or of power, or of a handsome husband, or of the paltry fruit of any action. It is the magical and mystical act of discovering and finally knowing the God-given talents and the artistry that is inside yourself and nurturing and expressing them rather than trying vainly to find out what "society," whatever that is, fashionably at that moment, wants. Aristotle said that happiness is an activity that is "in accordance with virtue." Vince Lombardi, more in tune with our times, said that "happiness is winning." Donald Trump carried it to the zenith of our times' senselessness and anomie, saying that it's not "whether you win or lose, it's winning."

Let me say right off that I think the search for joy—and, remember, that only in America is the "pursuit of happiness" assured in the very Constitution itself—is very difficult for all Americans, young and old, today. Dr. Joseph Plummber, an authority on values, recently put out a study listing profound changes in our basic American values. He found that more people in the developed Western nations were seeking self-actualization rather than security or traditionally defined success. He found a self-fulfillment ethic, individualized definitions of success, a growing sense of limits. . . .

Now, this is all right so long as it is associated with principles, with "good," and with the courage to carry it through, for, as Churchill said, "Courage is the most important virtue, because it *guarantees* all the rest." Instead, I see many Americans terrified by risk, thinking apparently that a life without risk really *is* possible. We see the mother who drank half a bottle of Jim Beam whiskey every day during her pregnancy and is suing the company because her poor child is deformed. I see a remarkable amount of lack of joy, of gamesplaying instead of principle and of cases where the grand principle of equality has been debased to no more than equality of appetite.

And I see the warning of Alexis de Tocqueville about excessive individualism being realized. Two centuries ago the brilliant Frenchman warned of the democracy that he so admired that it held within it the seeds of its own demise. "Not only does democracy make everyman forget his ancestors," he wrote, "but hides his descendants and separates his contemporaries from him, it throws him back forever upon himself alone and threatens in the end to confine him entirely within the solitude of his heart." That isolation, ladies and gentlemen, graduates and friends, is not democracy but a perverted democracy that looks to others desperately for approval, that looks not to a work one loves but to a lottery and to chance for succor, and that creates a person afraid to take the joy to live in one's arms, and equally incapable of living fully either in one's own self—or in community, for the common good.

Amidst all the good we have in our country, our churches and our lives, nevertheless today I also find this wanting. Where is joy? What is joy?

(continued)

> Permit me to muse, modestly, on what I have learned through living an unorthodox life, about joy.

So I was the first woman foreign correspondent and syndicated columnist in our time. So I had to break ground and sometimes face barriers put up against me. So I lost a number of fiancés because of my love for understanding other countries, because of my liking for hotels and plane rides across the Red Seas of the world. So one of them once said in irk, "Gee Gee, the most beautiful words in the world to you are not 'I love you' but 'Room Service, Please.'"

That meant that everybody was always and is still asking me, "Didn't you feel bitter about it?" I have thought about that. Bitter? It never crossed my mind to be bitter. I was having so much fun, I was so filled with spirit and joy, I thanked God every day for the very privilege of being able to know everyone in the world and for being able to do this work I so loved. And if the Sisters of Providence will forgive me a wicked aside, I will add that the one thing your enemies can never forgive you of is, not money, not even success, but having so much fun in life!

My joys were often the little things: Interviewing a Khomeini or a Castro, Sadat or a Duarte, yes, those were good professionally, and afterwards I felt a great sense of satisfaction for breaking through. . . . But I would often experience pure joy in odd and unexpected places. . . . Sitting at breakfast in Chile and quietly observing people and feeling so privileged to be there . . . being able to bring some message of truth about the world to my own people, something they didn't know . . . seeing an election in a war-torn El Salvador and watching the poor people dare everyone to go to vote . . . seeing Russia return to its own conscience—the inner conscience that was always there, waiting—as Gorbachev frees the Russian people these very days, before our eyes. . . .

I remember special messages that warmed me tremendously, like when I interviewed the late great Archbishop Oscar Romero of El Salvador in 1979. At one point, I asked this man, who seemed just to radiate goodness, whether it would not have been easier to have stayed out of all the fights for social justice he had entered. And his simple but profound words: "Well, I could have just stayed in the Archbishop's palace, but that would not have been very *easy*, would it?" It rang so very true. It would have been immeasurably harder, just as it will be immeasurably harder for you, if you choose to live a life without the components of joy.

But—what are those components? And why are they so hard to come by in our "fun-loving . . . non-risk-taking . . . gamesplaying . . . world?"

—*Risk taking.* First and very important, being able to feel joy involves risk taking, and I do not mean juggling monies around frenziedly in the stock market. It means risking your popularity by taking a genuinely unpopular stand, risking your life to do what it is that *you* want to do in life. Risks are going to be there anyway. It's just street sense to take them on your terms, not theirs. In warfare, it is called being on the offensive. In life, it is called embracing life with all your heart.

Along these lines, I recall one spring day seven years ago when I was going to Central America—again. I just had a gut feeling that I did not want to go to El Salvador, because there had been so much fighting there. Usually I don't obey fearful feelings, having found that they pass and are not

66 really accurate, but this time I did. So I took the plane to Nicaragua, and that week nothing at all happened in Salvador—and when I got to the Managua airport, I was standing second in line to pass through to the center of the airport . . . and the airport was blown up! I never tried to second-guess fate again after that!

—*Perspective*. What, you may ask, does perspective have to do with joy? Well, a whole lot!

Young people are always asking me how I "control" (a favorite word of your generation) my interviews. And I always answer, "Knowing more than they do." This is not, repeat not, a popular answer, but it is genuine and workable. I know history—so nothing surprises me. I know where things are, why and where they will be. The perspective of history—of all human life— gives me a terrifying confidence. Knowing the trajectory of mankind—its victories, its sordid defeats, its searchings for God and for meaning—I cannot be a utopian, which is dangerous anyway, but I also cannot be a pessimist. I see how far we have come; I can take joy in what we can accomplish in our lifetimes, because I know and understand the limits of what we can do.

Once I wrote a good friend, a Jesuit priest in Latin America, about how discouraged I was about how Latin America was going and he wrote back these very wise words, "Remember, Gee Gee, I am not responsible for the outcome, but I am responsible for my own fight." That's it. That's what I know. And that very simple perspective allows one to have joy in what one *is* able to do and not to moan and mourn over not being able to do the impossible. Because we cannot be perfect, that does not mean we cannot be good.

Perspective comes at you from the funniest, most unexpected places. In Finland last fall, I went to see this fine artist, Bjorn Weckstrom, and he explained to me, as no one else quite has, how we have come to this point, where so many search not for deeper meaning or for joy but "to do something, just to be someone for a moment." "A hundred years ago," Bjorn said, "people were living in small communities. Everyone had an identity known by the whole village. The group created the morals, the rules. . . . Even your name was taken from your father—you were 'son of. . . .' Now the frames are eliminated. People are desperate, living in this super tribe. The village was an enormous security for people. In a way it gave people stability and a kind of harmony in life. The problem has been to create something new which would replace this. . . . Before, it was enough to be recognized for what you do before the village. But now the borders of the tribe have been moving out. Now to be somebody, you have to be on television. It is the problem of the identity of man today, the need to be someone even for a short moment. Even if man knows he's almost at the end of his rope. . . ." And, of course, the amorphous, unseen, cruelly judgmental audience of the TV is a harsh audience indeed, compared to the village—and the person never really knows, in this new audience, whether what he has done is good or not. And it really doesn't matter, for this audience more than likely has already long succumbed to the lowest value of the collective will.

—*Timing*. Understanding the right time for an idea, for a painting, for doing something—it is critical. It is an instinct; it comes from within people in whom street sense has been blended blessedly with intellectual searching. It is critical for work and it is critical for personal relationships. Too often

(continued)

today, we want to rush work, rush relationships, become managing editor at thirty-two, editor at thirty-five. . . . And later, we wonder where we have been, or whether we've been anywhere at all.

I talked with a young man the other day, who happened to be a fundamentalist Christian. He spoke of how important the three years before marriage to his wife had been, when they were not making love. "We got to know each other in a way at that time that we could never have known otherwise," he told me. "When you go to bed too soon, you lose all kinds of precious levels of the development of a relationship." He was so right. The Bible has a lot about this. "There is a time . . . and a time . . ."

—*Choices*. I have found through life that a truly joyful person is willing to make choices on the basis of what he knows, then stick with them, and change them if he must. It is a terribly unjoyful life not to be able to make choices, not to have the inner confidence.

That recalls the most interesting evening I had, four years ago, when I was asked to drive the late Clair Booth Luce to a dinner party. I was delighted, for here was one of the truly great women of our time, a woman who had done just about everything. . . . Mrs. Luce was not, repeat not, a woman you contradicted or, as I soon found out, even questioned. As soon as she got in the car, she was throwing very pointed and brilliant one-liners at me. She obviously had a message for me. In fact, she repeated it several times.

"You did it right," she said. "You spent twenty years doing what you do best." When I tried to remonstrate with this woman who had been ambassador, playwright, journalist, novelist, wife, mother, she disdained the suggestion. "No," she said, "I could have been a great playwright, I could have been a great playwright. . . ."

I am not suggesting that Mrs. Luce was right. Personally, I feel deeply what I have had to give up for what I wanted most. I am suggesting that wise people at different times in their lives realize that we all make choices, even when we think we are not making them; so, again, it is better to embrace them than to run from them. I dedicate that story to our noble older women graduates here today, who I know have had to make many, many choices and are still courageously making them, as their presence here attests.

And think, women of my generation—think of what we have seen! We have seen the first age when women have sought to define *themselves*! All through history, men have defined us. Finally, we are taking responsibility for ourselves! Easy? How could it be easy? And yet, we have finally arrived at trying to know and understand the ultimate political relationship, which is the ecstatic but endlessly bedeviling relationship between men and women and we have finally arrived at the moment, as the poet Louise Bogan puts it so beautifully, of women giving back to the world "half of its soul." Which brings me to . . .

—*Love*. Finally, love! There is really only one thing that I know to tell you graduates—only one thing—and that is to *follow what you love!* Follow it intellectually! Follow it sensuously! Follow it with generosity and nobility toward your fellow man! Don't deign to ask what "they" are looking for out there. Ask what you have inside. I was blessed—I was blessed because I knew what I loved—writing, my countries, being a courier between cultures—and I had dogged determination to follow it. Doing what you love, whether it is having children, working in a profession, being a nun, being a journalist, is all encompassing, all engrossing; it is like a very great love affair

> occurring every day. It is principle and creation; you know why you are here; your personal life and your professional life is all one. It is not fun, not games, not winning or losing, not making money or having your fifteen minutes on television; it is what no one can ever, ever take away from you, it is . . . pure joy.
>
> In closing, I would like to ask you just to look around you today . . . to relish and preserve in your mind's eye and your memory this treasured moment at this quintessentially beautiful school.
>
> Never again will you graduates be at this pure moment of your existence, when all the roads are open to you. Perhaps never again will you have friends and comrades, and teachers and sisters, as pure in their friendship because no one is yet what he or she is going to become. Never again probably will your families be quite so specially proud of you.
>
> So, seize the moment joyfully. Follow not your interests, which change, but what you are and what you love, which will and should not change. And always remember these golden days.
>
> God bless you all, and may the gods of the winds and the seas be with you on your voyage. Thank you.

TURNING TO TECHNOLOGY

Critiquing Commencement Speeches

http://www.c-span.org/commencement/index.asp

ETHICS Select a professional commencement speech to watch. Critique it based on the guidelines offered in this chapter. Was it effective? Why or why not? Was it ethical? That is, did the speaker demonstrate honesty and respect for himself or herself and the audience? Explain.

Speeches to Entertain

A **speech to entertain** is a lighthearted speech that makes a serious point. Using humor, you invite listeners to agree with your opinion about an issue. Keep in mind that not all speaking to entertain qualifies as a speech to entertain. For example, a comedian's monologue that has no serious point cannot be considered a speech to entertain. There are five key guidelines to follow when preparing and presenting a speech to entertain.

First, make a point. Like an informative or persuasive speech, a speech to entertain has a clear thesis statement or serious point. The thesis may not be as bluntly stated in a speech to entertain, but by the end your point should be clear. Kim Roe (1987), for example, offered this serious point, or thesis statement, in her speech to entertain: "Don't act upon assumptions" (p. 135). It wasn't bluntly articulated this way, however, until her concluding remarks.

Second, be creative and unique in your use of humor. Avoid stale jokes and clichés. Like an informative or persuasive speech, a speech to entertain should offer a new perspective.

Third, use appropriate humor. This means it must be ethical. It must be related to the topic of your speech, should not offend or marginalize members of your audience, and should be positive in tone rather than, say, sarcastic. The choices should demonstrate both honesty and respect for yourself and the audience. Some comedians make a pretty good living delivering sarcastic monologues that almost always offend someone or some group. They are not, however, considered effective public speakers. Because the occasions for most speeches to entertain are festive, don't bring that mood down with inappropriate, offensive, or sarcastic humor.

Fourth, be organized. Like any public speech, a speech to entertain should have a clear introduction, body, and conclusion. It cannot be merely a smattering of jokes or a stream-of-consciousness humorous monologue. All the principles that guide effective public speech organization should guide this speech.

WHAT DO YOU THINK?

Think of a comedian you consider offensive. Why do you think so? Can an offensive comedian still be funny? Are they ethical? Why or why not?

PRACTICING THE PROCESS

Checklist for an Entertaining Speech

A speech to entertain does the following:

- ❏ Makes a serious point
- ❏ Is creative and unique
- ❏ Uses appropriate humor
- ❏ Demonstrates honesty and respect for the speaker and the audience
- ❏ Is organized
- ❏ Uses dynamic delivery

Finally, use a dynamic delivery style. This means your voice and body should convey an enthusiasm in keeping with your entertainment purpose. It also means using **comic timing**—pausing long enough to allow for applause and laughter. Generally, listen for the peak of laughter or applause before moving on. If you don't wait long enough, listeners will be inhibited from laughing or applauding by fear of missing what you have to say next. If you wait too long, however, it will create a sense of sluggishness, and you and your audience will lose momentum.

Consider Kim Roe's speech to entertain as it may or may not meet the six guidelines mentioned above:

> ## " NATIONAL CHAMPIONSHIP SPEECH, 1987
>
> *—Kim Roe*
>
> When I was about this tall, no, that was last year. [Laughter] When I was about this tall, my mom used to buy me story-records-with-*bing*-turn-the-page-go-along books. You know them, you loved them, you had them. Allow me to share with all of you one of my favorites. Three bears and a blonde bimbo meet in a bedroom. [Laughter] Goldilocks and the Three Bears

66 "And Goldilocks, trembling with anticipation, ran into her mother's arms and said, 'Bing, turn the page.'" [Laughter]

Naturally, I assumed that this was the ending, the climax, a Goldilocks catharsis. And even when I played it backwards it said: Mersh dea shea ner Goldilox is Satin. [Laughter and applause] Which wasn't as important to what I had done. I assumed.

And I am assuming that you're all assuming that my speech is on assuming. Can I make that assumption? I assume so. When an assumption is made it lays the foundation for disappointment. And I'm sure we've all heard that when we assume we make an ass out of you and well that's pretty much about it. [Laughter]

To better understand assumptions let's first take a look at, well, why we make asses out of ourselves, how it affects you, and ways to stop. Written, directed, and delivered by me. [Laughter]

Now I have to believe that each and every one of you here today already knows what an assumption is. And, if you don't, at least you have a good example of one. [Laughter] Some would go as far as to say, "What! Assumptions! Phaat." And if you're one of those you just might want to get that checked out. [Laughter] Or check out this true historical example. President Franklin Delano Roosevelt left a stack of papers on his desk with the top page saying, "Watch the borders." A presidential advisor, upon seeing this, quickly sent troops to secure the Mexican border. And, that wouldn't have been such a bad idea except that "Watch the borders" had been left for FDR's typist. And as my mother would've said, "Damn it to hell, somebody's going to get an ass-chewing." [Laughter]

One assumption. A potential disaster. One big question, why? Why do we make asses out of ourselves? Well, one reason is that we, for the most part being normal human beings, like very little surprise in our lives. [Not] knowing what is out there, or what's in store for the future, or what really goes into a hot dog, is frightening. We feel the need to fill the gaps in our lives with our assumptions.

Another reason why we assume is that there has been a lack of communication and understanding. Now, a prime example of this can be seen through the story of the Trojan Horse.

"Yo, fellow Trojans. A gift has been besto—A gift—We just got a present."

"Read the card, read the card!"

"Who's it from, who's it from?" [Laughter]

And as we all know that was one trick pony. [Laughter]

And finally, we assume because we rely on past experiences and knowledge. And it's fair to say that whenever Geraldo Rivera bursts on the screen to unveil another fast-breaking news story, the networks assume the ratings will go sky-high. So I too, like millions, tuned in to watch his riveting on-the-spot coverage of the uncovering of Al Capone's vault. Which turned out to be as entertaining as paste. [Laughter] But, tastes change. [Laughter] As did Geraldo's underwear when he opened that empty vault. [Laughter]

As children we are taught that monkeys live on bananas alone. But movies such as *Planet of the Apes* contradicted this assumption.

"Cornelius, [Laughter] would you like a Chicken McNugget?" [Laughter]

So right away we assume and fill in the gaps and probably don't know all the facts, and, hell, I like Roddy McDowell. [Laughter]

Now that we know why we assume let's see how it affects you, oh, what the heck, me too.

(continued)

Usually, negatively. Assumptions can hurt us interpersonally, inside, right here where it counts, because we read into something because deep down we want it to turn out our way. And when that doesn't happen we feel hurt and disappointed. And believe me, I know, because I have always thought that I could sing, so I naturally assumed that I was going to get a part in my ninth grade variety show, especially singing this beautiful love ballad. [Laughter]

I'd like to dedicate this to my boyfriend Chuck. [Laughter]

"Some say love, [Laughter] it is a river that drowns a tender reed. [Laughter] But with the sun's love, in the spring becomes a rose." [Applause]

I ushered. [Laughter]

Now, assumptions can not only affect ourselves but others as well through stereotyping. There was this guy in my high school—some called him Pete. He was president of the chess club, math club, Eagle Scout Troop 411, and head hall monitor. I don't think you understand; you see Pete monitored everyone in the hall. [Laughter]

What do you assume? (A) Pete's athletic, and besides his chess knowledge, he's one lady-killer. (B) Well, Pete's a partier, and after a tough day in the hall, hey, it's Miller time. (C) Ha. Ha. Ha. Pete's hung like a horse. [Laughter]

Now, although stereotyping can be harmful, or gosh, pretty darn entertaining as well, misdirected conclusions can lead to disaster. To illustrate, let's look at a page in history. [Laughter] You might want to stand up in the back. Okay, let's talk about it. Well, it's an average size piece of paper and it's got some bold letters on it and a lot of words on it. The year, 1948. The event, the presidential election. The assumer, the *Chicago Tribune.* Now this newspaper released over one hundred thousand copies each with the headline, "DEWEY DEFEATS TRUMAN." I'm sorry. I don't care how charismatic he was, who would ever vote for Donald Duck's nephew? I mean Huey and Louie maybe, but Dewey? He was like Pete. He was a dork of a duck.

And from this example we can see that assuming can lead to big problems. And because I said it was a problem, you probably think there's going to be a solution. Well look, I don't want you to leave empty-handed so let me give you some simple solutions, and I'm not talking saline. [Laughter] Well, I guess that one just lends itself to it. [Laughter] Oh, they were written by me.

First of all, our assumptions come from an alternate source, and it's important for us to evaluate and validate our sources. For example, my Aunt Beulah told me that professional wrestling is real. Now do I consider my aunt, who is also an ex—roller derby queen, to be a reliable source? Well, yeh. She's toothless, but she's family. [Laughter] And besides, to see Aunt Beulah fly across the room and complete that flying-scissor-hook-combination-body-slam makes you want to believe.

So after you have considered the source, get accurate information. Because acting upon an assumption can lead to real disaster. I didn't want to be in that show anyway!!! [Laughter]

If they could see me now. [Laughter]

So what's the point? An assumption in itself is harmless. It's harmful when acted upon. Quite simply don't act upon assumptions. Consider the source, find out the information, get the facts, and act upon well-thought-out, educated information. And, hopefully, with this information we can turn our misplaced assumptions into directed conclusions. So that we no longer have to hear that when we assume we make an ass out of you and, oh all right, me too. But only once.

Well, my, Kimberly. You certainly have filled us in on assumptions. And all in less than ten minutes. Simply amazing.

Don't put me on the spot silly-artificial-story-telling voice, just turn the page Bing. Kim's speech is over. [Applause]

TURNING TO TECHNOLOGY

Is This a Speech to Entertain?

http://www.mikemercury.com/free_samples.html

Listen to the audio clips at this site and read the transcript samples from comedian Mike Mercury. Based on the guidelines presented in this chapter, do you consider these excerpts to be speeches to entertain? Why or why not?

Student Workbook

Read through Chapter 6 in your student workbook. What rationale is provided for practicing impromptu speeches? Which "tips" will be most important for you to remember and why?

SUMMARY

Special occasion, or invitational, speeches are given at unique events. The goal is to invite listeners to agree with you about the value of a person, object, event, or place. There are various types of special occasion speeches; most are generally less than five minutes long.

Speeches of introduction are short and build enthusiasm for the main speaker and topic. To be effective, establish a welcoming climate, highlight the speaker's credibility, and generate enthusiasm for the speaker and topic.

Speeches of welcome are short and invite listeners to agree that the occasion is friendly and their attendance is appreciated. To be effective, respectfully catch your listeners' attention, graciously and thoughtfully set a friendly tone, and provide information about the occasion and those in attendance.

Speeches of nomination are typically short and given to propose an individual as a nominee for an elected office, honor, or award. The goal is to highlight the qualities that make this person the most credible candidate by clarifying the importance of the position, honor, or award and emphasizing the candidate's personal and professional qualifications. You then formally place the candidate's name in nomination.

Speeches of presentation present an award and recognize the accomplishments of the person or group receiving it. The goal is to invite listeners to agree that the person or group is worthy of the award. Do this by pointing out the achievements of the person or group, and perhaps explain the purpose of the award. Also acknowledge the worth of those not selected.

Speeches of acceptance express appreciation for an award. In addition to expressing appreciation for the honor and recognition, you might thank individuals who contributed to your success. To be effective, the speech should be brief, humble, and gracious.

Speeches of tribute praise or celebrate a person, group, or event. Eulogies, toasts, farewells, dedications, commemorative addresses, and commencement addresses are speeches of tribute. Beyond informing listeners, the goal is to invite them to appreciate the person, group, or event by arousing their sentiments. To achieve this, focus on the most notable characteristics, achievements, and influences.

Speeches to entertain are lighthearted but make a serious point. Using humor, they invite listeners to agree with your opinion about an issue. When preparing and presenting a speech to entertain, be sure to make a point, use creative and unique humor, use appropriate humor, be organized, and use a dynamic delivery style.

At various times in life, you may be asked to give a special occasion speech. By knowing what these speeches are and following the basic guidelines presented, you can be effective when those times arise.

The *Confident Public Speaking* CD-ROM is your one-stop point of access for not just the content on the CD itself, such as Speech Interactive, but also the many other resources on the *Confident Public Speaking* Web site, Speech Builder Express, and InfoTrac College Edition. Note that this chapter's key terms and activities are among the resources available in electronic format online. Additional information is included below.

SPEECH INTERACTIVE ON
THE *CONFIDENT PUBLIC SPEAKING* CD-ROM

Speech Interactive is your link to this text's speech videos. Offering opportunities to practice critiquing speeches by students and other public speakers, these videos will help you prepare for providing effective feedback to your peers and your own speech performances.

SPEECH BUILDER EXPRESS

The different combinations of prompt sequences that Speech Builder Express offers can help you prepare speeches for the full range of special occasions covered in this chapter.

KEY TERMS

Interactive flashcards for these key terms are available on the *Confident Public Speaking* Web site. You'll find the "Flashcards" link under the resources for Chapter 17.

ACTIVITIES

The activities below, as well as additional activities that include student speech outlines for analysis, are available in electronic format on the *Confident Public Speaking* Web site. You'll find the "Activities" link under the resources for Chapter 17.

1. **The Awards.** Form pairs. Then pick a favorite awards show (Oscars, MTV Awards, CMA Awards, Grammy Awards, Golden Globes, People's Choice Awards, or another). Brainstorm together what the award is for. You can make up the name of the song, program, or film. One of you will give a speech of presentation based on the guidelines in this chapter: Be brief (not more than two to three minutes). Point out relevant achievements. Explain unfamiliar awards. Acknowledge the worth of other candidates.

   The other partner will give a speech of acceptance, following the guidelines: Be brief (not more than one to two minutes). Acknowledge the competition. Thank those who've contributed to your achievement. Thank those who gave the award.

   Develop short speeches and present them to the class.

2. **Professional Speaker Critique.** Attend a guest lecture on campus. Pay special attention to the speech of introduction, and critique it based on the guidelines provided in this chapter: establishing a welcoming climate for the speaker, highlighting the speaker's credibility, and generating enthusiasm for listening to the speaker and topic. Be prepared to discuss your critique in class.

INFOTRAC COLLEGE EDITION ACTIVITY

Access InfoTrac College Edition and search for three to four articles that appeal to you on a specific type of special occasion speech. For example, you might use "humor" or "entertainment" and "public speaking" as your key words to find articles about the topic of humorous speeches. Make note of additional tips and considerations that you can keep in mind or use when you prepare and present a special occasion speech of the type you chose.

WORKING AND SPEAKING IN SMALL GROUPS

REFLECTIVE QUESTIONS

1. What are some reasons you like and don't like to work in a small group?

2. What task, relational, and housekeeping needs relate to leadership in small groups?

3. How are designated leaders, emergent leaders, and implied leaders different? How are they similar?

4. What are the responsibilities of group members?

5. What are the different formats for group presentations and how is each format unique?

WHAT'S AHEAD: FOCUSING YOUR READING

Why Work in Small Groups?

What Is a Small Group?

Effective Leadership in Small Groups

Responsibilities of Group Members

Systematic Group Problem Solving

Preparing Group Presentations

Group Presentation Formats

Evaluating Group Effectiveness

W ORK SESSION 1: JULIO, KRISTI, Luke, Bryn, and Nick have been asked to work as a small group to prepare a persuasive presentation that will account for one-third of their grade in the course. As the other members see it, Nick is a troublemaker because he has contradicted the instructor many times. Their impression might be compounded by the fact that Nick drives a Harley-Davidson motorcycle to school and wears black leather most days. Nick has also been absent frequently and seems less than fully committed to earning a good grade. In short, the other members are worried that Nick will cause them to earn a lower grade than they would otherwise get.

Work Session 2: After the instructor refused to move Nick into a different group, Julio, Kristi, Luke, and Bryn decided to restrict his participation and contributions. They agreed not to ask him for substantive help even though they realize he will earn a good grade for doing very little work. As the full group begins discussing the topic—the mandatory seat belt law—Nick explains that he has a lot of material on it since he is a fairly vocal opponent of the helmet law, which involves similar issues. Kristi and Luke become disgruntled because they plan to argue in support of the law and, as they suspected, Nick opposes it. Kristi asks Bryn how she feels about this conflict, expecting her support. But Bryn asks Nick to share some of his information. When he does, she discovers that much of it is highly relevant and can be used to strengthen the group's argument by enabling them to acknowledge and fairly treat objections. As Bryn explains this to the others, they begin to realize the hastiness of their judgments about Nick.

As this example suggests, working in small groups involves many complexities that group members need to know how to handle. This chapter is about ways to work and speak effectively in small groups. It examines the characteristics of small groups (especially problem-solving groups), effective leadership and the responsibilities of group members, systematic problem solving that groups can use to structure their work, preparing and formatting a group presentation, and how to evaluate group effectiveness.

WHAT DO YOU THINK?

Identify some of the small groups you've been in, such as social, classroom, or business groups. Did you enjoy working in them? Why or why not?

WHY WORK IN SMALL GROUPS?

When asked to work in small groups on a class project, many students respond—as Luke, Kristi, Julio, and Bryn did—with comments of frustration and resistance. The comments may focus on a group member or something else specific to the situation. Often, however, they reflect general concerns about group work. Some students are concerned that a few people will end up doing most of the work, that it will be impossible to find mutually acceptable times to meet, that the group process will slow them down and might even lead to getting a lower grade, or that they will be forced to compromise their ideas and values to reach group consensus. Some even plead to do the assignment alone.

Although small group work has disadvantages, it is the preferred problem-solving approach in business and industry (Ancona, 1990; O'Hair, O'Rourke, & O'Hair, 2001). You can expect to work in a group or on a team in professional life, sometimes in face-to-face settings and often in virtual settings through e-mail, chat rooms, discussion boards, and video conferences (Tullar & Kaiser, 2000). Business and industry leaders have come to realize that the advantages of small groups far outweigh the disadvantages. The advantages include deeper analysis of problems, greater breadth of ideas and of potential solutions, improved group morale, and increased productivity.

You can also expect to be asked to present group findings, perhaps to a small group of peers, a senior manager or management team, or a group of clients or customers. Some of the most common business presentations are progress reports, sales presentations, proposals, and staff reports (Lesikar, Pettit, & Flately, 1999). With increased terrorism and school violence, crisis-response presentations have become another common type of business presentation (Seeger, Sellnow, & Ulmer, 2003). Because small group participation is unavoidable today and in years to come, it makes sense to learn more about how to do it effectively.

WHAT IS A SMALL GROUP?

The **small group** can be difficult to define because there are so many types: families and friendship groups, self-help and therapy groups, problem-solving groups such as committees and task forces, and others. They have in common limited size and membership by people who have come together for a reason. This chapter focuses on problem-solving groups, such as those you participate in for class assignments.

A **problem-solving group** primarily carries out a task—usually figuring out solutions to problems. Business and professional organizations often refer to such groups as **work teams.** Most of them are self-directed; all members perform leadership functions as the group manages itself (Harris & Sherblom, 1999; Wellins, Byham, & Wilson, 1991). What makes a group effective or ineffective? Several factors—group composition, group size, group goal, and group history—appear to influence a group's likelihood of success.

TURNING TO TECHNOLOGY

Work Teams

http://www.workteams.unt.edu/

This site provides resources to learn more about work teams, which are widely used in the private sector. According to this site, in what ways are work teams effective? Do you agree or disagree? Why?

Composition of the Group

Groups can be relatively homogeneous or heterogeneous. In other words, their members can be similar to one another in cultural background, values and beliefs, age, and so on **(homogeneous groups)** or different **(heterogeneous groups).** Research shows that heterogeneous groups are often more effective. The reason is that differences bring broader perspectives and more ideas, thereby facilitating creative problem solving (Porter & Samovar, 1992). In our ever-more-diverse society, group heterogeneity is increasingly possible.

However, heterogeneity can impede the group process if members cannot see beyond their own cultural perspectives to respect and value other ideas and opinions. When Kristi and Luke became disgruntled with Nick, they were allowing heterogeneity to become a problem rather than an advantage. All members must agree to respect different perceptions and beliefs, including those

ETHICS

arising from different cultural backgrounds, or heterogeneity will be a disadvantage. Ideally, all members understand that multiple perspectives can enhance the quality of the group process and outcome.

Group Size

A small group must have at least three members but can have as many as twenty. Most communication specialists agree that the ideal size for a problem-solving group is from four to seven people (Bales, 1955). Groups of fewer than four tend to lack diversity of perspective. Groups of more than seven tend to develop hierarchies and subgroups. **Hierarchies** occur when members of a group are seen as having different ranks. They can damage the group's chances for success because, once they develop, members at the top of the hierarchy begin to dominate the discussion while those at the bottom become silent and dissatisfied with the group process (Wood, 2000). **Subgroups** are smaller groups within the group. For example, if three people in a group disagree with the others they might form a subgroup, which could begin to disagree on other issues as well. Ongoing disagreement could ultimately lead to failure.

Group Goal

A **group goal** is a collective purpose that unifies members. This purpose could be specific, such as persuading an audience to support coed dormitories on campus, or vague, such as improving campus safety. The more specific the goal, the more effective the group is likely to be. Thus groups that begin with a vague goal first work to make the goal more concrete. The students pursuing campus safety, for example, might decide to focus specifically on the possibility of a campus escort service between the hours of 11 p.m. and 6 a.m.

WHAT DO YOU THINK?

Recall a small group you were involved in where members disagreed about what to do. Why couldn't members agree on the goal? What was the outcome and how satisfied were you with it?

The group goal might be partially imposed from outside the group. In a speech class, for example, an instructor might require an informative or a persuasive speech on a campus or community issue. Even so, the group still determines its goal and how specific it is.

A group without a clear and specific purpose falters and ultimately fails. Just as a speech topic must be narrowed to a thesis statement, a group must focus on a goal—but it's important to make certain that all members understand and are committed to it.

Group History

Group history refers to members' perceptions of past work done by the group and its members. Every group begins developing a history from the first moment of the first meeting, and often before that. In a class, each small group is a subset of the entire class and so has a history that predates its first meeting. For example, Bryn, Julio, Kristi, and Luke's negative assumptions about Nick were based on Nick's behaviors in the group history of the class.

A positive group history increases the group's likelihood of success, which in turn leads to a yet more positive group history. Thus it's important to start off on the right foot. Research shows that initial successes give members confidence in the group's capacity to meet future challenges (Krayer & Fiechtner, 1984).

A group's history isn't always realistic. This can be a problem, especially when it takes the form of scapegoating. **Scapegoating** is the tendency to blame

The ideal size for a problem-solving group ranges between four and seven people.

one or more members for the failure of the group. Because assigning blame is not as productive as seeking solutions, scapegoating leads to poorer results. If Nick's group had scapegoated him, rather than figuring out what he had to offer, they would have developed a less effective presentation.

Many disadvantages of working in small groups can be reduced, avoided, or even turned into advantages by capitalizing on the group's composition, size, goal, and history. Following this advice will help make your small group experiences positive, both in the classroom and beyond.

WHAT DO YOU THINK?

Have you ever been falsely accused or blamed for something you didn't do? How did it make you feel? How was it resolved and how satisfied were you with it?

PRACTICING THE PROCESS

Guidelines for Forming Small Groups

- Strive for heterogeneity among members.
- Limit size to between four and seven members.
- Agree on a collective purpose or group goal.
- Focus on a positive history.

Dilbert reprinted by permission of United Feature Syndicate, Inc.

© Bill Varie/CORBIS

Group leaders function to meet the group's task, relational, and housekeeping needs.

EFFECTIVE LEADERSHIP IN SMALL GROUPS

To work well, a small group must have effective leadership. Traditionally leadership belonged to one person, but today **leadership** is considered a range of diverse functions, ideally shared by various group members. Have you ever been in a small group that failed because the "leader" could not lead? Sharing leadership functions avoids this problem and makes it possible for functions to be done by those who can do them most effectively. This is a matter of leadership functions, kinds of leaders, and leadership styles.

Functions of Leadership

There are three main kinds of leadership functions. Each meets a different set of group needs: task needs, relational needs, and housekeeping needs. Because these needs are too diverse to be met by one person, leadership is usually most effective when shared. It follows that all group members must understand the different needs and functions of leadership, as well as their own leadership strengths and weaknesses. For each of the roles described in the following paragraphs, there are counterproductive roles that must be avoided. These negative roles emerge when an individual focuses on his or her own desires over those of the group, such as being a "talk hog" by not allowing others a chance to speak; a "negativist" by responding to every idea with "it won't work"; a "naysayer" by continually bringing up issues that have already been settled; or a "know-it-all" by constantly calling attention to oneself rather than focusing on group tasks (Bramson, 1981).

Leadership Traits

http://www.sbaonline.sba.gov/managing/leadership/traits.html

This Web page sponsored by the U.S. Small Business Administration describes several leadership traits. Which trait seems most important to you and why? Do you disagree with any? If so, why?

Task Needs

Task needs are substantive actions that must be taken for the group to achieve its goal. To keep the group moving toward the goal requires managing the agenda, distributing workload, raising questions, and helping the group reach decisions.

To cover such a range of needs, someone usually assumes primary responsibility for each function. Consider which of the following roles you are especially suited to fill: initiator, expediter, information giver, information seeker, analyzer, and evaluator.

PRACTICING THE PROCESS

Checklist of Task Needs

- ❑ Setting and sticking to the agenda
- ❑ Distributing the workload
- ❑ Providing content for the discussion
- ❑ Raising questions and posing alternative perspectives
- ❑ Formulating criteria for evaluating possible solutions
- ❑ Helping the group reach a decision on its final solution

The **initiator** proposes new ideas and approaches, and distributes the initial workload. That is, you set the initial agenda in terms of what must be done and how to divide the workload into manageable pieces.

The **expediter** helps the group stick to the agenda, deciding when the group is going astray and leading it back to the problem at hand. In other words, you keep the group focused on the agenda and redirect discussion when necessary.

The **information giver** provides content for the discussion. You might do research, organize your findings, and bring them to the group to provide a foundation for the group discussion and problem-solving process.

The **information seeker** raises questions and probes into the contributions of others. As you listen to the research and conclusions presented, you might pose alternative points of view and ask questions that encourage group members to come up with yet other perspectives.

The **analyzer** helps the group relate evidence provided by the information seeker to the issues at the core of the problem. Ultimately, you help the group reach a decision about a conclusion, solution, or course of action.

The **evaluator** helps the group develop criteria for evaluating a conclusion, solution, or course of action and then makes an effort to apply those criteria to the group's decision.

Relational Needs

Relational needs involve interpersonal relationships among group members. Leadership functions that meet these needs foster and maintain positive interpersonal relationships. These functions include promoting self-esteem among group members, supporting divergent ideas, and dealing effectively with conflict.

As with task needs, the key is to meet each relational need in some way. Consider which of the following roles related to relational needs you are particularly suited to fill: supporter, harmonizer, and gatekeeper.

The **supporter** responds favorably when good points are made. The response can be verbal ("good point" or "that's an interesting idea") or nonverbal (a smile or nod). All members should be supportive, but by being particularly diligent about recognizing contributions, the supporter improves the group atmosphere.

The **harmonizer** recognizes and deals with misunderstandings and disagreements as they occur, noticing when someone appears upset, isolating the issues from the people, and refocusing discussion accordingly.

The **gatekeeper** helps keep the communication channels open for everyone, for example by noticing when someone wants to talk but can't break into the conversation, and helping them do so; or noticing when someone is withdrawing from the conversation and trying to bring them back in. Another role is redirecting the conversation when someone is monopolizing it.

PRACTICING THE PROCESS

Checklist of Relational Roles

❏ Promote self-esteem among members.
❏ Support divergent ideas.
❏ Encourage reticent members to participate and contribute to the discussion.
❏ Deal effectively with conflict among members.
❏ Ensure that all members feel satisfied with the group outcomes.

Housekeeping Needs

Housekeeping needs are the many details that need to be considered. Leadership functions here include deciding where and when the group will meet, taking notes during the meeting, and summarizing the group's progress at the end of the meeting.

As with the task and relational needs, different members might be better suited to fill each of these functions. Consider whether you are particularly suited to fill one of the two roles related to housekeeping needs: administrator and recorder.

The **administrator** determines where and when the group will meet. Schedules are solicited and coordinated in order to slate the meeting at a time when all members are available. The administrator finds and reserves a room and any equipment or special accommodations required, and tells all members in advance when and where the group will meet.

The **recorder** takes notes during the meeting and summarizes them for everyone at the end. This summary is often done both orally and in writing; the written version is distributed after each meeting in preparation for the next one.

Checklist of Housekeeping Needs

❑ Decide where and when the group will meet.
❑ Reserve a room for the meeting.
❑ Take notes during the meeting.
❑ Summarize the group's progress at the end of the meeting.

Fulfilling Leadership Functions

All three kinds of leadership functions are essential to the group process. A group can't function well unless necessary actions are taken, group members work together well, and details are attended to. Although everyone should do his or her part to fulfill the leadership functions to some degree, usually one person assumes primary responsibility for particular roles related to these needs. In fact, there may be a connection between excelling at a particular role and preferred learning style. If functions are divided, members can be responsible for those leadership functions they feel most capable of performing.

It is important that leadership functions be filled on this basis rather than on some arbitrary basis such as gender stereotypes. For example, although some studies have shown that women tend to meet the relational needs of a group slightly more effectively than men, that doesn't mean that in a given group the women would be the best relational leaders (Helgesen, 1990). Nor would it be appropriate to assume that all the men would perform task-related leadership functions better than the women. In fact, some studies indicate that women in general are more adept at keeping the group focused on its task than are men (Shimanoff & Jenkins, 1992). In short, each person should take on the leadership functions he or she can do best.

> **WHAT DO YOU THINK?**
> Consider the task, relational, and housekeeping leadership functions we've just discussed and the group member roles related to each of them. Which roles are you particularly suited to fill? Are there any you are not suited to fill? Are there any counterproductive roles you'll need to take care to avoid? Explain.

Kinds of Leaders

Although in many small groups today leadership functions are shared, in some groups most of these functions are concentrated in a single leader. When we look at why this occurs, we can distinguish three kinds of leaders: designated leaders, emergent leaders, and implied leaders.

A **designated leader** is appointed when the group is formed. Designated leaders can be effective for groups that meet once to perform a specific task. Under these circumstances, it's efficient to have a single leader, particularly one whose strengths lie in the area of task needs. However, designated leaders tend to be ineffective for other kinds of groups because rarely is one person most skilled at all the functions of leadership.

Sometimes a leader might emerge naturally during the group process. An **emergent leader** is someone who takes the initiative, filling such functions as arranging meetings, setting the agenda, and keeping discussion focused. These are task and housekeeping needs; typically, an emergent leader has strengths in such areas. An emergent leader can be effective as long as he or she is not authoritarian, as discussed in the next section.

WHAT DO YOU THINK?

Consider a group you have belonged to where the leader was designated. How effective was that group? Would the group have been more effective with shared leadership? Why or why not?

Most often the emergent leader is also an **implied leader,** the individual who has the highest status or whom the other members perceive as having the highest status or greatest expertise in the area. In a public speaking classroom, the implied leader might simply be the student who has delivered the best speeches or even the one who talks the most during class discussions. Unfortunately, the group members' perception of the individual's status or expertise may not be accurate. Someone who talks the most does not necessarily make the best leader.

Each of these leadership types has limitations and risks. Designating a leader or allowing an implied leader to emerge may not be as effective as dividing leadership functions among group members.

Leadership Styles

Any small group, regardless of the kind of leader it has or if it operates using shared leadership, develops a **leadership style**—that is, a style of communicating and operating. Research reveals that there are three main leadership styles: authoritarian, laissez-faire, and democratic. The style can affect both the group's atmosphere and productivity.

An **authoritarian leadership style** is directive, controlling, and dictatorial. This tends to occur in groups where someone takes on the role of leader rather than in groups where leadership is shared. Directions for discussion are clearly set and specific tasks are assigned to different members. Interaction among members is explicitly or implicitly discouraged. This style can be efficient and effective only under certain circumstances: for groups that meet once to complete a single task, or for groups with a leader much more knowledgeable than the other members (White & Lippitt, 1969). For example, coaches can work effectively using this style as long as the players respect their superior knowledge. However, this efficiency may come at the expense of a positive climate, good morale, and the quality of the outcome. Apathy and resentment are common responses to this leadership style (Gibb, 1969; Lewin, Lippitt, & White, 1939).

In contrast, a **laissez-faire leadership style** is nondirective and passive. No one provides specific guidance or direction; the group moves toward its goal without working out the details of how it will get there. This style can be effective when a group consists of members who are mature, experienced, and self-directed. But in most cases groups need guidance to sustain a good atmosphere and be focused and productive. Hence, this style is not recommended (Bass, 1990; White & Lippitt, 1960). Its inefficiencies typically leave group members feeling frustrated.

Although the best leadership style for a group depends on various factors, most researchers agree that generally it's a **democratic leadership style,** which is directive but not rigid. This style tends to encourage all members to take initiative and participate in decision making. Because democratic leadership generally leads to good communication among members, it promotes group morale and positive results (Gibb, 1969; White & Lippitt, 1969).

RESPONSIBILITIES OF GROUP MEMBERS

ETHICS

In a group with shared leadership, members must do two things to be ethical: respect and support the group and its goal, and value the contributions of each member. Everyone must do this for the group to meet its task, relational, and housekeeping needs. Each group member has five responsibilities: be commit-

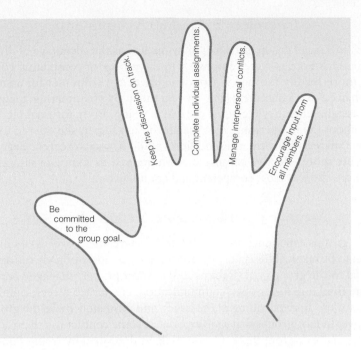

Keep the discussion on track.

Complete individual assignments.

Manage interpersonal conflicts.

Encourage input from all members.

Be committed to the group goal.

Figure 18.1 Responsibilities of group members

ted to the group goal, keep the discussion on track, complete individual assignments, manage interpersonal conflicts, and encourage input from all members (Figure 18.1).

Be Committed to the Group Goal

In public speaking class, being committed to the group goal means being committed to earning a good grade. In your career, it may mean working together to solve a work-related problem. In either setting, it means working together toward a solution and supporting it even if it doesn't fully fit your own position. Thus, in the example at the beginning of the chapter, the group took Nick's research and opinions into account and Nick agreed to support the group's ultimate recommendation—that seat belts be required. This might mean that, at some point, you must not be a naysayer or a negativist. For example, my university recently decided to move to Division I sports. In the discussion of whether to make the move, a variety of perspectives emerged and were taken into account. Now that the decision has been agreed upon, however, it is no longer appropriate to dredge up old issues that have already been settled. Being committed to the group goal means finding a way to align personal goals with the group goal as well as value the contributions of all members.

Keep the Discussion on Track

Although one member might most often perform the leadership function of keeping the discussion on track, this is a responsibility all members should share to a certain extent. It's irresponsible, unproductive, and ultimately unethical to get the discussion off track because you don't agree with what's being said, you want to talk about personal matters, or for any other reason. It is your responsibility to make sure that your input is relevant and to pitch in when necessary if other group members seem to be getting the discussion off track.

ETHICS

Complete Individual Assignments

Working in a small group instead of individually has the advantage of dividing up the work. However, you are responsible to the group for completing your share. This is more readily fulfilled if group members can volunteer for assignments rather than having assignments imposed on them. By volunteering, members can choose assignments they feel most capable of doing. Bryn, for example, has high anxiety about public speaking. As a graphic design major, she offered to prepare the visual materials for the presentation and do library research. Bryn and the group were more effective because she volunteered to complete assignments in areas where she was most competent and confident.

Manage Conflict among Group Members

All small groups experience some **conflict**—disagreement over issues or courses of action to be taken. This is normal, and if managed appropriately can actually be beneficial to the group goal (Rahim, 2001). Appropriately managed conflict can stimulate thinking, foster open communication, encourage diverse opinions, enlarge members' understanding of the issues, and ultimately make the group more productive. In fact, groups that *don't* experience some conflict run the risk of problems, especially of groupthink. Groupthink, as described by Irving Janis (1982), is the tendency to accept information and ideas without subjecting them to critical analysis. **Groupthink** occurs when group members' desire to agree with one another and get along keeps them from fully discussing the issues, raising questions, or posing alternatives. Behaviors that signal groupthink include:

- Avoiding conflict in order to avoid hurting the feelings of others
- Pressuring members who do not agree with the majority of the group to conform
- Reaching consensus without the support of all members
- Discouraging or ignoring disagreements
- Rationalizing a decision without testing it

Groups that succumb to groupthink are less likely to make the best decisions. The consequences might be minor, but can be devastating. Some have argued, for example, that the *Challenger* disaster came about in part because of groupthink (Seeger, Sellnow, & Ulmer, 2003). Thus it is the responsibility of all members to know the causes of conflict, not to avoid it but rather to help manage it productively when it surfaces.

TURNING TO TECHNOLOGY

Groupthink

http://www.afirstlook.com/archive/groupthink.cfm?source=archther

This site provides great information about Janis's concept of groupthink. What are the eight warning signs of groupthink described here and what can you do to enhance your group's chances for making the best decisions?

What are some causes of conflict? Conflict in groups often stems directly from lack of agreement on issues and goals. A member may feel his or her views are incompatible with those of the others. This is how Nick felt initially, as his opinions about seat belt laws were directly opposed to those of the others. Conflict may also stem from personal factors. For example, it might arise if a member feels his or her ego is being threatened, or is frustrated by the behavior of another member. Kristi and Luke initially felt frustrated because of Nick's behavior in previous class sessions.

How should conflict be managed? Shape the conflict so it is constructive rather than destructive. Destructive conflict is marked by a competitive focus, self-interest, and a win-lose orientation (where people think in terms of "winners" and "losers"). This negatively affects the atmosphere and members may be reluctant to share their ideas for fear of being personally attacked or criticized. But constructive conflict occurs when all members understand that disagreements are a natural part of a productive group process. Hence communication is cooperative. Members listen to opposing ideas openly and respectfully, and there is a collective win-win attitude.

ETHICS

To shape conflict so that it is constructive, begin by separating the issues from the people involved. This clarifies the issues and any misunderstandings that might have arisen, and then all members can offer productive input. To ensure that discussion is more productive, keep emotions in check and phrase comments descriptively, not judgmentally. Finally, seek a win-win compromise rather than a win-lose solution. Whereas Kristi and Luke wanted to institute a win-lose solution by ignoring Nick's ideas, Bryn listened to his ideas and argued that they should be incorporated into the speech, meaning Bryn managed conflict ethically and effectively. Once you accept that conflict in groups is natural, you can manage it in ways that better enable meeting the goal.

TURNING TO TECHNOLOGY

Conflict Management in Groups

http://www.onlinewbc.gov/Docs/manage/conflicts.html

This Web site offers tips for managing conflict. Which strategies will you try and why? Are there any you won't try? If not, why not?

PRACTICING THE PROCESS

Guidelines for Managing Conflict

- Focus on issues, not personalities.
- Clarify misunderstandings.
- Keep emotions in check.
- Phrase comments descriptively, not judgmentally.
- Seek ways to compromise.

Encourage Input from All Members

All too often in small group discussions, quiet members are overshadowed by extroverts. This doesn't mean quiet people have nothing to contribute. On the contrary, all members have valuable perspectives. If you are an extrovert, you have a special responsibility to refrain from dominating the discussion and to ask others

ETHICS

for their opinions. Bryn, for example, tends to be quiet during group discussions because of her speech anxiety, yet she was the one who realized how Nick's ideas could enhance the group's presentation. Because Kristi asked for Bryn's opinion, Bryn was able to offer the group a new perspective. Hence, it is the ethical responsibility of all members to both share their own ideas and encourage other members to participate.

Each group member must adhere to these five responsibilities, summarized in the next Practicing the Process box, for a couple of reasons. First, it ensures that the leadership functions are met, thus making the group more productive and effective. Second, it demonstrates ethical behavior to the group as a whole and to each member.

Student Workbook

Read through the "Group Speech Policies and Procedures" in Chapter 4 of your student workbook. Now complete the "Group Contract" based on the ethical responsibilities for group members.

PRACTICING THE PROCESS

Guidelines for Responsible and Ethical Group Membership

ETHICS
- Be committed to the group goal.
- Keep the discussion on track.
- Complete individual assignments.
- Manage interpersonal conflicts.
- Encourage input from all members.

SYSTEMATIC GROUP PROBLEM SOLVING

A group needs a concrete approach to problem solving in order to come up with productive solutions in a short time. The idea is to give the group a plan—a method to follow—for reaching its goal. When a group uses **systematic problem solving**, it identifies a problem and, through a process of reasoning, attempts to discover the best way to solve it. After generating a host of potential solutions, a process of elimination leads to the best solution. The plan has six steps (Dewey, 1933):

1. Identify and define the problem.
2. Analyze the problem.
3. Determine criteria for judging solutions.
4. Generate a host of solutions.
5. Select the best solution based on the criteria.
6. Implement the agreed-upon solution.

TURNING TO TECHNOLOGY

Honing Your Problem-Solving Skills

http://www.giftedcenter.com/creative_problem_solving__cps_mo.htm

This Web site offers tips for fine-tuning your problem-solving skills. Which skill will you try to refine in yourself? Why, and how?

Identify and Define the Problem

The first step is to identify the problem and define it in a way all group members understand and agree with. Groups begin by brainstorming a number of problems or felt needs and then narrow to a particular one. Questions can help groups identify and define the problem. For example, your group might ask the following questions: What is the problem? What is its history? Who is affected by it and how does it affect them? How many people are affected, in what ways, and to what degree? These are ways of learning how extensive the problem is. The group may find it must do research to be able to answer these questions.

Matt, Shannon, Pam, and Michelle, for example, identified gang violence as a problem in our country. To define the problem they used these kinds of questions to guide their research. They discovered that gang violence occurs all across the nation, not just in certain regions or densely populated communities. They also learned that victims can be of any age, race, ethnicity, or religion. And they discovered statistics on the growing number of gang-related crimes across the country, how many result in severe injury and death, and how family members of both victims and gang members are affected.

Analyze the Problem

Once the problem has been identified and defined, it can be analyzed. Again, questions can prove useful: Can the problem be subdivided into a series of smaller problems? Why has the problem occurred? What are the symptoms? What methods already exist for dealing with it? What are the limitations of those methods? Again, these questions are likely to lead group members to conduct additional research. Analyzing the problem this way helps groups discover underlying causes that need to be eliminated to solve the problem.

Matt, Shannon, Pam, and Michelle discovered two important reasons why young people join gangs: for a sense of belonging and for something to do. Analysis revealed how many young gang members come from dysfunctional homes, as well as how many are enticed to join because they aren't involved in other group-related activities such as sports and music. They also discovered two underlying reasons why gang members commit more violent crimes than gangs did twenty years ago: easier access to guns and less ability to control anger. These causes proved important to selecting a solution later.

Determine Criteria for Judging Solutions

Criteria are standards to use for judging the merits of proposed solutions—a blueprint for evaluating them. Without clear criteria, groups may select solutions that don't adequately address the real problem or that create a host of new problems. Questions you might ask when developing criteria include the following: Exactly what must the solutions achieve? Are there any factors that might limit the choice of solutions (cost, feasibility, location, complexity, expedience, risk/benefit ratio, or the like)? With criteria established, prioritize the list. Which factors are most important? Which are least important? Which must be addressed for an ideal solution? Which must be addressed for an adequate solution?

After a good deal of discussion, Matt, Shannon, Pam, and Michelle decided on these criteria:

- *Expedience.* The solutions should be ones that can be implemented quickly, since lives are at stake.
- *Complexity.* The solutions should be simple to implement so they are more likely to be enacted.
- *Cost.* The solutions should not raise taxes.
- *Freedom.* The solutions should not infringe on the constitutional right to bear arms.

Generate a Host of Solutions

Having gained a better understanding as a result of the analysis, members brainstorm a host of possible solutions to the problem. At least one group member should record all these as they are suggested. During brainstorming, it is imperative that group members withhold judgment and criticisms. To ensure that creativity is not stifled, no solution should be ignored or thrown out. Try to come up with at least six or seven solutions before moving on to the next step.

Matt, Shannon, Pam, and Michelle came up with these possible solutions:

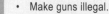

- Make guns illegal.
- Make gang participation a felony punishable by law.
- Make parents accountable for the actions of their children.
- Offer anger management training to children.
- Provide alternative activities for youth.
- Crack down on the illegal gun market.

Select the Best Solution

At this point, judgments come into play. These should be based on the criteria established by the group. Consider each solution as it addresses the criteria and eliminate solutions that do not meet them adequately. In addition to applying the criteria, the group might ask questions such as these when discussing each potential solution: How will the solution solve the problem? How difficult will it be to implement? How likely is it to be successful? What additional benefits might result from implementing it? What problems might be caused? The group can use the criteria and questions to eliminate solutions. Once all the possible solutions have been considered, the group can decide on the best one(s).

Here's what happened with the solutions Matt, Shannon, Pam, and Michelle came up with based on their criteria and these kinds of questions:

WHAT DO YOU THINK?

Have you ever encountered a problem you couldn't solve? Did you seek help or advice? How did it go?

- *Make guns illegal.* The group eliminated this solution because it infringes on the constitutional right to bear arms and because it would not be expedient to implement.
- *Make gang participation a felony punishable by law.* This solution was also eliminated because it would increase taxes, since more prisons would need to be built, and because making it into a law would take a great deal of time.
- *Make parents accountable for the actions of their children.* Because Florida has a model program for making parents accountable, this solution was selected. It meets the criteria adequately.
- *Offer anger management training to children.* Although this seemed like a good idea, it was rejected because it failed to meet three of the four criteria: expedience, complexity, and cost.
- *Provide alternative activities for youth.* This solution was selected because it meets three of the four criteria. Although such programs might increase taxes, the group determined that they could propose programs that would not. So although it did not meet one of the criteria, it did seem adequate.
- *Crack down on the illegal gun market.* Missouri has a program that could be modeled in other states. Hence it could be expedient and fairly simply to duplicate. It was also accepted because it meets three of the four criteria. The only criterion that seemed questionable was cost.

The group members decided to develop a three-part solution. They would argue for parental accountability, a crackdown on the illegal gun market, and alternative programs and activities for adolescents.

Implement the Agreed-Upon Solution

Finally, the group can implement the agreed-upon solution or, if it is presenting the solution to others for implementation, make recommendations for how the solution should be implemented. The group has already considered implementation in terms of deciding which solution(s) should be enacted, but must now fill in the details. What tasks are required by the solution(s)? Who will carry out these tasks? What is a reasonable time frame for implementation generally and for each of the tasks specifically? These details are important to consider before any solution(s) will likely be enacted. Matt, Shannon, Pam, and Michelle created implementation plans both for parental accountability (based on Florida's documents) and cracking down on the illegal gun market (based on Missouri's documents), which could be duplicated in other states. They also provided concrete program ideas and clear strategies for churches, businesses, and service groups to implement for alternative programs for area youth. As such, they didn't merely offer solutions; they provided plans for implementing them.

PRACTICING THE PROCESS

Guidelines for Systematic Problem Solving

- Identify and define the problem.
- Analyze the problem.
- Determine criteria for judging solutions.
- Generate a host of solutions.
- Select the best solution.
- Implement the agreed-upon solution(s).

Student Workbook

Complete the "Reflective Thinking Process Paper" as described in Chapter 4 of your workbook after each small group session you have.

Looking at the Learning Cycle

Systematic Problem Solving

- *Stage 1, feeling/watching:* Identify and define the problem.
- *Stage 2, watching/thinking:* Analyze the problem and determine criteria for judging solutions.
- *Stage 3, thinking/doing:* Generate a host of solutions and select the best solution.
- *Stage 4, doing/feeling:* Implement the agreed-upon solution.

PREPARING GROUP PRESENTATIONS

Once the group has worked through the systematic problem-solving process, it's time to prepare a group presentation. One way is to use a five-step process that starts with dividing the topic into areas of responsibility and practicing the presentation.

Divide the Topic into Areas of Responsibility

As a group, determine your thesis and main point design. Each member can then be responsible for researching and organizing the content necessary to develop a particular main point. If there are more group members than main points, assign more than one person to a topic area or assign one person to develop and integrate presentational aids.

Draft an Outline of Your Topic Area

Each group member should construct an outline for his or her main point. Even though the outline is for only part of the presentation it must still be thorough, so follow the steps for outline creation as detailed in Chapter 10.

Combine Member Outlines to Form a Group Outline

Once the individual outlines are completed, the group is ready to combine them into a single outline. Members should share their individual outlines and then, as a group, develop the transitions between main points and make any other changes needed for continuity and consistency. If no member was responsible for developing the introduction and conclusion, the group should create them now. Likewise, presentational aids should be integrated at this point.

Finalize the Details of Delivery

Because it's a group presentation, more than the usual number of decisions must be made about delivery. First, decide who will speak and when. The next section shows various presentation formats—oral reports, symposium presentations, and panel discussions. Which will you use? Also, details need to be determined if the presentation is to flow smoothly: Who will introduce the speakers and when? Where will group members sit when they are not speaking? How will presentational aids be displayed and who will be responsible for displaying them?

Practice Your Presentation

It is crucial to practice both individually and as a group. Use the delivery guidelines described in Chapter 12. But because group presentations pose additional complexities, there is more to be done and even more need for practice.

PRACTICING THE PROCESS

Guidelines for Preparing Group Presentations

- Divide the topic into areas of responsibility.
- Draft an outline of your topic area.
- Combine member outlines to form a group outline.
- Finalize the details of delivery.
- Practice the presentation.

GROUP PRESENTATION FORMATS

Many problem-solving groups are asked to present findings in both written and oral reports. In a public speaking class, you will probably be asked to present findings in a formal typed outline and some sort of oral presentation. Here are the most common formats for oral group presentations.

Oral Report

Groups that give an **oral report** select one person to present all the group's information in an individual speech. One speaker represents the group, its work, and its results.

Symposium Presentation

In a **symposium presentation,** all members of the group typically present a portion of the information. All members are seated in front of the audience. One member acts as moderator, offering the introductory and concluding remarks and providing transitions between speakers. In a way, the moderator provides the structure for the presentation. When introduced, each speaker moves to the lectern to deliver a speech on the aspect he or she is covering. Each individual speech can also stand on its own because it has its own introduction, body, conclusion, and transitions. After all speakers have finished, the moderator returns to the lectern to offer concluding remarks and possibly open the floor for questions and discussion. Questions can be directed to the group as a whole or to individuals within the group.

The way the group divides the content among speakers depends on how the material was organized. For example, each speaker might focus on one step of the problem-solving process, or on one major issue related to the topic. If the presentation is persuasive, successive speakers might focus on the problem, the cause, and the solution; if it's persuasive and uses Monroe's motivated sequence, successive speakers might demonstrate a need, offer a plan, and visualize the future. Regardless of the organizational pattern chosen, it is important to carefully plan each speaker's segment of the presentation to ensure that all aspects of the group's project are covered.

Panel Discussion

A **panel discussion** is a conversation among members of the group that takes place in front of an audience. Perhaps you've heard a panel of experts discuss a particular topic—for example, on radio or television talk shows such as *Larry King Live* or *SportsCenter.* As in a symposium presentation, a moderator introduces the topic and speakers. The moderator's role is to interject questions and comments throughout the discussion to clarify issues and keep the discussion on track. The panelists speak impromptu and keep their remarks brief. The panel discussion format is less formal than the oral report or symposium presentation, but it too is thoroughly researched in advance and the presentation is planned and practiced, even if in a looser way.

EVALUATING GROUP EFFECTIVENESS

Just as preparation and presentation are different for group speeches than for individual speeches, so is the process of evaluating effectiveness. Evaluations should focus on group dynamics during the preparation process as well as on the effectiveness of the presentation.

Student Workbook

Complete the "Group Dynamics Peer Critique" forms and "Summative Peer Critique" forms in Chapter 4 of your workbook. Turn these in to your instructor on the day your group presents their symposium.

© NBAE/Getty Images

Panel discussion and symposium presentation participants thoroughly research their topics in advance but speak impromptu.

Evaluating Group Dynamics During the Preparation Process

To be effective, groups must work together as they define and analyze a problem, generate solutions, and select a course of action. They also need to work together as they prepare their written report, which in some public speaking classrooms is the formal group outline, and practice the oral presentation.

Hence it is important to evaluate group dynamics as it relates to the eventual outcome—usually the oral presentation. This can be done by obtaining from each group member written feedback on other members' efforts. Such evaluations can be based on the five responsibilities of group members. You'll find a sample of this kind of evaluation form, as well as directions for writing a "Reflective Thinking Process Paper" that can help you assess your group's dynamics, including a self-critique of your role in the process, on this book's Web site under "Resources" for Chapter 18. Like the evaluations business managers make of employees, these document the efforts of group members. They can be submitted to the instructor, just as they would be submitted to a supervisor. In business, these documents provide a basis for determining promotion, merit pay, and salary adjustments. In the classroom, they can provide a basis for determining one portion of each member's grade.

Evaluating Effectiveness of the Presentation

Effective group presentations depend on quality individual presentations as well as the overall effectiveness achieved collectively. Hence evaluation of the presentation should be of each individual and of the group as a whole (Figure 18.2). Again, this is not unlike business, where teams are evaluated on the basis of the usefulness of the team's solution and of individual team members' efforts toward developing and implementing it.

Group Member Name: _____

Critic (your name): _____

Directions: Evaluate the effectiveness of each group member according to each of the following criteria for effective presentations individually and as a group.

Rating Scale:

1	2	3	4	5	6	7
(poor)						(excellent)

INDIVIDUAL PERFORMANCE CRITIQUE

_____ **Delivery** (Use of voice and use of body)
(rating) Critique (Provide a rationale for the rating you gave):

_____ **Structure** (Macrostructure and microstructure/language)
(rating) Critique (Provide a rationale for the rating you gave):

_____ **Content** (Breadth and depth and listener relevance)
(rating) Critique (Provide a rationale for the rating you gave):

GROUP PERFORMANCE CRITIQUE

_____ **Delivery** (Teamwork? Cooperation? Fluency? Use of aids?)
(rating) Critique (Provide a rationale for the rating you gave):

_____ **Structure** (Balanced? Transitions? Flow? Attn/Clincher?)
(rating) Critique (Provide a rationale for the rating you gave):

_____ **Content** (Thematic? Focused? Thorough? Construction of presentational aids?)
(rating) Critique (Provide a rationale for the rating you gave):

Overall Comments:

_____

Figure 18.2 Sample evaluation form for group presentations

Evaluating Your Own Participation

Effective group presentations depend on the combined efforts of individuals. So it's also a good idea to conduct self-evaluations to determine whether you ought to be doing something differently during the problem-solving process, as well as whether you contributed effectively during the presentation. Figure 18.3 is a sample self-evaluation form for your portion of the presentation.

Directions: Complete the items below with regard to your presentation in the group symposium.

1. In terms of delivery, I did the following things well in my oral presentation:

    a.

    b.

2. In terms of content, I did the following things well in my oral presentation:

    a.

    b.

3. In terms of structure, I did the following things well in my oral presentation:

    a.

    b.

4. If I could do my portion of the oral presentation over again, I would do the following things differently:

    a.

    b.

    c.

5. In terms of my role as a group member, I am most proud of how I:

6. In terms of my role as a group member, I am least proud of how I:

7. Overall, I would give myself a grade of _____ for the group speech because:

Figure 18.3   Sample self-critique form for group presentations

SUMMARY

Working in small groups is quickly becoming the preferred approach to solving problems and making decisions in both personal and professional settings. It is therefore important to learn how to work and speak effectively in small groups.

The potential advantages of small group work far outweigh the disadvantages; the ultimate advantage is better solutions. Successful small group work requires understanding leadership and group member functions as well as the processes of group problem solving and preparation of presentations. A problem-solving small group is more effective if it is heterogeneous, relatively small in size (five to seven members), and has a specific goal.

Leadership in small groups consists of a range of diverse functions, ideally shared by group members. These functions are related to meeting task, relational, and housekeeping needs. Although leadership is usually most effective when shared among group members, sometimes a small group does have a specific leader that is designated, emergent, or implied. Leadership styles can be authoritarian, laissez-faire, or democratic. A democratic leadership style generally is the most effective for problem-solving small groups.

All members have certain responsibilities to the group. They must be committed to the group goal, keep the discussion on track, complete individual assignments, manage conflicts among group members, and encourage input from all members.

Problem-solving small groups can also be most effective when they have a clear plan. The systematic problem-solving method consists of six steps designed for this purpose: Identify and define the problem, analyze the problem, determine criteria for judging solutions, generate a host of solutions, select the best solution based on the criteria, and implement the agreed-upon solution.

Group presentation formats include oral reports, symposium presentations, and panel discussions. Regardless of which format a group uses, several steps should be taken in preparing a presentation. Because group presentations differ from individual speeches, the evaluation process also differs: It looks at group dynamics during preparation and at the effectiveness of both the group's and the individual's presentation.

Several essential steps must be taken when preparing and presenting group speeches, whether an oral report, symposium, or panel discussion. Because group presentations differ from individual speeches, the means for evaluating group work also differ.

RETURNING TO TECHNOLOGY

The *Confident Public Speaking* CD-ROM is your one-stop point of access for not just the content on the CD itself, such as Speech Interactive, but also the many other resources on the *Confident Public Speaking* Web site, Speech Builder Express, and InfoTrac College Edition. Note that this chapter's key terms and activities are among the resources available in electronic format online. Additional information is included below.

SPEECH INTERACTIVE
ON THE *CONFIDENT PUBLIC SPEAKING* CD-ROM

Speech Interactive is your link to this text's speech videos. Offering opportunities to practice critiquing speeches by both other students and public speakers who are not students, these videos will help you prepare for providing effective feedback to your peers and your own speech performances.

SPEECH BUILDER EXPRESS

Speech Builder Express can help you prepare your portion of a group presentation, as well as help the group prepare its outline, manage time, and integrate sources and visuals.

KEY TERMS

Interactive flashcards for these key terms are available on the *Confident Public Speaking* Web site. You'll find the "Flashcards" link under the resources for Chapter 18.

ACTIVITIES

The activities below, as well as additional activities, are available in electronic format on the *Confident Public Speaking* Web site. You'll find the "Activities" link under the resources for Chapter 18.

1. **Group Member Role Self-Reports.** If you have formed a group to work on a presentation, review the discussion of group member roles in this chapter. Each member should then write a self-report indicating which

roles might be most appropriate in view of his or her strengths and weaknesses. Discuss the reports and, as a group, identify which members will be most responsible for each of the roles.

2. **Group Sales Pitch.** Form groups of about five persons. Pick an item that someone has with him or her (jewelry, school supply, chewing gum, or the like). As a group, devise a plan to sell that item to the class. To sell it, the group must generate a host of needs it may fulfill for their classmates and then convince classmates of it. After about ten minutes, group members should discuss how the leadership functions were or were not met and by whom. Also discuss how responsibilities of group members were met and how they could be better met in the future. Present your findings to the rest of the class in an oral report.

3. **Leadership Analysis.** Attend a meeting in your community. It can be a group to which you belong or one open to the public. Observe the group dynamics. Try to determine the degree to which each of the task, relational, and housekeeping needs are being met and by whom. That is, which roles are being played and by whom? (Task roles: initiator, expediter, information giver, information seeker, analyzer, evaluator. Relational roles: supporter, harmonizer, gatekeeper. Housekeeping roles: administrator, recorder.)

INFOTRAC COLLEGE EDITION ACTIVITY

Access InfoTrac College Edition to search for articles that present "best practices" for group presentations and accounts of successful group work.

APPENDIX A

LEARNING STYLES QUIZ

Step 1

For each question, circle the letter next to the response that is most like you. Remember there are *no wrong answers*. Work quickly. Record your first thought.

I.   When I purchase a kit that requires some assembly, I am likely to begin by
    A.   soliciting advice and possibly help from someone who has put together a similar item in the past.
    B.   studying the pieces, diagrams, and picture on the package or box.
    C.   reading through all of the directions.
    D.   putting the item together, referring to the directions only when I get stuck.

II.   When I try making a new recipe, I usually like to
    A.   taste it myself first.
    B.   see a picture of it.
    C.   follow the recipe carefully.
    D.   use the recipe as a general guide, modifying it as I go along.

III.   When I make decisions, I usually rely most on my
    A.   feelings.
    B.   observations.
    C.   thoughts.
    D.   actions.

IV.   I tend to enjoy classes most where
    A.   students interact with each other often.
    B.   professors use a lot of visual aids.
    C.   professors lecture most of the time.
    D.   students actively apply concepts themselves.

V.   I tend to be persuaded most when
    A.   I am presented with actual examples and experiences of people.
    B.   I have time to reflect about what I hear.
    C.   I am presented with specific facts and statistics related to the issue.
    D.   I experience issues firsthand.

VI.   If I were asked to choose only one, I'd say I am
    A.   intuitive.
    B.   careful.
    C.   logical.
    D.   responsible.

VII.   I am most likely to enjoy participating in extracurricular activities and functions
    A.   that are new and different.
    B.   that allow me to observe for awhile before joining in.
    C.   that require logical analysis.
    D.   that let me be actively involved.

VIII. I prefer working in an environment where
   - **A.** I can interact with others.
   - **B.** I am able to take time to reflect.
   - **C.** I am challenged to analyze logically.
   - **D.** I have opportunities to apply concepts and try things out.

IX. I especially dislike classes where the main focus is
   - **A.** professors lecturing about abstract concepts.
   - **B.** students doing lots of activities.
   - **C.** students engaging in open-ended discussions.
   - **D.** students taking lots of notes.

X. When discussing ideas with others, I am best at
   - **A.** considering a variety of points of view.
   - **B.** taking time to reflect before responding.
   - **C.** using logic to analyze and evaluate.
   - **D.** getting things done and accomplishing goals.

XI. When learning a new computer software program, I am most likely to begin by
   - **A.** asking for advice from people who've used the program before.
   - **B.** following the directions carefully.
   - **C.** reading through the manual.
   - **D.** experimenting with the program and using the manual only when I get stuck.

XII. When I take a vacation, I particularly enjoy
   - **A.** getting to know the people who live in the place I am visiting and learning from them about their customs and experiences.
   - **B.** taking time to plan each day carefully.
   - **C.** reading as much as possible about each place while I'm there.
   - **D.** experimenting with and trying out new customs, foods, and experiences.

Step 2

Count up the number of "A," "B," "C," and "D" responses you circled and record them in the space provided:

A _____ B _____ C _____ D _____

If you circled mostly As, you tend to prefer to learn by **feeling.**
If you circled mostly Bs, you tend to prefer to learn by **watching.**
If you circled mostly Cs, you tend to prefer to learn by **thinking.**
If you circled mostly Ds, you tend to prefer to learn by **doing.**

Step 3

Add your scores from Step 2 as follows:
A + B =   C + D =
B + C =   A + D =

Step 4

Circle the highest of the four sums from Step 3.
If you circled the A + B score: You tend to be a **diverger** (Stage 1 preference). You prefer to learn by some combination of watching and feeling.
If you circled the B + C score: You tend to be an **assimilator** (Stage 2 preference). You prefer to learn by some combination of watching and thinking.

If you circled the C + D score: You tend to be a **converger** (Stage 3 preference). You prefer to learn by some combination of thinking and doing.

If you circled the A + D score: You tend to be an **accommodator** (Stage 4 preference). You prefer to learn by some combination of doing and feeling.

Step 5

Consider how you will approach the speech preparation and presentation process in ways that address all of these learning styles. Remember, each learning style represents one stage on the cycle.

Stage 1 Preference. You probably want to know *why* you are learning things. You seek a personal connection with the content. So one of your public speaking strengths is the ability to consider things from many points of view. Another public speaking strength is your use of lots of actual *examples*, *testimonies*, and quotations from *interviews* with real people in your speeches.

Stage 2 Preference. You are likely to enjoy absorbing lots of information and strive for an understanding of *what* it means. Your public speaking strengths lie in providing clear *facts*, *statistics*, *definitions*, and *explanations* and in arranging them in a logical and orderly fashion.

Stage 3 Preference. You probably like to see if the facts you learn actually work in daily life. You want to know *how* an idea, strategy, or method works by trying it out. Your public speaking strengths lie in providing *practical applications* for using information to improve current situations, as well as in conceptualizing a *workable solution* to a problem.

Stage 4 Preference. You like to take what you've discovered and figure out *where else* you can use it to *make a difference* in your life and the lives of others. Your public speaking strengths lie in your ability to come up with *new solutions* to old problems. You enjoy interacting with others and probably excel at *delivering* your speech dynamically.

APPENDIX B

....

SPEECHES FOR ANALYSIS AND DISCUSSION

....

....

—Martin Luther King, Jr.
Washington, D.C., August 28, 1963

I am happy to join with you today in what will go down in history as the greatest demonstration for freedom in the history of our nation.

Five score years ago, a great American, in whose symbolic shadow we stand today, signed the Emancipation Proclamation. This momentous decree came as a great beacon light of hope to millions of Negro slaves who had been seared in the flames of withering injustice. It came as a joyous daybreak to end the long night of captivity.

But one hundred years later, the Negro still is not free. One hundred years later, the life of the Negro is still sadly crippled by the manacles of segregation and the chains of discrimination. One hundred years later, the Negro lives on a lonely island of poverty in the midst of a vast ocean of material prosperity. One hundred years later, the Negro is still languishing in the corners of American society and finds himself an exile in his own land.

And so we've come here today to dramatize a shameful condition. In a sense we've come to our nation's Capitol to cash a check. When the architects of our republic wrote the magnificent words of the Constitution and the Declaration of Independence, they were signing a promissory note to which every American was to fall heir. This note was a promise that all men—yes, black men as well as white men—would be guaranteed the unalienable rights of life, liberty, and the pursuit of happiness.

It is obvious today that America has defaulted on this promissory note insofar as her citizens of color are concerned. Instead of honoring this sacred obligation, America has given the Negro people a bad check—a check which has come back marked "insufficient funds."

But we refuse to believe that the bank of justice is bankrupt. We refuse to believe that there are insufficient funds in the great vaults of opportunity of this nation. And so we've come to cash this check—a check that will give us upon demand the riches of freedom and the security of justice.

We have also come to this hallowed spot to remind America of the fierce urgency of now. This is no time to engage in the luxury of cooling off or to take the tranquilizing drug of gradualism. Now is the time to make real the promises of democracy. Now is the time to rise from the dark and desolate valley of segregation to the sunlit path of racial justice. Now is the time to lift our nation from the quicksands of racial injustice to the solid rock of brotherhood. Now is the time to make justice a reality for all of God's children.

It would be fatal for the nation to overlook the urgency of the moment. This sweltering summer of the Negro's legitimate discontent will not pass until there is an invigorating autumn of freedom and equality. Nineteen sixty-three is not an end, but a beginning. Those who hope that the Negro needed to blow off steam and will now be content will have a rude awakening if the nation returns to business as usual. There will be neither rest nor tranquility in America until the Negro is granted his citizenship rights. The whirlwinds of revolt will continue to shake the foundations of our nation until the bright day of justice emerges.

But there is something that I must say to my people, who stand on the warm threshold which leads into the palace of justice. In the process of gaining our

66 rightful place, we must not be guilty of wrongful deeds. Let us not seek to satisfy our thirst for freedom by drinking from the cup of bitterness and hatred.

We must forever conduct our struggle on the high plane of dignity and discipline. We must not allow our creative protest to degenerate into physical violence. Again and again we must rise to the majestic heights of meeting physical force with soul force.

The marvelous new militancy which has engulfed the Negro community must not lead us to a distrust of all white people. For many of our white brothers, as evidenced by their presence here today, have come to realize that their destiny is tied up with our destiny. They have come to realize that their freedom is inextricably bound to our freedom. We cannot walk alone.

As we walk, we must make the pledge that we shall always march ahead. We cannot turn back. There are those who are asking the devotees of civil rights, "When will you be satisfied?" We can never be satisfied as long as a Negro is the victim of the unspeakable horrors of police brutality. We can never be satisfied as long as our bodies, heavy with the fatigue of travel, cannot gain lodging in the motels of the highways and the hotels of the cities. We cannot be satisfied as long as a Negro in Mississippi cannot vote and a Negro in New York believes he has nothing for which to vote. No, no, we are not satisfied, and we will not be satisfied until justice rolls down like waters, and righteousness like a mighty stream.

I am not unmindful that some of you have come here out of great trials and tribulations. Some of you have come fresh from narrow jail cells. Some of you have come from areas where your quest for freedom left you battered by the storms of persecution and staggered by the winds of police brutality. You have been the veterans of creative suffering. Continue to work with the faith that unearned suffering is redemptive.

Go back to Mississippi, go back to Alabama, go back to South Carolina, go back to Georgia, go back to Louisiana, go back to the slums and ghettos of our Northern cities, knowing that somehow this situation can and will be changed. Let us not wallow in the valley of despair.

I say to you today, my friends, so even though we face the difficulties of today and tomorrow, I still have a dream. It is a dream deeply rooted in the American dream.

I have a dream that one day this nation will rise up and live out the true meaning of its creed: "We hold these truths to be self-evident: that all men are created equal."

I have a dream that one day on the red hills of Georgia the sons of former slaves and the sons of former slave owners will be able to sit down together at the table of brotherhood.

I have a dream that one day even the state of Mississippi, a state sweltering with the heat of injustice, sweltering with the heat of oppression, will be transformed into an oasis of freedom and justice.

I have a dream that my four little children will one day live in a nation where they will not be judged by the color of their skin but by the content of their character. I have a dream today.

I have a dream that one day, down in Alabama, with its vicious racists, with its governor having his lips dripping with the words of interposition and nullifi-

(continued)

cation, one day right there in Alabama little black boys and black girls will be able to join hands with little white boys and white girls as sisters and brothers.

I have a dream today.

I have a dream that one day every valley shall be exalted, every hill and mountain shall be made low, the rough places will be made plain and the crooked places will be made straight, and the glory of the Lord shall be revealed, and all flesh shall see it together.

This is our hope. This is the faith that I go back to the South with. With this faith we will be able to hew out of the mountain of despair a stone of hope. With this faith we will be able to transform the jangling discords of our nation into a beautiful symphony of brotherhood. With this faith we will be able to work together, to pray together, to struggle together, to go to jail together, to stand up for freedom together, knowing that we will be free one day.

This will be the day—this will be the day when all of God's children will be able to sing with a new meaning, "My country 'tis of thee, sweet land of liberty, of thee I sing. Land where my fathers died, land of the pilgrim's pride, from every mountainside, let freedom ring." And if America is to be a great nation, this must become true.

So let freedom ring from the prodigious hilltops of New Hampshire. Let freedom ring from the mighty mountains of New York. Let freedom ring from the heightening Alleghenies of Pennsylvania!

Let freedom ring from the snowcapped Rockies of Colorado! Let freedom ring from the curvaceous peaks of California!

But not only that. Let freedom ring from Stone Mountain of Georgia!

Let freedom ring from Lookout Mountain of Tennessee!

Let freedom ring from every hill and every molehill of Mississippi. From every mountainside, let freedom ring.

And when this happens, when we allow freedom to ring—when we let it ring from every village and every hamlet, from every state and every city—we will be able to speed up that day when all of God's children, black men and white men, Jews and Gentiles, Protestants and Catholics, will be able to join hands and sing in the words of the old Negro spiritual, "Free at last! free at last! Thank God Almighty, we are free at last!"

Source: Delivered on the steps of the Lincoln Memorial in Washington, D.C. on August 28, 1963. Reprinted by arrangement with the Estate of Martin Luther King, Jr., c/o Writers House as an agent for the proprietor New York, NY. Copyright 1963 by Martin Luther King, Jr., copyright renewed 1991 by Coretta Scott King.

WHO THEN WILL SPEAK FOR THE COMMON GOOD?: DEMOCRATIC CONVENTION KEYNOTE ADDRESS

—Barbara Jordan, Congresswoman
New York, July 12, 1976

One hundred and forty-four years ago, members of the Democratic Party first met in convention to select a presidential candidate. Since that time, Democrats have continued to convene once every four years and draft a party platform and nominate a presidential candidate. And our meeting this week is a continuation of that tradition.

But there is something different about tonight. There is something special about tonight. What is different? What is special? I, Barbara Jordan, am a keynote speaker.

A lot of years passed since 1832, and during that time it would have been most unusual for any national political party to ask that a Barbara Jordan deliver a keynote address . . . but tonight here I am. And I feel that notwithstanding the past that my presence here is one additional bit of evidence that the American dream need not forever be deferred.

Now that I have this grand distinction what in the world am I supposed to say?

I could easily spend this time praising the accomplishments of this party and attacking the Republicans, but I don't choose to do that.

I could list the many problems which Americans have. I could list the problems which cause people to feel cynical, angry, frustrated: problems which include lack of integrity in government; the feeling that the individual no longer counts; the reality of material and spiritual poverty; the feeling that the grand American experiment is failing or has failed. I could recite these problems and then I could sit down and offer no solutions. But I don't choose to do that either.

The citizens of America expect more. They deserve and they want more than a recital of problems.

We are a people in a quandary about the present. We are a people in search of our future. We are a people in search of a national community.

We are a people trying not only to solve the problems of the present: unemployment, inflation . . . but we are attempting on a larger scale to fulfill the promise of America. We are attempting to fulfill our national purpose; to create and sustain a society in which all of us are equal.

Throughout our history, when people have looked for new ways to solve their problems, and to uphold the principles of this nation, many times they have turned to political parties. They have often turned to the Democratic Party.

What is it, what is it about the Democratic Party that makes it the instrument that people use when they search for ways to shape their future? Well, I believe the answer to that question lies in our concept of governing. Our concept of governing is derived from our view of people. It is a concept deeply rooted in a set of beliefs firmly etched in the national conscience of all of us.

Now what are these beliefs?

First, we believe in equality for all and privileges for none. This is a belief that each American regardless of background has equal standing in the public forum, all of us. Because we believe this idea so firmly, we are inclusive rather than an exclusive party. Let everybody come.

I think it no accident that most of those emigrating to America in the 19th century identified with the Democratic Party. We are a heterogeneous party made up of Americans of diverse backgrounds.

We believe that the people are the source of all governmental power; that the authority of the people is to be extended, not restricted. This can be accomplished only by providing each citizen with every opportunity to participate in the management of the government. They must have that.

We believe that the government which represents the authority of all the people, not just one interest group, but all the people, has an obligation to actively underscore, actively seek to remove those obstacles which would block individual

(continued)

" achievement . . . obstacles emanating from race, sex, economic condition. The government must seek to remove them.

We are a party of innovation. We do not reject our traditions, but we are willing to adapt to changing circumstances, when change we must. We are willing to suffer the discomfort of change in order to achieve a better future.

We have a positive vision of the future founded on the belief that the gap between the promise and reality of America can one day be finally closed. We believe that.

This, my friends, is the bedrock of our concept of governing. This is a part of the reason why Americans have turned to the Democratic Party. These are the foundations upon which a national community can be built.

Let's all understand that these guiding principles cannot be discarded for short-term political gains. They represent what this country is all about. They are indigenous to the American idea. And these are principles which are not negotiable.

In other times, I could stand here and give this kind of exposition on the beliefs of the Democratic Party and that would be enough. But today that is not enough. People want more. That is not sufficient reason for the majority of the people of this country to vote Democratic. We have made mistakes. In our haste to do all things for all people, we did not foresee the full consequences of our actions. And when the people raised their voices, we didn't hear. But our deafness was only a temporary condition, and not an irreversible condition.

Even as I stand here and admit that we have made mistakes I still believe that as the people of America sit in judgment on each party, they will recognize that our mistakes were mistakes of the heart. They'll recognize that.

And now we must look to the future. Let us heed the voice of the people and recognize their common sense. If we do not, we not only blaspheme our political heritage, we ignore the common ties that bind all Americans.

Many fear the future. Many are distrustful of their leaders and believe that their voices are never heard. Many seek only to satisfy their private work wants. To satisfy private interests.

But this is the great danger America faces. That we will cease to be one nation and become instead a collection of interest groups: city against suburb, region against region, individual against individual. Each seeking to satisfy private wants.

If that happens, who then will speak for America?

Who then will speak for the common good?

This is the question which must be answered in 1976.

Are we to be one people bound together by common spirit sharing in a common endeavor or will we become a divided nation?

For all of its uncertainty, we cannot flee the future. We must not become the new puritans and reject our society. We must address and master the future together. It can be done if we restore the belief that we share a sense of national community, that we share a common national endeavor. It can be done.

There is no executive order; there is no law that can require the American people to form a national community. This we must do as individuals and if we do it as individuals, there is no president of the United States who can veto that decision.

As a first step, we must restore our belief in ourselves. We are a generous people so why can't we be generous with each other? We need to take to heart the words spoken by Thomas Jefferson:

> Let us restore to social intercourse the harmony and that affection without which liberty and even life are but dreary things.

A nation is formed by the willingness of each of us to share in the responsibility for upholding the common good.

A government is invigorated when each of us is willing to participate in shaping the future of this nation.

In this election year we must define the common good and begin again to shape a common good and begin again to shape a common future. Let each person do his or her part. If one citizen is unwilling to participate, all of us are going to suffer. For the American idea, though it is shared by all of us, is realized in each one of us.

And now, what are those of us who are elected public officials supposed to do? We call ourselves public servants but I'll tell you this: we as public servants must set an example for the rest of the nation. It is hypocritical for the public official to admonish and exhort the people to uphold the common good. More is required of public officials than slogans and handshakes and press releases. More is required. We must hold ourselves strictly accountable. We must provide the people with a vision of the future.

If we promise as public officials, we must deliver. If we as public officials propose, we must produce. If we say to the American people it is time for you to be sacrificial; sacrifice. If the public official says that, we (public officials) must be the first to give. We must be. And again, if we make mistakes, we must be willing to admit them. We have to do that. What we have to do is strike a balance between the idea, the belief, that government ought to do nothing. Strike a balance.

Let there be no illusions about the difficulty of forming this kind of a national community. It's tough, difficult, not easy. But a spirit of harmony will survive in America only if each of us remembers that we share a common destiny.

I have confidence that we can form this kind of national community.

I have confidence that the Democratic Party can lead the way. I have confidence. We cannot improve on the system of government handed down to us by the founders of the Republic; there is no way to improve upon that. But what we can do is to find new ways to implement that system and realize our destiny.

Now, I began this speech by commenting to you on the uniqueness of a Barbara Jordan making the keynote address. Well, I am going to close my speech by quoting a Republican president and I ask you that as you listen to these words of Abraham Lincoln, relate them to the concept of national community in which every last one of us participates:

> As I would not be a slave, so I would not be a master. This expresses my idea of Democracy. Whatever differs from this, to the extent of the difference is no Democracy.

INAUGURAL ADDRESS

—John F. Kennedy
Washington, D.C., January 20, 1961

Vice President Johnson, Mr. Speaker, Mr. Chief Justice, President Eisenhower, Vice President Nixon, President Truman, reverend clergy, fellow citizens, we observe today not a victory of party but a celebration of freedom—symbolizing an end, as well as a beginning—signifying renewal, as well as change. For I have

(continued)

" sworn before you and Almighty God the same solemn oath our forebears prescribed nearly a century and three-quarters ago.

The world is very different now. For man holds in his mortal hands the power to abolish all forms of human poverty and all forms of human life. And yet the same revolutionary beliefs for which our forebears fought are still at issue around the globe—the belief that the rights of man come not from the generosity of the state, but from the hand of God.

We dare not forget today that we are the heirs of that first revolution. Let the word go forth from this time and place, to friend and foe alike, that the torch has been passed to a new generation of Americans—born in this century, tempered by war, disciplined by a hard and bitter peace, proud of our ancient heritage—and unwilling to witness or permit the slow undoing of those human rights to which this nation has always been committed, and to which we are committed today at home and around the world.

Let every nation know, whether it wishes us well or ill, that we shall pay any price, bear any burden, meet any hardship, support any friend, oppose any foe, in order to assure the survival and the success of liberty.

This much we pledge—and more.

To those old allies whose cultural and spiritual origins we share, we pledge the loyalty of faithful friends. United, there is little we cannot do in a host of cooperative ventures. Divided, there is little we can do—for we dare not meet a powerful challenge, at odds, and split asunder.

To those new states whom we welcome to the ranks of the free, we pledge our word that one form of colonial control shall not have passed away merely to be replaced by a far more iron tyranny. We shall not always expect to find them supporting our view. But we shall always hope to find them strongly supporting their own freedom—and to remember that, in the past, those who foolishly sought power by riding the back of the tiger ended up inside.

To those peoples in the huts and villages across the globe struggling to break the bonds of mass misery, we pledge our best efforts to help them help themselves, for whatever period is required—not because the Communists may be doing it, not because we seek their votes, but because it is right. If a free society cannot help the many who are poor, it cannot save the few who are rich.

To our sister republics south of our border: we offer a special pledge—to convert our good words into good deeds—in a new alliance for progress—to assist free men and free governments in casting off the chains of poverty. But this peaceful revolution of hope cannot become the prey of hostile powers. Let all our neighbors know that we shall join with them to oppose aggression or subversion anywhere in the Americas. And let every other power know that this hemisphere intends to remain the master of its own house.

To that world assembly of sovereign states, the United Nations, our last best hope in an age where the instruments of war have far outpaced the instruments of peace, we renew our pledge of support—to prevent it from becoming merely a forum for invective—to strengthen its shield of the new and the weak—and to enlarge the area in which its writ may run.

Finally, to those nations who would make themselves our adversary, we offer not a pledge but a request: that both sides begin anew the quest for peace, before the dark powers of destruction unleashed by science engulf all humanity in planned or accidental self-destruction.

We dare not tempt them with weakness. For only when our arms are sufficient beyond doubt can we be certain beyond doubt that they will never be employed.

But neither can two great and powerful groups of nations take comfort from our present course—both sides overburdened by the cost of modern weapons, both rightly alarmed by the steady spread of the deadly atom, yet both racing to alter that uncertain balance of terror that stays the hand of mankind's final war.

So let us begin anew—remembering on both sides that civility is not a sign of weakness, and sincerity is always subject to proof. Let us never negotiate out of fear. But let us never fear to negotiate.

Let both sides explore what problems unite us instead of belaboring those problems which divide us.

Let both sides, for the first time, formulate serious and precise proposals for the inspection and control of arms—and bring the absolute power to destroy other nations under the absolute control of all nations.

Let both sides seek to invoke the wonders of science instead of its terrors. Together let us explore the stars, conquer the deserts, eradicate disease, tap the ocean depths, and encourage the arts and commerce.

Let both sides unite to heed in all corners of the earth the command of Isaiah—to "undo the heavy burdens . . . and to let the oppressed go free."

And if a beachhead of cooperation may push back the jungle of suspicion, let both sides join in creating, not a new balance of power, but a new world of law, where the strong are just and the weak secure and the peace preserved.

All this will not be finished in the first one hundred days. Nor will it be finished in the first one thousand days, nor in the life of this administration, nor even perhaps in our lifetime on this planet. But let us begin.

In your hands, my fellow citizens, more than mine, will rest the final success or failure of our course. Since this country was founded, each generation of Americans has been summoned to give testimony to its national loyalty. The graves of young Americans who answered the call to service surround the globe.

Now the trumpet summons us again—not as a call to bear arms, though arms we need; not as a call to battle, though embattled we are—but a call to bear the burden of a long twilight struggle, year in and year out, "rejoicing in hope, patient in tribulation"—a struggle against the common enemies of man: tyranny, poverty, disease, and war itself.

Can we forge against these enemies a grand and global alliance, North and South, East and West, that can assure a more fruitful life for all mankind? Will you join in that historic effort?

In the long history of the world, only a few generations have been granted the role of defending freedom in its hour of maximum danger. I do not shrink from this responsibility—I welcome it. I do not believe that any of us would exchange places with any other people or any other generation. The energy, the faith, the devotion which we bring to this endeavor will light our country and all who serve it—and the glow from that fire can truly light the world.

And so, my fellow Americans: ask not what your country can do for you—ask what you can do for your country.

My fellow citizens of the world: ask not what America will do for you, but what together we can do for the freedom of man.

(continued)

> Finally, whether you are citizens of America or citizens of the world, ask of us here the same high standards of strength and sacrifice which we ask of you. With a good conscience our only sure reward, with history the final judge of our deeds, let us go forth to lead the land we love, asking His blessing and His help, but knowing that here on earth God's work must truly be our own.

" ADDRESS TO THE NATIONAL WOMEN'S RIGHTS CONVENTION, 1855

—Lucy Stone

The last speaker alluded to this movement as being that of a few disappointed women. From the first years to which my memory stretches, I have been a disappointed woman. When, with my brothers, I reached forth after the sources of knowledge, I was reproved with "It isn't fit for you; it doesn't belong to women." Then there was but one college in the world where women were admitted, and that was in Brazil. I would have found my way there, but by the time I was prepared to go, one was opened in the young state of Ohio—the first in the United States where women and negroes could enjoy opportunities with white men. I was disappointed when I came to seek a profession worthy of an immortal being—every employment was closed to me, except those of the teacher, the seamstress, and the housekeeper. In education, in marriage, in religion, in everything, disappointment is the lot of a woman. It shall be the business of my life to deepen this disappointment in every woman's heart until she bows down to it no longer. I wish that women, instead of being walking showcases, instead of begging of their fathers and brothers the latest and gayest new bonnet, would ask of them their rights.

The question of Women's Rights is a practical one. The notion has prevailed that it was only an ephemeral idea: that it was but women claiming the right to smoke cigars in the streets, and to frequent barrooms. Others have supposed it a question of comparative intellect; others still, of sphere. Too much has already been said and written about woman's sphere. Trace all the doctrines to their source and they will be found to have no basis except in the usages and prejudices of the age. This is seen in the fact that what is tolerated in woman in one country is not tolerated in another. In this country women may hold prayer-meetings, etc., but in Mohammedan countries it is written upon their mosques, "Women and dogs, and other impure animals, are not permitted to enter." Wendell Phillips says, "The best and greatest thing one is capable of doing, that is his sphere." I have confidence in the Father to believe that when He gives us the capacity to do anything He does not make a blunder. Leave women, then, to find their sphere. And do not tell us before we are born even, that our province is to cook dinners, darn stockings, and sew on buttons. We are told woman has all the rights she wants; and even women, I am ashamed to say, tell us so. They mistake the politeness of men for rights—seats while men stand in this hall tonight, and their adulations; but these are mere courtesies. We want rights. The flour-merchant, the house-builder, and the postman charge us no less on account of our sex; but when we endeavor to earn money to pay all these, then, indeed, we find the difference. Man, if he have energy, may hew out for himself a path where no mortal has ever trod, held back by nothing but what is in himself; the world is all before him, there to choose; and we are glad for you, brothers, men, that it is so. But the same society that drives forth the young man keeps woman at home—a dependent—working little cats on worsted, and little dogs on punctured paper; but if she goes heartily and bravely to give herself to some worthy purpose, she is out of her sphere and she loses caste. Women working in tailor-shops are paid one-third as much as men. Someone in Philadelphia has stated that women make fine shirts for twelve and a half cents apiece; that no woman can make more than nine a week, and the sum thus earned, after deducting rent, fuel, etc., leaves her just three and a half cents a day for bread. Is it a wonder that women are driven to prostitution? Female teachers in New York are paid fifty dollars a year, and for every such situation there are five hundred applicants. I know not what you believe of God, but I believe He gave yearnings and longings to be filled, and that He did not mean all our time should be devoted to feeding and clothing the body. The present condition of woman causes a horrible perversion of the marriage relation. It is asked of a lady, "Has she married well?" "Oh, yes, her husband is rich." Woman must marry for a home, and you men are the sufferers by this; for a woman who loathes you may marry you because you have the means to get money which she can not have. But when woman can enter the lists with you and make money for her self, she will marry you only for deep and earnest affection.

I am detaining you too long, many of you standing, that I ought to apologize, but women have been wronged so long that I may wrong you a little. [Applause]. A woman undertook in Lowell to sell shoes to ladies. Men laughed at her, but in six years she has run them out, and has a monopoly of the trade. Sarah Tyndale, whose husband was an importer of china, and died bankrupt, continued his business, paid off his debts, and has made a fortune and built the largest china warehouse in the world. [Mrs. Mott here corrected Lucy. Mrs. Tyndale has not the largest china warehouse, but the largest assortment of china in the world.] Mrs. Tyndale, herself, drew the plan of her warehouse, and it is the best plan ever drawn. A laborer to whom the architect showed it, said: "Don't she know e'en as much as some men?" I have seen a woman at manual labor turning out chair-legs in a cabinet-shop with a dress short enough not to drag in the shavings. I wish other women would imitate her in this. It made her hands harder and broader, it is true, but I think a hand with a dollar and a quarter a day in it, better than one with a crossed ninepence. The men in the shop didn't use tobacco, nor swear—they can't do those things where there are women, and we owe it to our brothers to go wherever they work to keep them decent. The widening of woman's sphere is to improve her lot. Let us do it, and if the world scoff, let it scoff—if it sneer, let it sneer—but we will go on emulating the example of the sisters Grimke and Abby Kelly. When they first lectured against slavery they were not listened to as respectfully as you listen to us. So the first female physician meets many difficulties, but to the next the path will be made easy.

Lucretia Mott has been a preacher for years; her right to do so is not questioned among friends. But when Antoinette Brown felt that she was commanded to preach, and to arrest the progress of thousands that were on the road to hell; why, when she applied for ordination they acted as though they had rather the whole world should go to hell, than that Antoinette Brown should be allowed to tell them how to keep out of it. She is now ordained over a parish in the state of New York, but when she meets on the Temperance platform the Rev. John Chambers, or your own Gen. Carey [Applause] they greet her with hisses. Theodore Parker said: "The acorn that the schoolboy carries in his pocket and the squirrel stows in his cheek, has in it the possibility of an oak, able to withstand, for ages, the cold winter and the driving blast." I have seen the acorn men and women, but never the perfect oak; all are but abortions. The young mother, when first the new-

(continued)

66 born babe nestles in her bosom, and a heretofore unknown love springs up in her heart, finds herself unprepared for this new relation in life, and she sends forth the child scarred and dwarfed by her own weakness and imbecility, as no stream can rise higher than its fountain.

66 ## GLORY AND HOPE: LET THERE BE WORK, BREAD, WATER, AND SALT FOR ALL

—Nelson Mandela, President of South Africa
Pretoria, South Africa, May 10, 1994

Your Majesties, Your royal highnesses, distinguished guests, comrades, and friends: Today, all of us do, by our presence here, and by our celebrations in other parts of our country and the world, confer glory and hope to newborn liberty.

Out of the experience of an extraordinary human disaster that lasted too long must be born a society of which all humanity will be proud.

Our daily deeds as ordinary South Africans must produce an actual South African reality that will reinforce humanity's belief in justice, strengthen its confidence in the nobility of the human soul, and sustain all our hopes for a glorious life for all.

All this we owe both to ourselves and to the peoples of the world who are so well represented here today.

To my compatriots, I have no hesitation in saying that each one of us is as intimately attached to the soil of this beautiful country as are the famous jacaranda trees of Pretoria and the mimosa trees of the bushveld.

Each time one of us touches the soil of this land, we feel a sense of personal renewal. The national mood changes as the seasons change.

We are moved by a sense of joy and exhilaration when the grass turns green and the flowers bloom.

That spiritual and physical oneness we all share with this common homeland explains the depth of the pain we all carried in our hearts as we saw our country tear itself apart in a terrible conflict, and as we saw it spurned, outlawed, and isolated by the peoples of the world, precisely because it has become the universal base of the pernicious ideology and practice of racism and racial oppression.

We, the people of South Africa, feel fulfilled that humanity has taken us back into its bosom, that we, who were outlaws not so long ago, have today been given the rare privilege to be host to the nations of the world on our own soil.

We thank all our distinguished international guests for having come to take possession with the people of our country of what is, after all, a common victory for justice, for peace, for human dignity.

We trust that you will continue to stand by us as we tackle the challenges of building peace, prosperity, nonsexism, nonracialism, and democracy.

We deeply appreciate the role that the masses of our people and their democratic, religious, women, youth, business, traditional, and other leaders have played to bring about this conclusion. Not least among them is my Second Deputy President, the Honorable F. W. de Klerk.

We would also like to pay tribute to our security forces, in all their ranks, for the distinguished role they have played in securing our first democratic elections and the transition to democracy, from bloodthirsty forces which still refuse to see the light.

The time for the healing of the wounds has come.

The moment to bridge the chasms that divide us has come.

The time to build is upon us.

We have, at last, achieved our political emancipation. We pledge ourselves to liberate all our people from the continuing bondage of poverty, deprivation, suffering, gender, and other discrimination.

We succeeded to take our last steps to freedom in conditions of relative peace. We commit ourselves to the construction of a complete, just, and lasting peace.

We have triumphed in the effort to implant hope in the breasts of the millions of our people. We enter into a covenant that we shall build the society in which all South Africans, both black and white, will be able to walk tall, without any fear in their hearts, assured of their inalienable right to human dignity—a rainbow nation at peace with itself and the world.

As a token of its commitment to the renewal of our country, the new Interim Government of National Unity will, as a matter of urgency, address the issue of amnesty for various categories of our people who are currently serving terms of imprisonment.

We dedicate this day to all the heroes and heroines in this country and the rest of the world who sacrificed in many ways and surrendered their lives so that we could be free.

Their dreams have become reality. Freedom is their reward.

We are both humbled and elevated by the honor and privilege that you, the people of South Africa, have bestowed on us, as the first president of a united, democratic, nonracial, and nonsexist South Africa, to lead our country out of the valley of darkness.

We understand it still that there is no easy road to freedom.

We know it well that none of us acting alone can achieve success.

We must therefore act together as a united people, for national reconciliation, for nation building, for the birth of a new world.

Let there be justice for all.

Let there be peace for all.

Let there be work, bread, water, and salt for all.

Let each know that for each the body, the mind, and the soul have been freed to fulfill themselves.

Never, never, and never again shall it be that this beautiful land will again experience the oppression of one by another and suffer the indignity of being the skunk of the world.

The sun shall never set on so glorious a human achievement!

Let freedom reign. God bless Africa!

“ THE SHAME OF HUNGER

—Elie Wiesel
Brown University
Providence, Rhode Island, April 5, 1990

A survivor of the concentration camps at Auschwitz and Buchenwald, Elie Wiesel has won a congressional medal and the 1986 Nobel Prize for Peace. He delivered the following speech at Brown University on April 5, 1990.

I have been obsessed with the idea of hunger for years and years because I have seen what hunger can do to human beings. It is the easiest way for a tormenter to dehumanize another human being. When I think of hunger, I see images: emaciated bodies, swollen bellies, long bony arms pleading for mercy, motionless skeletons. How can one look at these images without losing sleep?

And eyes, my God, eyes. Eyes that pierce your consciousness and tear your heart. How can one run away from those eyes? The eyes of a mother who carries her dead child in her arms, not knowing where to go, or where to stop. At one moment you think that she would keep on going, going, going—to the end of the world. Except she wouldn't go very far, for the end of the world, for her, is there. Or the eyes of the old grandfather, who probably wonders where creation had gone wrong, and whether it was all worthwhile to create a family, to have faith in the future, to transmit misery from generation to generation, whether it was worth it to wager on humankind.

And then the eyes of all eyes, the eyes of children, so dark, so immense, so deep, so focused and yet at the same time, so wide and so vague. What do they see? What do hungry children's eyes see? Death? Nothingness? God? And what if their eyes are the eyes of our judges?

Hunger and death, death and starvation, starvation and shame. Poor men and women who yesterday were proud members of their tribes, bearers of ancient culture and lore, and who are now wandering among corpses. What is so horrifying in hunger is that it makes the individual death an anonymous death. In times of hunger, the individual death has lost its uniqueness. Scores of hungry people die daily, and those who mourn for them will die the next day, and the others will have no strength left to mourn.

Hunger in ancient times represented the ultimate malediction to society. Rich and poor, young and old, kings and servants, lived in fear of drought. They joined the priests in prayer for rain. Rain meant harvest, harvest meant food, food meant life, just as lack of food meant death. It still does.

Hunger and humiliation. A hungry person experiences an overwhelming feeling of shame. All desires, all aspirations, all dreams lose their lofty qualities and relate to food alone. I may testify to something I have witnessed, in certain places at certain times, those people who were reduced by hunger, diminished by hunger, they did not think about theology, nor did they think about God or philosophy or literature. They thought of a piece of bread. A piece of bread was, to them, God, because a piece of bread then filled one's universe. Diminished by hunger, man's spirit is diminished as well. His fantasy wanders in quest of bread. His prayer rises toward a bowl of milk.

Thus the shame.

In Hebrew, the word *hunger* is linked to shame. The prophet Ezekiel speaks about "Kherpat raav," the shame of hunger. Of all the diseases, of all the natural

> diseases and catastrophes, the only one that is linked to shame in Scripture is hunger—the shame of hunger. Shame is associated neither with sickness nor even with death, only with hunger. For man can live with pain, but no man ought to endure hunger.

Hunger means torture, the worst kind of torture. The hungry person is tortured by more than one sadist alone. He or she is tortured, every minute, by all men, by all women. And by all the elements surrounding him or her. The wind. The sun. The stars. By the rustling of trees and the silence of night. The minutes that pass so slowly, so slowly. Can you imagine time, can you imagine time, when you are hungry?

And to condone hunger means to accept torture, someone else's torture.

Hunger is isolating; it may not and cannot be experienced vicariously. He who never felt hunger can never know its real effects, both tangible and intangible. Hunger defies imagination; it even defies memory. Hunger is felt only in the present.

There is a story about the great French-Jewish composer Daniel Halevy who met a poor poet: "Is it true," he asked, "that you endured hunger in your youth?" "Yes," said the poet. "I envy you," said the composer, "I never felt hunger."

And Gaston Bachelard, the famous philosopher, voiced his view on the matter, saying, "My prayer to heaven is not, 'Oh God, give us our daily bread,' but give us our daily hunger."

I don't find these anecdotes funny. These anecdotes were told about and by people who were not hungry. There is no romanticism in hunger, there is no beauty in hunger, no creativity in hunger. There is no aspiration in hunger. Only shame. And solitude. Hunger creates its own prison walls; it is impossible to demolish them, to avoid them, to ignore them.

Thus, if hunger inspires anything at all, it is, and must be, only the war against hunger.

Hunger is not a matter of choice. Of course, you may say, but what about the hunger striker? Haven't they chosen to deprive themselves of nourishment, aren't they hungry? Yes, but not the same way. First, they suffer alone; those around them do not. Second, they are given the possibility to stop any time they so choose, any time they will, any time their cause is attained. Not so [with] the people in Africa. Not so [with] the people in Asia. Their hunger is irrevocable. And last, hunger strikers confer a meaning, a purpose, upon their ordeal. Not so [with] the victims in Ethiopia or Sudan. Their hunger is senseless. And implacable.

The worst stage in hunger is to see its reflection in one's brother, one's father, one's child. Hunger renders powerless those who suffer its consequences. Can you imagine a mother unable, helpless, to alleviate her child's agony? There is the abyss in shame. There, suffering and hunger and shame multiply.

In times of hunger, family relations break down. The father is impotent, his authority gone, the mother is desperate, and the children, the children, under the weight of accumulated suffering and hunger, grow older and older, and soon, they will be older than their grandparents.

But then, on the other hand, perhaps of all of the woes that threaten and plague the human condition, hunger alone can be curtailed, attenuated, appeased, and ultimately vanquished, not by destiny, nor by the heavens, but by human beings. We cannot fight earthquakes, but we can fight hunger. Hence our responsibility for its victims. *Responsibility* is the key word. Our tradition emphasizes the question, rather than the answer. For there is a "quest" in question, but there is

(continued)

> "response" in responsibility. And this responsibility is what makes us human, or the lack of it, inhuman.

Hunger differs from other cataclysms such as floods in that it can be prevented or stopped so easily. One gesture of generosity, one act of humanity, may put an end to it, at least for one person. A piece of bread, a bowl of rice or soup makes a difference. And I wonder, what would happen, just imagine, what would happen, if every nation, every industrialized or non-industrialized nation, would simply decide to sell one aircraft, and for the money, feed the hungry. Why shouldn't they? Why shouldn't the next economic summit, which includes the wealthiest, most powerful, the richest nations in the world, why shouldn't they decide that since there are so many aircrafts, why shouldn't they say: "Let's sell just one, just one, to take care of the shame and the hunger and the suffering of millions of people."

So the prophet's expression, "the shame of hunger," must be understood differently. When we speak of our responsibility for the hungry, we must go to the next step and say that the expression "shame of hunger" does not apply to the hungry. It applies to those who refuse to help the hungry. Shame on those who could feed *the hungry*, but are too busy to do so.

Millions of human beings constantly are threatened in Africa and Asia, and even in our own country, the homeless and the hungry. Many are going to die of starvation, and it will be our fault. For we could save them, and if we do not, we had better have a good reason why we don't.

If we could airlift food and sustenance and toothpaste to Berlin in 1948, surely we could do as much for all the countries, Ethiopia and Sudan and Mozambique and Bangladesh, in the year 1990. Nations capable of sending and retrieving vehicles in space must be able to save human lives on earth.

Let our country, and then other countries, see in hunger an emergency that must be dealt with right now. Others, our allies, will follow. Private relief often has been mobilized in the past: Jews and Christians, Moslems and Buddhists have responded to dramatic appeals from the African desert. One of my most rewarding moments was when I went to the Cambodian border ten years ago and saw there the misery, the weakness, the despair, the resignation, of the victims.

But I also saw the extraordinary international community motivated by global solidarity to help them. And who were they? They represented humankind at its best: There were Jews and Christians and Moslems and Buddhists from all over the world. And if ever I felt proud of the human condition, it was then. It is possible to help, but private help is insufficient. Government-organized help is required; only governments can really help solve this tragedy that has cosmic repercussions.

We must save the victims of hunger simply because they can be saved. We look therefore at the horror-filled pictures, when we dare to look, day after day. And I cannot help but remember those who had surrounded us elsewhere, years and years ago. Oh, I do not wish to make comparisons. I never do. But I do have the right to invoke the past, not as a point of analogy, but as a term of reference. I refuse to draw analogies with the Jewish tragedy during the era of darkness; I still believe and will always believe that no event ought to be compared to that event. But I do believe that human tragedies, all human tragedies, are and must be related to it. In other words, it is because one people has been singled out for extinction that others were marked for slavery. It is because entire communities were wiped out then that others were condemned to die later in other parts of the planet. All events are intertwined.

> And it is because we have known hunger that we must eliminate hunger. It is because we have been subjected to shame that we must now oppose shame. It is because we have witnessed humanity at its worst that we must now appeal to humanity at its best.

CIVILITY WITHOUT CENSORSHIP: THE ETHICS OF THE INTERNET—CYBERHATE

—*Raymond W. Smith, Chairman of Bell Atlantic Corporation*
Los Angeles, California, December 1, 1998

Thank you, Rabbi Cooper, for the gracious introduction . . . and let me acknowledge the tremendous contributions the Museum and the Center have made toward harmonizing race relations and advancing equality and justice. We're truly honored that you would include us in today's program.

For the past two years, I've been using the "bully pulpit" to alert various civil rights leaders and organizations (like Martin Luther King III and the NAACP) of the dangers posed by cyberhate. If not for the early groundbreaking work by the Simon Wiesenthal Center, I doubt whether I would have even known of this growing threat. Thank you for warning us—and now, for showing us—how extremists are using the Internet for their own purposes.

When thinking about this morning's topic, I can't help but mention a cartoon that recently appeared in the newspapers. Through the doorway, a mother calls out to her teenager—who is surrounded by high-tech equipment—"I hope you're not watching sex stuff on the Internet!" To which her son replies, "Naw, I'm getting it on TV!"

Until recently, the chief concern of parents was pornography—kids' access to it over the Web and the fear of sexual predators cruising cyberspace. Now, we're worried about hate mongers reaching out to our children in digital space.

As we have just seen and heard, Neo-Nazis and extremists of every political stripe who once terrorized people in the dead of night with burning crosses and painted swastikas are now sneaking up on the public—especially our kids— through the World Wide Web.

As cyberhate is nothing less than the attempt to corrupt public discourse on race and ethnicity via the Internet, many people see censorship of Web sites and Net content as the only viable way to meet this growing threat.

I disagree.

Instead of fearing the Internet's reach, we need to embrace it—to value its ability to connect our children to the wealth of positive human experience and knowledge. While there is, to quote one critic, "every form of diseased intelligence" in digital space, we must remember that it comprises only a small fraction of cyberspace. The Internet provides our children unlimited possibilities for learning and education—the great libraries, cities, and cultures of the world also await them at just the click of a mouse key.

(continued)

"   In short, we need to think about ways to keep cyberhate off the screen, and more about ways to meet it head on: which translates into fighting destructive rhetoric with constructive dialogue—hate speech with truth—restrictions with greater Internet access.

This morning then, I would like to discuss with you the options that are available to combat cyberhate that don't endanger our First Amendment guarantees—and that remain true to our commitment to free speech.

That people and institutions should call for a strict ban on language over the Web that could be considered racist, anti-Semitic, or bigoted is totally understandable. None of us was truly prepared for the emergence of multiple hate-group Web sites (especially those geared toward children), or the quick adoption of high-technology by skinheads and others to market their digital cargo across state lines and international datelines at the speed of light.

One possible reason some people feel inclined to treat the Internet more severely than other media is that the technology is new and hard to understand. Also, the Internet's global reach and ubiquitous nature make it appear ominous. As Justice Gabriel Bach, of Israel, noted, this ability makes it especially dangerous. "I'm frightened stiff by the Internet," he said. "Billions of people all over the world have access to it."

My industry has seen all this before.

The clash between free speech and information technology is actually quite an old one. Nearly a century ago, telephone companies, courts, and the Congress debated whether "common earners" (public phone companies) were obligated to carry all talk equally, regardless of content. And in the end—though some believed that the phone would do everything from eliminate Southern accents and increase Northern labor unrest—free speech won out in the courts.

Whatever the technology, be it the radio or the silver screen, history teaches us that white supremacists, anti-Semites, and others will unfortunately come to grasp, relatively early on, a new medium's potential.

We simply can't condemn a whole technology because we fear that a Father Coughlin or a Leni Riefenstahl (early pioneers in the use of radio and film to advance anti-Semitism or Hitler's Reich) is waiting in the wings to use the latest technology to their own advantage. Nor can we expect the Congress, the federal government, or an international regulatory agency to tightly regulate cyberspace content in order to stymie language we find offensive.

The wisdom of further empowering such organizations and agencies like the FCC or the United Nations aside, it is highly doubtful even if they had the authority, that they would have the ability to truly stem the flow of racist and anti-Semitic language on the World Wide Web.

Anybody with a phone line, computer, and Internet connection can set up a Web site—even broadcast over the Net.

Even if discovered, and banned, online hate groups can easily jump Internet service providers and national boundaries to avoid accountability. I think cyber guru, Peter Huber, got it right when he said, "To censor Internet filth at its origins, we would have to enlist the Joint Chiefs of Staff, who could start by invading Sweden and Holland."

Then there is the whole matter of disguise. Innocent sounding URLs (handles or Web site names) can fool even the most traveled or seasoned "cybernaut."

As for efforts on Capitol Hill and elsewhere to legislate all so-called "offensive" language off the Internet, here again, we can expect the courts to knock down any attempts to curtail First Amendment rights on the Internet. As the Supreme Court

66 ruled last year when it struck down legislation restricting the transmission of "indecent" material online: (To Quote) "Regardless of the strength of the government's interest, the level of discourse reaching a mailbox simply cannot be limited to what is suitable for a sandbox."

In short, although the temptation is great to look to legislation and regulation as a remedy to cyberhate, our commitment to free speech must always take precedent over our fears.

So, cyberhate will not be defeated by the stroke of a pen.

Now, this is not to say that, because we place such a high value on our First Amendment rights, we can't do anything to combat the proliferation of hate sites on the Internet or protect young minds from such threatening and bigoted language.

Law enforcement agencies and state legislators can use existing laws against stalking and telephone harassment to go after those who abuse e-mail . . . parents can install software filtering programs (such as the Anti-Defamation League's HateFilter, or the one Bell Atlantic uses, CyberPatrol) to block access to questionable Internet sites . . . schools and libraries can protect children by teaching them how to properly use the Internet and challenge cyberhate . . . and Internet Service Providers can voluntarily decline to host hate sites. (Bell Atlantic Internet Services, for instance, reserves the right to decline or terminate service which "espouses, promotes, or incites bigotry, hatred, or racism.")

Given that today's panel has representatives from state government, law enforcement, the courts, and the Internet industry, we can discuss these initiatives later in more detail. The point is, there are other ways besides empowering national or international oversight agencies, or drafting draconian legislation, to lessen the impact of cyberhate.

Freedom, not censorship, is the only way to combat this threat to civility. In short, more speech—not less—is needed on the World Wide Web.

In fact, the best answer to cyberhate lies in the use of information technology itself. As a reporter for the *Boston Globe* recently concluded, (quote) "The same technology that provides a forum for extremists, enables civil rights groups and individuals to mobilize a response in unprecedented ways."

We totally agree.

Our prescription to cyberhate is therefore rather simple, but far-reaching in its approach:

The first component is access: if we're to get to a higher level of national understanding on racial and ethnic issues—and strike at the very roots of cyberhate—we must see that no minority group or community is left out of cyberspace for want of a simple Internet connection or basic computer.

At Bell Atlantic, we've been working very hard to provide the minority communities we serve with Internet access. Across our region, thousands of inner-city schools, libraries, colleges, and community groups are now getting connected to cyberspace through a variety of our foundation and state grant programs. Also, our employees have been in the forefront of volunteering their time and energy to wire schools to the Internet during specially designated "Net" days.

Internet access alone, however, won't build bridges of understanding between people—or level the playing field between cyber-haters and the targets of their hate.

The second thing we must do is make sure the Web's content is enriched by minority culture and beliefs, and that there are more Web sites and home pages

(continued)

" dedicated to meeting head-on the racist caricatures and pseudo history often found in cyberspace.

While cyberhate cannot be mandated or censored out of existence, it can be countered by creating hundreds of chatlines, home pages, bulletin boards, and Web sites dedicated to social justice, tolerance, and equality—for all people regardless of race, nationality, or sexual orientation.

Over the past two years, Bell Atlantic has helped a number of minority and civil rights groups launch and maintain their Web sites (like the NAACP, the Leadership Council on Civil Rights, and the National Council of La Raza), and we've done the same for dozens of smaller cultural organizations (like the Harlem Studio Museum and El Museo del Barrio).

We believe that kind of moral leadership can have a tremendous impact. Quite simply, we need more Simon Wiesenthal Centers, Anti-Defamation Leagues, and Southern Poverty Law Centers monitoring and responding to cyberhate.

If we're to bring the struggle for human decency and dignity into cyberspace, we must see that the two most powerful revolutions of the twentieth century— those of civil rights and information technology—are linked even closer together.

Finally, we need to drive real-time, serious dialogue on the religious, ethnic, and cultural concerns that divide us as a nation—a task for which the Internet is particularly suited.

Precisely because it is anonymous, the Internet provides a perfect forum to discuss race, sexual orientation, and other similar issues. On the Internet, said one user, "you can speak freely and not have fears that somebody is going to attack you for what comes out of your heart." It's the kind of open and heart-felt discussion that we need to advance and sponsor online.

Already, a number of small groups and lone individuals are meeting the cyberhate challenge through simple dialogue between strangers. I'm talking about Web sites run by educators to inform parents about online hate materials . . . sites operated by "recovering" racists to engage skinheads and other misguided kids in productive debate . . . Web sites run by concerned citizens to bridge the gap in ignorance between ethnic, racial, and other communities.

The "Y? forum," also known as the National Forum on People's Differences, is a wonderful example of a Web site where readers can safely ask and follow discussions on sensitive cross-cultural topics without having to wade through foul language or "flame wars."

As a columnist from the *Miami Herald* described the appeal of these kinds of sites: "As long as we are mysteries, one to another, we face a perpetuation of ignorance and a feeding of fear. I'd rather people ask the questions than try to make up the answers. I'd rather they ask the questions than turn to myth and call it truth."

In closing, my company recognizes that the Internet doesn't operate in a vacuum. We agree that those who profit from information technology have a special responsibility to see that its promise is shared across class, race, and geographic boundaries.

That's why we're working with the public schools and libraries in our region to see that they're all equipped with the pens, pencils, and paper of the twenty-first century . . . why we're helping to further distance learning and telemedicine applications that serve the educational and health needs of the disabled and isolated . . . why we're helping minority groups and civil rights organizations use information technology to spread their vision and their values to the millions of people electronically linked to the global village.

66 And that's the way it should be.

Let me leave you with a personal story. . . .

When growing up, my Jewish friends and I often swapped theology tales from the Hassidic Masters for stories from the Lives of the Saints. I remember from these discussions that one of the great Rabbis noted that the first word of the Ten Commandments is "I" and the last word is "neighbor." In typical Talmundic fashion, the Rabbi was telling us that if we want to incorporate the Commandments into our lives, we must move from a focus on ourselves to others.

At Bell Atlantic, the more we grow—in both scale and scope—the greater the emphasis we place on being a good corporate citizen, and the more we're driven to see that digital technology is used for purposes of enlightenment and education.

The Internet will fundamentally transform the way we work, learn, do commerce. It will also, if properly used and rightly taught, help bridge the gap in understanding between communities—becoming not a tool of hate, but one of hope.

Thank you again for the invitation to join you this morning.

Copyright 1999 City News Publishing Company Inc. Address by Raymond W. Smith, Chairman, Bell Atlantic Corporation. Reprinted with permission of Vital Speeches of the Day. Delivered at the Simon Wiesenthal Center/Museum of Tolerance, Los Angeles, California, December 1, 1998.

66 WHISPER OF AIDS

—Mary Fisher

Less than three months ago, at platform hearings in Salt Lake City, I asked the Republican Party to lift the shroud of silence which has been draped over the issue of HIV/AIDS. I have come tonight to bring our silence to an end.

I hear a message of challenge, not self-congratulation. I want your attention, not your applause. I would never have asked to be HIV-positive. But I believe that in all things there is a good purpose, and so I stand before you, and before the nation, gladly.

The reality of AIDS is brutally clear. Two hundred thousand Americans are dead or dying; a million more are infected. Worldwide, forty million, or sixty million, or a hundred million infections will be counted in the coming few years. But despite science and research, White House meetings and congressional hearings; despite good intentions and bold initiatives, campaign slogans and hopeful promises—despite it all, it's the epidemic which is winning tonight.

In the context of an election year, I ask you—here, in this great hall, or listening in the quiet of your home— to recognize that the AIDS virus is not a political creature. It does not care whether you are Democrat or Republican. It does not ask whether you are black or white, male or female, gay or straight, young or old.

Tonight, I represent an AIDS community whose members have been reluctantly drafted from every segment of American society. Though I am white, and a mother, I am one with a black infant struggling with tubes in a Philadelphia hospital. Though I am female, and contracted this disease in marriage, and enjoy the

(continued)

warm support of my family, I am one with the lonely gay man sheltering a flickering candle from the cold wind of his family's rejection.

This is not a distant threat; it is a present danger. The rate of infection is increasing fastest among women and children. Largely unknown a decade ago, AIDS is the third leading killer of young-adult Americans today—but it won't be third for long. Because, unlike other diseases, this one travels. Adolescents don't give each other cancer or heart disease because they believe they are in love. But HIV is different. And we have helped it along—we have killed each other—with our ignorance, our prejudice, and our silence.

We may take refuge in our stereotypes, but we cannot hide there long. Because HIV asks only one thing of those it attacks: Are you human? And this is the right question: Are you human? Because people with HIV have not entered some alien state of being. They are human. They have not earned cruelty and they do not deserve meanness. They don't benefit from being isolated or treated as outcasts. Each of them is exactly what God made: a person. Not evil, deserving of our judgment; not victims, longing for our pity. People. Ready for support and worthy of compassion.

My call to you, my Party, is to take a public stand no less compassionate than that of the President and Mrs. Bush. They have embraced me and my family in memorable ways. In the place of judgment, they have shown affection. In difficult moments, they have raised our spirits. In the darkest hours, I have seen them reaching out not only to me, but also to my parents, armed with that stunning grief and special grace that comes only to parents who have themselves leaned too long over the bedside of a dying child.

With the President's leadership, much good has been done; much of the good has gone unheralded; as the President has insisted, "Much remains to be done."

But we do the President's cause no good if we praise the American family but ignore a virus that destroys it. We must be consistent if we are to be believed. We cannot love justice and ignore prejudice, love our children and fear to teach them. Whatever our role, as parent or policy maker, we must act as eloquently as we speak—else we have no integrity.

My call to the nation is a plea for awareness. If you believe you are safe, you are in danger. Because I was not hemophiliac, I was not at risk. Because I was not gay, I was not at risk. Because I did not inject drugs, I was not at risk.

My father has devoted much of his lifetime to guarding against another holocaust. He is part of the generation who heard Pastor Niemoeller come out of the Nazi death camps to say, "They came after the Jews and I was not a Jew, so I did not protest. They came after the Trade Unionists, and I was not a Trade Unionist, so I did not protest. They came after the Roman Catholics, and I was not a Roman Catholic, so I did not protest. Then they came after me, and there was no one left to protest."

The lesson history teaches is this: If you believe you are safe, you are at risk. If you do not see this killer stalking your children, look again. There is no family or community, no race or religion, no place left in America that is safe. Until we genuinely embrace this message, we are a nation at risk.

Tonight, HIV marches resolutely toward AIDS in more than a million American homes, littering its pathway with the bodies of the young. Young men. Young women. Young parents. Young children. One of the families is mine. If it is true that HIV inevitably turns to AIDS, then my children will inevitably turn to orphans.

" My family has been a rock of support. My eighty-four-year-old father, who has pursued the healing of nations, will not accept the premise that he cannot heal his daughter. My mother has refused to be broken; she still calls at midnight to tell wonderful jokes that make me laugh. Sisters and friends, and my brother Phillip (whose birthday is today)—all have helped carry me over the hardest places. I am blessed, richly and deeply blessed, to have such a family.

But not all of you have been so blessed. You are HIV-positive but dare not say it. You have lost loved ones, but you dared not whisper the word AIDS. You weep silently; you grieve alone.

I have a message for you: It is not you who should feel shame; it is we. We who tolerate ignorance and practice prejudice, we who have taught you to fear. We must lift our shroud of silence, making it safe for you to reach out for compassion. It is our task to seek safety for our children, not in quiet denial but in effective action.

Some day our children will be grown. My son Max, now four, will take the measure of his mother; my son Zachary, now two, will sort through his memories. I may not be here to hear their judgments, but I know already what I hope they are.

I want my children to know that their mother was not a victim. She was a messenger. I do not want them to think, as I once did, that courage is the absence of fear; I want them to know that courage is the strength to act wisely when most we are afraid. I want them to have the courage to step forward when called by their nation, or their Party, and give leadership—no matter what the personal cost. I ask no more of you than I ask of myself, or of my children.

To the millions of you who are grieving, who are frightened, who have suffered the ravages of AIDS firsthand: Have courage and you will find comfort.

To the millions who are strong, I issue this plea: Set aside prejudice and politics to make room for compassion and sound policy.

To my children, I make this pledge: I will not give in, Zachary, because I draw my courage from you. Your silly giggle gives me hope. Your gentle prayers give me strength. And you, my child, give me reason to say to America, "You are at risk." And I will not rest, Max, until I have done all I can to make your world safe. I will seek a place where intimacy is not the prelude to suffering.

I will not hurry to leave you, my children. But when I go, I pray that you will not suffer shame on my account.

To all within the sound of my voice, I appeal: Learn with me the lessons of history and of grace, so my children will not be afraid to say the word AIDS when I am gone. Then their children, and yours, may not need to whisper it at all.

God bless the children, and bless us all.

Mary Fisher, Republican National Convention, Houston, Texas, August 19, 1992. Reprinted with permission

GLOSSARY

Academic journals: publish articles by professional researchers and educators

Accommodators: learners who tend to prefer concrete experience (feeling) and active experimentation (doing)

Accuracy: using words that precisely convey the meaning intended

Active sentence: the subject *performs* the action

Actual example: a short story about an event that actually occurred

Actuate: move someone to action

Actuation persuasive speech: designed to influence behavior

Ad hominem: fallacy in which a speaker attacks personal characteristics of the opponent rather than the issue at hand

Administrator: determines where and when the group will meet

Alliteration: the repetition of sounds at the beginning of words that are near one another

Analogical reasoning: strategy that links two concepts together and claims that what is true of one will—by comparison—also be true of the other

Analogy: an extended metaphor; a comparison drawn between two essentially unrelated concepts or objects

Analyzer: helps the group relate the evidence provided by the information giver to the issues that are at the core of the problem

Antithesis: combining contrasting ideas in the same sentence

Apathy barrier: the tendency of listeners to be indifferent toward a speech

Appeal to tradition: fallacy in which a speaker opposes change and defends the status quo simply because that's the way it's always been done

Appreciative listening: listening for enjoyment through the works and experiences of others

Argument: articulating a position with the support of evidence and reasoning

Assimilators: learners who tend to prefer abstract conceptualization (thinking) and reflective observation (watching and listening)

Assonance: the repetition of vowel sounds in the words of a phrase or sentence

Attention catcher: material in the introduction that grabs listeners' attention and relates to the topic

Attitude: a predisposition to respond favorably or unfavorably to something, to like or dislike it

Audience analysis: a process of finding out who the listeners are and adapting the speech to their needs and interests

Audience-based communication apprehension: a tendency to feel anxious about communicating with a certain person or group of people

Audience-centered: considering who the audience members are and tailoring the message to their interests, desires, and needs

Audience contact: a way of establishing eye contact in a large auditorium; speakers must create a sense of looking listeners in the eye even though they cannot actually do so

Audio aids: audiotaped excerpts of music, conversations, environmental sounds, speeches, and so on

Audiovisual aids: presentational aids that combine sight and sound

Auditory channel: what the receivers hear

Auditory distraction: associated with something someone hears

Authoritarian leadership style: directive, controlling, and dictatorial

Bandwagon: fallacy in which something is presented as popular and therefore good or desirable

Bar graphs: consist of parallel bars with lengths proportional to specific quantities; they highlight comparisons between two or more items

Belief: something one accepts as true or false, even though neither can be shown

Bias-free language: demonstrates through language choices a concern for fairness and respect for different groups, based on race, gender, or ethnicity, as well as different identities and worldviews

Brainstorming: a process of generating as many ideas as possible; used in the topic selection and narrowing process to generate ideas for potential topics

Breadth: the variety of different pieces of evidence used to explain the main points

Brief example: short, specific instance offered to illustrate a point

Browsers: a doorway into the World Wide Web, for example, Netscape Navigator, Internet Explorer, and Mosaic

Call to action: specific steps a persuasive speaker asks listeners to take to bring about a change

Card playing: a process of brainstorming in which ones put each idea on a separate index card or slip of paper

Causal pattern: main points are organized in a way that shows a cause-and-effect relationship

Channels: pathways through which messages are communicated between sender and receiver

Character: being perceived as trust-worthy, honest, and sincere, as well as engaging, likable, and attractive

Chronemics: socially constructed perceptions about time

Chronological pattern: the main points follow a time sequence

Claim of fact: states that something is true—that is, it takes a position on something that is not known but can be argued for

Claim of policy: states a position about whether a specific course of action should be taken

Claim of value: judges whether some concept or action is good, right, moral, fair, or better than some other concept or action

Cliché: an overused expression

Clincher: a final statement that reinforces the main ideas, provides closure to the speech, and ties back to the introduction

Closed-ended question: question that elicits a small range of specific answers

Coactive approach: a strategic method for confronting reluctant audiences intelligently and constructively

Cognitive distortions: unrealistic negative statements about oneself resulting in judging one's public speaking experience harshly, even if the experience goes well

Cognitive restructuring: a process to help a person systematically rebuild thoughts about public speaking

Comic timing: pausing the right length of time to allow for applause and laughter

Commemorative address: a speech of tribute that inspires listeners by remembering accomplishments and setting new goals

Commencement address: a speech of tribute praising graduating students and congratulating them on their academic achievements

Common ground: a technique for bolstering ethos by identifying with the audience by talking about shared beliefs and values related to the argument

Communication: the process of sending and receiving verbal and nonverbal messages to create shared meaning

Communication apprehension: the fear or anxiety associated with real or anticipated communication with others

Communication orientation: approaching a public speech as a message one are trying to get across to listeners rather than as a performance

Communication rules: guides for what is appropriate in a situation based on place, time, occasion, and cultural context

Communication situation: the particular context within which communication occurs

Comparative advantages pattern: a main point arrangement that leads the audience to agree with the disposition that one of two or more alternatives is better than the others

Competence: perception of being well informed, skilled, or knowledgeable about the subject

Comprehensive listening: listening for understanding

Concept mapping: a visual means of exploring connections between a topic and related ideas

Concrete words: refer to tangible people, places, and things

Conflict: disagreement over issues or courses of action to be taken

Connectives: words or phrases that serve as glue to hold the speech together

Connotation: what a word suggests or implies

Constructive criticism: criticism in which comments are specific, are about the speech rather than the speaker, are accompanied by a rationale, and are phrased as personal opinions using "I" language

Content: the actual ideas in the speech

Context-based communication apprehension: a tendency to feel anxious about communication in a particular setting

Controlled nervousness: to control anxiety and turn it into positive energy that can actually enhance delivery

Convergers: learners who tend to prefer abstract conceptualization (thinking) and active experimentation (doing)

Conversational: sounding and looking as though one is *talking with* listeners rather than presenting in front of them or reading to them

Credentials: pieces of evidence that qualify one as an authority

Credible evidence: information that seems both believable and reliable

Critical listening: listening that includes hearing, understanding, evaluating, and assigning worth to a message

Current evidence: information that is not outdated

Decoding: attaching meanings to symbols

Dedication: a speech of tribute that honors a worthy person or group by naming a structure such as a building, monument, or park after the honoree

Deductive reasoning: strategy that starts with a generally agreed-upon major premise and then demonstrates how a point or example—or minor premise—fits within that general principle

Definition: statement that clarifies the meaning of a word or phrase

Delivery: the way speakers communicate messages orally and visually through their voice, face, and body

Democratic leadership style: directive but not rigid

Demographic characteristics: characteristics of an audience such as age, sex, gender, sexual orientation, race, ethnicity, and sociocultural background

Denotation: the dictionary definition of a word

Depth: the level of detail of the evidence

Derived credibility: perception of credibility attained by what a speaker says and does during the speech itself

Description: statement that attempts to create a picture of something for listeners

Designated leader: a person who is appointed as leader

Diagram: a type of drawing used to show a whole and its parts

Dialect: a regional variety of a language

Direct question: a question that requests an overt response from listeners

Direct quotation: material lifted verbatim from a particular document

Directory: a human-edited Web search index

Discriminative listening: listening "between the lines"

Discussion board: an online "bulletin board" where people post, read, and respond to messages

Dispositional persuasive speech: designed to influence listeners' beliefs, attitudes, or values toward the topic

Divergers: learners who tend to prefer concrete experience (feeling) and reflective observation (watching and listening)

Either-or: fallacy in which a speaker argues that there are only two approaches to a problem when, in fact, more exist

Emergent leader: someone who takes the initiative to act as leader

Empathic listening: listening to support, help, and empathize with the speaker

Encoding: putting ideas into symbols

Enunciation: the act of speaking distinctly and clearly; how crisply vowel and consonant sounds are formed

Environmental characteristics: factors that influence why listeners attend and what they expect from a particular public speech

Ethics: our principles about what is right and wrong, moral and immoral, honest or dishonest, fair or unfair

Ethnocentrism: the tendency to assume one's own cultural values and beliefs are better than the values and beliefs of other groups

Ethos: the appeal of speaker credibility, in the sense of competence and character

Eulogy: a speech of tribute honoring someone who recently died

Evaluator: helps the group develop criteria for evaluating decisions

Evidence: any information that clarifies, explains, or in some way adds breadth or depth to the topic (also called *supporting material*)

Example: specific case used to illustrate or represent a concept, condition, experience, or group of some sort

Expanded personal inventory: a list of topics that interest you and why

Expediter: helps the group stick to the agenda

Expert testimony: a quotation or paraphrase from a recognized professional in a field related to the topic

Explanation: goes beyond definition to provide details about how and why

Extemporaneous method: speaking from a key word outline

Extended example: story or narrative developed at some length to illustrate a point

External interference: any distraction that originates in the communication situation

Eye contact: looking at the audience during the presentation

Facial expressions: facial movements that can reinforce a wide range of verbal messages

Fact: information established as accurate, usually concerning events, times, people, and places

Factual example: instance that actually occurred

False cause: fallacy in which a speaker claims that because one event follows another, the first event is the cause of the second

Farewell: a speech of tribute honoring someone who is leaving, for example, retiring, resigning, relocating, or being promoted

Feedback: those messages that listeners send back to a speaker about the clarity and acceptability of the speech

Figures of speech: language strategies that make striking comparisons between things or ideas that are not obviously alike

Flip chart: large pad of paper for display on an easel

Flowcharts: illustrate a sequence of steps

Focus group: a communication transaction with a small group of individuals for the purpose of gathering information from them

Formal outline: a typed outline, which labels and applies all macrostructural elements of the speech, using complete sentences and a complete reference list

Frame of reference: the listener's goals, knowledge, experience, values, and attitudes through which the message is filtered

Gatekeeper: helps keep the communication channels open

Gender: socialized tendencies of men and women to perceive, believe, and behave differently in the world

Gender-linked terms: words that somehow imply exclusion of either males or females

General purpose: to inform, to persuade, or to entertain

Government documents: documents and academic journals published by the federal government, often unavailable elsewhere

Graphs: representations intended to make statistics, statistical trends, and statistical relationships clearer

Group density: how crowded the room feels to audience members

Group goal: a collective purpose that unifies members

Group history: members' perceptions about the past work done by the group and its members

Groupthink: when a group opts for consensus over opposing alternative perspectives

Harmonizer: recognizes and deals with misunderstandings and disagreements among members

Hasty generalization: fallacy in which a speaker attempts to draw a conclusion based on too little evidence

Hearing: a physiological process

Heterogeneous groups: composed of members with different cultural identities

Hierarchies: members of a group are seen as having different ranks

Homogeneous groups: composed of members with similar cultural identities

Housekeeping needs: the many details that need to be considered in a group project

Human-edited index: Web search index edited by a human being (directory)

Hyperlinks: connections between two Web documents

Hypothetical example: a short story about a plausible event that never occurred; imaginary or fictitious instance or illustration

Impersonal communication: communication between two people about general information

Implied leader: an individual whom the other members perceive as having the highest status or greatest expertise

Impression formation and management: tendency to prejudge a speaker based on manner and appearance

Impromptu method: speaking with limited preparation

Inclusion: language choices that show respect for the audience and for all types of people

Incremental change: small movement in the direction of the ultimate goal

Inductive reasoning: strategy of arriving at a general conclusion from a series of specific facts or examples

Information giver: provides content for the discussion

Information seeker: raises questions and probes into the contributions of others

Informative speaking: a public speech in which one shares knowledge to create mutual understanding

Initial credibility: perception of credibility before one even begins to speak

Initial ethos: opening credibility of a speaker, achieved with a planned pause and taking a moment to establish eye contact with the listeners

Initiator: proposes new ideas and approaches, as well as distributes the initial workload

Intelligibility: capacity to be understood

Intelligible: clear enough to be understood

Interactive model of communication: accounts for the feedback receivers return to senders

Interference: anything that acts as a barrier to the communication of a message

Internal interference: any distraction that originates in the thoughts of the sender or receiver

Internal previews and summaries: connect pieces of supporting material to the main point or subpoints they address

Internet: a worldwide network of computers that links resources and people at colleges and universities, government agencies, libraries, corporations, and homes

Interpersonal communication: communication between two people who have a relationship

Interview: a communication transaction with one individual for the purpose of gathering information

Introduction: announces the topic and provides a brief road map of how the speaker will proceed

Invitational pattern: a main point arrangement designed to invite rather than convince listeners to agree with one's position

Irrational beliefs: beliefs that project harm onto events that are not harmful

Jargon: particular terminology of a trade or profession that is not generally understood by outsiders

Kinesics: how the body communicates through facial expressions, gestures, posture, and movement

Laissez-faire leadership style: nondirective and passive

LCD panel: a device connected to a computer and placed on top of an overhead projector that projects what is on the computer monitor to a screen in the front of the room

LCD projector: a unit that can be connected to a VCR or computer to project images onto a screen

Leadership: a range of diverse functions, which should ideally be shared by various group members

Leadership style: group's overall style of communicating and operating

Leading questions: questions phrased in such a way as to prompt a certain response

Learning style: a preferred way of receiving, organizing, and interpreting information

Line graphs: used to represent trends over time and sometimes compare trends over time

Linear model of communication: conceives of communication as a one-way process

Listener relevance link: a statement that reveals how and why the ideas offered might benefit listeners

Listening: multidimensional psychological process of receiving, attending to, constructing meaning from, and responding to spoken or nonverbal messages

Logos: appeals to logic, conveyed through structure, evidence, and reasoning

Macrostructure: the general framework for ideas in a speech

Main point summary: a brief statement in the conclusion that reminds listeners of the main points

Main topic: the subject of a speech

Major premise: a general principle that most people agree upon or for which the speaker provides support

Manuscript method: reading a speech that has been written out in its entirety

Maps: schematic representations of real or imaginary geographic areas

Marginalize: ignore or render illegitimate the experiences and values of some people

Mass communication: the mediated process whereby messages are transmitted to large publics

Master of ceremonies: an individual designated to set the mood of the program, introduce participants, and keep the program moving along

Media: the equipment used to display presentational aids

Memorized method: presenting from memory a script that was originally written out in its entirety

Mental distractions: wandering thoughts that occur while listening to a message

Message: any signal sent by one person and interpreted by another

Metaphor: an implied comparison between two unlike things made without using *like* or *as*

Metasearch engine: an Internet tool that searches for a key word through several search engines at once

Microstructure: language and style choices one makes to convey ideas

Minor premise: a specific point or example that fits within the major premise

Modeling: a learned response arising from watching the behaviors and reactions of those whom we admire

Models: scaled-down or scaled-up versions of actual objects

Monroe's motivated sequence: a five-step approach to structuring a persuasive speech, in which the main points consist of attention, need, satisfaction, visualization, and action

Motivated movement: reinforces the verbal message by emphasizing important points, referring to presentational aids, or clarifying structure

Narrative: a story used to support a point

Narrative pattern: a speech structure using a story or series of stories to convey an idea

Non sequitur: fallacy in which a speaker offers supporting material that is not related to the argument

Nonverbal communication: all those elements of a speech other than the words themselves that can contribute to the message

Nonverbal messages: those messages we send using nonlinguistic means

Object language: the concept of appearance as a form of communication

Onomatopoeia: the use of words that sound like the things they stand for

Open-ended question: asks respondents to reply in their own words

Oral footnotes: oral references to the original source of particular information at the point of presenting it during the speech

Oral reports: one person presents the findings of the group in the form of an individual speech

Oral style: language and style choices unique to oral communication, characterized by use of personal pronunciation, simple language and sentence structure, repetition, and descriptors

Organization: the process of putting ideas and information together in a way that will make sense to listeners

Organizational charts: illustrate hierarchical relationships among positions in organizations

Organizational mapping: a process of brainstorming in which you record as many ideas as you can think of related to your thesis as well as to each other

Outlining: a systematic process of placing ideas in a recognizable pattern that listeners can easily follow

Panel discussion: a prepared conversation among group members that takes place in front of an audience

Paralanguage: use of voice to communicate

Parallel treatment: to provide similar labels for the genders when referring to them together

Parallelism: repeating words or grammatical structures within or across sentences

Passive sentence: the subject *experiences* the action

Pathos: appeals to listeners' emotions

Pauses: wait time before, during, or after a phrase to add emotional impact

Peer testimony: a quotation or paraphrase from someone who has firsthand experience related to a topic

Performance orientation: approaching a public speech as a performer, in which a perfect speech must be delivered flawlessly to a hypercritical audience

Personal inventory: a list of topics that interest you

Personal narrative: a story about the speaker's experiences, told with the pronouns *I* or *we*, used to support a point

Personification: attributing human qualities to a concept or to an inanimate object

Persuasion: the process of influencing other people's attitudes, beliefs, values, or behaviors

Persuasive punch words: language choices that evoke emotion

Persuasive speaking: the process of influencing attitudes, beliefs, values, or behaviors through a public speech

Physical distractions: distractions associated with body aches, pains, and feelings

Pie graphs: show what proportions of a whole are represented by each of its parts

Pitch: the highness or lowness of the voice on the musical staff

Plagiarism: presenting another person's ideas as one's own

Poll: a quick method to find out where listeners stand on a topic

Posterboard: large piece of tag board or foam core for display on an easel

Posture: how one stands and carries oneself, which can convey confidence and commitment

Preparation outline: a rough draft of a speech

Presentational aids: visual, audio, and audiovisual supporting materials that help explain the ideas in a speech

Preview: a statement in the introduction that alerts listeners to the main points of the speech

Primacy-recency effect: the tendency to remember the first and last items conveyed orally in a series more than the items in between

Problem/cause/solution pattern: a main point arrangement with the first main point articulating the problem, the second analyzing its causes, and the third presenting multifaceted solutions

Problem (no solution) pattern: a main point arrangement that focuses on the depth and breadth of a problem in order to convince listeners that it is, in fact, a significant problem

Problem/solution pattern: an arrangement of two main points where the first main point examines the problem and the second presents solutions

Problem-solving group: small group primarily concerned with carrying out a task of determining appropriate solutions to problems

Progressive muscle relaxation therapy: when one systematically tenses and releases certain muscle groups while focusing on what a relaxed state feels like

Pronunciation: how the sounds of a word are said and which parts are stressed

Proxemics: the way in which space and distance communicate

Psychological characteristics: characteristics that motivate audience members to listen to and retain ideas presented in a message

Public communication: the process of sending messages to large audiences

Public speaking: a sustained formal presentation made by a speaker to an audience

Questionnaire: a series of questions designed to elicit particular information about a topic

Raised consciousness: sensitizing listeners to an issue and making them more receptive to persuasion in the future

Rate: the speed at which the speech is delivered

Reasoning fallacies: flawed reasoning

Receiver: a person to whom a sender communicates

Recorder: takes notes during meetings and summarizes them for everyone

Red herring: fallacy in which a speaker attacks an issue using irrelevant evidence or arguments as distractions

Refutative pattern: a main point arrangement that persuades by both disproving the opposing position and bolstering the speaker's

Reinforcement: a learning process in which the responses one gets shape future expectations and behavior

Relational needs: involve interpersonal relationships among group members

Relevant evidence: information that is directly related to the topic

Repetition: restating words, phrases, or sentences for emphasis

Research: the process of locating supporting material

Research interview: an interview conducted to gather information for a speech

Rhetorical question: a question phrased in a way that stimulates thought, but not an overt response

Rhetorical situation: the specific circumstances in which the speech is to be delivered—the speaker, the audience, and the occasion

Robot-generated index: comprehensive Web computer program that automatically visits a multitude of Web sites based on key words (search engine)

Scapegoating: the tendency to blame one or more members for the failure of a group

Search engine: robot-generated Web computer program that automatically visits a multitude of sites based on key words

Self-disclosure: sharing of personal information that is not generally known by others

Self-talk: those thoughts that go through our minds about our perceived success or failure in particular situations

Sender: a person who initiates communication

Sensory aids: appeal to senses such as sight, sound, taste, touch, or smell

Sex: biological differences between males and females

SIER model: a four-step process for understanding the dynamics of critical listening

Signposts: words or short phrases that mark where one is in a speech or help move the speech forward

Simile: a comparison between two unlike things using the words *like* or *as*

Situational acceptance: agreement that a certain policy, approach, or behavior is acceptable in some instances

Situational communication apprehension: a short-lived feeling of anxiety that occurs during a specific encounter

Skills training: a systematic method of breaking the speechmaking process into specific skills that can be mastered first in isolation and then together

Slang: a word arbitrarily assigned a meaning by a particular social group or subculture

Sleeper effect: the change emerges later after listeners absorb ideas into their own belief systems

Slide transition: style of moving from one slide to the next in a computerized slide show

Slippery slope: fallacy that is similar to false cause, but the speaker focuses on how a particular action will set forth a chain of events that will inevitably lead to a certain result

Small group: three to twenty people who come together for a reason

Small group communication: when three to twenty people meet to perform a task, reach a common goal, share ideas, or engage in a social experience

Socialization: a process of learning to fit within the rules of a society

Sociocultural background: differences in listeners' backgrounds such as ethnicity, culture, and even region

Solution: a way to solve a problem

Spatial pattern: main points help create a mental picture of what an object, person, place looks like based on location or direction

Speaker credibility statement: one or more sentences indicating what makes the speaker an authority on the topic

Speaking outline: a brief outline used solely as a memory aid while presenting the actual speech

Special occasion speeches: designed to fit the needs of some special occasion

Specific purpose: what the speaker hopes to accomplish in the speech

Speech of acceptance: a speech to express appreciation for an award or gift received

Speech of demonstration: speech to clarify a process or a procedure

Speech of description: speech to paint a clear picture in the minds of listeners

Speech of explanation: speech to generate a clear interpretation in the minds of listeners

Speech of introduction: a short speech, generally three to five minutes, to introduce the main speaker

Speech of nomination: a speech to propose an individual as a nominee for an elected office, honor, or award

Speech of presentation: a speech to present an award and recognize the recipient's accomplishments

Speech of tribute: a speech that praises or celebrates a person, a group, or an event

Speech of welcome: a formal public greeting to a visiting person or group to make the honoree feel comfortable and appreciated

Speech to entertain: a lighthearted speech that makes a serious point

Standard English: the language preferences described in the dictionary

Startling fact or statistic: a piece of information that is both little known and shocking

Statistics: the collection and arrangement of numerical facts

Stereotype: an assumption that all members of a certain group behave or believe a certain way solely because they belong to that particular group

Straw man: fallacy in which a speaker weakens some aspect of the opposing position by misrepresenting it and then attacks that weaker (straw man) argument

Stress: emphasis placed on words to indicate the importance of the ideas expressed

Structure: the overall framework used to organize content

Structures of speech: sentence strategies that combine ideas in a particular way

Subgroups: smaller groups within the primary group

Supporter: responds favorably, whether verbally or nonverbally, when good points are made

Supporting material: any information that clarifies, explains, or in some way adds breadth or depth to the topic (also called *evidence*)

Survey: a general or comprehensive view of a particular issue; a method of obtaining information from a large pool of people in a short amount of time

Syllogism: a three-part form of deductive reasoning

Symposium presentation: all members of the group orally present a portion of the findings in mini speeches

Systematic desensitization: a series of techniques focused around progressive relaxation, visualization, and participation

Systematic problem solving: the process of identifying a problem and, through a process of reasoning, attempting to discover the best way to solve it

Target audience: the portion of the audience that the speaker most wants to persuade

Task needs: substantive actions that must be taken in order for the group to achieve its goal

Terminal credibility: perception of a speaker's credibility at the end of the speech

Terminal ethos: closing credibility of a speaker, achieved with a planned pause and taking a moment to establish eye contact with listeners

Testimony: quotations or paraphrases used to support a point

Thesaurus: a book of synonyms

Thesis restatement: a reiteration of the thesis statement in the conclusion, usually offered in past tense

Thesis statement: a one-sentence summary of the speech

Third-person narrative: a story about someone else's experience, told using the pronouns *he, she,* or *they,* to support a point

Timbre: what distinguishes one's voice from other voices (also known as vocal quality)

Toast: a very short speech of tribute, usually delivered impromptu, often given at wedding receptions, graduation dinners, awards luncheons, holiday dinners, and so forth

Topical pattern: main point arrangement used when a topic is divided into subtopics or categories

Traitlike communication apprehension: a tendency to feel anxious about speaking in most situations

Transactional model of communication: concept of communication as a complex, multifaceted, and interactive process of creating shared meaning

Transition: a word or phrase that shows the relationship between two main points and lets the audience know the speaker has completed one main point and is moving on to another

Values: the enduring set of principles that shape one's beliefs and attitudes

Verbal immediacy: use of language to reduce the psychological distance between the speaker and the audience

Verbal messages: the words a speaker uses

Visual aids: pictures, drawings and diagrams, charts, graphs, and models

Visual channel: what the receivers see

Visual distractions: distractions associated with something someone sees

Vivid language and style: evokes feelings and images in the listeners' minds and thus invites them to internalize ideas

Vocal quality: what distinguishes one's voice from other voices (also known as timbre)

Vocal variety: changing rate, pitch, and volume in ways that reinforce the emotional meaning of the message

Vocalized pauses: unnecessary words, such as "um," "you know," that disrupt the fluency of the message

Volume: how loudly or softly one speaks

Work team: Common term for a problem-solving group in the workplace

Worldview: a way of looking at the world

World Wide Web: a software system that makes accessing information on the Internet simple

REFERENCES

Chapter 1

Adler, R., & Towne, N. (1996). *Looking Out/Looking In* (8th ed.). Fort Worth, TX: Harcourt Brace College.

Ancona, D. (1990). Outward bound: Strategies for team survival in an organization. *Academy of Management Journal, 33,* 334–365.

Astor, D. (1999, October 30). Cartoonists drawing more topical comics as century draws to a close. *Editor and Publisher,* 37.

Bakos, J. D., Jr. (1997). Communication skills for the 21st century. *Journal of Professional Issues in Engineering Education and Practice, 123*(1), 14–16.

Barbe, W., & Swassing, R. H. (1979). *The Swassing-Barbe modality index.* Columbus, OH: Waner-Bloser.

Brinson, S. L. (1992). TV fights: Women and men in interpersonal arguments on prime time television dramas. *Argumentation and Advocacy, 29*(2), 89–105.

Brown, T. (1997). The front line: Dilbert's message hits home. *HR Focus, 72*(2), 13.

Canfield, A. A. (1980). *Learning styles inventory manual.* Ann Arbor, MI: Humanics, Inc.

Capowski, G. (1997). We have seen Dilbert, and he is us. *HR Focus, 74*(2), 16.

Coffey, R. (1987, September 18). Biden's borrowed eloquence beats the real thing. *Chicago Tribune,* sec. 1, 23.

DeVito, J. (1993). *Messages: Building interpersonal communication skills* (2nd ed.). New York: Harper Collins.

Douglas, W. (1996). The fall from grace?: The modern family on television. *Communication Research, 23*(6), 675–703.

Dunn, R., Dunn, K., & Price, G. E. (1975). *Learning style inventory.* Lawrence, KS: Price Systems.

Ford, W. S. Z., & Wolvin, A. D. (1993). The differential impact of a basic communication course on perceived communication competencies in class, work, and social contexts. *Communication Education, 42*(3), 215–223.

Gardner, H. (1983). *Frames of mind: The theory of multiple intelligences.* New York: Basic Books.

Greenberg, B. S., Sherry, J. L., Busselle, R. W., Hnilo, L. R., & Smith, S. W. (1997). Daytime television talk shows: Guests, content and interactions. *Journal of Broadcasting and Electronic Media, 41*(3), 412–426.

Hahner, Jeffrey C., Sokoloff, M. A., & Salisch, S. L. (1993). *Speaking clearly: Improving voice and diction* (4th ed.). New York: McGraw-Hill.

Halone, K. K., Cunconan, T. M., Coakley, C. G., & Wolvin, A. D. (1998). Toward the establishment of general dimensions underlying the listening process. *International Journal of Listening, 12,* 12–28.

Honeycutt, J. M., Wellman, L. B., & Larson, M. S. (1997). Beneath family role portrayals: An additional measure of communication influence using time series analyses of turn at talk on a popular television program. *Journal of Broadcasting and Electronic Media, 41*(1), 40–57.

Jhally, S. (1995). *Dreamworlds II* [Video]. North Hampton, MA: The Media Education Foundation.

JobWeb (2003). *Job Outlook 2004.* National Association of Colleges and Employers. Retrieved December 4, 2003, from http://www.jobweb.com/joboutlook/2004outlook/outlook5.htm

Johannesen, R. (1990). *Ethics in human communication* (3rd ed.). Prospect Heights, IL: Waveland Press.

Kaus, M. (1987, September 28). Biden's belly flop. *Newsweek,* 23–24.

Kellermann, K. (1992). Communication: Inherently strategic and primarily automatic. *Communication Monographs, 59,* 288–300.

Kramer, M. W., & Hinton, J. S. (1996). The differential impact of a basic public speaking course on perceived communication competencies in class, work, and social contexts. *Basic Communication Course Annual, 8,* 1–25.

Kolb, D. (1984). *Experiential learning: Experience as the source of learning and development.* Englewood Cliffs, NJ: Prentice-Hall.

Landay, L. (1999). Millions "Love Lucy": Commodification and the Lucy phenomenon. *NWSA Journal, 11*(2), 25.

Larson, M. S. (1991). Sibling interactions in 1950s versus 1980s sitcoms: A comparison. *Journalism Quarterly, 68*(3), 381–388.

Littlejohn, S. (1989). *Theories of human communication* (3rd ed.). Belmont, CA: Wadsworth.

Maes, J. D. (1997). A managerial perspective: Oral communication competency is most important for business students in the workplace. *Journal of Business Communication, 34*(1), 67–80.

Margolis, J. (1987, September 17). Biden threatened by accusations of plagiarism in his speeches. *Chicago Tribune,* sec. 1, 3.

McCarthy, B. (1980). *The 4MAT system: Teaching to learning styles with right/left mode techniques.* Barrington, IL: Excel.

McCroskey, J. C. (1993). *An introduction to rhetorical communication* (6th ed.). Englewood Cliffs, NJ: Prentice-Hall.

Nagle, R. A. (1987). The ideal job candidate of the 21st century. *Journal of Career Planning and Employment,* 40.

Homosexual attraction is found in 1 of 5. (1994, September 6). *New York Times,* p. A14.

Nilsen, T. (1974). *Ethics of speech communication* (2nd. ed.). Indianapolis, IN: Bobbs-Merrill.

Nineteen nineties: As the 20th century comes to a close, the TV nation has grown into one big unhappy family. (1999, February 19). *Entertainment Weekly,* 96+.

Peterson, M. S. (1997). Personnel interviewers' perceptions of the importance and adequacy of applicants' communication skills. *Communication Education, 46*(4), 287–291.

Poole, M. (1998). The small group should be the fundamental unit of communication research. In J. Trent (Ed.), *Communication: Views from the helm for the 21st century* (pp. 94–97). Needham Heights, MA: Allyn & Bacon.

Renzulli, J. S., & Smith, L. H. (1978). *The learning styles inventory: A measure of student preference for instructional techniques.* Mansfield Center, CT: Creative Learning Press.

Richmond, V., & McCroskey, J. C. (1995). *Communication: Apprehension, avoidance, and effectiveness* (4th ed.). Scottsdale, AZ: Gorsuch Scarisbrick.

Seinfeld, J. (1993). *SeinLanguage.* New York: Bantam.

Shaw, M. (1981). *Group dynamics: The psychology of small group behavior.* New York: McGraw-Hill.

Stinson, L. M., & Asquith, J. (1997). Excellent communication skills are an essential part of being an accountant.

Journal of Technical Writing and Communication, 27(4), 385–390.

Trank, D. M. (1990). Directing multiple sections of the basic course. In G. Friedrich & A. Vangelisti (Eds.), *Teaching communication: Theory, research, methods* (pp. 403–413). Hillsdale, NJ: Erlbaum.

Trank, D. M., & Lewis, P. (1991). The introductory communication course: Results of a national survey. *Basic Communication Course Annual, 3,* 106–122.

Trenholm, S., & Jenson, A. (1992). *Interpersonal Communication* (2nd ed.). Belmont, CA: Wadsworth.

Ulmer, R., & Sellnow, T. (1997). Strategic ambiguity and the ethic of significant choice in the tobacco industry. *Communication Studies, 48*(3), 215–233.

Wallace, K. (1955). An ethical basic of communication. *The Speech Teacher, 4,* 1–9.

Wasserstein, W. (December, 1988). Streeping beauty: A rare interview with cinema's first lady. *Interview,* 90.

Wattenberg, B. J. (1991). *The first universal nation: Leading indicators and ideas about the surge of America in the 1990s.* New York: Free Press.

Weitzel, A. R. (1987). *Careers for speech communication graduates.* Salem, WI: Sheffield.

Willis, E. (1996). Bring in the noise. *The Nation, 262*(13), 19–21.

Wilson, T. (1996). Television's everyday life: Towards a phenomenology of the "televised subject." *Journal of Communication Inquiry, 20*(1), 49–67.

Wolvin, A. D. (1998a). The basic course and the future of the workplace. *Basic Communication Course Annual, 10,* 1–6.

Wolvin, A. D. (1998b). Careers in communication: An update. *Journal of the Association for Communication Administration, 27,* 71–73.

Wolvin, A. D., Berko, R. M., & Wolvin, D. R. (1999). *The public speaker/The public listener* (2nd ed.). Los Angeles: Roxbury.

Chapter 2

Ayres, J. (1986). Perceptions of speaking ability: An explanation of stage fright. *Communication Education, 35,* 275–287.

Bandura, A. (1973). *Social learning theory.* Englewood Cliffs, NJ: Prentice-Hall.

Behnke, R. R., & Beatty, L. W. (1981). A cognitive-physiological model of speech anxiety. *Communication Monographs, 48,* 158–163.

Bello, R. (1995, April). Public speaking apprehension and gender as predictors of speech competence. Paper presented at the annual conference of the Southern States Communication Association, New Orleans, LA.

Bourhis, J., & Berquist, C. (1990). Communication apprehension in the basic course: Learning styles and preferred instructional strategies of high and low apprehensive students. *Basic Communication Course Annual, 3,* 27–46.

Bourhis, J., & Stubbs, J. (1991, April). *Communication apprehension, learning styles, and academic achievement.* Paper presented at the Central States Communication Association annual meeting, Chicago.

Bourne, E. J. (1990). *The anxiety and phobia workbook.* Oakland, CA: New Harbinger Publications.

Daly, J. A., & Buss, A. H. (1984). The transitory causes of audience anxiety. In J. A. Daly & J. C. McCroskey (Eds.), *Avoiding communication.* Beverly Hills, CA: Sage.

Daly, J. A., & Stafford, L. (1984). Implications of quietness: Some facts and speculation. In J. A. Daly & J. C. McCroskey (Eds.), *Avoiding communication.* Beverly Hills, CA: Sage.

Davis, M., Echelon, E., & McKay, M. (1988). *The relaxation and stress workbook.* Oakland, CA: New Harbinger Publications.

Desberg, P., & Marsh, G. (1988). *Controlling stagefright: Presenting yourself from one to one thousand.* Oakland, CA: New Harbinger Publications.

Dwyer, K. (1998a). Communication apprehension and learning style preference: Correlations and implications for teaching. *Communication Education, 47,* 137–150.

Dwyer, K. (1998b). *Conquer your speechfright.* Orlando, FL: Harcourt Brace College.

Ellis, A., & Dryden, W. (1987). *The practice of rational emotive therapy.* New York: Springer.

Friedrich, G., & Goss, B. (1984). Systematic desensitization. In J. A. Daly & J. C. McCroskey (Eds.), *Avoiding communication.* Beverly Hills, CA: Sage.

Griffin, K. (1995, July). Beating performance anxiety. *Working Woman,* 62–65, 76.

Hahner, J., Sokoloff, M., & Salisch, S. (1993). *Speaking clearly: Improving voice and diction* (4th ed). New York: McGraw-Hill.

Hoffman, J., & Sprague, J. (1982). A survey of reticence and communication apprehension treatment programs at U.S. colleges and universities. *Communication Education, 31,* 185–193.

Jacobson, E. (1938). *Progressive relaxation.* Chicago: Chicago University Press.

McCarthy, B. (1987). *The 4MAT system: Teaching to learning styles with right/left mode techniques.* Barrington, IL: Excel.

McCroskey, J. C. (1972). The implementation of a large-scale program of systematic desensitization for communication apprehension. *Speech Teacher, 21,* 255–264.

McCroskey, J. C. (1977). Oral communication apprehension:A review of recent theory and research. *Human Communication Research, 4,* 78–96.

McCroskey, J. C. (1982). Oral communication apprehension: A reconceptualization. In M. Burgoon (Ed.), *Communication Yearbook 6.* Beverly Hills, CA: Sage.

McCroskey, J. C. (1984). The communication apprehension perspective. In J. A. Daly & J. C. McCroskey (Eds.), *Avoiding communication.* Beverly Hills, CA: Sage.

McCroskey, J. C., Ralph, D. C., & Barrick, J. E. (1970). The effect of systematic desensitization on speech anxiety. *Speech Teacher, 19,* 32–36.

Motley, M. (1991). Public speaking anxiety qua performance anxiety: A revised model and an alternative therapy. In M. Booth-Butterfield (Ed.) *Communication, cognition, and anxiety.* Newbury Park, CA: Sage.

Neer, M. R., & Kircher, W. F. (1991). Classroom interventions for reducing public speaking anxiety. *Basic Communication Course Annual, 3,* 202–223.

Pucel, J., & Stocker, G. (1983). A nonverbal approach to communication: A cross-cultural study of stress behaviors. *Communication, 12,* 53–65.

Richmond, V., & McCroskey, J. C. (1995). *Communication: Apprehension, avoidance, and effectiveness* (4th ed.). Scottsdale, AZ: Gorsuch Scarisbrick.

Rolfson, K. (1995). *An experiential learning group as treatment for high communication apprehensive students at NDSU.* Unpublished master's thesis. North Dakota State University, Fargo.

White, D. (1998, September). Smile when you say that. *Working Woman,* 94–95.

Wolpe, J. (1958). *Psychotherapy by reciprocal inhibition.* Stanford, CA: Stanford University Press.

Chapter 3

Decker, B. (1992). *You've got to be believed to be heard.* New York: St. Martin's Press.

Foss, S., & Foss, K. (1994). *Inviting transformation: Presentational speaking for a changing world.* Prospect Heights, IL: Waveland Press.

Gorham, J. (1988). The relationship between verbal teacher immediacy behaviors and student learning. *Communication Education, 37*, 40–53.

Jensen, V. (1985). Teaching ethics in speech communication. *Communication Education, 34*, 324–330.

National Speakers Association official Web site. (2003). Retrieved September 12, 2003, from http://www.nsaspeaker.org

Powell, R. G., & Harville, B. (1990). The effects of teacher immediacy and clarity on instructional outcomes: An intercultural assessment. *Communication Education, 39*, 369–379.

Reinard, J. C. (1988). The empirical study of the persuasive effects of evidence. *Human Communication Research, 15*, 3–59.

Shaw, C. C. (1997). *Critical issue: Educating teachers for diversity.* North Central Regional Educational Laboratory. Retrieved September 12, 2003, from http://www.ncrel.org/sdrs/areas/issues/educatrs/presrvce/pe300.htm

Whalen, J. D. (1996). *I see what you mean: Persuasive business communication.* Thousand Oaks, CA: Sage.

Chapter 4

Active listening (1997). *Public Management, 79*(12), 25–28.

Adler, R., & Towne, N. (1996). *Looking out, looking in* (8th ed.). Fort Worth, TX: Harcourt Brace College.

Barker, L., Edwards, C., Gaines, K., & Holley, F. (1980). An investigation of proportional time spent in various communication activities by college students. *Journal of Applied Communication Research, 8*, 101–109.

Bostrom, R. N. (1990). *Listening behavior: Measurement and application.* New York: Guilford Press.

Cissna, K., & Sieburg, E. (1981). Patterns of interactional confirmation and disconfirmation. In C. Wilder-Mott & J. H. Weakland (Eds.), *Rigor and imagination: Essays from the legacy of Gregory Bateson* (pp. 253–282). New York: Praeger.

Coakley, C., & Wolvin, A. (1991). Listening in the educational environment. In D. Borisoff & M. Purdy (Eds.), *Listening in everyday life: A personal and professional approach.* Lanham, MD: University Press of America.

DeWine, S., & Daniels, T. (1993). Beyond the snapshot: Setting a research agenda in organizational communication. In S. A. Deetz (Ed.), *Communication Yearbook 16* (252–330). Thousand Oaks, CA: Sage.

Gitomer, J. (2000). Good listening skills open doors to closing sales. *The Business Journal—Serving Phoenix and the Valley of the Sun, 20*(32), 33.

Gunderson, T. (1999). Listen and learn. *Restaurant Hospitality, 83*(3), 26.

Halone, K. K., Cunconan, T. M., Coakley, C. G., & Wolvin, A. D. (1998). Toward the establishments of general dimensions underlying the listening process. *International Journal of Listening, 12*, 12–28.

Hiam, A. (1997). Is anybody listening? *Workforce, 76*(8), 92.

Horowitz, A. (1996). Hey! Listen up! *Computerworld, 30*(27), 64–67.

Hunsaker, R. (1991, November). Critical listening—a neglected skill. Presentation to the 77th annual meeting of the Speech Communication Association, Atlanta, GA.

International Listening Association official Web site. (1996). Retrieved December 5, 2003, from http://www.listen.org/

Kaye, S. (1998). Effective communication skills for engineers. *IIE Solutions, 30*(9), 44–47.

Kearney, P. (1994). Affective learning. In R. B. Rubin, P. Palmgreen, & H. E. Sypher (Eds.), *Communication research measures: A sourcebook* (pp. 81–85). New York: Guilford Press.

Kearney, P., Plax, T. G., & Wendt-Wasco, N. J. (1985). Teacher immediacy for affective learning in divergent college courses. *Communication Quarterly, 33*, 61–74.

Kiewitz, C. (1997). Cultural differences in listening style preferences: A comparison of young adults in Germany, Israel, and the United States. *International Journal of Public Opinion Research, 9*(3), 233–248.

Kiewra, K., DuBois, N., Christian, J., & McShane, A. (1988). Providing study notes: Comparison of three types of notes for review. *Journal of Educational Psychology, 80*, 595–598.

Legge, W. (1971). Listening, intelligence, and school achievement. In S. Duker (Ed.), *Listening: Related readings* (pp. 121–133). Netuchen, NJ: Scarecrow Press.

Linowes, J. G. (1998). Listening between the lines. *Journal of Management in Engineering, 14*(6), 21–23.

Luiten, J., Ames, W., & Ackerson, G. (1980). A meta-analysis of the effects of advance organizers on learning and retention. *American Educational Research, 17*, 211–218.

Mayer, L. (1996). *Fundamentals of voice and articulation* (11th ed.). Madison, WI: Brown & Benchmark.

Messmer, M. (1998, March). Improving your listening skills. *Management Accounting, 14*.

Miccinati, J. L. (1988). Mapping the terrain: Connecting reading with academic writing. *Journal of Reading, 31*, 542–552.

Morgan, G. (1983, August). Therapeutic listening: A communication tool. *Training and Development Journal, 44*.

Mulvaney, S. (1998). Improving listening skills. *Journal of Property Management, 63*(4), 20.

Ritts, V., Patterson, M., & Tubbs, M. (1992). Expectations, impressions, and judgments of physically attractive students: A review. *Review of Educational Research, 62*, 413–426.

Ross, R. (1983). *Speech communication: Fundamentals and practice* (6th ed.). Englewood Cliffs, NJ: Prentice-Hall.

Salopek, J. J. (1999). Is anyone listening? *Training and Development, 53*(9), 58–60.

Steil, L. K., Barker, L. L., & Watson, K. W. (1983). *Effective listening.* Reading, MA: Addison-Wesley.

Stephens, M. (1999). The new TV: Stop making sense. In R. E. Hiebert (Ed.), *Impact of mass media: Current issues* (4th ed.) (pp. 16–22). New York: Longman.

Temple, L., & Loewen, K. (1993). Perceptions of power: First impressions of a woman wearing a jacket. *Perceptual and Motor Skills, 76*, 339–348.

Treinen, K. (1998). *The effects of gender and physical attractiveness on peer critiques of a persuasive speech.* Unpublished master's thesis. North Dakota State University, Fargo.

Watson K., & Barker, L. (1984). Listening behavior: Definition and measurement. In R. N. Bostrom & B. Westley (Eds.), *Communication Yearbook 8.* Beverly Hills, CA: Sage.

Wolvin, A., & Coakley, C. (1991). A survey of the status of listening training in some Fortune 500 corporations. *Communication Education, 40*, 152–164.

Wolvin, A., & Coakley, C. (1992). *Listening* (4th ed.). Dubuque, IA: W. C. Brown.

Chapter 5

Ball, P. (1999). What works for me. *Teaching English in the Two-Year College, 26*(3), 313–318.

Callison, D. (2001). Concept mapping. *School Library Media Activities Monthly, 17*(10), 30–32.

Clark, C. H. (1958). *Brainstorming, the dynamic way to create successful ideas.* Garden City, NY: Doubleday.

Lamb, M. (1991). Animal behavior processes. *Journal of Experimental Psychology, 17*, 45–54.

Richmond, V. P., & McCroskey, J. C. (1995). *Communication: Apprehension, avoidance, and effectiveness* (4th ed.). Scottsdale, AZ: Gorsuch Scarisbrick.

Siau, K. (1999). Internet, world wide web, and creativity. *Journal of Creative Behavior, 37*(3), 191–201.

Suskind, R., & Lublin, J. (1995, January 26). Critics are succinct: Long speeches tend to get short interest. *Wall Street Journal,* A1–A5.

Trocco, F. (2000). Encouraging students to study weird things. *Phi Delta Kappan, 81*(8), 628–631.

Weiten, W. (1986). *Psychology applied to modern life* (2nd ed.). Belmont, CA: Wadsworth.

Chapter 6

Aristotle. (1954). *Rhetoric* (W. Rhys Roberts, Trans.). New York: Modern Library.

Bashi, V., & McDaniel, A. (1997). A theory of immigration and racial stratification. *Journal of Black Studies, 27*(5), 668–683.

Berko, R., Wolvin, A., & Ray, R. (1997). *Business communication in a changing world.* New York: St. Martin's Press.

Canary, D. J., & Dindia, K. (1998). *Sex differences and similarities in communication.* Mahwah, NJ: Erlbaum.

Canary, D. J., & Hause, K. S. (1993). Is there any reason to research sex differences in communication? *Communication Quarterly, 41,* 129–144.

Caplan, S. E. (1999). Acquisition of message-production skill by younger and older adults: Effects of age, task complexity, and practice. *Communication Monographs, 66*(1), 31–48.

De Ciantis, S. M., & Kirton, M. J. (1996). A psychometric reexamination of Kolb's experiential learning cycle construct: A separation of level, style, and process. *Educational and Psychological Measurement, 56*(5), 809–821.

DiMartino, E. C. (1989). Understanding children from other cultures. *Childhood Education, 66,* 30–32.

Di Santa Ana, J. (1996). Cultures in tension and dialogue. *International Review of Mission, 85*(336), 93–103.

Donavan, J. M., & Rundle, B. A. (1997). Psychic unity constraints upon successful intercultural communication. *Language and Communication, 17*(3), 219–236.

Dunn, R. S., & Dunn, K. J. (1979). Learning styles/ teaching styles: Should they . . . can they . . . be matched? *Educational Leadership, 36,* 238–244.

Faludi, S. (1991). *Backlash: The undeclared war against American women.* New York: Doubleday.

Gudykunst, W. B., Matsumoto, Y., Ting-Toomey, S., Nishida, T., Kim, K., & Heyman, S. J. (1996). The influence of cultural individualism-collectivism, self construals, and individual values on communication styles across cultures. *Human Communication Research, 22*(4), 510–544.

Hummert, M. L., Shaner, J. L., Garstka, T. A., & Henry, C. (1998). Communication with older adults: The influence of age stereotypes, context, and communicator age. *Human Communication Research, 25*(1), 124–153.

Hummert, M. L., Wieman, J. M., & Nussbaum, J. F. (Eds.). (1994). *Interpersonal communication in older adulthood: Interdisciplinary theory and research.* Thousand Oaks, CA: Sage.

Iino, M. (1993). The trap of generalization: A case of encountering a new culture. *Working Papers in Educational Linguistics, 9,* 21–45.

Ivy, D. K., & Backlund, P. (1994). *Exploring genderspeak.* New York: McGraw-Hill.

Kemper, S., & Harde, T. (1999). Experimentally disentangling what's beneficial about elderspeak from what's not. *Psychology and Aging, 14*(4), 656.

Kim, M., Hunter, J. E., Miyahara, A., Horvath, A., Bresnahan, M., & Yoon, H. (1996). Individual- vs. culture-level dimensions of individualism and collectivism: Effects on preferred conversational styles. *Communication Monographs, 63*(1), 29–50.

Kirtley, M. D., & Weaver, J. B. (1999). Exploring the impact of gender role self-perception on communication style. *Women's Studies in Communication, 22*(2), 190.

Kolb, D. (1984). *Experiential learning: Experience as the source of learning and development.* Englewood Cliffs, NJ: Prentice-Hall.

Lustig, M. W., & Koester, J. (1993). *Intercultural competence: Interpersonal communication across cultures.* New York: Harper Collins, 37–50.

Magolda, M. B. (1989). Gender differences in cognitive development: An analysis of cognitive complexity and learning styles. *Journal of College Student Development, 30,* 213–220.

Marshall, C. (1990, October). The power of the learning styles philosophy. *Educational Leadership, 48,* 62.

Maslow, A. (1970). A theory of human motivation. *Psychological Review, 50,* 370–396.

Masterson, J., Watson, N., & Cichon, E. (1991). Cultural differences in public speaking. *World Communication, 20,* 39–47.

McAdoo, L. (1999). *Gender and student critiques.* Unpublished master's thesis, North Dakota State University, Fargo.

McGuire, W. (1985). Attitudes and attitude change. In G. Lindzey & E. Aronson (Eds.), *The handbook of social psychology* (2nd ed.). New York: Random House.

Merriam, A. H. (1982, April). *Comparative chronemics and diplomacy: American and Iranian perspectives on time.* Paper presented at the Annual Meeting of the Southern Speech Communication Association, Hot Springs, AR.

Nussbaum, J. F., & Coupland, J. (Eds.). (1995). *Handbook of communication and aging research.* Mahwah, NJ: Erlbaum.

Petronio, S., Ellemers, N., Giles, H., & Gallois, C. (1998). (Mis)communicating across boundaries. *Communication Research,* 571.

Plotnik, R. (1993). *Introduction to psychology* (3rd ed.). Belmont, CA: Wadsworth.

Reeder, H. M. (1996). A critical outlook at gender difference in communication research. *Communication Studies, 47*(4), 318–331.

Reinard, J. C. (1988). The empirical study of the persuasive effects of evidence. *Human Communication Research, 15,* 3–59.

Reisman, J. (1990). Intimacy in same-sex friendships. *Sex Roles, 23,* 65–82.

Richmond, V. P., & McCroskey, J. C.(1995). *Communication: Apprehension, avoidance, and effectiveness* (4th ed.). Scottsdale, AZ: Gorsuch Scarisbrick.

Rogers, C. (1983). *Freedom to learn for the '80s.* Columbus, OH: Merrill.

Sellnow, D., & Golish, T. (2000). The relationship between a required self-disclosure speech and public speaking anxiety: Considering gender equity. *Basic Communication Course Annual, 12,* 28–59.

Sprague, J. (1993). Why teaching works: The transformative power of pedagogical communication. *Communication Education, 42,* 349–366.

Suzuki, S. (1998). In-group and out-group communication patterns in international organizations: Implications for social identity theory. *Communication Research, 25*(2), 154–184.

Tannen, D. (1992). *You just don't understand.* New York: Ballantine Books.

Thimm, C. (1998). Age stereotypes and patronizing messages: Features of age-adapted speech in technical instructions to the elderly. *Journal of Applied Communication Research, 26*(1), 66–83.

Weatherall, A. (1998). Re-visioning gender and language research. *Women and Language, 21*(1), 1–9.

Williams, A. (1997). Young people's beliefs about intergenerational communication: An initial cross-cultural comparison. *Communication Research, 24*(4), 370–394.

Wood, J. (1994). *Gendered lives: Communication, gender, and culture.* Belmont, CA: Wadsworth.

Chapter 7

American Psychological Association. (2001). *Publication manual of the American Psychological Association* (5th ed.). Washington, DC: Author.

Basch, R. (1996). *Secrets of the super net searchers: The reflections, revelations, and hard-won wisdom of 35 of the world's top Internet researchers.* Wilton, CT: Pemberton Press.

Frances, P. (1994). Lies, damned lies . . . *American Demographics, 16,* 2.

Kent, P. (1998). *The complete idiot's guide to the Internet* (5th ed.). Indianapolis, IN: Alpha Books.

Munger, D., Anderson, D., Benjamin, B., Busiel, C., & Paredes-Holt, B. (1999). *Researching online* (2nd ed.). New York: Longman.

Quaratiello, A. R. (1997). *The college student's research companion.* New York: Neal Schuman.

Reddick, R., & King, E. (1996). *The online student: Making the grade on the Internet.* Fort Worth, TX: Harcourt Brace College.

Reinard, J. (1991). *Foundations of argument.* Dubuque, IA: W. C. Brown.

Shalala, D. (1994, May 15). Domestic terrorism: An unacknowledged epidemic. *Vital Speeches of the Day,* 451.

Tyson, L. D. (2003, April 28). The wrong time for ballooning deficits. *Business Week,* 26.

Whitely, S. (Ed.). (1994). *The American Library Association guide to information access.* New York: Random House.

Young, G. (Ed.). (1998). *The Internet.* New York: H. W. Wilson.

Chapter 8

Connor, U., & McCagg, P. (1987). A contrastive study of English expository prose paraphrases. In U. Connor & R. B. Kaplan (Eds.), *Writing across languages: Analysis of L2 text.* Reading, MA: Addison-Wesley, 73–86.

Darnell, D. (1963). The relation between sentence-order and comprehension. *Speech Monographs, 30,* 97–100.

Dwyer, K. K. (1998). *Conquer your speechfright.* Fort Worth, TX: Harcourt Brace College.

Foss, S., & Foss, K. (1994). *Inviting transformation: Presentational speaking for a changing world.* Prospect Heights, IL: Waveland Press.

Hoffman, R. (1992). Temporal organization as a rhetorical resource. *Southern Communication Journal, 57,* 194–204.

Smith, R. (1951). Effects of speech organization upon attitudes of college students. *Speech Monographs, 18,* 292–301.

Tayler, J. (1999, May 26). The sacred grove of Oshogbo. *Atlantic Abroad.* Retrieved from http://www.theatlantic.com/unbound/abroad/jt990526.

Thompson, E. (1967). Some effects of message structure on listening comprehension. *Speech Monographs, 34,* 51–57.

Chapter 9

Humes, J. C. (1988). *Standing ovation: How to be an effective speaker and communicator.* New York: Harper & Row.

Slan, J. (1998). *Using stories and humor to grab your audience.* Needham Heights, MA: Allyn & Bacon.

Trenholm, S. (1989). *Persuasion and social influence.* Englewood Cliffs, NJ: Prentice-Hall.

Chapter 10

Beatty, M. J. (1988). Public speaking apprehension, decision-making errors in the selection of speech introduction strategies and adherence to strategy. *Communication Education, 37,* 297–311.

Sharp, Jr., H., & McClung, T. (1966). Effects of organization on the speaker's ethos. *Speech Monographs,* 182.

Thompson, E. (1960). An experimental investigation of the relative effectiveness of organization structure in oral communication. *Southern Speech Journal, 26,* 59–69.

Chapter 11

Braithwaite, D., & Braithwaite, C. (1997). Viewing persons with disabilities as a culture. In L. Samovar & R. Porter (Eds.), *Intercultural communication: A reader* (8th ed.). Belmont, CA: Wadsworth, 154–164.

Browner, C. M. (1998). Cleaner air and economic progress. Cited in C. M. Logue & J. DeHart (Eds.), *Representative American speeches: 1997–1998.* New York: H. W. Wilson, 187–192.

Duck, S. W. (1994). *Meaningful relationships.* Thousand Oaks, CA: Sage.

Fisher, M. (1994). A whisper of AIDS. In M. Fisher, *Sleep with the angels: A mother challenges AIDS.* Wakefield, MA: Moyer Bell.

Gastil, J. (1990). Generic pronouns and sexist language: The oxymoronic character of masculine generics. *Sex Roles, 23,* 629–643.

Gorham, J. (1988). The relationship between verbal teacher immediacy behaviors and student learning. *Communication Education, 37,* 40–53.

Hamilton, M. C. (1991). Masculine bias in the attribution of personhood: People = male, male = people. *Psychology of Women Quarterly, 15,* 393–402.

Legette, G., Mead, C., Kramer, M., & Beal, R. (1991). *Prentice-Hall handbook for writers* (11th ed.). Englewood Cliffs, NJ: Prentice-Hall.

Maggio, R. (1988). *The nonsexist word finder: A dictionary of gender-free usage.* Boston: Beacon.

Miller, C., & Swift, K. (1991). *Words and women: New language in new times.* New York: Harper Collins.

Motley, M. (1991). Public speaking anxiety qua performance anxiety: A revised model and an alternative therapy. In M. Booth-Butterfield (Ed.), *Communication, cognition, and anxiety.* Newbury Park, CA: Sage.

MTV Video Music Awards (2003, August 28). Retrieved September 18, 2003, from http://www.mtv.com/onair/vma/2003/

Political correctness makes sense, helps fight racism. (1997, April 29). *USA Today,* p. 12A.

Powell, R. G., & Harville, B. (1990). The effects of teacher immediacy and clarity on instructional outcomes: An intercultural assessment. *Communication Education, 39,* 369–379.

Shotter, J. (1993). *Conversational realities: The construction of life through language.* Newbury Park, CA: Sage.

Switzer, J. Y. (1990). The impact of generic word choices: An empirical investigation of age- and sex-related differences. *Sex Roles, 22,* 69–82.

Trebbe, A. (1993, July 21). Puncturing the PC principle. *USA Today,* p. D1.

Treinen, K., and Warren, J. (2001). Antiracist pedagogy in the basic course: Teaching cultural communication as if whiteness matters. *Basic Communication Course Annual 13.* Boston: American Press, 46–75.

Wood, J. (1994). *Gendered lives: Communication, gender, and culture.* Belmont, CA: Wadsworth.

Chapter 12

Barker, L. L., Cegala, D. J., Kibler, R. J., & Wahlers, K. J. (1979). *Groups in process.* Englewood Cliffs, NJ: Prentice-Hall.

Bate, B. (1992). *Communication and the sexes.* Prospect Heights, IL: Waveland Press.

Blouin, D., Summers, T., Kelley, E., Glee, R., Sweat, S., & Arledge, L. (1982). Recruiter and student evaluation of career appearance. *Adolescence, 17*(68), 821–830.

Bremer, J. (2002). Proxemics—How we use space. *Bremer Communications*. Retrieved September 21, 2003, from http://www.bremercommunications.com/Proxemics_How_We_Use_Space.htm

Cherulnik, P. D. (1989). *Physical attractiveness and judged suitability for leadership* (Report No. CG 021 893). Chicago: Annual Meeting of the Midwestern Psychological Association. (ERIC Document Services No. ED 310 317).

Decker, B. (1992). *You've got to be believed to be heard.* New York: St. Martin's Press.

Drogosz, L. M., & Levy, P. E. (1996). Another look at the effects of appearance, gender and job type on performance-based decisions. *Psychology of Women Quarterly, 20,* 437–445.

Hall, E. T. (1968). Proxemics. *Current Anthropology, 9,* 83–108.

Lawrence, S. G., & Watson, M. (1991). Getting others to help: The effectiveness of professional uniforms in charitable fund raising. *Journal of Applied Communication Research, 19,* 170–185.

Lustig, M. W., & Koester, J. (1993). *Intercultural competence: Interpersonal communication across cultures.* New York: Harper Collins.

Mayer, L. V. (1994). *Fundamentals of voice and diction* (10th ed.). Madison, WI: W. C. Brown.

Molloy, J. T. (1975). *Dress for success.* New York: Warner.

Morris, T. L., Gorham, J., Cohen, S. H., & Huffman, D. (1996). Fashion in the classroom: Effects of attire on student perceptions of instructors in college classes. *Communication Education, 45,* 135–148.

Phillips, P. A., & Smith, L. R. (1992). *The effects of teacher dress on student perceptions* (Report No. SP 033 944). (ERIC Document Services No. ED 347 151). Temple, L. E., & Loewen, K. R. (1993). Perceptions of power: First impressions of a woman wearing a jacket. *Perceptual and Motor Skills, 76,* 339–348.

Watzlawick, P., Bavelas, J. B., & Jackson, D. D. (1967). *Pragmatics of human communication.* New York: W. W. Norton.

Chapter 13

Anderson, G. Z. (2003). *Adding value with visual aids.* Presenters University. Retrieved October 18, 2003, from http://www.presentersuniversity.com/courses_visual-aids_adding_value.php

Antonoff, M. (1990). Meetings take off with graphics. *Personal Computing,* 62.

Booher, D. D. (2003). *Speak with confidence [electronic resources]: Powerful presentations that inform, inspire, and persuade.* New York: McGraw-Hill. Retrieved from http://www.netLibrary.com/urlapi.asp?action=summary&v=1bookid=81800.

Brody, M. (2003). *Seeing is believing and content counts.* Presenters University. Retrieved October 17, 2003, from http://www.presentersuniversity.com/visuals_designforclose_visuals_seeing.php

Currid, C. (1995). *Make your point: The complete guide to successful business presentations using today's technology.* Rocklin, CA: Prima.

Dwyer, K. (1998). *Conquer your speechfright.* Orlando, FL: Harcourt Brace.

Heinich, R., Molenda, M., & Russell, J. D. (1993). *Instructional media and new technologies of instruction* (4th ed.). New York: Macmillan.

Hotch, R. (1992, August). Making the best of presentations. *Nation's Business,* 37–38.

Kurnoff, J. (2003). *Generate results with PowerPoint.* Presenters University. Retrieved October 18, 2003, from http://www.presentersuniversity.com/visuals_designforclose_Visuals_generate_results.php

Long, K. (1997, August 12). *Visual aids and learning,* University of Portsmouth. Retrieved October 16, 2003, from http://www.mech.port.ac.uk/av/ALALearn.htm

Mitchell, G. (1987). *The trainer's handbook.* New York: American Management Association.

Pearce, J. (2003. *The seven deadly sins of visual presentations.* Presenters University. Retrieved October 18, 2003, from http://www.presentersuniversity.com/visuals_designforclose_visuals_7_Deadly_Sins.php

Shaw, G. R. (2003). *Can you see what I see?* Presenters University. Retrieved October 18, 2003, from http://www.presentersuniversity.com/visuals_designforclose_visuals_See.php

Tufte, E. R. (2003). *The cognitive style of PowerPoint.* Chesire, CT: Graphics Press.

Vogel, D. R., Dickson, G. W., & Lehman, J. A. (1986). *Persuasion and the role of visual presentation support: The UM/3M study.* Commissioned by Visual Systems Division of 3M.

Wangen, C. (1999). *The effects of PowerPoint visual aids on communication apprehension in public speaking situations.* Unpublished master's thesis, North Dakota State University, Fargo.

Chapter 14

Baker, L. (1998). The Illongot headhunters. Unpublished speech. Used by permission.

Banach, W. J. (1991, March 15). Are you too busy to think? *Vital Speeches of the Day, 57*(11): 351–353.

Ledbetter, C. (1995, July 1). Take a test drive on the Information Superhighway: Unmasking the jargon. *Vital Speeches of the Day,* 565–569.

Sev'er, A., & Ungar, S. (1997). No laughing matter: Boundaries of gender-based humor in the classroom. *Journal of Higher Education, 68*(1): 87–105.

Swift, W. B., & Swift, A. T. (1994, March). Humor experts jazz up the workplace. *HR Magazine on Human Resources, 39*(3): 72–76.

Wallinger, L. (May 1997). Don't smile before Christmas: The role of humor in education. *NASSP Bulletin, 81,* 27–34.

Wanzer, M., & Frymier, A. (1999). The relationship between student perceptions of instructor humor and students' reports of learning. *Communication Education, 48,* 48–62.

Chapter 15

Anton, M. L. R. (1994). Sexual assault policy a must. *Winning orations.* Mankato, MN: Interstate Oratorical Association.

Cook, J. S. (1989). *The elements of speechwriting and public speaking.* New York: Collier Books.

Foss, S. K., & Foss, K. A. (1994). *Inviting transformation: Presentational speaking for a changing world.* Prospect Heights, IL: Waveland Press.

Foss, S. K., Foss, K. A., & Griffin, C. L. (1999). *Feminist rhetorical theories.* Thousand Oaks, CA: Sage.

Frisby, T. (1998). Floss or die. *Winning orations.* Mankato, MN: Interstate Oratorical Association.

Johannesen, R. L. (1990). *Ethics in human communication* (3rd ed.). Prospect Heights, IL: Waveland Press.

Lewis, H. (1998). I spy, with my high tech eye. *Winning orations.* Mankato, MN: Interstate Oratorical Association.

McCombs, M. E. (1981). The agenda-setting approach. In D. D. Nimmo & K. R. Sanders (Eds.), *Handbook of political communication.* Beverly Hills, CA: Sage.

Monroe, A. H. (1935). *Principles and types of speech.* Chicago, IL: Scott Foresman.

Perloff, R. M. (1993). *The dynamics of persuasion.* Hillsdale, NJ: Erlbaum.

Simons, H. W. (1986). *Persuasion: Understanding, practice, and analysis.* New York: Random House.

Sonnenberg, F. K. (1988, September/October). Presentations that persuade. *Journal of Business Strategy,* 55.

Ziegelmueller, G. W., Kay, J., & Dause, C. A. (1990). *Argumentation: Inquiry and advocacy* (2nd ed.). Englewood Cliffs, NJ: Prentice-Hall.

Chapter 16

Aristotle. (1954). *Rhetoric* (W. Rhys Roberts, Trans.). New York: Modern Library.

Benjamin, J. (1997). *Principles, elements, and types of persuasion.* Fort Worth: Harcourt.

Booth-Butterfield, S., & Gutowski, C. (1993). Message modality and source credibility can interact to affect argument processing. *Communication Quarterly, 41,* 77–89.

Buck, S., & Tiene, D. C. (1989). The impact of physical attractiveness, gender, and teaching philosophy on teacher evaluations. *Journal of Educational Research, 82,* 172–177.

Cherulnik, P. D. (1989). *Physical attractiveness and judged stability for leadership* (Report No. CG 021 893). Chicago: Annual Meeting of the Midwestern Psychological Association. (ERIC Document Services No. ED 310 317).

Drogosz, L. M., & Levy, P. E. (1996). Another look at the effects of appearance, gender and job type on performance-based decisions. *Psychology of Women Quarterly, 20,* 437–445.

Eagly, A. H., & Chaiken, S. (1993). *The psychology of attitudes.* Fort Worth, TX: Harcourt Brace Jovanovich.

Ericson, J. M., Murphy, J. J., & Zeuschner, R. B. (1987). *The debater's guide* (Rev. ed.). Carbondale: Southern Illinois University Press.

Frisby, T. (1998). Floss or die. *Winning orations.* Mankato, MN: Interstate Oratorical Association, 67–70.

Grammer, R. (1986). *Teaching peace* [CD]. Brewerton, NY: Red Note Records.

Hamilton, S. (1999). Cruise ship violence. *Winning orations.* Mankato, MN: Interstate Oratorical Association, 92–94.

Kracht, K. (1998). Including Joshua: What's the big deal? *Winning orations.* Mankato, MN: Interstate Oratorical Association, 96–98.

Krishnan, A. (1998). Is Mr. Goodwrench really Mr. Rip Off? *Winning orations.* Mankato, MN: Interstate Oratorical Association.

Labor, R. (1998). Shaken baby syndrome: The silent epidemic. *Winning orations.* Mankato, MN: Interstate Oratorical Association, 70–72.

Maloney, S. R. (1992). *Talk your way to the top.* Englewood Cliffs, NJ: Prentice-Hall.

McCroskey, J. C., & Teven, J. (1999). Goodwill: A reexamination of the construct and its measurement. *Communication Monographs, 66,* 90–103.

Miller, L. C., Cook, L. L., Tsang, J., & Morgan, F. (1992). Should I brag? Nature and impact of positive and boastful disclosures for women and men. *Human Communication Research, 18,* 364–399.

Morley, D. D., & Walker, K. (1987). The role of importance, novelty, and plausibility in producing belief change. *Communication Monographs, 54,* 436–442.

Morris, T. L., Gorham, J., Cohen, S. H., & Huffman, D. (1996). Fashion in the classroom: Effects of attire on student perceptions of instructors in college classes. *Communication Education, 45,* 135–148.

Mulholland, R. (1998). Nuclear scare: What's happening out there? *Winning orations.* Mankato, MN: Interstate Oratorical Association, 149–152.

Murphy, B. O., & Zorn, T. (1996). Gendered interaction in professional relationships. In J. Wood (Ed.), *Gendered relationships.* Mountain View, CA: Mayfield, 213–232.

The New York Public Library Desk Reference (2nd ed.). (1993). New York: Stonesong-Simon.

O'Keefe, D. (1990). *Persuasion: Theory and research.* Newbury Park, CA: Sage.

Perloff, R. M. (1993). *Dynamics of persuasion.* Hillsdale, NJ: Erlbaum, 145–149.

Reardon, K. K. (1991). *Persuasion in practice* (2nd ed.). Newbury Park, CA: Sage.

Reinard, J. C. (1988). The empirical study of the persuasive effects of evidence: The status after fifty years of research. *Human Communication Research, 15,* 3–59.

Robinson, D. L., Stack, D. W., & Nelson, W. H. (1989). *The effect of physical attractiveness and spokesperson sex on perceived source and organization credibility* (Report No. CS 506 642). San Francisco: Annual meeting of the International Communication Association. (ERIC Document Services No. ED 306 622).

Slater, D. (1998). Sharing life. *Winning orations.* Mankato, MN: Interstate Oratorical Association, 63–66.

Slan, J. (1998). *Using stories and humor: Grab your audience.* Boston: Allyn & Bacon.

Stewart, R. (1994). Perceptions of a speaker's initial credibility as a function of religious involvement and religious disclosiveness. *Communication Research Reports, 11,* 169–176.

Treinen, K. (1998). *The effects of gender and physical attractiveness on peer critiques of a persuasive speech.* Unpublished master's thesis. North Dakota State University, Fargo.

Waddell, C. (1990). The role of pathos in the decision-making process: A study in the rhetoric of science policy. *Quarterly Journal of Speech, 76,* 381–400.

Witte, K. (1992). Putting the fear back into fear appeals: The extended parallel model. *Communication Monographs, 59,* 329–349.

Ziegelmueller, G. W., Kay, J., & Dause, C. A. (1990). *Argumentation and advocacy* (2nd ed.). Englewood Cliffs, NJ: Prentice-Hall.

Chapter 17

Bellefante, G. (1994, March 14). People. *Time,* 109.

Bush, L. (2002, October 2). Laura Bush's introduction to the President at White House Conference on Missing, Exploited and Runaway Children. Retrieved October 23, 2003, from http://www.whitehouse.gov/news/releases/2002/10/20021002-17.html

Cooper, C. (2003, March 23). Chris Cooper's acceptance speech. Retrieved October 23, 2003, from http://www.oscar.com/oscarnight/winners/win_32287.html

Geyer, G. A. (1989, August 15). Joy in our times. *Vital Speeches of the Day,* 666–668.

Lee, R. E. (1865, April 10). Farewell to the Army of Northern Virginia. Retrieved October 23, 2003, from http://americancivilwar.com/south/lee.html

Matsumaga, M. (2002, May 5). Dedication of Spark M. Matsumaga Elementary School. Retrieved October 23, 2003, from http://www.steveokino.com/speechwriting.html

Reagan, R. (1993). Tribute to the *Challenger* astronauts. In L. E. Rohler, & R. Cook (Eds.), 1993. *Great Speeches for Criticism and Analysis* (2nd ed.) (pp. 314–315). Greenwood, IN: Alistair Press. (Speech delivered January 28, 1986)

Roe, K. (1987). After dinner speaking final round winner. In J. K. Boaz and J. R. Brey (Eds.), *1987 Championship debates and speeches* (Vol. 2). Normal, IL: American Forensic Association.

Sellnow, D. (1999). Success. Speech delivered at the Society of Women Engineers Spring Banquet, April 17, 1999.

Stratton, S. (2000, July 1). Pioneer Presenter Speech. Retrieved October 23, 2003, from http://ebbs.english.vt.edu/sfra/awards.htm#pilgrimA

Volunteer State Community College Humanities Department. (2003, December 10). *Department Course Manual, COM 103, Public Speaking.* Retrieved December 30, 2003, from http://www2.volstate.edu/humanities/comm/ManualCOM103.doc

Chapter 18

Ancona, D. G. (1990). Outward bound: Strategies for team survival in an organization. *Academy of Management Journal, 33,* 334–365.

Bales, R. F., & Borgatta, E. F. (1955). Size of a group as a factor in the interaction profile. In A. P. Hare, E. F. Borgatta, & R. F. Bales (eds.), *Small groups: Studies in social interaction.* New York: Knopf.

Bass, B. M. (1990). *Bass and Stodgill's handbook of leadership: Theory, research, and managerial applications* (3rd ed.). New York: Free Press.

Bramson, R. M. (1981) *Coping with difficult people.* New York: Bantam Doubleday.

Dewey, J. (1933). *How we think.* Boston: Heath.

Gibb, C. (1969). Leadership. In G. Lindsey & E. Aronson (Eds.), *The Handbook of Social Psychology* (2nd ed.). Reading, MA: Addison-Wesley.

Harris, T., & Sherblom, J. (1999). *Small group and team communication.* Boston: Allyn & Bacon.

Helgesen, S. (1990). *The female advantage: Women's ways of leadership.* New York: Doubleday.

Janis, I. L. (1982). *Groupthink: Psychological studies of policy decision and fiascos* (2nd ed.). Boston: Houghton Mifflin.

Krayer, K. J., & Fiechtner, S. B. (1984). Measuring group maturity: The development of a process-oriented variable for small group communication research. *Southern Speech Communication Journal, 50,* 78–92.

Lesikar, R., Pettit, Jr., J., & Flately, M. (1999). *Basic business communication* (8th ed.). New York: McGraw-Hill.

Lewin, K., Lippitt, R., & White, R. K. (1939). Patterns of aggressive behavior in experimentally created "social climates." *Journal of Social Psychology, 10,* 271–299.

O'Hair, D., O'Rourke, J., & O'Hair, M. (2001). *Business communication: A framework for success.* Cincinnati, OH: South-Western.

Porter, R. E., & Samovar, L. A. (1992). Communication in the multicultural group. In R. S. Cathcart and L. A. Samovar (Eds.), *Small group communication* (6th ed.). Dubuque, IA: W. C. Brown.

Rahim, M. A. (2001). *Managing conflict in organizations* (3rd ed.). Westport, CT: Greenwood.

Seeger, M., Sellnow, T., & Ulmer, R. (2003). *Communication and organizational crisis.* New York: Praeger.

Shimanoff, S. B., & Jenkins, M. M. (1992). Leadership and gender: Challenging assumptions and recognizing resources. In R. S. Cathcart and L. A. Samovar (Eds.), *Small group communication* (6th ed.). Dubuque, IA: W. C. Brown.

Tullar, W., & Kaiser, P. (2000). The effect of process training on process and outcomes in virtual groups. *Journal of Business Communication, 37,* 408–427.

Wellins, R., Byham, W., & Wilson, J. 1991. *Empowered teams: Creating self-directed work groups that improve quality, productivity, and participation.* San Francisco: Jossey-Bass.

White, R., & Lippitt, R. (1960). *Autocracy and democracy.* New York: Harper & Row.

White, R., & Lippitt, R. (1969). Leader behavior and member reaction in three social climates. In D. Cartwright and A. Zander (Eds.), *Group dynamics* (3rd ed.). New York: Harper & Row.

Wood, J. T. (2000). *Communication in our lives* (2nd ed.). Belmont, CA: Wadsworth.

INDEX

Logos (*continued*)
    inductive reasoning, 388–389
    persuasive speeches and, 380
    reasoning fallacies, 391–396
    strategies for conveying, 387–396
LookSmart, 169
Lotus' Freelance Graphics, 306, 314. *See also*
    Computerized slide shows
Love needs, 137–138
Lublin, J., 114
Luiten, J., 83
Lung, K., 302
Lustig, M. W., 135, 271
Lycos, 169

Macrostructure, 60–66
    introductions highlighting, 211–212
    organization and, 184–185
    preparation outlines, 64
Maes, J. D., 7
Magazines
    APA style reference for, 174
    oral footnotes for, 177
    supporting material in, 166–167
    topics from, 108
Maggio, R., 254
Magolda, M. B., 139
Main points. *See also* Logos; Main point
        summaries
    in actuation persuasive speeches,
        365–374
    anxiety about, 184
    in body of speech, 62–63
    causal pattern for, 190
    chronological pattern for, 188
    compare-and-contrast pattern for,
        191–192
    conclusions reinforcing, 214
    connectives, linking, 194–196
    in dispositional persuasive speeches,
        358–365
    internal previews and, 195–196
    introductions previewing, 210–213
    learning cycle and, 193
    narrative pattern for, 188–189
    pattern, selecting, 185–193
    for persuasive speeches, 358–374
    in preparation outlines, 225–226
    relevance of supporting material, 194
    signposts for, 196
    spatial pattern for, 190–191
    subdivisions, adding, 193
    supporting material, integrating, 58,
        193–194
    topical pattern for, 191
    transitions for linking, 194–195
Main point summaries, 195–196
    in conclusions, 63, 64, 214
Main topic, 58
Major premises in deductive reasoning,
    389–390
Maloney, S. R., 396
Mandela, Nelson, speech by, 475–476
Manuscript method of delivery, 289
Maps as presentational aids, 306
Marginalizing, 17
    audience analysis and, 128
    with biased language, 254
    stereotypes and, 132
Marsh, G., 38
Marshall, C., 139
Mary Tyler Moore show, 289
Maslow, A. H., 137–138, 398
Maslow's hierarchy of needs, 137–138

Mass communication, 10–11
Master of ceremonies, speeches by, 411–412
Masterson, J., 135
Matsumaga, M., 422–423
Mayer, L. V., 87, 284, 285
McAdoo, L., 131
McCagg, P., 184
McCarthy, B., 18, 38
McClung, T., 223
McCombs, M. E., 352
McCroskey, J. C., 4, 35, 37, 38, 41, 106,
    127, 384
McDaniel, A., 135
McGuire, W., 130
McKay, M., 42
Media for presentational aids, 312–315
Memorized method of delivery, 289
Memory, conclusions enhancing, 214–215
Mental arguing and listening, 92
Mental distractions, 87
Merriam, A. H., 142
Messages, 7, 15–16. *See also* Nonverbal
        communication; Verbal messages
    discriminative listening and, 81
    empathic listening and, 82
    guidelines for presenting, 16
    nonverbal messages, 8
Metacrawler, 170
Metaphors, 260
    in informative speeches, 336
Metasearch engines, 170
Miccinati, J. L., 89
Microsoft PowerPoint presentations, 301,
        306, 314. *See also* Computerized
        slide shows
Microstructure, 67–68, 184–185
    guidelines for using, 68
    language and, 244
Miller, C., 254
Miller, L. C., 384
Milosevic, Slobodan, 22
Minor premises in deductive reasoning,
        389–3912
Mirror, practicing with, 292
Miscommunications, 5–6
Mitchell, G., 300
Models
    communication, models of, 11–13
    as presentational aids, 306
    socialization and, 37
Modern Language Association (MLA), 173
Modified comparative advantages pattern,
        368–369
Molenda, M., 302
Molloy, J. T., 274
Monroe, A., 369–374
Monroe, Marilyn, 284
Monroe's motivated sequence, 187, 369–374
*Monthly Catalog of United States
        Government Publications,* 167
Moore, Demi, 284
Moore, M., 143
Morgan, G., 82
Morley, D. D., 384
Mosaic, 169
Motivated movement, 282–283
Motley, M., 39, 47, 247
MSN Search, 169
Mudslinging fallacy, 395
Mulholland, R., 400–401
Mulvany, S., 87
Munger, D., 168, 170
Murphy, B. O., 384
Murphy, J. J., 391

Music
    APA style reference for, 175
    appreciative listening to, 81

Nagle, R. A., 7
Name-calling fallacy, 395
Narrative pattern
    for explanation speeches, 332
    for main points, 188–189
Narratives as supporting material, 159–160
Nasality Reduction exercise, 285
Nasal voices, 285
National Communication Association, 173
Needs
    Maslow's hierarchy of, 137–138
    in Monroe's motivated sequence,
        370–371
Neer, M. R., 38
Negative self-talk. *See* Self-talk
Negativist cognitive distortion, 46
Netscape Navigator, 169
Newspapers
    APA style reference for, 174
    oral footnotes for, 177
    supporting material in, 166–167
    topics from, 108
Nicholson, Jack, 284
Nilsen, T., 22
Nixon, Richard, 273
Nolte, Nick, 284
Nomination speeches, 412–413
Non sequitur fallacy, 395
Nonverbal communication, 8
    believability and, 269–270
    and closure, 216
    as culturally bound, 269
    and delivery, 268–270
    of message, 16
    multiple cues in, 270
    posture, 281–282
    principles of, 268–270
    as situationally bound, 269
    space, use of, 270–272
    time and, 273–274
    types of, 270–284
    voice and, 284
Note-taking
    as listening strategy, 89
    outlining method of, 90
Nussbaum, J. F., 129

Object language, 276
Objects as presentational aids, 12
Observations for audience analysis,
        144–145
Occasion for speech, 142
Occasion of communication, 13
O'Hair, D., 438
O'Hair, M., 438
O'Keefe, D., 386, 387
Online encyclopedias, 166
Onomatopoeia, 247, 258
Open Directory, 169
Open-ended questions
    for audience analysis, 144
    in research interviews, 164
Opposing arguments, acknowledgment of,
        25, 352
Oprah, 5
Oral footnotes, 176–177
Oral presentations, 6
Oral reports by small groups, 455
Oral style, 248–249
    integrating language and, 260–261

PHOTO CREDITS

2 © The Kobal Collection/Null, Gary; 8 © Len Rubenstein/Index Stock; 11 © Mark Richards/PhotoEdit; 27 © David Wells/The Image Bank; 27 © The Kobal Collection/Null, Gary; 32 © Chris Hardy/CORBIS; 42 © Ricardo Azoury/CORBIS; 50 © Chris Hardy/CORBIS; 54 © Gary Walts/Syracuse Newspapers/The Image Works; 57 AP/Wide World Photos; 71 © Larry Lawfer/Index Stock; 73 © Gary Walts/Syracuse Newspapers/The Image Works; 76 © Jeff Greenberg/PhotoEdit; 79 © Werner Krutein Liaison/Getty Images; 82 © The Everett Collection; 83 © Rhoda Sidney/Stock Boston, LLC; 100 © Jeff Greenberg/PhotoEdit; 104 © Ranald Mackechnie/Getty Images/Stone; 107 © George Shelley/CORBIS; 116 © Columbia/Courtesy Everett Collection; 120 © Ranald Mackechnie/Getty Images/Stone; 124 © Chabruken/Getty Images/The Image Bank; 129 © Bob Daemmrich/The Image Works; 130 © Mark Richards/CORBIS; 133 © Deborah Davis/PhotoEdit; 147 © Chabruken/Getty Images/The Image Bank; 150 © Bonnie Kamin/PhotoEdit; 178 © Bonnie Kamin/PhotoEdit; 182 © Tim Hall/Getty Images/Taxi; 186 © REUTERS/Anthony P. Bolante/CORBIS; 189 © Stephan Faris; 190 © David Leeson/The Image Works; 192 © Bruce Burkhardt/CORBIS; 196 © Tim Hall/Getty Images/Taxi; 200 © Jim Naughten/Getty Images/Stone; 204 © Michael Newman/PhotoEdit; 207 © CBS/EC/Everett Collection; 217 © Jim Naughten/Getty Images Stone; 220 © Rachel Epstein/PhotoEdit; 229 © Jennifer Levy/FoodPix/Getty Images; 240 © Rachel Epstein/PhotoEdit; 244 © Bettmann/CORBIS; 255 © Jeroboam; 259 © Ken Redding/CORBIS; 263 © Bettmann/CORBIS; 264 © Lucidio Studio Inc./CORBIS; 271 © Dennis MacDonald/PhotoEdit; 273 © Alberto Incrocci/Getty Images/The Image Bank; 278 © Columbia/The Kobal Collection; 279 © Michael Newman/PhotoEdit; 280 © David Young-Wolff/PhotoEdit; 282 © Rick Friedman/CORBIS; 291 © Dwayne Newton/PhotoEdit; 298 © Jim Erickson/CORBIS; 301 © Bob Daemmrich/Stock Boston, LLC.; 318 © Romily Lockyer/Getty Images/The Image Bank; 322 © Jim Erickson/CORBIS; 324 © Javier Pierini/CORBIS; 326 AP/Wide World Photos; 331 © Bettmann/CORBIS; 333 The Everett Collection; 336 The Everett Collection; 342 AP/Wide World Photos; 346 The Everett Collection; 349 © REUTERS/Shannon Stapleton/CORBIS; 353 © Phil Schermeister/CORBIS; 354 © Tom Keck/Getty Images; 355 © Laura Dwight; 356 © Rachel Epstein/The Image Works; 367 © A. Ramey/PhotoEdit; 374 The Everett Collection; 378 AP/Wide World Photos; 381 © NBC TV/The Kobal Collection; 383 The Everett Collection; 386 AP/Wide World Photos; 400 left © Gregory Pace/CORBIS; 400 right © CORBIS; 402 top © Bob Daemmrich/PhotoEdit; 402 bottom AP/Wide World Photos; 406 AP/Wide World Photos; 410 The Everett Collection; 413 © Newsmakers/Liaison Agency; 416 © Marc Serota/CORBIS; 420 © CORBIS; 421 © Susan Van Etten PhotoEdit; 424 AP/Wide World Photos; 433 AP/Wide World Photos; 436 © Bill Bachman/PhotoEdit; 441 © Rob Lewine/CORBIS; 442 © Bill Varie/CORBIS; 456 © NBAE/Getty Images; 458 © Bill Bachman/PhotoEdit